slavery

slavery

the story of
joão
wally
oopjen
paulus
van bengalen
surapati
sapali
tula
dirk
lohkay

eveline sint nicolaas
valika smeulders

maria holtrop
stephanie archangel
lisa lambrechts
karwan fatah-black
martine gosselink

RIJKS MUSEUM | ATLAS CONTACT

contents

lenders

Alkmaar, Regional Archives
Amersfoort, Cultural Heritage Agency
Amsterdam, Allard Pierson Museum, Archaeological Museum of the University of Amsterdam
Amsterdam, Amsterdam Museum
Amsterdam, Mrs. T. van Andel
Amsterdam, Collectie Monumenten en Archeologie
Amsterdam, De Nederlandsche Bank Nationale Numismatische Collectie
Amsterdam City Archives
Amsterdam, Stichting Werkspoormuseum
Brussels, Royal Museums of Fine Arts of Belgium
Cambridge, St Catharine's College
Cape Town, Iziko Museums of South Africa
Cape Town, Western Cape Archives
Commewijne, L. Tjin-A-Djie jr Family, Wederzorg Plantation
Copenhagen, SMK, The National Gallery of Denmark
Copenhagen, The National Museum of Denmark
Dokkum, Gemeente Noardeast-Fryslân
Dordrecht, on loan from Huis Van Gijn, Atlas Van Gijn
E. van Drecht collection
Hong Kong, The Mari-Cha Collection Limited
Jakarta, Arsip Nasional Republik Indonesia (ANRI)
Leiden, Leiden University Libraries
Leiden, Naturalis Biodiversity Center
Leiden, Stichting Nationaal Museum van Wereldculturen
London, British Museum
London, The Royal Collection / HM Queen Elizabeth II
Middelburg, Zeeuws Museum, KZGW collection
Oranjestad, Sint Eustatius, Collection St. Eustatius Historical Foundation
Oranjestad, Sint Eustatius, Collection St. Eustatius Monuments Foundation
Oranjestad, Sint Eustatius, private collection
Oudeschild, Museum Kaap Skil
Paris, Bibliothèque nationale de France
Paris, Musée du Louvre
Rotterdam, Atlas van Stolk
Rotterdam, Maritime Museum Rotterdam
Rotterdam, Museum Rotterdam
Siegen, Evangelische Nikolai-Kirchengemeinde
Sint Maarten (NH), Swellengrebel-Boekee Archive
Soest, National Military Museum
The Hague, City Archives
The Hague, Kunstmuseum Den Haag
The Hague, The Royal Collections of the Netherlands
The Hague, National Archives of the Netherlands
Wiesbaden, Hessian State Archives
Willemstad (Curaçao), National Archaeological Anthropological Memory Management
Zeist, Museum Het Hernhutter Huis

think tank

Reggie Baay, Raul Balai, Aspha Bijnaar, Mitchell Esajas, Karwan Fatah-Black, Dienke Hondius, Wayne Modest, Ellen Neslo, Matthias van Rossum, Maurice San A Jong, Alex van Stipriaan, Jennifer Tosch, Urwin Vyent, Simone Zeefuik, Suze Zijlstra

with thanks to

Sarah Adams, Helen Ajentoena, Gerard Alberga, Saida si Amer, Tinde van Andel, Ana Lucia Araujo, David Bade, Romy Beck, Leonard Blussé, Anthony Bogues, Remy Bonjasky, Irma Boom, Leonoor Broeder, Bea Brommer, Raymond Buve, Titas Chakraborty, Alissandra Cummins, Mingus Dagelet, Joy Delima, Philip Dikland, Ida Does, Piet Emmer, Christiaan van der Eijk, Felicia Fricke, Stephan van Galen, Jerzy Gawronski, Alexander van Geelen, Carl Haarnack, Gijs van der Ham, Romuald Hazoumè, Glenn Helberg, Jeanne Henriquez, Colin Higgins, Everon Jackson Hooi, Ranjith Jayasena, Afaina de Jong, Nancy Jouwe, Geralda Jurriaans-Helle, Reza Kartosen-Wong, Arthur Kibbelaar, Richard Kofi, Elmer Kolfin, Christian Korbeld, Anastacia Larmonie, Tessa Leuwsha, Sri Margana, Tirzo Martha, Cynthia McLeod-Ferrier, Daphina Misiedjan, Simba Mosis, Susi Mosis, Murth Mossel, Henk Niemeijer, Gert Oostindie, Ruud Paesie, Tim van Polanen, Thomas Polimé, Mark Ponte, Zaira Pourier, Clara Reyes, Raimie Richardson, Yosina Rumajauw, Angelie Sens, Janneke Stegeman, Gijs Stork, Vinod Subramaniam, John Thorton, Jörgen Tjon a Fong, Jose Tojo, Joris van den Tol, Annemieke van der Vegt, Linda Volkers, Anne Marieke van der Wal, Gloria Wekker, Mark Welland, Bart Westenbroek, Matthea Westerduin, Hans Zijlstra

together we write history

What did a woman living and working in slavery know about her 'owner' over in the Dutch Republic? What did a sugar refiner in Amsterdam know of the conditions in which the raw sugar he processed was produced? And what did a freedom fighter on Curaçao know of the struggle for equal rights being waged in Europe? The exhibition *Slavery* examines the positions of ten people within the system of Dutch colonial slavery. What were their lives like? What knowledge did they possess, and how did they relate to a system in which human beings considered other human beings as their property? These questions are not easy to answer, but they do compel us to think about the meaning of colonial slavery.

Slavery is an essential part of the colonial history of the Netherlands, a history that concerns every one of us. By collectively delving into the history of slavery, we can arrive at a better understanding of today's Dutch society. With the exhibition *Slavery*, the Rijksmuseum, as the national museum of art and history of the Netherlands, aims to provide a more complete picture of that history, so that we can truly be a museum for everyone. Studying the history of slavery reveals how interwoven the slave trade and slavery are with the economic and social history of the Netherlands and how this history continues to influence society in our country, as well as those of the former colonies and overseas parts of our kingdom.

This exhibition was produced in a time of drastic social change. The outbreak of the Covid-19 pandemic has had an unprecedented effect on our everyday lives, and it also influenced the making of this exhibition. Lenders and partners worldwide collaborated on this exhibition under often difficult circumstances. Funders, sponsors and individuals gave us their full support. The *Slavery* exhibition has been made possible in part by the Mondriaan Fund, Blockbuster Fund, Fonds 21, DutchCulture, Democracy and Media Foundation, Stichting Thurkowfonds, Scato Gockinga Fonds/Rijksmuseum Fonds, Fonds de Zuidroute/Rijksmuseum Fonds, Zusjes Nieuwbeerta Fonds/Rijksmuseum Fonds, Fonds Dirk Jan van Orden/Rijksmuseum Fonds, Henry M. Holterman Fonds/Rijksmuseum Fonds and Boomerang Agency. The Rijksmuseum is grateful to these patrons for their contribution.

Our team of curators made grateful use of the knowledge, suggestions and critical observations of the many individuals who were asked, based on their expertise and background, to provide input into the exhibition. These individuals brought together the history of 'East and West', in the same way the exhibition does. We thank them, and we hope to continue to collaborate in this way with so many people from outside the museum. A multiplicity of voices is not just important when it concerns subjects like colonial history and slavery; it is essential in order for us to be able to optimally fulfil our role as the national museum of art and history of the Netherlands.

Taco Dibbits
General Director, Rijksmuseum

eveline sint nicolaas
valika smeulders

slavery

an exhibition of many voices

The Rijksmuseum is the national art and history museum of the Netherlands; its mission is to be of broad social relevance to all Dutch people. The colonial past of the Netherlands is part of this; it spans, after all, a lengthy period during which a significant portion of the foundations of the present-day Netherlands were laid. Slavery was an essential component of the colonial period, and many generations suffered unimaginable injustice as a result. This past has long been insufficiently examined in the national history of the Netherlands, including at the Rijksmuseum.

In February 2017, the Rijksmuseum announced it would programme an exhibition about slavery for the first time in its history. This exhibition would focus on the people who were part of that history, rather than be an overview of the economic history of slavery with figures and dates. This required in-depth research into a social history that has until now only scarcely been studied by the museum but which is still a living past for many people beyond its walls. A living past that, moreover, cannot readily be found in the collection of the Rijksmuseum.

A vital first step in the development of the exhibition was approaching people and bringing them together. New staff members with relevant professional as well as personal backgrounds were hired; a think tank was assembled; and there was an extensive exchange of ideas with national and international experts with various specialisms within the history of slavery. Artists and other creatives were also recruited, and contact was made with potential lenders of objects in the Netherlands and abroad. At the same time, numerous emails came in, with reactions, suggestions and proposals for collaboration or loans. The exhibition turned into an intensive four-year process, during which people in many capacities engaged in dialogue around diverse themes. Every department of the museum was involved, from management to security, personnel and communications. The resulting plans for the exhibition were discussed internally with staff and externally with Friends of the Rijksmuseum and many other stakeholders. Sometimes these were groups who were already in significant agreement; on other occasions these were groups that had not previously reflected together on how to represent this complex, controversial history. This produced a broad palette of input as well as questions such as 'Can slavery in the transatlantic region be compared to slavery in Asia?' 'As a white visitor, should I feel guilty about colonial slavery?' 'Can the museum really tell the story of my ancestors in slavery?' and 'Is the Rijksmuseum building an appropriate venue in which to present the history of slavery?' These are questions that had not previously been posed in such clear terms; questions that gained particular relevance once all these diverse parties came together around this exhibition.

The fact that the subject of slavery was to a large extent absent from the permanent presentation of the Rijksmuseum was long explained based on the idea that there was no collection available to tell the story. But is this true? Had the museum taken a good enough look at its collection? One apt example is the handsome tortoiseshell and gold box that the Dutch West India Company (WIC) presented to stadtholder William IV of Orange, in 1749 (fig. 1). This was the luxurious packaging that housed the document in which William IV was

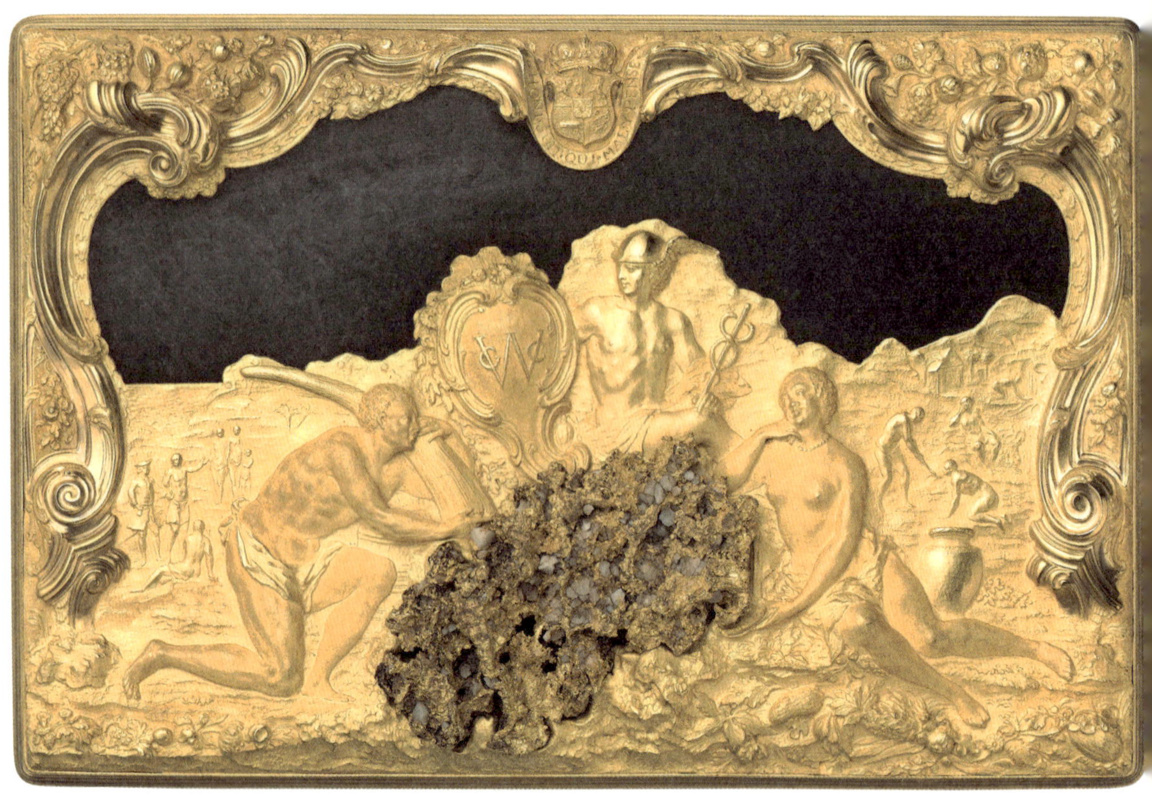

fig. 1 **Lid of a box made for the Dutch West India Company, depicting the trade in ivory and gold as well as people, attributed to Jean Saint, 1749**

offered supreme command of the WIC. For a long time, this box was described as a magnificent example of the Rococo style, the stadtholder's favourite art movement. No heed was paid, however, to what was depicted in this style: the trade in ivory, gold as well as people, and a map showing part of West Africa and important posts for human trafficking, like Elmina Castle in the Gulf of Guinea and the island of Curaçao in the Caribbean.[1] The subject of slavery was there, presented on a platter, as it were, yet it remained long unnoticed.

Proceeding from the idea that the collections might contain more such links with slavery, the museum's collections and permanent presentation were critically examined in parallel with the research for the exhibition. A surprisingly high number of points of reference emerged. Under the title *Rijksmuseum & Slavery*, the results of this research will be on show in the permanent display for one year, with extra text labels explaining each object's connection to slavery. These links vary from portraits of people who owned plantations or occupied administrative functions in the WIC or Dutch East India Company (VOC), to depictions of stimulants like coffee and tobacco, produced in slavery, to the use of Black people as a stylistic device in applied art. The research makes clear that the history of slavery is inextricably bound with the national history of the Netherlands in its full scope and diversity. Slavery was not something that merely took place far away, on the other side of the world; it also left traces in the Netherlands. It did not only enrich the elite in their canal houses; many artisans also made a living from it as subcontractors and suppliers. This happened in Holland and Zeeland in particular, but in other provinces too. The history of slavery also extends beyond the transatlantic slave trade: in the collection objects were found with links to regions around the Indian Ocean as well.

The research for *Rijksmuseum & Slavery* produced a large number of stories, and at the same time the results made it painfully clear that these stories mainly focus on the slaveholder and not the enslaved person or people. Indeed, the collection of the Rijksmuseum was not originally assembled with a view to conveying the stories of people in slavery; a large proportion of its holdings come from the wealthy elite. What we can do, however, is point out to the visitor what may not be apparent, or is not shown, in a painting of a plantation; the awkward contrast between idyllic representation and harsh reality; and the stereotyped depictions of and lack of real faces given to enslaved people. With these added insights we reveal how intertwined slavery is with the history of the Netherlands. Yet is this openness about what these objects do not show sufficient to contribute to a sense of connection for visitors who are descended from enslaved people?

Connection or recognition is an important aspect of any visit to a museum. An inhabitant of Wijk bij Duurstede will recognize a depiction of the town's windmill; a mother will be affected by a painting of a sick child. That sense of recognition, of being able to relate to the objects on display – and therefore to history – is vital. It arouses curiosity and makes a visit to a museum worthwhile. There is a reason many people have recently been taking group photographs in front of the painting of the militia company that hangs to the right of Rembrandt's *Night Watch*. The painting is part of the Black Heritage

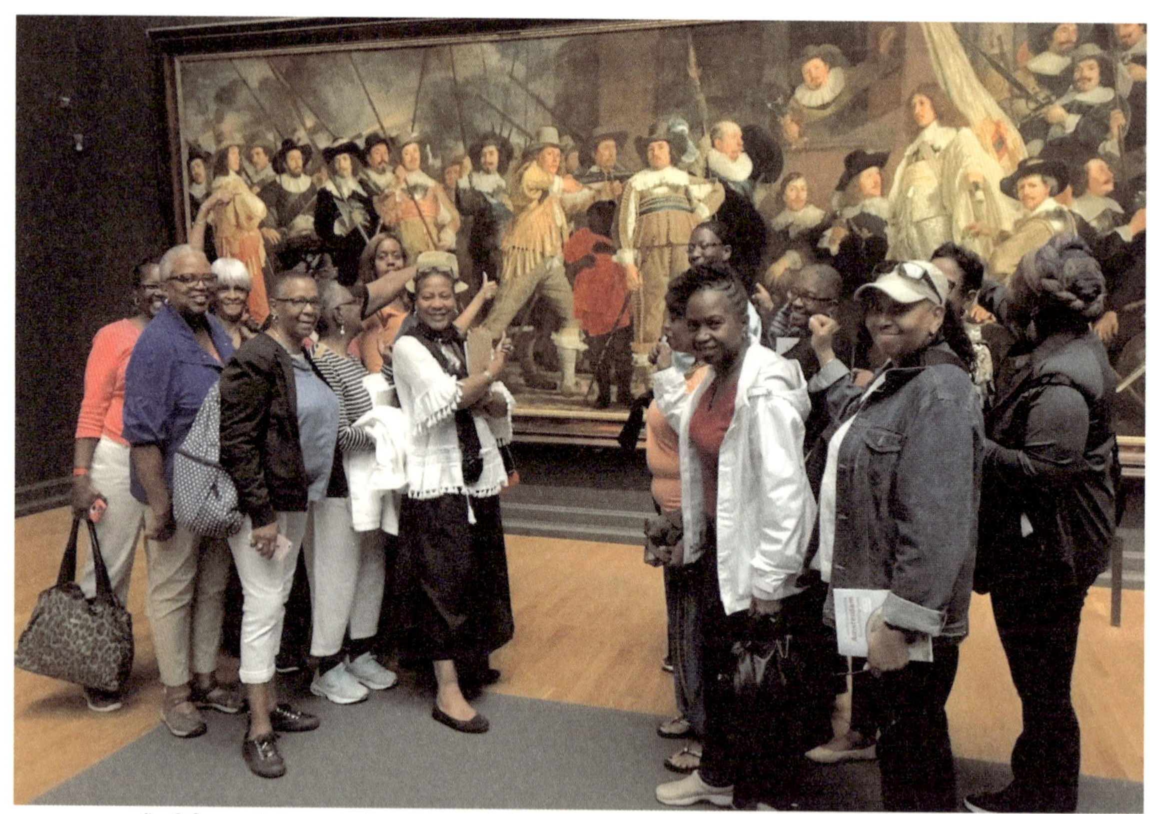

fig. 2 **Group photograph of participants in Jennifer Tosch's Black Heritage Amsterdam Tour in front of the militia company portrait by Bartholomeus van der Helst from c. 1640–1643**

Amsterdam Tours, organized by Jennifer Tosch. During these walks around the city, Tosch takes her groups to the Rijksmuseum and points out to them the young man of African origin who stands next to the painting's central figure, Roelof Bicker.[2] The young man, like the militiamen portrayed, is a person of flesh and blood. We do not know his name, but he must have walked around in seventeenth-century Amsterdam. He remained unnoticed by many white museum staff and visitors for years, until Jennifer Tosch changed this. She *did* notice him, and so did many other people of colour, who might even recognize part of themselves or their history in his image in the Gallery of Honour and so wish to include him in their group photos (fig. 2). We aim to continue to work on this recognition in the museum so that we can tell a more complete story of the Netherlands, a story in which a broad national audience can see itself reflected and that also appeals to an international audience. There is still a great deal of work to do, for it is clear that telling a shared history cannot be done based on the existing collection. With the exhibition *Slavery*, therefore, we go one step further.

a story of many voices

At an early stage, the museum decided to make people the focus of its *Slavery* exhibition: ten different lives in the period of slavery. People who were related in all sorts of ways to the greater system of power and money; who were part of it or suffered because of it; people who had to adapt to it or who dared to rise up against it; slaveholders and enslaved people in the transatlantic context, around the Indian Ocean and in the Netherlands. In order to tell their stories, the museum went in search of as many sources as possible, sources that do justice to these people's lives – that tell *their* stories instead of telling stories *about* them.

We looked for objects outside the direct context of slavery, because the history of people in slavery does not begin at the moment they were enslaved. The seventeenth-century head-covering from the Congo, for instance, woven with palm and pineapple leaf fibres, is related to the hierarchy within the powerful Congolese royal house (p. 80, fig. 9). We also looked for objects that say something about forming and preserving one's own culture within the system of slavery, such as a musical instrument used during Winti rituals on plantations in Suriname (p. 101). There are very few, if any, personal possessions of enslaved people. People in slavery were not allowed to own anything, and whatever they might have possessed has rarely survived. Some objects therefore represent immaterial heritage. Fifty dried plants in the herbarium of the botanist Paul Hermann, dating from around 1687, for instance, attest to the crucial knowledge people had for surviving in the forest (p. 211). They were collected during the period of Dutch slavery and make it possible to show intangible knowledge about the medicinal effects and nutritional value of plants.

Direct testimonies from enslaved people are rare in written sources as well. In most colonies there was a ban on reading and writing, and people often had no access to paper and ink; it was also unwise to commit one's thoughts to paper. So the autobiographical documents that are known were practically always written by formerly enslaved people looking back on their lives. The texts were often published in the context of the anti-slavery movement in Britain and the United States.[3] In the Dutch context, we know the letters of Boston Band, a man who negotiated between escaped enslaved people in the forests of Suriname and the colonial authorities there. They were preserved in their Dutch translations, but his own letters in English were lost.[4] Another written source is the will of Angela van Bengalen, a formerly enslaved woman who died a wealthy freewoman in Cape Town in 1720. In order to tell the stories of the individuals at the centre of the exhibition, written colonial sources were used as well: a journal kept on a slave ship, administrative documents or judicial records, for example. These colonial documents sometimes provide a literal account of what was said by people in slavery. Father Schinck quotes the words of Tula, a captured resistance fighter on Curaçao. And in one of the interrogation reports sent to the Society of Suriname, we can read the words spoken by the enslaved man Wally, who was arrested in 1707. Reading them gives a researcher gooseflesh, because for a moment you get very close to the person in slavery. But they remain words spoken and written down within an unequal power relationship.

In a system in which property and writing were forbidden, histories passed down orally from generation to generation were of course of vital importance. Singing is storytelling in the language of music.[5] Everywhere in the world where people lived in slavery, there was singing and dancing: to celebrate an event or to give each other strength in times of sorrow; while pounding the coffee beans or rowing the tent boat; as an outlet for frustrations; to call for resistance; or to pass stories on to the next generation. But it is not only songs that bring us closer to some of the ten individuals whose stories are told here. Interviews with elderly people, recorded in the twentieth century, provide us with access to the experiences of people in slavery. What did people who escaped the system pass on to their children? How did they phrase their story? And how do their descendants look back on this history?

'How do you keep it from remaining too comfortable for the visitor?' someone asked in the run-up to the exhibition. This is a legitimate question, for how can you give an accurate impression of a system based on brutal violence, exploitation and fear in a museum setting? A foot restraint, made for use in colonized territories and recently gifted to the museum, makes it possible to show something of the physical violence that was inflicted on enslaved individuals (pp. 72–73).[6] *Troncos* like these were used on plantations to punish people or to chain them down if the slaveholder feared they would escape during the night. At least four people, lying on the ground, could be bound by the feet between the wooden beams, their freedom of movement further impeded by heavy iron shackles.

During preparations for the exhibition, the Rijksmuseum also acquired a *kappa*, a cast iron kettle like those used on sugar plantations in Suriname. The kappa provides a counterpoint to the romanticized paintings of plantation landscapes in the collection (p. 95, fig. 6). This utensil, used by enslaved people on plantations, symbolizes not only the harsh working conditions but also the skill connected with it. Slaveholders were often entirely dependent on the knowledge and experience of the people who worked for them in slavery. A *sirih* box made in Batavia at the end of the eighteenth century brings us close to the hands of an enslaved man (p. 162). Silversmith Hendrik Rennebaum put his hallmark on it, but it is probable that the enslaved man Januarij van Bengalen did the actual work, as well as make a significant contribution to the design. With this knowledge, we get closer to Januarij as a person and not as an enslaved individual.

We will never know the names of millions of people who lived in slavery, nor will we ever see their faces. To do justice to their stories, contemporary art by Benin-born artist Romuald Hazoumè has been included in the exhibition (pp. 58–61). In his installation *La Bouche du Roi*, Hazoumè brings to life the 'Middle Passage', the forced crossing from Africa to the Americas. In this he reflects on archival documents from the period, in which people are reduced to commodities. The installation, which calls upon several senses (sight, hearing, smell), offers a powerful counterpoint to the visual might of the colonial objects. It also adds an important element: the lingering effect of colonial relations in the present. Hazoumè brings to the fore not only the experiences of those who were taken away but also those of the descendants of the people left behind in Africa.

In an exhibition, visual language is important, but the language in which the story is told is just as important. We have opted to speak of enslaved men, women and children and not of slaves, except in quoted material or in text clearly written from the point of view of the slaveholder. This decision is in line with the premise of the exhibition, in which people in slavery are seen not as an anonymous category of merchandise in an inventory but as human beings. People are more than their skin colour or ethnic background, but in writing about colonial slavery, a system in which the social construct of race was an important instrument, it is sometimes unavoidable to use terms that are sensitive, or to speak in general descriptions when the subject is a person of flesh and blood. We are aware that the term 'Black' does not do justice to the skin colour of individual people, but it is sometimes used to differentiate from 'white'. By capitalizing Black when referring to people in ethnic or cultural terms, or in terms of 'race', we acknowledge the fact that this term connects people of African descent around the world, in the absence of identifiable ethnicities that have been erased by the system of slavery.

During one of the meetings about the exhibition, the Rijksmuseum was described as a temple of colonial self-aggrandizement, and the architect Afaina de Jong described the building as the physical representation of the Dutch national identity. In a museum building whose visual programme presents the former Dutch colonies solely in the context of the supposed motherland's self-sacrifice (fig. 3), one cannot organize an exhibition on slavery without acknowledging that building. And so that acknowledgment is reflected in De Jong's exhibition design, such as the application of colour on some wall sections, while other sections are deliberately left white as a reference to the Rijksmuseum as an institution (fig. 4). Through materiality and scale, the design also refers to the role of architecture in the slavery system: the

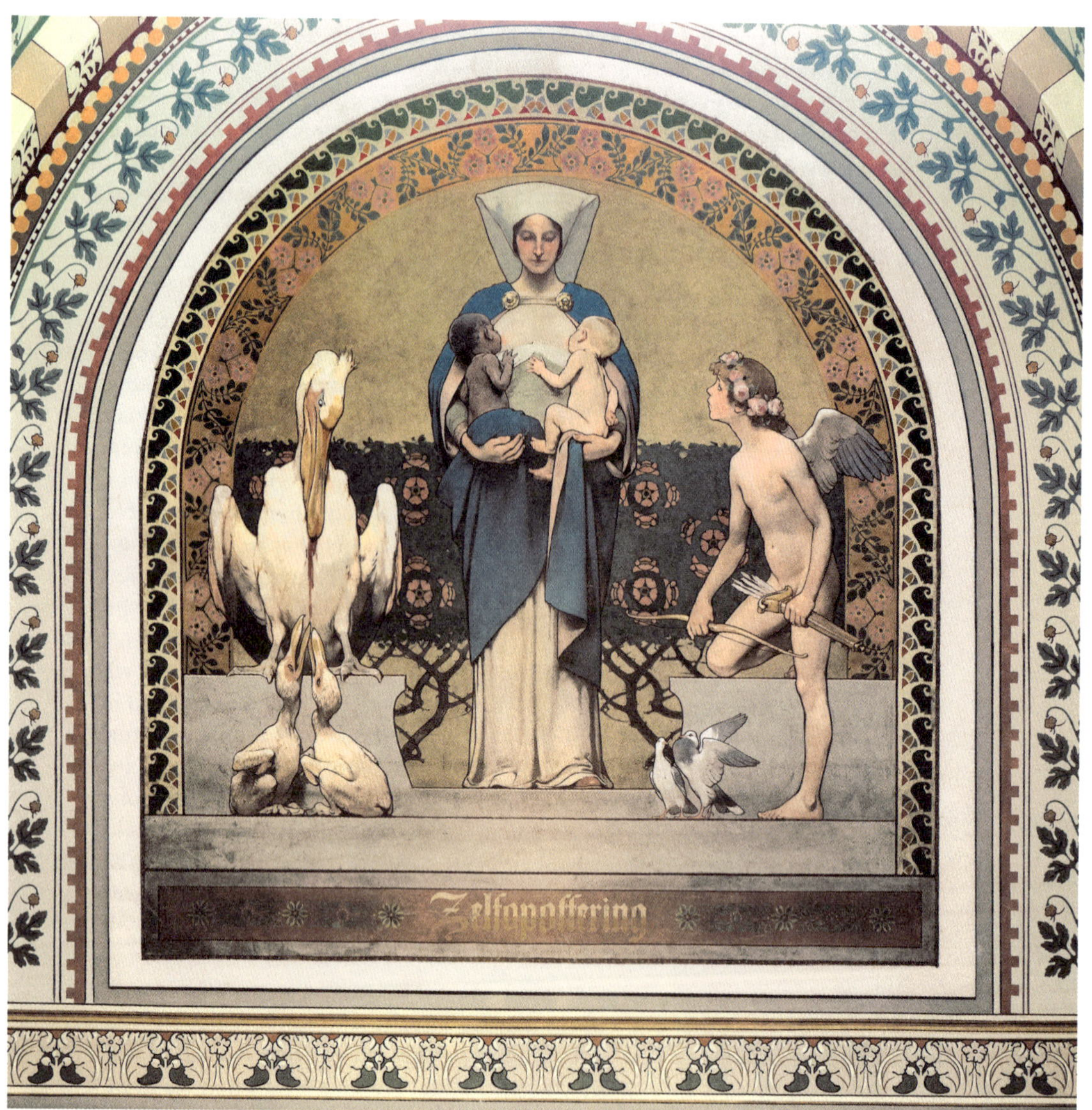

fig. 3 ***Self-Sacrifice*, painting in the Great Hall of the Rijksmuseum, Georg Sturm, 1885**

difference in space between rooms for slaveholders and those for enslaved people. In the first galleries, the visitor feels the oppressiveness of a dungeon or a ship's hold, and the design has a directional quality. In the later galleries, the round shapes instead provide more opportunity to find one's own way, and therefore a greater sense of freedom. The use of mirrors influences what the visitor does or does not (immediately) see, an allusion to the invisibility of slavery in people's perceptions, both then and now. On the reverse of the reflecting walls we find the stories that remained unheard for so long.

ten stories, millions of lives

The exhibition tells the stories of ten historical persons using the diverse sources mentioned earlier: objects, archival documents and oral sources. The objects come from various collections – collections assembled to tell the story of the wealthy bourgeoisie and the Dutch artisan, as well as anthropological collections that have traditionally been more focused on 'the Other'. Careful reading of the archival documents reveals a little of the dark side of the colonial story. And the oral sources give us a glimpse into what was discussed by people in slavery, and the life lessons they passed down to their descendants. Each story features a different combination of sources and has different focal points. Each story is unique and is not necessarily representative of a particular group. In selecting the ten individuals, consideration was given to geographical distribution and an effort was made to achieve a certain gender balance. The ten historical figures also take the visitor through time and along the exhibition's themes: from life in slavery, or profiting from it, to diverse stories of resistance and, ultimately, to freedom.

Slavery is not a closed, resolved history. Abolition has been followed by a long path towards greater equality in society and greater openness about the lingering effects of inequality from the past. That past must still be examined from a variety of angles today. In an effort to do justice to these many voices, we have opted to have each of the ten stories told by means of an audio tour by people who feel a close bond to that specific person.[7] In this way, we show how our society today is made up of the descendants of the people from back then. The surname of the actress Joy Delima, like the name of João Mina, alludes to the African slave fortress of Elmina. Genealogist Annemieke van der Vegt is a descendant of an African servant in the Netherlands, like Paulus. And due to his partly Indonesian heritage, writer Reza Kartosen-Wong feels an affinity with the story of Surapati.

At the end of the exhibition, the visitor returns to the here and now. What have the ten stories from the past conveyed? Have we gained a better insight into a system that was conceived, implemented, maintained and resisted by people? What can you do yourself to break through the system? What is your place in its history? With these questions in mind, the visitor is invited to join artist duo Tirzo Martha and David Bade, as well as other visitors, in giving shape to ten new 'images' of the ten people from the exhibition (fig. 5).

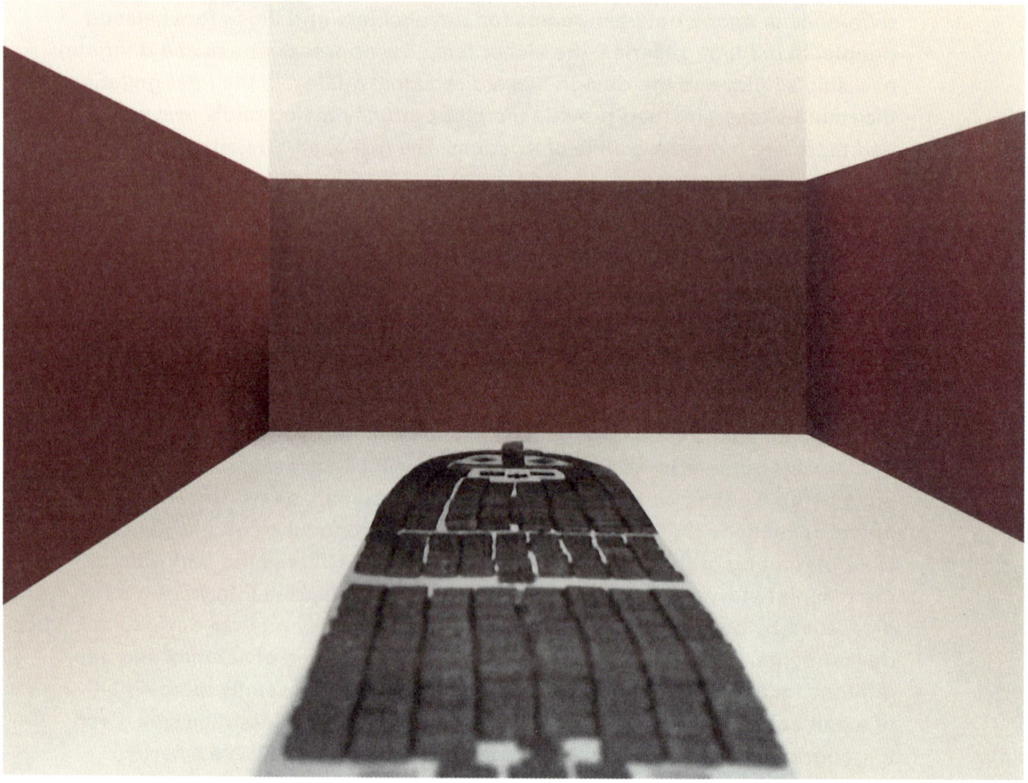

fig. 4 **Visualization of one of the galleries of the *Slavery* exhibition by Afaina de Jong, with the work *La Bouche du Roi* by Romuald Hazoumè (see pp. 58–61). The use of colour in this gallery emphasizes the oppressiveness of the ship's hold**

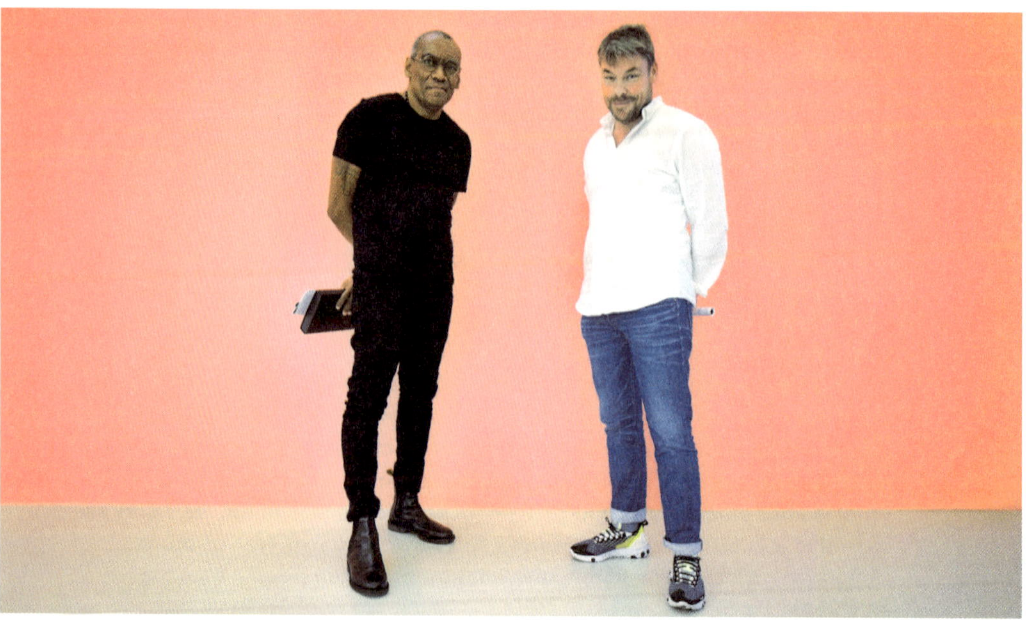

fig. 5 **A closing art project by artists Tirzo Martha and David Bade, both from Curaçao, allows visitors to interact with the exhibition**

João, Wally, Oopjen, Paulus, the Van Bengalens, Surapati, Sapali, Tula, Dirk and Lohkay are only ten of the many millions of people who lived during the 250 years of Dutch colonial history. Through them, the museum aims to promote a broader picture of our common ancestors: those who were part of the system, those who suffered from it and those who helped put an end to it. Their lives inspire reflection about the past, present and future.

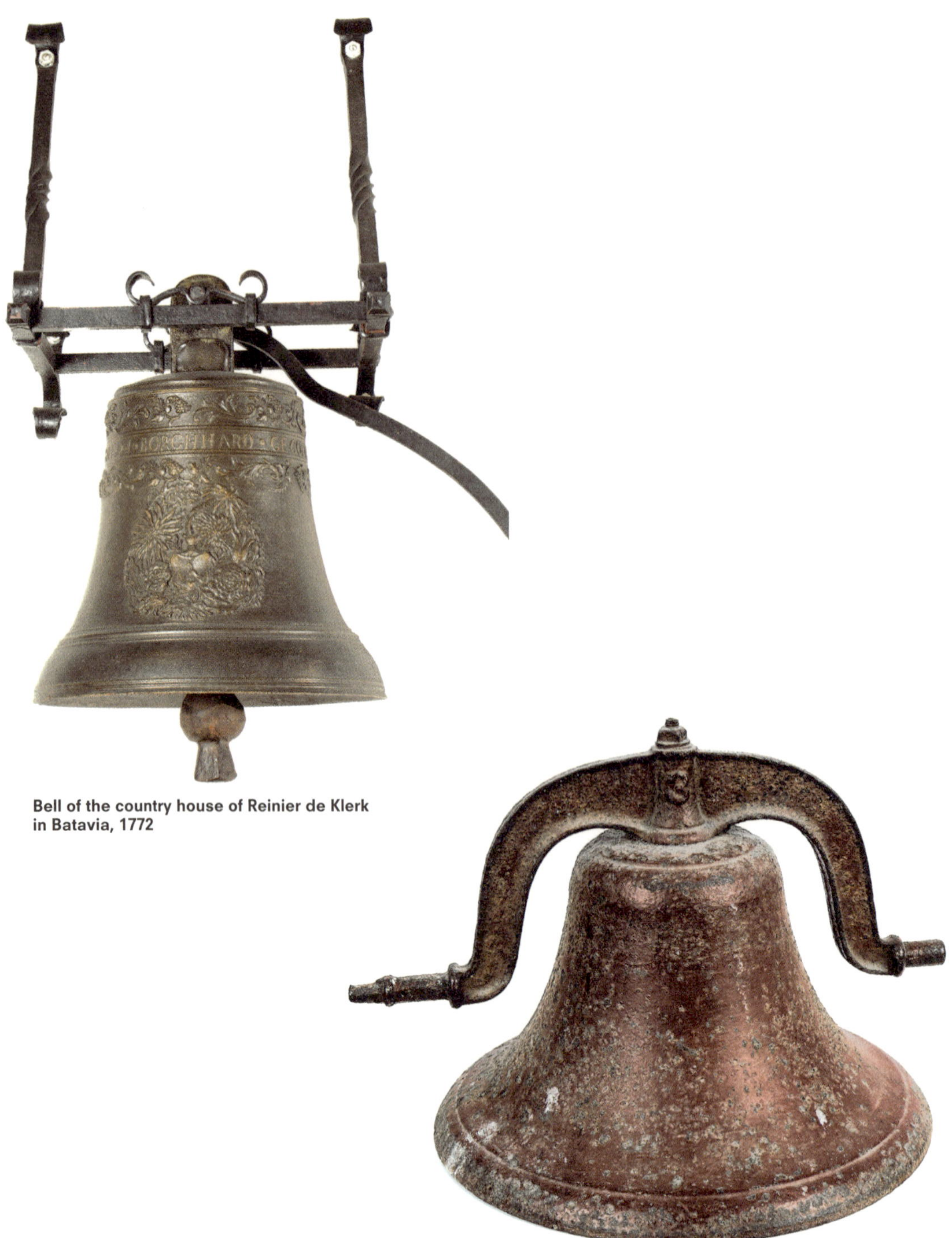

Bell of the country house of Reinier de Klerk in Batavia, 1772

Bell of the Santa Catharina estate, Curaçao, before 1750

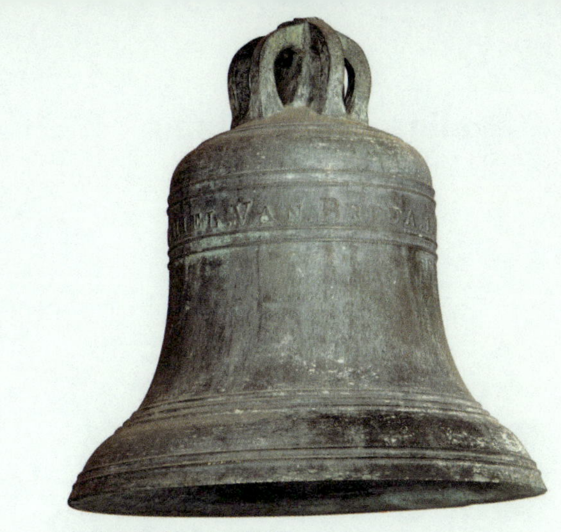

Bell of the Oranjezicht farm near Cape Town, c. 1775

Bell of the Wederzorg plantation in Commewijne, Suriname, 18th century

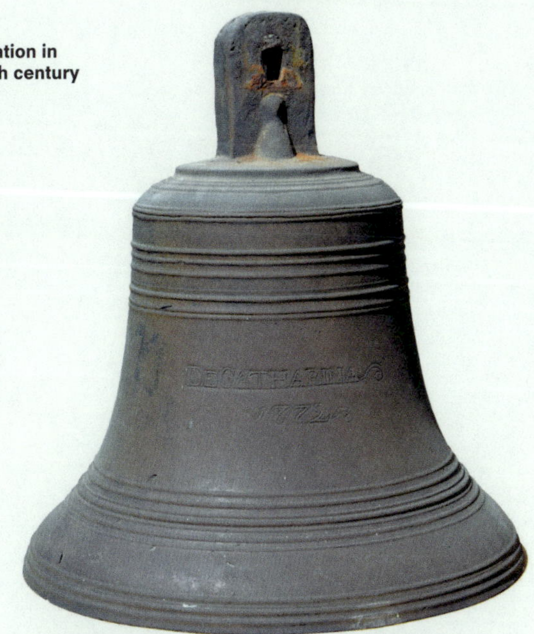

Bell of the De Catharina plantation in Demerara (in present-day Guyana), 1772

eveline sint nicolaas

dutch colonial slavery

Faya siton,
No bron mi so!
No bron mi so!
Adyen Masra Jansi kiri suma pikin

Red-hot stones,
Don't burn me so!
Don't burn me so!
Again Mister Jansen murdered someone's child

The well-known Surinamese song *Faya siton* tells of the punishment that would follow at the end of a long workday on the plantation if not enough coffee beans had been picked. The enslaved workers were forced to hold red-hot stones in their hands until the overseer said they could drop them. The stones caused severe burns that could be fatal.[1] The song also relates how even children were not spared this punishment. Born into slavery, they were automatically the possession of the slaveholder, and as soon as they were old enough they had to work in the fields.

Faya siton has been passed down from generation to generation and is often sung as a lullaby. It contains echoes of fear, but also of anger at the disproportionally severe punishments that were part of the slavery system. This was a system based on hard labour from early morning to late evening, following the rhythm of the plantation bell; a system in which a human being became a tool that could be used, exploited and punished according to the whims of the slaveholder, as long as it did not break. This chapter takes a closer look at that system: who was enslaved, in what way, by whom and in what circumstances, and what kinds of labour they were forced to do. Rather than a complete history of slavery, it presents frameworks within which the lives of the ten people central to the *Slavery* exhibition and publication can be placed and understood.

ringing the bell

'I work all the time; I have to rest a little too,' replied Slammat van Bougis, who laboured in slavery on a plantation on the Cape in South Africa. The overseer had asked him why he was sitting down and smoking a pipe instead of working.[2] Every workday on a plantation began with the ringing of the bell, audible across the whole estate and an irrevocable signal that the day had started (fig. 1). Showing up late or taking a break without permission meant risking a severe punishment. The working day ended with the same sound, often at the moment when the day's harvest was weighed and the overseer decided whether the labourers had worked hard enough. Again there was the threat of punishment.

The ringing of a bell is a method of communication used since time immemorial all over the world to summon people to church services, weddings or funerals, to mark working hours or the closing of city gates, or as a warning of fire or shipwreck. The sound carries far and is a practical and universal means of reaching large numbers of people. In the colonial world, in addition to this practical function, the sound also came to be associated with exploitation and violence. In Batavia (present-day Jakarta), at the house of the governor general Reinier de Klerk, there hung a bell that had been cast on site in 1772 by a gun-founder from Enkhuizen (p. 20).[3] Its ringing meant the start of the workday for about 200 people.[4] Joseph, who played clarinet in the De Klerk family's 'slave orchestra', would have heard this bell, as would the violinists Ratea van Batavia, Pas-op and Djoeroemoedi van Malaya and the thirteen other members of the orchestra.[5] The other enslaved labourers worked primarily in the De Klerk garden and house, and in the warehouse used for the substantial private commerce of this high functionary of the Dutch East India Company (VOC). Long stone buildings flanked the garden on two sides. These were the living quarters of this large group of enslaved people, beyond the immediate view of the house yet close enough that they could be set to work quickly.

On the other side of the ocean, on Curaçao, a bell likewise set the arduous and merciless rhythm of the day on the Santa Catharina plantation, where cotton, beans, corn and peanuts were cultivated (p. 20).[6] Every plantation, farm or government building in the Dutch colonies had such a bell, often referred to as a slave bell. Sometimes this bell would have a dual function. The bell at the Oranjezicht farm, an estate owned by the Van Breda family on the Cape, for instance, was used not only to signal the start and end of the workday but also to announce the sale of the harvest at the gate (p. 21).[7] While the sound of the bell might have been a welcome invitation to someone wanting to buy fruit, for people in slavery it was unequivocally linked to hard labour and violence, or the threat thereof.

To this day, the ringing of a former plantation bell can elicit strong emotions. At St Catharine's College at the University of Cambridge, a discussion began in May 2019 about the use of a former plantation bell. The bell of the De Catharina plantation in Demerara (in present-day Guyana), dating from 1772, had been used since 1960 by the college porter to call students to meals or prayers (p. 21).[8] The bell had already been moved to a less prominent location in 1994, and in 2019 it was definitively removed. On hearing the bell at the Wederzorg plantation in Suriname, meanwhile, the present owner is reminded of the fact that one of its former overseers would use it to 'order' the company of a female labourer in the 1960s (fig. 2).[9]

Most of the bells found in former Dutch colonies or trading posts were cast in the Netherlands. Artillery founders who produced cannons during wartime used their workshops in quieter periods to cast bells and screw pumps. Along with merchandise, provisions, tools and building materials, the bells were placed in the holds of ships in Dutch harbours, to be dispatched all over the world. They were instruments within the slavery economy, deployed with the aim of maximizing profit. The bells of plantations and other colonial buildings can be seen as an invisible hand – the representation of a system disseminated, controlled and promoted from the Netherlands. Aspects of this system would vary according to the local situation, yet at its core it was uniform all across the world: it made people into objects.

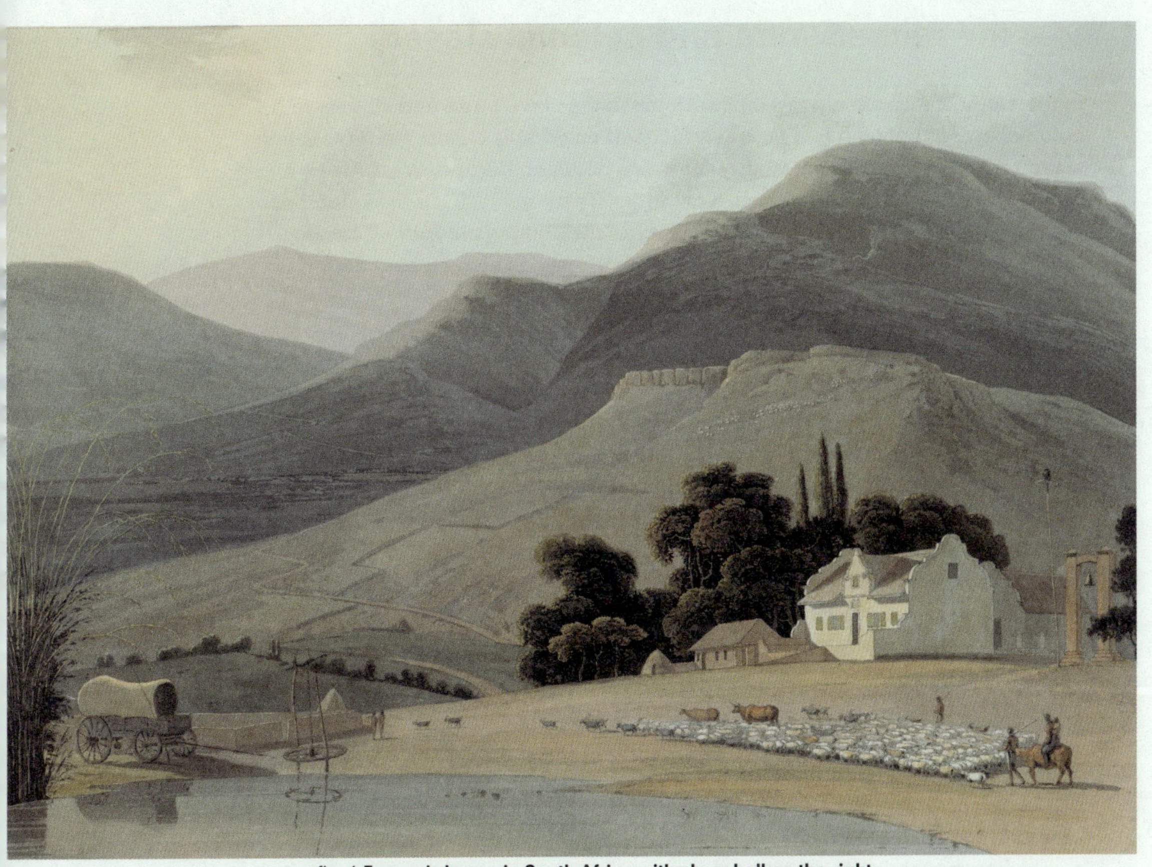

fig. 1 **Farmer's house in South Africa with slave bell on the right**
Samuell Daniell, 1804

the netherlands and colonial slavery

In the study of the role played by the Dutch in the slave trade and slavery in the colonial era, attention has long been focused on what is called the transatlantic slave trade, referring to the triangular trade between Europe, West Africa and the Americas, in which the Dutch West India Company (WIC) was a significant player. Less well known is that the history of the Dutch East India Company (VOC), the trading company that was active in Asia, is also closely bound up with the slave trade and slavery.

Both trading companies were established with both private and state capital, and their authority was likewise partially governmental; they had the right to wage war, for example. This means that studying the history of the VOC and WIC provides not just insights into the trials and tribulations of a commercial enterprise but also a view of a substantial section of the society and economy of the Netherlands. The slave trade and slavery were a significant component of the activities of both trading organizations, but the differing positions occupied by the VOC and WIC in the territories in which they operated, and the different forms of slavery they employed, make a comparison complicated. In the transatlantic territory, human trafficking was carried out to a significant extent under the aegis of the WIC, which claimed a monopoly on the slave trade until 1730.[10] The VOC did not claim such a monopoly. The company was mainly involved in the slave trade at the beginning of the seventeenth century, but thereafter it was primarily VOC functionaries who pursued this trade, outside their official work, using the Asian network and the infrastructure of the VOC itself (figs. 3, 4). The VOC did however endeavour to facilitate the monitoring and auditing of this trade via legislation, as it did with other commodities.

There were also reciprocal connections between the two trading companies. For example, cowrie shells collected in the Maldives, in the Indian Ocean, were transported by the VOC to the Dutch Republic, where they were purchased by the WIC for use as currency in the slave trade on the coast of West Africa.[11] Asian textiles and saltpetre served as links between the VOC and WIC as well.[12] Moreover, shareholders often had a financial interest in both companies.

As well as the slave trade itself, the production of goods by enslaved people varied greatly in form and scope, from the large-scale plantations of the Atlantic region (or 'gardens', as plantations were described in the VOC archives), to the use of enslaved labourers in the silver mines of Sumatra, or as artisans in cities like Paramaribo (in Suriname) and Batavia. Beyond the direct production of consumer goods such as nutmeg, pepper, sugar, silver, gold, coffee and tobacco, enslaved people were also employed in the transport of products, in military expeditions, in households or orchestras, to row tent boats or carry parasols, or simply to raise the status of the slaveholder.

people become objects

What the various forms of slavery and the slave trade in the Dutch colonial empire have in common is that they are part of a system that makes people into

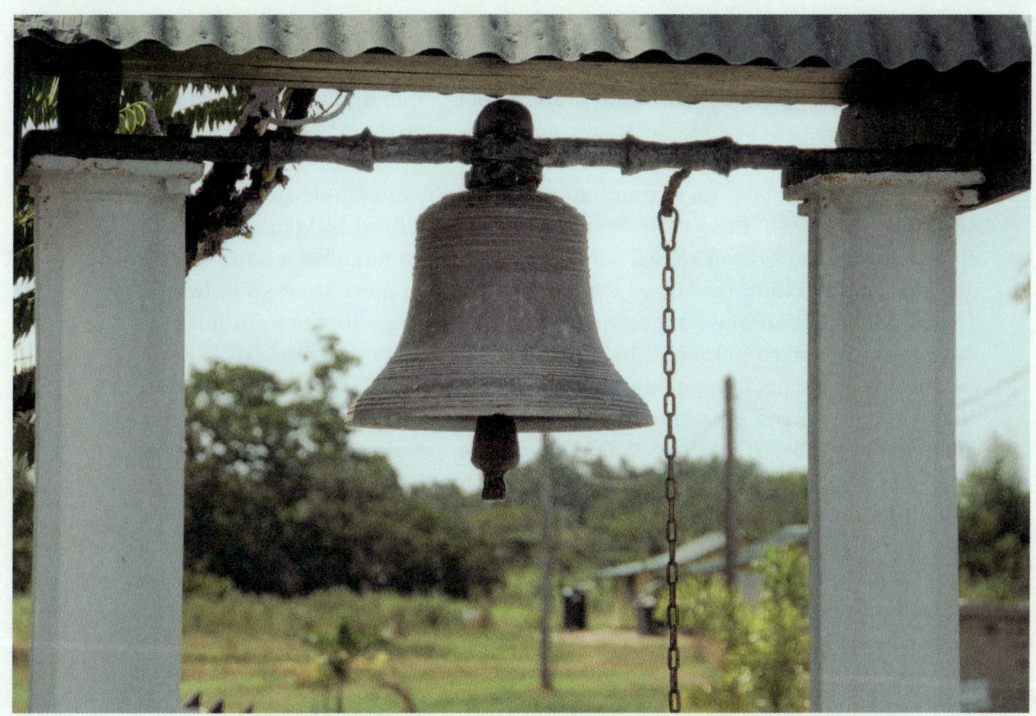

fig. 2 **Bell at the Wederzorg plantation in Commewijne, Suriname, 18th century**

objects, severs their bonds of kinship and reduces them to commercial property, to an economic unit. At its core, slavery can be defined as a relationship in which one human being is or becomes the property of another and in which authority over the treatment of that human being, such as forcing them to perform labour, lies with the other, owning party.[13]

Enslaved people no longer had any authority over their own body. The slaveholder could use their body to make it work hard, to take care of the slaveholder or to perform sexual acts – all actions that required a body – while the person inhabiting that body was legally nothing more than an object. This situation is part of what has been called slavery's ultimate paradox.[14] Because an enslaved person in the Dutch colonial system was property in legal terms, they could not be considered to have been robbed, raped or murdered. Neither could an enslaved person own any possessions or have rights over their families. The VOC stipulated that the children, money and any other items of an enslaved person belonged to no one but his or her master, both in life and after death.[15] Conversely, slaveholders could not be held responsible for any misdemeanours or felonies committed by their enslaved workers.

Once enslaved, a person typically remained so until death. In some cases, however, individuals were able to escape this lifelong, hereditary form of servitude. Someone might be ransomed, for example, or find another way to freedom. Various societies based on slavery featured a form of manumission, or release from slavery.[16] Sometimes, release followed a predetermined number of years in slavery or the slaveholder stipulated the release of certain people in his or her will.[17] These would likely be the children of a male slaveholder and an enslaved woman, or other enslaved people for whom a certain affection was felt. Perhaps the slaveholder hoped to secure a place in heaven in this way. But release could also be a practical way of not having to bear the expense of looking after older people who had lost their usefulness in the eyes of the slaveholder.[18] Ironically, manumission preserved the system rather than undermined it. In an otherwise hopeless existence, the possibility of release provided a spark of hope, and therefore could be a reason to work hard after all. The possibility of release varied widely from one society and from one type of slavery to another. The vast majority of the millions of enslaved men and women remained someone else's property their entire lives, as did their children and grandchildren, and *their* children and grandchildren.

Many different forms of slavery existed in Asia and Africa prior to the arrival of Europeans. Sometimes people were enslaved for life, but there was also slavery of a temporary nature, for instance until a debt was repaid. Slavery within local communities did not often involve a market. Rather, people were assigned to wealthy families, for whom they worked as domestics, farm labourers or artisans.[19] The European expansion resulted in an unprecedented scaling up and hardening of the existing systems. Moreover, the Europeans implemented a thorough uniformization of the slavery system's legal parameters, which had hitherto featured many local variations and therefore many different rules as well.

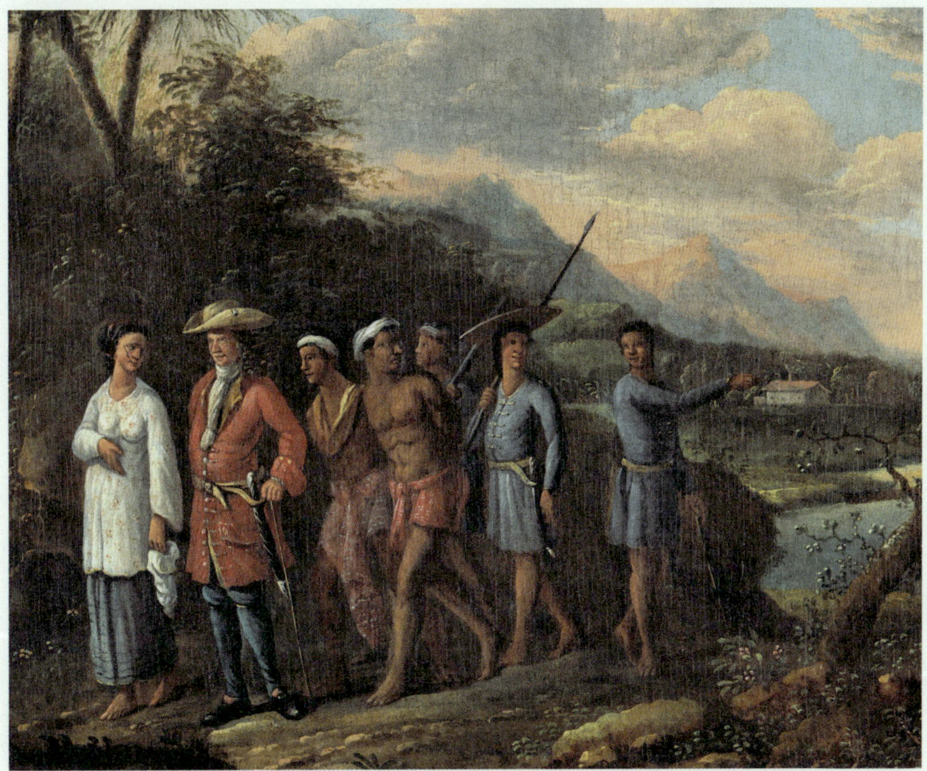

fig. 3 **Dutch merchant and his wife with enslaved servants in a hill landscape, anonymous, 1700–1725**

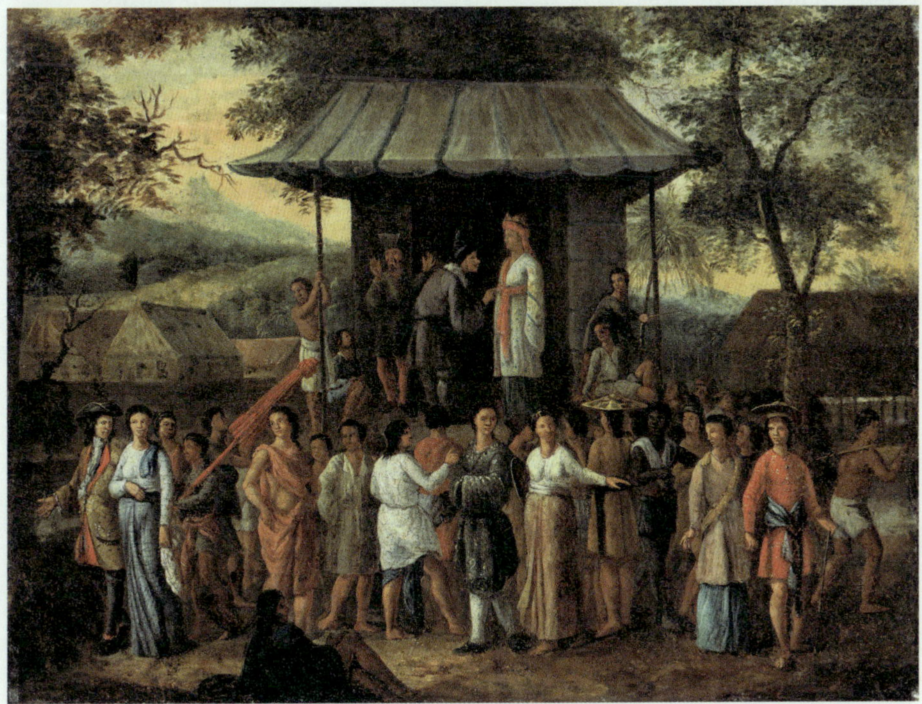

fig. 4 **Slave market, possibly in the environs of Batavia, anonymous, 1700–1725**

displacement as instrument

Displacement was an important instrument within the colonial system of slavery. People were violently taken out of their environments and moved to different, distant lands, forced to leave behind their family ties, languages, cultures and religion. This displacement made resistance to the system virtually impossible and exacerbated the anonymity of enslaved people. Throughout the history of the transatlantic trade, millions of people were transported from the west coast of Africa to the Americas. In the area around the Indian Ocean, millions of people were similarly shipped by sea: from Southeast Asia to South Asia and vice versa; and from East Africa or Madagascar to South and Southeast Asia, and vice versa. And from all of these areas, people were transported to South Africa as well. Once they arrived, a life in slavery awaited them, with no guarantee that whatever they might build up in terms of social structure and culture would not have to be left behind again if they were sold on. Slammat van Bougis was well aware of this: 'If the boss wants to sell me, let him sell me,' he replied to the overseer when reprimanded for smoking a pipe. Slammat probably felt he had nothing to lose, but it was also the case that enslaved people, after a time, became attached to their new soil: the soil on which new relationships were forged and children were born. So slaveholders who wished to sell part of their 'slave stock' after several years to another slaveholder had to reckon with mass protests.[20]

Such large-scale forced relocations had a major impact on the lives of the people who had to endure this, as well as on the lives of those left behind. In songs passed down from generation to generation, we sometimes hear echoes of the experiences of the enslaved people themselves, of the tension of being simultaneously person and property. They counterbalance colonial sources, such as inventories in which enslaved people are listed as anonymous units in the categories 'man', 'woman', 'boy', or 'girl', among the livestock and the tools. A song from Curaçao, for instance, conveys the pain of parents who had no say over what happened to their children. They could not protect their children because, in the colonial system, they did not belong to them. Children could be sold by the slaveholder and thereby separated from their mother and father, with no consideration given to the children's despair.

Katibu ta galiña, mama
Katibu ta galiña
Shon ta bende nos, mama
Katibu ta galiña

Slaves are chickens, mama
Slaves are chickens
The landlord sells us, mama
Slaves are chickens

The song *Kanaldorp se mense* (The people of Canal Town) from South Africa tells of enslaved people who had to leave their family and friends behind when they were sold to a new 'owner'.[21] The song is sung from the perspective of the enslaved worker Aderjan's lover and ends with the wish that the female slaveholder (the *nonna*) lie in a *taaibos*, a thorny shrub common to the area.

Hoor wat sê die mense,
Kanaldorp se mense:
Al wil my ma nie hê nie,
Al wil my ma pa nie hê nie,
Maar Aderjan bly nie hier nie.
Wat word dan van my?
Die nonna wat die bolla dra,
Laat sy in die taaibos lê.[22]

Listen to what the people are saying,
The people of Canal Town:
Even if my mother doesn't want to,
Even if my father doesn't want to,
But Aderjan cannot stay here.
What will become of me?
The madam with her hair in a bun,
Let her lie in the taaibos.

who could be enslaved?

At the time of the founding of the trading companies in the early seventeenth century, slavery officially no longer existed in the Dutch Republic. Papal decrees at the end of the Middle Ages had outlawed the enslavement of Christians, and serfdom and slavery had largely become a thing of the past in western Europe. The conquest and colonization of overseas territories, however, made the question of whether a human being could be made a slave relevant once more. The Spanish and Portuguese, who preceded the Dutch in the colonization of the world, employed slavery on a massive scale. It soon became clear to those in power that the position of Spain and Portugal in Asia and the Atlantic region could only be overtaken if the Dutch Republic also made use of slavery. But was this legitimate?

An incident in Middelburg in 1596 shows that allowing the slave trade was not initially a self-evident proposition to all. A group of 100 enslaved African people were captured from a Portuguese ship by Zeelanders. The captain brought the captive men and women to Middelburg to sell them, but the city authorities refused to grant permission. The Estates of Zeeland took the same point of view and explicitly pointed out that these people were baptized Christians and therefore could not be sold as slaves. The fact that in all probability the Portuguese had baptized the captives before the sea voyage as a matter of routine made no difference to the Middelburg authorities: baptized meant baptized.

Neither was the VOC, at its founding in 1602, immediately interested in human trafficking and slave labour. Gerard Reynst, the VOC's first governor general, asked the Heren Zeventien (Lords Seventeen, the company's central board of shareholders) for permission to enslave people in 1614. The governor general represented the company's highest authority in Asia, but the VOC was run from the Dutch Republic by the Lords Seventeen. Reynst wanted to put enslaved men to work in the recently conquered territories, but approval from Amsterdam was not forthcoming. He reiterated his request the following year:

> We and those of our nation ... are not able to perform the labour in these quarters. The heat is too great and the drink in almost all places too plentiful. I have already found that a slave can do more work than two or more of our nation would do, if only I could obtain and employ slaves as others have done, they would be useful in our service.[23]

Increasing numbers of Dutch people in Asia were in favour of slavery, but there was still resistance back in the Republic.[24] After the founding of Batavia as the company's headquarters in 1619, however, a steadily growing demand for cheap manpower emerged. Demand grew still more when the VOC, having waged war on and massacred the local inhabitants of the Banda Islands in 1621 in order to take over the production of nutmeg, needed labourers to work on the plantations.[25] And with the founding of the WIC in 1621 and expansion in the Atlantic region, it also became clear that the Dutch could only take over the territories of the Portuguese and hold on to it if they participated in the slave trade.

The Dutch jurist Hugo de Groot argued in his *De iure belli ac pacis* (On the law of war and peace) in 1625 that a person is free by nature but can be enslaved if he or she is taken prisoner in a legitimate war, or when a sentence of death is commuted to slavery. According to De Groot, therefore, slavery could not be objected to on legal grounds. Ethnicity played no role in his thesis, but such an argument was intrinsic to the viewpoint of some Protestant church leaders beginning in the second quarter of the seventeenth century. In the late sixteenth and early seventeenth centuries, slavery was still rejected by Protestants and described as a 'popish aberration' of the Spanish and Portuguese. Their eighth commandment, after all, stated, 'Thou shalt not steal' – and that implied 'human theft' as well.[26] This view changed after the establishment of the trading companies, when governors of the colonized territories asked permission to make use of enslaved people. From the same pulpit, many pastors now argued that the Old Testament said that slavery was acceptable because African people were predestined to slavery. Reference was made to the story of Ham, who mocked his father Noah when the latter, drunk after the Flood, lay naked and sleeping it off in his tent. When Noah later heard of Ham's behaviour, he cursed Ham's son Canaan and with him condemned all Africans to eternal servitude.[27] Although there is no explicit mention in the Bible of Ham being Black, he came to symbolize 'the cursed Black', which referred to Asians as well as Africans, and his 'curse' was used to legitimize the slave trade.[28] Only a few clergymen called this 'Biblical evidence' into question from the pulpit and pointed out the inequity of the system.[29]

The Dutch populace was nonetheless aware that a life in slavery was nothing to be envied. In the seventeenth and eighteenth centuries, Dutch people devoted themselves to freeing 'Christian slaves', European men enslaved after their ships were raided by pirates from the North African coast. Collections were organized and taxes levied to provide the 'slave fund' with enough money to free these unfortunate sailors from slavery.[30] These fellow Christians deserved to be rescued at all costs, and as long as there were sufficient funds, this was in fact possible. Enslaved Africans, on the contrary, were predestined to serve the white man – this was the conclusion drawn from the story of Ham. This destiny carried over from generation to generation and meant exclusion from equal participation in society. In this way, skin colour became a factor within colonial society that made it possible to identify 'the Other' – in other words, to determine which people could be made into slaves. It is an aspect of colonial slavery that continues to be felt to this day. The creation of the concept of 'the Other' also played a role on the other side of the world, in the places where the VOC operated. Throughout VOC territory, the question of whether people were 'enslavable' hinged on whether they were Christian or not. In the southwest of India, the caste to which a person belonged played a part as well.[31]

In the process, an increasingly clear hierarchy among continents and population groups was constructed based on elements such as skin colour and religion, a hierarchy that legitimized who could be enslaved and who could not. But what did people back in the Republic know of life in slavery? The question of how extensive people's knowledge was of slavery in the Dutch colonies, as well as the degree to which they were interested in its application, is difficult to answer. Until the early seventeenth century, travellers' accounts focused primarily on local forms of slavery in Africa and Asia; the slave trade was seldom discussed.[32] This changed with the publication of Olfert Dapper's *Naukeurige Beschrijvingen der Afrikaensche gewesten* (Precise descriptions of the African regions) in 1668. The reader found in the book mainly a justification for the slave trade, as Dapper made reference to most African peoples' natural predisposition towards slavery – to European eyes – and the local application of slavery.[33]

Newspapers had a larger audience at this time than books and were also more up to date with current developments, thanks to news brought back by sailors, among others. Recent research into reporting on slavery through this medium clearly shows that there was a growing awareness from 1630 to 1650 of the struggle against the Portuguese in order to expand colonial possessions overseas, but that there was no attention paid to the use of enslaved people, let alone the conditions in which they were forced to work.[34] This was in sharp contrast to the fate of the Christian slaves. For a long period, any visual image that people in the Republic might have had of the work on a plantation was defined by the Brazilian sugar mills drawn on location by Frans Post, which had found their way to a wider audience in etchings (see p. 70, fig. 4). At the beginning of the eighteenth century, this information was effortlessly transferred into publications about Suriname.[35] These pictures showed nothing of the harsh working conditions, and the slave trade – except for the drawing Zacharias Wagener made in Recife, Brazil (see pp. 66–67) – also remained out of the field of vision of most Dutch people.

For those who were interested, therefore, books and newspapers provided some information in the course of the seventeenth century. And of course there were also people who could relate stories first hand – returning VOC and WIC functionaries; people who had been brought to the Dutch Republic in slavery to work there as servants; and free Black people who made their living as sailors, for example. Many Dutch cities and towns were home to people with dark skin; they were part of the social landscape and would have contributed to the wider awareness of what was taking place in the country's colonies (fig. 5).[36]

A great deal of research still needs to be done to get a better insight into what people in the Dutch Republic were able to know about slavery, but it is clear that the idea of enslaving people was not immediately self-evident or accepted. From the beginning, there were opposing voices and debates. And although it is not possible to pinpoint the precise moment the Dutch decided to stop seeing slavery as a 'popish aberration', it is clear that they made deliberate use of slavery in order to be able to play a role in global trade.[37]

expansion of a colonial empire

The Portuguese, in the sixteenth century, were the first European power in Asia to attempt to conquer a trading position, followed by the Dutch, under the flag of the VOC, from 1602 onwards. The States General had granted the VOC the exclusive right to carry out trade in the name of the Dutch Republic in Asia and, if necessary, to deploy military operations there for the purpose. Shares of stock were sold to anyone who could afford them, and provincial offices were established in the six cities of Amsterdam, Middelburg, Rotterdam, Delft, Hoorn and Enkhuizen, each with its own directors. Delegates from these chambers formed the Lords Seventeen, who jointly set central policy from Amsterdam.

The lands around the Indian Ocean and the Indonesian archipelago already had a long and varied history of international trade, with routes over land and sea, when the Europeans appeared on the scene. The VOC made use of these routes and established, often by savage force, a vast network of trading posts all around the Indian Ocean. The initial expansion in the Moluccas (Maluku Islands in Indonesia) was followed by the conquest and destruction of Javakarta (or Jacatra), Java, in 1619. On the remains of this city, the company founded Batavia as its headquarters in Asia. With the massacre of the inhabitants of the Banda Islands (1621) and the conquest of Formosa (present-day Taiwan, 1622–1663), the company was quickly able to expand its sphere of power. Attention subsequently turned to the regions around the Indian Ocean. First, the strategic port of Malacca in present-day Malaysia was captured (1641), followed by a series of conquests that gave the VOC control over the coast of Sri Lanka (Galle, 1641; Colombo and Jaffna, 1654–1658). In the second half of the seventeenth century, the empire further expanded with the establishment of a trading post at the Cape of Good Hope, South Africa (1652); the conquest of Kochi and the setting up of strategic settlements on the Malabar and Coromandel coasts, in southern India (1663); and the continuing expansion of power in the Indonesian archipelago. In addition, the VOC was granted permission to build forts or trading offices in major trading hubs, including Bengal and Surat in northeast and northwest India, respectively (fig. 6).

While the VOC strongholds in the Moluccas, Banda Islands and Sri Lanka were significant production areas for spices like nutmeg, cloves and cinnamon, the Cape of Good Hope and the region around Batavia quickly developed into production areas for sugar, rice, coffee, livestock and wine.[38] After a time, slavery and the slave trade were present in all the trading posts. But slavery was also used in VOC activities connected to military expansion, administration, and production and transport of trading goods. Large numbers of enslaved Asian and African people were disseminated across an area that stretched from Japan to South Africa, with focal points in southern India, Sri Lanka and parts of Indonesia. The VOC, but other European parties as well, traded alongside and in competition with Asian, African and Arab administrators and merchants. The arrival of the Dutch provided a strong stimulus to the slave trade and the production of merchandise through slavery.

trade in the atlantic

The first Dutch trading activities in the Atlantic region date from the end of the sixteenth century and arose from a shortage of salt and sugar on the European market as a result of the Eighty Years' War. Spain and Portugal had long been active in this area and claimed a monopoly on trade. The Dutch needed salt to pickle North Sea herring, a major export. When Portugal and Spain formed a single political entity, the Iberian Union, in 1580, the Dutch Republic was at war not only with Spain but also with its most important salt supplier, Portugal. Sugar was primarily purchased in Antwerp, where refineries processed and marketed the raw sugar from the Atlantic region. The occupation of Antwerp by the Spaniards in 1585 meant the loss of this supply as well. The shortage of salt for the herring fleet was so acute that the Dutch decided to extract salt themselves on the salt flats of Venezuela. For sugar, they explored the Caribbean. They also ventured to the west coast of Africa for *grein* (a kind of pepper), ivory and gold. And in North America they sailed up the North River (the Hudson) to obtain beaver and otter pelts. All of these trading activities proved lucrative for the Dutch, which provided an impetus to investigate whether, following the model of the Dutch East India Company, forces might be joined in a Dutch West India Company.

Like the VOC, the WIC was a commercial enterprise that was founded partly using private capital and which had been granted by the States General a number of political powers, stipulated in a charter. There were five chambers: Amsterdam, Zeeland, Maze (Rotterdam), Stad en Lande (Groningen) and the Noorderkwartier (Hoorn), and a board of directors, the Heren XIX (Lords Nineteen), which consisted of delegates from these chambers. All Dutch trade west of the Cape of Good Hope fell under the monopoly of the WIC. The main trading activities took place in Africa, Brazil, Suriname, the Antilles and parts of North America. Privateering (the capture of enemy ships in wartime) was also one of the WIC's tasks, as was the expansion of overseas territories.

The first main objective of the WIC was the conquest of Brazil, which was in the hands of the Portuguese. The Brazilian provinces of Paraíba, Itamaracá and Pernambuco in the northeast were particularly sought after because of the vast profits that could be made there from the production of and trade in sugar. The indigenous inhabitants of the area occupied by the Portuguese were Tupi. When, in the view of the Portuguese, enslaved Tupi people no longer sufficed on the plantations, enslaved Africans were put to work. The first Dutch conquest over the Portuguese took place in San Salvador (Bahia), in 1624, but this did not last long. In the meantime, the WIC was also fighting the Portuguese on the west coast of Africa, but there too it was initially unable to defeat them definitively. The largest slave depot of the Portuguese, in Luanda, Angola, was attacked in vain, like the slave depot at Elmina (in present-day Ghana) in 1625. The conflict with the Portuguese was costing the WIC a great deal of money for very little result. In 1628, admiral Piet Heyn captured the Spanish 'silver fleet' in Cuba's Bay of Matanzas. The battle brought in enough money to outfit a war fleet, in order to make a new attempt to defeat the Portuguese in Brazil. This time, the Dutch were successful. In 1630, Olinda, the Portuguese capital of Pernambuco, was conquered. This is considered the founding of the colony of Dutch Brazil.

At the end of 1636, Johan Maurits of Nassau-Siegen was appointed governor general of Dutch Brazil by the States General, in order to bring the continuing conflict with the Portuguese to an end and to expand the Dutch colony and make it profitable. Like the Portuguese before them, the Dutch set enslaved African people to work cultivating and processing the sugar cane. Johan Maurits therefore urged the Lords Nineteen to resume military operations against the Portuguese on the west coast of Africa, in order to guarantee the supply of manpower. In 1637, the Portuguese fort of Elmina was captured, followed by the conquest of the slave market in Luanda in 1641. The Dutch were now active in the slave trade from Senegal to Angola (fig. 7).[39]

The sugar plantations in Dutch Brazil were initially the most important market for the people transported from Africa. From 1630 to 1650, approximately 25,000 enslaved people were shipped to Brazil.[40] In 1654, the Portuguese were able to retake the last parts of Brazil occupied by the Dutch. The end of this colony did not however mean the end of the Dutch slave trade in the Atlantic region. The WIC controlled important forts and support points on the west coast of Africa, and Essequibo, Demerara and Berbice (in present-day Guyana) were conquered around 1618, followed by Curaçao (1634), Aruba, Bonaire and Sint Eustatius (1636), Saba (1640) and Sint Maarten (1648) in the Caribbean. Curaçao became a major destination for the slave ships, along with Sint Eustatius and the coast of Guyana. The natural harbour made the island suitable as a transhipment port for goods and enslaved people, and furthermore Curaçao was favourably situated in relation to the colonies in the Atlantic region. In 1667, Suriname was conquered from the British by the Zeelanders, after the country had been successively occupied by the French, the Dutch and the British since 1630, ending up in British hands in 1650. Suriname did not deliver the Zeelanders the profits they had hoped for, and in 1683 they sold the colony to the Society of Suriname, a joint venture between the city of Amsterdam, the WIC and the Van Aerssen van Sommelsdijck family.

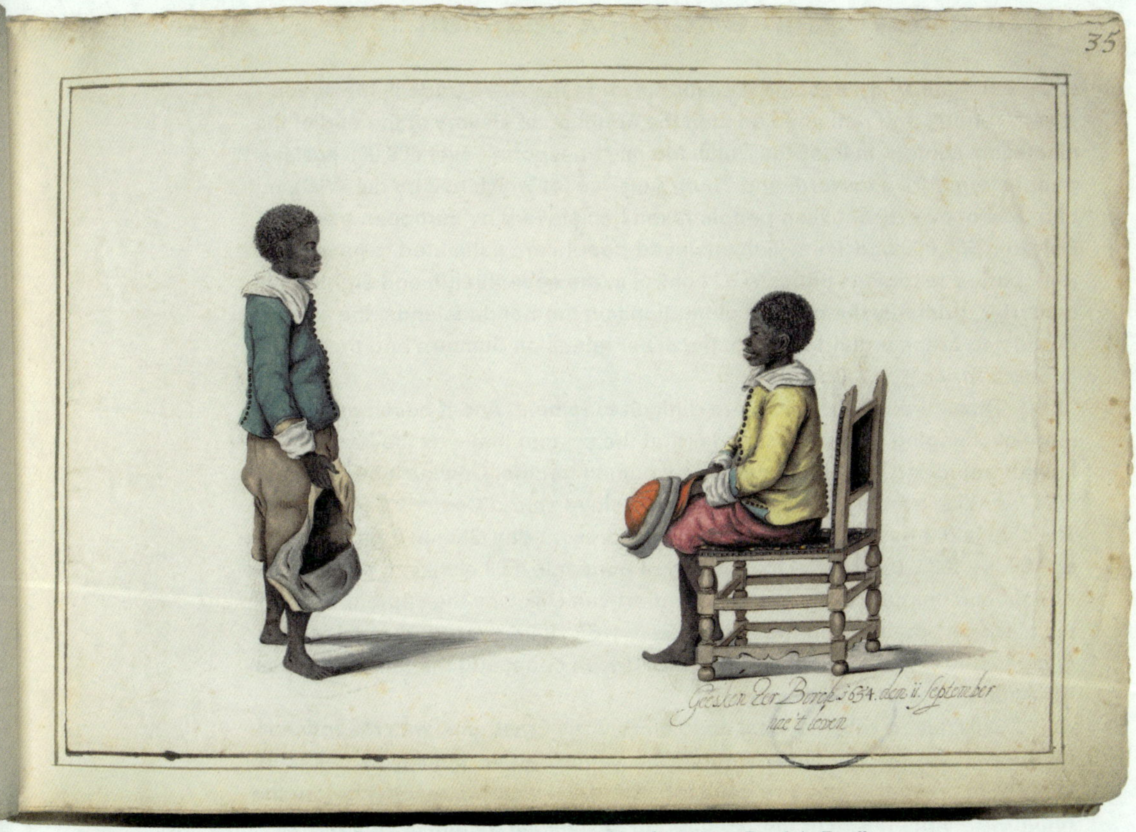

fig. 5 **These two young men posed for Gesina ter Borch in Zwolle on 11 September 1654**

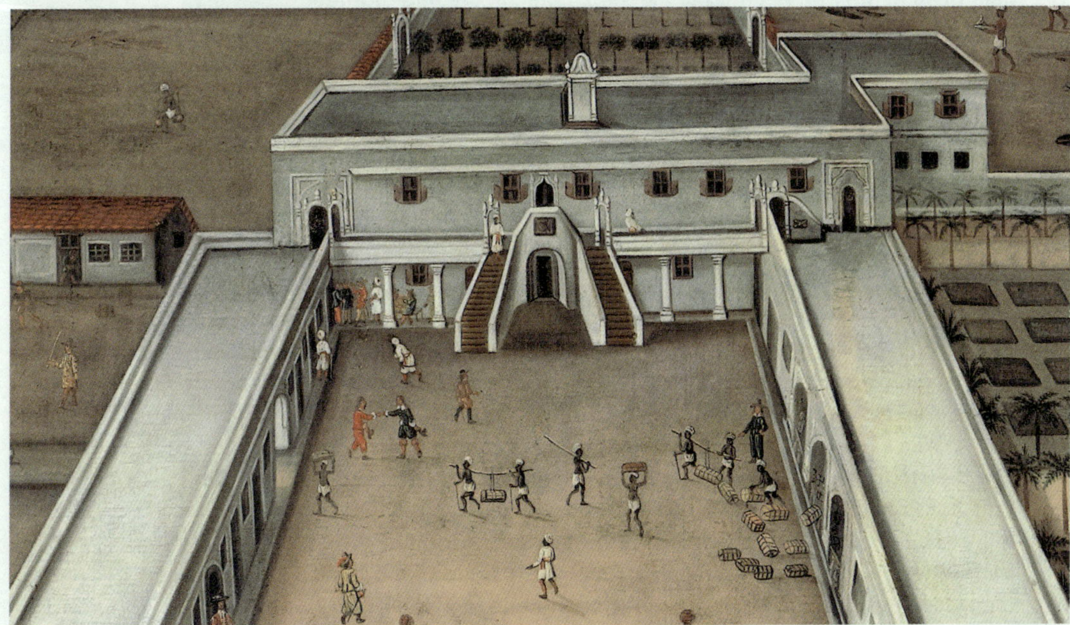

fig. 6 **Courtyard of the trading post of the Dutch East India Company in Hooghly in Bengal, 1665. The slave quarters are probably located in the building at rear left (detail of pp. 154–155)**

the slave ship *d'coninck salomon*

The Netherlands had become a major player in the slave trade in the seventeenth century and remained so until the abolition of slavery at the end of the nineteenth century. In total, the Dutch forcibly transported over 600,000 enslaved people from Africa to North and South America (of which half by the WIC), out of a total of over 12.5 million people taken into slavery by European traders.[41] Between 660,000 and 1.1 million enslaved people are estimated to have been transported to regions under VOC control in the seventeenth and eighteenth centuries, primarily the nutmeg plantations on the Banda Islands, the sugar-producing areas around Batavia, the silver mines on Sumatra and the farms in South Africa.

These are numbers that are difficult to fathom. And it becomes even more challenging when we consider that the system that was the basis of this human trafficking was implemented by human beings. One such human pawn was Jan Wils, a member of the crew of the slave ship *d'Coninck Salomon*.[42] The ship had arrived in the port of Accra (in present-day Ghana) from Rotterdam on 10 May 1686. By order of the Society of Suriname, 508 enslaved people were bought and shipped to Suriname. Leendert van Dijk was the captain, Jan Wills the clerk who maintained the ship's log (fig. 8). His daily report provides a glimpse into the passing of days off the African coast and the journey across the Atlantic Ocean to Suriname.

Wils, along with the local head clerk, Joris Ernsthuijs, was responsible for the purchase of people in West Africa, preferably as quickly as possible in order to prevent premature death on board.[43] It was two months before the required 500 people were loaded onto the *d'Coninck Salomon*. This was a horribly long time for those who had been brought aboard first and had to spend their days in the low, hot hold of the ship. Later, in the mid-eighteenth century, it could sometimes be up to six months before a ship had enough people on board. Wils and Ernsthuijs tried to trade in different places along the coast. The first fourteen men and nine women came aboard in Accra. The hold of the ship contained a supply of cowrie shells, red coral, French brandy, muskets, gunpowder, bedsheets and tobacco, which must have been enough to buy 500 African people in Guinea, the coastal region of present-day Ghana, Togo and Benin. Most of these men, women and children would have been captured in inland areas by African or Arab slave traders operating on behalf of local rulers. When the captives got to the coast, they had often already been marching in the broiling sun for several weeks. The men, women and children were then gathered in the Dutch forts, examined and branded. After this the captives often had to wait weeks, sometimes months, until there were enough people, before they were sold to European traders who shipped them to the Atlantic region.

Wils's report shows how company and personal interests intertwined. The director general of the WIC in Elmina, Nicolaas Sweerts, and his head clerk Ernsthuijs also tried to make a profit for themselves, for instance by exchanging the payment goods shipped from the Netherlands for other commodities, under the pretext that the latter were more in demand on the Gold Coast (in present-day Ghana), or by purchasing old and sometimes sick people

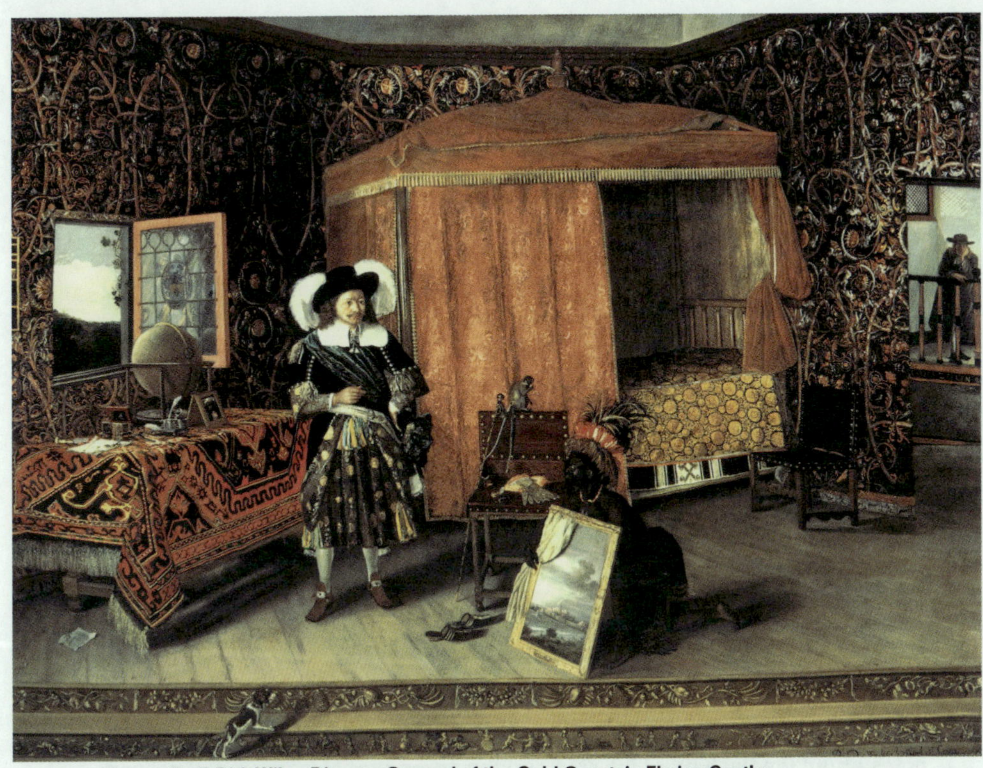

fig. 7 **Dirk Wilre, Director General of the Gold Coast, in Elmina Castle**
Pieter de Wit, 1669

cheaply, since they had no personal interest in healthy and strong labourers ending up on the other side of the ocean. On Monday 3 June 1686, Wils notes: 'bought 6 men and 3 women. And 2 of the men slaves who arrived half dead have died.' Wils protested against these practices, not out of compassion but out of fear that his client, the Society of Suriname, would not be satisfied. His objections were brushed aside by Sweerts, who relied on his higher position within the WIC.[44]

On board, the men were usually separated from the women and children, and then the two groups were packed into spaces in which they could scarcely sit or move. Since the enslaved men and women came from different parts of Africa, they were often unable to understand one another. The voyage across the sea – a vast, raging body of water that the people from inland regions of the continent had never seen – must have only magnified the fear and despair. Ripped away from family, land and possessions, they faced a precarious and miserable existence.

On 15 June the *d'Coninck Salomon* sailed for her final destination of Paramaribo, and Wils drew up the balance in his journal. Aboard were 333 men, 3 boys, 167 women and 5 girls, a total of 508 enslaved Africans. A man had died earlier that day, and quite a few people had died in the preceding days as well. They would not experience the dreadful voyage across the ocean and a hopeless life in slavery.[45] Another 54 members of the group would die on the journey – a little over 10 per cent.[46] 'Threw overboard this day 4 men slaves who had died,' Wils writes on Wednesday 26 June. In the journal, Wils makes notes about the flushing of the ship and the spreading of incense, the delivery of provisions, the daily recording of people ill with pox, mange, scurvy or exhaustion, and the crew's efforts to deliver as many people as possible alive in Suriname by giving them citrus fruits, some extra food, or a pipe and some jenever. On Thursday 20 June he writes:

> We freed 30 of the most emaciated men slaves from the shackles and we also had the cook give them double rations of food and palm oil. Also unshackled the previous group, of 80 men slaves, because they were in very dire shape, and this day 3 men slaves died. We had spread incense aboard our ship this morning as previously noted and we gave every slave a drink of jenever.[47]

The journal provides a glimpse into the daily routine on board and, unintentionally, into the lives of the African people who had become merchandise. However, these remain practical notations from Wils's perspective. He does not record any personal thoughts or remarks that would indicate he saw the merchandise as people as well. And what the enslaved people aboard the *d'Coninck Salomon* themselves thought is entirely unknown. The many stories about the collective resistance of enslaved people on board the slave ships, and about men and women who jumped overboard out of desperation, tell us enough, however. Surviving documents record 493 slave ship uprisings that took place over the entire period of the slave trade, but there must have been many more.[48] If the crew managed to regain the upper hand, the uprising would

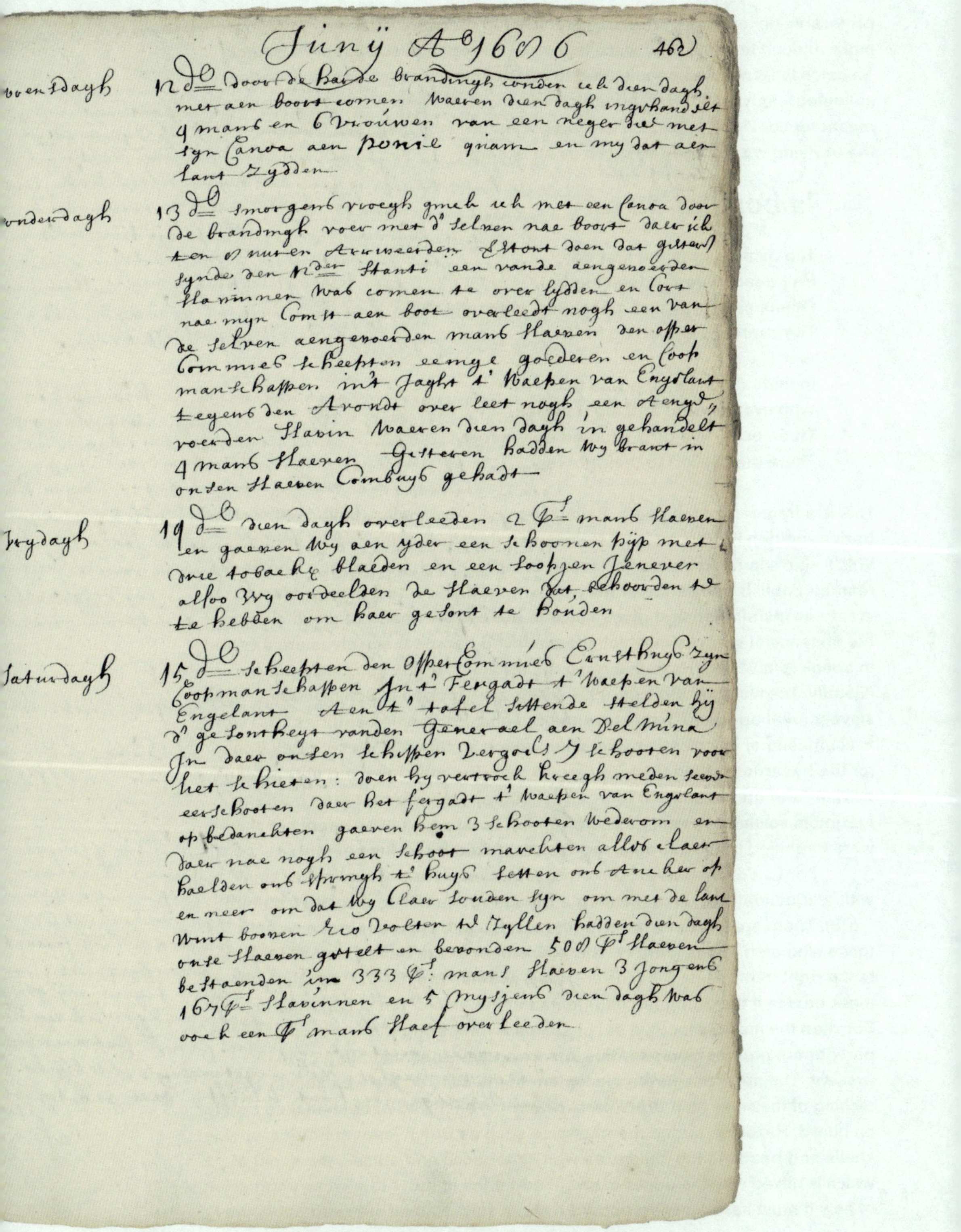

Junij Ao 1686 462

oensdagh 12 do Door de harde brandingh conden ick dien dagh met aen boort comen waeren dien dagh ingehandelt 4 mans en 6 vrouwen van een neger die met syn Canoa aen boort quam en my dat aen lant zydden

onderdagh 13 do smorgens vroegh ginck ick met een Canoa door de brandingh voer met d' selven nae boort daer ick ten 8 uuren arriveerden Etstont doen dat gestervt synde den 12den stanti een vande aengevoerden slavinnen was comen te overlyden en cort nae myn Comst aen boort overleedt nogh een van de selven aengevoerden mans slaeven den opper Commies scheepten eenige goederen en Coopmanschappen in't Jaght t' Waepen van Engelant tegens den Avondt over leet nogh een aengevoerden Slavin waeren dien dagh ingehandelt 4 mans slaeven Gesterven hadden wy brant in onsen slaeven Combuys gehadt

Vrydagh 14 do dien dagh overleeden 2 Ps mans slaeven en gaeven wy aen yder een schoonen pyp met drie tobackx blaeden en een soopjen Jenever alsoo wy oordeelden de slaeven het schoorden te te hebben om haer gesont te houden

Saturdagh 15 do scheepten den opper Commies Constbuys zyn Coopmanschappen Jnt' Fergadt t' Waepen van Engelant Aen t' tafel settende stelden hy d' gesontheyt vanden Generael aen Delmina Jn daer onsen schipper Vergoels 7 schooten voor het schieten: doen hy vertrock kreegh meden seven eerschooten daer het fergadt t' Waepen van Engelant op bedanckten gaeven hem 3 schooten wederom en daer nae nogh een schoot maeckten alles claer haelden ons springh t' huys setten ons Ancker op en neer om dat wy claer souden syn om met de lant wint booven Rio Volter te zyllen hadden dien dagh onse slaeven getelt en bevonden 500 Ps slaeven bestaende in 333 Ps mans slaeven 3 Jongens 167 Ps slavinnen en 5 mysjens dien dagh was oock een Ps mans slaef overleeden

fig. 8 **Journal of the ship *d'Coninck Salomon* by clerk Jan Wils, 1686**

preferably be left unreported in the ship's log, because enslaved people were more difficult to sell if they were known to be rebellious. On the *d'Coninck Salomon* too, enslaved people tried to seize control. However, the weapons they collected – knives, sharpened nails and pieces of firewood that were actually meant for cooking – were discovered prematurely by the crew. The leader of the uprising was hanged to serve as an example.

la bouche du roi

The dying began the first day,
Half dead were fourteen loaded,
Others sick, grey and emaciated, without a smile
The captain summed up his loss

In thirty days the ship was full
With five hundred and eight slaves,
Three boys, five girls counted on the roll:
There they sailed to their graves

This is a fragment of the poem 'Ballade van de slavenhaler' (Ballad of the slave trader), written in 1963 by Jan Marinus van der Linde after he had studied Wils's ship's log.[49] Romuald Hazoumè, an artist of Yoruba heritage from Benin, read an English translation of the poem in the 1990s and it inspired him to create an installation that gives voice to the people aboard a slave ship, in the absence of sources in which the enslaved people themselves are allowed to speak (pp. 58–61). Hazoumè gave the artwork the title *La Bouche du Roi* (literally, The mouth of the king, 1997–2005), after a place in Benin where a major slave market operated in the seventeenth and eighteenth centuries. The work is composed of 304 plastic petrol cans, which are used in present-day Benin for the hazardous, illegal smuggling of fuel. The men involved in this black market heat up the cans to increase their capacity, so that they hold the maximum volume of petrol possible without bursting – just as people in slavery were exploited to the extreme and then replaced by a new person.

For *La Bouche du Roi*, the artist turned each petrol can into a 'mask' with unique features, representing a person with a name, a voice, a culture (fig. 9). There are smaller masks for the women and children; broken masks for those who died on the journey. The black mask at the back of the installation, to the right, represents the (current) king of Benin (pp. 60–61), and the yellow mask next to it the European middleman at the time of the slave trade (fig. 10). Between the masks stands a set of scales, symbolizing the question of which party bears greater blame for this history and its continuing legacy in the present. The artist based the placement of the cans on the well-known 1789 etching of the slave ship *Brookes*, showing the enslaved people packed tightly on board. Hazoumè added merchandise such as Dutch jenever bottles, cowrie shells and beads to the masks, as well as tobacco and spices, the scent of which is mixed with the odour of sweat and urine in order to give an impression of how it must have smelled aboard a slave ship. Names are read out in the

African languages Yoruba, Mahi and Wémé, alternated with an elegy with a repeated refrain in English: 'Where are we going? What is our destination? Deign, Oshoun, to bring us back home. Help! Help! Obatala, come and rescue us! Can you bring us back home?'

With this installation, Hazoumè is not just explicitly looking to the past but examining the present, as evidenced by the black mask of the king of Benin and the short accompanying film of young men carrying petrol over unpaved roads on their mopeds. These allude to the problematic legacy of the colonial past in modern-day Benin, a message that is also found in the motto given by the artist to his installation:

> They didn't know where they were going, but they knew where they had come from.
> Today they still don't know where they are going, and they have forgotten where they come from.

an imposed name

How a person could be made into merchandise is made painfully clear by an archival document registering a slavery transaction on the other side of the world. It is a '12-stiver document' that tells the story of China, a girl of nine or ten (fig. 11).[50] On 24 January 1768 she arrived with her mother, Silidana, at a VOC office in Bimilipatnam (Bheemunipatnam), on the east coast of India. Jan Christiaan List, a trumpeter serving the VOC, was also present, as were two witnesses he had brought along. Silidana probably belonged to a lower caste in India and was forced by 'dire poverty, and a lack of victuals' to sell her daughter.[51] She received 15 silver rupees for her child.

The VOC itself was not a party to this transaction, but it did make money from the registration and the collection of 'slave tax'.[52] These '12-stiver documents' were intended for the VOC administrative records and always contained the person's original name, their 'new' name, their gender and age, as well as the name of the seller and the name of the new 'owner'. In addition, it recorded that this was someone of a lower caste and who moreover was not of the Christian faith. The document was stamped with a seal costing 12 stivers, payable by the buyer. A '6-stiver document' was the actual sale receipt or original deed. This was kept with the enslaved person and had to be turned over to the new slaveholder at the next sale.[53] Under her new name, Rosa, China accompanied Jan List to Nagapatnam (Nagapattinam). Six years later she was sold there to Hendrik Hilmand, who sold her within six months in the same city to one Mackiel Sanders. We do not know whether this was his reason for the sale, but Hilmand made a profit from it. Rosa did not stay long with her new 'owner'; after a month she was sold to Captain Cornelis Bosch, who took her aboard his ship from Nagapatnam to South Africa, over 8,000 kilometres away. It is a striking example of the private trade by which VOC functionaries made money. On 30 March 1775, Rosa was sold for probably the last time, to Mr Jan Serrurier, owner of the Groot Constantia winery on the Cape. Her transport deed is in the archives of this family, which would seem to indicate that she was not sold again, but this is not entirely certain. Three years later, Groot Constantia came into the possession of Hendrik Cloete, including the sixteen enslaved men listed like merchandise in the inventory along with wine barrels, the wine press and other equipment. Rosa is not listed in the inventory. Perhaps she died in the intervening time, or possibly she remained in Serrurier's possession and ended up on yet another continent upon his return to Hanover in 1783.

In this history of slavery, names seem interchangeable – with a turn of a page, China became Rosa on 24 January 1768. Sometimes a slave trader would add a toponym to a person's new name, a reference to a place. It is a custom that seems mainly to have been prevalent in the context of the VOC, such as with the enslaved man Augustus van Bengalen (named after Bengal), but we also find it in WIC practice, such as with João Mina (after Elmina). For both individuals, this part of their name says nothing about the place or region where they were born; it is a reference to the place where they were sold. We do not find sources like the VOC's 6- and 12-stiver documents with the WIC, which fulfilled no regulatory role and levied no slave tax like the VOC, but rather operated as a trader itself. The archives of the WIC, when it comes to people, primarily contain categories and numbers. Ironically, we know that the ship that sailed from the west coast of Africa to Paramaribo in 1686 was called the *d'Coninck Salomon*, as well as the names of the handful of crew members. But we do not know the names of the 508 men, women and children who were aboard as merchandise. Those who survived the crossing were sold upon arrival and given new names, short and easy to pronounce, like Flora, Geluk (Luck) or Fortuijn (Fortune). These are slave names, not names chosen in freedom by parents for their children. In the Atlantic region these names were not centrally recorded, but they can be found in wills, estate inventories and legal documents describing specific events or transactions. Only at the beginning of the nineteenth century does this change, with the slave registers.[54]

Enslaved people who were sold within the transatlantic region were not only given a new name but also branded again. In Africa the brand of the trading company had been burned into their body; now it was the 'owner' who had his initials or an abbreviation of the plantation name applied, like a farmer branding livestock (fig. 12).[55] Once more it was made horrifyingly clear to these men and women that they no longer had full authority over their own bodies. Their skin was smeared with oil, whereupon the hot branding iron was briefly applied to the body and the wound cleansed with lemon juice and gunpowder.[56] Branding enabled the slaveholder to see which people were part of his property, and if an escapee was caught, it could quickly be determined to whom this person 'belonged'. For the people in slavery, branding must have been not just a physical but also a mental disfigurement.

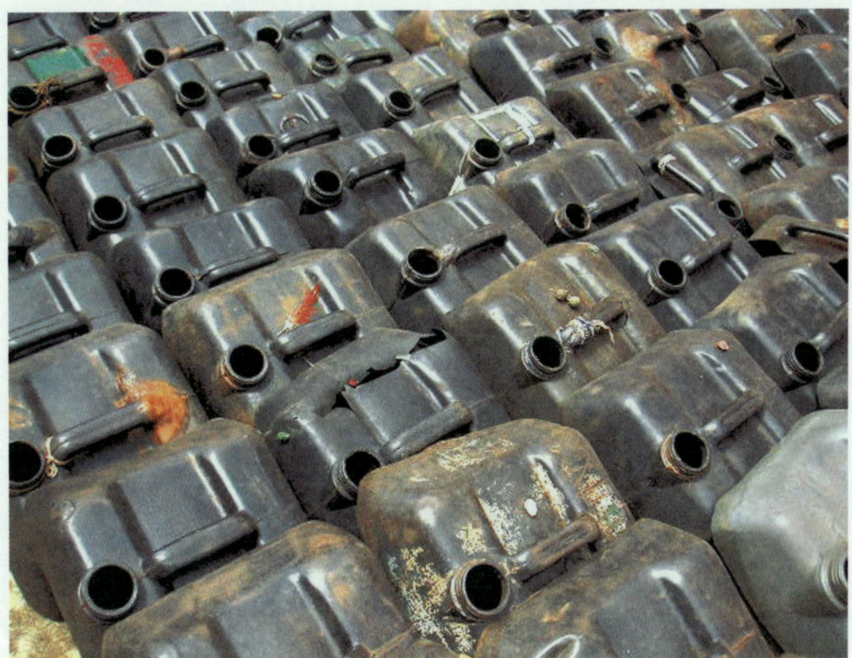

fig. 9 **Petrol cans in the installation *La Bouche du Roi*, Romuald Hazoumè, 1997–2005 (see pp. 58–61)**

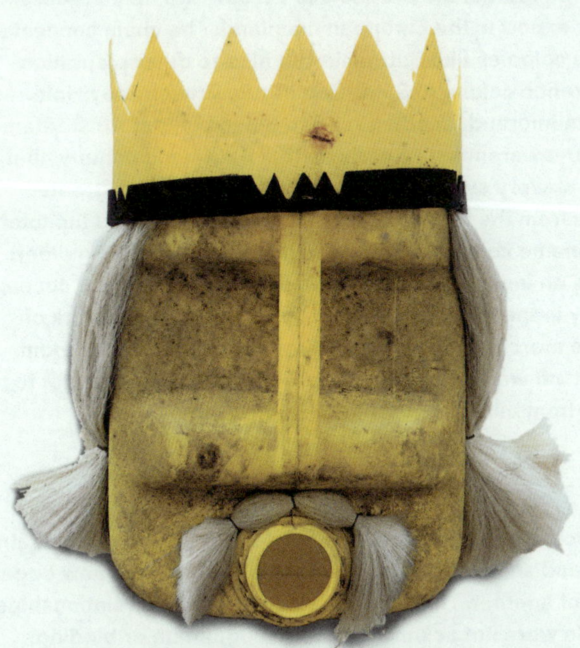

fig. 10 **'Mask' representing a European in the time of the slave trade, made from a yellow petrol can. The mask is part of the installation *La Bouche du Roi*, Romuald Hazoumè, 1997–2005 (see pp. 58–61)**

economic advantage

It was not only those directly involved, like merchants and plantation owners, who made money from the slave trade and goods produced in slavery. Anyone could participate financially, from wealthy regents to their servants (fig. 13).[57] An artisan could also make money as a supplier of products for the slave trade or for everyday life in the colonies: a founder cast the bells and carpenters worked on the shipping wharves, and we know of a blacksmith who received an order of 200 shackles from the WIC, intended for Guinea and Angola.[58] Moreover, a list of products from 1770 shows that the provinces of Holland and Zeeland were not the only ones to profit economically from the slave trade and slavery. Cheese, bacon and ham was exported from Frisian villages, printed cotton from Nigtevecht and linen from Eindhoven and Borculo; so-called *neegerhoeden* (the hats worn by the enslaved labourers) were manufactured in Den Bosch and iron pots in Deventer.[59] All of this was necessary to keep the colonies going, and it stimulated the national economy. For that same year, 1770, recent research has shown that 5.2 per cent of the gross domestic product of the Netherlands, and in fact 10.36 per cent of that of the wealthiest province of the Netherlands, Holland, was related to slavery in the Atlantic region.[60] And this does not even take into account the trade in Asia. The research looked at the distribution chains of consumer goods like sugar, coffee and tobacco that were produced in slavery. These chains ran from the supplying of the slave ships in the Netherlands, via the slave trade, to the plantations, the transport of the products to Europe and their processing in the Republic, to their export to the European mainland. The chain connected the Republic not just to colonies like Suriname but also to other plantation colonies such as the French colony of Saint-Domingue, present-day Haiti.

An anonymous memorandum addressed to the mayors of Amsterdam shows that there was an awareness, as early as the eighteenth century, that the contribution of the slavery system to the Dutch economy was greater than simply the income from the slave trade.[61] The author estimated the total contribution of the Suriname colony to the city's income at 2,238,755 guilders per year. He based this on income from the trade in sugar, coffee and cocoa; the processing industry in the city, such as sugar refineries; all the work of suppliers; and from the merchant fleet. The author ends his memorandum with the statement that 'no working man ... was found in Amsterdam not to earn some of his living from this Colony'.

in slavery

Forcibly ripped away from their home environment, language and culture, and given a different name and sometimes a brand, an enslaved person now began their life in the service of another. This was a life in which social relationships among enslaved people were not acknowledged as legitimate or binding. This did not mean, of course, that such ties did not exist, although slaveholders deliberately endeavoured to prevent their being forged. On opposite sides of the world, enslaved people were used to monitor or punish their fellow

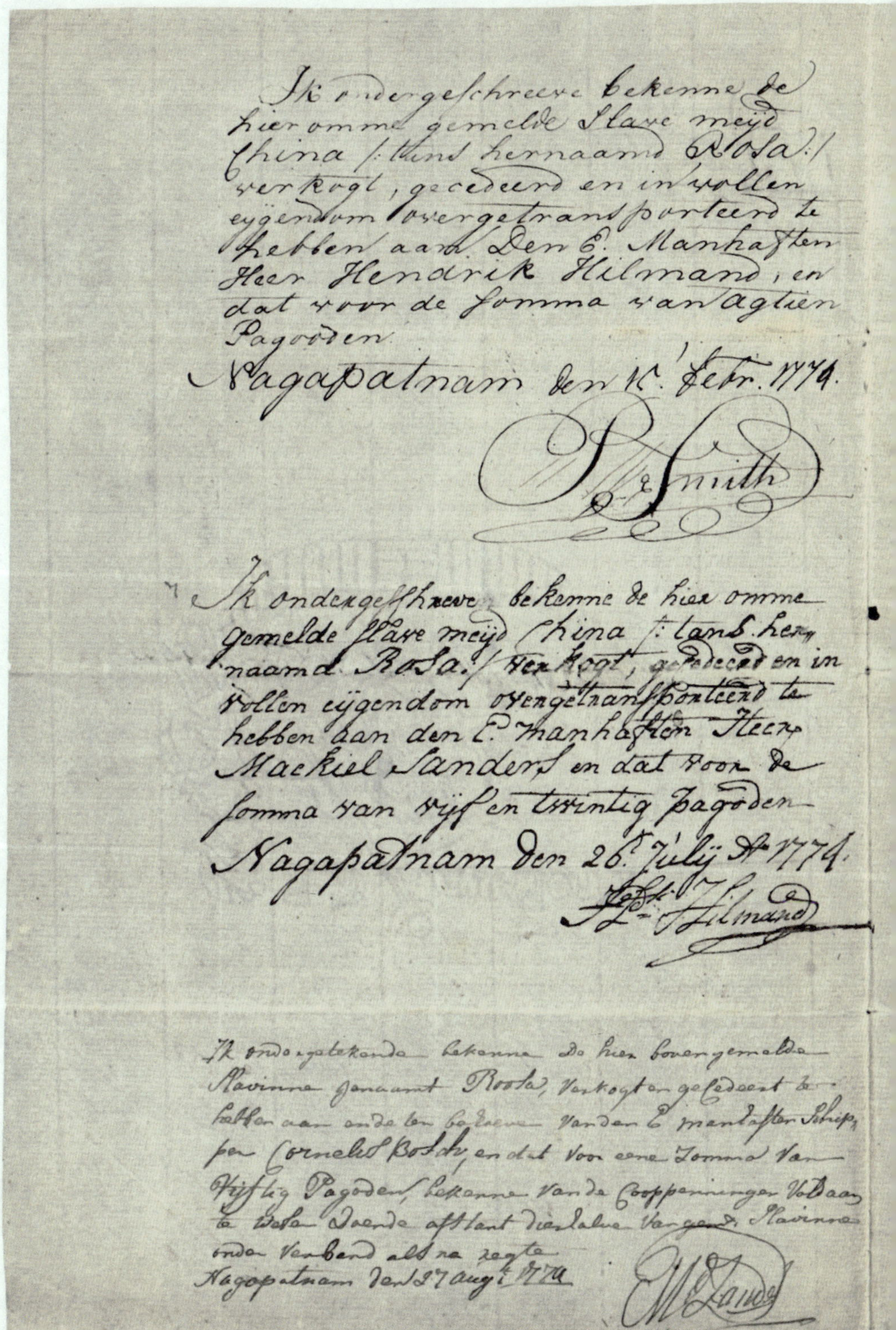

Ik ondergeschreeve bekenne de
hier omme gemelde Slave meyd
China / thans hernaamd Rosa /
verkogt, gecedeerd en in vollen
eygendom overgetransporteerd te
hebben aan Den E. Manhaften
Heer Hendrik Hilmand, en
dat voor de somma van agtien
Pagoden.

Nagapatnam den 15. Febr. 1774.

P. Smith

Ik ondergeschreeve bekenne de hier omme
gemelde slave meyd China / thans hernaamd Rosa. / verkogt, gecedeerd en in
vollen eygendom overgetransporteerd te
hebben aan den E. manhaften Heer
Mackiel Sanders en dat voor de
somma van vijf en twintig Pagoden

Nagapatnam den 26. Julij Ao 1774.

H. Hilmand

Ik ondergeteekende bekenne de hier bovengemelde
Slavinne genaamt Roosa, verkogt en gecedeert te
hebben aan ende ten behoeve van den E. manhafte Schipper
Cornelis Bosch, en dat voor eene somma van
vijftig Pagoden, bekenne van de Coopenningen voldaan
te wesen doende afstant derselve van gemelde Slavinne
onder verband als na regte
Nagapatnam den 27 aug. 1774

M. Sanders

fig. 11 **This 12-stiver document of the East India Company records that the girl China was sold to a new 'owner' multiple times, second half of the 18th century**

labourers, for instance, which led to suspicion rather than solidarity. The wide geographic distribution in the origins of the people who were enslaved, as well as an imbalance between the number of men and women on plantations, also hindered the formation of a new society with a shared culture from which comfort and strength could be drawn.[62] The fact that people were nevertheless able to build a social life under such difficult circumstances attests to their enormous courage and resilience. All over the world, new forms of music and dance emerged, as did new forms of religion and new languages in which elements from different cultures came together. Those in power were often unable to get a handle on this, felt threatened by it or responded with contempt. People in slavery drew strength and a sense of self-worth from these expressions of cultural identity: the sense of being a person and not a machine.

Violence was a constant factor in the daily lives of people in slavery. Along with the enactment of a sophisticated divide-and-rule strategy and the inculcation of a deep sense of inferiority upon the minds of the enslaved people, violence was a significant instrument for the small groups that wished to have and retain power over the majority. The punishments meted out were often cruel and numerous. Punishments were imposed by the official judicial authorities and by the slaveholders themselves, on their far-flung plantations. In both situations the enslaved person enjoyed little if any protection under the law. Serious abuse by plantation owners was occasionally punished, but it was the slaveholders who determined the punishment among themselves. Often this punishment came down to a monetary fine, and the judgement was given as little publicity as possible. This contrasts with the horrific corporal punishments that enslaved people had to endure publicly.

In the seventeenth and eighteenth centuries, slave laws were primarily focused on the maintenance of public order and peace, and not so much on the protection of enslaved people. In the eighteenth century, an increasing number of rules about physical characteristics were promulgated in the Atlantic region, designed so that those in power could continue to distinguish enslaved people from free people. In the beginning this had been a fairly simple matter: dark skin unequivocally meant that the person in question was enslaved. However, as a result of both manumission and an increase in the number of multiracial people, this distinction became less and less definitive, and administrators and slaveholders felt they needed clear rules to which they could refer. Enslaved people in Suriname, for example, were not allowed to wear shoes, a rule that was also applied in Indonesia. From the outset in colonial society in Asia, it had been far more difficult to identify enslaved people based on external characteristics. There, specific groups of free people were required to possess a 'licence', and there were clothing requirements for enslaved people and for formerly enslaved people, such as the Mardijkers in Indonesia, identifiable by their striped clothing (fig. 14).[63]

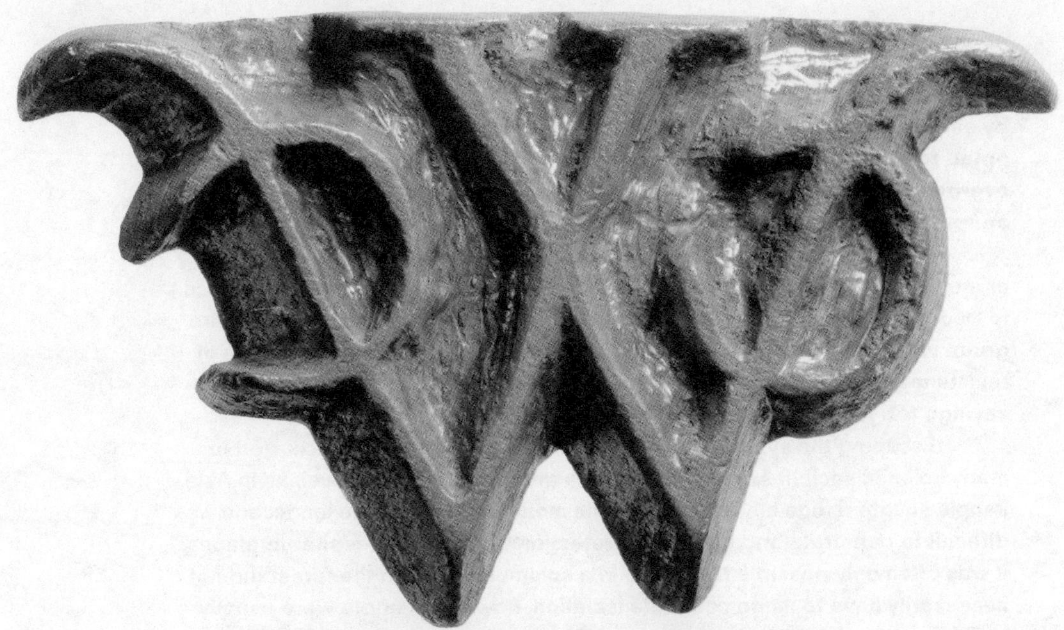

fig. 12 **Branding iron with the letters 'GWC', probably the logo of the Geoctroyeerde West-Indische Compagnie (Chartered West India Company)**

in resistance

People forced into slavery have always resisted it, as individuals or as a group: by sabotaging the system, escaping it or fighting it. Sometimes individuals opted for the most extreme way out. Acts of desperation such as jumping overboard during the crossing, suicide or the murder of their own children are poignant examples of this.

Means of sabotage used by people in slavery included working slowly or inefficiently, actions that resulted in smaller harvests but were often difficult to trace to an individual. There was, however, a significant risk that the entire group would be punished if the sabotage were discovered. Another form of resistance was to feign stupidity, a tactic alluded to in a Surinamese *odo*, or saying: *'téki joe kóni, hóli joe dom'* (be smart, act stupid).[64]

Escaping the system by building a new, parallel society occurred in many colonial societies, in South America and South Africa as well as in Asia. People sought refuge in the forests or the mountains, where the landscape was difficult to penetrate and provided protection.[65] In such inhospitable places, it was often only possible to survive in a community. Life in the forest did not necessarily have to mean complete isolation, however. People were usually well informed about what was taking place beyond their immediate environment. Information was shared – through music, among other means – about refugees, about uprisings elsewhere, and about the political developments in other colonized places and in Europe. There were also enslaved people who sought the solution in changing the colonial system from the inside out. The uprising on the French colony of Saint-Domingue in 1791 is a powerful example of resistance by enslaved people that led to the abolition of the system and inspired many other enslaved people, giving them the courage to continue their struggle.[66]

Stories about the many uprisings of enslaved people in the Atlantic region found their way into Dutch newspapers and topical illustrations. The atrocities of the struggle were often described in detail in ways that seemed to confirm for these European readers the constructed image of 'the Other', with enslaved people depicted as irrational 'creatures' far removed from 'civilized' humanity and useful only as slaves. These ideas were underpinned by racial and racist classifications produced by physicians and naturalists regarding supposed racial differences, based on the study of human remains.[67] In the hierarchy that emerged from this, the white man was always on top, while people of colour were at the bottom. Only a few preachers and a handful of patriots advocated freedom and human equality for their brothers and sisters in the Dutch colonies.[68] In plays, novels and poems, and pamphlets and publications by various enlightened societies, increasingly louder and more direct criticism of the trade in human beings and of slavery was expressed, but this did not lead to concrete steps towards abolition. It was mainly developments abroad that influenced the changing attitude towards slavery in the Netherlands.

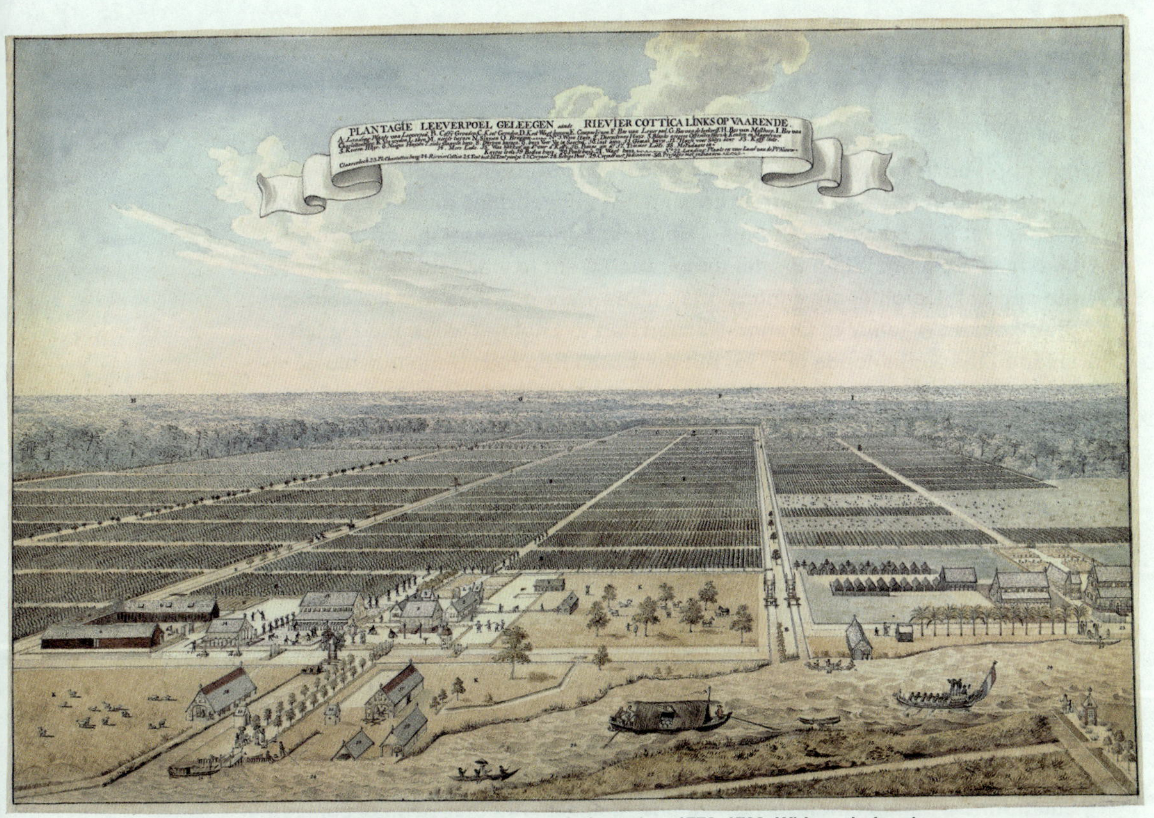

fig. 13 **View of the Leeverpoel plantation, 1772–1792. With such drawings, investors in the Netherlands could form a picture of their future property**

abolition of the slave trade and slavery

The WIC was dissolved in 1791, after the company had already given up its monopoly on the slave trade in 1730. In the Dutch Republic, a Council of Colonies was formed in order to centrally administrate the various areas (Essequibo, Demerera, Sint Eustatius, Curaçao, Berbice, Suriname and the forts on the coasts of Guinea). When Britain and France went to war with each other at the end of the eighteenth century, their allies were dragged into the conflict. Stadtholder William V of Orange-Nassau fled to England when the French invaded the Netherlands in 1795, but the Dutch Republic (from that moment known as the Batavian Republic) chose the side of the French. The definitive end of the VOC, after a long decline, followed in 1799. As a result of the conflict with Britain, the Dutch colonies in the Atlantic region and around the Indian Ocean were occupied by the British. From that point on, English laws were in force, such as the prohibition on the slave trade that went into effect in 1807. A subsequent power shift took place at the Congress of Vienna (1814–1815), where the future of Europe was discussed. William Frederick, the son of the last stadtholder, William V, had returned to the fatherland when Napoleon's triumphal progress seemed to be coming to an end. He had declared himself King William I of the United Kingdom of the Netherlands, and Duke of Luxembourg. The Dutch kingdom wanted its colonies back from the British, but immediate agreement on this was not achieved at the congress. Essequibo, Demerara and Berbice would eventually remain in British hands, as would South Africa, parts of India, Sri Lanka and Malacca. Another point of contention was the abolition of the slave trade. The British feared unfair competition if its prohibition were to be dropped the moment the colonies came into the possession of the Netherlands once more.

As a result, international pressure led to a prohibition on the slave trade – that is to say, the importation of newly enslaved men, women and children from Africa to the Dutch colonies – in 1814. Traders and plantation owners then constantly searched for loopholes in the law. They delivered enslaved people who were already in the Caribbean, used alternative routes, or were able to circumvent the rules by using forged papers. Only with the introduction of the slave registers in 1826 in Suriname and in 1839 on Curaçao was progress made in combatting human trafficking. The prohibition on the slave trade also led to a significant increase in illegal trade in the Dutch East Indies, and as a result the conditions under which enslaved people were transported and sold deteriorated even further. Slave registers were introduced there in 1819.[69]

The growing international debate on the practice of slavery, meanwhile, led the government and plantation owners to consider alternative systems of (forced) labour. In Indonesia, the Culture System (or Cultivation System) was introduced in 1830. The Javanese population was forced into unpaid labour and the mandatory supply of crops for the European market. In Suriname, a group of Chinese contract labourers arrived from Java in 1853, to work on a sugar plantation. In the last quarter of the nineteenth century, Indians and Javanese followed.

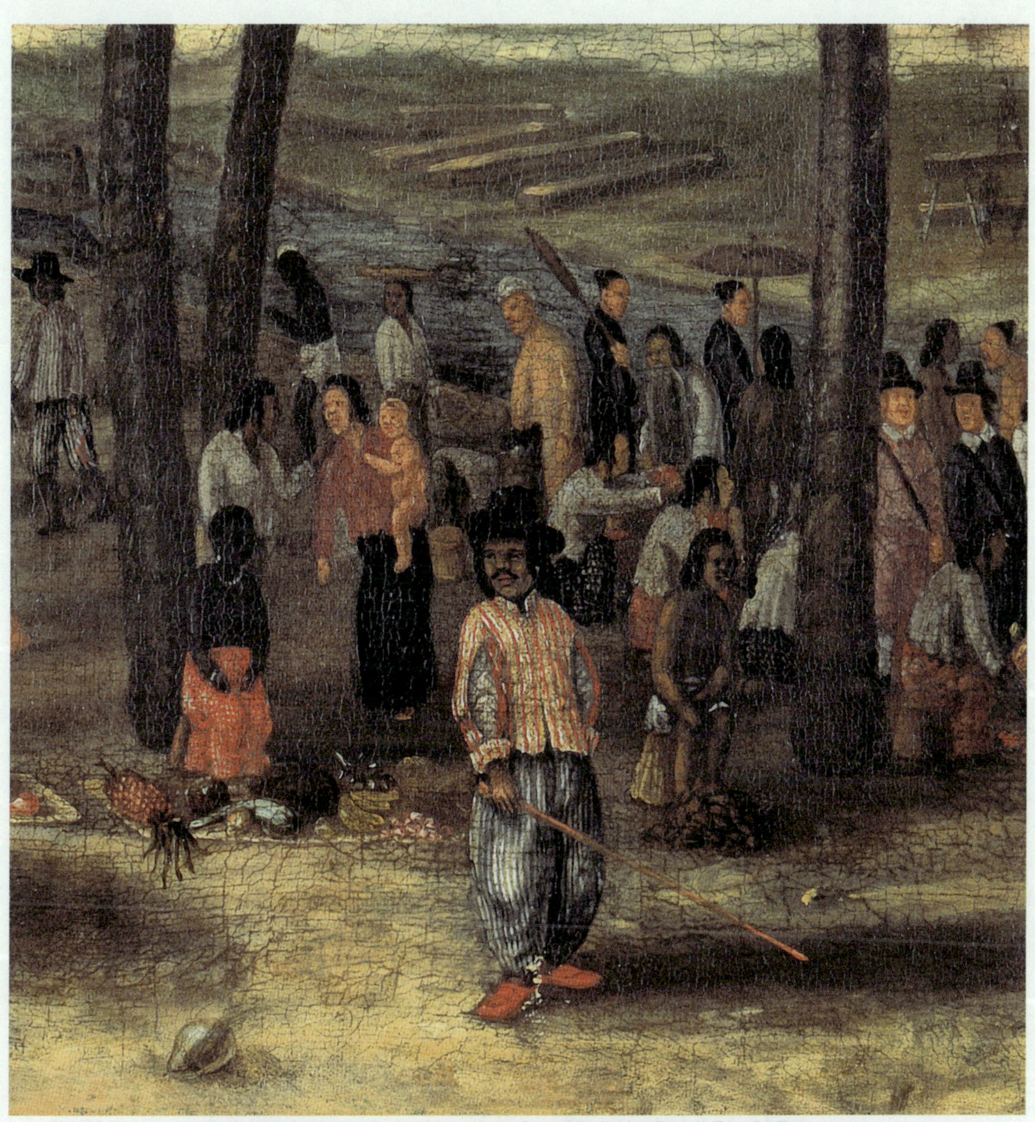

fig. 14 **Mardijkers, formerly enslaved people in the Dutch East Indies, were identifiable by their striped clothing and the fact that they were permitted to wear a hat and shoes (detail of** fig. 6**, p. 160)**

External influences continued to determine Dutch policy in relation to slavery. After Britain abolished slavery in 1834, France also opted for definitive abolition, in the revolutionary year of 1848. This gave enslaved people in the surrounding Dutch colonies the courage to keep resisting and to fight for a life of freedom and equality.[70]

The call to abolish slavery was gradually taken up in the Netherlands, although the effect remained limited because abolitionists did not join forces. The Netherlands Society for the Promotion of the Abolition of Slavery (NMBAS), founded in 1824, proved insufficiently decisive in countering the economic objections of the slaveholders, and protest faded for a few years. By then the debate had taken a paternalistic tone. Under the influence of international developments, the prohibition of the slave trade and the continuing and multi-faceted resistance of people in slavery, the establishment had gradually come to realize that it was more advantageous to treat enslaved people not as machines but as people, albeit not as equals. Not much improved for people in slavery. Policy may have become a bit more humane, but it was still based on the idea that enslaved people were less civilized and therefore inferior. This kept the old racial hierarchy in place.

An interesting voice in this period is that of W.R. van Hoëvell, a statesman and former pastor on Java.[71] In the revolutionary year of 1848, he wrote *De Emancipatie der Slaven in Nederlands-Indië* (The emancipation of slaves in the Dutch East Indies), a publication that called for the abolition of slavery in the Dutch East Indies because, he wrote, this was 'no more defensible in the East Indies than anywhere else'. In 1855 he also published his findings on Suriname in *Slaven en vrijen onder de Nederlandsche wet* (Slaves and free people under Dutch law). He denounced the treatment of enslaved people in the colony, offering a song as a source. *Basya fon* tells of a white man on a plantation who has an enslaved woman – by whom he has a son – mistreated daily by the *basya*, the overseer. This song, Van Hoëvell reports, could be heard in the colony almost every day.[72]

> *Ai, Basya fon! Mi taki fon!*
> *A wenke meki mi ati bron.*
>
> Basya, whip! I said whip!
> That girl has made me so angry.

In the closing chapter, Van Hoëvell rebuts the oft-heard arguments for the preservation of slavery, including the claim that many labourers in the Netherlands were materially less fortunate and went hungry more often than people in slavery. That might well be true, Van Hoëvell said, but this argument ignored something priceless that the labourer in the Netherlands possessed and people in slavery did not, namely freedom.

It took until 7 May 1859 before the abolition law intended to end slavery in the Dutch East Indies was signed. Its implementation followed in phases, and slavery continued to exist in parts of Indonesia far into the twentieth century.[73] At the end of 1859, enslaved people on Java and Madura were emancipated; their 'owners' were financially compensated for the release of people they considered their property.[74] On 1 January 1860 the abolition of slavery on the Banda Islands followed, here without the option for former slaveholders to submit a claim for their losses. The formerly enslaved people were informed of their rights and duties and allowed to dispose of their clothing and other modest possessions. Many of them could now live in freedom, but they had to made do, at least initially, without shelter or food, and sometimes without income either.

On the islands of Sulawesi, Sumatra, Borneo, the Moluccas, Bali and Lombok, everything stayed virtually the same after 1860. The Dutch administration was less firmly established on these islands; European slaveholders were in the minority in relation to Asian slaveholders and a large number of people in slavery were not registered, and slaveholders were therefore unable to request financial compensation for them. The situation was much more complex than on Java and Madura, and as a result, even after the legal abolition of slavery in 1860, hundreds of thousands of enslaved people still worked in involuntary servitude for Europeans, Eurasians and Asians in the Indonesian archipelago. Through a lack of political will, slavery continued to exist in these areas into the twentieth century.

In Suriname and the Netherlands Antilles, the abolition law also finally came into force on 1 July 1863. Far more than in Indonesia, the interests of private individuals who owned shares in plantations or other property played a role here. For a long time, attention was focused on safeguarding their status quo, including providing financial compensation for the loss of their 'property'. A large number of free Surinamese people of colour, meanwhile, decided not to wait for the official abolition of slavery and began to buy their family members' freedom. Manumission had become an instrument in the struggle against slavery.[75] In 1863, slaveholders received a set amount per enslaved man or woman, an arrangement that was made possible by the income from forced labour under the Culture System in Indonesia.[76] The formerly enslaved people in Suriname and the Netherlands Antilles were not yet truly free, however. The Staatstoezicht (State Supervision) legislation stipulated that men and women between fifteen and sixty years of age were required to work, for pay, for their former 'owner' for another ten years. In this way the Dutch government hoped to prevent a complete collapse of the plantation economy. Because no mass demand for the supply of labourers was expected on Curaçao, Bonaire, Aruba, Sint Eustatius, Saba and Sint Maarten, enslaved people there were not placed under state supervision upon their emancipation. Other systems of cheap labour did develop, such as the *paga tera* system on Curaçao: in exchange for a few days of unpaid labour per year, formerly enslaved people were allowed to keep living on the plantation. A lack of alternatives led many to opt for this.

The abolition laws meant the legal end of the slavery system as it had been applied by the Dutch in all sorts of variants across its colonized territories. The people who lived and worked in slavery had had to wait for this for generations. Political decision-making was constantly postponed out of fear of letting go of the existing financial and social structures of the system, and was ultimately only forced by international pressure. In some places, (formerly) enslaved people had already forced the end of the system through their unrelenting resistance. With small acts or large-scale insurgencies, they had taken charge of their own destiny.

There was no genuine closure, however; the system upon which slavery was based was too tightly bound to the Dutch economy and the social structure of Dutch society. The physical and mental traces of this history can be found, in the Netherlands as well as in its former colonies, in historical buildings like warehouses and canal-side mansions, and in businesses that build on the activities of the trading companies. They are audible to everyone in the public debate and visible in museum collections, monuments and street names. And, not least, they can be found in thoughts, customs and family histories. The slavery past is interwoven with the present of us all.

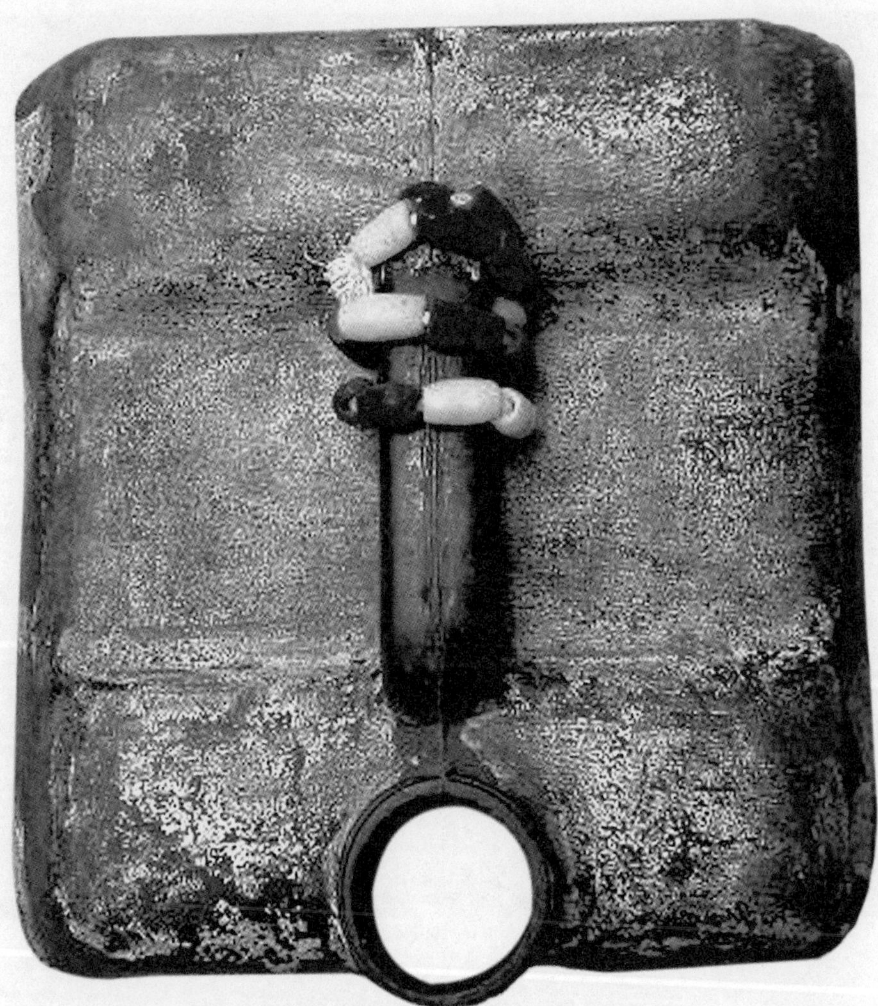

Petrol can from the installation *La Bouche du Roi*
Romuald Hazoumè, 1997–2005 (see pp. 58–61)

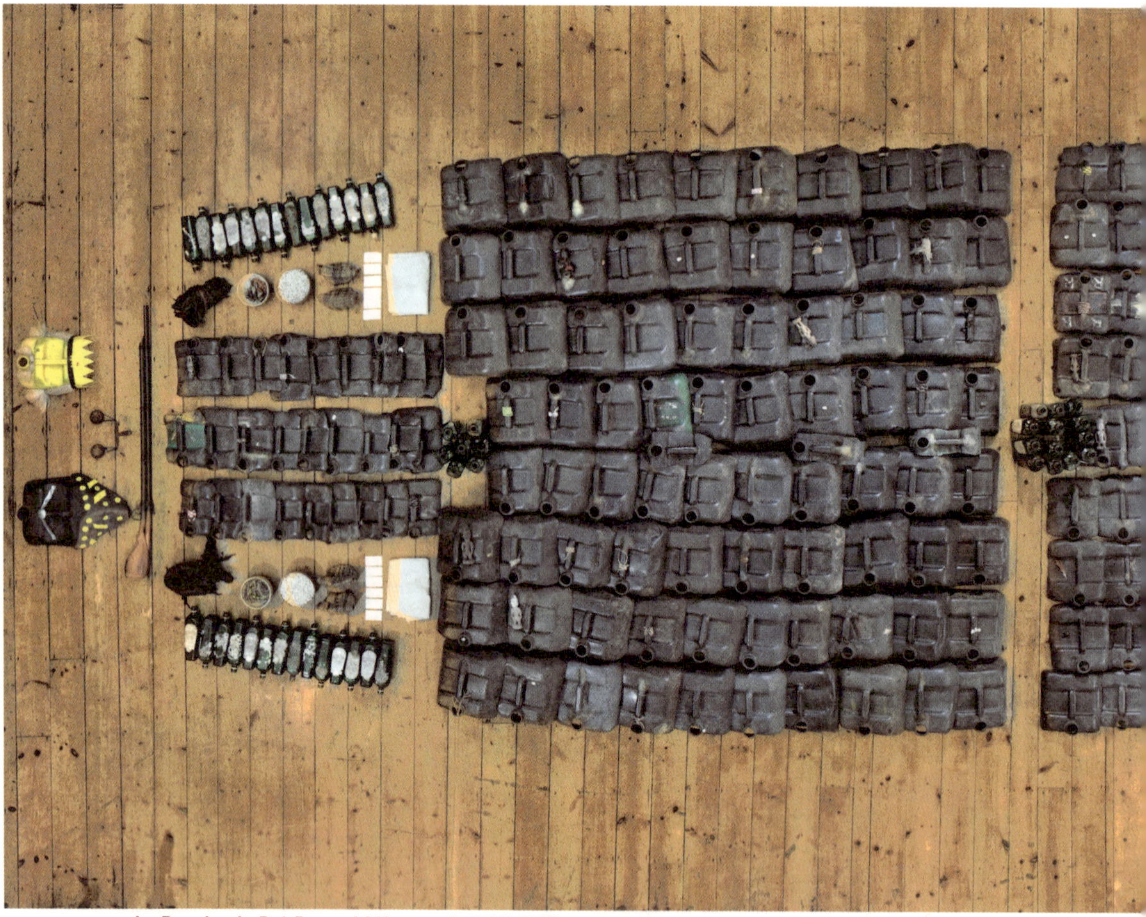

La Bouche du Roi, **Romuald Hazoumè, 1997–2005**

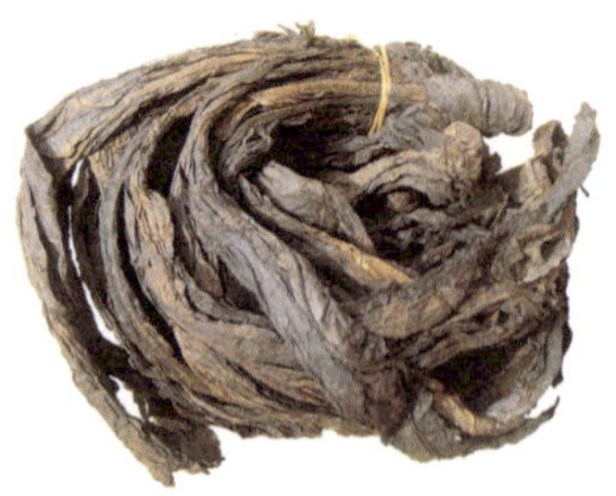

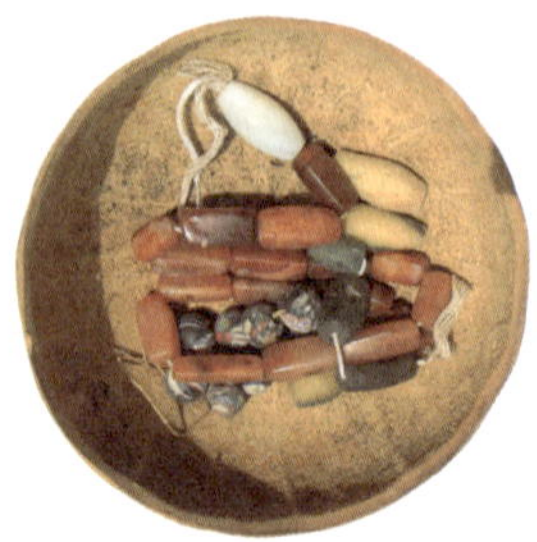

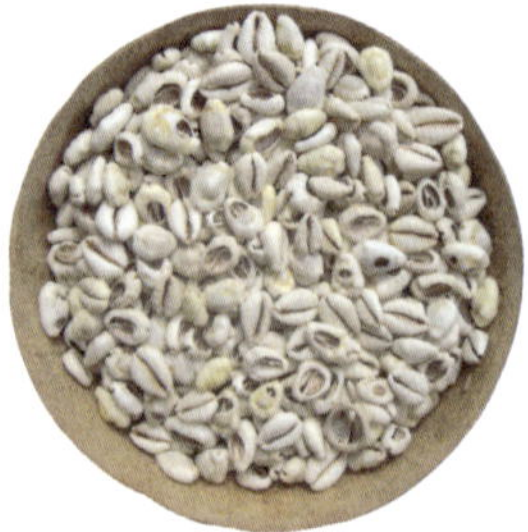

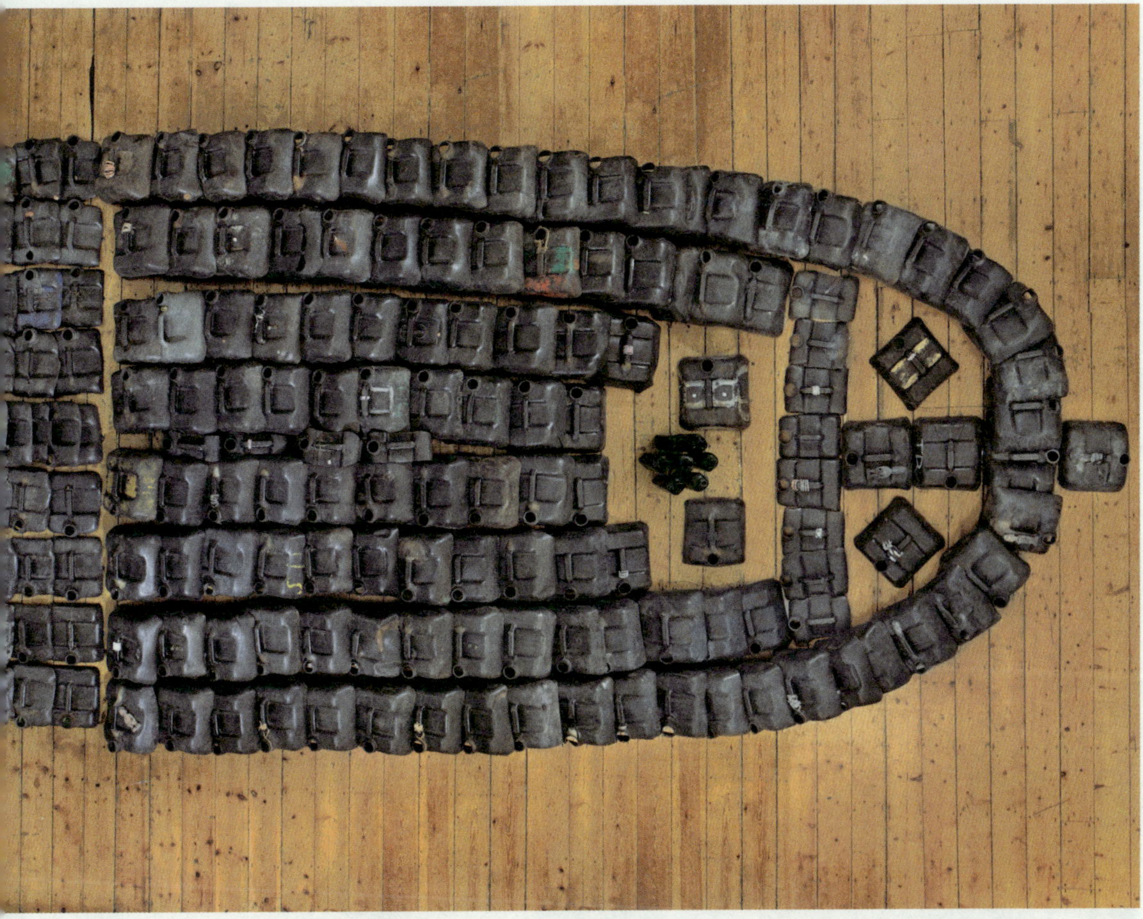

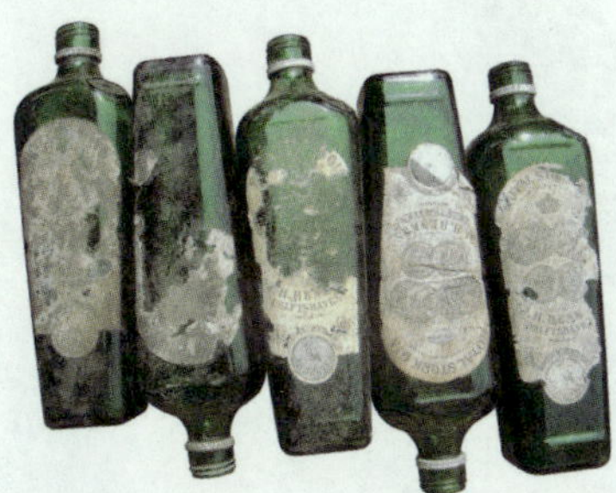

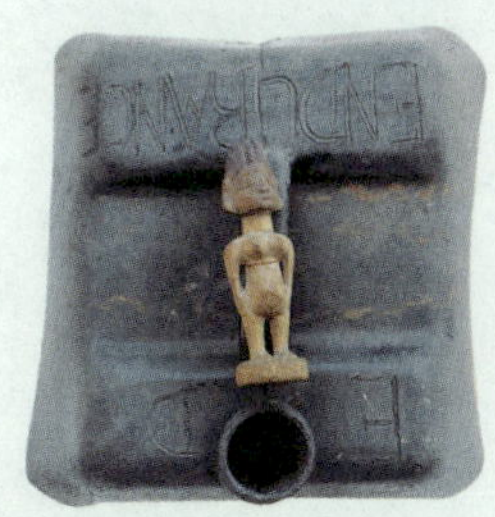

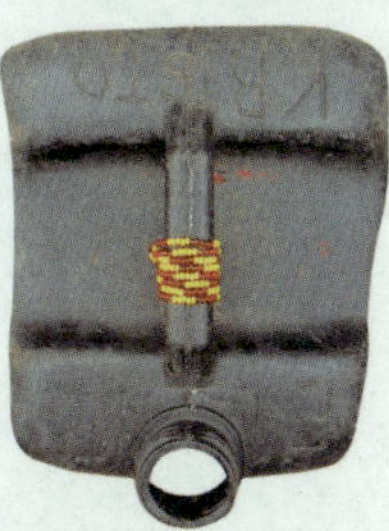

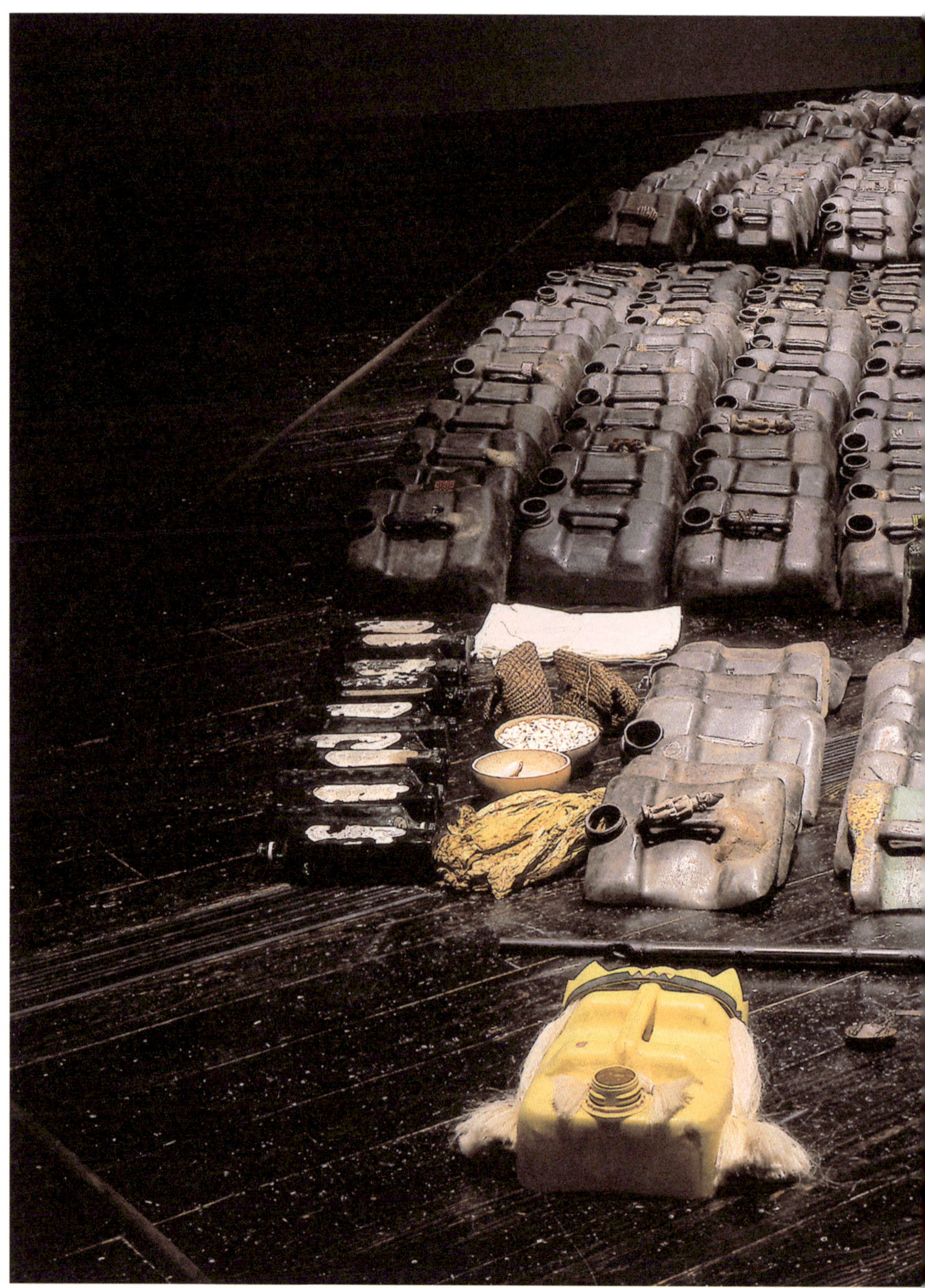

La Bouche du Roi, **Romuald Hazoumè, 1997–2005**

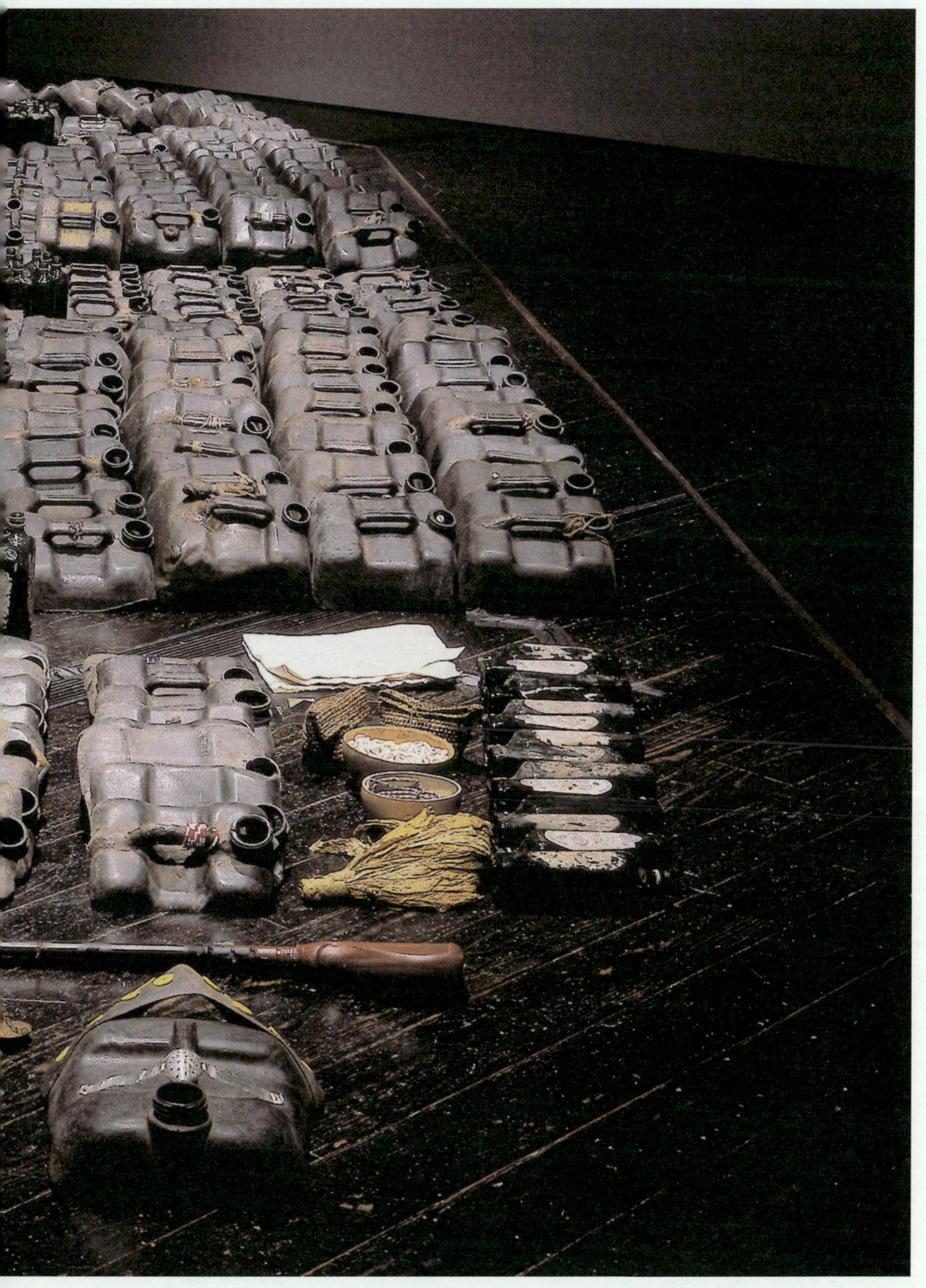

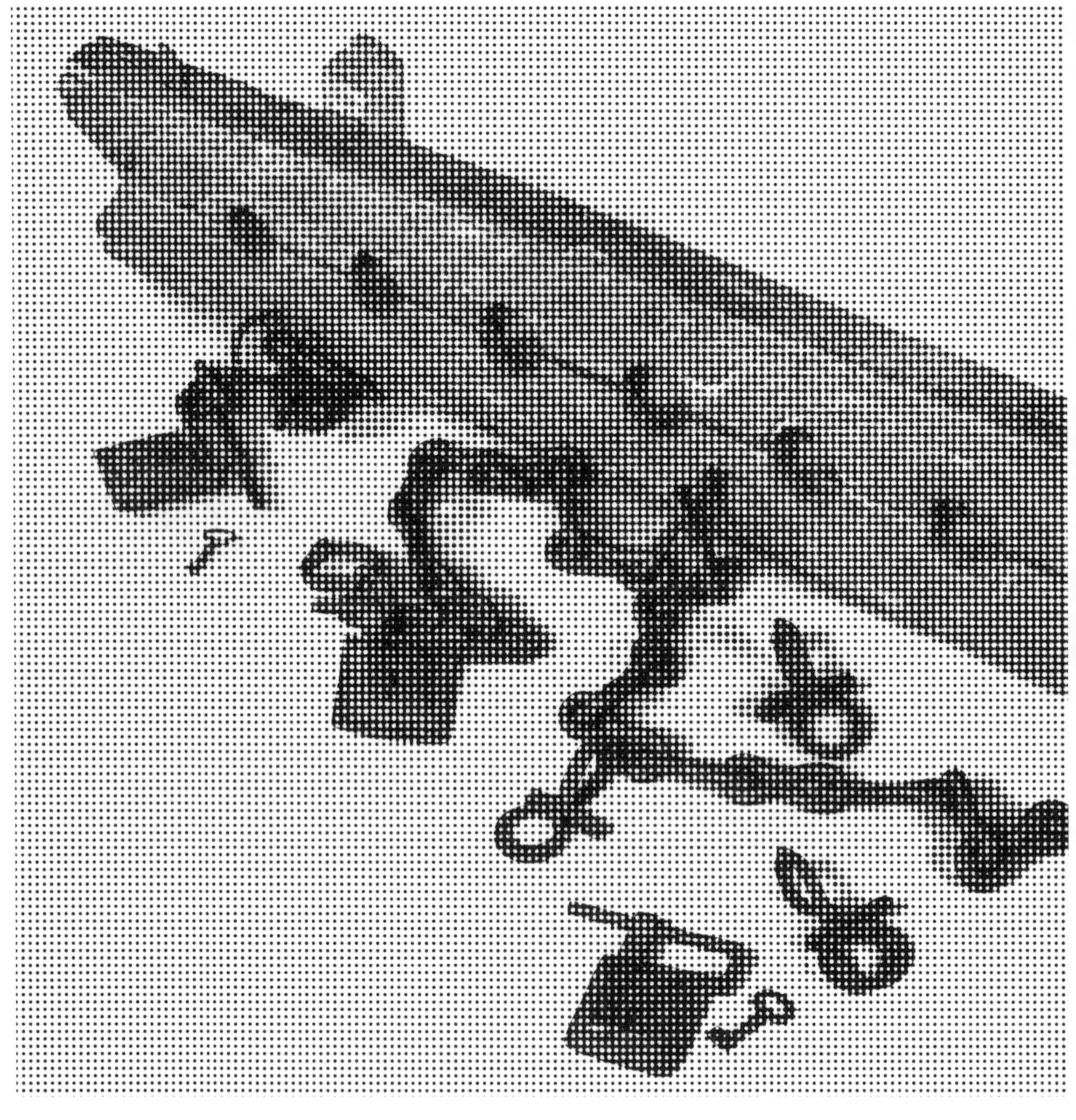

stephanie archangel

joão

caught in the crossfire in dutch brazil

> On the appointed day, these poor people, half dead from hunger and thirst, are taken one by one, as if pigs or sheep leaving the pen, better to be counted; Portuguese and Dutch traders examine them in front and behind ... When eight, ten or more have been chosen from this crowd and found to be perfect, the trader undertakes to pay for each one of them, be he a child of 6 or 7 years or an adult male.[1]

In his *Thierbuch* (Book of animals, c. 1641), Zacharias Wagener, a German quartermaster of the Dutch West India Company (WIC), records his observations of the people, flora and fauna of Brazil, accompanying them with his own watercolour illustrations. One of his pictures shows a slave market on Jodenstraat, in central Recife (fig. 1). European men are scattered about the square, holding their walking sticks, some chatting with one another. It would be a leisurely scene were it not for the clusters of African people, huddled together both in the foreground and further along the square, with one man using a cane to make a beating gesture at them. Wagener witnessed with his own eyes the scene of African men, women and children being herded into the market square after a brutal sea voyage, to be vetted and sold to traders to work on their sugar plantations.

It is likely that João Mina was sold at this slave market, or one very similar to it. He was an enslaved man whose name has been passed down to us through records of his interrogation in Dutch Brazil in 1646. His last name tells us that he was sold into slavery at Elmina, on the Gold Coast (now the coast of Ghana). In the period around 1640, the WIC used the toponym 'Mina' to name African people shipped off from the Gulf of Guinea region to the Dutch colony in Brazil.[2] Precisely where João originally came from in Africa is now impossible to know. What we do know is that most enslaved people had to trek long distances from inland areas before being forced onto European ships.

The WIC's occupation of parts of Brazil from 1630 to 1654 was an outcome of the Eighty Years' War between the Dutch Republic and Spain (1568–1648). From 1580 to 1640, Portugal was part of the Iberian Union and ruled by Spain, and was therefore regarded by the Netherlands as an enemy in this period. The war spread to the territories colonized by Spain and Portugal, and in 1630 the WIC captured the coastal cities of Olinda and Recife and the island of Antônio Vaz in northeast Brazil. Soon afterwards the Dutch also captured a number of Portuguese Brazilian *capitanias* (administrative provinces). By 1635 the Dutch trading company had occupied a 600-kilometre coastal strip of land stretching from Cabo de Santo Agostinho to the Rio Grande and containing many sugar plantations and sugar mills.[3]

From the outset, these Dutch-occupied territories remained under attack from the *moradores* (Portuguese settlers in Brazil), whose troops included Portuguese soldiers, Indigenous Brazilians, and free and unfree people of African origin. During the hostilities, some of the enslaved Africans took opportunities to escape from their Portuguese slaveholders. Some, known as Maroons, settled in the forests and formed communities of their own. Others fled to WIC territory, where some were forced to fight alongside the Dutch against the Portuguese.[4]

Although the Dutch Republic and Portugal signed a peace treaty in 1641, in 1645 the Portuguese plantation owners rebelled against the WIC authorities. During the ensuing guerrilla war, large numbers of African men, women and children fled Portuguese territory. In 1645 the WIC retreated to the coastal city of Recife and its defensive positions, the islands of Itamaracá and Fernando de Noronha, and various forts along the coast. Henceforth, the WIC would not venture outside these areas except to carry out military operations.[5]

Africans who fled Portuguese-run territories were able to pass on information about the enemy, so their testimonies were of great importance to the WIC. Judicial interrogations of such individuals were sometimes attended by a large number of interested parties. In fact, the importance of an interrogation can be judged by the number of signatories to the report and the rank of the WIC officials who were present. The officials still regarded the stories with some caution, however. On his departure from the colony, Johan Maurits of Nassau-Siegen, the WIC-appointed governor general of Dutch Brazil from 1636 to 1644, warned against being too quick to believe refugees from Portuguese Brazil: 'Suspect the good faith of the defectors,' he wrote, 'for they repeat the words of the leaders.'[6]

A collection of letters in the WIC archive contains 76 reports on interviews with 110 refugees,[7] one of whom was João Mina.[8] The reports reveal how João and others in his position strategically manoeuvred between the two conflicting sides. The interview report and other historical sources give us some small insights into João's life.

the hearing

In September 1646, or thereabouts, João Mina made a successful escape from his Portuguese slaveholder to Dutch territory. To attempt to flee was dangerous, according to Zacharias Wagener, because those who were captured and returned to their plantation in either Portuguese or Dutch Brazil could be brutally whipped.[9] João reached the Dutch colonial settlement in Recife on 4 October, whereupon a WIC official subjected him to a judicial interrogation. The report describes him as a man named Joan: 'Examination carried out on the fourth of October 1646 of the negro Joan Mina belonging to Gabriel Castanio' (fig. 2). We can be fairly certain that his Portuguese name would have been João, since this was the name most commonly given to male Africans in Portuguese Brazil.

The report is not signed, so we do not know the identity of the person who questioned João, but interrogations were almost always conducted by lawyers or members of the colonial government. The hearing was conducted in Dutch, but there is no record of what language João spoke. Little interest was expressed in the personal lives of the African people under interrogation. Instead they were usually questioned about their reasons for escaping, and how they had reached Dutch territory. The underlying purpose of this questioning was to identify weaknesses in the enemy defences by obtaining information about the military situation and living conditions in the Portuguese colony.

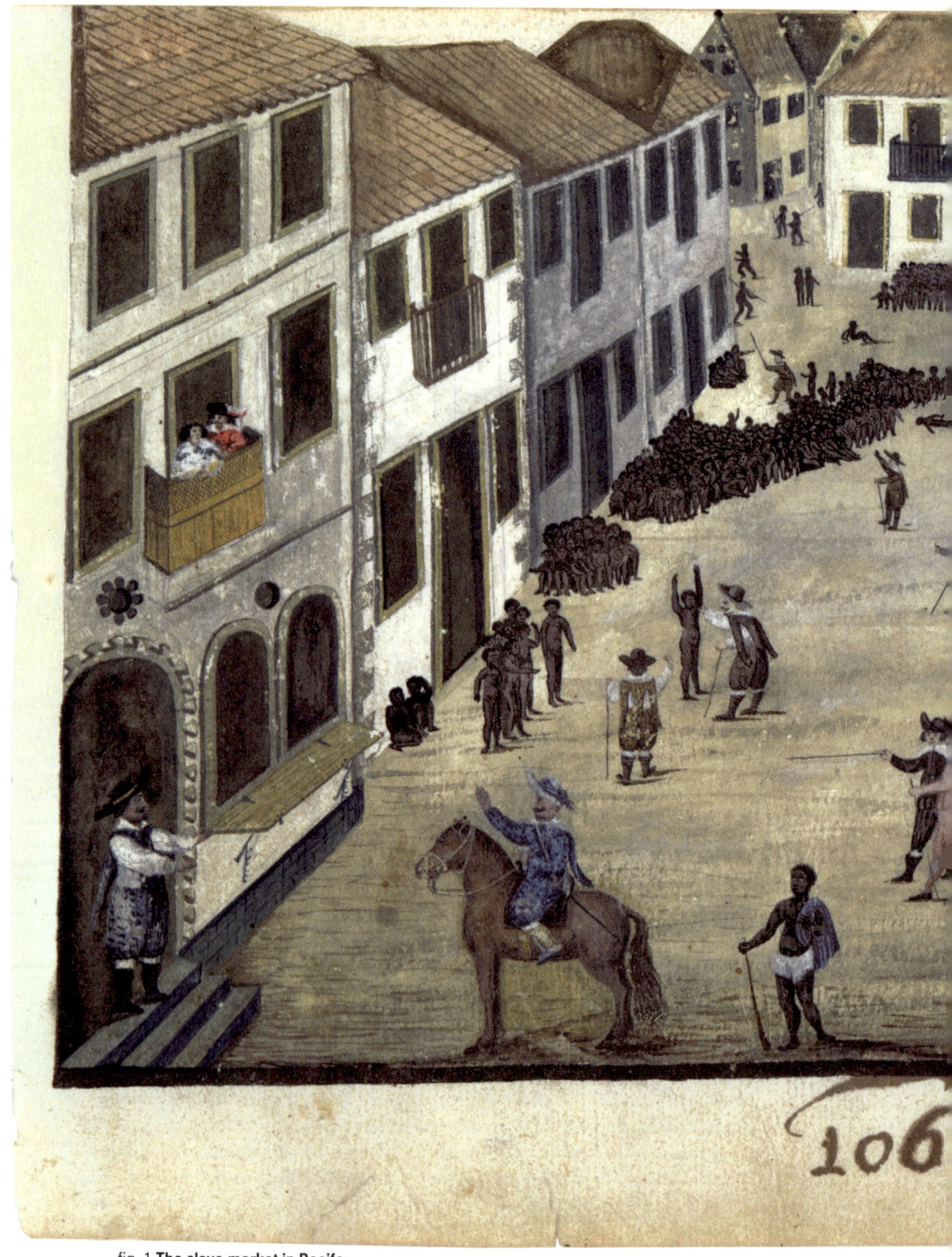

fig. 1 **The slave market in Recife**
Zacharias Wagener, c. 1637–1641

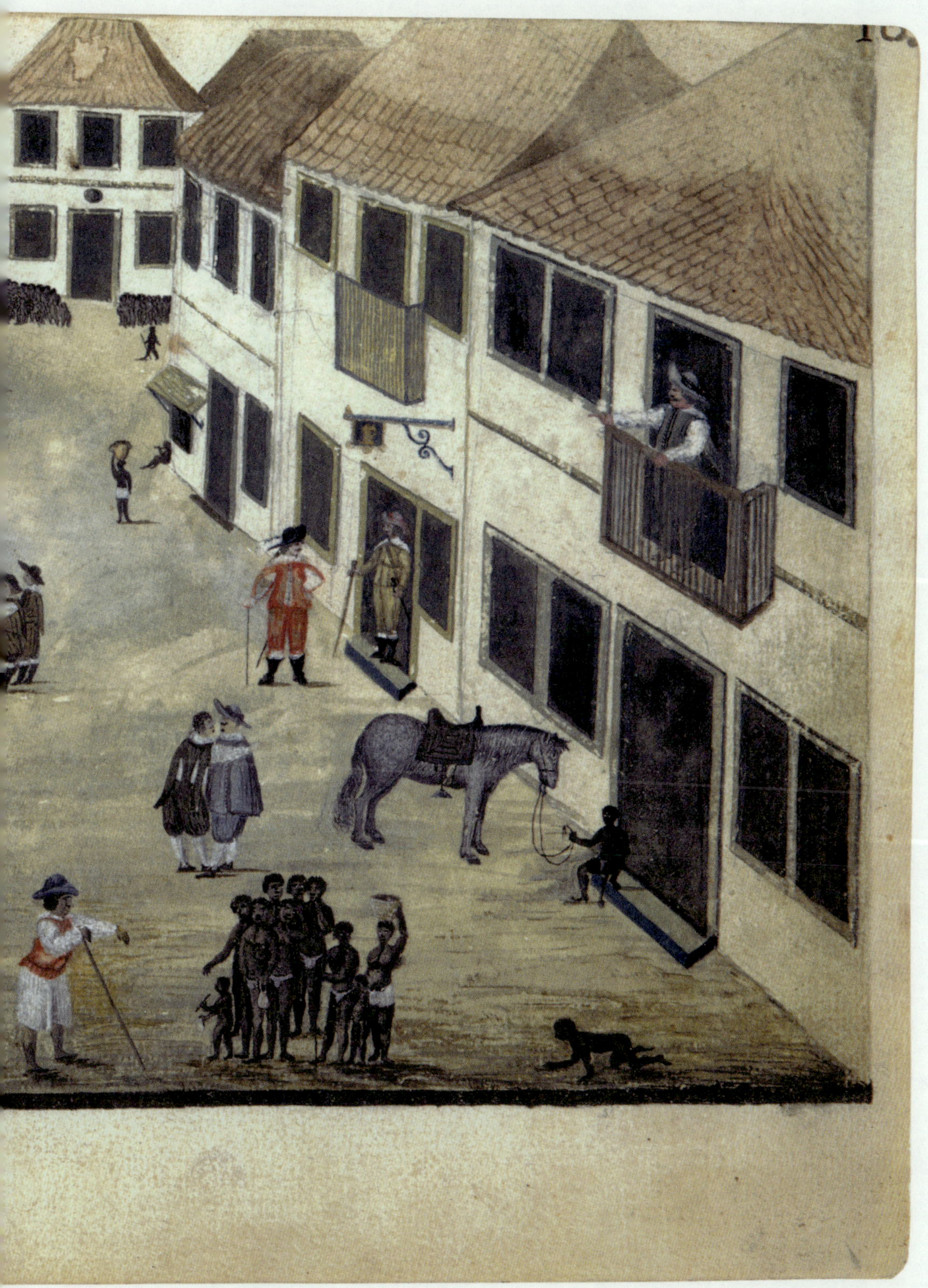

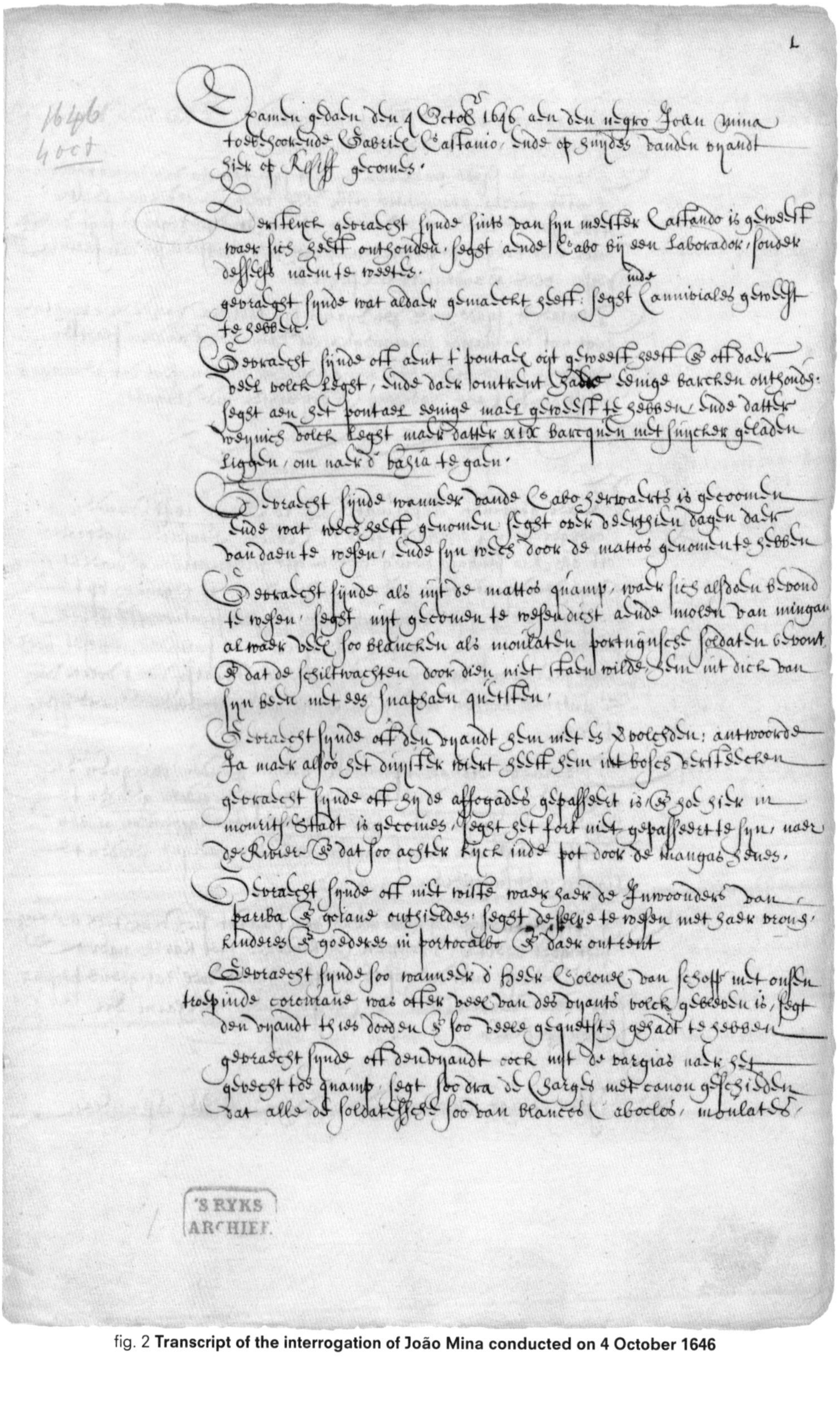

1

1646
400t

Examen gedaen den 4 Octob. 1646 aen den negro Joan Mina toebehoorende Gabriel Castanio, ende op huyden vanden vyandt hier op Reciff gecomen.

Eerstelyck gevraecht synde hoe hy van syn meester Castando is geweecken waer hy hem heeft onthouden, segt aende Cabo by een Laborador, sonder deselfs naem te weeten.

gevraecht synde wat aldaer gemaeckt heeft: segt Cannibiales ende gewrocht te hebben.

Gevraecht synde off aent Pontael uyt geweest heeft & off daer veel volck legt, ende daer omtrent hadde eenige barcken onthouden. segt aen het pontael eenige maelen geweest te hebben, ende datter weynich volck legt maer datter XIX barquen met suycker geladen liggen, om naer de Bahia te gaen.

Gevraecht synde wanneer vande Cabo herwaerts is gecomen ende wat wech heeft genomen segt over veerthien dagen daer vandaen te wesen, ende syn wech door de mattos genomen te hebben.

Gevraecht synde als uyt de mattos quam, waer hy alsdoen bevond te wesen. segt uyt gecomen te wesen dicht aende molen van Mingau alwaer veel soo blancken als moulaten portugesche soldaten bevont, & dat de schiltwachten door dien niet staen wilde hem int dick van syn been met een snaphaen quetsten.

Gevraecht synde off den vyandt hem niet en vervolchden: antwoorde Ja maer alsoo het duyster wiert heeft hem int bosch versteken.

gevraecht synde off hy de affogados gepasseert is & hoe hier in Mauritsstadt is gecomen, segt het fort niet gepasseert te syn, maer de Rivier & dat soo achter Kyck inde pot door de mangas is comen.

Gevraecht synde off niet weet waer haer de Inwoonders van Pariba & Goiana onthielden: segt deselve te wesen met haer vrouw, kinderen & goederen in Portocalbo & daer ontrent

Gevraecht synde soo wanneer d' Heer Colonel van Schoppe met onsen troupe inde Coromans was offer veel van des vyants volck gebleven is, segt den vyandt thien dooden & soo veele gequetsten gehadt te hebben

gevraecht synde off den vyandt oock uyt de vargias naer het gevecht toe quam, segt soo dra de Chargie met canon geschieden dat alle de soldatessen soo van blancos, abocles, moulatos,

fig. 2 **Transcript of the interrogation of João Mina conducted on 4 October 1646**

The questions put to João mostly concerned military troops, supplies and the sugar trade. The records show that he was aware of a WIC military campaign that took place in the same period as his escape. João was asked if, on his travels, he had encountered Sigismund von Schoppe, the general of the artillery and the Dutch navy commander in Brazil.[10] João responded that 'when the attacks with cannon took place, all the soldiers – white, *caboclos* [people of mixed Indigenous Brazilian and European origin], mulattoes and negros alike – marched to the beach, and the *vergas* [the fertile plantation region around Recife] was empty but for women and children.'[11] He goes on to explain that during the attack, ten men on the Portuguese side were killed and many more wounded. On the subject of supplies, he notes that there were only meagre rations 'of *farinha* [cassava flour], fresh meat and other foodstuffs'. João also tells his interrogator that he hid out in Cabo de Santo Agostinho (35 kilometres from Recife) at a *lavrador*, a small independent sugar producer. From there he trekked through the forest for fifteen days and emerged at the small town of Mingao, where he was apprehended by Portuguese soldiers. João would not be stopped, however, and he walked on, whereupon they shot at him and 'wounded him in the flesh of his leg with a snaphance [flintlock musket]'.[12] João managed to escape his pursuers by hiding in the woods until after sundown.

João's reasons for leaving the Portuguese settlement do not appear in the record of his interrogation. Wagener, however, notes that the Portuguese badly mistreated the people they enslaved: Black people 'are treated very miserably by these, receiving little food and being forced to work without rest in the mills and cane-fields, hardly having time to breathe.'[13] Those who did not cooperate were punished, writes Wagener:

> It is necessary to whip and humiliate these blacks if you want them to work and gain their goodwill as they are very stubborn and obstinate by nature. I saw many, due to the errors they had made, be hung up by their wrists and [have] their naked bodies terribly beaten with switches.[14]

Another punishment that enslaved men and women were subjected to in Brazil was to be locked in a foot stock known as a *tronco* (tree trunk), which had multiple notches into which people's ankles could be clamped. Its two timber sections were connected by an iron hinge at one end and an iron lock at the other (fig. 3). Stocks of this kind have survived at former sugar plantations in the northeast of Brazil. The oak foot stocks shown here were probably made in the Netherlands, possibly in Zeeland province, but were never actually shipped to Dutch Brazil. The metal locks have been dated to somewhere between the end of the sixteenth century and the third quarter of the seventeenth century. This tronco is 2.65 metres long and has nine holes, allowing multiple individuals to be shackled at the ankles at the same time with very little room for movement (fig. 5).

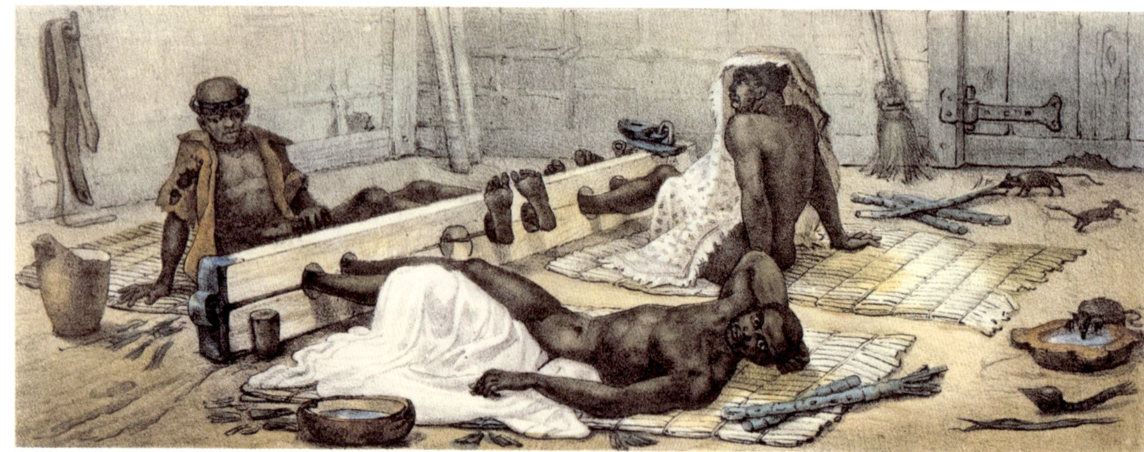

fig. 3 **Enslaved people, constrained in foot stocks**
Jean-Baptiste Debret, c. 1830

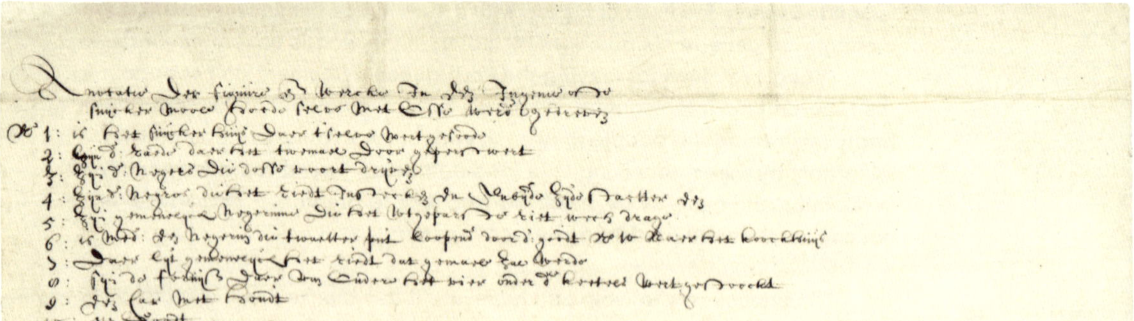

fig. 4 **Ox-driven sugar mil**
Frans Post, c. 1640

the sugar trade

In 1636, Johan Maurits of Nassau-Siegen, a grand nephew of William I the Silent, was appointed to rule the colony of Dutch Brazil. He was tasked with ending the ongoing hostilities between the Dutch and the Portuguese in the region and safeguarding the sugar trade for the Dutch Republic. At this time, insufficient numbers of North European farmers had chosen to relocate to the colony to run Dutch plantations, so it was crucial for the Dutch that they remained on good terms with the Portuguese colonists.[15] To this end, Johan Maurits decreed that the High Council (Hoge Raad, akin to a judicial council) reserve two days a week for the handling of petitions submitted by these colonists. Furthermore, those who pledged an oath of obeisance to the WIC now had their estates returned to them.[16] Abandoned plantations were confiscated and auctioned off. The WIC issued long-term loans to Portuguese plantation owners to buy these estates.[17]

The Portuguese representatives of the *capitanias*, many of them wealthy owners of sugar mills, still had a part to play in WIC decision-making in the colony. They were allowed to submit petitions to the High Government in Brazil (Hoge Regering, which resembled a political government), and a large proportion of them were granted.[18] Another factor that may well have played a part in this strategy was that the Dutch were vastly outnumbered by the Portuguese colonists: in 1640 there were 25,000 Portuguese in the colony and only about 10,000 WIC officials, sailors and soldiers, the majority of whom were mercenaries originating from England, France, Scotland and Germany, and of the 3,000 inhabitants of the colony who had come from the Dutch Republic, fully a third had a Portuguese-Jewish background.[19]

Johan Maurits took with him to Brazil a number of scientists and artists to study and document the colony's landscape, flora and fauna. One of the artists was Frans Post, who made a drawing of a sugar mill and described the various phases of the production process (fig. 4).[20] It shows men driving the oxen that powered the mill, and the three roll presses at the heart of the mill used to double-press the sugar cane. Enslaved men manually fed the sugar cane into the rollers to produce the juice, which was then carried, usually by enslaved women, to boilers at the side of the building, where the juice was reduced and refined. The syrup produced in this way was then shipped in crates to Europe for further refining processes.[21] The pressing and boiling of sugar cane was a hard and dangerous task for João and enslaved sugar workers like him.[22] Planting and harvesting the crop – done in the burning sun – was also exceptionally hard work.

João mentions during his hearing that on several occasions he visited Pontal de Nazaré, a fort from which the Portuguese shipped sugar. It is likely that João went there on the orders of the plantation owner Castanio. This offered the Dutch interrogators an excellent opportunity to glean more information about the sugar trade, so they questioned him on matters such as the number of ships and people there. João explained that there were not many people, but 'barques loaded with sugar ... ready for delivery to the Bahia'.[23] At Bahia, the colonial capital of Portuguese Brazil, most of the sugar would have been loaded onto tall ships and transported across the ocean to Europe.

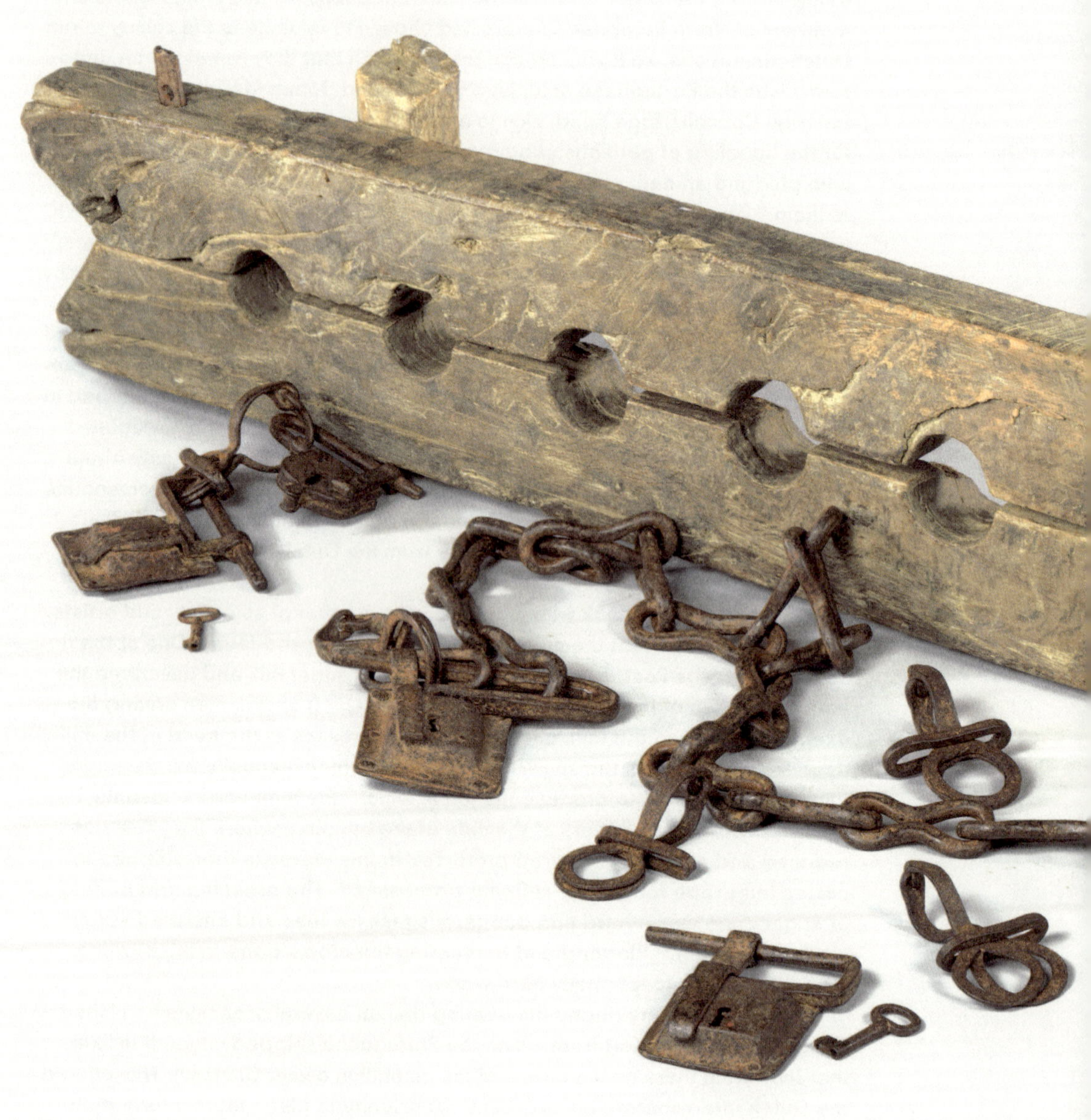

fig. 5 **Foot stocks designed for the constraint of multiple enslaved people, c. 1600–1800**

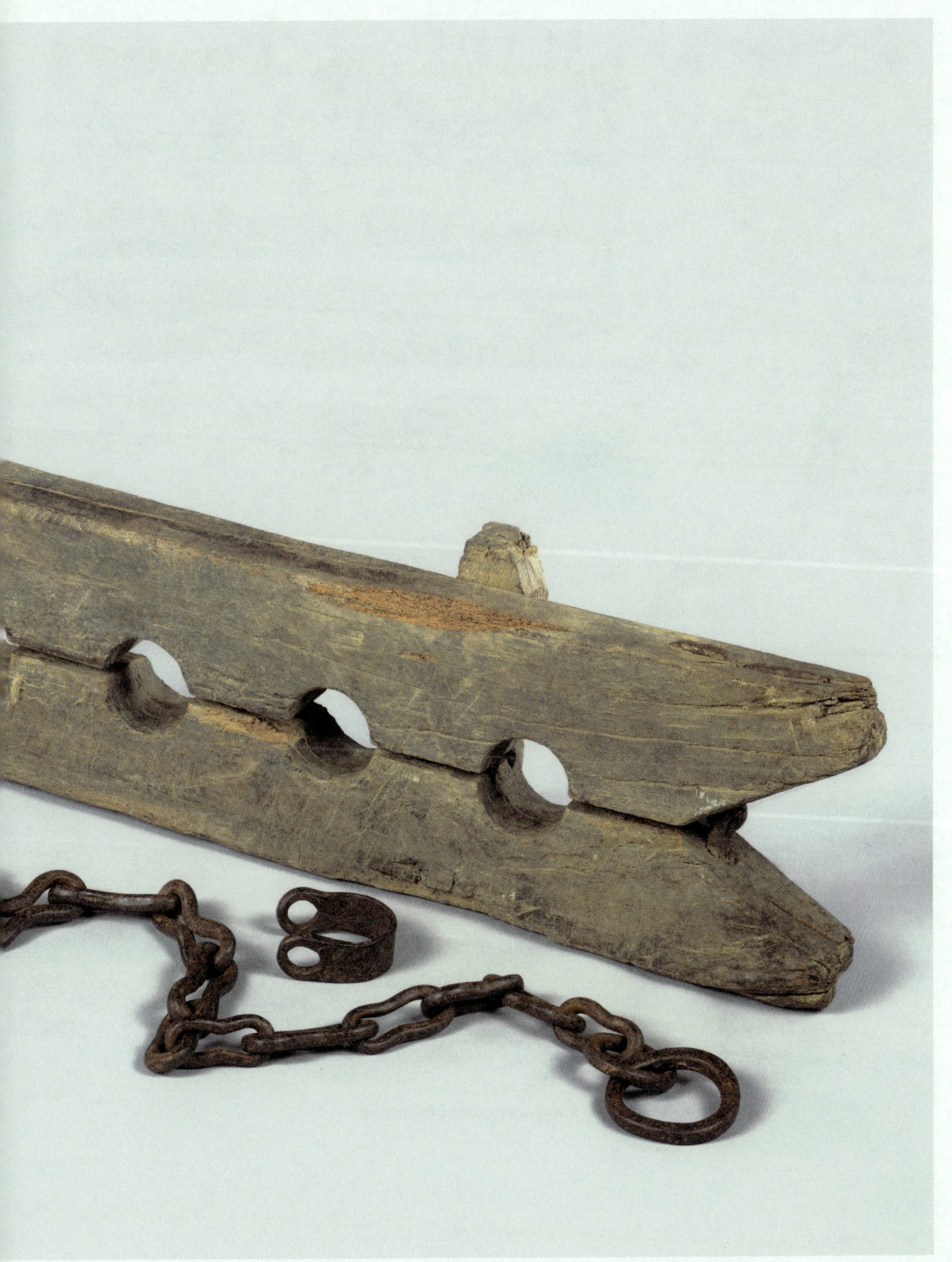

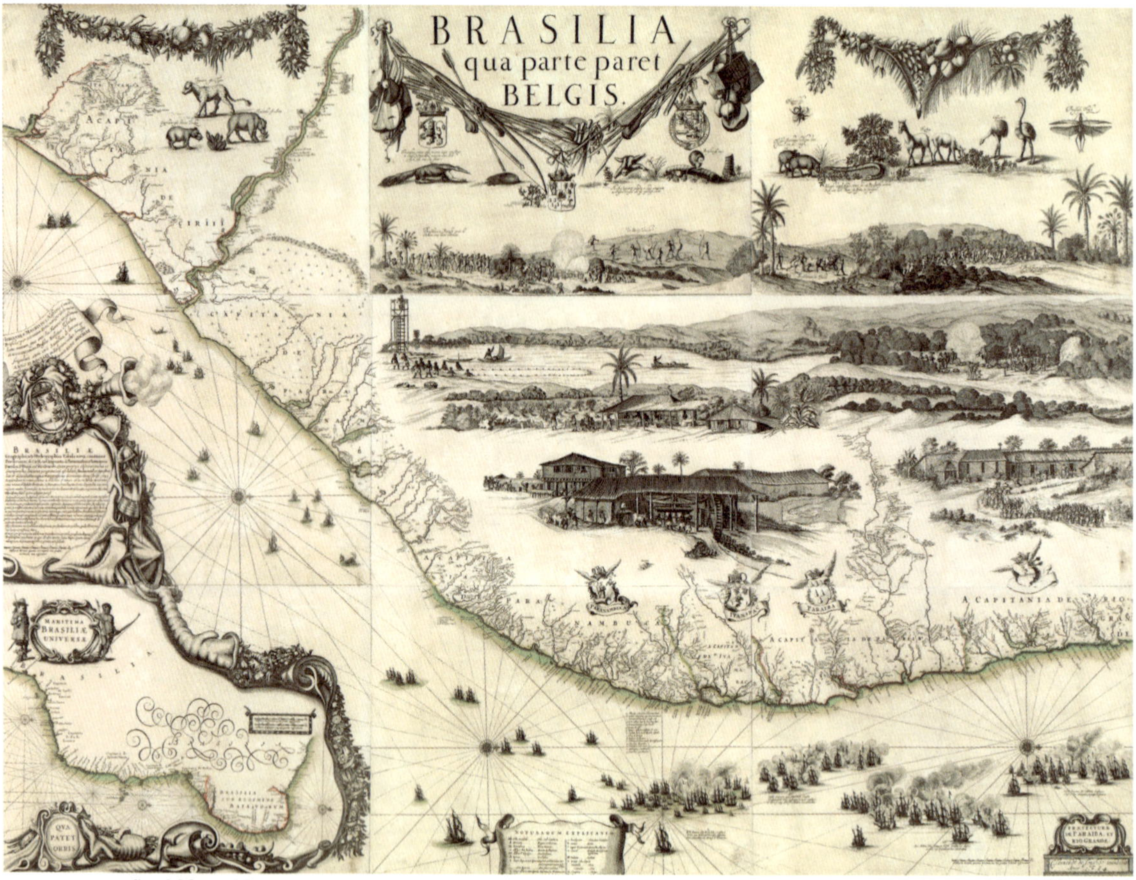

fig. 6 **Map of Dutch Brazil, Georg Marcgraf, 1664**

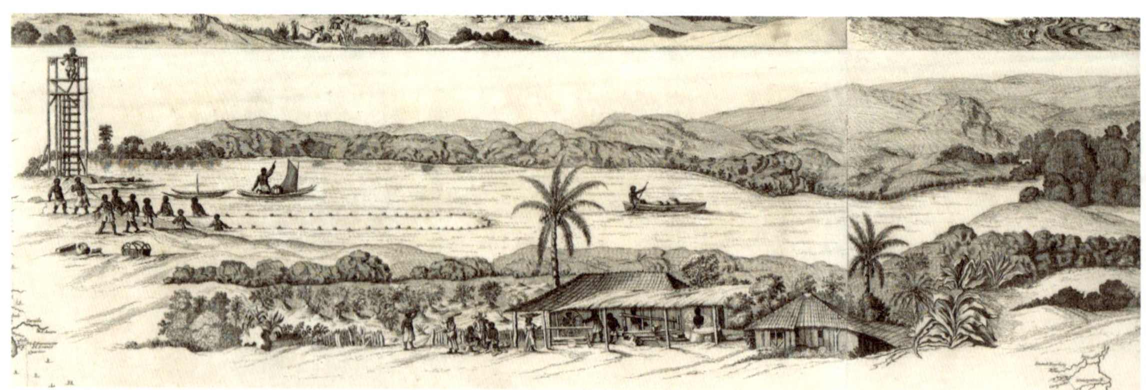

fig. 6a **Detail of the map with boats transporting sugar, Frans Post**

Illustrations made by Post on a detailed map of Brazil show how the sugar was carried out to the barques (figs. 6, 6a). The map itself was made by the German astronomer and cartographer Georg Marcgraf, who was part of the same entourage that sailed with Johan Maurits to Brazil. He embarked on various expeditions in the colony to collect mapmaking data. The illustrations show packages of raw sugar being transported on small boats. On the far left of the image, we can see an enslaved man in a lookout tower, probably keeping an eye on the workers and watching for approaching enemies.

slavery

By the time the WIC established a colony in Brazil, there were already 40,000 people of African descent living in slavery there.[24] In 1637, Johan Maurits and the other members of the colonial government in Recife took the decision to continue under the Dutch flag the policy of enslaving Africans for forced labour.[25] In a report to the directors of the WIC in the Dutch Republic, they indicated that although they knew 'that the work would be better if the sugar mills were operated by white people', it could not be expected that workers from the Dutch Republic or Portugal would emigrate en masse to Brazil.[26] Johan Maurits argued that regular shipments of enslaved people would be necessary to ensure that sugar production increased and remained profitable.[27] Unlike the Portuguese traders, the WIC had managed to come to an agreement with the Potiguara (one of the largest indigenous populations in northeast Brazil) that they would not be enslaved.[28] The conditions for this agreement were established in 1630, when the Dutch arrived in Brazil and the Potiguara provided them with strategic and cartographic information that was crucial to their successful conquest of colonial territory.[29] Later, in 1642, the WIC reneged on this agreement.

The Dutch needed workers for their plantations. First they attacked Portuguese slave ships to capture enslaved people. But they still needed greater numbers, and in 1637 they attempted to conquer from the Portuguese the most important trading post in West Africa: Elmina Castle, on the Gold Coast. The WIC had tried to take the castle once before, in 1625, but even before the attack could be initiated the fleet was captured by Elminese allies of the Portuguese.[30] Some years later, a WIC merchant named Hans Propheet made a sketch of this foiled attack, showing the castle and its strategic location (fig. 7). Because of this map, the WIC was better prepared for its second attempt in 1637.

The WIC set up cannon positions on the high hill of St Jago, shown in the left background of the Propheet sketch, and proceeded to attack the castle from many sides.[31] The raid was successful, bringing to a close the Portuguese occupation of Elmina after a period of 155 years. The Portuguese had used the castle primarily as a trading post for gold and provisions for further trade.[32] Now, it was also used for the purpose of human trafficking, with the full endorsement of the States General, the Dutch parliament.[33] Elmina Castle became the Dutch administrative headquarters in West Africa from 1637 to 1872.[34] For a period of nearly 150 years, African people were shipped from the west coast of Africa to South America. A WIC report about

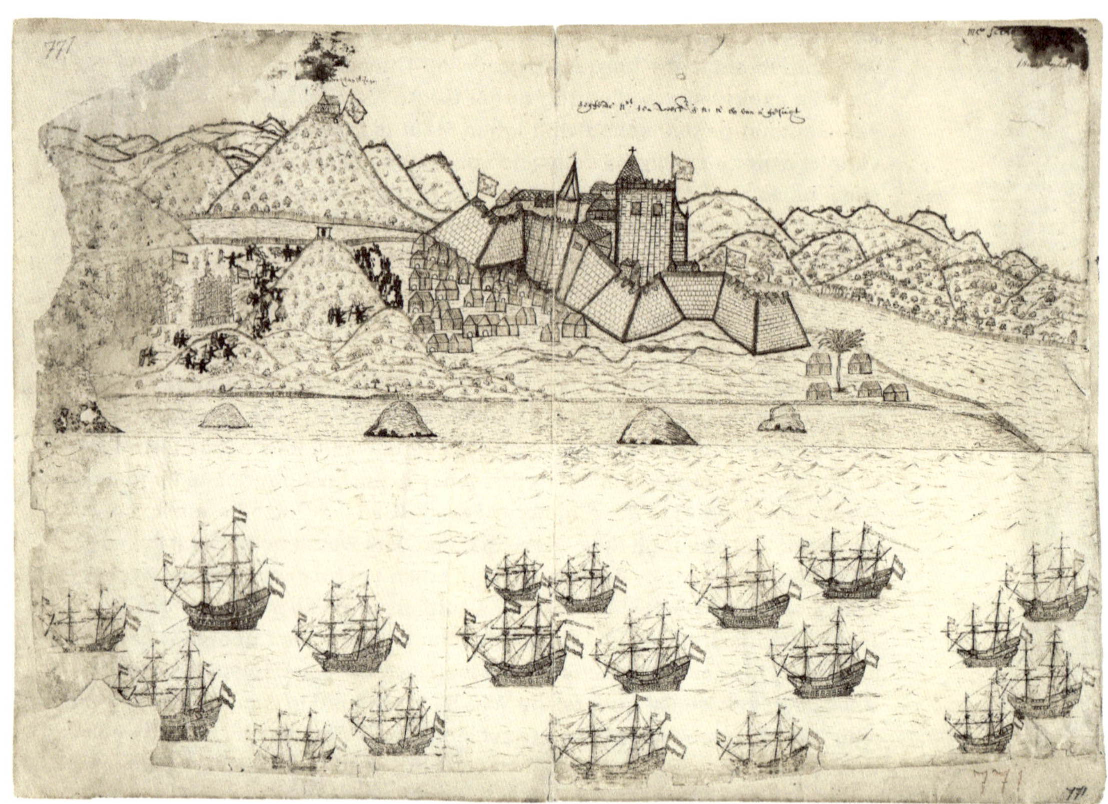

fig. 7 **Attack of Elmina Castle by the West India Company in 1625**
Hans Propheet, 1629

the colony stated in 1639: 'Without these slaves it is impossible to achieve anything in Brazil ... and if anyone finds himself feeling conscience-stricken by this, [these feelings] would merely be unnecessary scruples'.[35]

the slave trade

After his initial capture in Africa, João was probably taken to Elmina Castle, where, after being sold, he would have stayed in a barracks or goods warehouse until the time came to be shipped out.[36] He would have been branded prior to departure and then taken out to the slave ship by canoe. The 200 or so prisoners on each ship had their hands and feet shackled before being loaded as cargo into the lower decks.[37] João must surely have wondered what was to become of him during the long voyage on the overcrowded ship. A direct crossing would have taken five to eight weeks, but in many cases a ship would first sail for several months along the coast of Africa, searching for more men, women and children. Only when sufficient human cargo had been collected did the ship set sail for the other side of the Atlantic.[38] Crammed as it was with people, the longer the voyage took, the greater the chance that disease would take hold and that people would not survive the crossing.

Precisely how João came to be enslaved in Africa is unknown. A Dutch trader named Pieter de Marees travelled to the west coast of Africa and in 1602 wrote a travelogue that included descriptions of the local slavery systems, to help other traders. He explained, for example, that there were differences between forms of enslavement in the coastal region of Guinea (from the coast of modern Senegal to the mouth of the Niger River, an area that included the Gold Coast) and in Angola or Congo: people could be enslaved in all these places, but in Guinea it was not common for enslaved people to be loaded onto ships, while in Angola and Congo it was.[39]

Marees also explains that it was possible to enslave people locally because they were poor, were unable to earn a living or were unable to repay debts to the king. In some cases, lacking the resources to look after them, parents had no choice but to sell their young children.[40] And in wartime, prisoners of war were enslaved: 'According to an ancient right of the peoples, those that defeat the others in battle take them and consider them as their slaves and servants.'[41]

In the early seventeenth century, the Gold Coast was made up of several mutually hostile mini-states. This is clearly illustrated in another map by Hans Propheet (fig. 8). Europeans wanting to conduct trade in the region needed to be acquainted with its various communities and able to take advantage of their political differences if necessary. They forged multiple alliances with the various African powers. In exchange for weapons and soldiers that could be deployed in local conflicts, they received permission to conduct trade.[42] The agreements, requirements and obligations were stipulated in contracts. The African rulers were the dominant parties in these alliances, and the Europeans needed to be tough negotiators to achieve anything at all; Propheet even added descriptions of the communities in each area – 'traders', 'very wealthy', 'warlike' – to give an indication of what approach to negotiation was most likely to be successful.

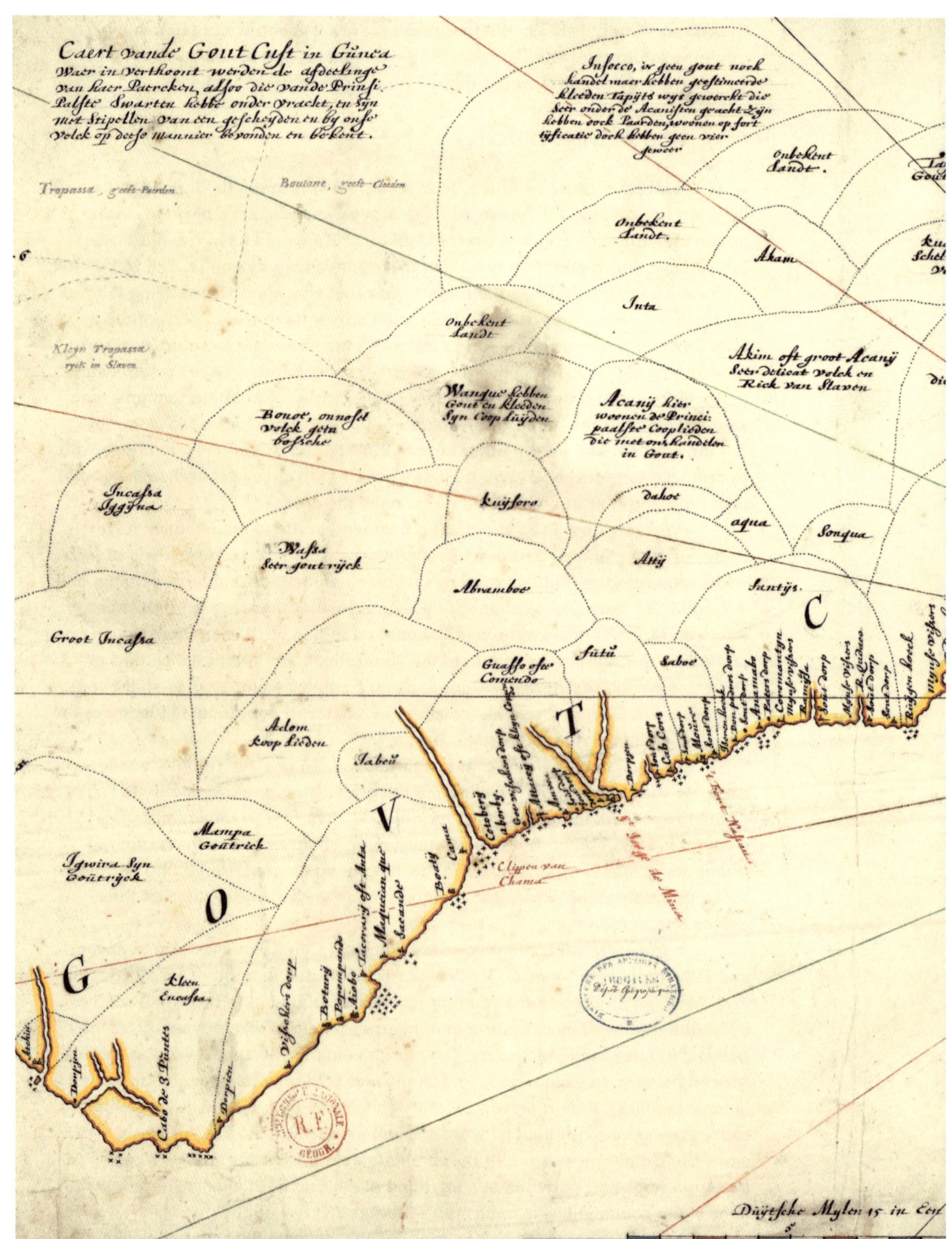

fig. 8 **Detail of a Dutch map of Gold Coast kingdoms, with notes for trading, attributed to Hans Propheet, c. 1629**

In this way the WIC gained access in the seventeenth century to coastal trading posts and to the prisoners of war of these African states, whom it enslaved. On 20 August 1642, a contract was drawn up between the WIC and 'Ockij, king of the great Accra', stating that Ockij granted the WIC permission to conduct trade with his kingdom and to establish a trading post without hindrance from his subjects.[43]

It soon became clear following the WIC's capture of Elmina Castle that the supply of enslaved people could not satisfy the demand for workers in Brazil, so the trading company made efforts to gain access to the slave market in other parts of Africa. The WIC took its first step towards this goal in 1641 by capturing from the Portuguese their castles in Luanda (Angola) and on the island of São Tomé. They achieved this by joining forces with the Congolese king Nkanga a Lukeni a Nzenze a Ntumba, better known as Garcia II of Congo.

The next step was to develop trading relations. Around this time, the WIC received an anonymous and undated letter written in French advising the trading company to give gifts to various rulers in order to gain a foothold in the Angolan slave trade: 'Ask the king [of Congo] to send envoys to collect these gifts and do not treat these envoys like slaves. Do the same with Queen Ginga [Nzinga], of the kingdom of Matamba in Angola.'[44] In October 1642, the director of the recently captured trading post in Luanda, Pieter Mortamer, passed on a similar message to Johan Maurits in a letter concerning 'gifts to the King of Congo'.[45] Mortamer supplemented his advice with a warning that the Congolese were quite aware of the quality of gifts they received and could not be easily fooled. The African traders were pulling all the strings: levying excise duty on the Europeans and rejecting low-quality goods.

Before Johan Maurits could follow this advice, he was visited by delegations from Africa seeking a political alliance against the Portuguese. In 1642–1643, Garcia II sent five envoys from Congo to Recife. Albert Eckhout, one of the artists in Johan Maurits's entourage, painted their portraits.[46] Their clothing and jewellery indicate the men's respective status. Three of them are wearing the prestigious *mpu* cap, which was worn exclusively by members of the royal family or other elite groups. Mpu were hand-woven from raffia palm or pineapple fibre and featured complex motifs. They also served as diplomatic gifts: a cap catalogued in 1674 in Denmark as part of the country's royal collection probably arrived in the country through a similar channel (fig. 9).[47] Mpu also feature in a print by Jacob van Meurs in the 1668 book *Naukeurige Beschrijvingen der Afrikaensche gewesten* (Precise descriptions of the African regions) by the historian Olfert Dapper, showing European traders kneeling before Garcia II to ask for permission to conduct trade in Congo (fig. 10).

The king wanted the alliance with the Dutch Republic so he could get military support for his war with the Portuguese. In a 1642 letter to Johan Maurits, written in Portuguese, Garcia II writes that 'under the pretext of peace and friendship, [the Portuguese] seek to take my kingdom from me, to profit from my mines.'[48] Elsewhere in the letter he describes 'the cruelty of the Portuguese, which is founded on ambition' and explains that he wishes to expel them to liberate his kingdom, despite it being inconsistent with his Catholic faith to expel other Catholics.[49]

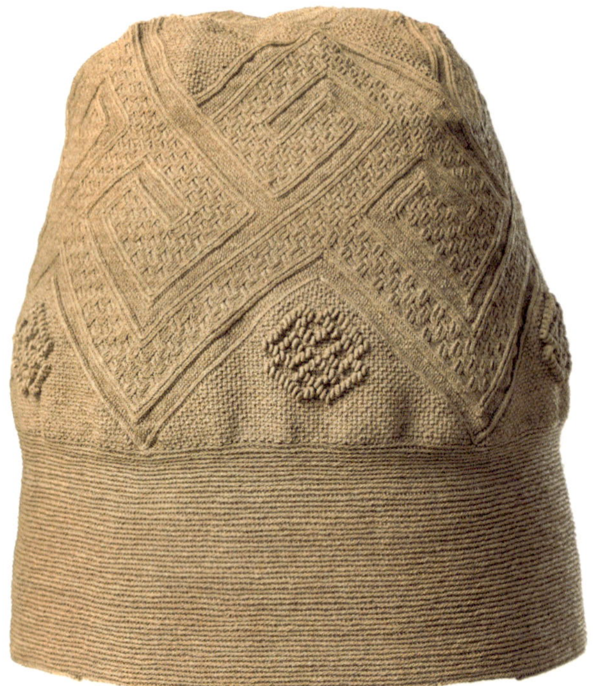

fig. 9 **Congolese *mpu* cap, before 1674**

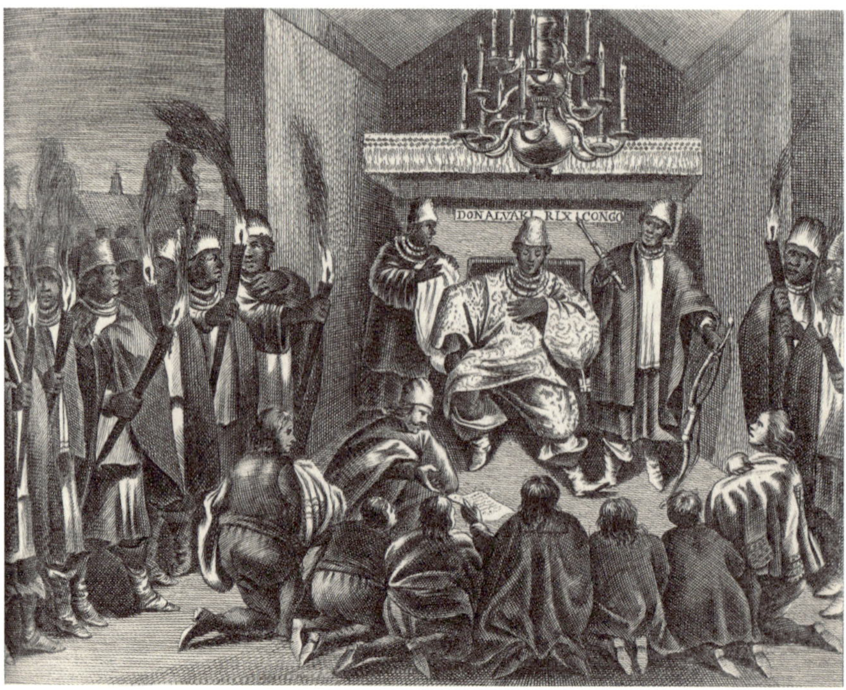

fig. 10 **European traders at the court of Garcia II, King of Congo**
Jacob van Meurs, 1668

The envoys delivered the letter, accompanied by several gifts 'in acknowledgement of loyal friendship'.[50] Notes written by Johan Maurits himself confirm that he received the following gifts: 'a large gold chain and a silver water basin, which [I] have donated to the church at Siegen as a baptismal font, and 200 slaves or moors'.[51] This large basin is still used to this day for baptisms at St Nicholas Church in Siegen (fig. 11). Indeed, it already had a long history before it was offered as a gift to Johan Maurits in Brazil. The basin, weighing a full 5 kilograms, was made by a silversmith in Peru around 1586,[52] and in the same century the Spanish gave it to Portuguese traders in exchange for enslaved people. The Portuguese, in turn, traded the basin in Luanda, again for enslaved people. This is how it came into the possession of Garcia II, who sent it back across the ocean to Brazil as a diplomatic gift in 1642.

Garcia II also lists all the gifts in his letter to Johan Maurits, with the exception of the '200 slaves or moors'. Did the king do this on purpose? In later letters to Filipe Franco, a Jesuit rector in Luanda, Garcia blamed the Portuguese in Luanda for the slave trade, pointing out that 'rather than the gold or silver or other goods that serve as money elsewhere ... these coins are not gold or textile, but living beings.' He saw that his kingdom was jeopardized by the international demand for forced labour and wrote that, to his sorrow, he and his ancestors had 'in our humility given way to that from which all evil grows in our country'.[53]

In the period from 1636 to 1645, alliances between African rulers and the WIC led to more than 23,000 people being deported from Guinea and Angola to the northeast Brazilian state of Pernambuco.[54] These regions (along with the Caribbean island of Curaçao, which the WIC conquered in 1634) were now part of a triangular trading route: the Dutch Republic transported copper, cotton, textiles, gunpowder and, later, alcohol and weapons from Europe to West Africa, where textiles and other products were exchanged for gold, ivory and people; these people were then shipped to the Americas, where they were forced to work in wretched conditions; and the triangle was completed by the export of sugar, brazilwood, cochineal, coffee beans and tobacco from South America to Europe.

the end of dutch brazil

Portugal and the Netherlands signed a peace treaty in 1641. Although it was effective in Europe itself, Portuguese colonists in Brazil, Angola, São Tomé and elsewhere continued to wage guerrilla wars against the Dutch.[55] This is one of the reasons that the Dutch eventually pulled out of Brazil. The WIC was suffering unsustainable losses as a result not just of the continuing wars but also the millions of guilders in loans to Portuguese plantation owners that were never paid back. By 1654, all of Brazil was once again in Portuguese hands and almost all the Dutch colonists had vacated the plantations. Some of them went to Suriname, where they resumed sugar cultivation.

What the end of Dutch rule in Brazil meant for João Mina is unknown. Did he manage to stay out of the hands of the Portuguese? Did he join a Maroon forest community with whom he could build a life for himself? Or did

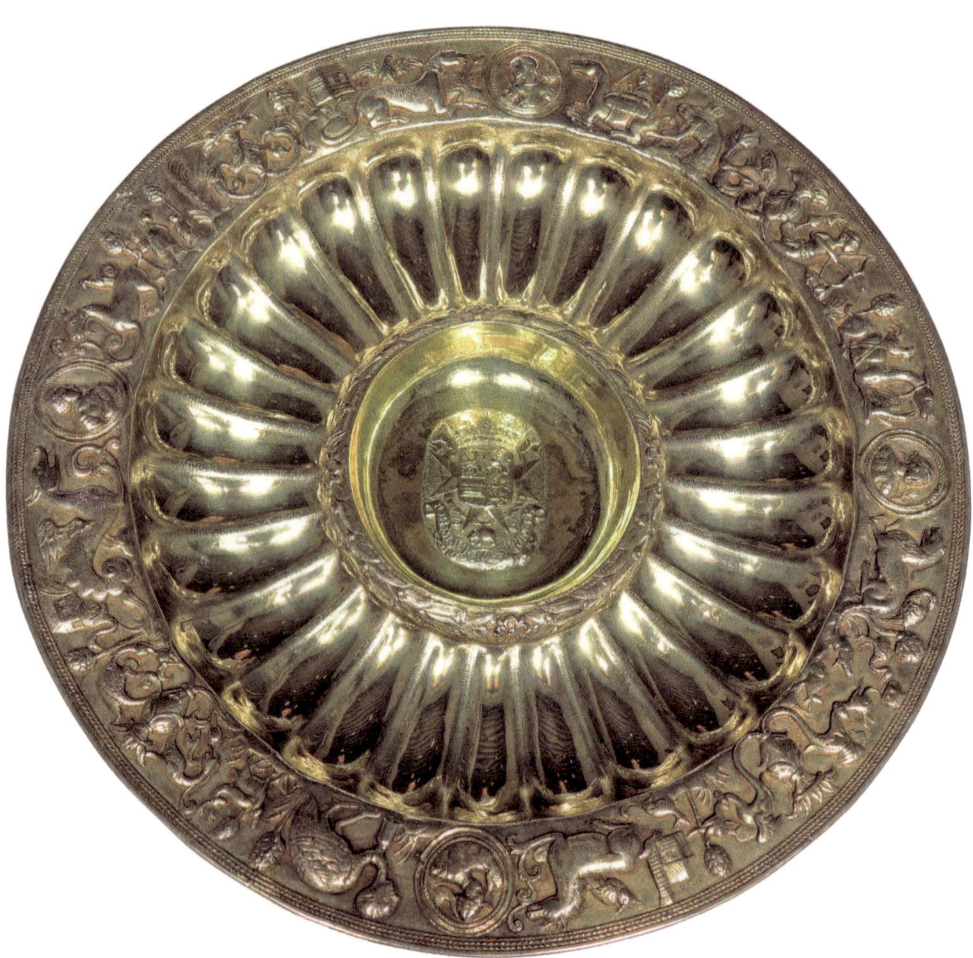

fig. 11 **Gilt silver basin, 1586**
Gift of Garcia II to Johan Maurits

he find himself in the Dutch Republic or some other region? Unfortunately, we have no personal information about João beyond what appears in his testimony. Nonetheless, the fact that we do have a few details about his life makes him (along with the other enslaved people whose testimonies have survived in the archives) a rarity; no trace remains of millions of enslaved men, women and children. For them, we have no stories, no names, no faces, no voices.

eveline sint nicolaas

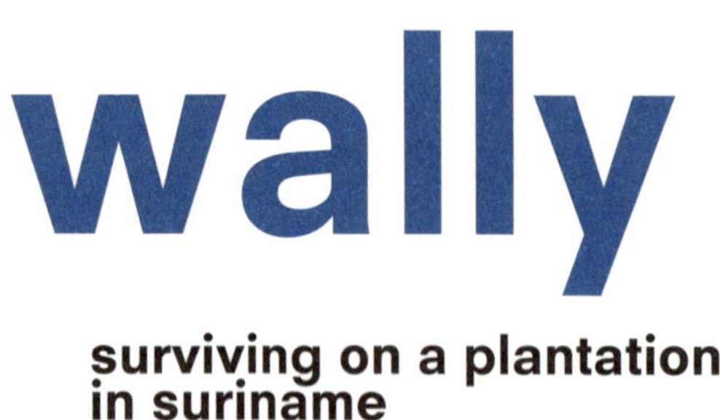

surviving on a plantation in suriname

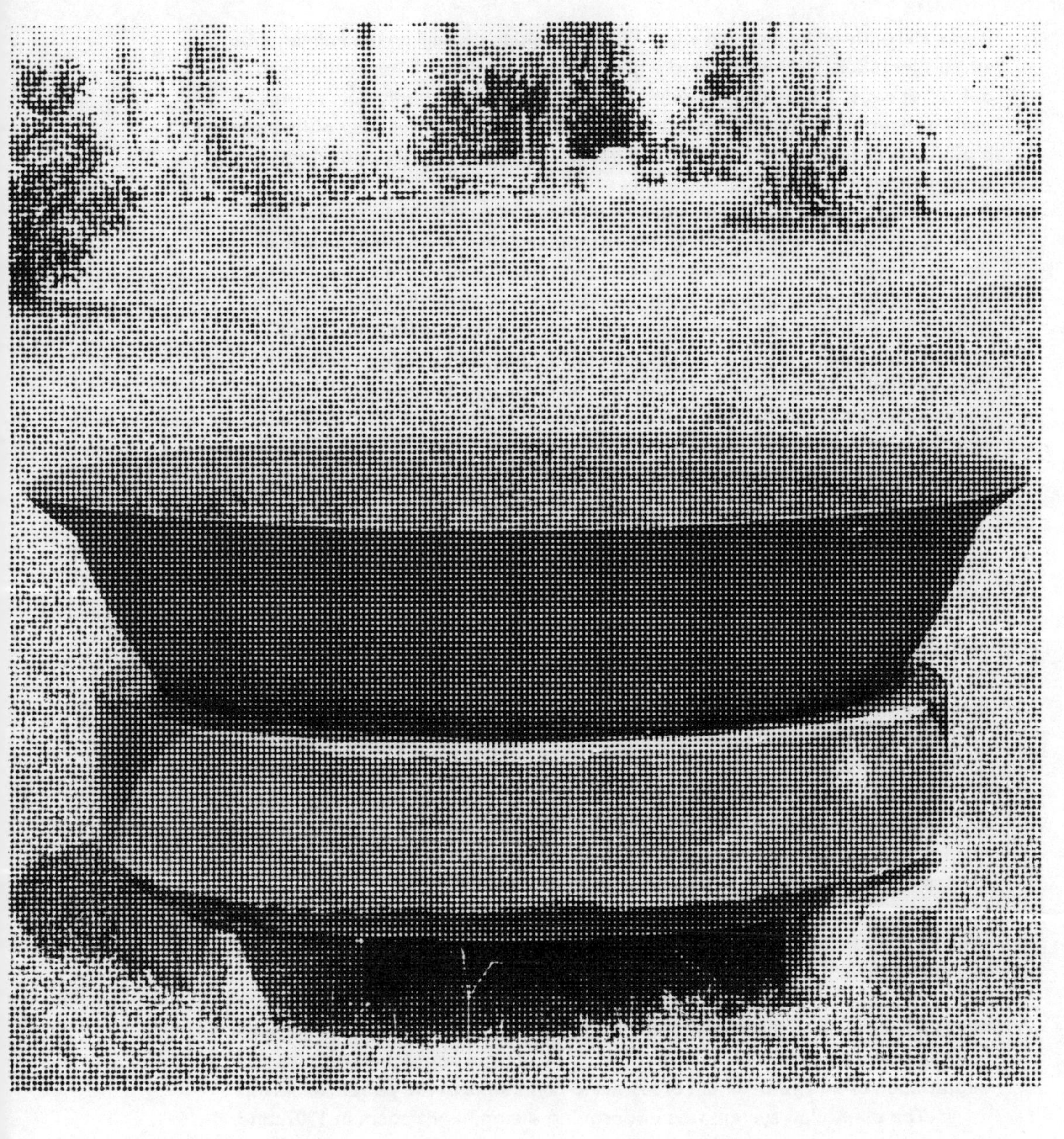

It was still early in the morning when Wally walked to the mill on the Palmeneribo sugar plantation, where he found a group of men setting off for the fields to cut sugar cane. This was hard work and often resulted in nasty cuts to the arms and legs. Why go to work so early, Wally asked the men: 'Our old master in Holland is dead; our new master is rich enough; you fellows don't need to work so hard.'[1]

Hard labour was an everyday reality on a sugar plantation, from early morning to deep into the night. The slaveholder decided what each worker was to do and where and when it had to be done. Absolute submission was required. In the colonial system, administration, law and infrastructure were entirely dedicated to extracting as much profit as possible from land and labour. Within that system – conceived and maintained by human beings – Wally and other enslaved human beings were considered property. Property that was tallied in the records along with tools and livestock. Property that was forced to work to exhaustion during the harvest, day and night, in order to process the sugar cane on time. Property that was not considered human and which therefore could find no recourse in the courts, for by law the body of an enslaved person belonged not to him or her but to the slave owner, meaning that from a legal point of view there was no such thing as abuse or rape of an enslaved person.

In 1707, 156 enslaved people lived and worked on Palmeneribo, one of the sugar plantations along the upper reaches of the Suriname River, a day's journey by boat from Paramaribo, the capital. The plantation was run by three European men reporting to Jonas Witsen, the owner in Amsterdam. They were expected to produce maximum profit, and this demanded total exertion and submission from the people in slavery.

Maintaining the system required constant dedication on the part of the slave owners, which was undoubtedly accompanied by a fear of the enslaved people, who vastly outnumbered them. This system could only function through the use of extreme violence, the application of a sophisticated divide-and-rule strategy and the profound sense of inferiority drilled into people in slavery. This latter aspect came into play at specific moments such as branding, when they were literally marked as the property of another human being, and through daily punishments and bullying.[2] The situation on any given plantation was highly dependent on the owner or the local manager and their implementation of the system. A change of management or ownership could therefore mean a degradation or an improvement of the living conditions of the people in slavery.

The plantation system was undergoing a significant boom in 1707, and there was little chance that the situation of Wally and the others would change in the foreseeable future. Perhaps they found comfort in the idea that after death their souls would travel across the ocean back to Africa, to their birthplaces or those of their families. Or they may have derived hope from the fact that some men and women had managed to escape the plantation and survive in the forest, proof that life outside slavery was possible. But at what price? In order to protect themselves and their children, most enslaved people accommodated themselves as well as they could to the slavery system, perhaps in part in the hope of slightly improving their own positions within that system.

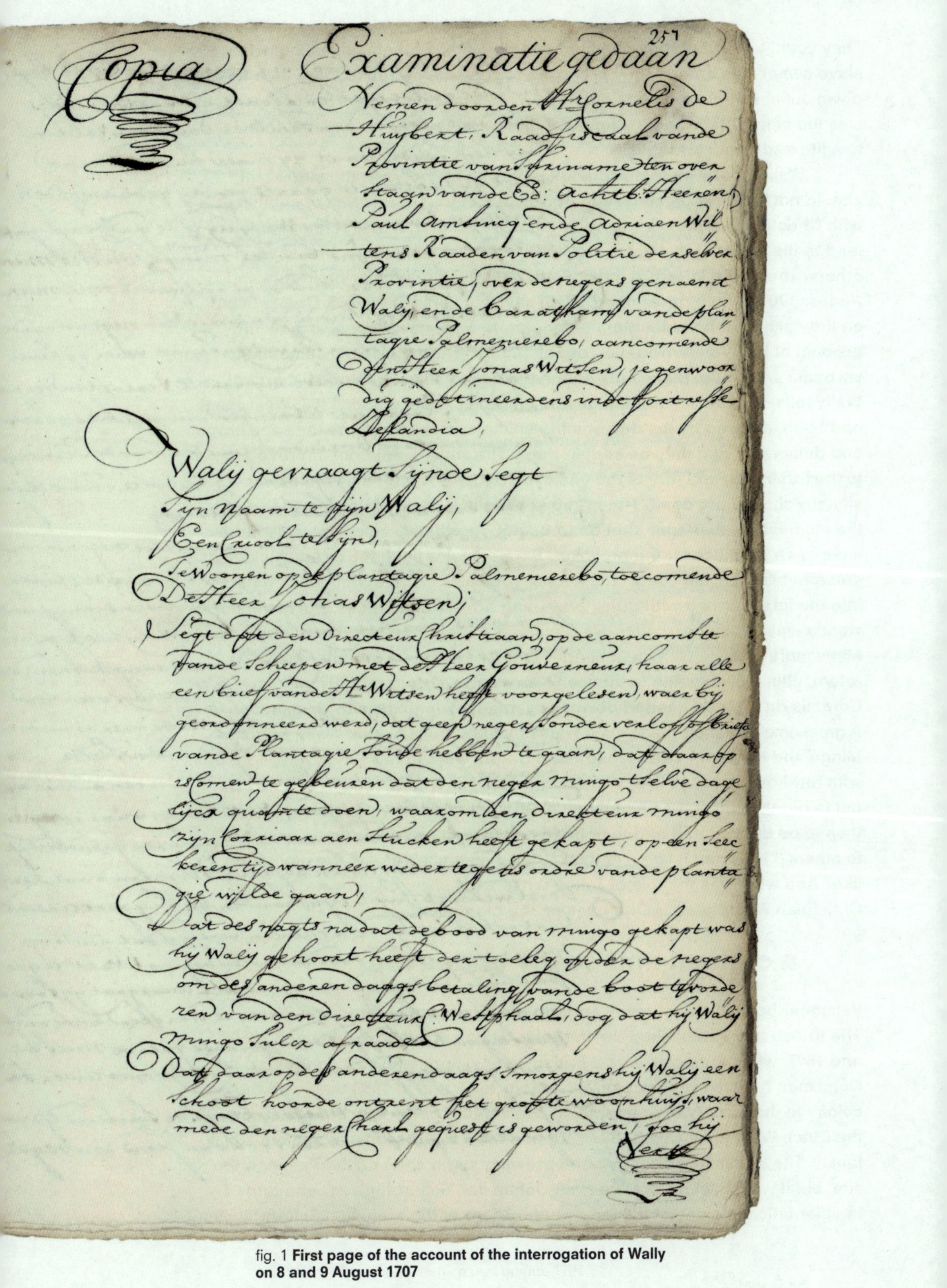

257

Copia

Examinatie gedaan

Nemen door den Hr Cornelis de Huybert, Raadfiscaal vande Provintie van Suriname ten overstaan vande Ed: Achtb: Heeren Paul Amsincq ende Adriaen Wiltens Raaden van Politie derselver Provintie, over de negers genaamt Waly, ende Barathamf vande plantagie Palmeniereb o, aancomende den Heer Jonas Witsen, jegenwoordig gedetineerd en in de fortresse Zeelandia,

Waly gevraagt synde segt

Syn naam te syn Waly,

Een Criool te syn,

Te woonen op de plantagie Palmeniereb o, toecomende den Heer Jonas Witsen;

Segt dat den directeur Christiaan, op de aancomste vande scheepen met de Heer Gouverneur, haar alle een brief vanden Hr Witsen heeft voorgelesen, waer bij geordonneerd werd, dat geen neger sonder verlof of briefje vande Plantagie soude hebben te gaan, dat daar op is comen te gebeuren dat den neger Mingo tselve dagelijcx quam te doen, waarom den directeur Mingo zyn corriaar aen stucken heeft gekapt, op den seeckeren tijd wanneer weder tegens ordre vande plantagie wilde gaan,

Dat des nagts na dat de bood van Mingo gekapt was hy Waly gehoort heeft der toeleg onder de negers om des anderen daags betaling vande boot te vorderen van den directeur Westphaal, dog dat hy Waly Mingo sulcx afraade

Dat daar op des anderen daags 's morgens hy Waly een schoot hoorde ontrent het grootste woonhuys, waar mede den neger Charl gequetst is geworden, soo hy

Verte

fig. 1 **First page of the account of the interrogation of Wally on 8 and 9 August 1707**

They could talk about their common suffering among themselves, but when a slave owner was around they preferred to keep silent. Yet keeping their heads down out of self-preservation did not always work. Sometimes the provocation was too much. An ordinary altercation about something trivial might then lead to a life-and-death struggle.

Wally's early morning conversation with his peers at the sugar mill should not be viewed in isolation. It was in fact part of a series of conflicts with Christiaan Westphaal, the plantation's manager, that would eventually lead to the arrest of Wally, his brothers Baratham and Mingo, and several others. They were interrogated at Fort Zeelandia in Paramaribo in July and August 1707. 'When questioned, Walij says his name is Walij, a Creole living on the Palmeniriebo plantation, belonging to Mr Jonas Witsen', is how the account of Wally's interrogation opens (fig. 1).[3] There follows a sometimes verbatim account of the events on the plantation since Westphaal's arrival. Wally tells of a conflict about pigs and chickens in December 1706: Westphaal had been annoyed by the damage the animals were causing to the cane crops and demanded that they be kept in pens. The situation did not improve and, to the frustration and fury of the enslaved people, Westphaal would occasionally shoot a pig dead. The group kept calm in spite of this injustice, until the moment the manager shot dead one of Baratham's chickens. This must have been too much for the provoked Baratham. He flung the dead chicken in Westphaal's face, shouting, 'You shot it, you eat it.' Whereupon 22 men fled into the forest armed with guns, bows and arrows and lances. But life in the woods was difficult and after five days they all returned to Palmeneribo.[4] Many more clashes with the manager followed in the period after their return, ultimately leading to the men's arrest. On 11 August 1707, magistrate Cornelis de Huijbert handed down his sentence: death by slow immolation. A gruesome sentence, made even worse by the stipulation that Wally, Baratham, Mingo and their comrades Joseph and Charle were to have their flesh torn off with red-hot pincers as they were burned alive in public, 'and in this way be put to death in the most painful and most protracted way possible. They were then to be decapitated and their heads displayed on spikes as an example to others.'[5] How had it come to this? What was Wally's life on the plantation like? And what was the role of Jonas Witsen, the slave owner who, through Christiaan Westphaal, set the rules on the plantation?

'a difficult and costly endeavour'

Palmeneribo was one of many sugar plantations on the Suriname River. The British had established the first plantations in this area between 1650 and 1667, when Suriname was a British colony. Suriname was conquered by Dutchmen from the province of Zeeland in 1667, and in 1683 they sold the colony to the Society of Suriname, a joint venture of the City of Amsterdam, the Dutch West India Company (WIC) and the Van Aerssen van Sommelsdijck family. The British had already been growing sugar cane on the Palmeneribo site, but it was Witsen's predecessor, Johan van Scharphuijzen, who turned the plantation into one of the larger enterprises in the area. Van Scharphuijzen was from Middelburg, in Zeeland, and had been living in Suriname since the period of British rule. He was both governor of the colony and a slave owner. Besides Palmeneribo he owned the Waterland plantation, also on the Suriname River. His brother-in-law, pastor Joan Basseliers, had started the sugar plantation Surimombo on the plot of land next to Palmeneribo in 1671.

To start a plantation, all one needed to do was drive a few posts into the ground; the area circumscribed by these was then recorded by the authorities. No payment was required and ownership was automatically inheritable. There was, however, a limit on the width of any such plot of land along the river: all transport took place over water, so the river had to be accessible to all. There was also a requirement to cultivate the land and build a house. Finally, in the event of a foreign invasion of Suriname, plantation owners were required to help defend the country. All in all, the policy of the colonial administration was quite flexible, in the hope of attracting large numbers of people and generating as much profit as possible.

The land appropriated in this manner was not, incidentally, uninhabited or unused. The indigenous Kalina, or Caribs, who lived in the coastal region along the Atlantic Ocean, and the Arawak, who lived along the rivers of the interior, suffered most at the hands of the Europeans, who not only took their land but also attempted to enslave them. The Arawak and the Kalina put up fierce resistance by burning cane fields and plantations, and their uprising was so successful that by 1679 the Zeelanders had nearly given up hope. 'If we get no assistance and continue to be denied God's help, I fear that we shall have to abandon Suriname ... for they say that they want us to leave their country, which belonged to them', a Zeelander official wrote to the States of Zeeland.[6] Finally, in 1686, governor Cornelis van Aerssen van Sommelsdijck made peace with the Arawak and Kalina and the devastating warfare came to an end. The original inhabitants were given the guarantee that they would not be enslaved unless they committed a crime, and from now on their interests had to be considered when land was distributed to newcomers.[7]

The enforced peace opened the way for the establishment of new plantations. After a hesitating start, the number of sugar plantations rose from 50 in 1683 to almost 200 in 1713, a growth that could only take place by bringing over enslaved men and women from Africa to work on the plantations. Approximately 125,000 people are estimated to have been taken into slavery and transported to Suriname on ships sailing under Dutch flags during this period.[8] The children of these people, like Wally and his brothers Baratham and Mingo, were born in slavery and put to work on the plantations as well.

To administer the land, the Society of Suriname drew up a charter comprising 32 articles.[9] This was the new colony's constitution. The entire policy was predicated on turning a profit for the Dutch Republic back home, not for the overseas colony. This began with the importation of enslaved Africans to work on the plantations. When the society was established, it was stipulated that the WIC was to provide 'manpower' for the colony every year. Other parties were allowed to take part in this only if the company was unable to supply enough people. The WIC would hold on to this monopoly until 1730. Another stipulation was that all raw materials and semi-finished products were to be sold in the Netherlands. Further, Dutch ships were always to be used to transport the plantation products to the 'motherland', a stipulation that would only be rescinded in 1848. In addition, all products essential to the plantation economy and everyday life in the colony were to be imported from the Netherlands, from simple nails and machetes to shackles, to victuals for the inhabitants (fig. 2). Only tobacco, salted fish and livestock were allowed to be imported from North America. These stipulations leave no margin for doubt: Suriname was a productive colony for the Dutch Republic, and the plantations played a central role in this (fig. 3).

At the beginning of the eighteenth century, to help newcomers develop land in Suriname, the widow Magdalena Boxel-van Gelre wrote the practical guide *Aanwijzingen voor plantage-onderneming in Suriname* (Instructions on plantation management in Suriname).[10] After the death of her husband, she owned the Boxel sugar plantation – which like Palmeneribo and Waterland was situated on the Suriname River – until 1709. Her instructions date from the period when Witsen owned Palmeneribo and provide an impression of the work that Wally and the other enslaved workers were made to do, from the point of view of the slave owner.

Boxel-van Gelre begins her guide with the following advice: 'Establishing a new plantation is a difficult and costly endeavour – in the beginning, with new and unskilled slaves, nearly impossible for newcomers, but if one has old, trained slaves it goes well enough.' Even for enslaved workers with experience, however, the reclamation of land, with which the establishment of a plantation began, was one of the most exhausting operations. Broad canals and narrow trenches, intended for drainage and the transport of crops, were dug in the broiling sun using nothing more than a shovel. It is no coincidence that today, in the oral tradition of the Maroons,[11] the digging of canals and trenches (and their biannual dredging) is still cited as one of the principal reasons for fleeing from a plantation (fig. 4).[12]

The guide also describes how, after the initial drainage, the fields had to be set on fire in order to cleanse them of weeds and vermin and make them ready for planting. This burning had to be repeated regularly in order to maintain the quality of the cane. Every three or four years, the planting of cane had to be done all over again from scratch. Newly cultivated soil often resulted in a first harvest of poor quality. The juice of the first cane had to be boiled much longer and often produced a brown rather than a clear mass. In such cases it was advisable to burn off the cane and start over.

According to the guide, it was also vital to monitor water levels constantly. The mill trench had to be deep enough that, during the spring tide, sufficient water could be let in for the mill to operate through the entire harvest season. If there was too little water and the mill stopped prematurely, the process would come to a halt too early and the harvest would be lost (fig. 5). Timing and pace were therefore of crucial importance in harvest season: if too much cane was brought to the mill, the excess would sit idle for too long and would go sour, producing poor-quality sugar. In practice this meant an unrelenting schedule of working day and night to press all the cane in time. The next phase of processing followed immediately: reducing the juice in the boiling

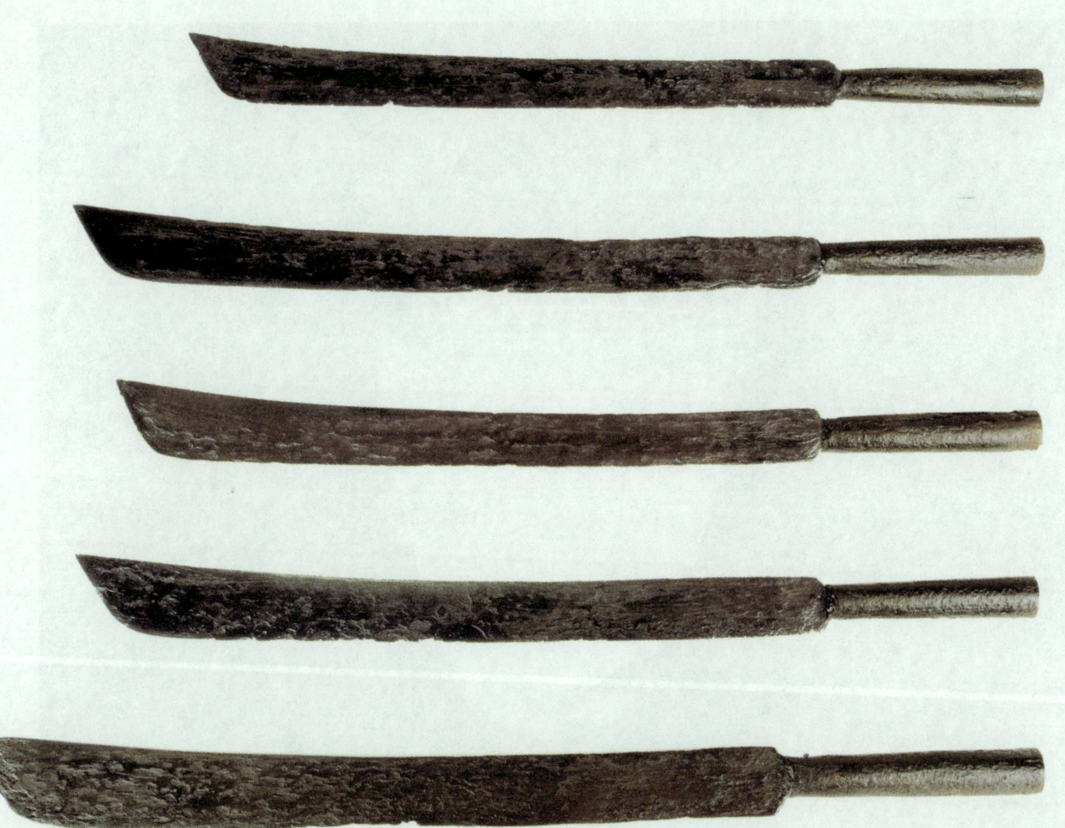

fig. 2 **Sugar cane machetes, manufactured in Europe and lost in a shipwreck on the way to Suriname, c. 1800–1850**

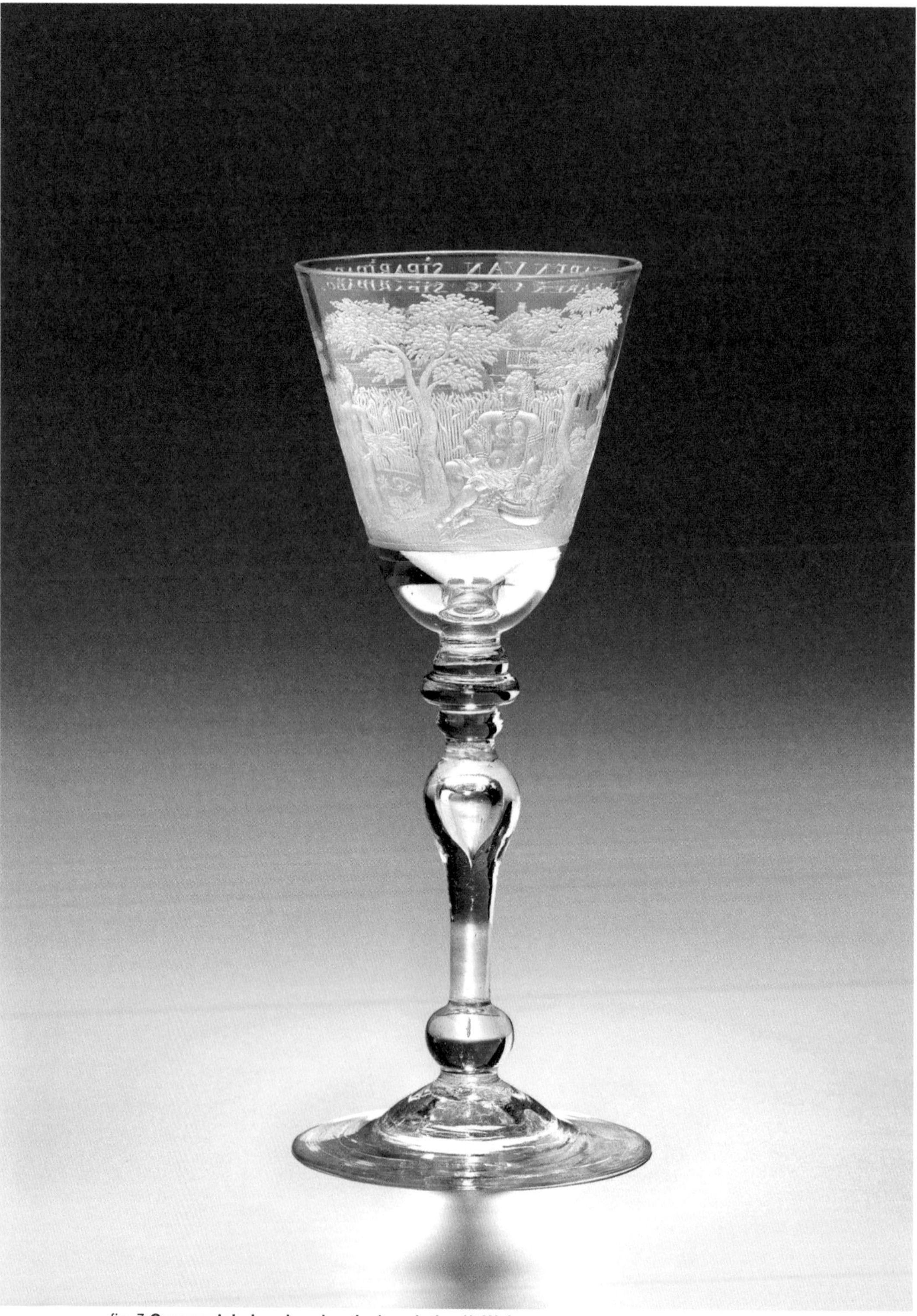

fig. 3 **Ceremonial glass bearing the inscription '*'t Welvaren van Siparipabo*' (The prosperity of Siparipabo), c. 1725–1750. With this kind of glass, slave owners would raise a toast to celebrate the ownership and profitability of their plantation**

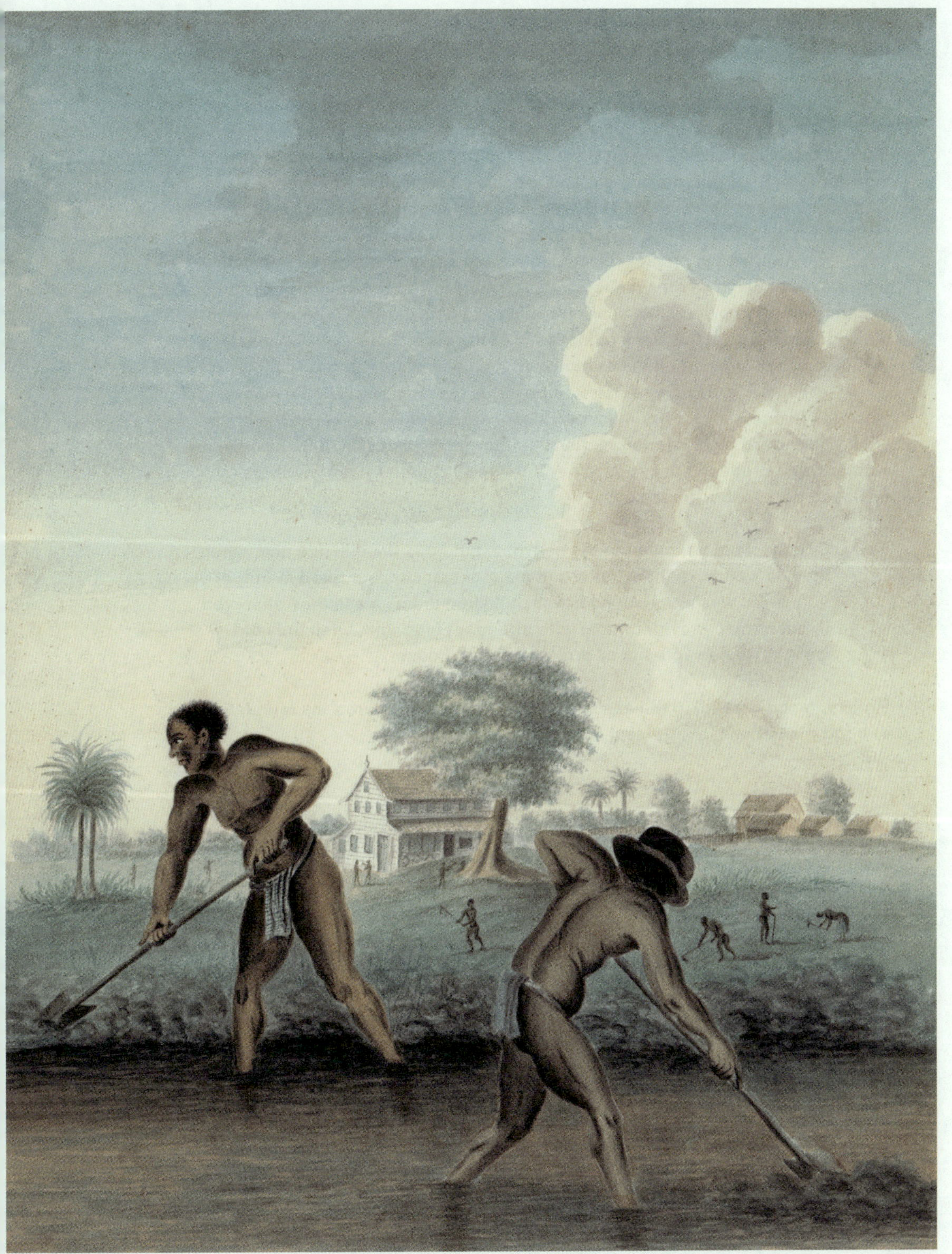

fig. 4 **Enslaved men digging trenches, c. 1850**

house. This was a hazardous occupation, and exhaustion greatly increased the risk of burns. The sugar cane juice, known as *lika* (derived from the Portugese *liquor*), was mixed with quicklime in a *kappa*, a cast-iron kettle, and boiled (fig. 6). These kappas often stood in a row, arranged from large to small, on the fire. During the boiling process, the crystals that formed along the rim of the kappa were swept back into the boiling cane juice with a brush in order to prevent caramelization, and the thick, greyish-brown layer of scum was regularly removed with a skimmer to keep the liquid clear. When the boiling had reduced the lika enough that the mass began to crystalize, the kappa was emptied in phases. Once cooled, the sugar was poured into vats to drain. After six to seven weeks, enslaved men rowed the solidified sugar to Paramaribo. From there the vats were shipped to Amsterdam, where the sugar was purified in one of the many refineries.[13] As the sugar cane was often planted in phases, the workload on the sugar plantation was always high.

In her guide, Boxel-van Gelre emphasizes the crucial role of the manager, who was responsible for optimum production on site. In practice, however, he would have been highly dependent on the knowledge and skill of the enslaved workers who produced the sugar year after year. On the treatment of the enslaved people, the guide says:

> One must not be unjust to the negroes, but keep them in line and, when they do well, give them some salt meat or salt cod; our good manager Van der K. was strict but he never punished them unless they deserved it, but always provided them with abundant food and when they did well they received a hat or dress or pair of trousers.

Punishing and rewarding the enslaved workers was considered the foundation of good plantation management.

the new slaveholder's strict policy

Palmeneribo, along with the Waterland and Surimombo plantations, came into the possession of Jonas Witsen of Amsterdam in 1702. From that point on, the plantations were no longer run locally by the owner himself as had been the case under Van Scharphuijzen and his sister and brother-in-law Sara and Joan Basseliers, but remotely, from Amsterdam. How had the 25-year-old Witsen come to own these three plantations in Suriname?

Basseliers, the owner of Surimombo, had died in 1689, whereupon his wife, Sara, had taken over the running of the plantation. At the time she was one of the largest sugar producers in Suriname. When in 1693 Sara died as well, the plantation became the property of her brother, Johan van Scharphuijzen. He died in 1699 in Amsterdam, and Elisabeth Basseliers, daughter of Sara and Joan (and therefore Van Scharphuijzen's niece), inherited his three plantations. Elisabeth was nineteen years old and placed under the guardianship of mayor Nicolaes Witsen, a friend of her uncle in Amsterdam. The Witsen family was an influential patrician family whose interests included the municipal

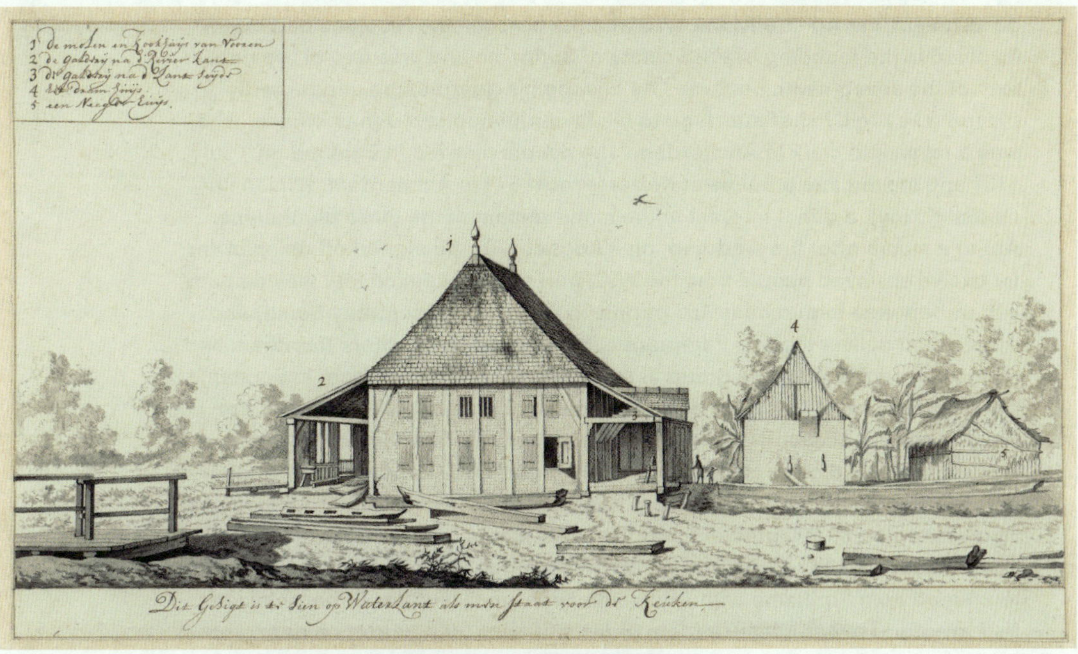

fig. 5 **View of the mill and the boiling house of the Waterland plantation, Dirk Valkenburg, 1708**

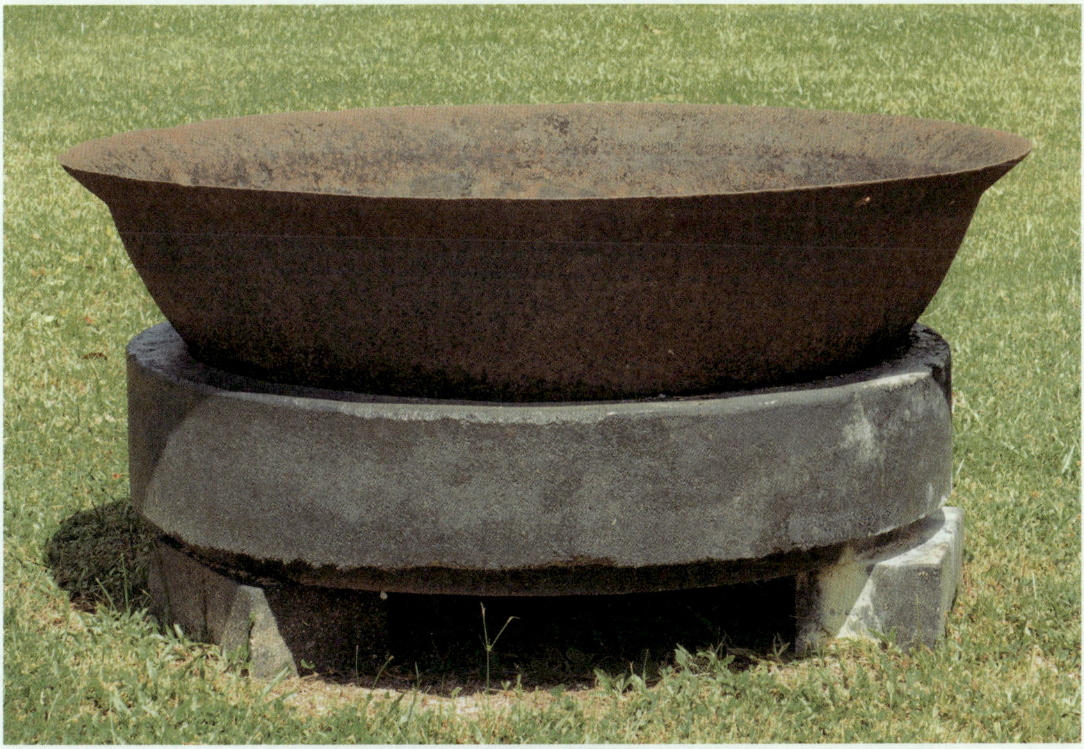

fig. 6 **A *kappa*, a cast-iron kettle for boiling down sugar cane juice, 19th century**

government, the Admiralty, the WIC and the civic militia. Nicolaes had been involved in the founding of the Society of Suriname and was one of the richest men of the seventeenth century.[14] As Elisabeth's guardian he undoubtedly played a key role in her marriage to his favourite nephew, Jonas Witsen, who was a municipal clerk in Amsterdam. The couple married in Egmond on 1 July 1701 and moved into a house at Keizersgracht 674 in Amsterdam. Witsen immediately took a direct interest in the management of the three plantations. About a month after the wedding, on 8 August 1701, he signed off on an order for twelve enslaved people from the WIC, part of an obligation that the company had undertaken to purchase 165 people in Ardra (in present-day Benin) and Angola and deliver them to Paramaribo.[15] Wally and his brothers Baratham and Mingo were not among this group of twelve, as they had been born in Suriname, but perhaps one of the other enslaved men and women whose names are recorded in the accounts of the interrogations was part of this shipment.

Elisabeth died in childbirth on 23 February 1702, less than a year after her wedding. Mother and child were buried in the Nieuwe Kerk in Amsterdam. Jonas inherited 88,000 guilders and the three plantations. And there was one more legacy for him to take charge of: the young man Trawatte, who had journeyed from Suriname with Johan van Scharphuijzen. Van Scharphuijzen had granted Trawatte his freedom in his will, plus 200 guilders a year, and he had entered the service of Elisabeth and Jonas upon the former governor's death.[16] Trawatte is not the only enslaved person mentioned in Van Scharphuijzen's will. A number of 'old and faithful slaves' in Suriname were given 100 guilders each, and the document stipulated that they were to be punished less severely than the other enslaved labourers. Van Scharphuijzen had lived with these people in Suriname for years and knew them by name. They include the first overseer Marq and his wife; the former cook Cacoe and his wife; head cooper James and his wife; head carpenter Jacob and his wife; the wood turner Ackan; and Hanna, who was born in Van Scharphuijzen's house, the daughter of an indigenous man and an African woman. Arthur, the overseer on the Waterland plantation, also received 100 guilders, but he was not exempted from harsh punishments.[17] Here, in writing, are the differences in reward and treatment typical of the divide-and-rule principle applied on the plantations.

Once Elisabeth died, there was no one in Jonas Witsen's immediate circle with direct experience of any of the three plantations. Jonas, like his uncle Nicolaes, was a great art lover and was on good terms with the painter Dirk Valkenburg, owning eighteen of his paintings by this point.[18] To find out more about the nature and condition of his inheritance, Jonas Witsen commissioned Valkenburg to travel to Suriname and document his property. A contract was drawn up by the Amsterdam solicitor Henrick Outgers on 24 and 27 February 1706, stipulating that Valkenburg was to go to Suriname for four years to take charge of their bookkeeping and to paint 'all three plantations from life, as well as other rare birds and crops', and that he 'agrees not to sell any paintings, watercolours or drawings or other art he makes during the stipulated time, or to paint for anyone else than for Mr Witsen' (fig. 7).[19] The business details are efficiently arranged. For the first two years Valkenburg is to earn 500 guilders a year, and thereafter 600, with the prospect of a bonus at the end of the contract's term. He is to be given a good room and may dine at the manager's table. Witsen shall supply Valkenburg 'with anything he might need to produce his art and services as stipulated above, namely canvas, brushes, paint and oil; a boy shall also be assigned to serve him, to be treated not as a slave but as a child and not harshly'.[20] Treating the boy as a child and not as a slave: this is a stipulation that chills the reader to the marrow, for how was an enslaved human being supposed to be treated?

In late 1706, Christiaan Westphaal, who had served as surgeon at Palmeneribo since May 1701, was promoted to manager. The ship that brought the new governor, Wilhelm de Gruijter, to Suriname in early 1707 also carried a letter from Witsen to Westphaal, containing instructions for a stricter regime. Wally talked about this during his interrogation: '[He] Says that the manager, Christiaan, on the arrival of the ships carrying the governor, read them out all a letter from Mr Witsen, in which it was ordered that no negro was to leave the plantation without a pass.'[21] Westphaal probably read out the letter in the hope of inspiring deference to and acceptance of the new rules. It might have been his responsibility to carry out the new policy, but he enjoyed little authority himself. Charle had told him this directly to his face: Westphaal might be a master in medicine, but that did not make him master of the plantation.

The stricter regime that Witsen wished to impose would constrain the freedom of the enslaved people even further. Their private lives were very circumscribed – everything was predicated on the work on the plantation, and they had scarcely any time or space for themselves. The people in slavery were usually given permission to celebrate once a year, most commonly after the harvest. They came together to make music, to dance and to practise their own religious rituals (fig. 9). Valkenburg recorded one such rare moment of togetherness and relaxation in one of the paintings he produced for Witsen (fig. 8). It is a unique representation of people in slavery, with portraits that display a variety of expressions and emotions. It is quite possible that the people we have met in this chapter are represented in this painting.

Only on the weekends was there time for contact with family and the cultivation of their own subsistence crops. Witsen, however, had stipulated in his letter that even the free Saturday, specified in Van Scharphuijzen's will, was to be rescinded. The owner felt the regular free Sunday provided more than enough opportunity for the enslaved people to work their small fields and visit friends and family on nearby plantations.

mingo's *korjaal*

On many plantations, due to the difficulty of the physical labour, there were one and a half times as many men as women. Because of this, enslaved men might begin relationships with women outside the plantation on which they lived; Mingo was married to a woman on the nearby plantation owned by Josua Serfatijn Pina. To visit her on his free days he had to take his *korjaal* (a small open canoe made out of a hollowed-out tree trunk) some way up the Suriname River.

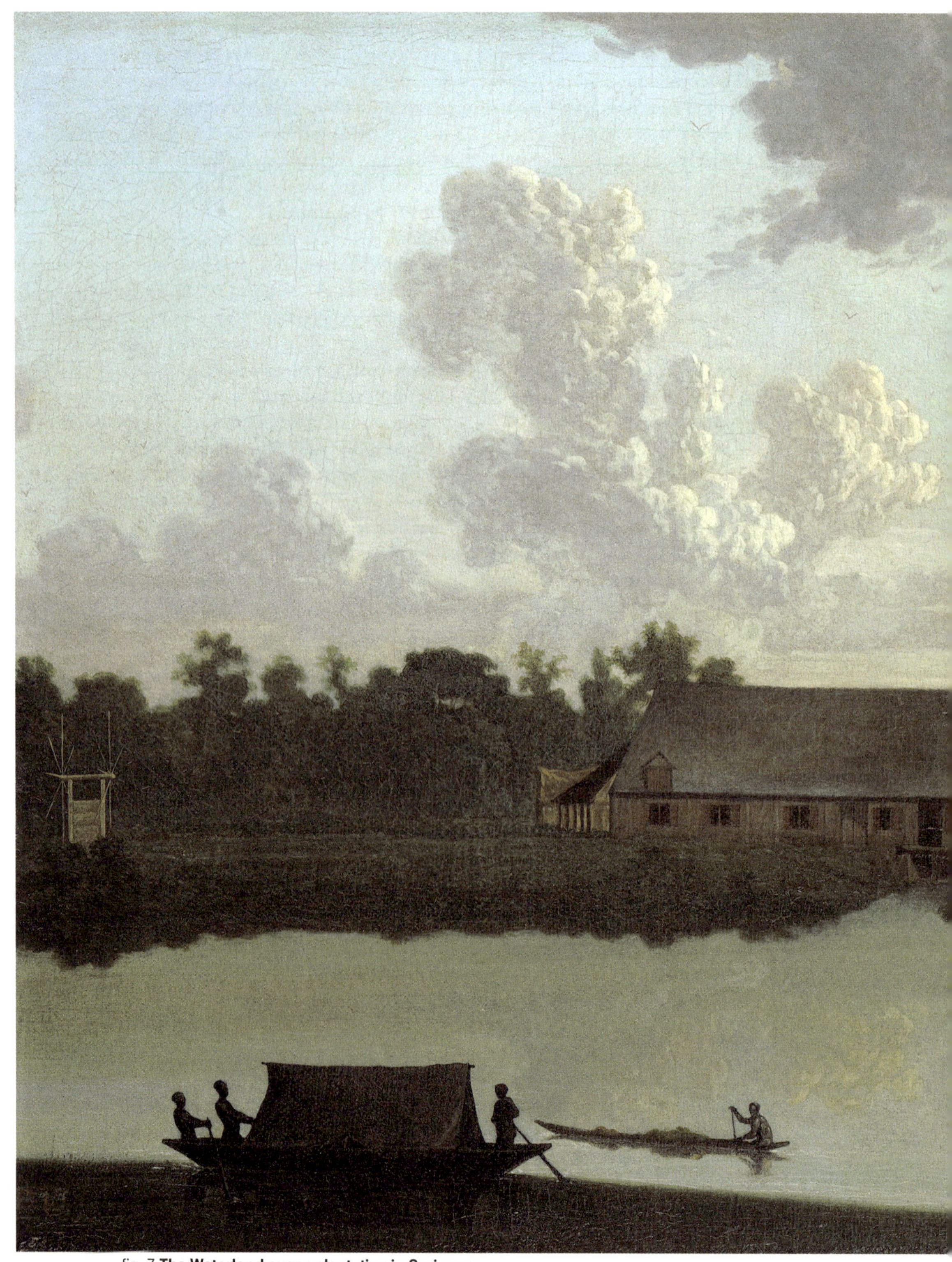

fig. 7 **The Waterland sugar plantation in Suriname**
Dirk Valkenburg, c. 1698–1718

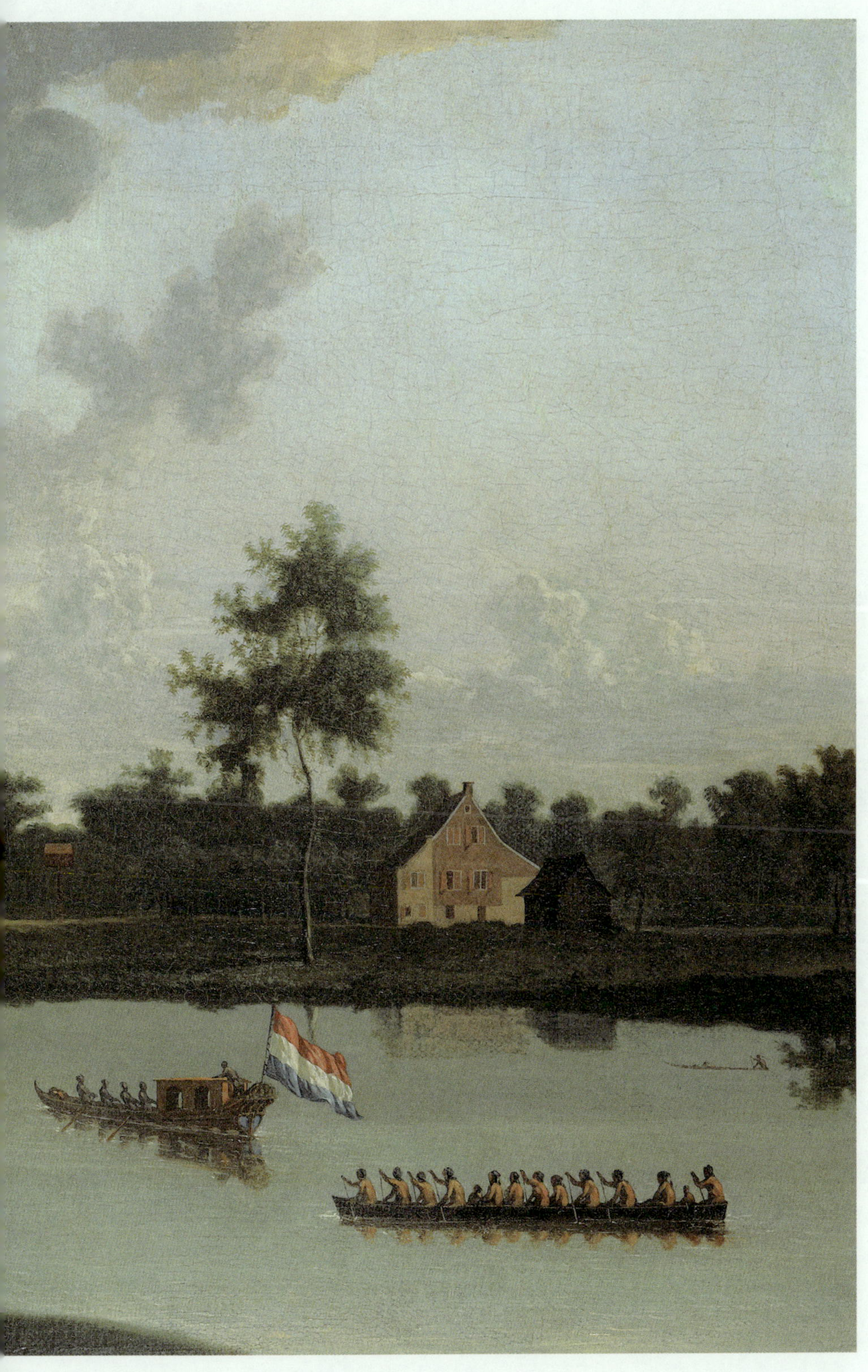

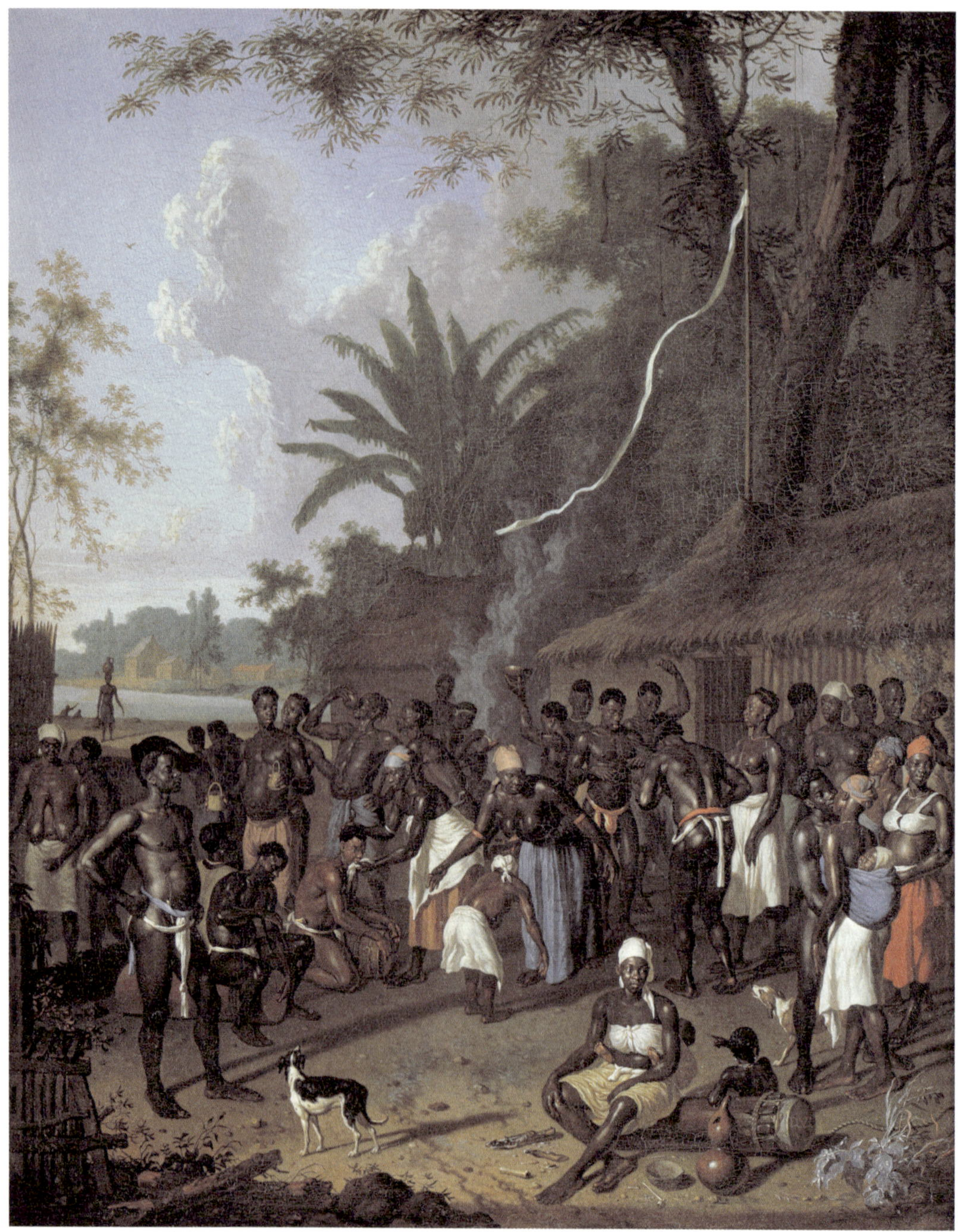

fig. 8 **Gathering on one of the sugar plantations of Jonas Witsen**
Dirk Valkenburg, 1708

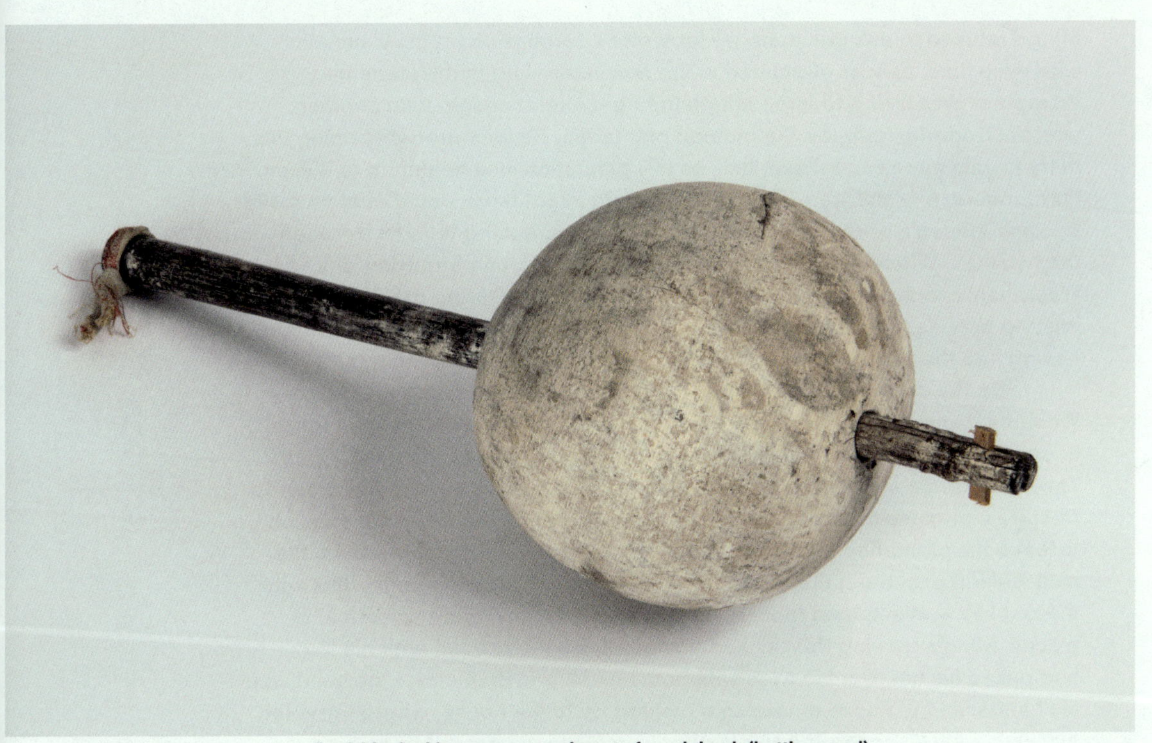

fig. 9 **Musical instrument made out of a calabash (bottle gourd), used in Winti rituals, before 1938**

Mingo refused to ask the manager for written permission for his visits to his wife each time, as was stipulated in the new rules. And in the meantime, Westphaal was trying to force Mingo to begin a relationship with another woman: Dorinda, from the Surimombo plantation. He was probably doing this to try to gain more control over him, as this plantation also belonged to Witsen.[22] Furthermore, any children Mingo and Dorinda might have would automatically become Witsen's property. The situation led to increasing tension between the two men. When Mingo's wife was at Palmeneribo one Saturday, she saw Westphaal coming and tried to hide in Wally's house. During the fight that ensued between the manager and Wally, she fled from Palmeneribo, without having had the chance to spend the free Saturday with her husband.

On the morning of Saturday 18 June 1707, things came to a head. Westphaal and Valkenburg were sitting in the front gallery of the manager's house at Palmeneribo, from where they had a good view of the river (fig. 10). They saw Mingo and his friend Tam moor the korjaal and walk up the grounds. Despite a promise to reform, Mingo had once again failed to get permission to leave the plantation. Furthermore, and to Westphaal's great irritation, the men walked past the gallery without greeting him. For the manager, this was the last straw. Westphaal took up his axe and smashed Mingo's korjaal to pieces. Mingo, 'seeing this, kicked and stamped the ground with his legs, and pulled his hat over his eyes with both hands, and then struck his head with his hands, and in this manner came rushing up to the house, where I greeted him with a stick', according to Westphaal in his testimony.[23] Mingo then ran off cursing. Westphaal and Valkenburg made sure they had their rifles within reach throughout the rest of the day. Their fears were not unfounded. The next day, Mingo, Joseph and Charle stood in front of the main house along with the full group of enslaved workers to demand an explanation from Westphaal for the destruction of the korjaal and to negotiate compensation for Mingo. Westphaal erupted in anger; he said the men always managed to avoid punishment and were proud of it, but now he would show them who was boss: 'You cur, I can never catch you to punish you as you deserve, and you brag about that, and say that I am not man enough to be your master; I'll get you right here and now.'[24] He grabbed his rifle, which was ready by the door, and blasted Charle in the legs with buckshot. He called to Valkenburg to come help him. Stones were thrown. The painter joined in the struggle: he gave Wally 'a slap in the face' and said to him: 'You cur, you're always the cause of this trouble and rebellion with your brother Mingo etc., and you've so long been the ruin of such good negroes, and the fools are punished many times because of your rogue practices.'[25] After this the group withdrew, and calm returned to the plantation. The next day, Westphaal attempted to placate them with a few bottles of rum, to stop them from fleeing again. It was to no avail: on the Monday the group left the plantation en masse. They were arrested shortly thereafter by a military commando dispatched from Paramaribo.

In the transcripts of the interrogation we read that the men had not wanted to leave the plantation at all, but had felt compelled to when Westphaal refused to compensate Mingo for his korjaal, the boat that had made contact with his wife possible and was so essential for the little bit of freedom left to the

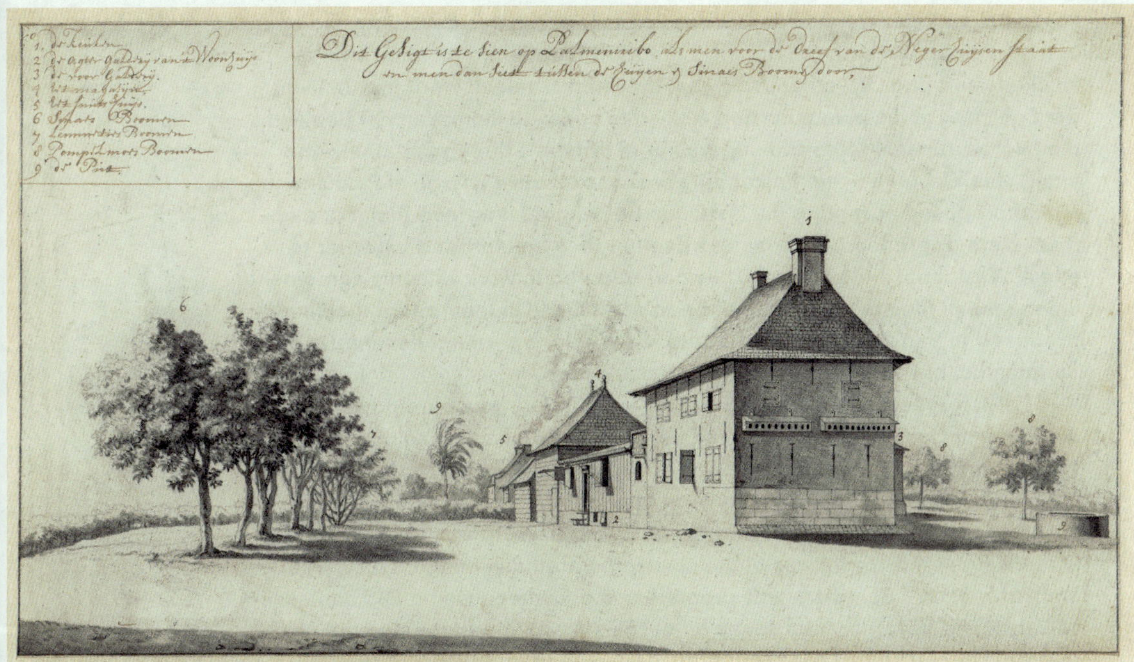

fig. 10 **The residence on the Palmeneribo plantation**
Dirk Valkenburg, 1708

enslaved workers. We also get a better picture of the five days they had spent in the forest in December 1706 after the aforementioned incident with the chickens and pigs. Baratham said that they had received word that Jan van der Beek was at the plantation and wished to speak to them. Van der Beek was the overall administrator and supervisor of Witsen's three plantations and along with Westphaal and Valkenburg was in executive charge of Palmeneribo. Mingo proposed accepting the invitation but wanted it agreed that if one of them were apprehended or taken prisoner, they would band together to attack Westphaal and kill him.[26] They had returned to work with this agreement among them; their escape had not been punished. On their return they had proposed to Van der Beek that he replace Westphaal with the manager of Surimombo, but Van der Beek had not acquiesced.

The gruesome sentence, death by immolation, was pure power display by governor De Gruijter. He wavered between forceful action so that the unrest would not spread further along the river and preventing worse developments at Palmeneribo itself, where there were another nineteen men classified as accomplices, and a great fear that things would flare up again. After the sentencing of the key figures of the uprising, Baratham, Mingo, Wally, Charle and Joseph, only Baratham was granted clemency because he had confessed willingly. The governor then sent a letter to Palmeneribo pardoning the nineteen men left behind on the plantation. In this instance, the fear of more unrest and resistance in reaction to the carrying out of the sentence weighed more heavily than the desire to punish also these enslaved of Palmeneribo. The governor later declared before the Court of Police that after the letter had been read out at the plantation, the men had 'duly resumed their work and the plantation is now at peace'.[27] The free Saturday granted to the enslaved people of Palmeneribo by Van Scharphuijzen was definitively abolished for all plantations by the government in August 1707. As usual, the slaveholders had come out on top.

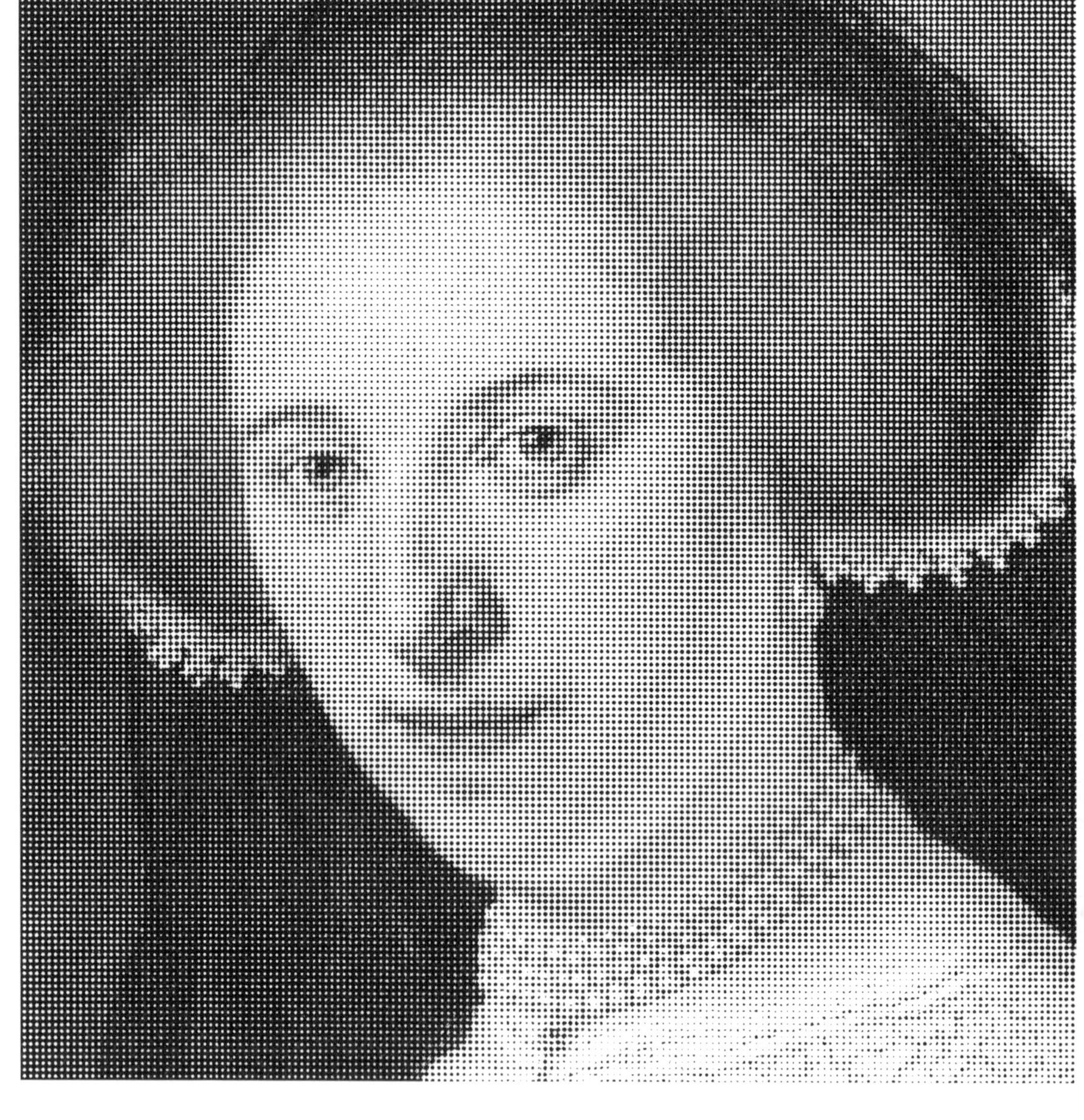

eveline sint nicolaas

oopjen

wealth in the dutch republic

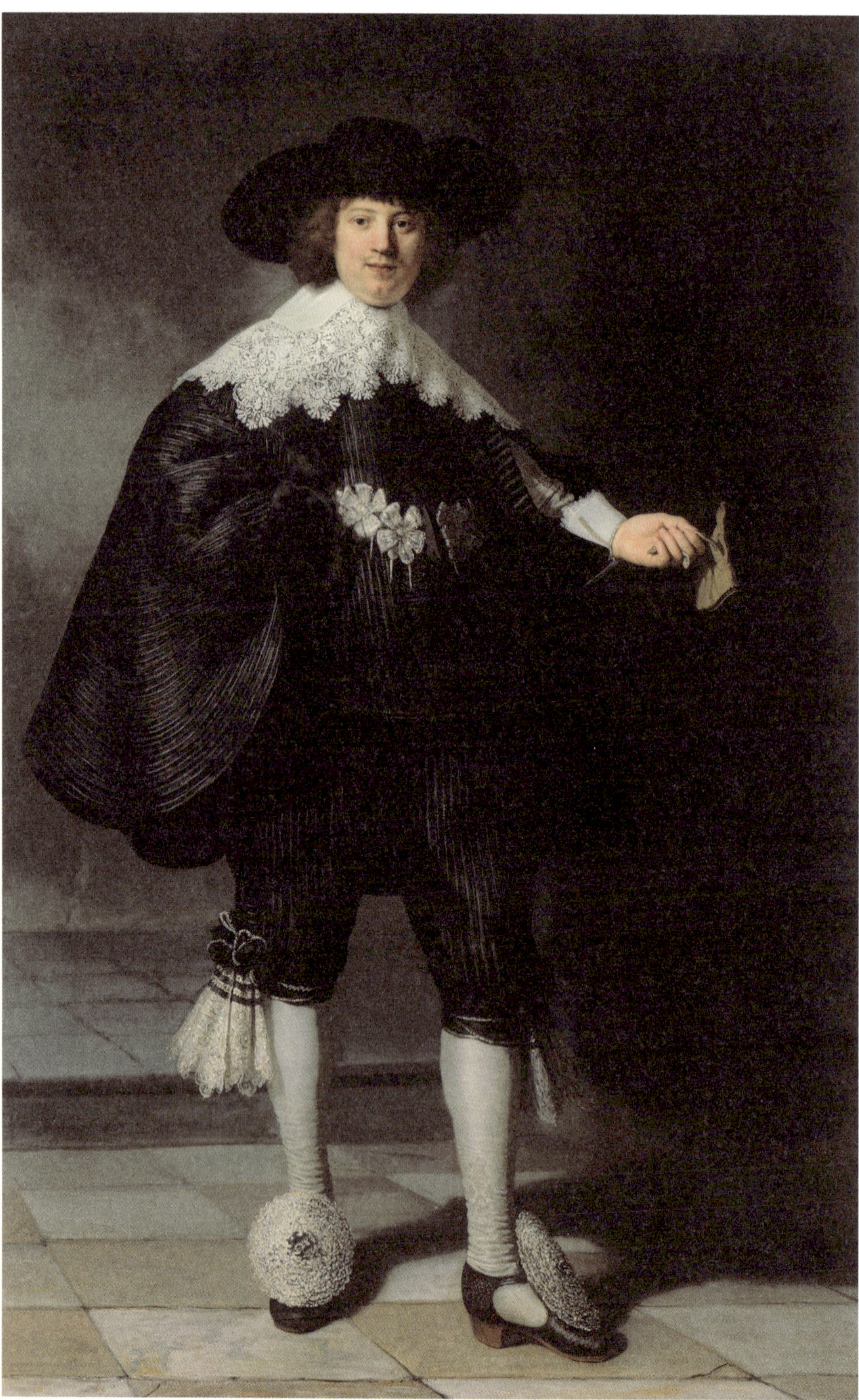

fig. 1 **Portrait of Marten Soolmans**
Rembrandt, 1634

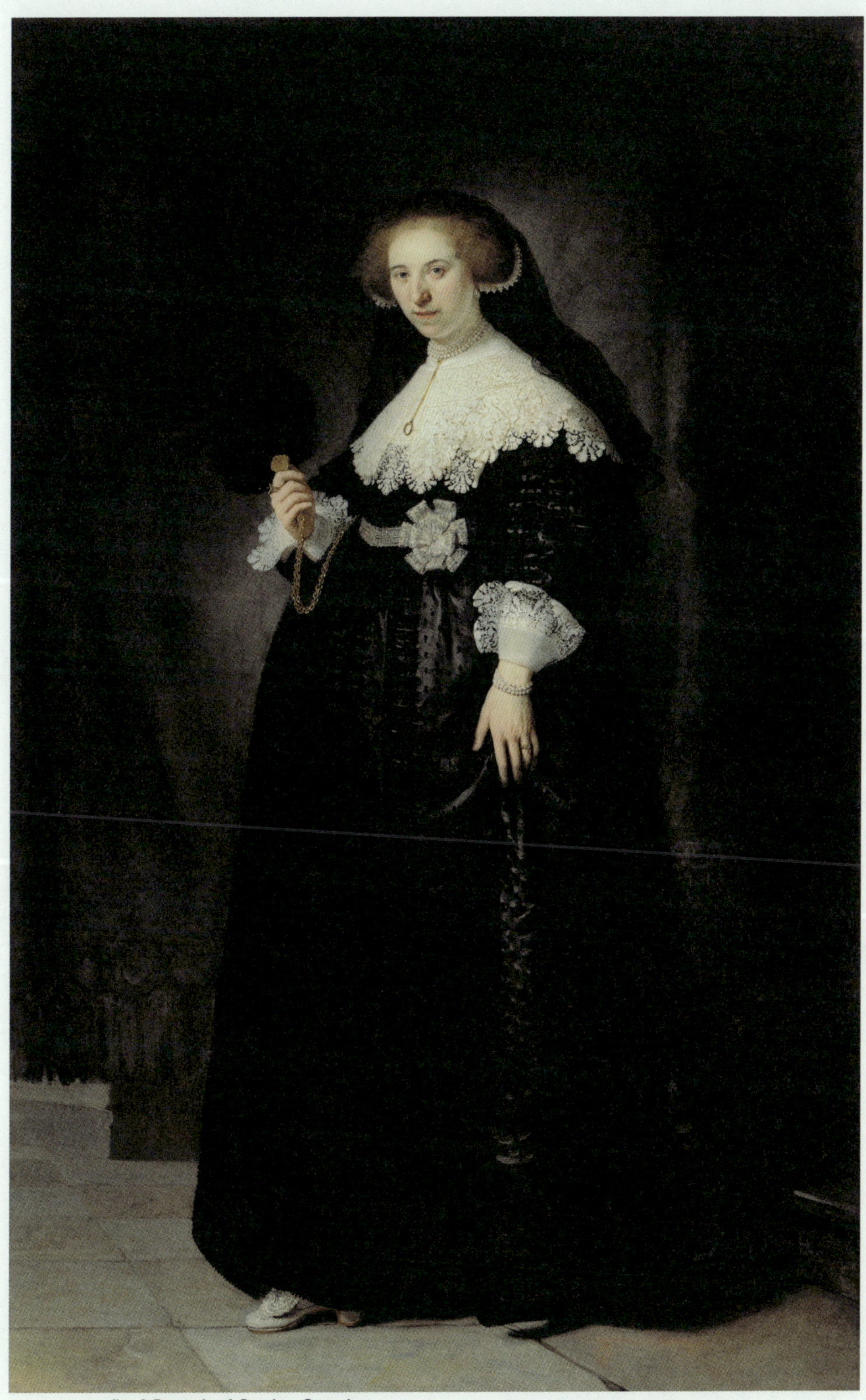

fig. 2 **Portrait of Oopjen Coppit**
Rembrandt, 1634

There they stand, radiating utter self-confidence: Oopjen Coppit and her husband Marten Soolmans (figs. 1, 2). She is 22 years old; he is two years younger. They have been married for just a year, and Oopjen is expecting their first baby. Rembrandt's full-length portraits show a couple with the world at their feet, dressed in costly clothing. All attention is on Oopjen and Marten; there are no distracting vistas or symbolic objects. Oopjen and Marten are the stars of the show.

Given the prevailing Protestant culture in Amsterdam when this painting was made in 1634, it is quite extraordinary that two such young people who had yet to achieve anything of note in society should choose to have themselves portrayed in such regal fashion. The pattern of the closely woven white collar of Flemish bobbin lace draped over Oopjen's black quilted satin and tulle dress is echoed in the cuffs. Her necklace and bracelets, each comprising four rows of pearls, perfectly complement the white lace. Oopjen wears a single gold ring set with a large diamond on the ring finger of her left hand, and two gold rings on the index finger of her right: one set with a single black stone and the other banded with small diamonds – these are almost certainly her engagement and wedding rings. Another ring, hanging from the chain around her neck, is probably a memento of a beloved relative. Oopjen's feather fan, frizzy hairstyle and artificial mole, or *mouche*, on her left temple are all in keeping with the fashions of the day. Her husband, Marten, looking at us with a somewhat aloof expression, is wearing a black suit composed of narrow embroidered bands and decorated around the waist with silver-white ribbon rosettes with silver points. His large, flat collar has a broad bobbin lace border, and the knees of his britches are adorned with pleated silver lace. The most striking elements of all are the huge lace rosettes on his shoes.

Their self-assurance is matched by their wealth. Oopjen's dowry amounted to 35,000 guilders, and Marten received assets worth 12,000 guilders when they married. In modern terms, their total shared capital was equivalent to almost 600,000 euros.[1] The young couple had not accumulated this fortune themselves, a fact that perhaps explains the absence of the references customary in such portraits to the origins of the subjects' wealth. Where did all that money come from? And what connects these two masterpieces by Rembrandt to slavery? To answer these questions, we must first explore the background story of Marten and his father, Jan.

soolmans, sugar-baker

Marten Soolmans grew up in the Amsterdam sugar refinery 't Vagevuur (The Fires of Purgatory) belonging to his father, Jan.[2] Standing on the current site of the Dominicus Church at Spuistraat 12–14, it was the largest such sugar house in the city in the seventeenth century. Others in the neighbourhood bore names such as Groot Hemelrijck (Great Heavenly Kingdom) and de Hel (Hell). The latter bore a sign that read: 'This is de Hel, where all is well. Our sugar does cost more, but 't Vagevuur's is poor.'[3] It is a message that reflects the business atmosphere in this period: competition among these concerns was intense because there was a great deal of money to be made from processing raw sugar. In the sixteenth century it had been primarily refineries in Antwerp that supplied sugar to Western Europe, with most production taking place on Madeira, São Tomé and the Canary Islands, and in Brazil.

In 1585, during the Eighty Years' War, the port of Antwerp was blockaded and the city fell into Spanish hands, prompting Protestant business owners and merchants in particular to flee the city for Amsterdam. They brought their expertise and networks with them to the city, which led to a flourishing of economic activity there. Jan Soolmans was one of these newcomers. He was about 30 years old in 1591, the year in which he was entered in the Amsterdam records as a *poorter,* a citizen from outside the city who had gained the rights necessary to live within its gates (*poorten*).[4] For the first few years he probably traded in pepper and sugar, benefiting from his contacts from Antwerp. In 1598 he and his business partner Peter Garet became co-owners of a sugar house in Amsterdam's Nieuwe Nieuwstraat. Garet was responsible for the day-to-day management of the refinery and lived in, or adjacent to, the company premises. Soolmans, meanwhile, focused on maintaining the records of the purchases of raw sugar and sales of refined sugar. Three years later the company declared bankruptcy. It seems likely that this was part of a ruse on Soolmans's part to dupe his business partner. Shortly afterwards, Soolmans bought two houses as well as grounds on Amsterdam's Nieuwezijds Achterburgwal (now Spuistraat), where, in 1607, he founded the Fires of Purgatory sugar refinery.[5] In his work as a sugar-baker, and prior to that as a merchant, he dealt with sugar on a regular basis, but would he have been aware of the enslaved labour involved in the harvest and initial processing of sugar cane?

slave labour in brazil

Soon after Jan Soolmans founded The Fires of Purgatory in 1607, trade between the Dutch Republic and Brazil received a huge boost thanks to the Twelve Years' Truce between the Netherlands and Spain during the Eighty Years' War. Following the blockading of the port of Antwerp in 1585, Dutch sugar merchants decided that they would themselves go to the source of the product: Brazil. The Portuguese owners of the plantations there were soon supplying a large proportion of their sugar to the Dutch, and by the time The Fires of Purgatory was in operation, the Dutch Republic had a considerable interest in the Brazilian sugar trade. By 1621, the year the Dutch West India Company (WIC) was founded, Dutch traders were responsible for bringing to market more than half the sugar produced in Brazil. The exceptional profitability of this business lay behind the decision taken by the Dutch in 1623 to embark on a major military campaign dubbed the Groot Desseyn (Great Plan). The ultimate goal of the attack was to conquer from the Portuguese the northeast Brazilian provinces of Paraíba, Itamaracá and Pernambuco and to take over production of sugar in the region. The Portuguese had more than 350 sugar cane mills in these provinces at the time and were annually exporting sugar with a value of 5 million guilders.[6] This scale of production was only possible through the widespread use of enslaved labour. The Groot Desseyn did not succeed as planned, but in 1628 the Dutch admiral Piet Heyn captured a Spanish treasure fleet – whose cargo included

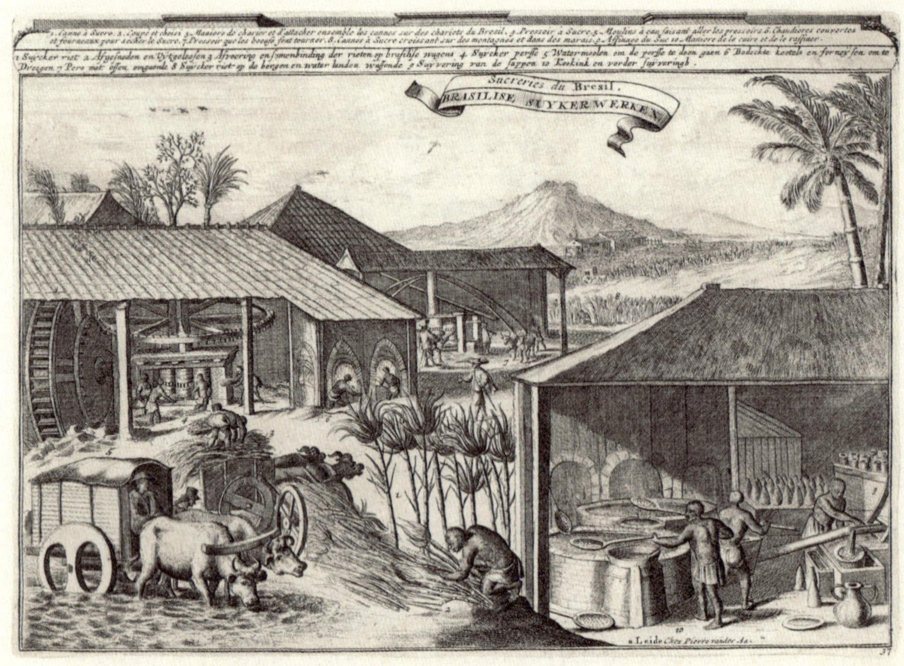

fig. 3 **Enslaved men process sugar cane on a plantation in Brazil Romeyn de Hooghe, before 1682**

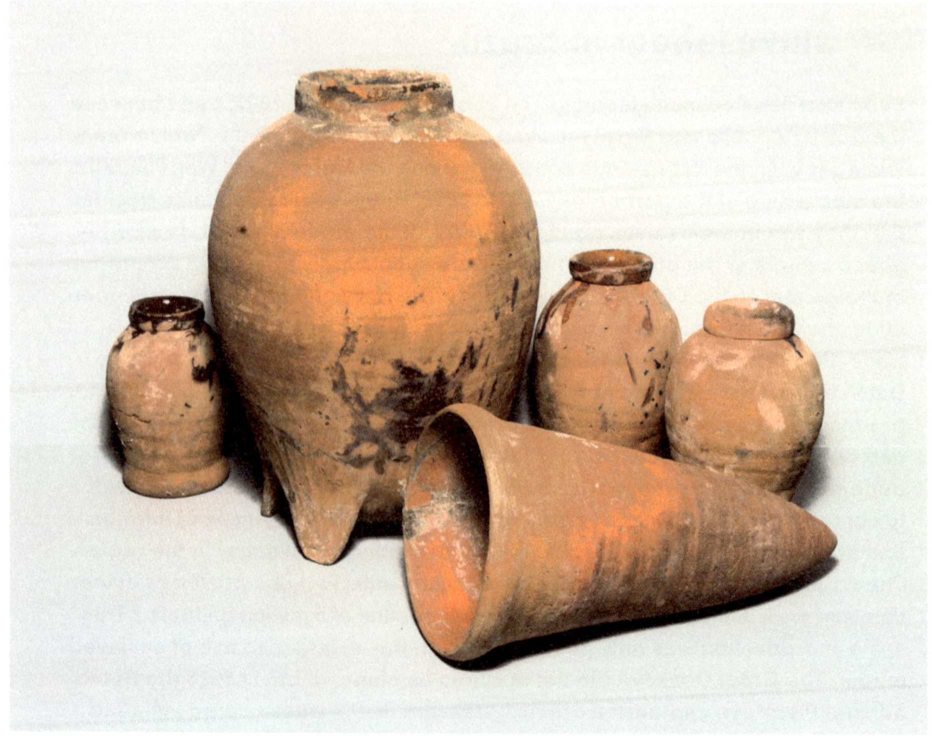

fig. 4 **Earthenware sugar funnel and collecting jars, archaeological finds, Amsterdam, 17th and 18th centuries. These earthenware vessels were made in specialized potteries that provided employment to large numbers of Amsterdammers**

361 crates of sugar – and this provided the WIC with sufficient financial resources to embark on a renewed attack on the Portuguese. In 1630 the Dutch ousted the Portuguese from Olinda, in Pernambuco, an event that is generally seen as marking the beginning of the Dutch colony in Brazil. The Dutch were going to need cheap labour to make big profits from the production of sugar, so the WIC set their sights on capturing the Portuguese 'slave castles' in West Africa. In 1637 they captured Elmina Castle (in present-day Ghana) from the Portuguese and in 1641 they took the Luanda slave market in Angola.

Work on sugar plantations is exceptionally labour-intensive. The sugar cane deteriorates rapidly after harvesting, so it has to be processed immediately, *in situ*. This was the work carried out by enslaved labourers. First they pressed the freshly harvested sugar cane in mills, generally driven by oxen, and the juice this produced was reduced by boiling before being refined further (fig. 3). The raw sugar was then transported to Europe in the form of cones. The further processing of the raw sugar to produce refined sugar was lengthy and expensive, and for this reason it was mostly carried out in Europe. Splitting the processes meant the benefits to the Dutch economy were maximized, the colony remained dependent on the colonizing nation, and the economic consequences of any loss of sugar during transport – due to shipwreck, for example – were mitigated.

Sugar refiners in early seventeenth-century Amsterdam would not have been directly connected with sugar plantations in Brazil, so Jan Soolmans almost certainly bought his raw sugar on the open market, possibly through a specialist broker – the lines of communication between producer and refiner would shorten dramatically in the 1630s when the WIC had complete control of the sugar trade for a number of years. In Soolmans's time, however, the sugar passed through many hands on its way from the fields of Brazil, where it was harvested and pressed by enslaved men and women, to the businesses in Amsterdam that oversaw its further refining. This long chain of middlemen included the plantation owner, the colonial administrators coordinating exports, the merchant or trading company purchasing and transporting the sugar, and the broker in Amsterdam.

Newspapers and illustrated news sheets were crucial sources of information for businesspeople like Soolmans. In 1618, two newspapers were founded in Amsterdam that invariably prioritized reports of events abroad.[7] The first news articles about Brazil were published in 1624, and henceforth Soolmans would have been able to stay informed about any issues relating to the supply of raw sugar. News coverage focused on the war with Portugal and not on the deployment of enslaved people on plantations, however, and certainly not on the conditions in which they had to work. Wherever the word 'slave' does appear in newspapers of this period, it pertains to Dutch compatriots who had been enslaved in the Mediterranean region, rather than Dutch colonial slavery.[8] Furthermore, there were as yet no European painters or draughtsmen in Brazil to document life on the plantations. This would change with the founding of the Dutch Brazil colony. The Dutch artist Frans Post, for example, made a very detailed drawing of a sugar cane mill in 1640 (see p. 70, fig. 4).

Whether Soolmans was aware of the conditions under which his raw sugar was produced is impossible to state with certainty. We can conclude, however, that at the start of the seventeenth century there was no direct contact between plantation owners and sugar-bakers, and there was little information available in print media about the plantations in Brazil.

the fires of purgatory

There are no surviving details about the building in which The Fires of Purgatory was housed, but the set-up was almost certainly similar to that of other sugar refineries of the day. There would have been a wide door opening on the ground floor where the large crates containing cones of raw sugar were brought into the building and where the crates containing refined sugar were dispatched. On the same floor was the fire pit, in which the sugar cones were melted and slaked lime and egg added to the syrup to further refine it (fig. 5), producing a sticky mass that was poured into inverted cone-shaped earthen moulds in the filling room (fig. 6). The moulds, each of which had a small hole at the narrow end, were placed upright in collecting jars. When the moulds were filled, excess syrup flowed through the holes into the jars, leaving behind the crystallized sugar, or sugarloaf, in the mould (fig. 4); large sugar houses would sometimes be filled to the rafters with thousands of such jars of varying sizes, which were produced at specialist potteries. Sugar refineries would generally have several storeys so there was enough space for all the sugarloaves to be left to dry out.[9] The floors of the upper storeys had to be strong to bear the load of all the heavy jars, so they were constructed using sturdy timber and firmly anchored to the walls. A manual hoist was used to haul each of the jars into or out of each storey through a hatch in the floor. Several stoves and the flue of the sugar furnace provided the heat needed for the drying process. Once dry, the sugarloaves were packed in blue paper to keep off flies and then dispatched for sale on domestic and international markets. Besides the sugar refiner and a foreman, the workforce usually comprised no more than ten men, who carried out the heavy work in the filling room and the drying attics. Jan Soolmans was a certified sugar refiner from 1598 to 1609, so it is possible that he did this work himself at The Fires of Purgatory. After 1609 he was registered as a financier.[10]

Amsterdam was a major supplier of sugar to the rest of Europe in the mid-seventeenth century.[11] Sugar quickly became very popular, although it remained a luxury product until the nineteenth century. It was used as a medicine, spice, preserving agent, decoration, and sweetener for beverages such as coffee, tea and hot chocolate, all of which were introduced to the region in this period. Less wealthy people were able to afford syrup, a cheaper by-product of the refining process that was thought to be highly nutritious.

the soolmans family

The popularity of sugar propelled a rapid growth in the number of sugar-bakers in the city, but Jan Soolmans was well able to cope with the competition. The fact that his name appears no fewer than 80 times in the church council minutes in connection with fighting and cursing suggests he did not shy away from confrontation. His conflicts were not limited to those with colleagues and fellow citizens of Amsterdam; he was violent at home as well. Soolmans married Willemina Salen in 1608, and they lived together in or near The Fires of Purgatory. It was here that their son Marten was born in 1613. Their first spouses had died, so this was the second marriage for both of them,[12] and it is doubtful that it was a happy one. Church minutes from 1623 record that Soolmans 'leads a most quarrelsome existence with his wife and has caused great vexation of late'. A year later, it was noted that he 'lives in great turmoil with his wife' and that he 'beats her and has also harmed his maid'.[13]

The situation for the family was much brighter on the financial front: the Soolmanses moved among the economic elite of Amsterdam, as evidenced by their purchase of a tomb in the central nave of Amsterdam's Oude Kerk.[14] Space was very limited in the church, and a grave there was expensive and therefore limited to the uppermost echelons of society – a grave in the choir was the most costly and prestigious of all. The fact that Soolmans could afford to buy a tomb in the nave, just outside the choir, says a great deal about his position in the social hierarchy. In 1622, when Marten was about nine years old, his father bought Sterrenburg, a house on Keizersgracht (now number 231). The family moved out of their home at or near the sugar refinery and moved into this residence on Amsterdam's prestigious canal belt. Herengracht and Keizersgracht were second only to Warmoesstraat as the most expensive streets in the city in this period.

Jan Soolmans died in 1626, and ownership of The Fires of Purgatory passed to his widow, Willemina. Soon afterwards, she moved with the now thirteen-year-old Marten to the city of Amersfoort, some 50 kilometres southeast of Amsterdam. Two years later, Marten enrolled at Leiden University to study law – he was clearly keen to be thought of as older, because he gave his age as twenty in the university register. Willemina and Marten seem not to have been actively involved in day-to-day operations at the sugar refinery. Although no bookkeeping records for The Fires of Purgatory have survived, a number of other sources shed some light on the family's financial situation. Marten brought assets with a value of 12,000 guilders into his marriage in 1633. This would suggest that even after the purchase of the Keizersgracht house (which Marten's mother still owned at the time of his marriage), there was still plenty of money left over. Archival documents also reveal that Willemina owned shares in the WIC, which she redeemed during the 1630s.[15]

oopjen and marten

On 28 June 1633, Marten Soolmans and Oopjen Coppit were married at the Nieuwe Kerk in Amsterdam. The wealth that The Fires of Purgatory had generated for Marten and his mother was now supplemented by Oopjen's dowry. Oopjen's family were members of the wealthy ruling elite who had accumulated capital through trade in grain and gunpowder. In contrast to Marten's family, the Coppits had been members of Amsterdam's political upper class for generations. Oopjen, the first of Hendrick Coppit and Silleken Princen's three daughters, was born in January 1611 and grew up in De Spiegel, a residence on Warmoesstraat (now number 70). The two families were connected to one

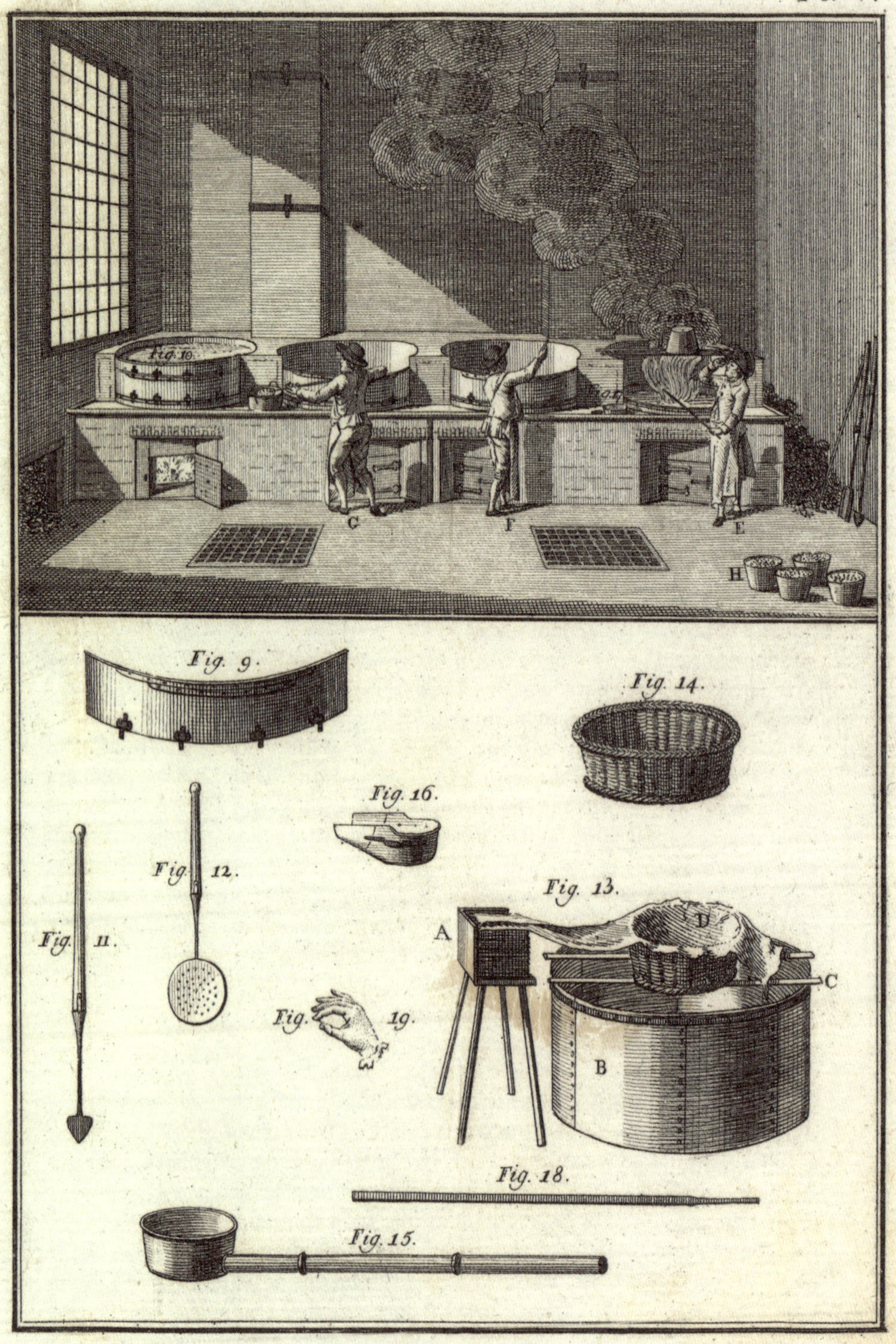

fig. 5 **Interior of a sugar refinery, showing boiling kettles and associated tools, 1793**

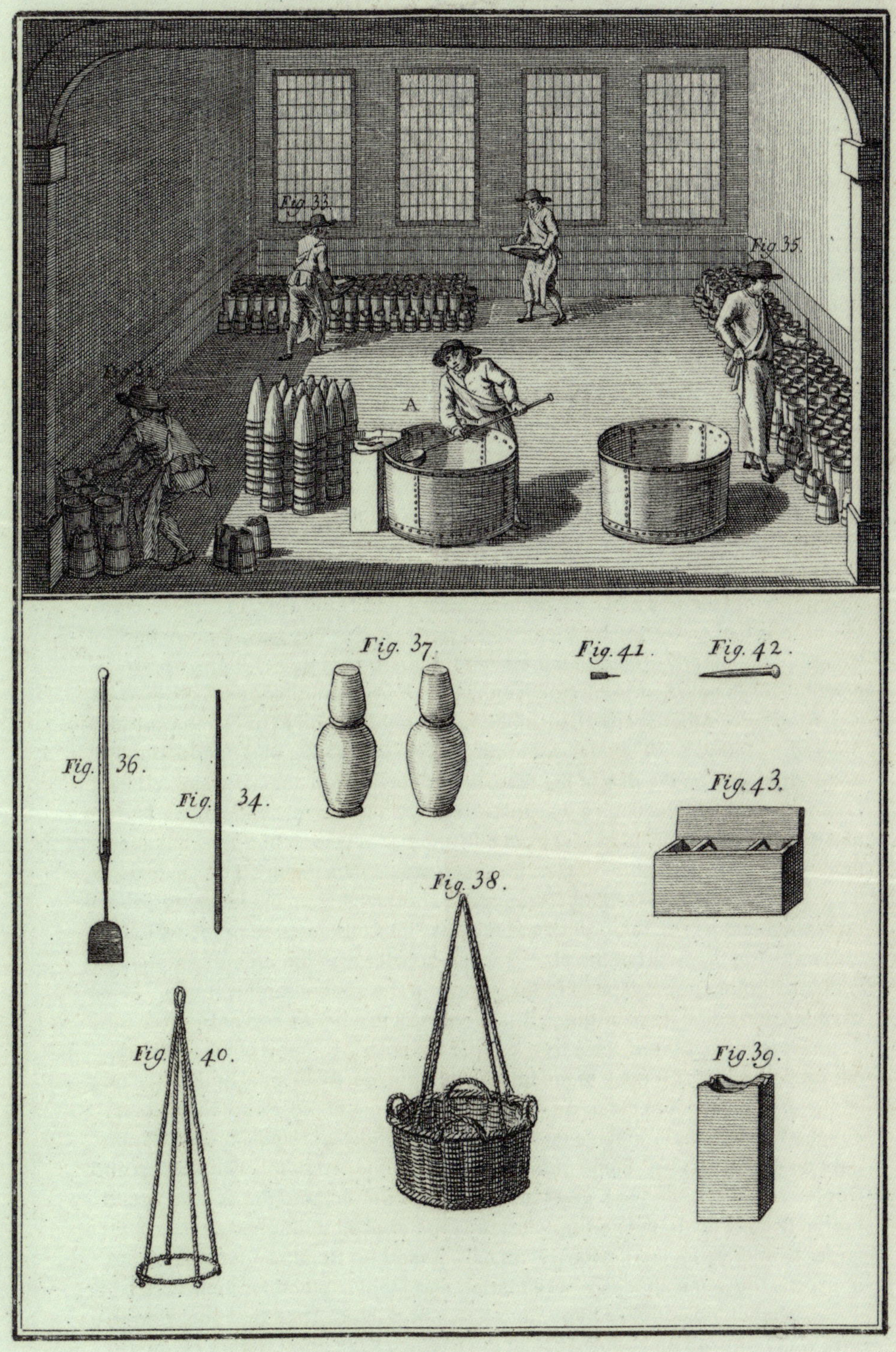

fig. 6 **Interior of a sugar refinery, showing collecting jars and associated tools, 1793**

another in many ways. Marten's uncle, for example, also lived on Warmoesstraat.[16] Once married, Oopjen and Marten moved in with the parents of the bride, who at this point lived in a house called De Levantsvaarder (now Nieuwe Hoogstraat 9). With Oopjen being the eldest daughter, her parents now getting on in years, and Marten being an only child, it is likely that both families would have very much welcomed a grandchild at this point. And Oopjen was indeed soon pregnant with their first child. Fortune was smiling upon them, and Rembrandt captured that moment.

This was to be the first and only occasion on which Rembrandt would paint a pair of life-size, full-length portraits. In preceding centuries, only members of royal or noble families would commission artists to paint portraits of this kind. Nonetheless, there are some cases of prosperous citizens having themselves portrayed in a similar way before Marten and Oopjen. An early example is a pair of portraits painted by Cornelis Ketel around 1588, but they are lost to history. In 1618, the later director of the WIC and subsequent mayor of Amsterdam Cornelis Bicker commissioned Cornelis van der Voort to paint full-length portraits of himself and his wife, Aertgen Witsen. Several years later, Pieter Jansz Hooft and his wife Geertruyt Overlander were portrayed in a similar manner by an anonymous artist. And others followed their example. The Coppit family would certainly have been aware of this trend: it was a great uncle of Oopjen's who commissioned the double portrait by Cornelis Ketel, and Pieter Jansz Hooft was a neighbour of the Coppits on Warmoesstraat – and Hooft was, in turn, related to Cornelis Bicker. By having themselves portrayed in this way, Marten and Oopjen were clearly staking their claim to a position of power in the upper echelons of Amsterdam society. Given their relative youthfulness, this could be regarded as a rather pretentious ambition. Their decision to have the portraits painted by Rembrandt, whose reputation as an innovative and exceptionally good artist was on the rise at the time, would have been controversial. While it is conceivable that the choice was influenced by a personal connection – Marten and Rembrandt had lived not far from one another in Leiden and may have met there – it is more probable that Rembrandt's status as a rising star was decisive.

For Marten and Oopjen, it was just a short walk from the family residence on Warmoesstraat to Rembrandt's studio on Sint Anthonisbreestraat, which as well as being the heart of the city's Jewish quarter was the area of Amsterdam with the highest population of Black people in the seventeenth century,[17] some of whom had come from Portugal, Spain or Brazil to work as servants, often for Sephardic Jews; others were free people from Africa, many of whom were mariners or soldiers for one of the trading companies. All of them had either lived in slavery or seen it at close quarters. Those who worked as servants, in a country far from their families and own communities, were still largely dependent on their 'masters'. Some of them probably crossed paths with Marten and Oopjen as they made their way to Rembrandt's studio, and the couple would probably have heard the Portuguese language spoken during their walks. A little under twenty years later, two African men posed for Rembrandt at his studio, at exactly the same spot as where Marten and Oopjen stood for their portrait.[18]

The young couple's happiness was short-lived. Their first son, Hendrik, who was baptized on 25 July 1634 at the Nieuwe Kerk, died before his first birthday. In 1636 they had a second son, Jan, and the following year a daughter, Cornelia, who also died at a young age. Around 1637, Oopjen, Marten and Jan moved to the small fort city of Naarden, some 20 kilometres west of Amsterdam, where the Coppit family owned land. They moved into a house on what is now Kloosterstraat and kept two gardens with summerhouses just outside the city walls. Fate struck the family again in 1641, when, unexpectedly, Marten died at the age of just 28. He was buried in the family grave in the Oude Kerk in Amsterdam, and Oopjen and Jan continued to live in Naarden. Willemina Salen also survived her son, but we know that she died in or shortly before 1647, because her name does not appear on that year's tax returns for The Fires of Purgatory – by now its registered owners were Oopjen, Antonij Pietersz and Marten Soolmans, a nephew and grandnephew of Jan Soolmans, respectively.

oopjen and maerten

Oopjen remarried in 1647. Her second husband, Maerten Daey, was a soldier who had served in Dutch Brazil from 1629 to 1641, partially under the colonial governorship of Johan Maurits of Nassau-Siegen.[19] Daey, a widower with three children, lived on an estate in the village of Groenekan, near Utrecht. It is possible that Oopjen got to know him through Johan Stachouwer, who had served in Brazil at the same time as Daey. Stachouwer was married to Oopjen's cousin Sybrich Appelman, the daughter of Tryntje Coppit, the sister of Oopjen's father. They lived fairly close to Naarden and it is quite likely that Oopjen was in regular contact with them. Stachouwer owed his great wealth to his two sugar plantations in Brazil, the Sint Anna and the Iseliettes, which yielded him assets of 180,000 guilders.[20] Johan's brother Jacob also spent several years in Dutch Brazil, where he was a member of the High Government (Hoge Regering) that ran the colony. Jacob's name appears in the archives in transcripts of interrogations of enslaved people.[21] The brothers would have been able to tell Oopjen (who was still a co-owner of the Fires of Purgatory sugar refinery at the time) first-hand about what went on at a sugar plantation in Dutch Brazil.

It is quite possible that it was Johan Stachouwer who introduced Maerten to Oopjen. She would certainly have known that he had previously been married to a Dutch woman and that he had lived with her in Recife, Brazil. The question remains, however, whether Maerten told her about his daughter by an African woman named Francisca. We can read about Francisca in the Paraíba church council minutes (fig. 7), because a Johannes Hartman, a pastor, and mayor Jacques van der Neusen submitted a complaint to the church about the treatment of 'a Negress named Francisca coming from the island Illha de Fernando'.[22] The minutes record that Francisca had spent four months in the city of Olinda with Daey – he held her captive in the house and raped her and she became pregnant. Pastor and mayor declared that Daey was undoubtedly the father, because Francisca was still menstruating during her captivity and was not permitted to see other men afterwards. Daey then took Francisca to Recife, where he kept her imprisoned for another month and abused her horribly. When he discovered that she was pregnant, due to 'the swelling of her belly', he informed her that she must not give birth in his house but that the child

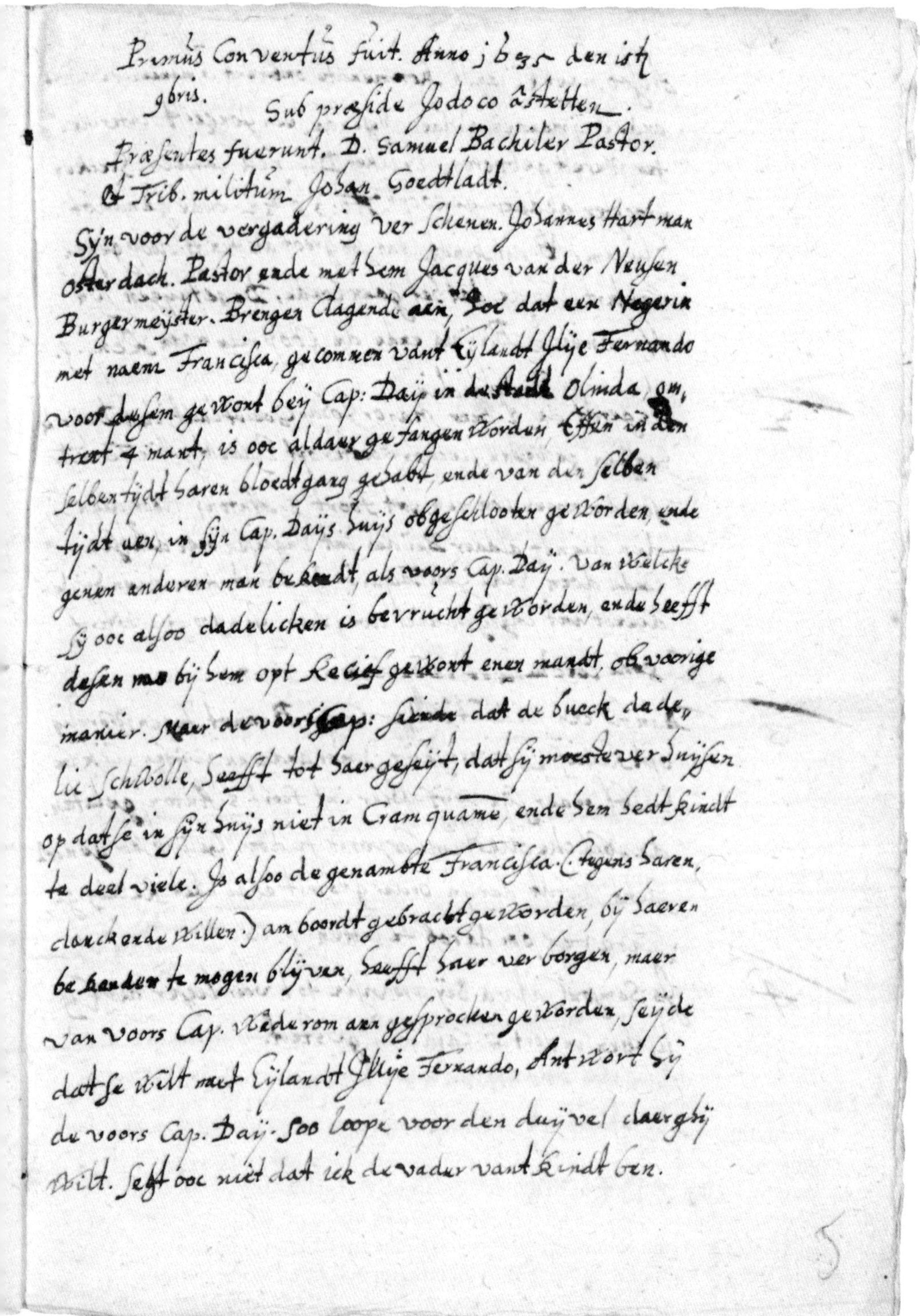

Primus Conventus fuit. Anno 1635 den 15 9bris.
Sub præside Jodoco à Stetten.
Præsentes fuerunt. D. Samuel Bachiler Pastor.
& Trib. militum Johan Goedtladt.
Sijn voor de vergaderingh verschenen. Johannes Hartman
Osterdach. Pastor ende met hem Jacques van der Neusen
Burgermeijster. Brengen clagende aen, hoe dat een Negerin
met naem Francisca, gecomen vant Eijlandt Ilije Fernando
voor desen gewoont bij Cap: Daij in de stadt Olinda, om
trent 4 maent, is ooc aldaer gevangen worden. Effen in den
selven tijdt haren bloedtgang gehadt, ende van der selben
tijdt aen, in sijn Cap. Daijs huijs opgesloten geworden, ende
genen anderen man bekendt, als voors Cap. Daij. Van welcke
sij ooc alsoo dadelicken is bevrucht geworden, ende heefft
desen mo bij hem opt Recief gewoont enen maendt, op voorige
manier. Maer de voors Cap: siende dat de buyck dade,
hie schbolle, heefft tot haer geseijt, datsij moeste verhuijsen
op datse in sijn huijs niet in cram quame, ende hem hedt kindt
te deel viele. Js alsoo de genamde Francisca. tegens haren
danck ende willen) an boordt gebracht geworden, bij haeren
behanden te mogen blijven, heefft haer verborgen, maer
van voors Cap. wederom aen gesprocken geworden, seijde
datse wilt met Eijlandt Ilije Fernando, Antwoort hij
de voors Cap. Daij. Soo loopt voor den duijvel daer gij
wilt. Seght ooc niet dat ick de vader vant kindt ben.

fig. 7 **Minutes of the church council in Paraíba, containing an account of Maerten Daey's maltreatment and rape of Francisca, 1635**

would be his. Francisca managed with the help of acquaintances to hide from him, but Daey eventually found her. When Francisca told Daey that she wanted to return to the island Fernando de Noronha, he replied: 'Go where the devil takes you, but tell no one that I am the father of the child.' Three months later, in 1632, Francisca gave birth on Fernando de Noronha to a daughter, who was baptised Elunam.[23] In 1633, Maerten Daey visited the Dutch Republic for several months before returning to Recife on 5 February 1634 with a Dutch wife. The couple were witnesses at two baptisms held in the Paraíba church.[24] Apparently, Daey was at this time free to go about his life without suffering any repercussions for his rape of Francisca. It was in 1635, three years after these crimes took place, that the pastor and mayor attempted to remedy this situation by bringing their indictment. We do not know whether Daey was actually ever reprimanded by the church council. In 1641 he returned to the Dutch Republic with his wife and three children; his wife died there in 1646.

Oopjen and Maerten married on 21 March 1647. Oopjen was three months pregnant at the time, and the desire to conceal this may have been behind their move to Amsterdam. Maerten was given the command of a company of soldiers in 1650, when they moved into a rented house on the city's Singel canal. Oopjen bore a son, Hendrick, but he died in infancy. Their second son, also named Hendrick, was baptized in 1651, and it was he who would later look after the marriage portraits of Oopjen and Marten. Oopjen also survived her second husband, who died in 1659. Initially she continued living in Amsterdam with Jan Soolmans, her unmarried son from her first marriage, but they later moved together to the city of Alkmaar, north of Amsterdam, where Oopjen died in 1689 at the age of 78. The Fires of Purgatory was by this time well past its heyday as a flourishing business. In fact, the contemporary historian Melchior Fokkens was already referring to the refinery in the past tense in 1662: 'There stands the once-famed Vagevuur,' he wrote, 'where for many a year an icy, sugary furnace blazed.' The dilapidated premises on Nieuwezijds Achterburgwal were finally demolished in 1737.

The inventory of the estate of Maerten Daey reveals that the house on Singel canal contained a large collection of art, including almost a hundred paintings, as well as all sorts of craftwork objects such as doll paraphernalia and a model of a 'West Indies sugar cane mill'.[25] For Maerten, this is likely to have been a memento of his years in Dutch Brazil; for Oopjen it perhaps triggered thoughts of the crates of raw sugar that were once delivered to The Fires of Purgatory.

The number of ways in which the lives of Marten, Oopjen and Maerten were entangled with the history of slavery is quite remarkable. They owed their wealth to slave labour in Brazil. Maerten lived in Brazil for some time; he sired a child there, and had seen the sugar plantations with his own eyes. In Amsterdam they crossed paths with people who had left the days of slavery behind, and with others who were still working in unfree conditions. Close scrutiny of the lives of Oopjen and her husbands reveals the extent to which the history of slavery is bound up with the history of the Netherlands. Do we now look differently at the portraits of Oopjen and Marten? Probably, we do. New pieces have been added to their story that pique our curiosity even more – about their lives and about the thoughts stirring behind those confident expressions.

valika smeulders
lisa lambrechts

paulus

a ‘moor’ in the dutch republic

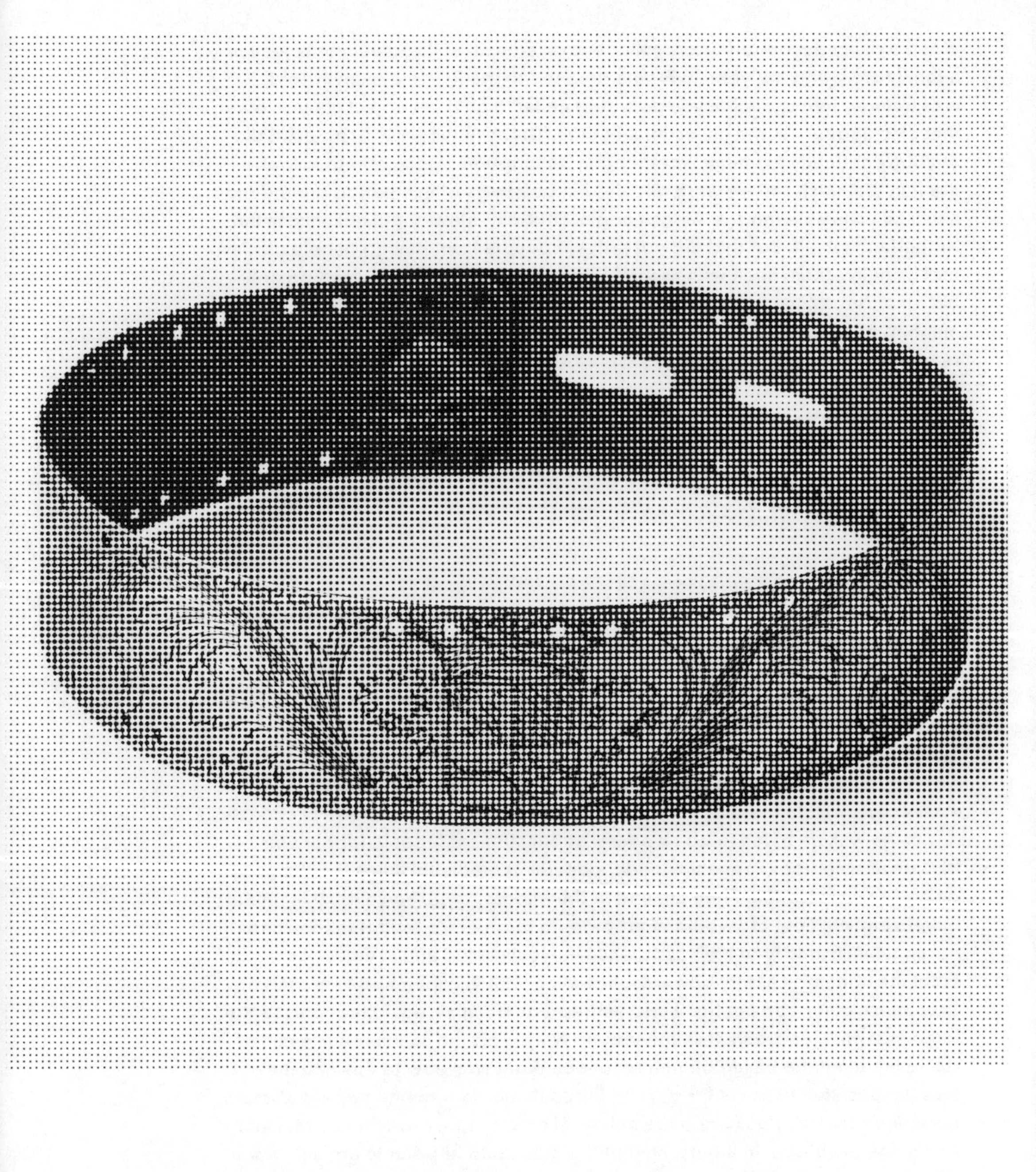

When a richly decorated brass collar engraved with stylized acanthus leaves, a family crest and the year 1689 was donated to the Rijksmuseum in 1881, it was entered into the collection as a 'dog collar' (fig. 1), an object classification that also appears in the collections of other Dutch museums.[1] At no point did anybody critically examine whether this description was accurate, despite the fact that such collars were depicted in paintings of this period around the necks of young servants of African origin. Officially, slavery did not exist in the Netherlands itself, but that did not prevent people from buying people abroad and bringing them back with them. Legally speaking, any enslaved person became free as soon as they set foot in the Netherlands, but it remains very much in question whether they were treated as such. Archival documents reveal that young Black servants were generally referred to as 'Moors', a reference to their skin colour. One of these servants was Paulus Maurus, a young man who can be traced back to the same household as that from which the 'dog collar' came. Is it possible that it was Paulus Maurus who wore the collar? What would life in the Netherlands have looked like for him?

marked

Slavery, serfdom and other forms of unfree labour have existed since time immemorial. There are ancient Roman collars inscribed with texts such as: 'I have escaped. Bring me to my master'.[2] Such a collar could be placed around a person's neck to certify authority over them, as well as to reduce the risk of fleeing. The forced wearing of a collar could also be used as a form of punishment. The inscription on a brass collar found in Scotland and dating from 1701 indicates that its wearer had been convicted of robbery and murder and been given as a gift to serve as a permanent servant to a member of the nobility.[3] A sentence of lifelong slavery was second only in severity to a sentence of death.

As well as being used as a form of punishment, unpaid labour was also used as part of a revenue model popular in medieval times that focused on profit maximization. From the end of the Middle Ages, however, this model increasingly fell out of favour in Europe, with large-scale feudal landowners no longer willing to feed their serfs when harvests failed and in times of scarcity. From the fifteenth century onwards, however, with European powers starting to colonize other parts of the world, entrepreneurs once again recognized the huge potential for profits through unpaid work. This led to the resurgence of the revenue model based on unfree labour. What was new to this situation was the decision to travel far beyond Europe's borders to find unpaid workers, something that would change the nature of slavery forever. Where previously being enslaved was, in theory, something that could happen to anyone, from this point onwards slavery was increasingly inflicted upon specific regions and peoples. Under European dominance of the transatlantic region, skin colour was introduced as an identifying and differentiating characteristic of enslavement. Europeans transported people from Africa to the Americas, where they were forced to work involuntarily, generation after generation. The idea that dark-skinned people should be in permanent service to Europeans was legitimized through a biblical reference to Ham, Noah's son, whose

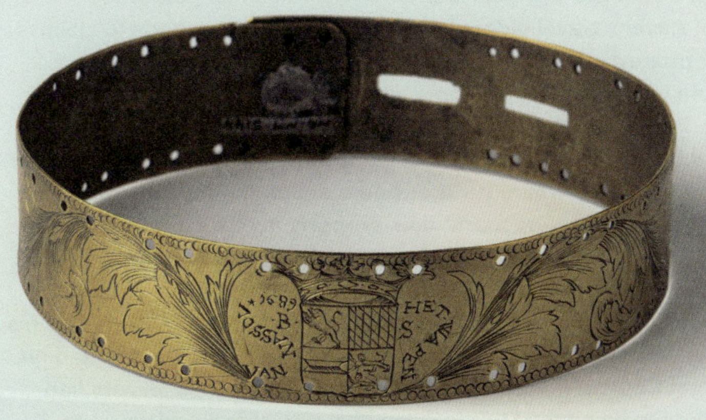

fig. 1 **Brass collar, 1689**
This neck band was originally categorized as a dog collar, but was possibly worn by a human being

descendants were cursed to serve their brothers for all eternity.[4] In this way, words such as 'slave', 'negro' and 'black' were made increasingly synonymous. In the area controlled by the Dutch East India Company (VOC), the phenomenon of slavery was also coupled to a notion of 'the Other'. The onset of the colonial period marked the start of an era in which people of colour were subjugated and defined as naturally subordinate to Europeans, who henceforth regarded themselves as superior.

Although distinctive physical characteristics became part of the legitimization of slavery, slaveholders held on to additional methods to claim people as their property. The primary purpose of these methods was to ensure the return of any enslaved people who fled, through the use of collars or by branding. Before being shipped off to faraway destinations, people were branded with the identifying mark of the trading company concerned. When they were sold they would be branded a second time, with the mark of the new 'owner'. People were marked as property in this way primarily in colonized territories, but the phenomenon was not unknown in Europe. In 1532, for example, a Portuguese commercial representative asked the Antwerp court of justice to arrest and return an escaped man whom he regarded as his property. The man was described as having the letters 'P' and 'M' branded on his jaw. The Great Court of Mechelen, however, ruled that since slavery had not existed in Europe since the Middle Ages, the man concerned was free. This information has survived in the exchange of letters between Mary, Governor of the Habsburg Netherlands and Hungary, and her brother Charles V, Holy Roman Emperor. It was by this means that the governor informed her brother of the extent of the verdict.[5]

The Dutch colonial slavery system operated exclusively outside the Netherlands, and enslaved people brought into the country were in principle free under domestic law. Servants taken to the Netherlands from 'the East' or 'the West' by Dutch slaveholders were able to apply for documents attesting to their free status (*vrijheidspapieren*). Without them they ran the risk of being treated as a 'slave', because in the colonial system their physical appearance was made synonymous with slave status.[6]

paulus maurus, 'moor'

The plantation economy boosted Dutch prosperity. Some members of the nobility and other elite groups were able to strengthen their positions, while a new wealthy class emerged. The addition of a dark-skinned servant to one's domestic staff was one way in which members of the elite could signal that they were part of a select group exerting global power. Given the fact that slavery was illegal in the Netherlands, the decision to have one's Black servant wear a metal collar – an indication of slavery and ownership – could be regarded as a form of provocation.[7] Was the collar a visual signal advocating the incorporation of colonial relations in Dutch society and legislation, or was it simply a mimicking of a practice that was common in Britain?[8] What is certain is that various former 'masters' who claimed ownership over servants went to court to claim that right, and the legislation was amended on various occasions. In 1776, for

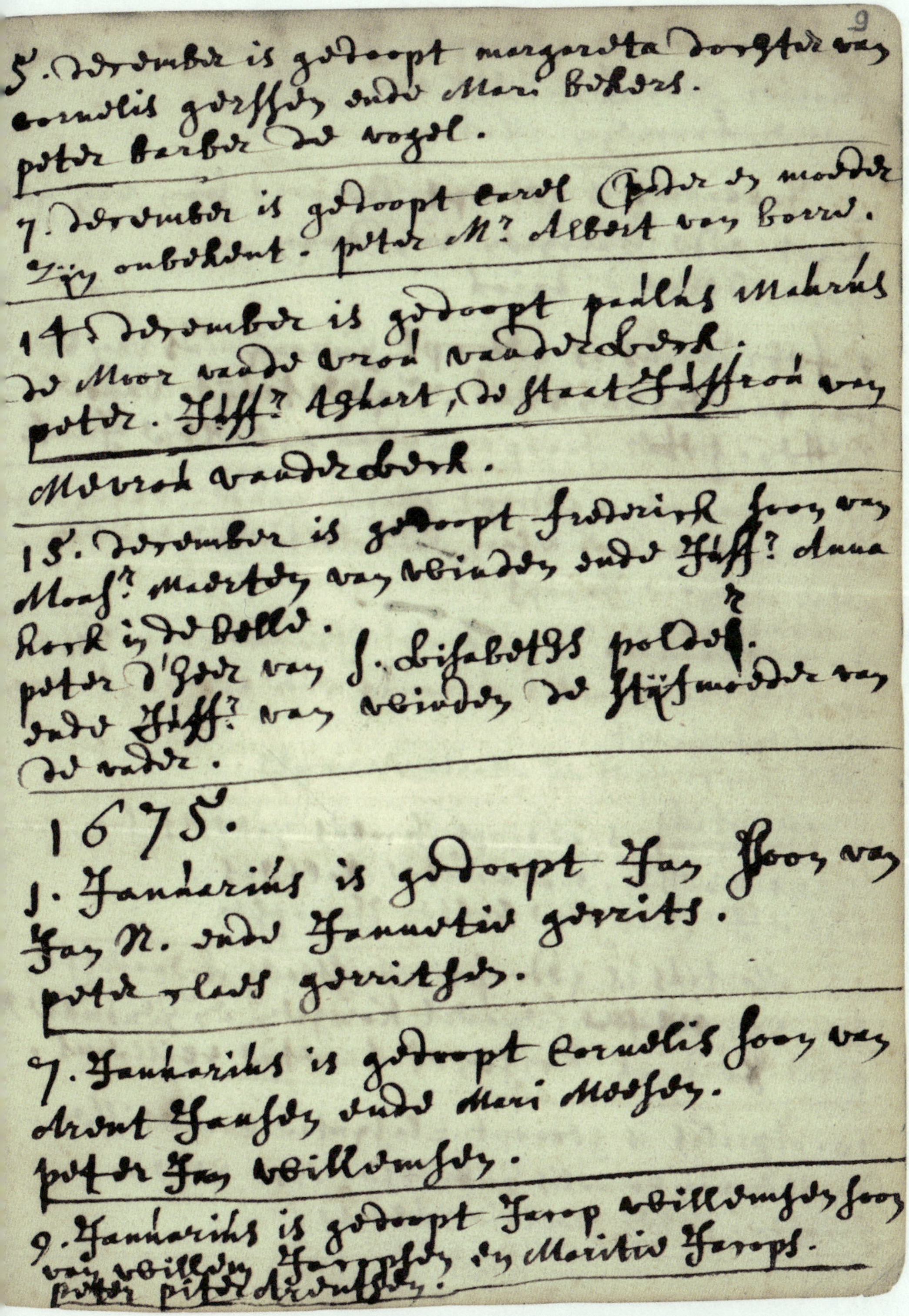

9

5. december is gedoopt margareta dochter van
cornelis gerritsen ende Mari bekers.
peter barber de vogel.

7. december is gedoopt carel (Peter en moeder
zijn onbekent. peter Mr. Albert van borre.

14. december is gedoopt paulus Maurus
de Moor vande vrou vanderleck.
peter. Juffr. Aghert, de staet juffrou van
Mevrou vanderleck.

15. december is gedoopt fredrick soon van
Mons. Maerten van winden ende Juffr. Anna
Kock in de Bolle.
peter d'heer van S. Elisabeths polder.
ende Juffr. van winden de stiefmoeder van
de vader.

1675.

1. Januarius is gedoopt Jan soon van
Jan N. ende Janneke gerrits.
peter claes gerritsen.

7. Januarius is gedoopt Cornelis soon van
Arent Jansen ende Mari Moesen.
peter Jan willemsen.

9. Januarius is gedoopt Jacop willemsen soon
van willem Jacobsen en Maritie Jacops.
peter pieter Arentsen.

fig. 2 **Paulus Maurus was registered as 'the Moor of Mrs Vanderleck' in a baptism and marriage book in The Hague on 14 December 1674**

example, a law was enacted that permitted a slaveholder to keep a person from the colonies in slavery for six months.[9]

The assumption that the brass collar inscribed with the year 1689 in the Rijksmuseum collection was intended for a dog is a reflection of the art historical gaze in the late nineteenth century. In English newspapers, however, we do find references to the use of similar collars not only for dogs but also people.[10] Might this also apply to this collar?

Close study of this elaborately embellished neck collar reveals the striking level of care and attention that was given to the application of the inscriptions. The entire surface is decorated, with opulent symmetrical tendrils of acanthus leaves and a family crest at the centre. The crest is quartered, with the first, third and fourth quarters referring to sections of the crests of the Nassau, Vianden and Dietz families, respectively, and the second containing part of the Beieren family crest.[11] The letters 'B' and 'S' are positioned on either side of the crest, along with the words 'Het wapen van Nassov' (The Nassau crest). This combination of signs probably refers to Anna Isabella van Beieren van Schagen, the Roman Catholic wife of Maurits, Count of Nassau La Lecq.

Church registers in The Hague reveal that a young Black man worked in the couple's household. Did he perhaps wear this brass collar? We encounter him for the first time in the archives in 1674, when he appears under the name Paulus Maurus in a baptism and marriage book. He is mentioned in the records for 14 December of that year as 'the Moor of Mrs Vanderleck'.[12] He was baptized in the Roman Catholic chapel in The Hague's Hofkwartier (Court Quarter) (fig. 2).[13] In the time of Moor rule over Spain, the word 'Moor' was used to refer to people from North Africa, in particular those with dark skin and Muslims. In Dutch records, however, terms such as 'Moor', *moriaan, moorinne, swart* (black), *swartin, nigri* and *negro* were increasingly used interchangeably to refer to skin colour and non-European descent.[14] In addition to this use of the term 'Moor' as a categorization, in the colonial period the term also served as a job title. By describing him as a 'Moor of', Paulus Maurus was both othered and objectified, as belonging to the wife of Nassau La Lecq and being different from the other servants.

Precisely where Paulus Maurus was originally from we do not know, but it is highly unlikely that his parents gave him the name Paulus Maurus. In many cases, the young men of African origin who found themselves working as domestic servants in the Netherlands were brought to the country by people who visited Africa's west coast and came into contact with human traffickers. We can only guess at why these young men, instead of being enslaved on colonial plantations, were selected to be put to work as servants in Dutch households. Possibly, it was a combination of factors, including age, an endearing appearance and intelligence. Jacobus Elisa Johannes Capitein, for example, a young African man living in the Netherlands in the household of Jacobus van Goch in 1728, was encouraged to study theology in Leiden. He was named after the captain who had bought him, after Van Goch himself and after his sister and niece.[15] It is possible that Paulus Maurus's surname is derived from the first name of his 'master', Maurits, Count of Nassau La Lecq. We could infer from this that Paulus was perhaps well loved within the family. On the other hand, the name may have been used for its meaning in Latin, 'Moor', in which case his name was a symbol of ethnic hierarchization.

An African child was regarded by the lady of the house as a kind of plaything, a form of entertainment; as he grew older, his role would increasingly become that of a servant.[16] This relationship characterized by domination and servitude is reflected in many portraits painted in the period 1650 to 1750, in which young African men were featured near the female subject, helping her to put on jewellery, offering her food or flowers, or holding her parasol.[17] These young men were often portrayed wearing a neck collar. With Paulus Maurus in their household, the Nassau La Lecq family signalled to the outside world that they belonged to a prosperous, internationally oriented class. At the same time, they were displaying their intention to educate the young man and convert him to the Christian faith by having him baptized. In the visual arts as in life, people like Paulus were degraded to the position of an exotic status symbol used by the white elite to reinforce their position in society.

The way in which Black servants were regarded by women of the upper classes, and the importance attached to the collar, are manifested in the seventeenth-century doll's house designed by Petronella Oortman and on permanent display in the Rijksmuseum (fig. 3). In curating the building of doll's houses, ladies of the affluent bourgeoisie indicated what they thought a decent and proper Dutch household should look like.[18] Having a doll's house made was an exceptionally costly pastime: at the time of its making, the value of this example was comparable with that of an actual canal house on Herengracht.[19] In her role as commissioner of the doll's house, Oortman oversaw its making and was responsible for fundamental decision-making.[20] She made every effort to ensure the final result was true to life and perfect, which makes the doll's house a reliable reference source for the ideal interior, household and social conventions of the period.[21] The Rijksmuseum collection also contains a painting of this doll's house from 1710, which gives us a reliable impression of its original state, including the dolls that have since been lost (fig. 4).[22]

Oortman made the striking choice to position an African servant in the 'best room', the most prestigious reception room of the house, situated on the left of the middle storey (fig. 4a).[23] The servant is dressed in sumptuous livery and wears a shiny silver collar around his neck.[24] He stands on the right, in front of a row of chairs, his hands stretched out before him – they probably once held a serving tray. He is depicted as a far smaller figure than the other people in the room. This possibly reflects his young age, but his limited height was also a characteristic of the stereotypical depiction of African servants in the colonial period. This situating of him in the most important room of the house, where appearances were all-defining, suggests that women such as Petronella Oortman and Anna Isabella van Beieren van Schagen regarded the presence of a Black servant as essential. It was a social convention in the homes of the elite.

The manner in which the room is decorated further underlines the conclusion that servants such as Paulus Maurus were status symbols that could be flaunted. The walls and ceiling are entirely covered with paintings depicting a panoramic Italian landscape and a sky dotted with clouds and birds. The painted parrot on the tea table in the right corner and the parrot on the over-

fig. 3 **Petronella Oortman's doll's house, c. 1686–1710**

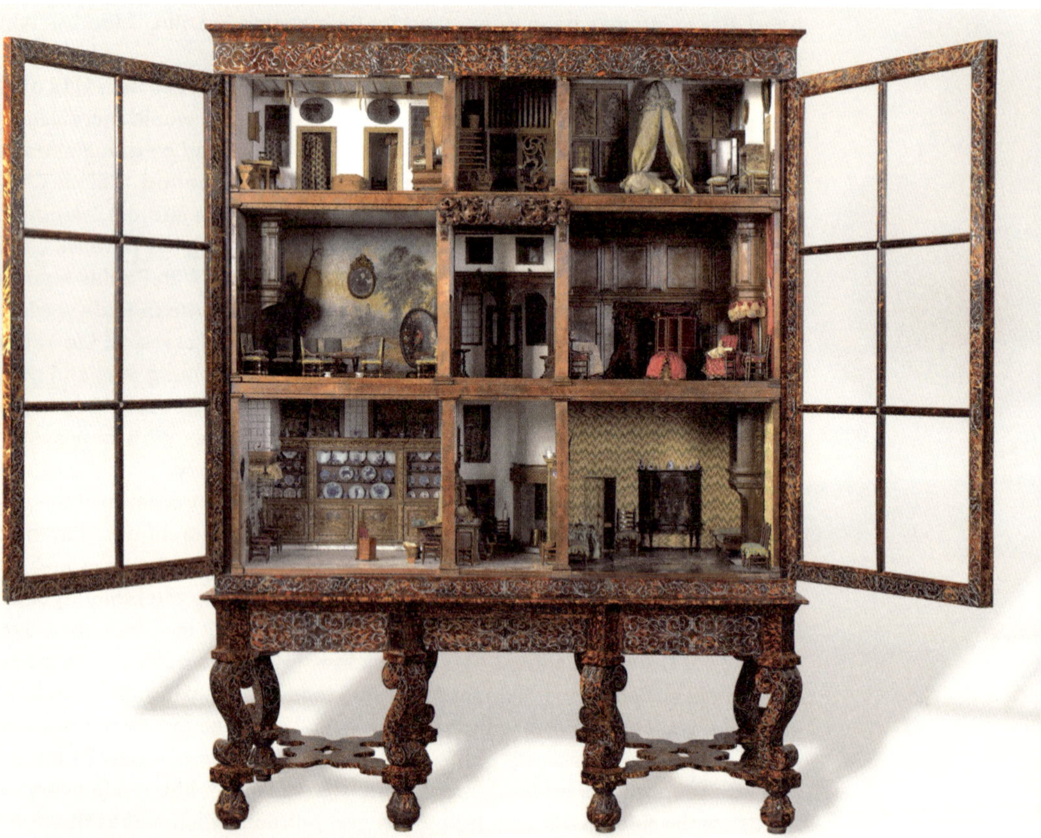

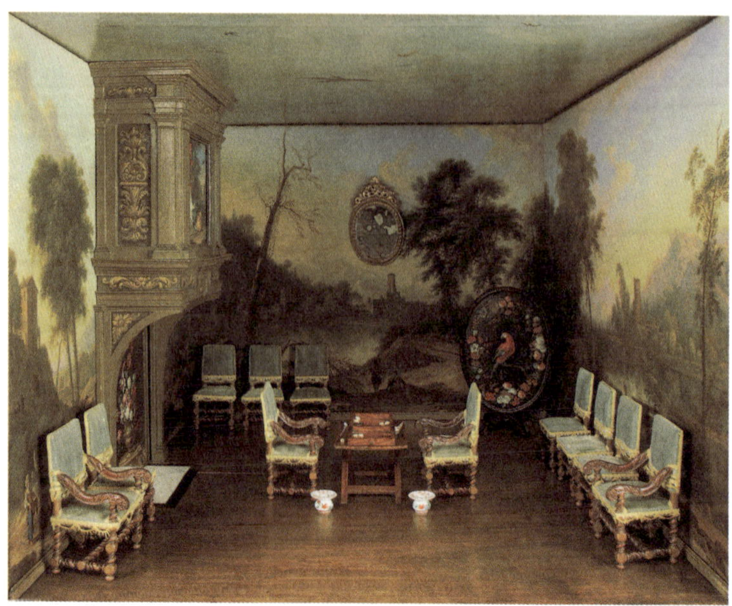

fig. 3a **Two spittoons in the doll's house**

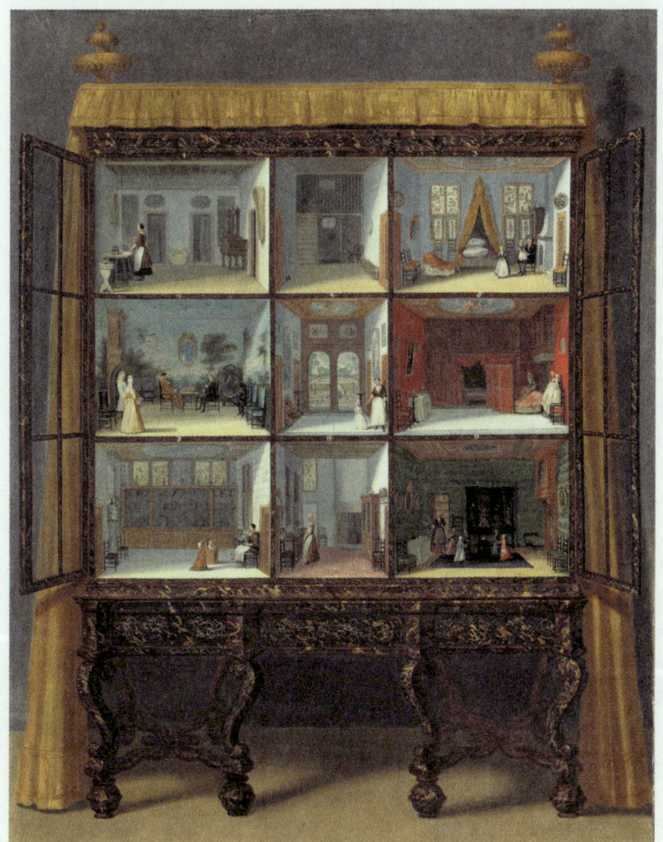

fig. 4 **Painting of Petronella Oortman's doll's house Jacob Appel (I), c. 1710**

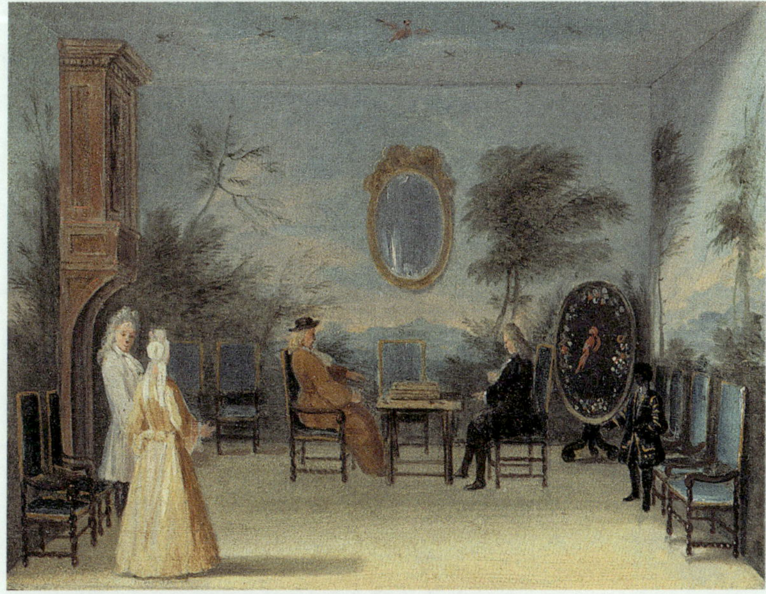

fig. 4a **Originally, a figurine of an African servant was positioned on the right-hand side of the most prestigious reception room in the doll's house**

mantel reinforce the overall 'exotic' ambience.[25] A reception room decor of this kind gave the visitor the illusion of walking into a landscape, providing an experience of being in nature that was amplified by the presence of the African servant owing to the stereotypical associations of his 'natural' and 'primitive' origins.[26]

The use of tobacco as presented in the doll's house also testifies to the role played in European notions of luxury by the products and servitude of people from the colonized world. The painting shows two men playing a game of draughts or backgammon while smoking long golden tobacco pipes.[27] In the doll's house itself, two decorated porcelain spittoons can be seen on the floor next to the table (fig. 3a). The tobacco caused the smoker to produce a large amount of saliva, which could be discharged into one of these receptacles. The smoking or chewing of tobacco, a plant native to the tropical Americas, became popular in the Dutch Republic in the second half of the seventeenth century. The Rijksmuseum collection contains a pair of early eighteenth-century spittoons featuring depictions of enslaved people cultivating tobacco. The depiction on the spittoons connects the iconographic tradition of the 'master and servant' on display in the doll's house with plantation slavery. The group shown smoking at the table are being served by an enslaved man (fig. 5).

Paulus clearly lived in a world in which people who looked like him were the exception, and were invariably depicted in one way: in a servile position. It was a world of exorbitant luxury, elitist pastimes and the consumption of products such as tobacco, which was accompanied by the aestheticization of slavery in decorations and utilitarian objects such as the spittoon. He must surely have been aware that he was himself a component in a luxury decor; an exceptional piece in an extravagant game. The stake of the game was prestige, and the presence in the household of an African servant adorned with a collar of precious metal scored high points. Could Paulus still remember his original social environment and his identity before he found himself in this subservient role? In the course of his journey from boyhood to manhood, did he come to accept the European world and make the best of a situation from which there was barely any hope of escape? And could he free himself of the collar – was it merely part of the uniform of a young domestic servant, or did he have to wear it outdoors when he was older?

paulus maurits, timpanist

Life would have been very different for a man of colour in the Netherlands than for an enslaved labourer in the colonized territory. Under the colonial system, an enslaved person was an object without rights. In the Netherlands, Paulus could shape his own life, to a degree. He could marry, for example.[28] The Hague court archives of 1684, ten years after Paulus's baptism, contain the record of his marriage. On 11 June that year, the wedding took place of 'Paulus Maurits, Herpaucker [military timpanist] of the Mounted Bodyguard Company of His Highness, and Maria Sauls, young daughter, both residing in the Hague' (fig. 6).[29] This could be read as an indication that he had found a place in society and was able to create a 'home' of his own.

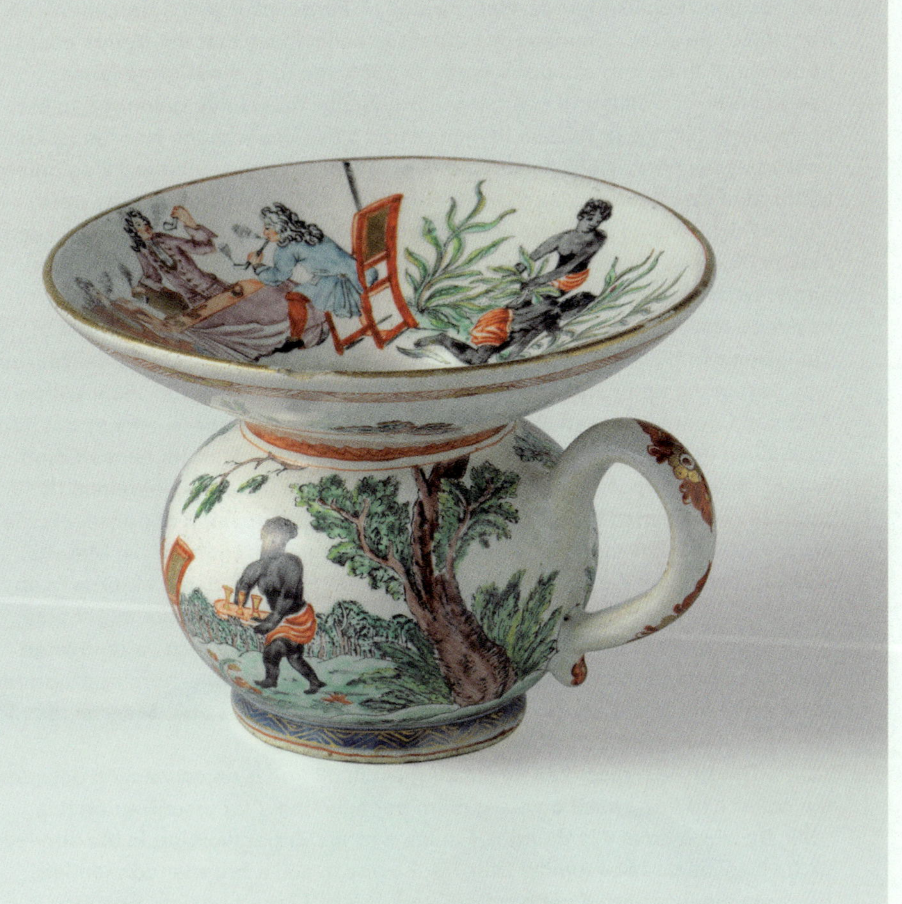

fig. 5 **Spittoon featuring depictions of enslaved people cultivating tobacco, c. 1715–1725**

These two lines of archival text further testify to a change of Paulus's name and position: 'Paulus Maurits, Herpaucker'. A *herpaucker* was a drummer who translated the army commander's orders in such a way that the troops could understand them and act upon them. In 1684, the title His Highness was used to refer to William III of Orange, and Paulus must have belonged to his bodyguard (his army). William III maintained close ties with the Nassau La Lecq family because they were descendants of one of the acknowledged illegitimate children of stadtholder Maurits of Orange. As William's cousins, they were handed high-ranking positions under his authority. The Count of Nassau La Lecq, Paulus Maurus's 'master' Maurits, was in 1672 a cavalry lieutenant general and was known to be a highly capable military man.[30] Maurits's brother Henry de Nassau, Lord Overkirk, saved the life of William III at the Battle of Saint-Denis in 1678 and was henceforth the prince's confidant. Henry de Nassau was part of the army that accompanied William III to England in 1688. Willem Adriaan, Count of Nassau-Odijk, another of Maurits's brothers, was appointed by William III as a special envoy to the English court.[31] Maurits himself died in 1683. Maurits's position as cavalry commander in the army of William III probably contributed to Paulus's appointment to the position of *herpaucker* in his army. The following year, 1684, Paulus's name was recorded as 'Maurits', shifting away from the possible ethnic connotation of the name Maurus to an association with the first 'master' whom he served. The new name might also have been a reference to Maurits's ancestor Maurits of Orange, a renowned military commander. The second name Maurits was probably more appropriate for a man with a military position than Paulus's previous one, Maurus, associated as it was with a position in domestic service.

This archive record seems to suggest that there is no connection between the collar and this specific young man, because the year inscribed on it is 1689, by which time, it is thought, Paulus was no longer working in the service of the Nassau La Lecq family. There is, however, still a broader connection between the wearing of neck collars and Paulus's new position, because it was not unknown for the position of military drummer to be occupied by African men, who are sometimes portrayed in the visual arts wearing a collar around their neck.[32] It is possible that military commanders chose to assign these men to this specific function due to European ideas about African people's sense of rhythm. But the presence of an African man also promoted the image of the army as a world power – in this sense, African men in the army fulfilled a similar role to their counterparts at the royal court or in the domestic sphere. The troops that accompanied William III to Exeter, England, in 1688 included many Africans, a fact that attracted the attention of the print press: '200 Blacks brought from the Plantations of the *Netherlands* in *Americ*[*a*], [with embroider'd] Caps lined with white Fur, and plumes of white Feathers, to attend the Horse'.[33] Perhaps Paulus Maurits was also part of this military passage to England, as timpanist in William's household cavalry.

A slightly later painting whose central subject is a noble or royal personage shows just how image-defining a timpanist could be. The figure at the centre of the painting, wearing a red coat, is shown on horseback in front of a carriage, with soldiers on the march in the background. The area of the

fig. 6 **Registration of the marriage of Paulus Maurits and Maria Sauls on 11 June 1684, indicating that in 1684 Paulus was a timpanist with William III's mounted bodyguard**

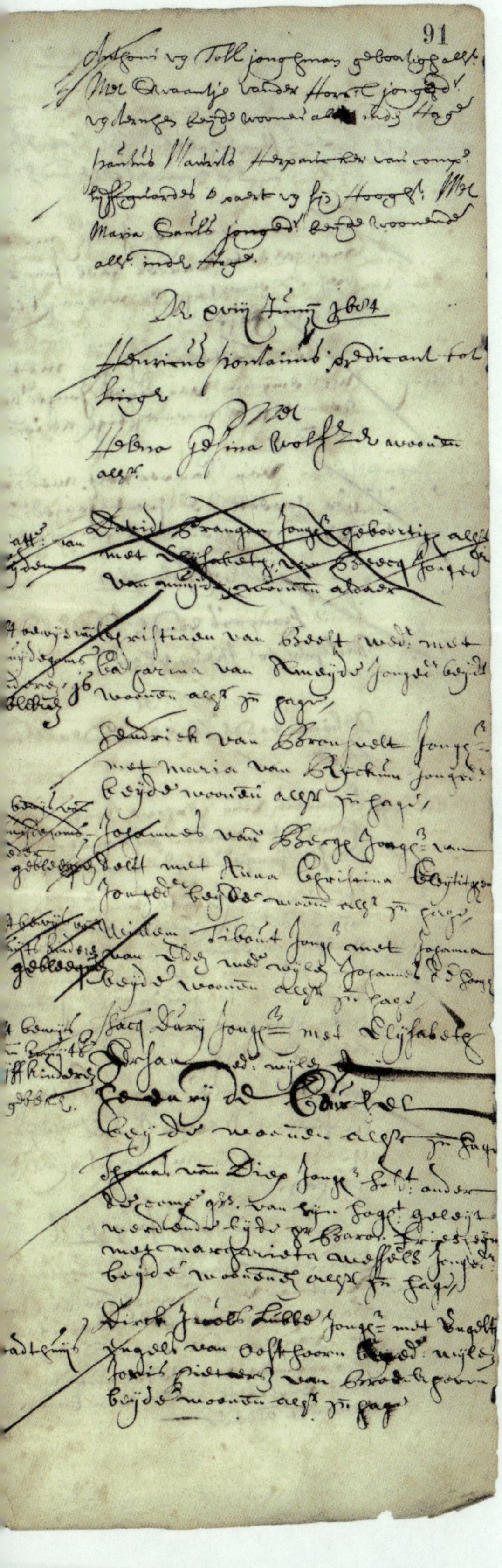

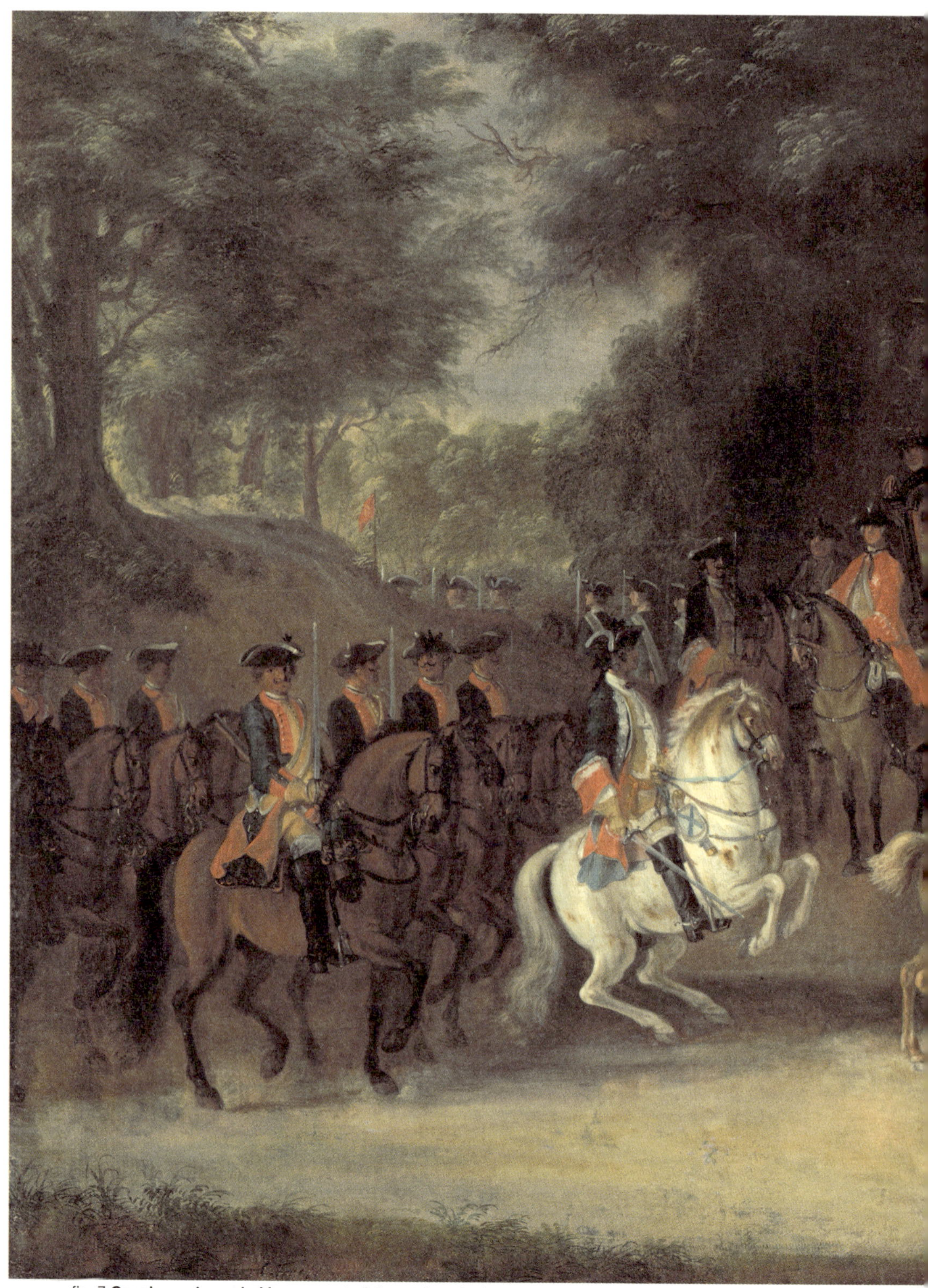

fig. 7 **Cavalry regiment led by a mounted timpanist who beats a marching rhythm on the timpani drums, Cornelis Troost, 1742**

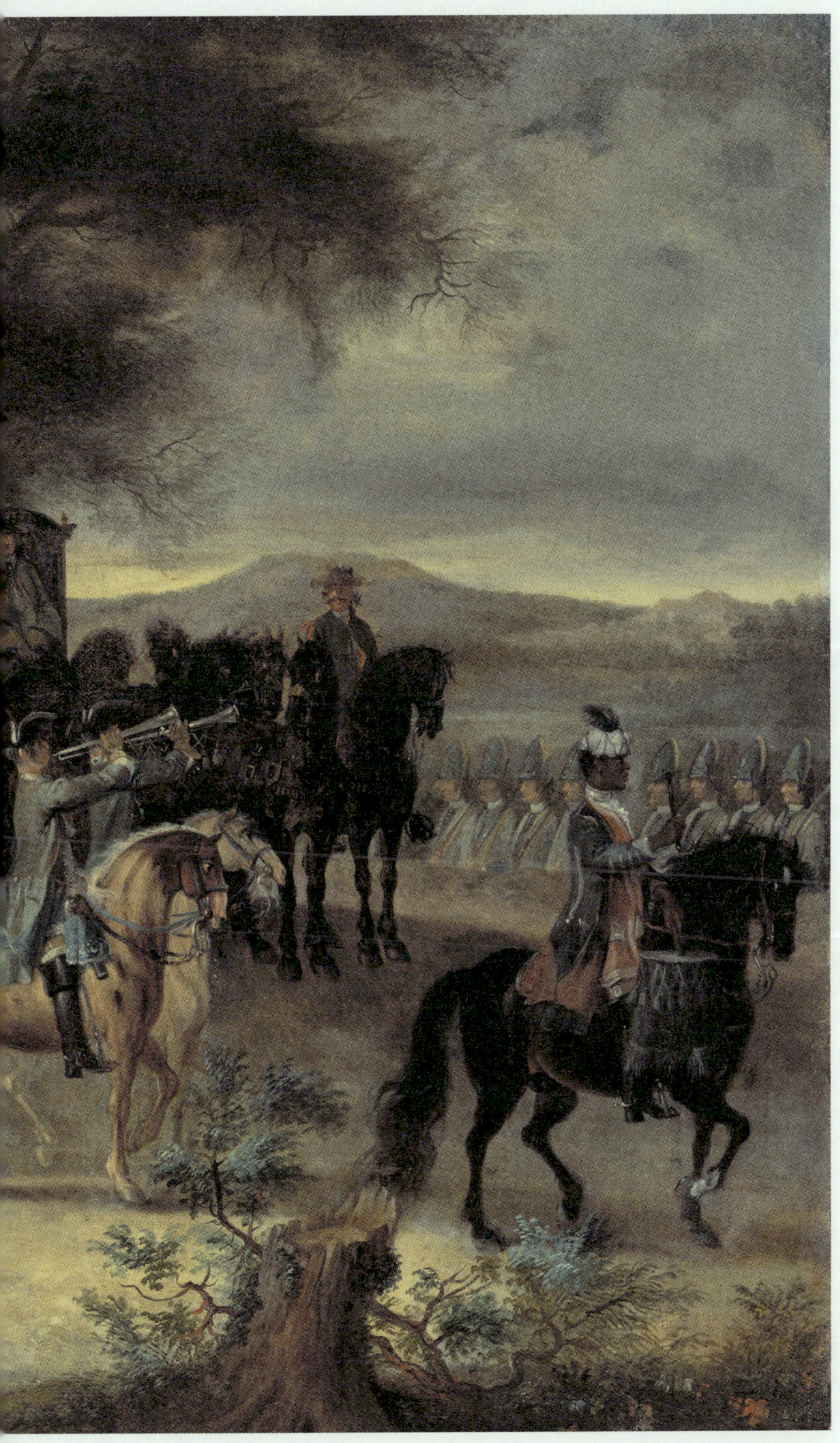

composition directly in front of him is completely filled by a group of officers on horseback preceded by two trumpeters and, at the very front, an African man. He is beating his drums to set the marching pace, a task that demanded great skill, for while playing the drums he had to control his horse solely with his feet. Seated proudly erect, this man leads the troops out. At first sight, this seems to epitomize upward social mobility for a Black man in a predominantly white environment. But even in this more responsible position, this man is depicted wearing a silver collar (fig. 7).

William III had Black men at his side from a young age. While studying in Leiden in 1659, for example, he had a Black assistant – he appears in a 1675 print by Romeyn de Hooghe (fig. 8).[34] It is also documented that in 1667, someone named Jan (van) Dam de Moor was working at the court.[35] Might he be the person portrayed in this print, holding in his hands the helmet belonging to William III (fig. 9)? These are prints in which young Black men are again placed in a supporting role, while William III takes centre stage. This could not be said of an exceptional life-size bust by John Nost the Elder (fig. 10). It is said that this impressive work of art is a portrait of William III's favourite servant.[36] The idea that this sculpture was likely made from life elevates the work to a personal portrait of a man of flesh and blood. The man is shown wearing a fanciful and stereotypical kind of costume – described in the period as 'Oriental' or 'Eastern' – that includes a feathered turban, a common feature of portrayals in the visual arts of young Black men in domestic or military service.[37] Around his neck he wears a conspicuous collar. What can we read from the expression in his eyes?

This juxtaposition of the costume and the collar combines two periods: before and after 1492. In the first, medieval, period, European Christians embarked on crusades to conquer countries ruled by people they called 'Moors': Islamic leaders who controlled parts of North Africa and the Mediterranean region, including Spain and Portugal. Although these 'Moors' were in fact ethnically diverse, Europeans often portrayed them as dark-skinned. Many Dutch family crests incorporated depictions of 'Moors'. Standardized representations of dark-skinned men wearing 'turbans', pearls and gold earrings were a familiar sight on Dutch streets. Pharmacies would hang these figureheads on their shopfronts in a reference to medical knowledge from 'the East'. Representations such as these constructed a contrast between the European and 'the Other' that was based on fantasies and preconceptions. This contrast is inherent to a system of representation that propagates the unequal power relationship that literary scholar Edward Said termed 'Orientalism'.[38] There was no question yet of institutionalized racism in the Middle Ages, however.

In 1492, the 'Moor' rulers of Spain were ousted and Columbus embarked on his first voyage west. He mistakenly landed in the Caribbean region, a chance event that would lead to European exploration and colonization of the Americas in the centuries that followed. It marked the beginning of the colonial period, one in which slavery was for the first time coupled to the notion of 'race', a European social construct that legitimized the subjugation of 'the Other'. Henceforth, 'black' was structurally subordinated to 'white', and a collar around the neck of a Black man stood for something much more

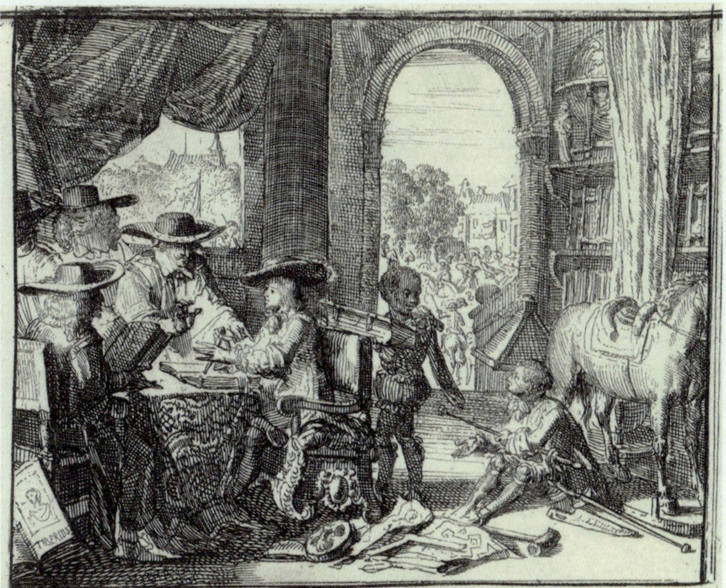

fig. 8 **Portrait of William III of Orange as a student, with a young Black man at his side, Romeyn de Hooghe, 1675**

fig. 9 **Portrait of William III of Orange with a Black servant, Romeyn de Hooghe, 1668–1688**

far-reaching than punishment of the individual: it represented the subjugation of African people.[39]

The combination of the fanciful 'Oriental' costume and the collar unites references to the defeat of 'Moorish' rule and to European hegemony, and symbolizes an entirely new 'racial' hierarchy that became increasingly institutionalized on a global scale. With dark skin becoming more and more synonymous with slavery, the collar gradually lost its pre-colonial practical function and came to serve purely as a luxury display of dominance. If William III did indeed choose to have a bust made of his favourite servant, the result was not simply a portrait but also a statement about the sovereign's power.

Maurits, Count of Nassau La Lecq, also chose to have himself portrayed with a Black servant (fig. 11). The young man, positioned in the corner of the painting, holds in his hands Maurits's plumed helmet as he looks upwards in awe and admiration to his 'master', seated high on his horse (fig. 11a). Maurits had himself portrayed in armour as the commander of the troops in the background. He holds the reins in both hands and a ceremonial baton in his right. The anonymous artist chose to compose the painting in such a way that the servant appears smaller than the main figure. This ensures that the latter appears to be larger and more powerful.[40] This equestrian portrait is a manifestation of the construction of a self-image, one in which Maurits presented himself to the outside world as he wished to be perceived – as he believed himself to be. Paintings of this kind idealize and normalize the notion of the 'master' and the 'black servant'.[41] But how did Paulus himself perceive his relationship with Nassau La Lecq?

monsieur paul maurice agulard

Although Paulus Maurus joined William III's army in 1684, he stayed in contact with the Nassau La Lecq family. In 1690, Anna Isabella van Beieren van Schagen became godmother to his son. The baptism took place in the French Roman Catholic chapel in The Hague, where Van Beieren van Schagen's chambermaid Elisabeth Weltins acted on her behalf. Weltins carried the one-day-old baby to the baptismal font.[42] Paulus and Maria Sauls baptized their child with the name Maurice (fig. 12).[43]

Intriguingly, in the archival record of the baptism of Paulus's son in 1690, he is again registered under a different name from what appears in the record of his marriage six years earlier, and his own baptism in 1674. Having first appeared in the archive as 'Paulus Maurus' and then as 'Paulus Maurits', in 1690 he is referred to as 'monsieur Paul Maurice Agulard'. This change can be explained, at least in part, by the fact that the French language was used in the chapel and therefore in this document. The additional name Agulard is however striking because it gives the impression of being a full-fledged last name – whereas Maurus and Maurits could both serve as either first or last names. Possibly, the prospect of fatherhood prompted in Paulus a desire for a name that he would be proud to pass on to future generations, a name untainted by associations with a racialized social position. It is appealing to consider that the choice of 'Maurice' possibly alludes to yet another Maurice,

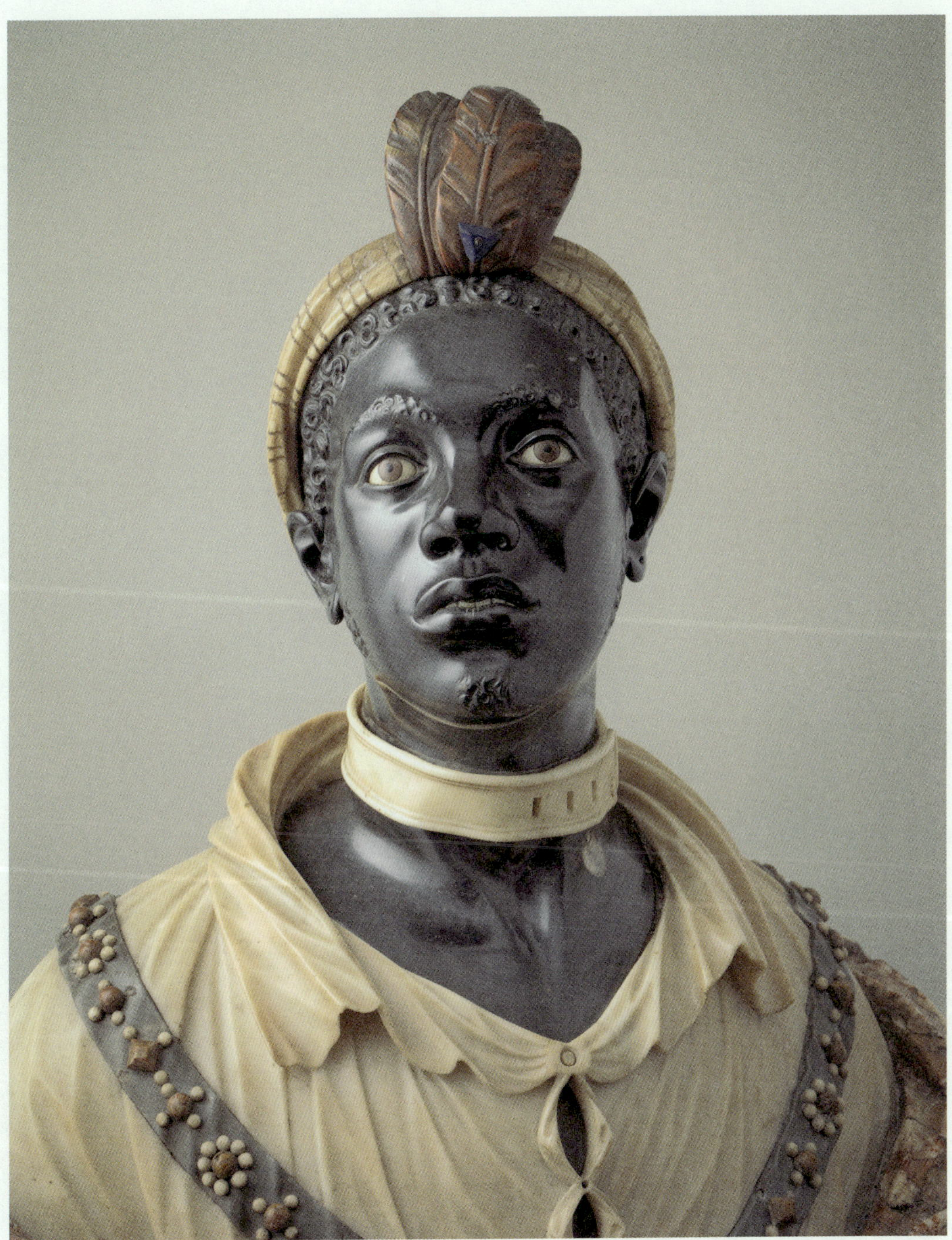

fig. 10 **Detail of a bust of an African man**
John Nost the Elder, 1701

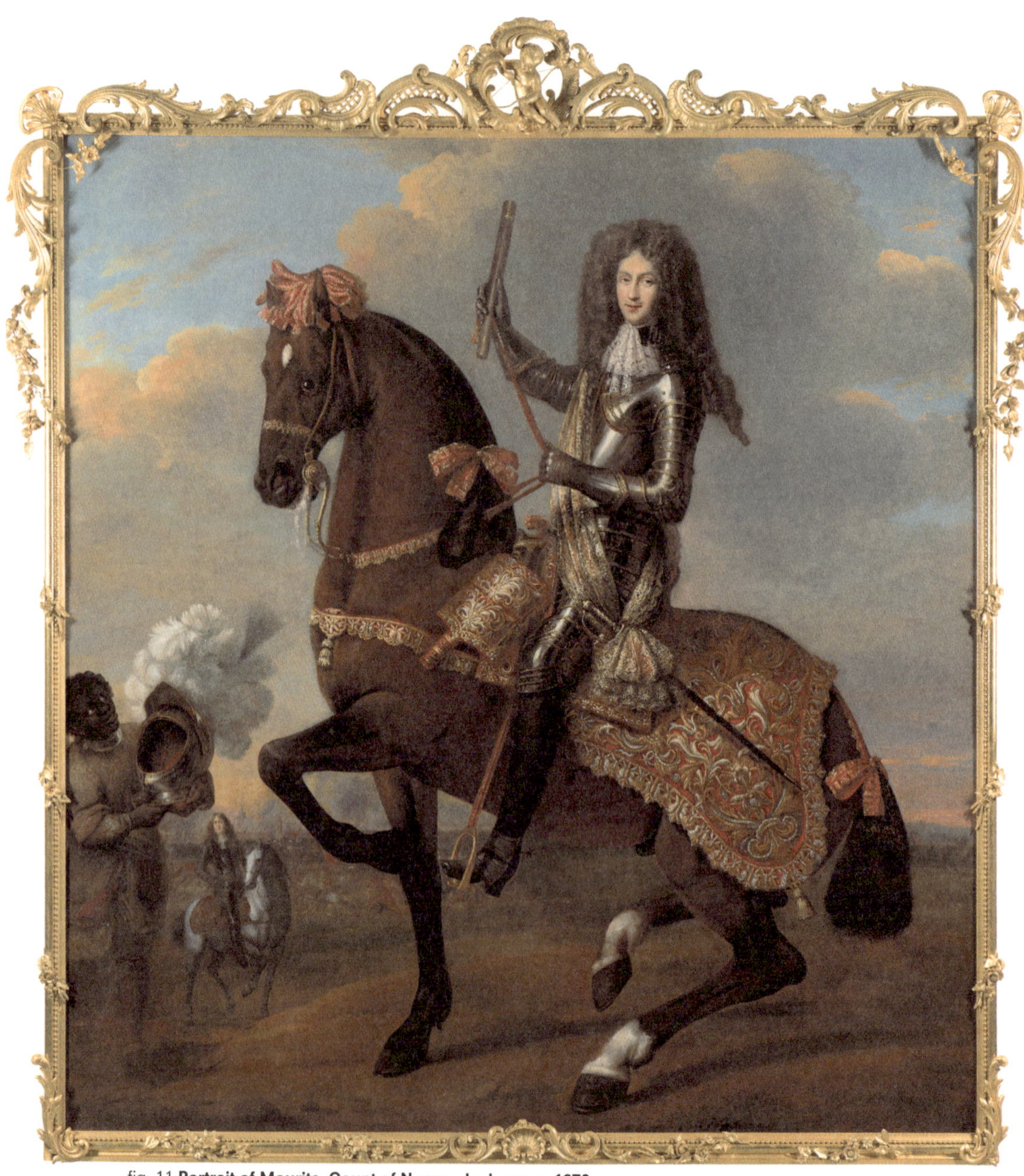

fig. 11 **Portrait of Maurits, Count of Nassau La Lecq, c. 1670**

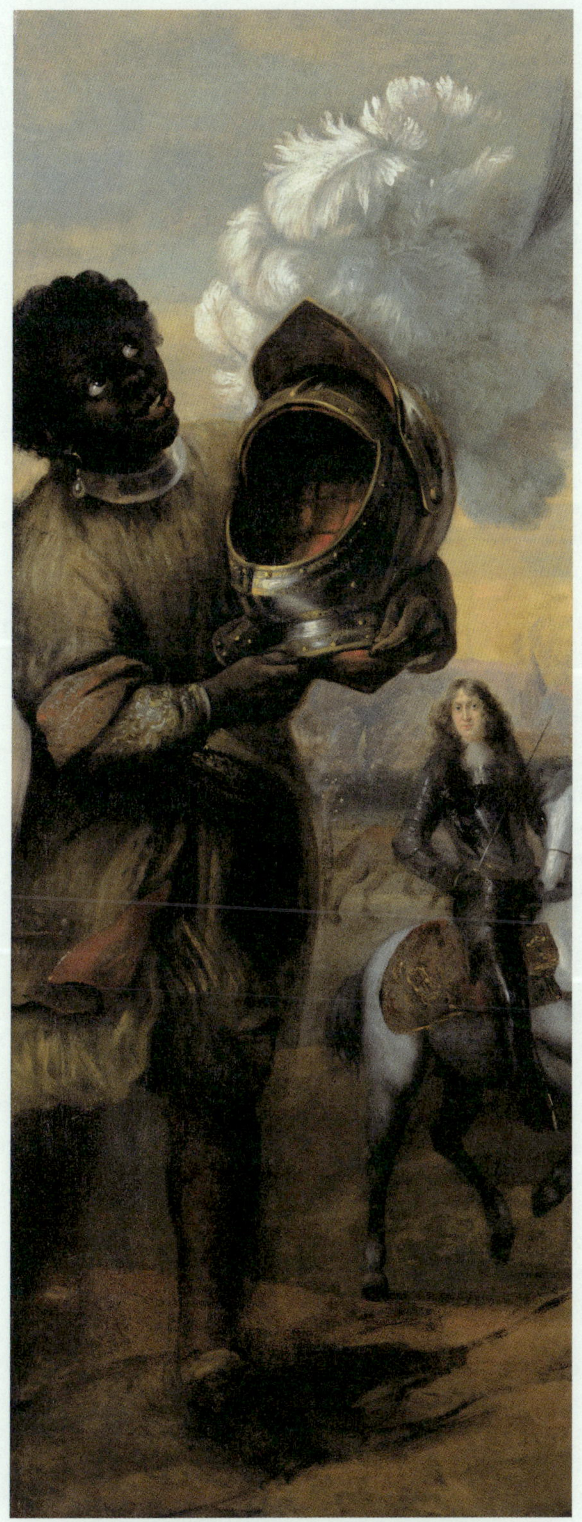

fig. 11a **An African young man is portrayed in the lower left corner of the painting, holding Maurits's helmet**

a great military commander with a name of mythical proportions who was, furthermore, a Black man. According to tradition, the Christian Saint Maurice was a high-placed commander in the Imperial Roman army in the third century. He came from Thebes in Egypt and he and his legion had, unlike the Romans themselves, converted to Christianity, and they refused to execute fellow Christians.[44] Later, in the thirteenth century, the Egyptian Saint Maurice was increasingly portrayed as a Black man in European armour. Images of him were used by the Catholic Church as part of its efforts to disseminate the Catholic religion more widely, and they became popular in Europe.[45]

The evidence suggests that Paulus was able to rise out of his position as a servant, and to enjoy a private life as a husband and father. From the little we know about Paulus, it is difficult to infer the nature of his continued contact with the Nassau La Lecq family and whether it was born out of personal choice or necessity – in a society where families could exert great power, the ability to adapt and conform may have been a valuable one. Nonetheless, the name that Paulus adopted in his later life and passed on to his son – a name associated with a Black saint – gives some reason to believe that he was aware of realities other than solely those of a man whose status was signalled by a collar.

paulus's legacy

What do we know about what life was like for Paulus and other people like him in similar situations in the Dutch Republic? Although the visual sources depict scenes constructed by the European elite, they do reveal the environment in which Paulus moved. Within these constructions, these young men appear to accept their role obediently and willingly. We can safely assume, however, that the relationship between 'master' and 'servant' was more complex than this, and that the servant did not always simply accept all aspects of the position imposed upon him. It was, in short, an ambivalent experience. Life as a servant in the Netherlands was certainly not comparable to the life of an enslaved labourer on a plantation in the Americas, where people were treated as nothing more than instruments with no connection to the society around them. In the Dutch Republic, people such as Paulus were church members; they married and they had families of their own. While this demonstrates that they enjoyed many of the same rights as white Europeans, the use of the collar shows that in the Netherlands of the colonial era there were Black people who were nonetheless branded, even if their 'brand' took the form of a precious metal collar. Given that the collar was a symbol of slavery, it can hardly be otherwise than that Paulus and people like him were continually aware that they were being categorized by those around them as a 'slave'.

Who are the descendants of Paulus and Maria, and their son Maurice? Do they know that they have roots in Africa? Various studies indicate that there are more descendants of early African Dutch people than is often assumed.[46] It is not only in formerly colonized territories that there are many descendants of people who occupied a wide variety of positions in the colonial system – the current population of the Netherlands is also more diverse in origin than first impressions might suggest.[47]

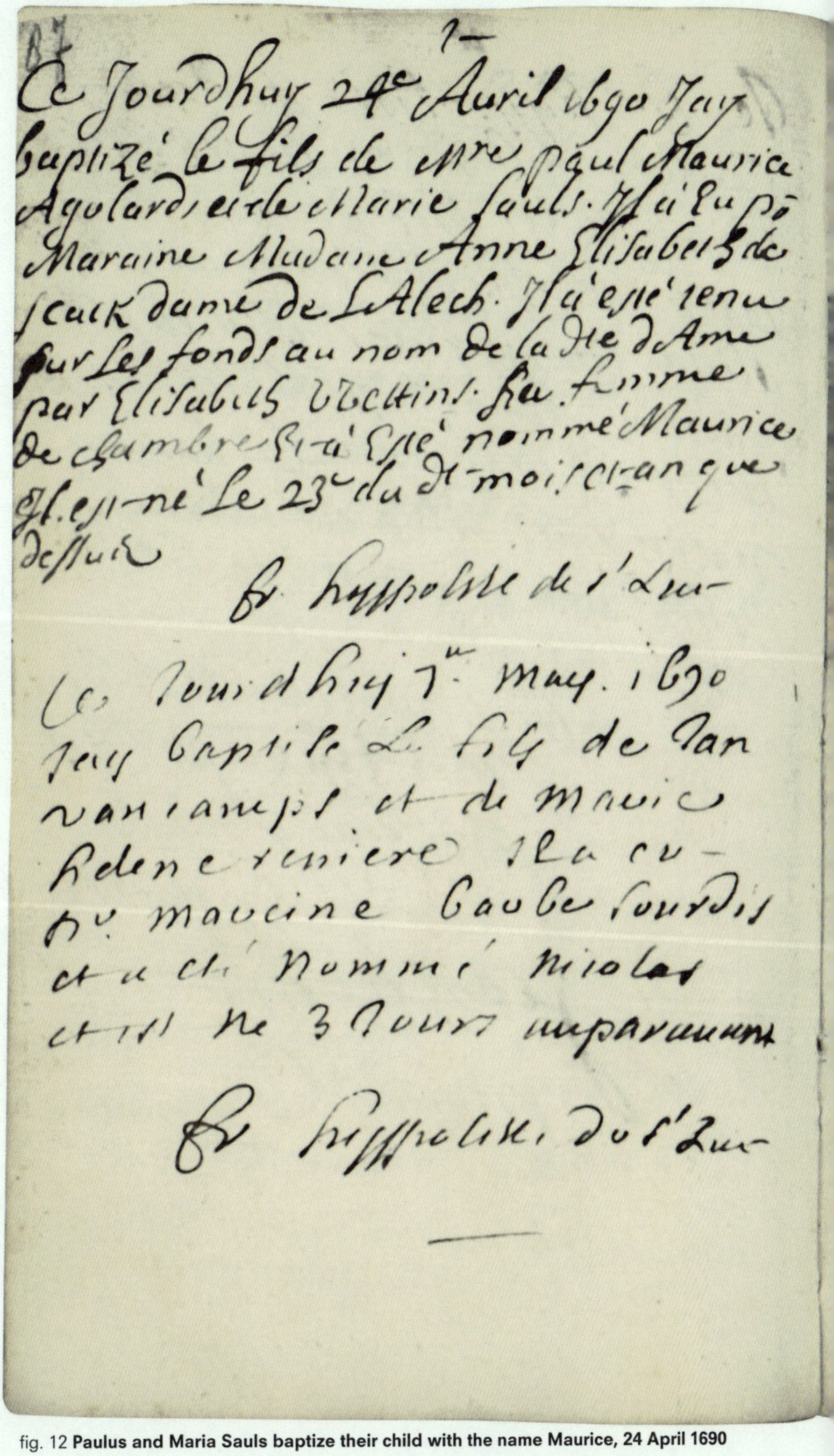

1

Ce Jourdhuy 24e Avril 1690 Jay
baptizé le fils de Mre paul Maurice
Agolardi et de Marie Sauls. Il a eu pô
Maraine Madame Anne Elisabeth de
Seulk dame de La Alech. Il a esté tenu
sur les fonds au nom de la dte dame
par Elisabeth Vrettins sa femme
de chambre. Et a esté nommé Maurice
Il est né le 23e du dt mois et an que
dessus

fr. hippolitte de s'Lu—

Ce Jourdhuy 7e may. 1690
Jay baptisé le fils de Jan
van iamps et de marie
hedene reniere ila eu
p. maraine Barbe Jourdis
et a esté nommé niolas
et il est né 3 Jours auparavant

fr. hippolitte. de s'Lu—

fig. 12 **Paulus and Maria Sauls baptize their child with the name Maurice, 24 April 1690**

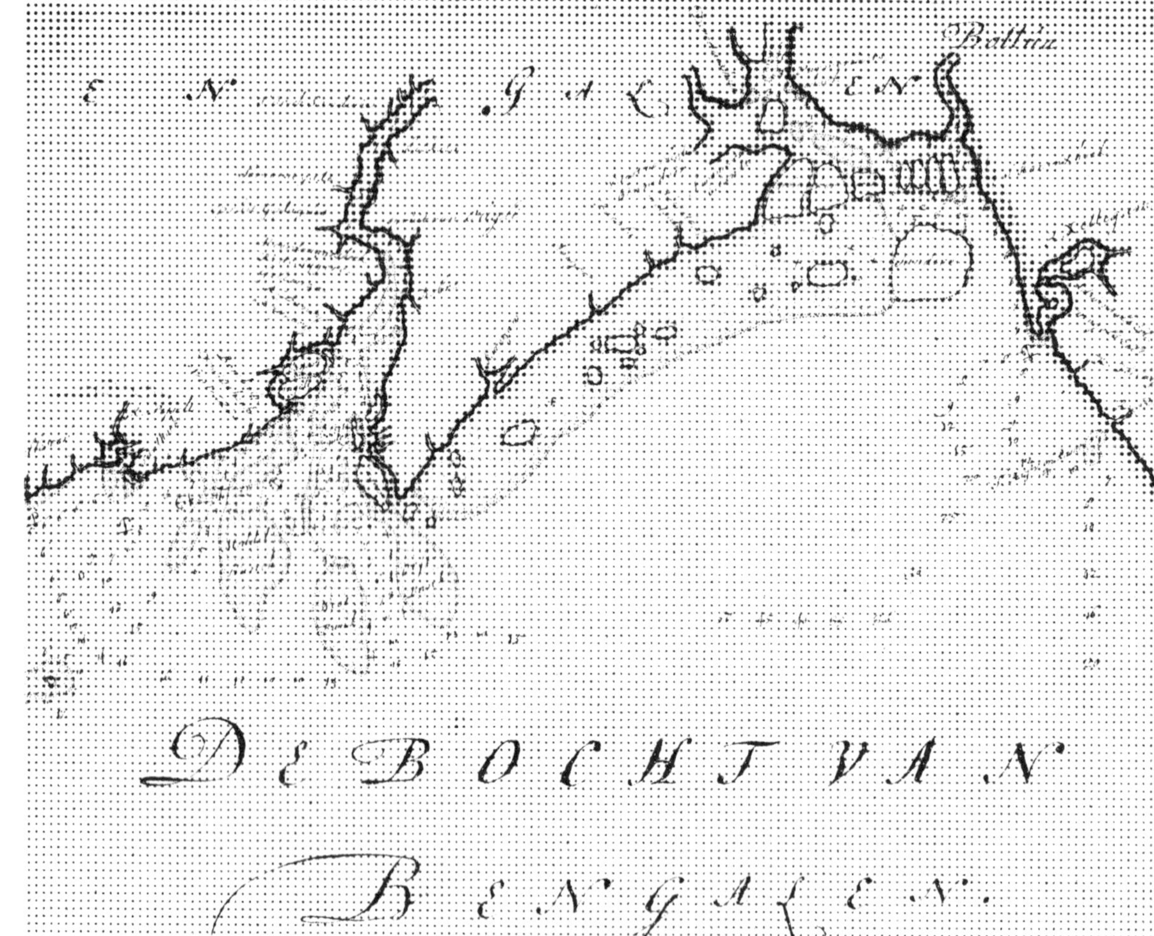

DE BOCHT VAN
BENGALEN.

maria holtrop

van bengalen

shipped to batavia, banda, cape town and dokkum

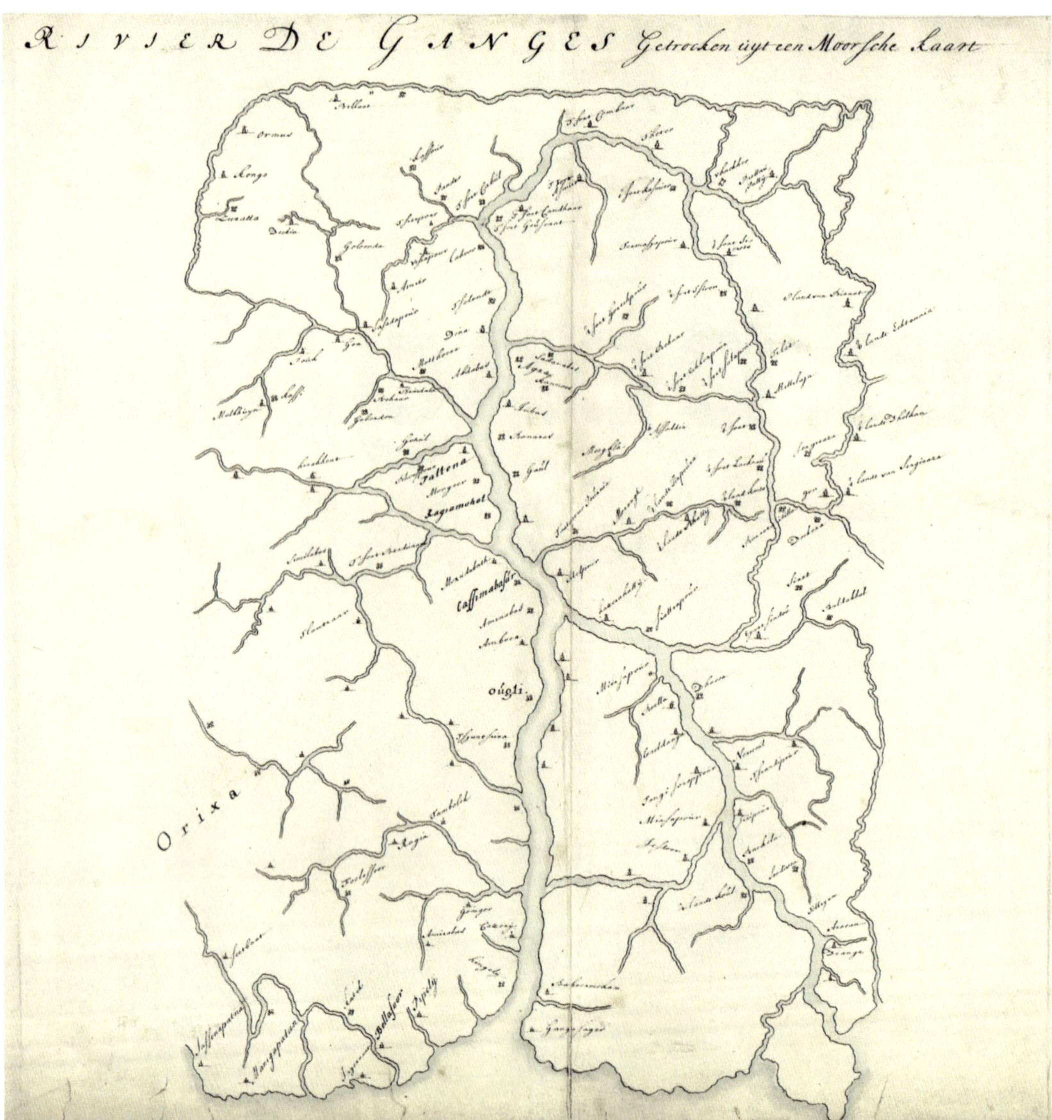

fig. 1 **Map of the Ganges River basin, c. 1695**

In the early morning of 22 January 1662, the Dutch surgeon Wouter Schouten stands on the shore in the Bengali city of Pipeli. Looking out over the river, he sees ten *jelias*, narrow rowing boats, approaching in the distance. The boats are packed with people. Schouten describes in his travelogue how 'these unfortunates' lie sprawled on their backs, bound with nooses around their necks and arms, and can barely move.[1]

> Anyone can imagine what a miserable groaning, weeping and heartbreaking whimpering these unfortunates utter. Forlorn people who only days before lived in comfort and freedom, were now robbed of everything, tied up and beaten, taken, poor and naked, into slavery. For a pittance they are sold to Christians, Moors and all kinds of heathen peoples and so forever separated from each other and scattered across the whole earth.[2]

These boats were piloted by armed men from Arakan (now Rakhine, Myanmar), a kingdom on the east side of the Bay of Bengal. Under the leadership of Portuguese captains, they would travel up the Ganges River, kidnapping the people of the villages along the shore in violent raids and then selling them in Pipeli. A map of the Ganges basin shows how extensive this hinterland was (fig. 1). According to Schouten, the boats were mainly filled with women and girls – the men had managed to escape. For only 20 rupees, or 10 rix-dollars, per person, these people were sold.[3]

> It was touching to see how these wretched people were sold and freed from the awful bonds and shackles of their arch-enemies, the raiders. Once brought aboard our ships, they knew not how to show their joy and happiness, grateful for the clothing and food given to them.[4]

One wonders how much joy and happiness they still felt once they realized that they were now the property of the Dutch. They were transported to households in Batavia (present-day Jakarta, Indonesia), nutmeg plantations on the Banda Islands in the Moluccas (Maluku Islands), and farms on the Cape in what is now South Africa, where they would have to work in slavery for the rest of their lives.

People like these feature in great numbers in the various archives of the Dutch East India Company (VOC). The VOC and its employees considered enslaved men, women and children to be personal property that could be bought, sold, bequeathed and inherited. Their own names were stripped from them and new, European names forced on them. These new names were taken, for example, from the Bible, the classics of antiquity or the months of the year. To this new first name a toponym was added, referring to the place from which they came or where they were sold. The people who were captured in the area around the Bay of Bengal were called 'Van Bengalen' – 'of Bengal' – by the Dutch.

These VOC archives reveal a network sprawling all around the Indian Ocean. The archive documents afford us a glimpse into the lives of these people.

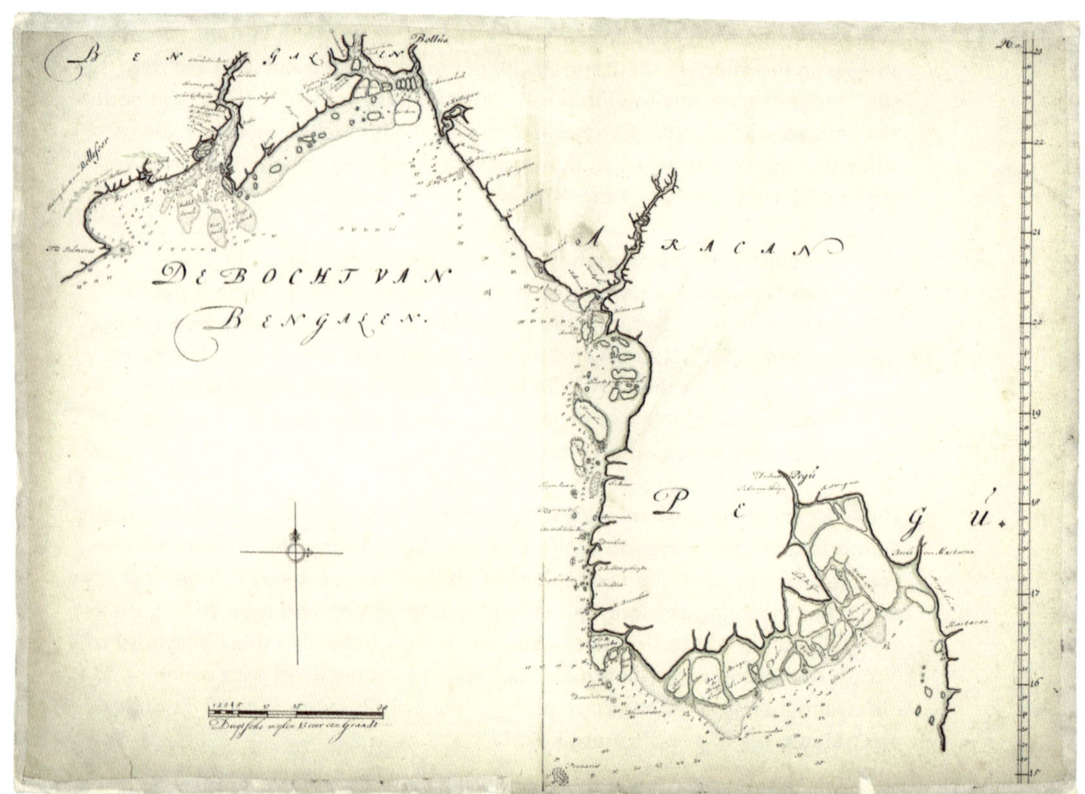

fig. 2 **Map of the Bay of Bengal, c. 1695**

What did it mean to be enslaved in the VOC period? The Dutch traveller Johannes Olivier wrote in the nineteenth century that 'in no colony on the face of the earth are slaves so humanely treated and given such easy work as in the Dutch East Indies.'[5] But there is no such thing as a gentle system of slavery. Enslaved men and women had no rights whatsoever. The slaveholder decided everything for them, and they could be sold at any time without having any say in it. They owned no property, were allowed to bequeath nothing, and even their children belonged to the slaveholder. They were not allowed to defend their honour and therefore could not rise up against humiliations or mistreatments without dire consequences.

For some of the enslaved people with the toponym Van Bengalen, only their name and position have survived in the VOC archives; for others, parts of their lives can be reconstructed. Maart, Calistra, Amon, Horij, Francina, Januarij, Marij, Angela, Susanna, Abraham, Augustus and Baron van Bengalen all lived in slavery, in different places and in different circumstances, and we can follow them across the entire territory of the VOC, all the way to the Dutch Republic. Maart was taken from Bengal to Batavia, where Calistra, Horij, Francina, Januarij and Amon also ended up. Marij was forced to work on the nutmeg plantations of the Banda Islands. Susanna, Angela, Augustus and Abraham ended up at the Cape of Good Hope. Finally, Baron van Bengalen and his son Filander de Baron were brought to Alkmaar and Dokkum, in the Netherlands.

As the headquarters of the VOC, Batavia was a way station or a terminus for many people in slavery. Maart, Horij, Calistra, Amon, Januarij, Francina, Susanna, Angela, Baron and Filander all spent a certain amount of time in Batavia. It is reasonable to assume that Marij, Augustus and Abraham were also there at some point. All of them were presumably born, enslaved and sold in the area around the Bay of Bengal. That was the starting point of their journey.

the bay of bengal

This map of the Bay of Bengal shows the area where the Van Bengalens, according to their toponym, came from: present-day northeast India and Bangladesh (fig. 2). At the time, this region was part of the vast Mughal Empire. Southeast of Bengal lay the kingdom of Arakan, around the river of the same name. Dutch accounts from the early seventeenth century mention trading opportunities here in rice and textiles, but, remarkably, nothing is noted about the slave trade. However, slavery definitely existed in the area around the Bay of Bengal, even before the arrival of the Dutch. Slavery had been a custom in Southeast Asia for centuries, and to varying degrees, long-term or temporarily. One could end up in slavery for a number of reasons: through poverty, debt, by selling oneself, as a punishment, as a prisoner of war, through kidnapping during raids or by birth. The Dutch, and the Portuguese before them, manipulated these customs to their advantage.

The Van Bengalens were enslaved after being kidnapped from the villages around the Ganges and other rivers in this region and brought to the slave market in Pipeli or Arakan. Portuguese slave traffickers in particular

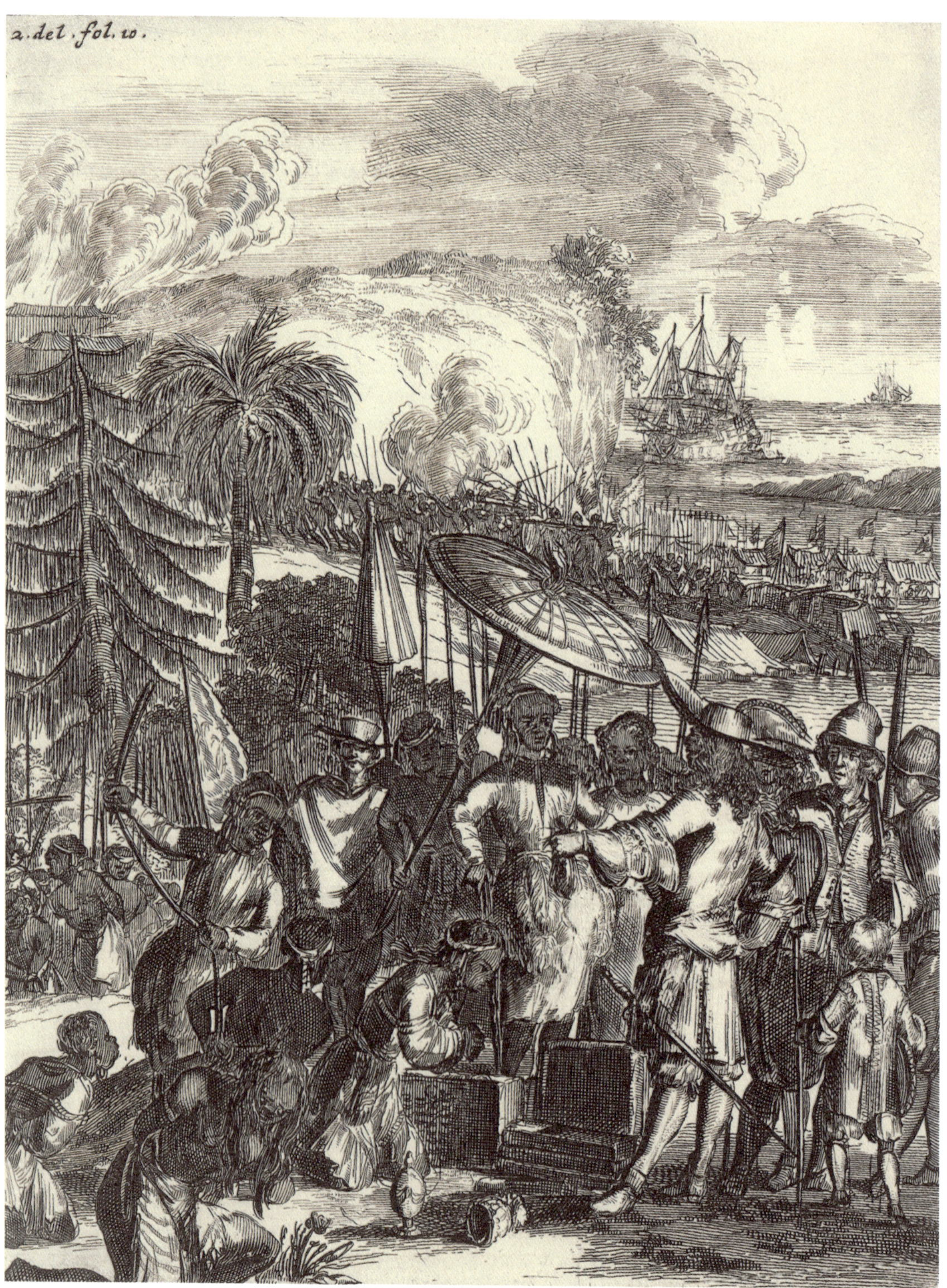

fig. 3 **Enslaved Bengalis being sold to Dutch buyers, 1676**

played a central role in this process. They had been in this area long before the Dutch and were hired by the kings of Arakan as pirates, to attack ships and kidnap and sell people. They were called Harmads in the local language, derived from the Portuguese word *armada*, meaning fleet.[6] The populace lived in constant fear of losing all their property, being enslaved or even losing their lives at a stroke. The menace of the Harmads was sung about in long ballads. The text below comes from the popular Bengali ballad *Nasar Malum*:

> The Harmads were seen at a distance busy observing their ship with the help of telescopes. Nasar felt a shudder at the sight of the miscreants. Ten or twelve of them, dressed in black trousers, approached Nasar. Some of them wore red coats and turbans on their heads. In the belt of their waists, they had scabbards bound tightly and they had guns in their hands. The blood flowing through the veins of Nasar became frozen in fear. The captains and sailors found their limbs paralysed and could not move their hands and feet. The first thing that the robbers did was to hold Nasar tightly by the neck. They slapped his cheeks and the blows were so sudden and severe that Nasar fell down on the deck. His sailors and other men lay more like dead than living beings viewing with their timid eyes the action of the robbers.[7]

The Dutch first set foot in Bengal around 1600. In the early days of the VOC, after its founding in 1602, there was still a great deal of aversion to slavery in the Netherlands.[8] The directors of the VOC differed in their opinions about the use of enslaved workers, but due to the high cost of labour in Southeast Asia, objections were eventually set aside and a structural source of enslaved people was sought. That source was found in 1623 in Arakan.[9] The arrival of the VOC meant a constant demand for enslaved people, and this provided a great stimulus to the slave market in Bengal and Arakan.[10] The people captured by the Portuguese traffickers were sold to the VOC in Pipeli – as described above by Wouter Schouten – or Arakan. An illustration in Schouten's account depicts a richly attired Dutch trader with a sack of money in his hand. He appears to want to buy a group of chained enslaved people from the Bengali trader or ruler who stands in the centre. Another European, with a striking hat and moustache, can be seen in the trader's retinue – probably one of the Portuguese who practised human trafficking in Arakan and Bengal (fig. 3). Once sold, the enslaved individuals were registered in the VOC archives.
To make the human trafficking process possible, the kings of Arakan issued various *firmans*, documents through which they gave the Dutch the right to trade in people. The VOC archive contains a translation of one of these *firmans* from 1642.[11] With it, the king permitted the Dutch to buy 'new Bengali slaves'. The word 'new' is crucial here. The king did not want his own subjects to be sold in slavery to the Dutch; these had to be 'new slaves': men, women and children from the area around the Ganges in Bengal.[12] The first 88 people were shipped from Arakan to Batavia aboard the *Jager* and *Muijs* in 1624. Evidently this trade was a success, for in 1634 officials in Batavia decided to establish a permanent post in Arakan for the trading of slaves and rice.

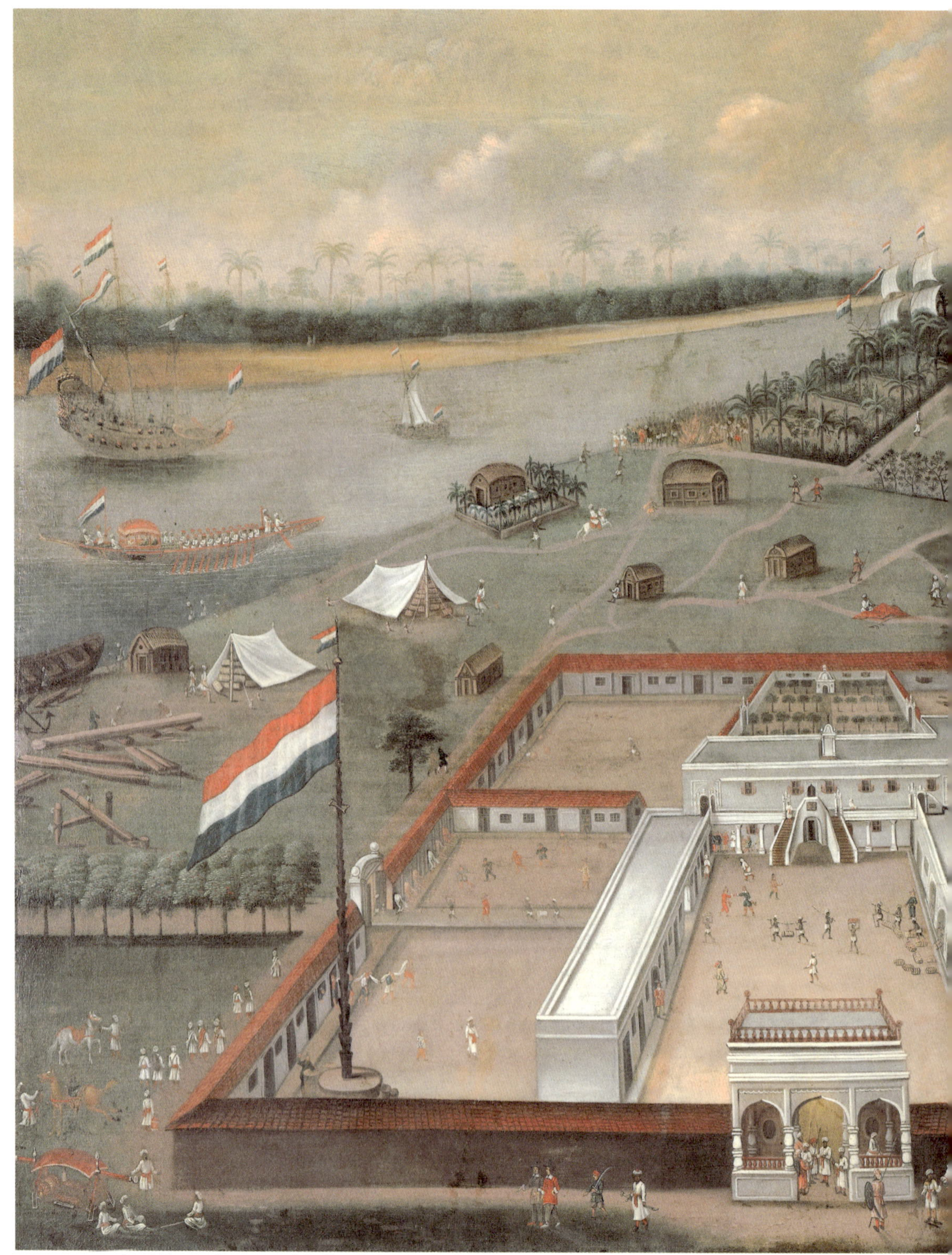

fig. 4 **The trading post of the Dutch East India Company in Hooghly, Bengal, Hendrik van Schuylenburgh, 1665**

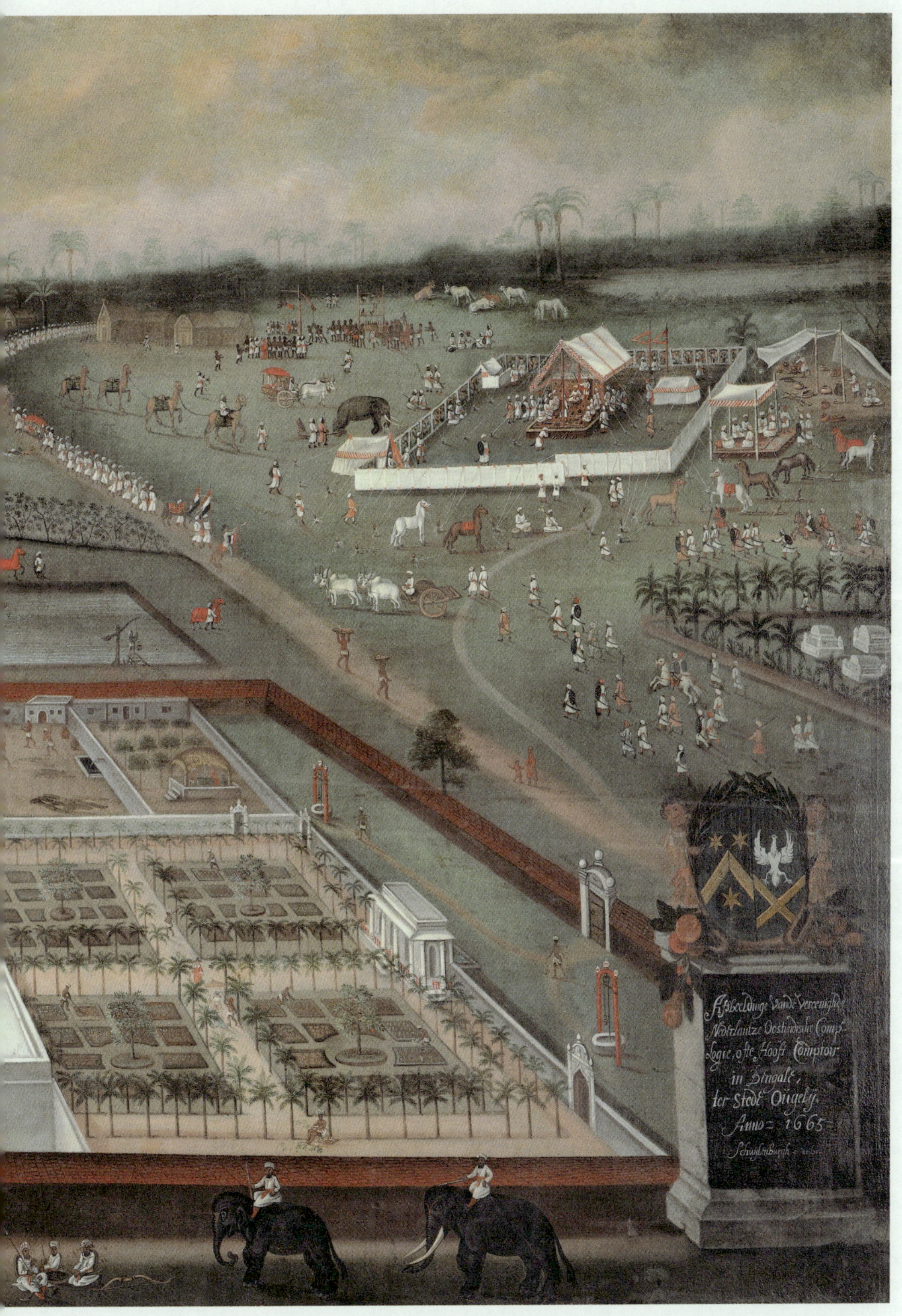
Afbeeldinge vande Vereenighde
Nederlantze Oostindische Comp.
Logie, ofte Hooft Comptoir
in Bengale,
ter Stede Ougely.
Anno = 1665 =

By 1635 this trading post was a reality. Between 1624 and 1665, the Dutch bought and transported 26,885 people from Arakan to Batavia.[13] Many of them did not survive the voyage. The annual missive from the governor general in Batavia to the VOC directors in the Netherlands, for instance, notes that of the 1,300 men, women and children bought by the VOC in Bengal and Arakan in 1625, only half made it to Batavia alive.[14] The VOC's great demand for enslaved people stimulated the slave trade in Arakan and kept it going. When the VOC temporarily withdrew from Arakan in the early 1650s, the Portuguese traffickers stopped bringing people to the slave market. After the VOC's return in 1653, the market slowly recovered. The VOC left Arakan for good in 1665, and the importance of the slave trade there declined rapidly.[15]

In Bengal, the situation was different. There is no evidence that the VOC, as a company, was directly involved in the slave trade here. As Schouten's account and the illustration show, enslaved people were bought and sold by Dutchmen; but it was not the company itself that organized these shipments. In Bengal, private traffickers played a significant role.[16] These were VOC functionaries who earned a tidy income by dealing in the slave trade outside their work for the VOC. After 1665 – throughout the remainder of the seventeenth century and the entire eighteenth century – they ensured the supply of people from Bengal to Batavia and the rest of VOC territory. This kind of private trade was common not just in Bengal but everywhere the VOC was active in Asia and Africa. With this trade, VOC employees were responsible for the transportation and trafficking of hundreds of thousands of men, women and children.[17]

Maart van Bengalen was one of the victims of these private traffickers. On 21 April 1778, she was sold at a public auction in Hooghly in Bengal to Johannes Plusker, the VOC chief surgeon, for 80 sicca rupees (fig. 4).[18] Maart's previous slaveholder had died, and all his property, including enslaved people, was sold. Plusker sold her two years later in Batavia at a profit of 35 sicca rupees.[19] On purchase, Maart's new 'owner', Adrianis Weyding, received a document meticulously recording the transaction.[20] This document certified Maart's lack of freedom.[21]

It is not known how Maart ended up in slavery. She was presumably captured from one of the villages around the Ganges. The name Maart probably alludes to the month (March) in which she was first bought by someone. Nothing more is known of her life in Batavia.

batavia

Calistra van Bengalen came from the same area as Maart, or at least was sold there. Calistra ended up in Batavia, in the household of Willem Ferdinandus, the junior verger of the Portuguese Inner Church. He mistreated his enslaved servants on a daily basis. In the case of Calistra, he took this so far that she died of her injuries. In order to cover up this atrocity, he ordered the other servants to bury her in secret.

Slavery in Batavia was often centred in and around the house. In domestic situations, slavery led to significant tensions. In a relatively small setting, enslaved servants were put to work, monitored, rewarded and punished.

The punishments could easily get out of control and degenerate into systematic maltreatment or even death. Officially, enslaved people could register complaints about their ill-treatment with the authorities, but this happened only in rare instances, because in practice it was made almost impossible for them.[22]

Yet it is because of this complaints procedure that we know something of the fate of Calistra van Bengalen. One Augusto van Balie lodged a complaint against Willem Ferdinandus in 1765. He testified about the daily mistreatments he received and, as evidence, displayed his own back and face, where the welts from the whip were visible. His main complaint, however, was that Ferdinandus had beaten Calistra so viciously and for so long that 'she had given up the ghost that same night as a result'.[23] A few days later, another enslaved servant from Ferdinandus's house gave a similar testimony. Their brave statements accomplished nothing, however. They were contradicted by someone else from Ferdinandus's household, who may have testified under duress. He stated that Ferdinandus did administer punishments occasionally, but only when it was really necessary. Since Calistra had tried to flee, her punishment was deemed to be deserved.

Of course, many enslaved people tried to flee from their difficult circumstances. Fleeing was viciously punished by the slaveholders and the authorities.[24] Enslaved people sometimes lived in such hopeless conditions that they sought another way to escape from their misery. So it was with Amon van Bengalen: his body was found behind the Dutch church in Batavia on 1 February 1729. He had hanged himself from a tree in the garden of the house where he worked. Amon was an enslaved man in the household of the Mardijker Dirk Jansz.[25] His name is listed in the notebook of the municipal surgeon Benjamin van der Haak, whose task it was to examine corpses in Batavia and make a brief annotation of what he saw. His notebook lists many other enslaved men and women who had hanged themselves or slit their own throats. For instance, in the nine months after 1 February 1729 he encountered five dead Bengalis: Coridon, Calister and (another) Januarij had hanged themselves, and Catharina had slit her own throat. The body of 'an unidentified vagabond, to all appearances a Bengali, who died of poverty and deprivation' was also found.[26]

This depressing record is a powerful testament to the despair that people in slavery must have experienced. The cruel abuse they suffered and the hopelessness of their existence drove them to commit suicide or to 'run amok' – to run out into the street with a *kris* dagger or other weapon in order to kill as many people as possible. The travel writer Jacob Haafner vividly described these conditions at the end of the eighteenth century:

> Early on Saturday mornings the house would echo with the lamentations of poor slave women who, from the discontented looks of their torturers during the preceding week, had to fear that very soon the split reed would tear their skin ... Who then can blame these people ... when at long last, driven by rage and despair and intoxicated by opium, they decide to free themselves of their suffering through suicide, after having satisfied their rightful lust for vengeance on their white tyrants?[27]

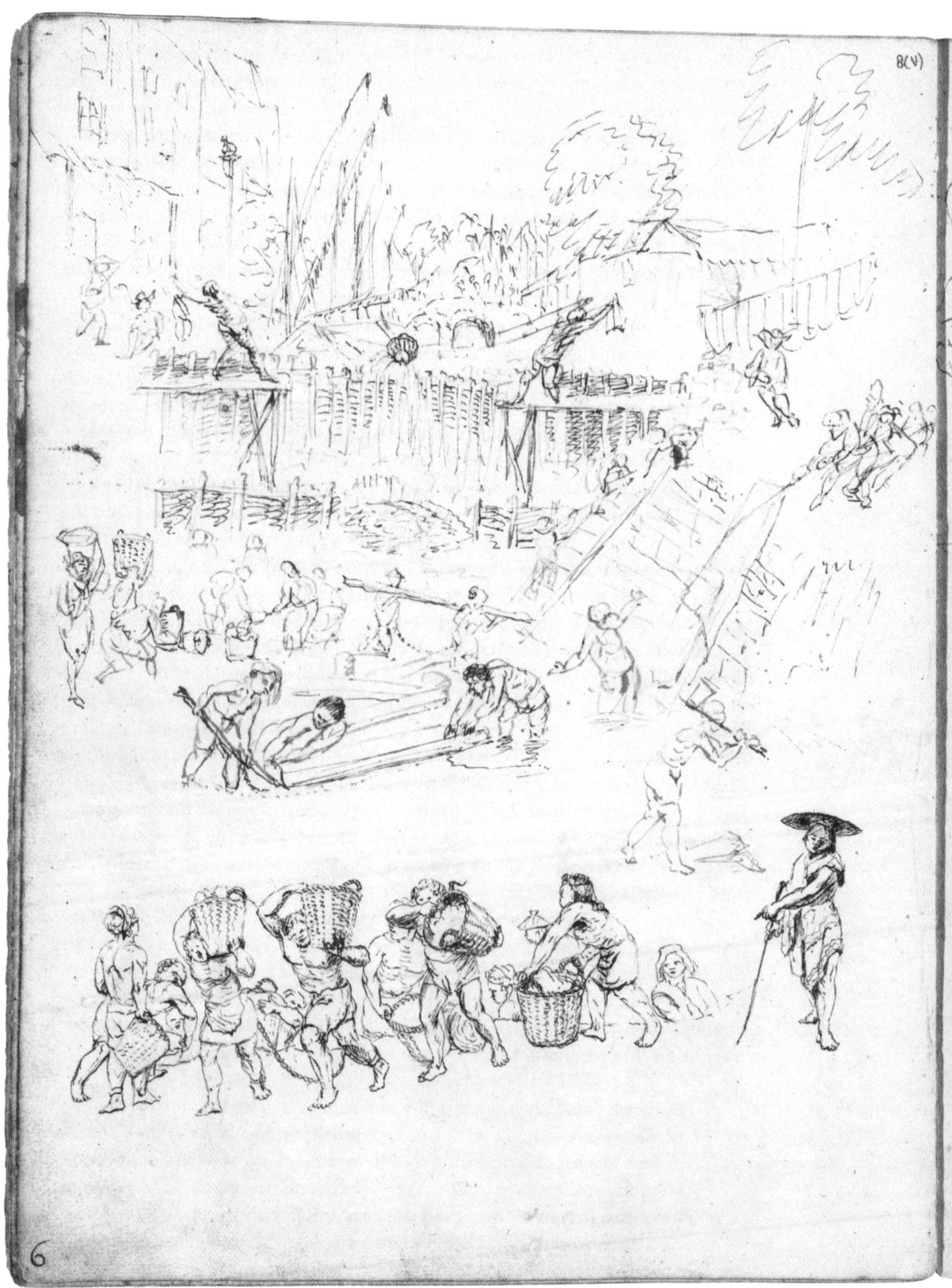

fig. 5 **Construction labourers in Batavia, several of them chained together**
Wouter Schouten, c. 1660

Free and enslaved people lived in Batavia from its founding by the Dutch in 1619 (fig. 6). The construction of the city and its defences was primarily done by enslaved labourers. Gerard Reynst, Governor General of the Dutch East Indies in 1614–1615, found the use of slave labour indispensable because, he believed, people in slavery worked twice as hard as the Dutch themselves.[28] Until 1660, the enslaved labourers mainly came in large slave transports from India, Bengal, Arakan and Madagascar. Subsequently, many people were taken from the islands around Java as well. At the end of the seventeenth century, more than half of the inhabitants of Batavia were enslaved men, women and children.[29] This slowly but surely turned Batavia into a central slave market for the region, where both Europeans and Asians engaged in human trafficking.[30]

A sketch by Wouter Schouten shows the hard work involved in building cities, defence structures and forts (fig. 5). It looks like canals are being excavated. Some of the men are carrying baskets of rubble; others are shoring up the retaining walls with thick planks. Warehouses are visible high above them. Several of the men pictured are bound to one another with heavy chains. The *mandoer*, or overseer, is issuing orders. These labourers were the property of the VOC. The company usually had between 1,000 and 3,000 people in its possession. The precise number depended on the amount of work to be done. When a large job was completed, people who were no longer needed were sold to reduce costs. If the amount of work unexpectedly increased again, enslaved people had to be hired in a hurry from private individuals. The VOC always retained a number of people as property for the hard work in the warehouses or on the lumber wharves. In the transhipment port and the shipyard of the small island of Onrust, just off the coast of Batavia, for instance, around 200 forced labourers would normally be working.[31]

The daily accounts of the VOC record that Horij van Bengalen was released from slavery on 23 January 1682. He had worked as a sawmill worker on Onrust since about 1632. He was probably brought to Batavia on one of the large transports from Arakan and then put to work on Onrust. Fifty years later, Horij asked the company to set him free, due to old age and a weakening body. It was 'agreed to grant him freedom',[32] but only on condition that his son-in-law, who was a choirmaster, would take care of him so that Horij did not end up dependent on parochial relief for the poor. This was an advantageous arrangement for the VOC as it no longer bore any responsibility for him. While people in slavery were not paid wages, the VOC did incur expenses. Enslaved people serving the VOC were given new clothes twice a year: blue-and-white-striped trousers for the men, short trousers or a piece of cloth for the children, and a cloth for the women plus a piece of fabric. In addition, each received a monthly ration of rice, salt, pepper, lamp oil and firewood. It was also stipulated that they should receive money to provide for their sustenance: half a rix-dollar per month for the men, three-eighths of a rix-dollar for the women, a quarter of a rix-dollar for boys and girls aged between eight and twelve, and one-eighth of a rix-dollar for children up to the age of seven. For comparison, a soldier serving the VOC earned 22 rix-dollars per month.[33]

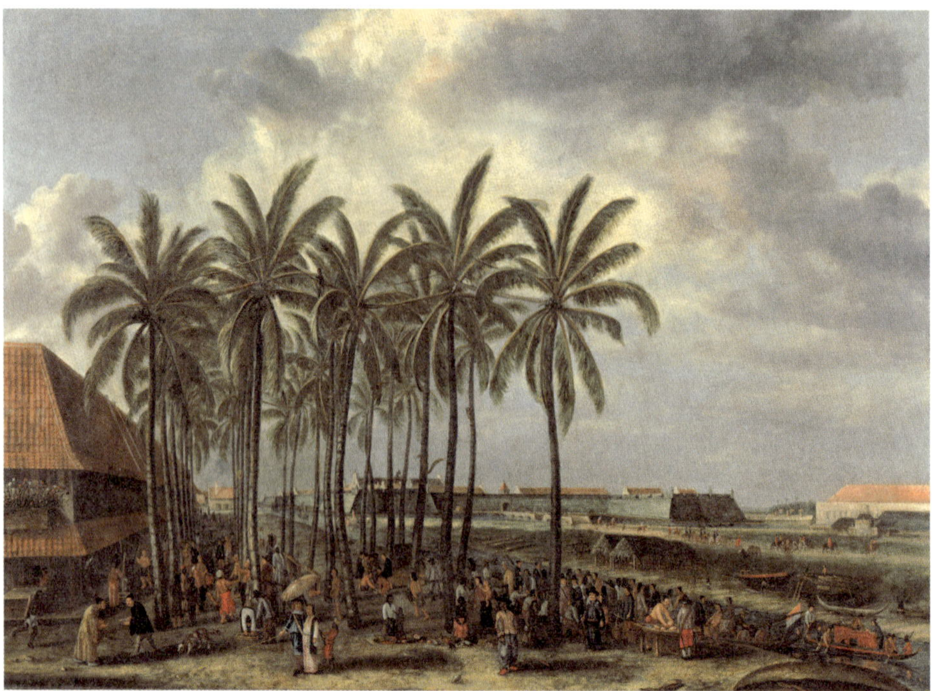

fig. 6 **The market of Batavia with the fortress of the Dutch East India Company in the background, Andries Beeckman, c. 1661**

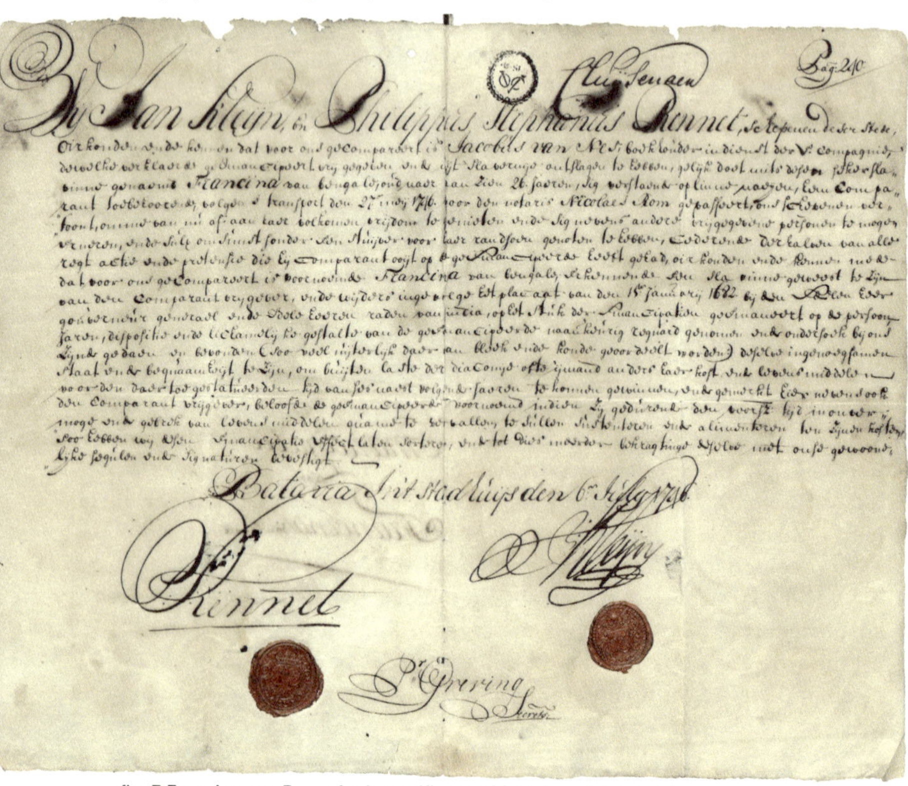

fig. 7 **Francina van Bengalen's certificate of freedom, 6 July 1746**

As noted earlier, the Dutch in Batavia adopted customs concerning slavery that already existed in Southeast Asia and adapted them to their own ends. One of the most radical changes was the institutionalization of existing practices. The notary played an important role in this. He drew up the documents that defined freedom and enslavement.[34] Francina van Bengalen, a woman about 26 years of age, obtained her freedom on 6 July 1746 with one such official document (fig. 7). She was set free by Jacobus van Nes, a bookkeeper at the VOC in whose 'possession' she had been until that point. She had to promise that she could provide for her own sustenance and would not become a burden to the diaconia. Her health was also examined. This had been required since 15 January 1682,[35] because there was a fear of 'Lazarus's disease', or leprosy, a disease that was apparently prevalent among formerly enslaved people. Francina had been bought by Van Nes only nine days before the document was drawn up. Did he set her free because he wished to marry her? We do not know, but enslaved women often had their freedom redeemed for that reason. This document must have been very important to Francina, for, not being European, without a licence attesting her freedom she would likely be suspected of having fled from her slaveholder. Francina's freedom was redeemed for her, but there are also many cases of people who saved up to purchase their own freedom. Enslaved people were sometimes put to work for someone else by their 'owners'. Their pay was collected for the most part, but occasionally there was something left over to put aside.[36]

Notaries were responsible for various documents that influenced the lives of people in slavery. Maart van Bengalen's document, for example, defined her enslavement and the ownership that someone else had over her. Ownership is also a feature of a third example of a legal document: the estate inventory of a silversmith in Batavia. An inventory like this would be drawn up in the event of divorce or death. Because the silversmith in question, Hendrik Rennebaum, was no longer of sound mind, the inventory was drawn up several years before his death. The majority of the document consists of a list of the pieces of silver in his possession, but at the end, his *lijfeijgenen* (bondsmen) are mentioned, enslaved people who like the objects in the inventory could be bequeathed and inherited. The list includes a certain Januarij van Bengalen. Januarij, it is noted, was a 'silversmith for Mr Rennebaum'. He lived with his wife Dina and their two children on Rennebaum's grounds. He is not the only one. October van Boegies was 'chief silversmith', and the 'young man Julij van Soembawa' also worked as a silversmith for Rennebaum.[37] This meant that Rennebaum came up with the designs and was responsible for the shop and contact with customers, but October, Julij and Januarij were the ones who made the objects in the workshop behind the shop. As 'chief', October ran the workshop and coordinated the work. It is highly unusual that we know the names of the individuals in the workshop of a silversmith, for in general the people in such workshops remained anonymous, in Europe as well as in Batavia.

The collection of the Kunstmuseum in The Hague includes a *sirih* box bearing Hendrik Rennebaum's silver hallmark (fig. 8). This box dates from between 1775 and 1780. The design and technique are European. In Europe, a box like this would be machine-made, but in Batavia this was done by hand.

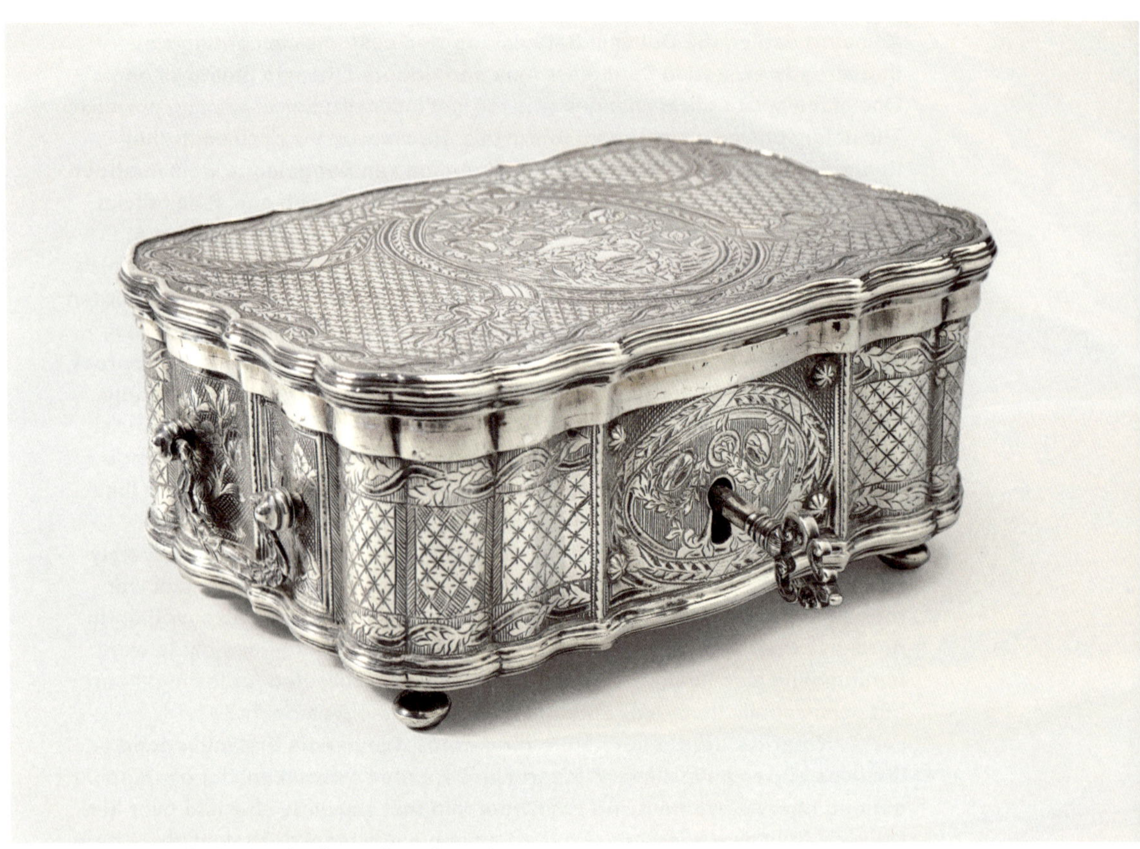

fig. 8 **A *sirih* box that Januarij van Bengalen may have worked on, 1775–1780**

It was a labour-intensive job, mainly carried out by enslaved silversmiths. Each employee in a workshop had his own specialism and therefore worked on the same types of objects. It is therefore very probable that Januarij handled and worked on this box.

banda islands

The Banda Islands were among the first places where the VOC decided to make use of enslaved people (fig. 9). The indigenous people of the Banda Islands, part of the Moluccas, refused to sell their nutmeg exclusively to the VOC. In retaliation, a genocide was perpetrated on the Bandanese in 1621, under governor general Jan Pietersz Coen: some 14,000 of the approximately 15,000 inhabitants were massacred. Subsequently, in order to harvest the nutmeg, a plantation system using enslaved labourers was instituted. The islands were divided into *perken* (perks), or plantations, administered and operated by *perkeniers*, primarily Dutchmen who had previously served for the VOC. Each *perk* was 25 *zielen* (souls) in size, where a *ziel* represented the amount of land a labourer could farm per day. The labourers were brought from Bengal and other parts of India, Madagascar and the Indonesian archipelago. The number of people in slavery on the Banda Islands in 1638 was about 2,200. This number rose to 3,700 in 1688 and reached 4,100 in 1794.[38]

The VOC archives include thick volumes from the period 1697–1704, listing the number of perken for each year, the condition of the perken and the number of enslaved labourers per week. In some years the names and toponyms of enslaved people are listed. Marij van Bengalen is included at the bottom of a list of 39 women who worked on the perk of Lucas Claasz de Jong. In 1697, 68 men, women and children worked on this plantation, which was 84 zielen in size.[39] The Dutch pastor and historian François Valentijn, who travelled in the Banda Islands in 1687, wrote in his travelogue that this same perk was then 50 *zielen* in size, totalled 90 enslaved labourers and produced 28,000 pounds (12.5 tonnes) of nutmeg plus 7,000 pounds (3 tonnes) of mace per year.[40] Ten years later, there was more land but fewer people working on it. Someone like Marij must therefore have had to work much harder.

Valentijn describes what the day was like for the enslaved workers: 'The slaves in each Perk find their work the whole day.' This proves to be an understatement upon reading the rest of the description. According to Valentijn, they set off for the forests of nutmeg trees early in the morning and spent the whole day picking the fruits (fig. 10). At the end of the day they returned home with their harvest, whereupon the nuts had to be cracked open, the mace removed and the nutmegs and mace laid out together to dry.[41]

This description of the work on Banda is reminiscent of descriptions of plantations in the Americas and how enslaved people were put to work there. But this was not the usual situation in VOC territory. In general, the company bought its spices from local merchants or producers. Banda was the only place where the company itself was responsible for the production of spices. The VOC introduced a plantation system, within which someone like Marij was forced to work until she died.[42]

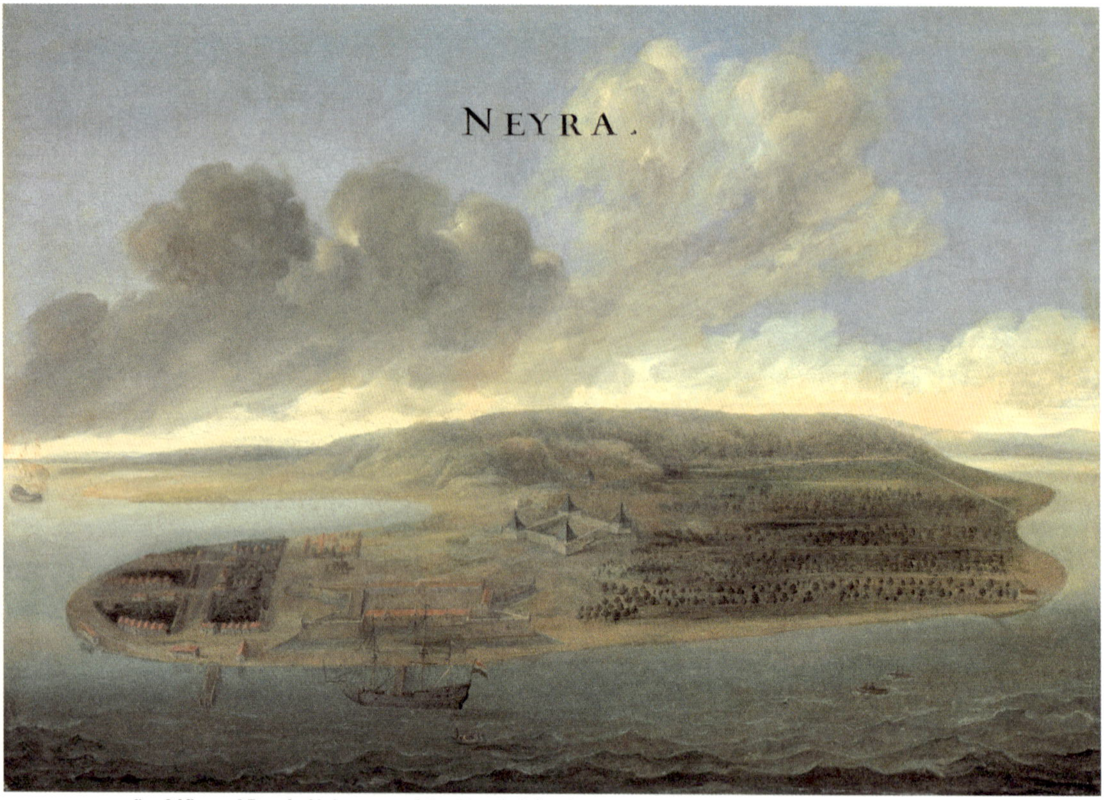

fig. 9 **View of Banda Neira, one of the Banda Islands**
Johannes Vinckboons, c. 1662–1663

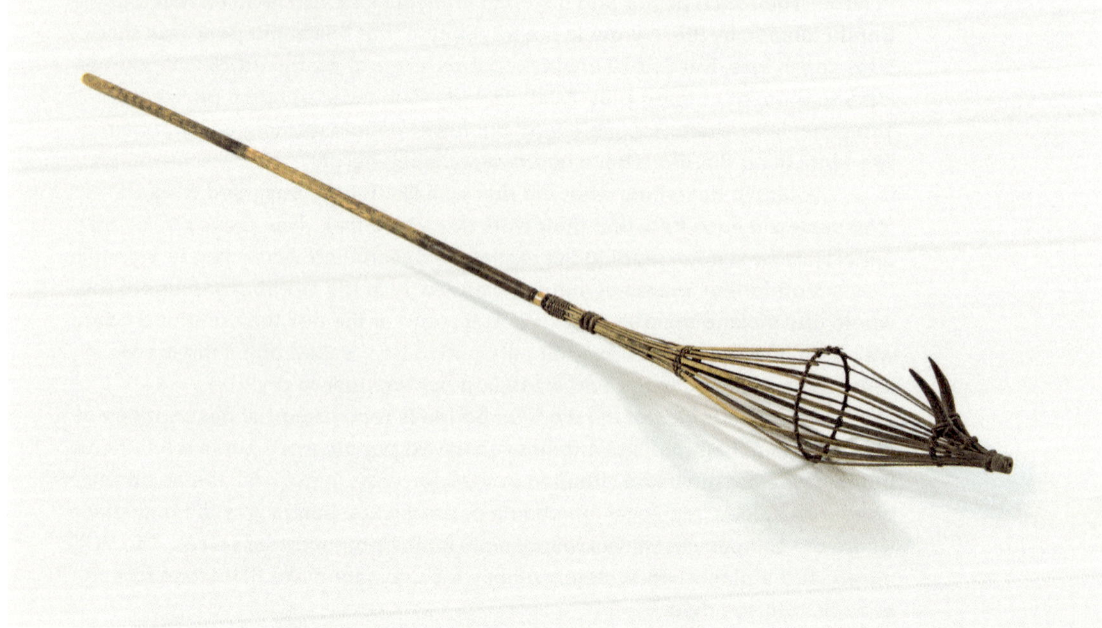

fig. 10 **Tool for harvesting nutmeg, consisting of a bamboo stick with two sharp wooden hooks, above a basket in which to catch the picked nuts, before 1897**

the cape

In 1720, Angela van Bengalen died a wealthy woman in Cape Town. Her will lists her numerous children and grandchildren. They occupied important positions in Cape Town. She left them 14,000 guilders altogether, which equates to about 150,000 euros today.[43] Angela was the first woman in South Africa to own land. As a widow, she was independent, and she played an important role in Cape Town society. In South Africa, Angela van Bengalen is considered the foremother of many South Africans.[44]

Originally she came from the area around the Bay of Bengal, where she was captured, enslaved and shipped to Batavia. In Batavia she came into the service of the Dutchman Pieter Kemp. In 1656, Kemp took her and her three children with him to Cape Town on his way to the Netherlands, probably so that she could attend to him during the voyage. In Cape Town he sold her to Jan van Riebeeck, commander of the Cape colony, because taking enslaved people to the Dutch Republic was forbidden by law.[45] This is how Angela van Bengalen ended up on the southern tip of Africa, at the VOC post Van Riebeeck had established there four years earlier along with a victualing station for the ships sailing to and from Batavia. Like the early governors general in Batavia, he complained to his superiors about the lack of manpower to truly build something on the Cape. He felt slavery was indispensable for this. Van Riebeeck got his way: groups of enslaved men, women and children were brought to the Cape. Many were trafficked from Madagascar or Angola, while others were brought by VOC functionaries from Batavia. Many people in these first groups fled or died in the cold of the Cape. For the VOC, this was no reason to abolish the slavery system. The VOC continued to bring enslaved people to the Cape long into the eighteenth century (fig. 11).[46]

When Van Riebeeck left for Batavia several years later, Angela and her children were sold to a certain Abraham Gabbema, who decided to set her free in 1666 'out of pure affection'.[47] Angela was the third woman to be set free from slavery on the Cape. As a free woman, she prospered. She set up a small business selling fruit and vegetables to passing ships. In 1669 Angela married a certain Arnoldus Willemsz van Wesel, also known as Basson, with whom she had a further six or seven children. Arnoldus Basson died twenty years later and left her possessions valued at 6,495 guilders. She managed to more than double this sum in the last 30 years of her life.

Susanna van Bengalen also ended up in Cape Town via Batavia. She was called Susanna Een Oor ('one ear') because of her mutilated ears, probably suffered as punishment for an infraction she supposedly committed. Her banishment to the Cape in 1658 was also part of this punishment. Nothing about the nature of the alleged crime can be found in the archives. At the Cape she ended up in what was called the 'slave lodgings', a windowless building in which the VOC housed enslaved men, women and children. The slave lodgings stood next to the company gardens, where these people were put to work growing fruit and vegetables; Susanna too worked in these gardens.[48]

In December 1669, she returned to the slave lodgings after a day's hard work. Her little daughter, Elsje, was ill and would not stop crying.

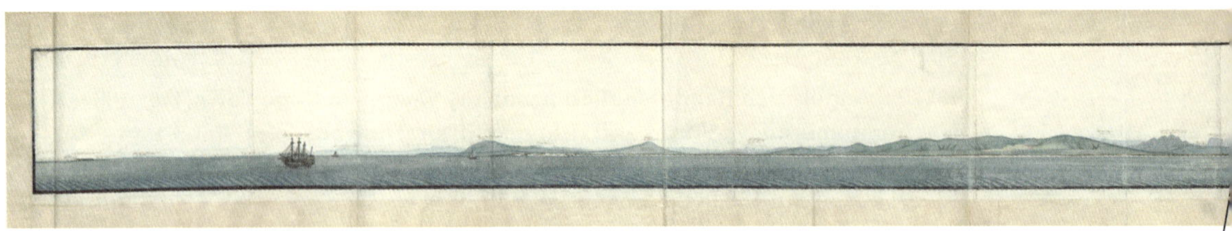

fig. 11 **Panorama of Cape Town and its surroundings, attributed to Robert Jacob Gordon, 1778, with the locations of the Van Bengalens indicated**

Abraham van Bengalen worked on the Overveen farm

Susanna, who was herself gravely ill with the pox, was at the end of her tether and had no mother's milk to feed the child. None of the other women in the lodgings were willing to help her feed the baby, who continued screaming. What happened next is not entirely clear. There was a struggle among the women, and eight days later the child died of the injuries she sustained that evening. An investigation was launched. The women in the lodgings said that Susanna had tried to strangle the child with three strips of cloth and that they had then snatched the baby out of Susanna's arms. Susanna herself denied this version of events. However, after an application of the thumbscrews, she confessed and was charged with infanticide. The surgeon confirmed the strangulation, and the sentence was signed (fig. 12)**. It noted that she, like a God-forsaken, murderous pig, went so far as to raise her hands to her young infant (who was a mestizo out of wedlock) and bound three strong cloths around her throat to strangle her.[49]**

Susanna was deemed to deserve gruesome punishment: 'the murderess, upon having her breasts torn from her body with red-hot pliers, shall be burnt to ashes here outside the fort.'[50] Ultimately it was decided to cast her in a sack into Table Bay, so that she would die from drowning. All the residents of the slave lodgings were present at the execution of this sentence.[51]

Incidents like this give us an impression of what the lives of enslaved people at the Cape must have been like. Susanna's baby, Elsje, is described as 'a mestizo out of wedlock', meaning she had a white European father who did not acknowledge her. This was a common occurrence; the slave lodgings

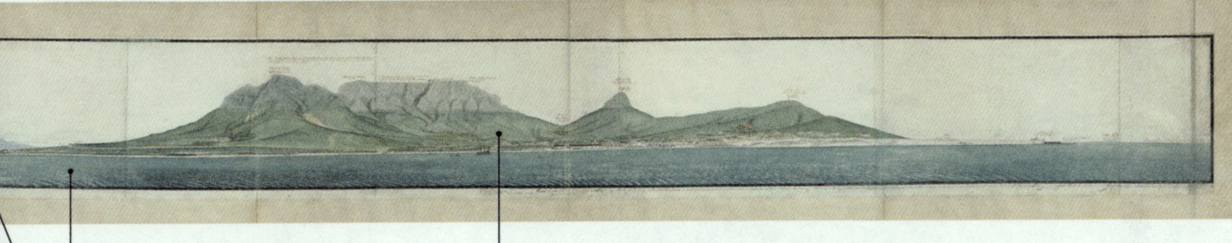

also served as a brothel and the women were sexually abused on a regular basis. In 1730, a German resident of Cape Town described how:

> as evening falls, a series of soldiers and sailors can be seen entering the slave quarters, where they spend their time until the clock strikes nine ... The Company does nothing to prevent this ... since it seems to increase the slave population.[52]

The story also shows the despair of enslaved women. Sick herself and with a sick child, Susanna was perhaps driven to kill her own child, and then was tortured until she confessed to the murder. We also see here an example of the grisly punishments the VOC meted out to people in slavery. The other residents of the slave lodgings being made to watch indicates that this kind of punishment was meant to serve as an example. A culture of fear was created, because the VOC wanted to prevent mass uprisings or other disturbances.

People in slavery in South Africa did not live only in Cape Town; the number of enslaved people also increased in the region behind Table Mountain. Development of the hinterland of Cape Town for agriculture began at the end of the seventeenth century. The VOC granted pieces of land to *vrijburghers* (free burghers), former employees of the VOC. Slavery, the administration in Cape Town declared in 1717, had become indispensable, and 'Europeans are, as befits their position, not as diligent in carrying out their work as in the

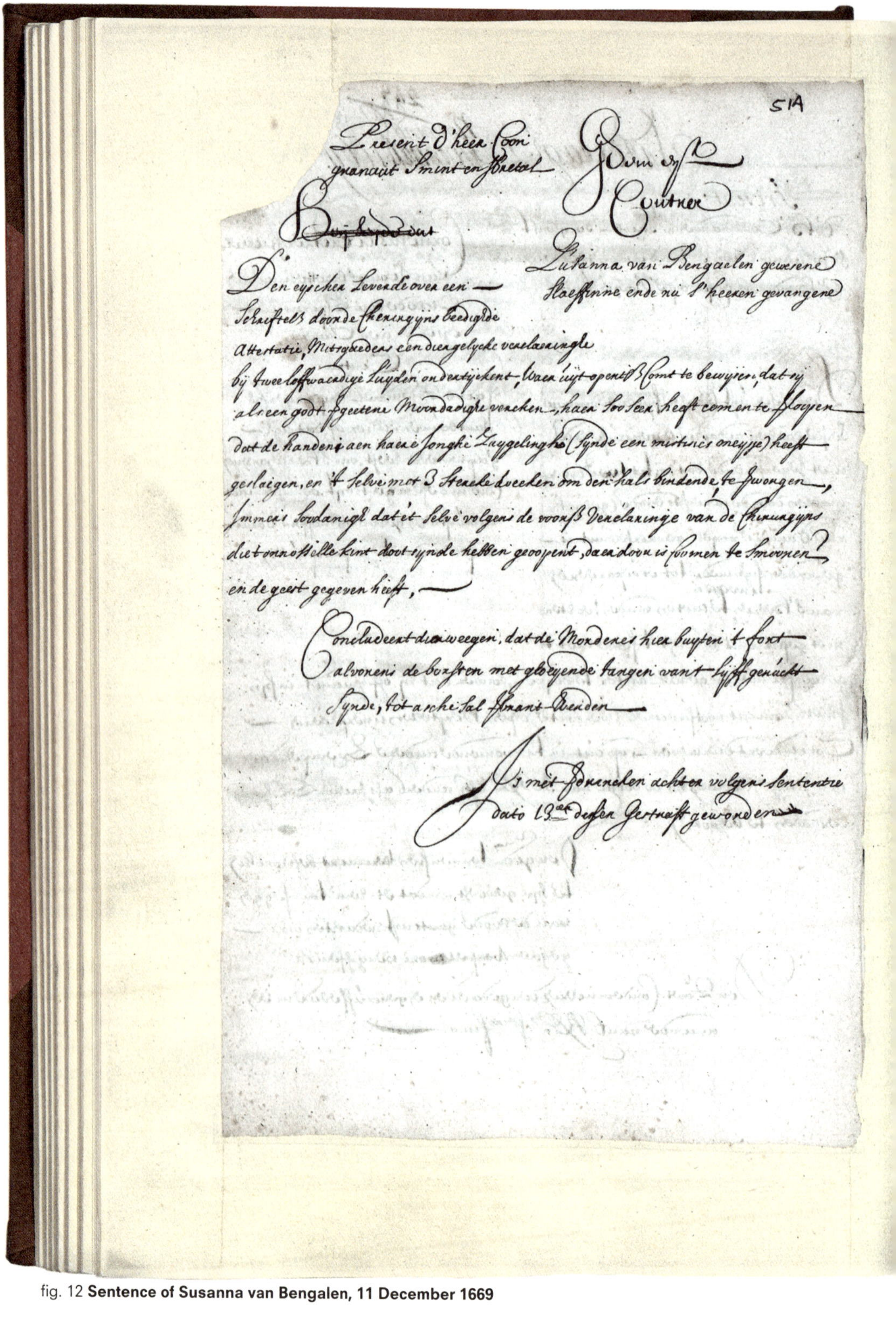

51A

Present d'heer Com[mandeu]r
granaat Smint en Hetel

~~Bewijsgeest~~

Eysch contra

Susanna van Bengaelen gewesene
Slaeffinne ende nu 's heeren gevangene

Den eyscher leverde over een —
schriftelt door de Chirurgyns beedigde
Attestatie, Mitsgaeders een dergelycke verclaringhe
bij twee loffwaerdige luyden onderteykent, waer uyt openlijck komt te bewijsen, dat sij
als een godt vergeetene Moordadige vrachen, haer soo seer heeft comen te vergeten
dat de handen aen haer jonghe zuygelinghs (synde een mistiecs oneyjje) heeft
geslaegen, en 't selve met 3 steerke doecken om den hals bindende te worgen,
immers soodanigh dat 't selve volgens de voorss verclaringe van de Chirurgyns
die t onnosselle kint doot synde hebben geopent, daer door is koomen te smooren
en de geest gegeven heeft, —

Concludeert dienweegen, dat de Moorderes hier buyten 't fort
alvoorens de borsten met gloeyende tangen van 't lijff genucht
synde, tot asche sal verbrant werden —

Is met swaerden achter volgens sententie
dato 13en dessen gestrafft geworden

fig. 12 **Sentence of Susanna van Bengalen, 11 December 1669**

land of their birth. However poor someone is, he will not want to get used to doing the work of a slave, because he feels this distinguishes him from a slave.'[53]

In the eighteenth century, most of the enslaved people in South Africa lived on farms in the hinterland of Cape Town. Their lives were regulated by the bell rung at the beginning and end of each workday.[54] Someone like Abraham van Bengalen must have heard this bell every day. In 1750 he was working on the Overveen farm or its lands. The inventory of this farm lists 21 enslaved labourers. Their toponyms give an indication of their origins. Eleven of them came from Africa: nine people were born at the Cape, and two came from Madagascar. Four people came from the area that encompasses present-day India: three men from Malabar, on the southwest coast of India, and one man from Bengal. There were six men from the present-day Indonesian archipelago: two from Boegies (South Sulawesi), one from Bali, one from Timor, one from Damme (Damar, one of the Lesser Sunda Islands) and one from Batavia, the son of enslaved people who originally came from elsewhere.

This enormous cultural and geographic diversity provides insight into the sprawling slave trade network of the VOC. How must Abraham have felt as the only one from Bengal? Would he have felt most at ease with the people from Malabar, or would they too have been foreign to him? And how did these people communicate with each other? Probably they had no choice but to adopt the language of the Dutch slaveholders of the farm, Aletta Keijser and Hendrick Willem van der Merwe. The great diversity of cultural backgrounds here was not unique. There was no homogeneous population of enslaved men, women and children at the Cape. There was little they could do other than adapt to one another and to the Europeans. In practice, three languages were spoken: Dutch, Portuguese and Malay (an Austronesian language with loanwords from Portuguese and Dutch). The latter two languages served as the lingua franca in the area around the Indian Ocean. Afrikaans is a mixed language with influences from these three languages as well as the Khoisan languages, a group of languages indigenous to southern Africa.[55]

Of the 21 enslaved labourers on the Overveen farm, 15 were men and 6 were women. The six women were all born at the Cape, while most of the men came from outside the Cape. The skewed ratio of men and women is not exceptional. More men than women worked in slavery at the Cape. This led to significant interpersonal tensions and murders committed out of jealousy. Few children were born, and a common culture never developed. People usually came to the Cape individually; and seldom in large groups. As a result, they formed few communal bonds, something that was further hampered by the great cultural diversity among them.[56]

The enslaved people at Overveen probably worked on the land. They developed the area to make it ready for farming and they planted and harvested. This was not true of all enslaved people in the hinterland of Cape Town. Augustus van Bengalen was the personal domestic of the wine grower Hendrik Cloete and probably worked in the main house at the famed Groot Constantia vineyard. Augustus is one of the few people in slavery at the Cape

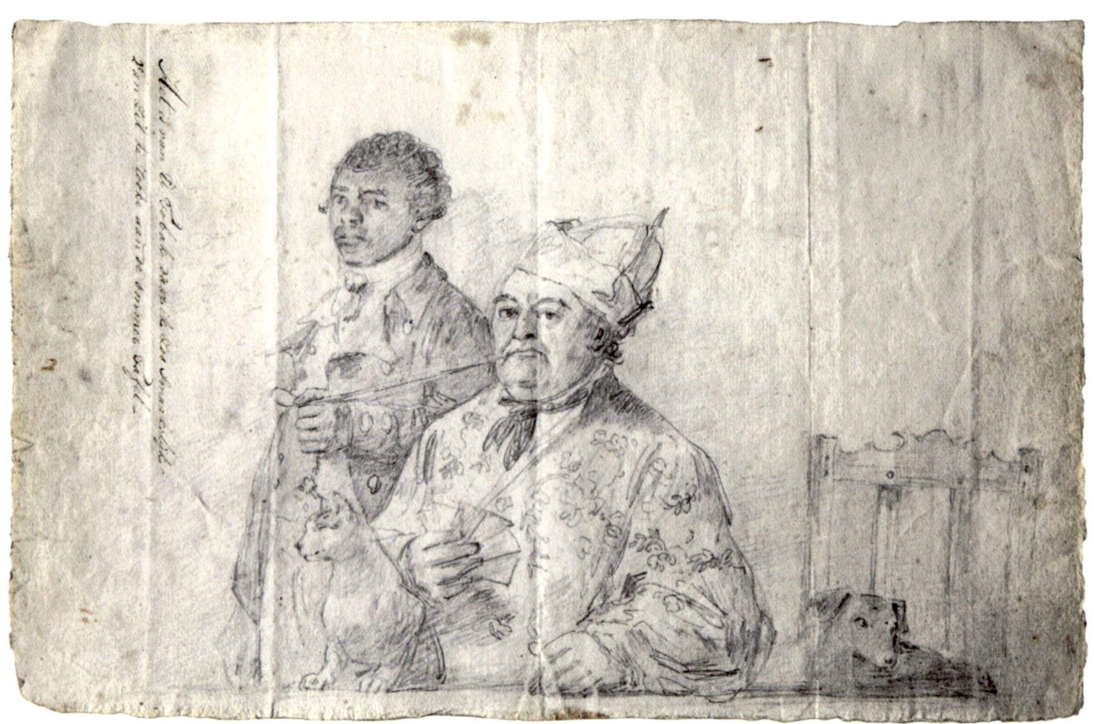

fig. 13 **Augustus van Bengalen holding the pipe of slaveholder Hendrik Cloete, c. 1778**

whose name and portrait have survived. In a small sketch, he stands in the fashionable livery of a domestic, holding a long pipe (fig. 13). He must be between 15 and 25 years old at this point. His dark curly hair is mid-length and he has a small moustache. He stares into the distance. In Cloete's will of 18 August 1789, Augustus van Bengalen is listed as his 'valet', someone who had to be by Cloete's side day and night – and therefore probably held his pipe as well.[57] Of the rest of his life we know only that he spent another ten years in Cloete's service.[58]

the netherlands

The Cape was often a victualing station for the ships on their way to the Netherlands from Batavia. For repatriates, this was the place where they sold the servants they had taken on the journey. In general, it was forbidden to bring enslaved people to the Netherlands. Special requests to bring back servants were occasionally submitted, however, and sometimes such a request was granted. Often, enslaved 'servants' were brought back clandestinely, without the VOC's knowledge.

Baron van Bengalen, for example, travelled to the Netherlands from Batavia via the Cape in 1689 with Rosette van Sambauwa (Sumbawa, another of the Lesser Sunda Islands) and a number of other enslaved servants. They were brought along by the high-level VOC official Gualther Zeeman and his wife, Sara van den Broecke. At the Cape, the fleet's last stop on the way to the Dutch Republic, Zeeman and several others submitted a request to bring along a number of enslaved people 'for the benefit and service of their wives and infant children'.[59] This request was granted, and Rosette van Sambauwa, Baron van Bengalen, Grietje van Tominij, Michel Cochin, Matij van Punto de Gale, Martha van Makassar, Calamatacke and an unnamed woman from the slave lodgings travelled from Cape Town to the Netherlands. The sum of 68 rix-dollars was paid into the company coffers for each of them.[60] Baron and Rosette were taken to Alkmaar, in Holland, where Gualther Zeeman was from. They had their daughter Magdhalena baptized there on 3 January 1690, a little less than nine months after leaving Cape Town. The baptismal records note that 'both are Indians, the father a Christian' (fig. 14). Baron van Bengalen had apparently been baptized in Batavia. Gillis van den Broecke, a brother of Sara, is listed as a witness.[61]

Baron and Rosette already had a son, named Filander de Baron. He must have been at most two years old at the time of the voyage to the Netherlands. We know of his existence because he was immortalized in a painting of 1697 that now hangs in the town hall of Dokkum, in Friesland, a northern province of the Netherlands (fig. 15). The painter, Gerard Wigmana, depicted Filander as a servant of Sara van den Broecke and her second husband, Julius Schelto van Aitzema. After the death of her first husband in 1692, Van den Broecke moved to Dokkum with Van Aitzema and took her Indian and Southeast Asian servants with her. In the painting, the couple is dining with an unidentified guest. They are being served by a child of about ten with black wavy hair. That is Filander; he stands prominently in the foreground holding a silver platter

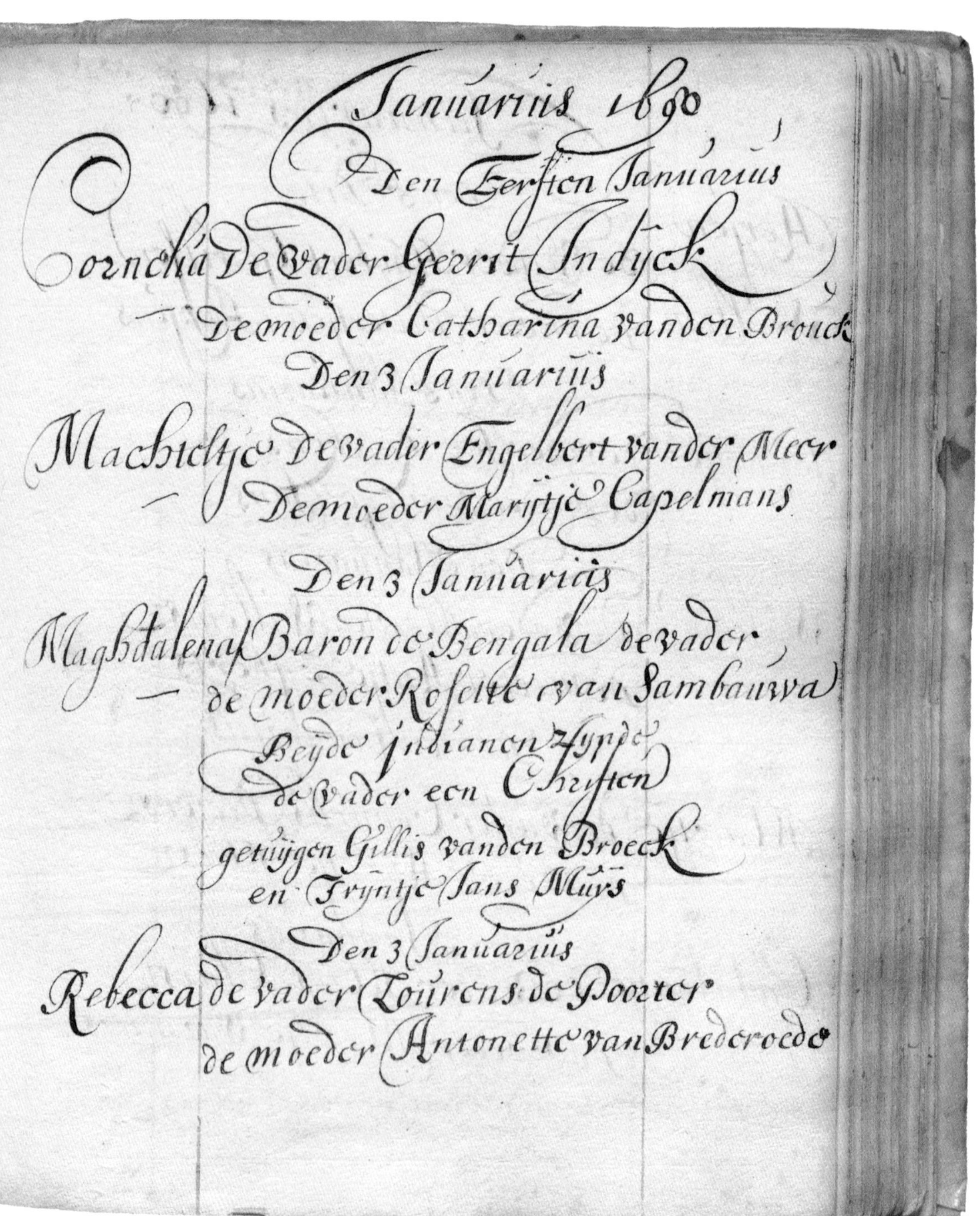

Januarius 1690

Den Eersten Januarius

Cornelia de vader Gerrit Indyck

de moeder Catharina vanden Broeck

Den 3 Januarius

Machteltje de vader Engelbert vander Meer

de moeder Marytje Capelmans

Den 3 Januarius

Magdalena Baron de Bengala de vader

de moeder Rosette van Sambauwa

Beyde indianen zynde

de vader een Christen

getuygen Gillis vanden Broeck

en Trijntje Jans Muys

Den 3 Januarius

Rebecca de vader Lourens de Poorter

de moeder Antonette van Brederode

fig. 14 **Baron van Bengalen and Rosetta van Sambauwa baptize their daughter with the name Magdhalena de Baron, 3 January 1690**

with a look of concentration. He wears a grey livery, set off with red piping, and shiny black shoes decorated with a silver buckle. He is dressed in the same way as two other servants pictured standing to his right. In the corner to the right, at the back, stands a woman with Southeast Asian features. She is probably his mother, Rosette van Sambauwa. She stands out because of her penetrating, somewhat disconsolate gaze.

We know that the people portrayed here represent Filander and Rosette because of a newspaper article from the nineteenth century. The painting was sold at an English auction, leading a London newspaper to interview the Dokkum municipal clerk about it. He described the people in the painting, identifying Sara van den Broecke and her husband and saying that 'they are being served by a servant named Philander de Baron ... originally from the East Indies (whose daughter, known as Black Rosette, I knew personally) ... and another named Martha, also originally from the East Indies.'[62] Extensive research made it possible to connect the names Filander and Rosette with the servants in the painting. The municipal clerk also suggested that the woman on the left, 'Martha, also originally from the East Indies', might be Martha van Makassar, who had made the journey to the Netherlands with Baron and Rosette.[63]

High-level VOC officials took hundreds, perhaps thousands, of enslaved people back with them to the Dutch Republic as servants. They can be found in the baptism, marriage and burial registers. This did not mean that the VOC permitted them to be brought over without question. Multiple edicts were issued forbidding the transport of people in slavery to the Netherlands. In this way, the company hoped to avoid significant costs if these people wanted to return to Batavia, which was often the case. There was also a fear of *voorttelinge* (reproduction). Why this was a concern is not explained.[64] A *minnemoer*, or wet nurse, for a baby was allowed on the journey as long as she was paid for. This woman had to 'bring a receipt for that money to the Netherlands, in which case her passage to Batavia would be permitted, and otherwise not'.[65] Officially, Asian servants no longer worked in slavery once in the Republic since this was forbidden by law.[66] What this meant in practice, however, and whether the servants themselves were aware of this law, is not known.

That we are able to trace part of the histories of Baron van Bengalen and Rosette van Sambauwa is quite unusual. We do not know, however, whether Baron came to Dokkum as well. Might he have died in Alkmaar, and is that why he is not depicted in the painting? His son's life is better documented. Filander became a chief of police and married a Frisian woman, with whom he had five children. He named his daughter Rosette, after his mother. All the children were given his surname, De Baron, named after his father. It is not known whether any of them had issue. Magdhalena, the other child of Baron and Rosette, turns up in the archives one more time in a census in 1744.[67] She is in fact living in Dokkum and is receiving poor relief. She does not seem to have had any children either. With these descendants of an enslaved man from Bengal and an enslaved woman from Sumbawa, the history of Dutch slavery left its mark in Dokkum as well.

A story that began with human trafficking in the basin of the Ganges and other rivers around the Bay of Bengal ends with a brother and sister in the

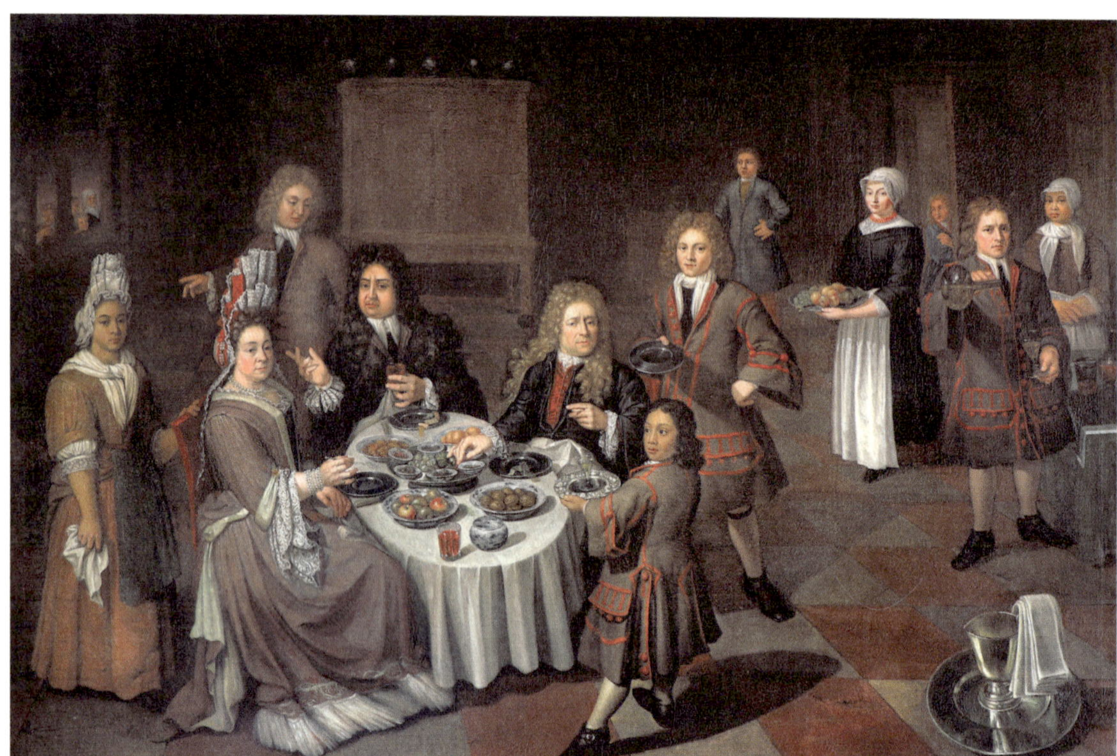

fig. 15 **Filander van Baron, with two other domestics, serves Sara van den Broecke and Julius Schelto van Aitzema. The woman standing to the right, in the background, is probably his mother, Rosette van Sambauwa, Gerard Wigmana, 1697**

Frisian village of Dokkum. Unlike their parents, this brother and sister were no longer bound by slavery. They were able to dispose of their own lives and own property, and their children were free as well. Their connection with Bengal had become invisible. Not much more is known about them or the other people in this chapter who were called Van Bengalen than what is written here. They were scattered throughout the entirety of VOC territory, and their children were given other toponyms referring to the place where they were born or sold. As a result, their origins could scarcely be traced any longer. But who knows what Bengali songs were still sung at home as they were rocked to sleep, and who knows what stories they were told and went on to tell their own children and grandchildren.

maria holtrop

surapati

from enslaved servant to sovereign

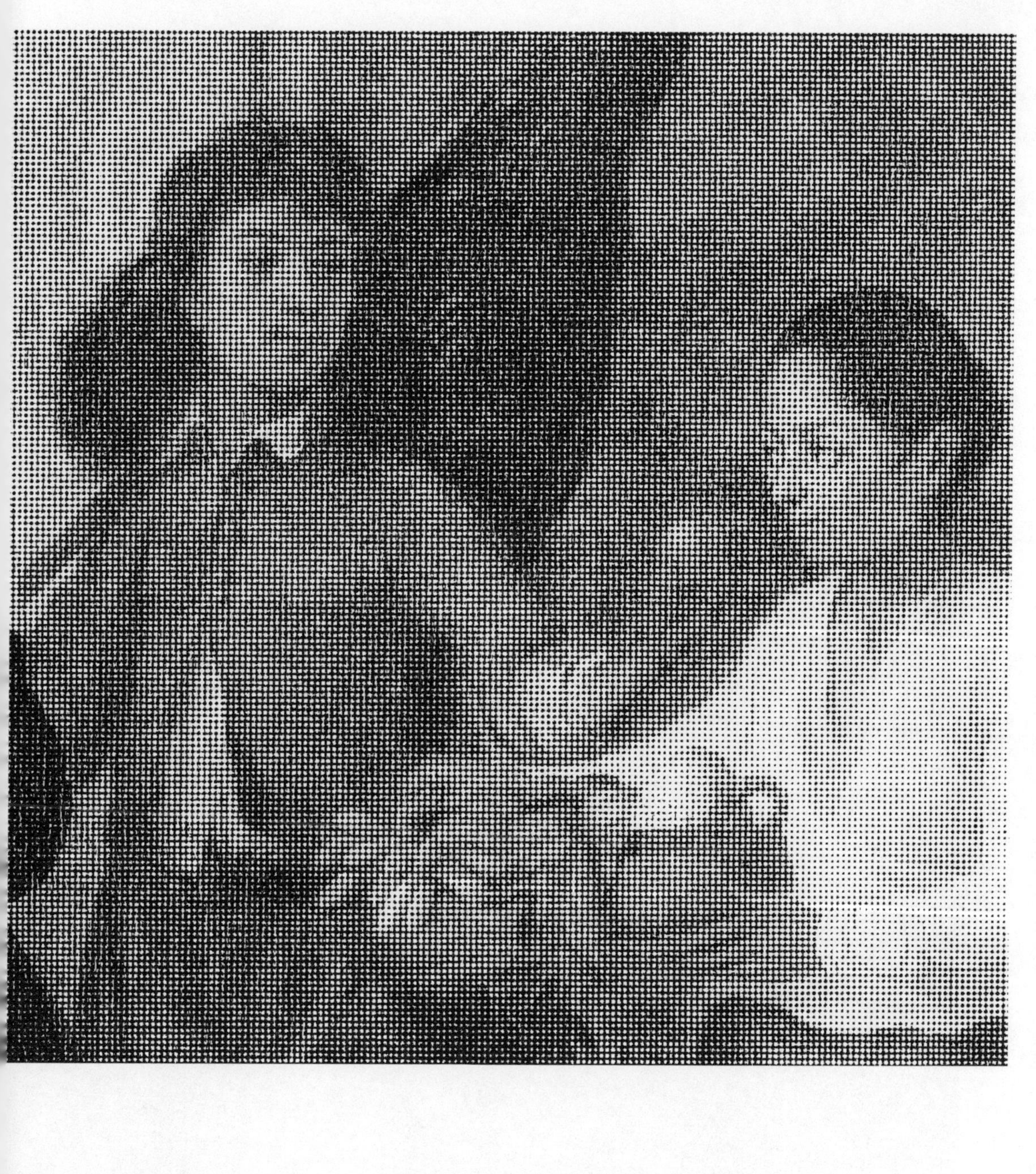

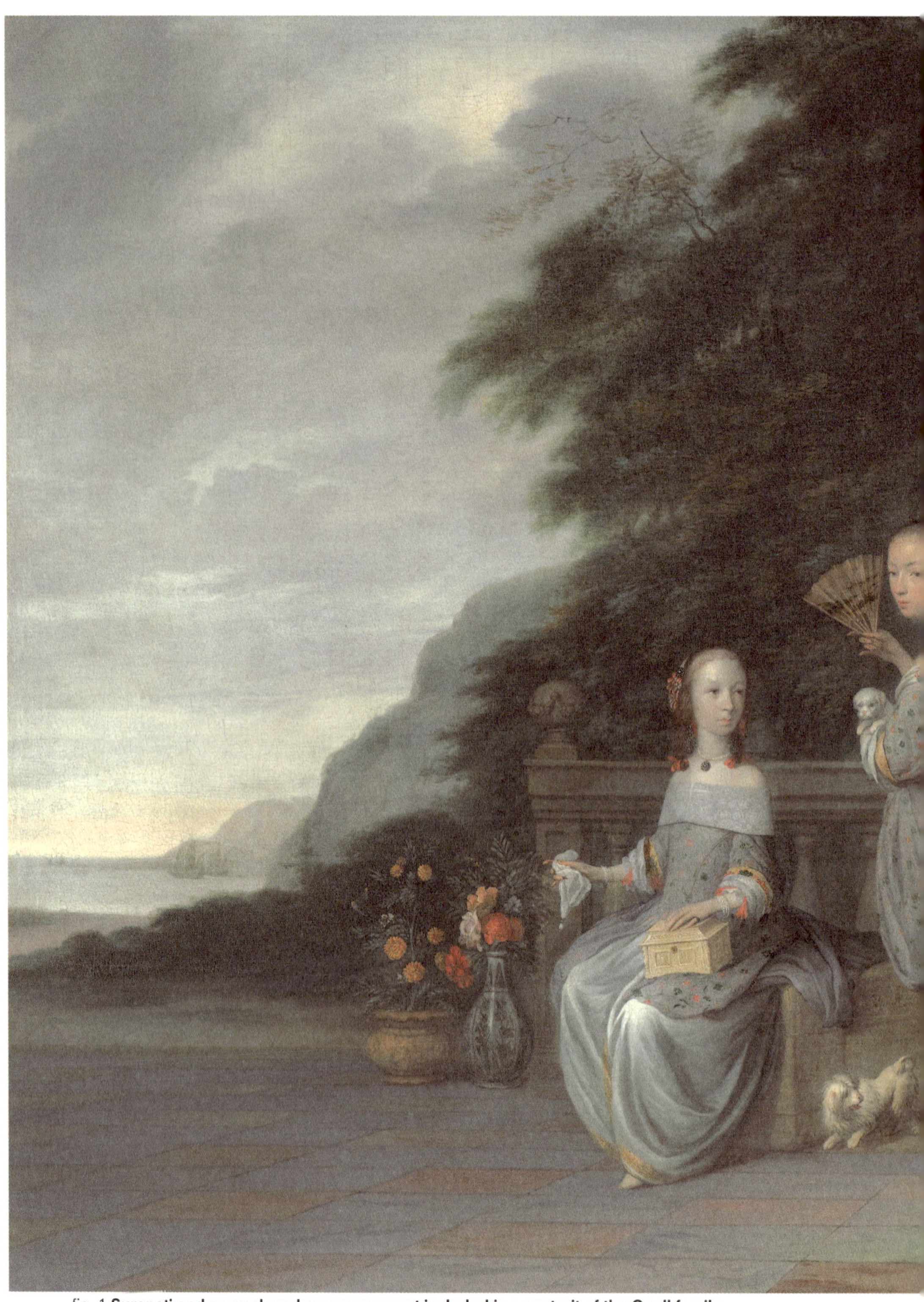

fig. 1 **Surapati and an enslaved woman servant included in a portrait of the Cnoll family**
Jacob Coeman, 1665

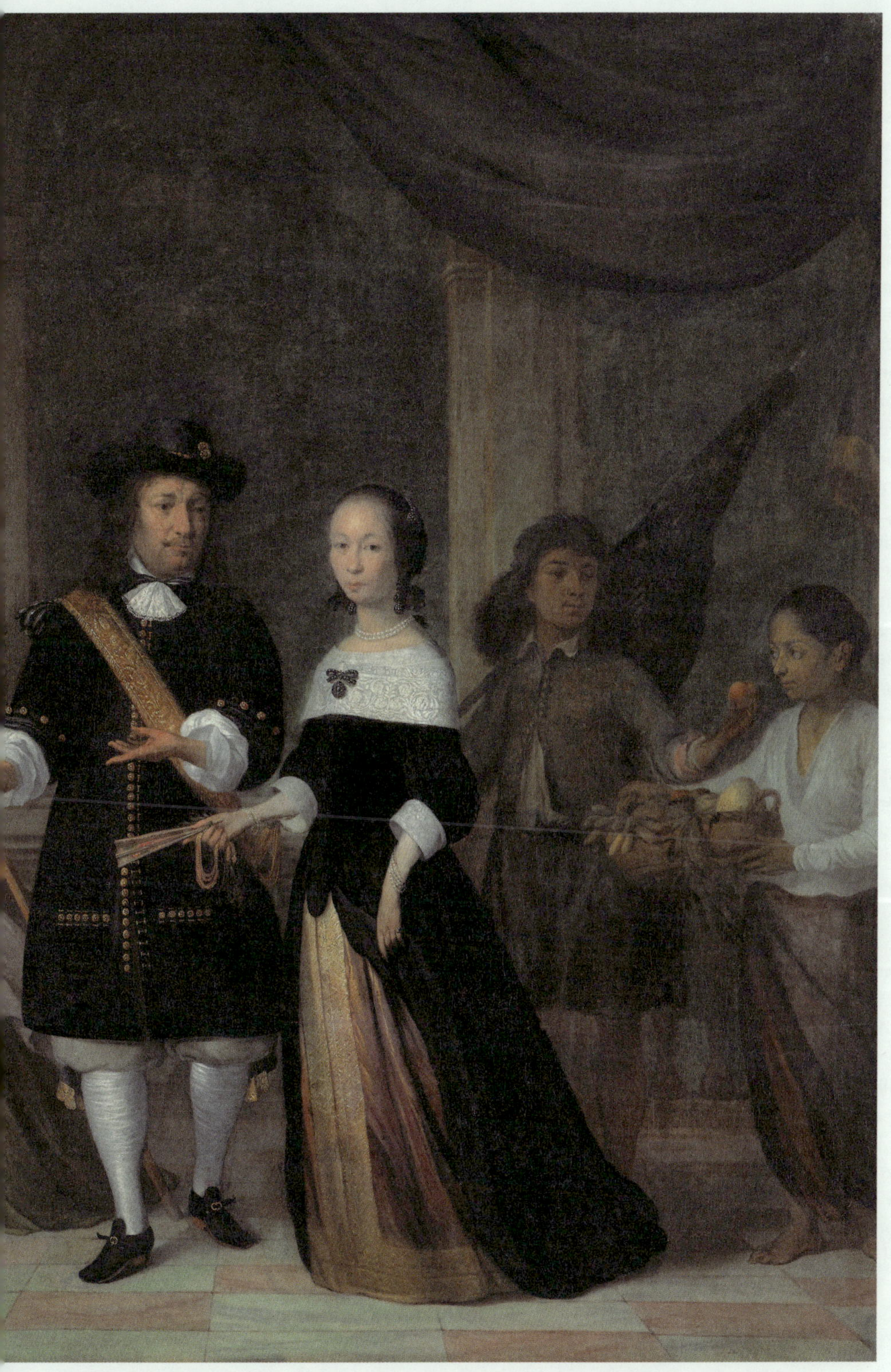

An enormous seventeenth-century family portrait in the Rijksmuseum includes a young man with black curly hair that falls loosely over his shoulders. He wears pleated knee breeches, a light shirt and an open jacket. A banner rests on his right shoulder. His feet are not visible but he is probably not wearing shoes, like the woman beside him. She gives him an arch look as he takes a piece of fruit from her basket. His gaze is averted from the viewer (fig. 1). He is not the first figure that stands out in the painting; as an enslaved servant, he stands in the shadow of a luxuriously attired family. Yet this boy is not just anyone. He is most probably Surapati, a National Hero of Indonesia, famed for his struggle against the Dutch in the seventeenth century.[1] His name inspired some to the greatest of deeds and filled others with fear.

Surapati was already so famous in his own lifetime that his life story was recorded in numerous writings. He appealed so much to the imagination that not only the Javanese wrote about him, but Europeans as well. While the stories from these various sources do not always match, together they make it possible to reconstruct Surapati's life to a large extent: he was an enslaved Balinese man in the service of a Dutchman in Batavia and later succeeded in escaping slavery. He became the leader of a group of fugitive Balinese people and initially fought for the Dutch East India Company (VOC) but eventually against it. Ultimately he became the ruler of an area of East Java, where he died of wounds sustained during a battle with the VOC.

In Java, Surapati's life story was described in *babads*, chronicles in verse meant to be sung and performed before an audience.[2] These *Surapati babads* were written down on *lontars*, booklets made of palm leaves. They are accounts of heroic deeds, supplemented with mystical or fantasy elements, that describe Surapati's life in broad outline and contain a great deal of information about the Java of the seventeenth and eighteenth centuries. The European sources are often travelogues or documents from the VOC archives. Surapati's youth and life as a servant rarely feature in these sources. Rather, he appears from the moment when he begins fighting against the VOC and inspires fear in the Dutch, usually as a marginal figure, in contrast to the central role he plays in the Javanese sources.[3]

To reconstruct his life, *Surapati babads* from three different parts of Java were consulted: West Java, East Java and Balambangan (at the time a small state in East Java). The West Javanese babad was probably written around the middle of the eighteenth century and is based on a manuscript by a contemporary of Surapati (fig. 2). The Balambangan babad dates from about 1730–1740. One of the East Javanese babads (from the early eighteenth century) is a copy of a manuscript by a poet at the court of Surapati, or that of his son; the other is a copy from the first half of the nineteenth century.[4] It becomes clear that different aspects of his life story are emphasized in different regions.[5] Together with the Dutch sources, the Javanese writings provide a picture of this colourful man and his time.

It is remarkable how differently Surapati is depicted in the various sources. The significance attached to his person is demonstrated by the fact that the *Surapati babads* are devoted entirely to him, rather than to a large region or dynasty, and that he is written about throughout Java. For the Javanese

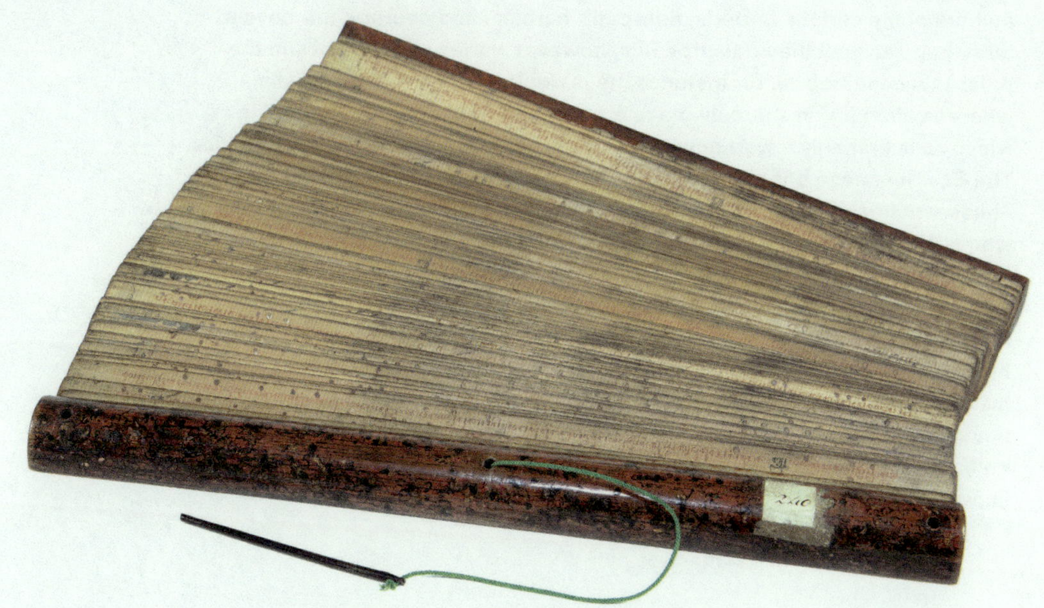

fig. 2 **West Javanese *Surapati babad*, c. 1750**

authors of the various babads, Surapati's heroism and courage are beyond question. The way they describe him, however, varies significantly. In the West Javanese babad, for instance, he is depicted as a devout Muslim, whereas his religion scarcely plays a role in the Balambangan babad, in which he is primarily a warrior who aims to achieve peace and is above politics. The East Javanese babads are those that depict Surapati most as a person. These writings characterize him mainly as a just, decent and forgiving ruler who solves problems himself and does not leave difficult matters to others.[6] In VOC sources, Surapati is primarily characterized as a rebel. Ruys, a VOC captain, is very negative about the Balinese 'scum' in general, but Reynier Adriaensen, a soldier, is more positive: according to him, Surapati is uncommonly brave and has fought with the VOC more than 48 times.[7] The Dutch pastor and historian François Valentijn praises Surapati, who in his view is 'a virtuous, unusually alert, God-fearing soldier' who 'was never wont to offend anyone'.[8] Valentijn drew this conclusion based on what he heard from people who had known Surapati personally.

enslaved servant

Jacob Coeman painted the group portrait, described above, of senior merchant Pieter Cnoll, his wife, Cornelia van Nijenrode, and their two daughters Catharina and Hester in Batavia in 1665. Surapati must have been one of the family's many enslaved servants, but the fact that he is featured in the family portrait says something about his prominent position in the household. Moreover, he carries Cnoll's banner, a task exclusive to the most important servants. A contemporary of Cnoll, the German Georg Meister, describes in his book *Der Orientalisch-Indianische Kunst- und Lust-Gärtner* (The Oriental-Indian art and pleasure gardener) the origins of 'the rebel Surapati', who he says was an enslaved Balinese man and as Cnoll's servant had the privilege of carrying the *pajong* (parasol). Meister also writes that it would have been logical for Cnoll to free Surapati in his will. In Batavia, people in slavery could be bequeathed to an heir as part of an inheritance, but the custom was for a servant to be freed on the death of his 'master', after years of faithful service. Cnoll, however, left the servant to his son, Cornelis. According to Meister, Surapati lost his privileged position in his new household, leading him to run away.[9] Meister's story is corroborated by the description by François Valentijn, who wrote that: 'In the region of Karawang ... a certain Surapati, a Balinese, and a runaway slave of the senior merchant Cnoll, with 70 or 80 like him, was based' (fig. 3).[10]

Both Meister and Valentijn thus claim Surapati was from the island of Bali. The writers of the babads, however, make no mention of this; for them, it was vital to state that Surapati was of Javanese royal blood, in order to legitimize his eventual position as a Javanese ruler. A connection with Bali is nevertheless noted in the Javanese writings. In several texts, Surapati flees there in his youth and remains on the island for some time.[11] In the Balambangan babad, for example, he says: 'I am a son of Sunan Pugĕr, and I have become a Balinese, for the Balinese saved me when I was in dire trouble, and made it possible for me to become a Prince.'[12]

It is therefore quite possible that Surapati really did come from Bali. After all, many enslaved Balinese people lived in Batavia. Balinese women were sold for large sums because of their beauty,[13] but the men struck fear in the VOC. So much so that in 1665 the sale of men was outlawed: 'Balinese slaves were found to be of an angry nature, causing great trouble to the Indies republic, and nothing good could be expected of them.' In addition, it was said that the slave collectors in Bali 'often risked life and limb from the brutality and murderousness of that nation'.[14]

Nevertheless, Bali was one of the principal sources of enslaved people in the Indonesian archipelago in the seventeenth and eighteenth centuries. Most of them were shipped to Batavia; roughly a thousand people suffered this each year. Balinese rulers made a lot of money from the slave trade, reinforcing their own positions in the process. On Bali, someone might end up in slavery as a prisoner of war, because of debts or as punishment. The numerous wars and battles on the island resulted in many prisoners of war, and raids were undertaken during which large numbers of people were enslaved. Balinese rulers also organized cockfights in which the populace was required to take part. If people were unable to pay the debts they incurred as a result, they were enslaved and sold. Judicial sentences on Bali often took the form of fines, which also led to slavery if they could not be paid. This mostly happened among the poorer populace. Once enslaved, it was difficult to escape.[15]

But how did Surapati end up in slavery? Nothing about this can be found in the European sources; the Europeans likely attached no importance to such information. According to the Javanese writings, Surapati was the son of a ruler who ended up in the hands of a Dutchman, who took him to Batavia, where he resided as an enslaved servant in the Dutchman's household. (This period of slavery is missing from the West Javanese badad.) The daughter of the Dutchman subsequently fell in love with Surapati, and according to most writings he had an affair with her; only in the Balambangan babad does he reject her advances. Eventually he left Batavia, by fleeing, according to some, and simply of his own free will according to others.

In the babads, Surapati in his youth is called Untung. Untung is a name that Europeans gave to many enslaved men. People in slavery did not keep their own name; they were given one that was easier for Europeans to pronounce. In both the Balambangan babad and the East Javanese babads, Untung is given the name Surapati by the ruler of Cirebon (on the north coast of West Java) after winning a battle. In the West Javanese babad, a Dutch captain gives the young man the name out of affection. In European sources, he is consistently called Surapati, in every possible spelling. It is therefore reasonable to assume that Surapati was still called Untung during the period that he was in Cnoll's household. Cnoll's will has survived, but the enslaved servants are not specifically mentioned in it.[16] Given the fact that Surapati was only documented in European writings after his period in slavery, his 'slave name' was probably not known. Only Meister wrote about this period, but he probably used the later name because of the fame Surapati had already attained as 'the rebel Surapati'.[17]

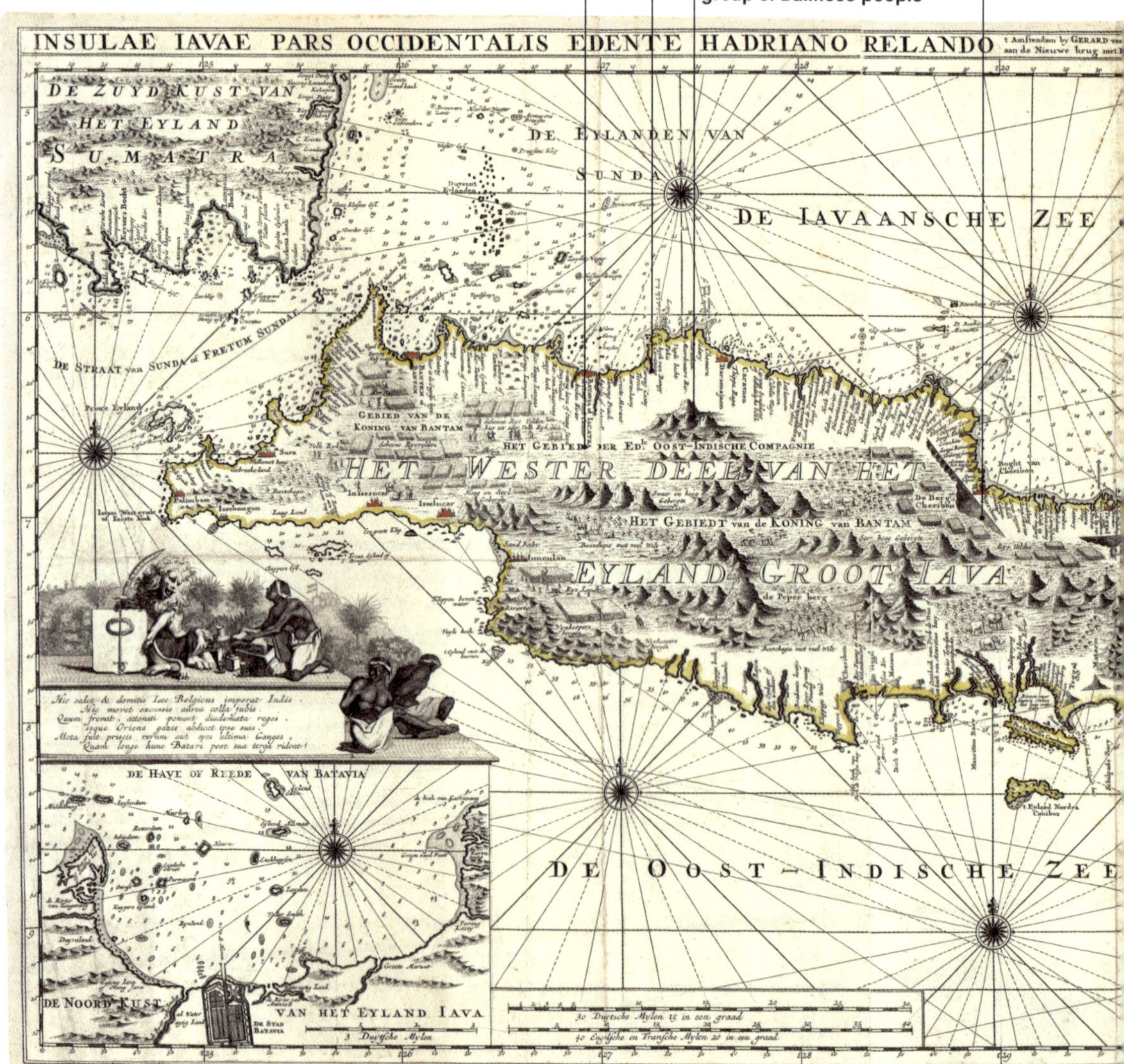

fig. 3 **Map of Java, 1734, with important places in Surapati's life marked**

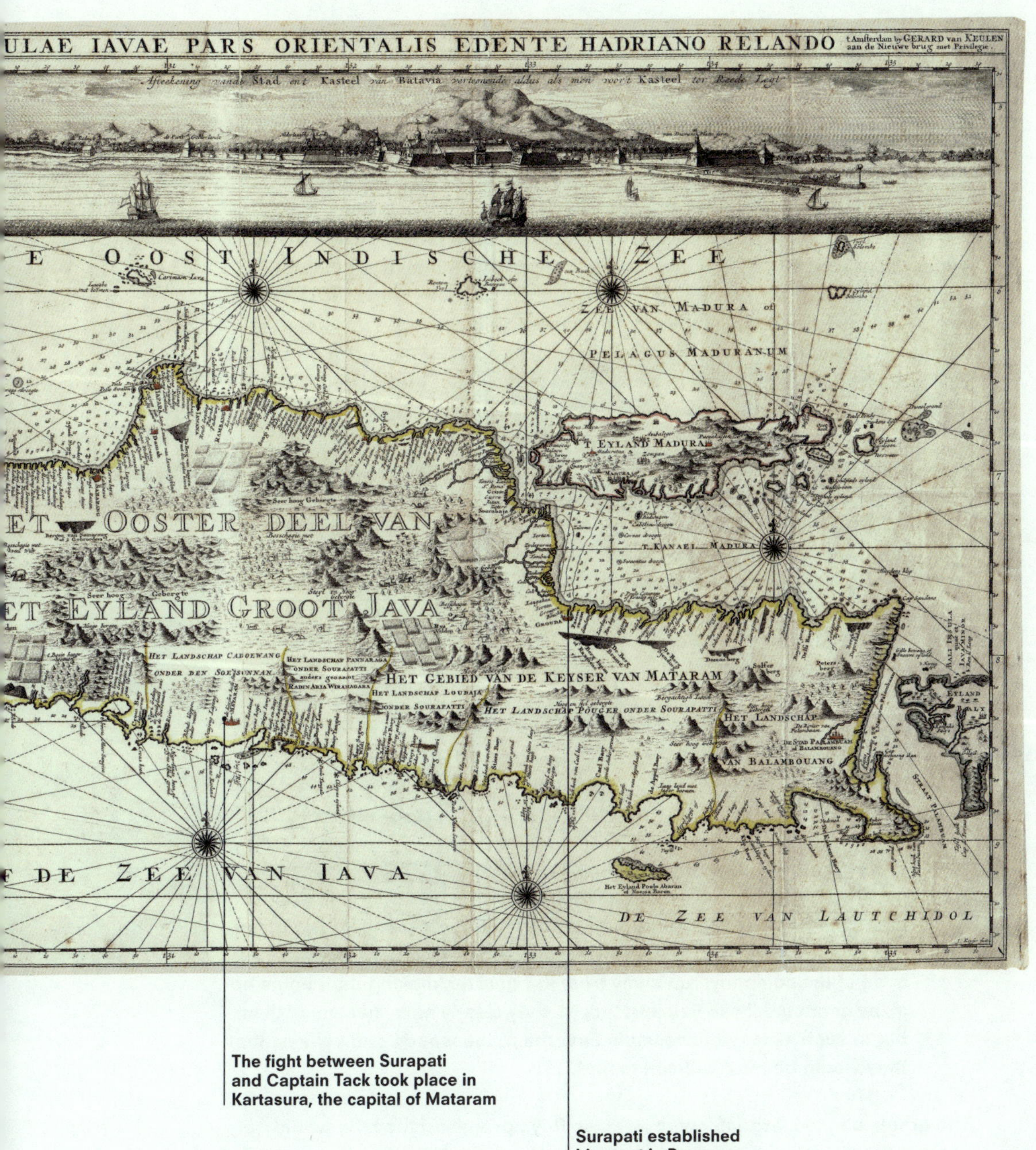

The fight between Surapati and Captain Tack took place in Kartasura, the capital of Mataram

Surapati established his court in Pasuruan

In all the *Surapati babads*, Surapati is adopted by a Dutchman who has become fond of him. This might be an allusion to the prominent position he held, according to the European sources, in the Cnoll household. The story of the relationship between Surapati and the daughter of his 'owner' also appears in all the *Surapati babads*. This story, however, is not corroborated by European sources (which nevertheless says nothing about its veracity).[18]

warrior

About seven years after he was painted by Coeman, Surapati appears for the first time in the daily accounts of the VOC. By now he is the leader of a group of Balinese who have escaped slavery and are based near Batavia. The Balinese were fierce warriors and were able to survive in inhospitable areas. They possessed knowledge and skills that the Dutch lacked. It was for this reason that the VOC was keen to enlist them. Surapati too joined the VOC military. The accounts record that 'Soura Patty' swore allegiance to the VOC on the Quran on 24 November 1672.[19] Surapati and his men were subsequently deployed to subdue hostile rulers in Java, because they were skilled at penetrating mountainous territory. The West Javanese *Surapati babad*, for instance, describes how the VOC soldiers were afraid of the water that flowed in a deep ravine around a fort and only dared to attack once Surapati took the lead.

Despite their important role, the Balinese did not have a stable position in the military. Mutual trust was precarious. The Dutch were afraid they would switch sides and join the enemy. The Balinese, on the other hand, were afraid the Dutch would enslave them again. Slavery was always held over their heads as a threat, and often that threat became reality. If they tried to desert the army and were caught, for instance, they were enslaved by the VOC and put to work carrying heavy provisions. Reynier Adriaensen, a soldier in the VOC army, described in his travelogue what these men had to do to be released from slavery once more: 'only once they chop off the head of one of the enemy soldiers are they allowed to fight as soldiers again.'[20]

Surapati and his men too must have deserted the VOC army, for eleven years after his mention in the daily accounts, the VOC captain Ruys describes a group of escaped Balinese people whom he came across on one of his expeditions, in the mountains of Tjikalong:

> this is ... scum ... a rabble of thieves and wretches, some of whom have held out for twenty years and sustained themselves on nothing other than pillaging and robbing travellers, among them many known male slaves and who knows how many female slaves of various persons, yes, even of the company, run away from the quarter, making their home not in, by or around those hamlets, though they clearly have mastery of them, but in such almost inaccessible caverns of the woods and valleys, that they would be most difficult to find.[21]

The group was too large to overpower, so Ruys promised them he would not enslave them again if they joined his troops. He went on to write that he hoped he could 'tame' them in his army and that he would be able to get rid of them later. He expected nothing but the worst from them. One of the leaders of this 'rabble' was Surapati. He was made a lieutenant – probably because of his demonstrated leadership – and was assigned to capture an enemy of the VOC, Purbaya. It was not clear to him, however, what was supposed to happen to this Purbaya afterwards. Was he to be brought to Batavia or handed over to one of the VOC functionaries? An ensign, a certain Kuffeler, ordered Surapati to turn over Purbaya to him, whereupon the captive managed to escape as a result of Kuffeler's actions. Kuffeler blamed Surapati for this and ordered him to pursue Purbaya again. Surapati refused, for as a lieutenant he was the superior in rank. Kuffeler then threatened and slapped him.[22] This was an affront to Surapati's honour. He could not let this pass and attacked Kuffeler's camp, and 53 people were killed. Kuffeler, however, managed to escape.

The foregoing episode is included both in the West Javanese *Surapati babad* and in the history written by the previously mentioned Valentijn. Valentijn claimed to have got his information from Purbaya himself, who later gave himself up and was brought to Batavia, where Valentijn supposedly spoke to him. Valentijn described how Kuffeler's slap and threats had caused an enormous commotion among Surapati's men, who 'told Surapati that they no longer wanted to serve under a commander who allowed himself be so insulted and would not seek revenge, nor did they want to become slaves again, which they feared, as Kuffeler berated them'.[23] Surapati is alleged to have said, according to Adriaensen: 'Are these the thanks for my faithful services to the Dutch?'[24]

This conflict would prove the definitive break between Surapati and the VOC, although the VOC attempted to persuade Surapati to rejoin their army in the months that followed. Multiple letters were exchanged, some friendly, others of a menacing tone. When Surapati remained adamant, the VOC officially declared him an enemy on 21 May 1684 and put a price on his head.[25] By then Surapati had fled to Kartasura, in East Java, where Amangkurat II, Sunan (ruler) of Mataram, had his court. One of the East Javanese *Surapati babads* describes how Surapati arrived before Amangkurat II: 'Prince Pugĕr came before the sunan to inform him that the Patih [vizier] had a refugee from Batavia, originally a slave, and ill-treated by the Dutch.'[26] The sunan admitted Surapati to his court, but the VOC demanded his extradition. Amangkurat II still had a large debt outstanding with the VOC for assistance the company had lent his father in 1677 in eliminating his opponents and retaining his throne. The VOC let the sunan know that captain François Tack would be dispatched to Kartasura as an ambassador to discuss both matters. His true assignment, however, was to seize Surapati at all costs. The Mataram court had no illusions about the mission and prepared for battle.[27]

Battle did break loose when the VOC arrived, culminating in a direct encounter between Tack and Surapati. An East Javanese *Surapati babad* describes how Amangkurat II and his three younger brothers sat on a balcony watching the duel.[28] This scene is depicted in a painting (fig. 4). The large man in red is Tack; his hat lies on the ground. The man to his right is Surapati. Behind them, their followers stand poised to attack. Sunan Amangkurat II looks on with a spyglass from a raised platform.

The fight was long and intense and ended with a fatal assault on Tack by Surapati (fig. 5). In the words of the West Javanese *Surapati babad*:

> Surapati attacked fiercely, heedless of danger. He sought out Raja Tack, and seized him, striking him with his sword, so that he fell from his horse. He got up to retaliate, taking aim. Raden [Surapati] struck blow after blow with his sword. Raja Tack staggered as he tried to stand – he had been wounded and was too dazed to fight back. He was vomiting blood and looked like a buffalo calf trying to stay on its legs. [Surapati] seized him by the hair and thrust his sword into his neck. Raja Tack was dead, and so were his soldiers, those who survived fleeing away.[29]

The battle cost 75 Europeans and about 80 Balinese their lives. The VOC collected the dead and retreated. Surapati and his men left the court, apparently on horses from Amangkurat II and with several good weapons, as a gift of the ruler. To the VOC, Amangkurat II always insisted that he too considered Surapati a rebel.[30]

ruler

Surapati withdrew to the east and established his court in Pasuruan, situated between Mataram and Balambangan – possibly this territory too was a gift of Amangkurat II, as a reward for driving off the VOC. Surapati had become a ruler, and the VOC had to take him into consideration. Valentijn describes Pasuruan as a city of 10,000 inhabitants, one of the strongest cities in Java, ruled 'sovereignly and tranquilly' by Surapati.[31]

In 1706 the conflict between the VOC and Surapati flared up with a new campaign, which Valentijn documented. The campaign consisted of three major battles. Surapati was killed in the last of them. His body was buried in Pasuruan. A year later, the VOC again sent troops to Pasuruan, this time to fight against Surapati's sons, who had taken over from their deceased father. The sons lost the battle and spread out across Java. They would remain fierce opponents of the VOC for most of the eighteenth century.[32]

The VOC commander who led the 1707 expedition had Surapati's bones exhumed and burnt and his ashes scattered at sea. Apparently he had been such a dangerous opponent to the VOC that they wished to erase him from history forever; as the authoritative nineteenth-century Dutch historian Conrad Busken Huet colourfully wrote:

> Surapati's spirit could be content that it had taken two campaigns and two armies to bring him down, and the Company, to erase his legacy, had found the help of wind and waves necessary.[33]

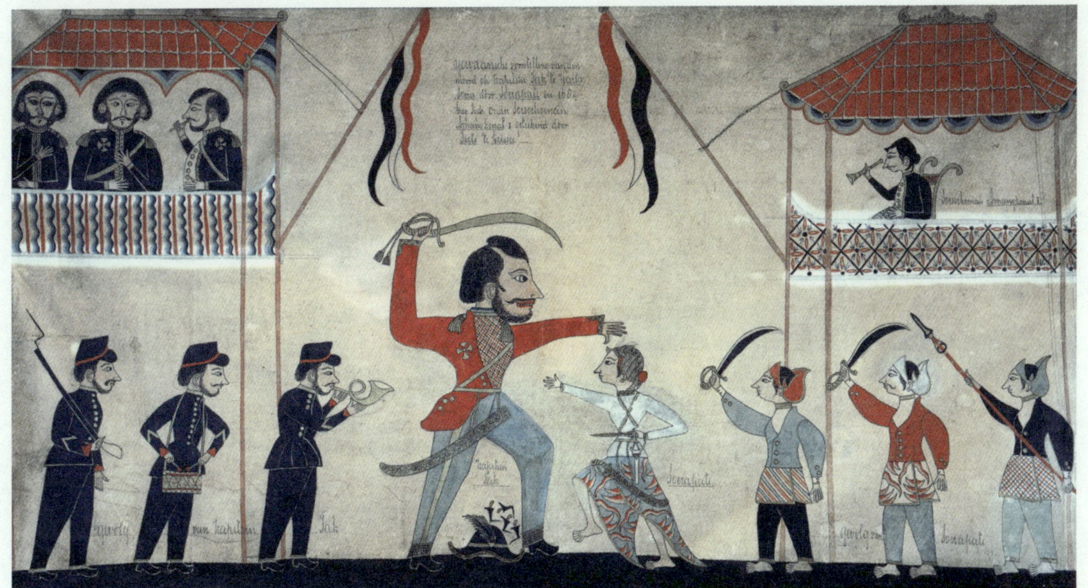

fig. 4 **The murder of Captain Tack in Kartasura, 1890–1900**

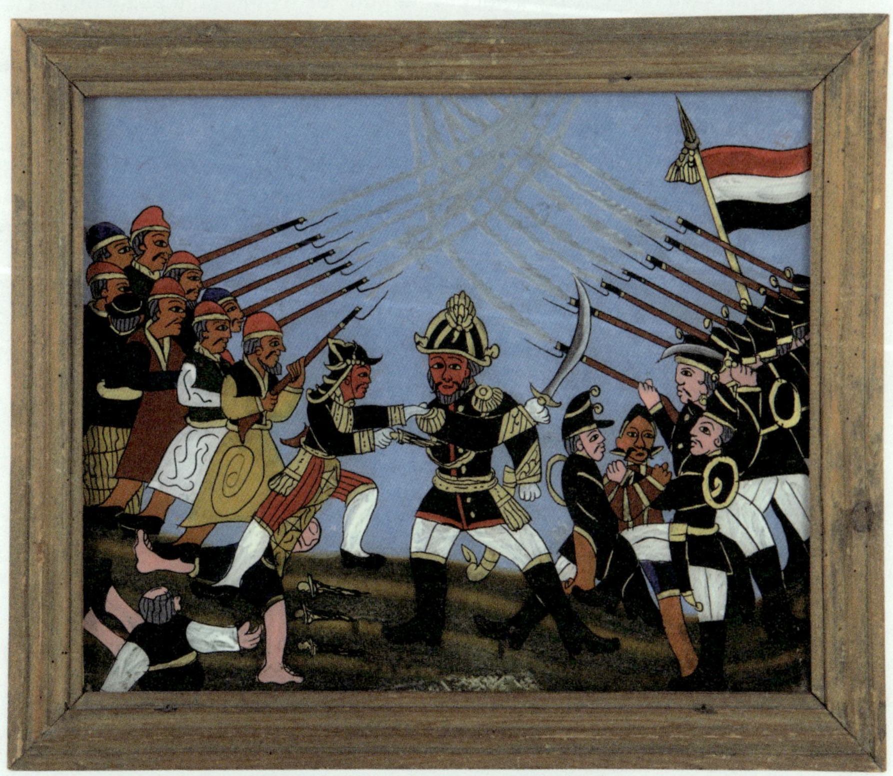

fig. 5 **The attack on Captain Tack by Surapati during the battle in Kartasura, 1900–1950**

national hero

The VOC did not succeed in erasing Surapati's legacy, however. On 3 November 1975, the Indonesian government declared him a National Hero, the highest honour an Indonesian can be given by the state. Surapati was given this title of honour for his struggle against the Dutch colonial military.[34] He never faded from the collective memory. After his death, the *Surapati babads* were written down and reproduced numerous times. In the Netherlands, Busken Huet included him in his *Het land van Rembrand* (Rembrandt's country).[35] He owes his hero status in the twentieth century mainly to the book *Surapati* (1950) by Abdoel Moeis (fig. 6),[36] a politically active journalist who played an important role in the nationalist movement in Indonesia that emerged after 1900.[37]

Surapati's life story as Indonesians know it today comes primarily from Moeis's novel, in which he largely follows the history as it is told in the babads, but with a clear emphasis on anticolonial aspects. In his book, Si Untung (as Moeis calls him) marries Suzanne, the daughter of the Dutch merchant (named Moor in this book) in whose service he is an enslaved domestic, and has a child with her. When Moor has him jailed for this, Si Untung becomes embittered about his fate and the way in which people like him are treated by the colonists. After his escape and work for the VOC military, this distrust is once again confirmed by his conflict with Kuffeler. By this time Suzanne has returned to the Netherlands, whereupon Si Untung definitively turns against the VOC and establishes his own court as Surapati. Robert, the son of Surapati and Suzanne, has in the meantime enlisted in the VOC military and become engaged to Tack's daughter. Father and son do meet again but are never reconciled. When Surapati is mortally wounded in a battle with the VOC, he tries to reach out to his son one last time, on his deathbed, to no avail.[38]

In Moeis's novel, the emphasis lies on the unbridgeable chasm between the Dutch and the Indonesians, entirely in the nationalist spirit of the early twentieth century. Moeis's *Surapati* borrows from the late nineteenth-century novel *Van slaaf tot vorst* (From slave to ruler, 1887) by Melati van Java, a pseudonym of the Dutch Indies-born Dutch writer Nicolina Maria Christina Sloot (fig. 7). The broad outlines of the two narratives are virtually identical.[39] However, whereas the Javanese and Balinese possess only good qualities in Moeis's book, in Melati van Java's they are often portrayed as having bad ones as well. In her book, Surapati tries, tragically alone, to overcome the conflicts between the Europeans and Javanese but is undermined by both parties. Moeis places the emphasis on Surapati's positive character traits, contrasting them with the negative qualities of the colonial Dutch. The image conjured in Moeis's book probably contributed to a large extent to Surapati being declared a National Hero of Indonesia.[40]

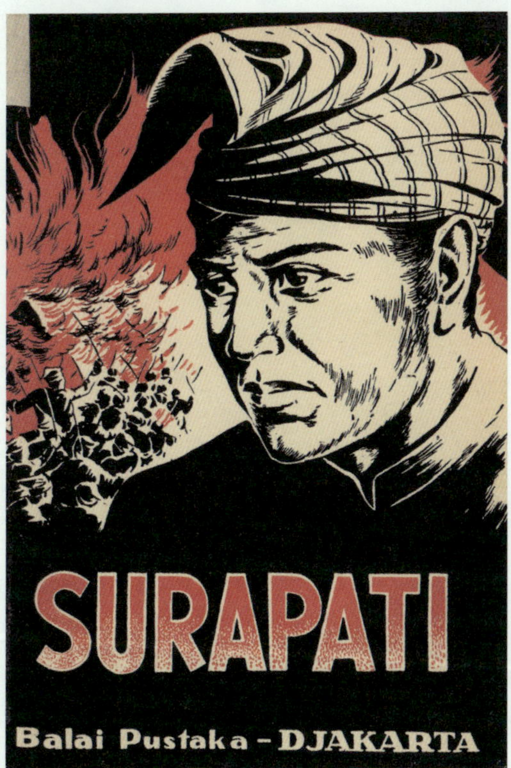

fig. 6 ***Surapati*, Abdoel Moeis, 1965 edition**

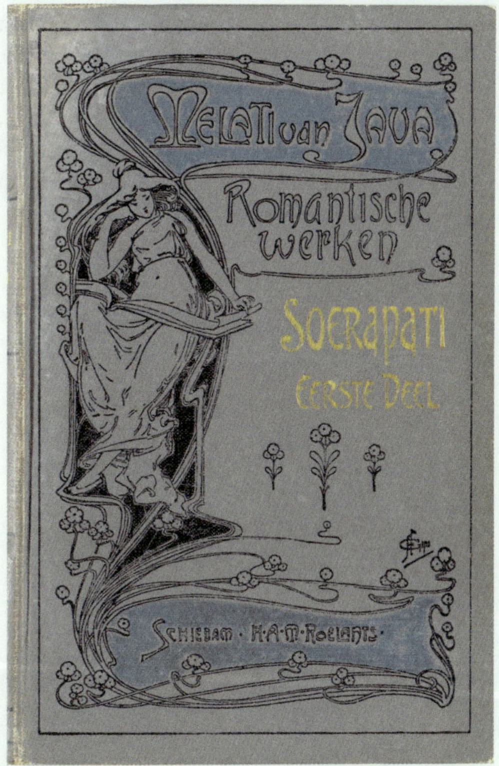

fig. 7 **'From slave to ruler: Historical romantic sketch from the history of Java' Melati van Java, 1907 edition**

In today's Indonesia, Surapati appears in a number of places. The Universiti Surapati in Jakarta is named after him, and various streets in the country bear his name. He has also featured as a character in comic books, television series and on the stage (fig. 8)**. As a result, his legend lives on. What is known of his life is indeed remarkable. Someone who managed to escape slavery, rally large groups of people to a united cause and ultimately establish a realm of his own deserves to be remembered as a hero, in Indonesia and beyond.**

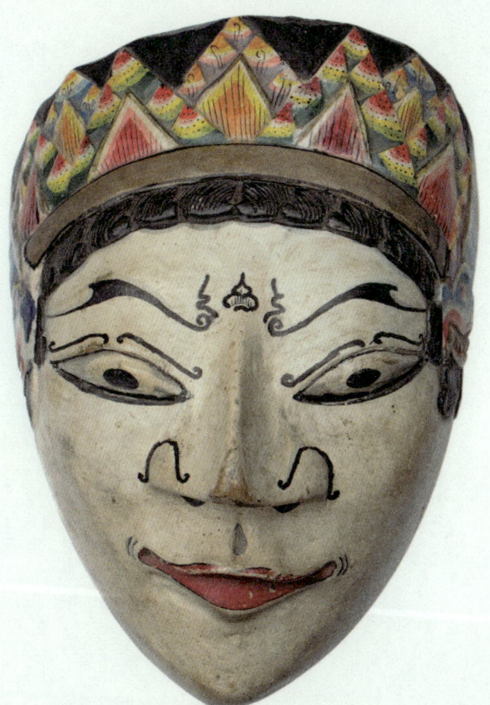

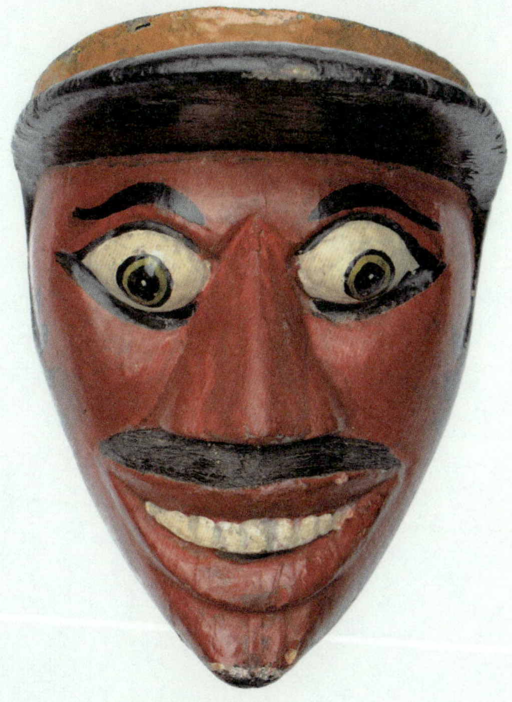

fig. 8 **Masks representing Surapati and Tack, before 2003**
Such masks are used in classical Javanese *wayang topéng* dance and theatre performances

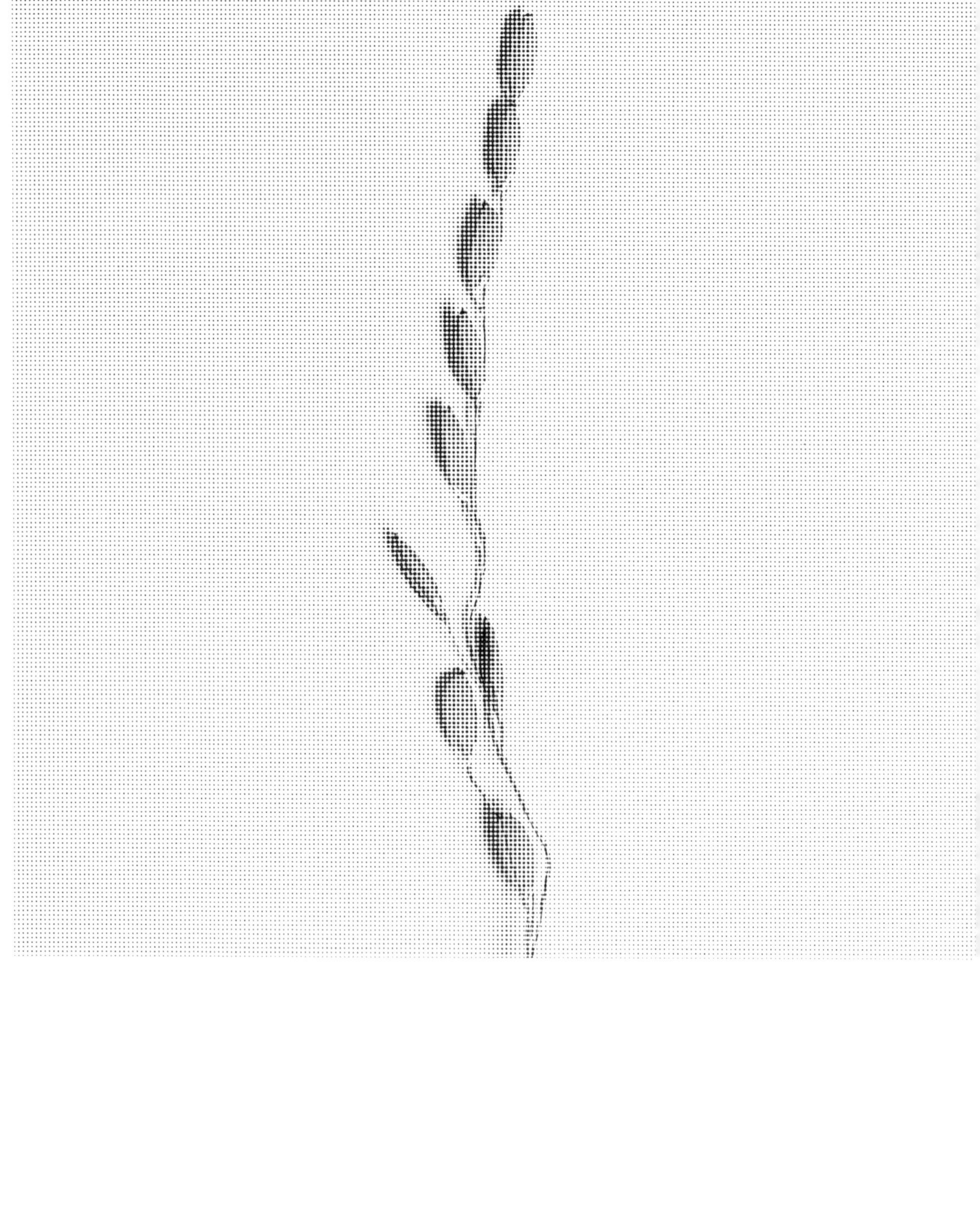

valika smeulders

sapali

an independent society

What do you do if you are kidnapped by human traffickers and have no idea what awaits you? And if you then end up in a faraway, unknown land, on a plantation where you are forced to work to exhaustion and are humiliated every day, but where wide-open nature calls out to you? Many knew what to do: flee. Flight, however, was full of risks. Not just because it was subject to harsh punishment, but also because of the uncertainty of how to survive in an unfamiliar environment. In spite of these dangers, some people managed to escape colonial oppression and start up autonomous communities. These people are called Maroons. In Suriname, women played a significant role in this new beginning by taking with them a sustainable food source: rice seeds. Sapali, for instance, was able to vouchsafe the survival of a group of Maroons called the Ndyuka or Aukan. These were names given by the colonists, after the nearby creek Mama Ndyuka and the Auka plantation; the people themselves use the name Okanisi.[1] Because of her strategic thinking and care for the greater group, Sapali is called Ma Sapa among the Okanisi. She is cherished as a founding mother in the collective memory, living culture and spirituality. Her story has not hitherto been told in Dutch museums. Can colonial museum objects and present-day research into rice varieties confirm this oral history and perhaps cast new light on it?

oral sources

In a video filmed in 2018, Edith Adjako demonstrates an age-old survival strategy passed down to her by the elders of the Maroon group to which she belongs. She makes a parting in the hair of the girl sitting in front of her. Edith takes a handful of dry, unpeeled rice grains and sprinkles them carefully in the channel the comb has formed. Her fingers deftly divide the girl's hair into three sections, and she starts to braid it. As the braid pattern grows, the grains vanish from sight, well hidden within the hair. As she works, Edith talks about the concealment and secret transport of rice, a story passed from generation to generation by the Okanisi.[2]

This far-sighted way in which women provided their community with food has also become famous outside Maroon communities, for instance through songs. Humbert Oosterwolde and Ricardo Mateda, members of NAKS, the African-Surinamese organization for socio-cultural awareness and the Ko Haika music school in Jaw Jaw, Suriname, perform a Saramaccan song whose words include: '*U tya nyanya ko o, e! U tya nyanya ko o, baa! Gaanlanti mi begi un baya, e! Tye, ma u tya nyanya ko o! U tya nyanya ko o, baa! Gaanlanti mi begi un baa!*'[3] Vinije Haabo, an expert in Saramaccan language and culture, explains that the first word of the lyrics can mean 'you' as well as 'we' and 'I'; 'I' is thus made subordinate to 'you' or 'we'. The first line means 'I have brought food with me'. The second line means, 'People, I beg you'. This might be the plea of a woman asking to be accepted into the group. Because of the dangerous conditions, escapees would set high demands for those who wanted to flee with them. To have food at their disposal was an important contribution.

In European society, authority in the colonial period is often associated with men, but this is not the case among Maroons. As in many West African societies, kinship is traced through the female line. In these matrilineal societies, women play a fundamental, authoritative role. Furthermore, Maroon women traditionally bear responsibility for the cultivation of crops and food supplies, thereby making a vital contribution to society. These were crucial roles that inspired respect and pride among the group as a whole. The fact that this group was able to survive – in spite of efforts at suppression by the colonial system – is in part due to female leadership. Today, about 120,000 Maroons live in Suriname, forming the country's third-largest population group.

Women, for example, decided when one would be able to eat. Waiting for the rice seeds, the unhulled grains of rice, to germinate in the soil, to grow and become ready for harvest must have seemed long for people who were hungry. This is still sung about today. André Mosis, formerly Ede-Basiya, head of the assistants and right-hand man of the Ede-Kabiten (the Okanisi leader), performs this with his daughters Susi and Simba Mosis: '*Alesi lepi, Ba Dé no no. Alesi gung oo, goo Ba Dé no no jeee*'. Susi relates: 'This song was sung by women returning from their farming plots. We know the men want to eat rice, they sing, but the rice is not ripe. They are telling the men to be patient, however difficult that is; the rice cannot be harvested yet.'

For the Maroons of today, commemoration of the role of women extends beyond oral traditions and the acknowledgement of female leadership. There are names of specific women that have been passed down, surviving in ceremonial customs, for example. During religious gatherings, people are sometimes possessed by the spirit of Ma Sapa, says Helen Ajentoena, Ede Kabiten, one of the highest authority figures and spiritual leaders of the Okanisi in the Netherlands. At such moments, a connection is felt with the woman who stood at the founding of all Okanisi by providing them with a sustainable food source, by first taking rice from Africa to Suriname, and then in Suriname from the plantation to freedom. During ceremonial moments, people reflect in gratitude on the significance of the founding mother and on their spiritual and ancestral connection with Africa.

In Africa, in colonial times, people lived with the reality of human traffickers, including nomads on horseback who organized nightly raids to kidnap people. In a number of areas, housing was adapted to hinder entry by kidnappers in order to gain time to escape. Houses were built with lower doors, in mazes or over water. Women, responsible for growing food, anticipated uncertain situations by carrying on their person crops that might be useful in an escape. They did not know what might happen, but the need for food was a certainty. In this way, crops like rice, cassava, sesame and okra found their way to various countries in South and North America. There too, the cultivation of crops, in addition to hunting and gathering, proved indispensable to the self-sufficient survival of larger groups. The names of specific women who brought rice with them live on in specific rice varieties. The Okanisi grow rice varieties called Sapali (Ma Sapa) and Milly. The inhabitants of Saramacca grow a rice called Ma Pansa. The prefix 'Ma' was added as a sign of respect and indicates that Pansa is seen as the founding mother of all Saramaccans.

Precisely how far back in time these historical songs telling the stories of Maroon women go has not been determined. The Ndyuka signed a peace treaty with the colonial authorities of Suriname in 1760. Sapali must have lived before that. Whether the songs date from this time cannot be ascertained. What is known is that these songs and stories are passed down from parents to children. Each new generation chooses to lend significance to the historical challenges faced by the group and to those of their ancestors who demonstrated leadership. The practice of oral history is a living cultural heritage, one that also changes over time. New songs are composed, for instance. One example is the song sung by women in Saramacca in the film *Stones Have Laws* (2018) by Lonnie van Brummelen and Siebren de Haan:

> Foremother Pansa brought rice seeds to feed her people
> She multiplied the seeds and shared them with her people
> Foremother Pansa did she bring her wisdom from Africa?
> She planted one stalk's seeds it became a bundle
> One bundle became more bundles
> Ma Pansa multiplied the seeds and shared them with her people.[4]

The song brings together information from other songs and stories, in order to clearly pass the history on to the next generation.

Stones Have Laws shows how the rice harvest is performed by women, just as women in Africa often bear the responsibility for farm plots. The cultural entrepreneur Jose Tojo, who has ancestral ties to a number of Maroon people, called attention on social media to a short film showing a long line of women working in a vast rice paddy, bounded in the distance by trees. Their right hands dart from the plants to their left hands, in which they collect the stalks. They sing, long notes alternating with short ones, fast notes that tumble over one another. One singer leads: she supplies one line, to which the rest respond. It is a typical work song, like those kept alive across the Americas and in the Caribbean, on plantations and elsewhere. By singing together, people support one another and help each other through the work. In the video, the women seem to become so absorbed in their communal singing that it is as if the work becomes merely the backdrop to their being together.

In this way, immaterial heritage, from oral history and spirituality to expertise about farming and food, forms the main source of information about Ma Sapa. It is knowledge that has been kept alive for centuries by Sapali's descendants, first in Suriname and later in the Netherlands. In the wider Surinamese community, the story has become more famous thanks to the work of organizations such as NAKS, and in the Netherlands Ma Pansa became known through *Stones Have Laws* and a digital programme by the national broadcaster NOS.[5] Museums, archives and libraries, meanwhile, have mainly preserved objects and written sources, in which the names of these women were still unknown until recently, but bringing together immaterial and material sources produces a much clearer picture of the past and the role therein of women like Sapali.

rice from africa

The majority of the written sources we know about attest to the introduction of rice by European seamen, colonists and scientists, mostly from Asia to the Americas. As a result, a one-sided picture was long maintained. Rice was supposed to have been developed as an agricultural product in Asia and disseminated by Europeans as part of the globalizing economy during the colonial period. Yet there were also early mentions of other possible ways in which (as well as other reasons why) rice found its way into colonized areas. In 1726, the Swiss correspondent Jean Watt wrote that rice had been brought to Carolina in North America by a woman.[6]

Recent research into the DNA profile of the many rice varieties produced in Suriname provides further insight. Tinde van Andel, a professor at Leiden and Wageningen universities, has applied modern techniques to map the DNA of 50 rice varieties. Her research group concluded that fifteen of these had not previously been scientifically documented. For instance, the researchers determined that Baaka Alisi, the black rice grown by the Okasini along the Marowijne and Lawa rivers in Suriname, originates from Ivory Coast.[7] The Okanisi told Van Andel that this rice is difficult to de-husk and little of it is eaten; it is mostly used for medicines and in ancestor rituals. Other rice varieties were also found to occur only in Africa and Suriname. There is thus genetic evidence of the direct route of rice between the two areas.

The research also made it clear that Maroons have traded rice seed for centuries, even between villages difficult to access and far away from one another. Geographer Judith Carney had already written that, among communities outside Suriname, in a vast area of Brazil and French Guyana, oral tradition tells of a woman who brought rice from Africa.[8] This raises the question of whether there might have been many women who did this or whether groups in South America might have passed the rice seeds on to one another. The genetic research confirms the latter theory. It turns out that Maroons have been cultivating many rice varieties for centuries, because variation contributes to crop resistance to a range of conditions. This includes Asian rice varieties and, from the Second World War onwards, varieties that were 'improved' in the United States. At the same time, traditional rice varieties have also been maintained. These are prized for their taste and nutritional content, but are above all also protected because of their spiritual value.[9] In addition, Van Andel's research established that, rather than having a single origin in Africa, the rice varieties originated from different parts of the continent.[10] This also seems to validate the idea that multiple women may have taken rice with them on their transatlantic crossings. In other words, the genetic research provides support to the claims in the oral tradition regarding the deeds and significance of Ma Sapa, Ma Pansa and Milly.

Van Andel brought many of these rice varieties back to the Netherlands, including a Ma Sapa stalk (fig. 1). Since this is unprocessed biological material with a limited shelf life, its historical value does not reside in the fact that this specific rice stalk is 300 years old. But we can assume, based on the combination of genetic research and oral sources, that this rice stalk is directly descended

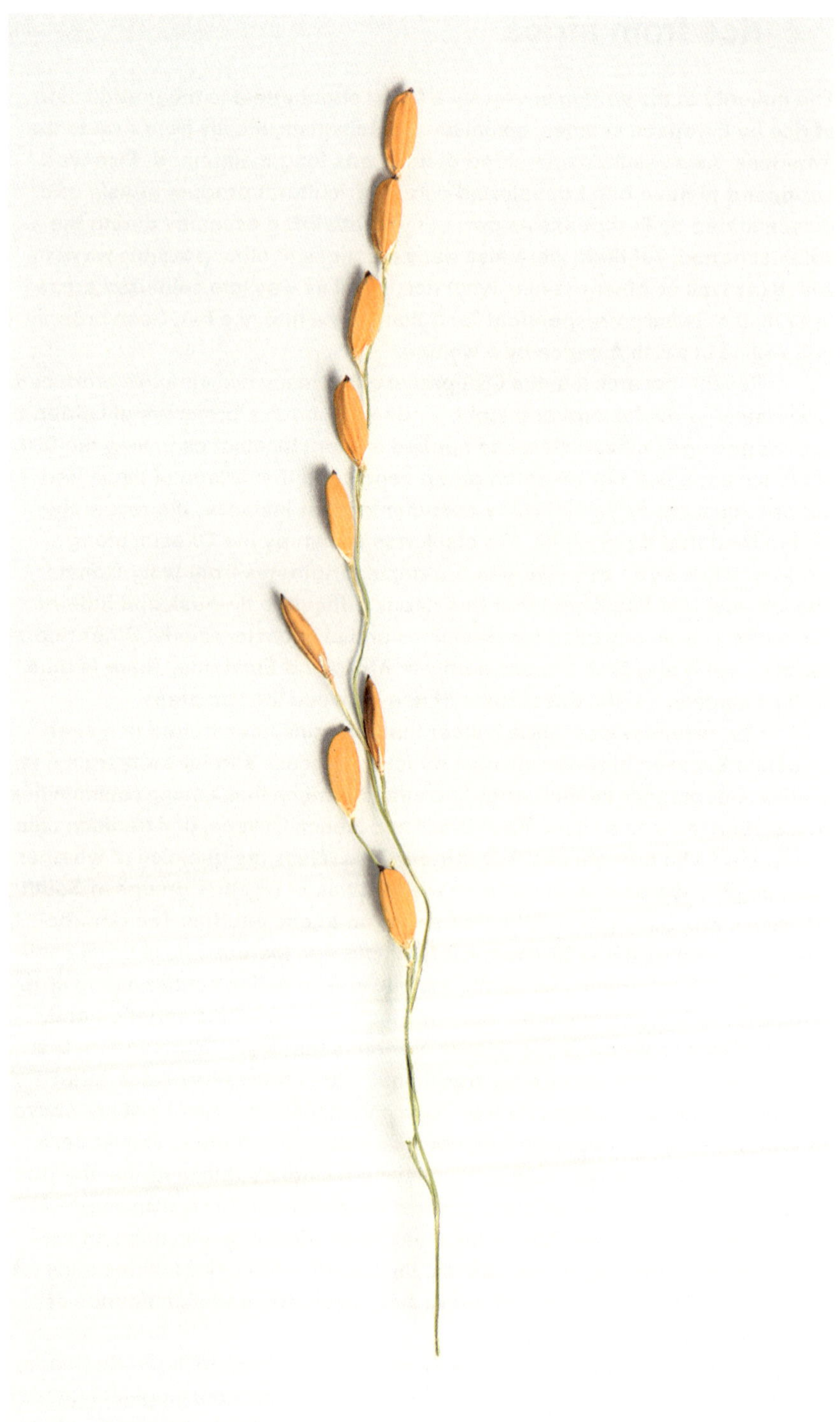

fig. 1 **Stalk of a rice variety named after Ma Sapa or Sapali**

from the rice that Ma Sapa braided into her hair 300 years ago. This gives us a sense of closeness to a woman who was forced three centuries ago to leave behind her home and undertake an unknown voyage filled with danger. While we will never know what she looked like, through the rice, her presence is made palpable.

It is difficult to picture the individuals behind the large, anonymous groups of people who were documented only as property using colonial museum objects. People taken into slavery were very seldom the subject of portraits. Further, Maroon peoples make beautiful art, but portraits do not form part of this tradition. Yet the search for objects that can convey Sapali's story has produced more than we initially expected. It is not quite true, it turns out, that no pictures of women like Sapali were made. There is even a representation to be found in the collection of the Rijksmuseum, even though when it was assembled this collection was never intended to contribute to the telling of stories like Ma Sapa's.

a closer look at objects

The museum's collection began to be assembled about 1800, towards the end of the colonial period. The objects, to a large extent, derive from the possessions of the upper classes. This focus on the wealthy meant that, on the one hand, the history of slavery was neglected in the first centuries of the museum's existence, but on the other hand, paradoxically, the link between the collection and slavery is evident. The elite of the Netherlands was, after all, closely connected economically to the plantation system in this period. These links varied from the ownership of plantations to financial relations through mortgages or insurance, to all manner of administrative functions. Nor can the art in which the working classes are depicted be seen separately from the colonial system. Many labour activities were after all directly connected with the international economy, from supplying the shipping sector to processing colonial products, from bakers to the blacksmiths who made shackles.

The Rijksmuseum has in its possession an unusual map, made of silk and more than 2 metres wide (fig. 2). The map, depicting Suriname, was produced in a limited edition and intended as a gift for the members of the board of directors of the Society of Suriname in Amsterdam in 1737. A substantial proportion of the map is taken up by its richly ornamented border. The crest of the Society features prominently in the lower centre, flanked by two muscular, armed men. The one on the left has long hair and probably symbolizes the original inhabitants of Suriname. The one on the right is dark-skinned and is also depicted as a warrior, and probably symbolizes the African continent. The rest of the border consists of a luxuriant profusion of tropical products and the twelve family crests of the eleven directors and the secretary of the Society. The top of the map reads, 'General Map of the Province of Suriname'. The map is meant as a display of ownership: this is Dutch territory, consisting of 400 plantations. It also indicates military expeditions. These were intended to hunt down people who had escaped the plantations and freed themselves from slavery. At least seven such expeditions had been undertaken under

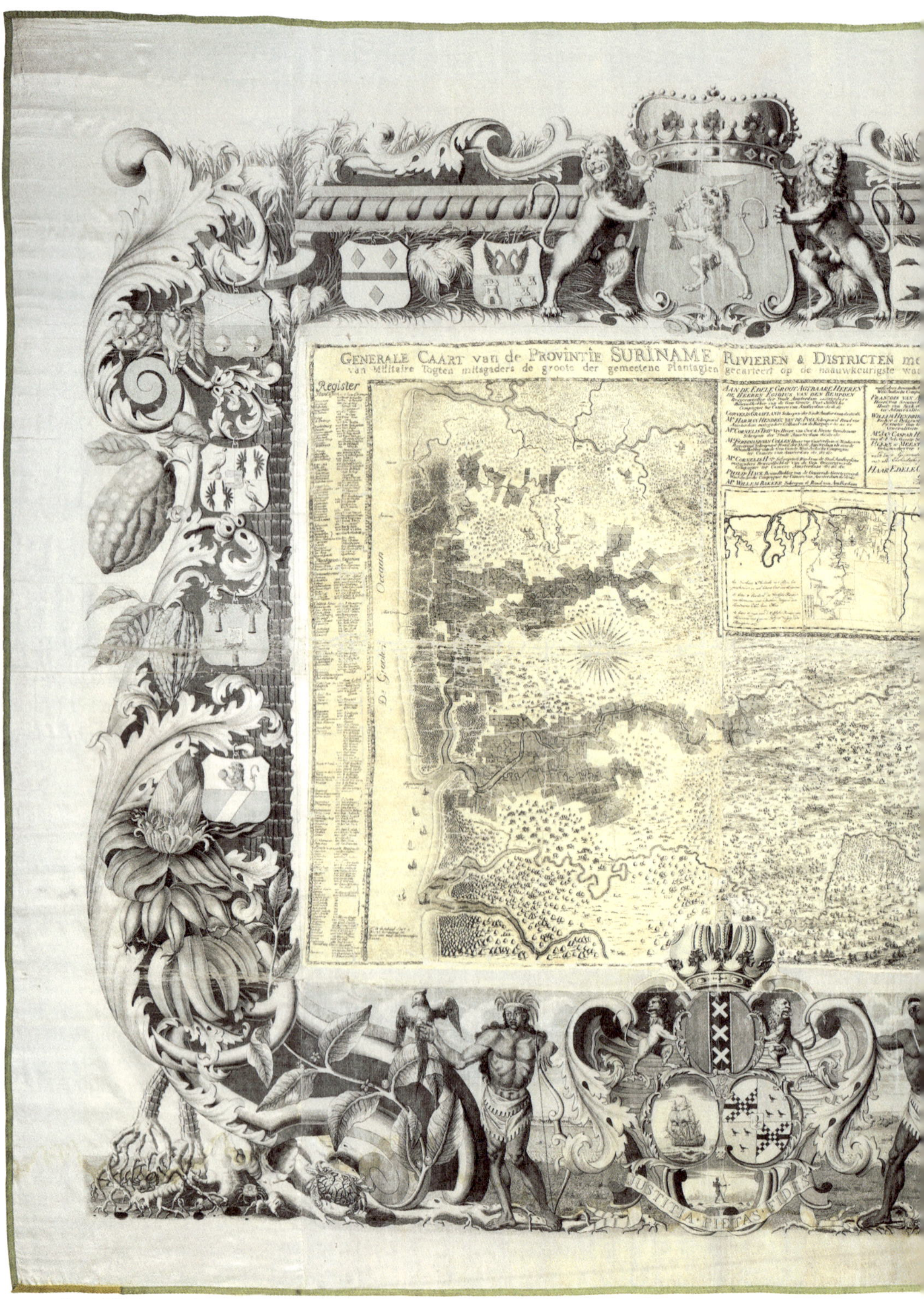

fig. 2 **Silk map of Suriname, Alexander de Lavaux, 1737**

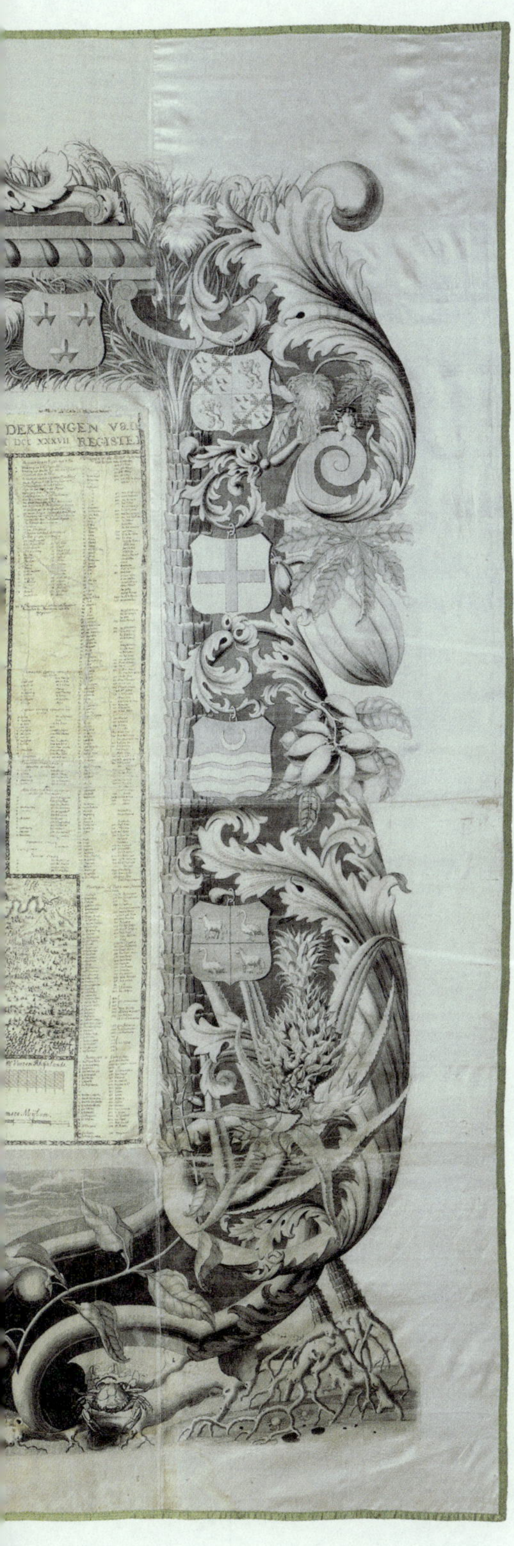

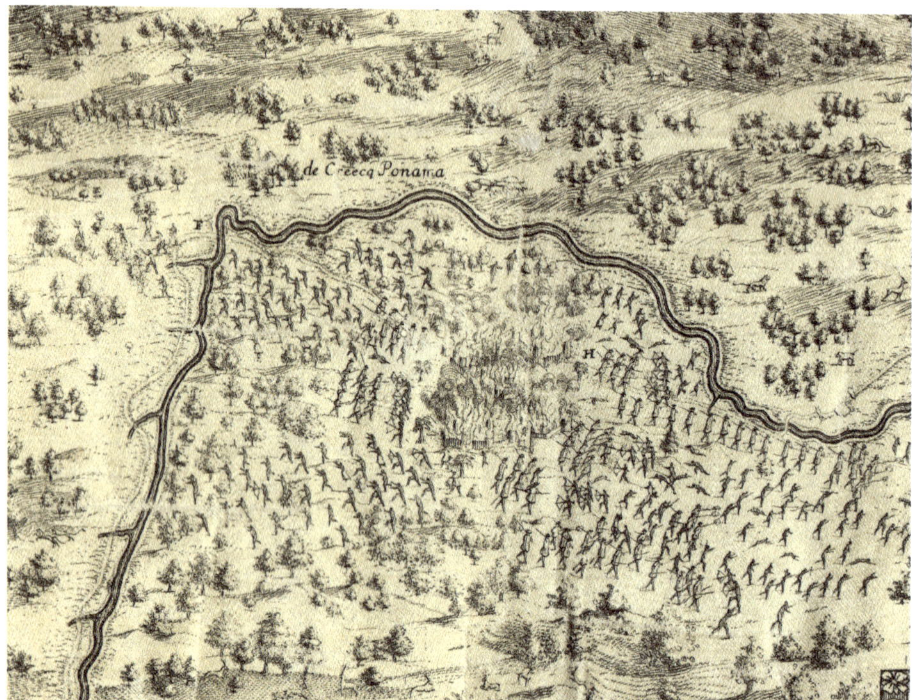

fig. 2a **Detail of the map: Maroons forced to defend or flee their villages**

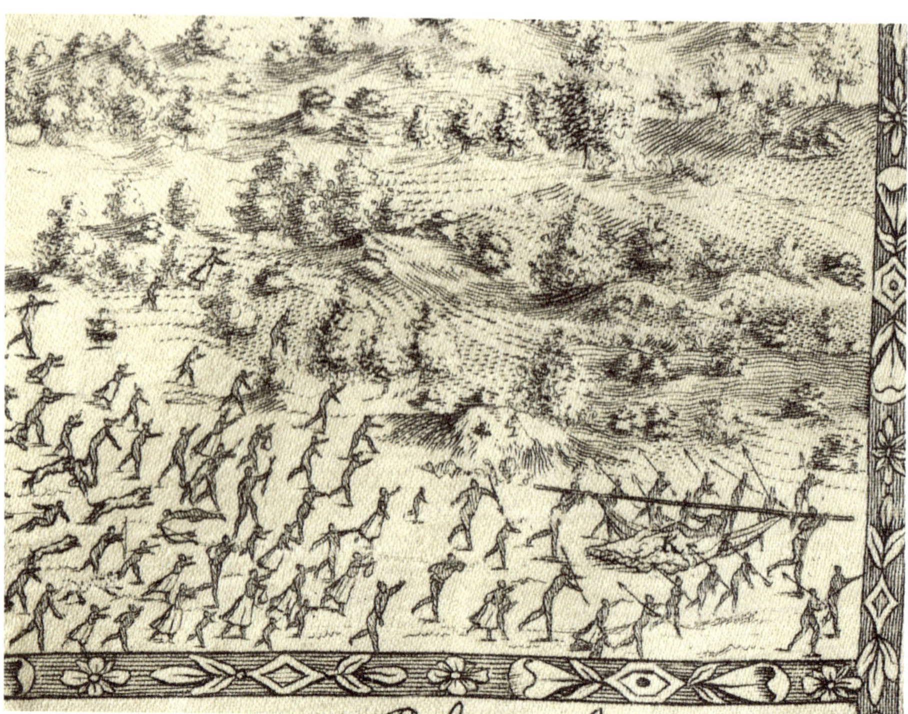

fig. 2b **Detail of the map: Fleeing women, identifiable by their wraps; two of them are taking goods with them**

the command of the governor of Suriname in 1730 and 1731. Alexander de Lavaux, the maker of this map, took part in two of these.

De Lavaux was an officer but also a land surveyor. Thus he not only held a military function in Suriname but also recorded what he observed. He began this documentation of his own volition; later, he produced maps commissioned by governor Jacob de Cheusses and the Society's board of directors.[11] The result is thus not simply a schematic rendering of the geography of the country; it is also a representation of the struggle De Lavaux took part in as a military man. On the map, he indicates the locations of 'villages of runaway rebel slaves'. He drew the army taking action against these 'runaways' and depicted how the villages they had built were set on fire. This shows the people defending their homes but sometimes having to run for their lives as well, leaving behind what they had built (fig. 2a).

This is not simply a generalized depiction of the struggle; De Lavaux indicates specific events and names. In the legend under 'F' and 'G', for example, he drew the discovery of the 'villages of Claas' and 'the flight of Claas with most of his Negroes'. The villages in that area were referred to as 'Claas and Pedro Villages' as early as 1717, presumably named after known individuals within these groups. This area, between the Suriname and Saramacca rivers, is where the Saramaccans later settled.[12] Women can also be seen among the fleeing figures, identifiable by their wraps (fig. 2b). Might Ma Pansa have been among them? Might De Lavaux have seen her? Two of these women definitely hold something in their hands that looks like a knapsack. In the event of an attack, it was the responsibility of the women to secure the harvest and food supplies.[13] It seems not unlikely that cloths were used as knapsacks for this purpose. But De Lavaux probably had no idea that women also used their hair as a hiding place.

What is certain is that the colonial authorities were aware of the fact that rice was taken by people who escaped the system. The rice increased the Maroons' chances of survival and as such threatened the continuation of the plantation economy. Maroonage, the existence of settlements of people who had freed themselves from slavery, was a constant threat to the slavery system in Suriname, including when the Dutch conquered the country from the British in 1667. Each year, 200 to 300 people escaped the repressive system. By 1679, about 700 to 800 such people lived in freedom, while the colonial army never exceeded 1,000 to 1,200 men.[14] The strategic importance of destroying the Maroons' food supply is also confirmed by other visual sources. This is shown on a map drawn by another military man, John Gabriël Stedman, at the end of the eighteenth century (fig. 3). The map shows villages of the native inhabitants of Suriname as well as Maroon villages. In the northeast of the country, two sites are labelled 'destroyed abode of the mutineers'. Nearby is a 'field sown with rice' (fig. 3a). This is where the Boni lived, one of the Maroon groups who never made peace with the colonial regime. Even after the peace treaties concluded by the regime with the Ndyuka, among others, in 1760, they continued to resist.

Neither map shows the area where Sapali lived. On De Lavaux's map, this part of the country is hidden from view by a text box containing the legend, consisting largely of the list of plantation names. The fact that the colonial

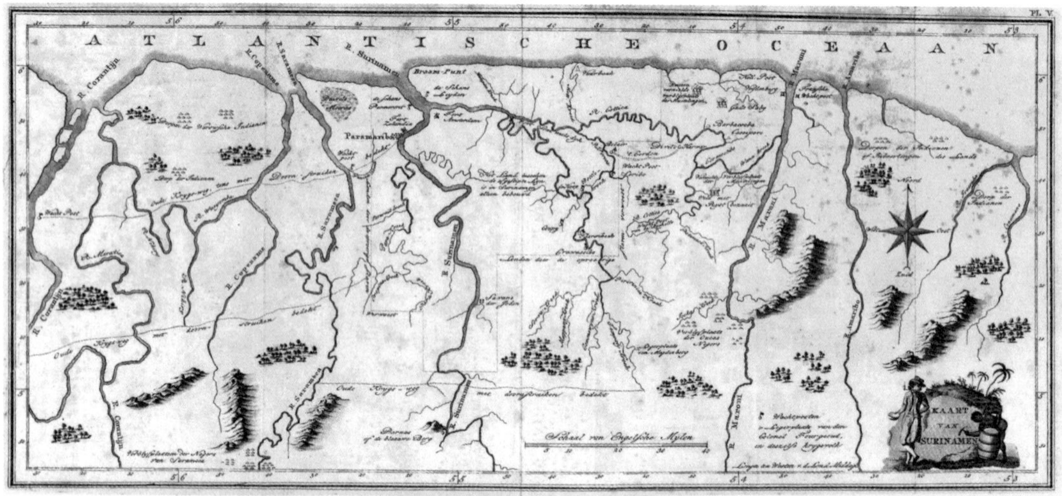

fig. 3 **Map of Suriname, John Gabriël Stedman, 1799**

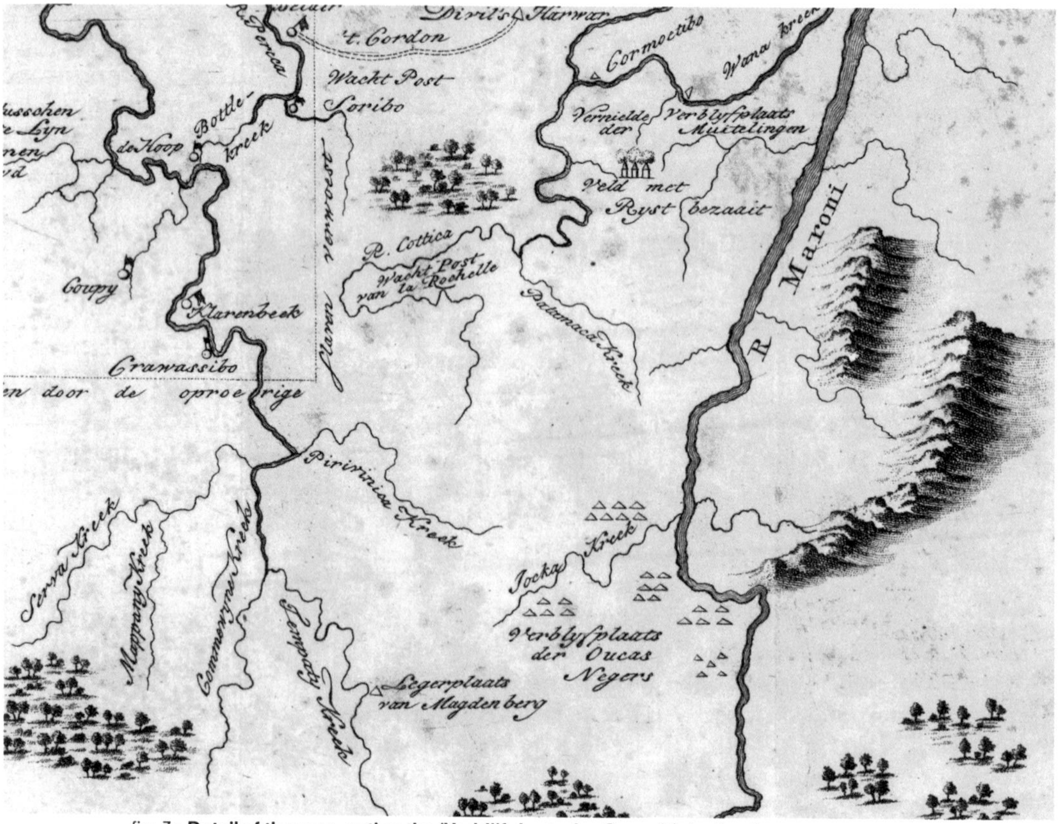

fig. 3a **Detail of the map, noting the 'Verblijfplaats der Oucas' (abode of the Okanisi), 'Veld met Rijst bezaait' (field sown with rice) and 'Vernielde Verblijfplaats der Muitelingen' (destroyed abode of mutineers)**

administration blocks our view of the story of this woman in this way can almost be deemed symbolic. Yet it is surprising that an object like a colonial map has a connection with a perspective that has long been neglected in the history museums of the Netherlands.

One object that brings us a step closer to Sapali and the way she concealed rice in her hair is a comb from the collection of the Zeeuws Museum in Middelburg (fig. 4). In 1817, five 'ethnological objects' were donated to the Royal Zeeland Society of Sciences, including this comb. The object was described as having been made by 'Bokanese', a pejorative generalization referring to the Buginese, or Bugis, of South Sulawesi.[15] The donor was judge A.F. Lammens, a man from the province of Zeeland who lived in Suriname for a while, and therefore the comb could originate from that country. Anthropologist Thomas Polimé has studied the object and declared it quite probable that it was made by Maroons. In addition, he indicated that it must date from a time in which the maker did not have access to the improved instruments that would later produce finer combs. Helen Ajentoena's grandfather has also confirmed that the technique was consistent with that used by Maroons, which differs from the technique used by descendants of enslaved people. The making of combs, according to Ajentoena, is a social activity among Maroons. While family members gather and converse, their hands perform the chores that take up time, such as pressing oil from seeds. A comb is a labour-intensive project, the shaping of each of its long teeth requiring a great deal of time, patience and technique.

The most important legacy that Ma Sapa left her descendants was life and time: the ability to feed, physically and spiritually, with rice representing an inexhaustible source of life. This legacy can be symbolically represented by historical rice spoons in the collection of the Nationaal Museum van Wereldculturen (fig. 5). These are calabash (bottle gourd) spoons, or *soepoeng kaabasi* in the Okanisi language. These specific spoons were decorated by women. This can be seen in the decorations present on the inside of the spoons: decorations here are always made by women, using shards of glass. Men decorate the outsides, using different tools. These spoons date from the late nineteenth century; they were probably made shortly after the abolition of slavery. The smaller rice spoons are used to consume the meal, the mid-sized ones to prepare it, and the largest to prepare large, communal repasts, such as for festive occasions. In this way, Ma Sapa's care for others lives on in her descendants' shared meals.

a society alongside colonial society

It would take a very arduous journey, however, before these spoons could be used to celebrate life in the nineteenth century. The Maroons had to struggle long and hard to be able to create their own settlements alongside those of the colonists. Colonial authorities fought and threatened the autonomy of the Maroons throughout virtually the entire colonial period. As noted earlier, the colonial army did not have much superiority in terms of numbers. The greatest danger lay in the soldiers' weapons. This is shown in depictions from the late

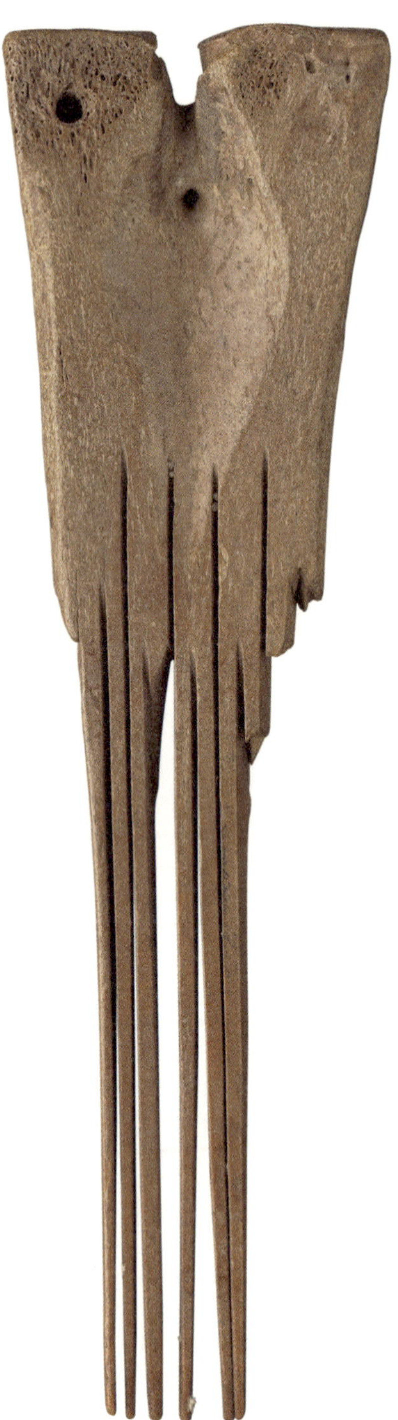

fig. 4 **Bone comb, probably made by Maroons in Suriname, before 1817**

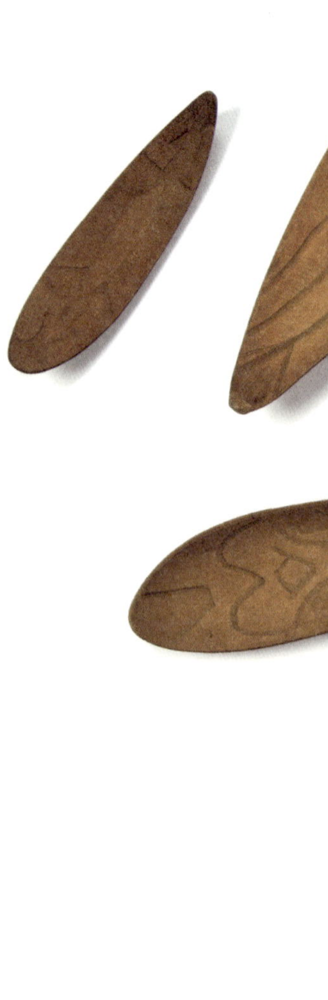

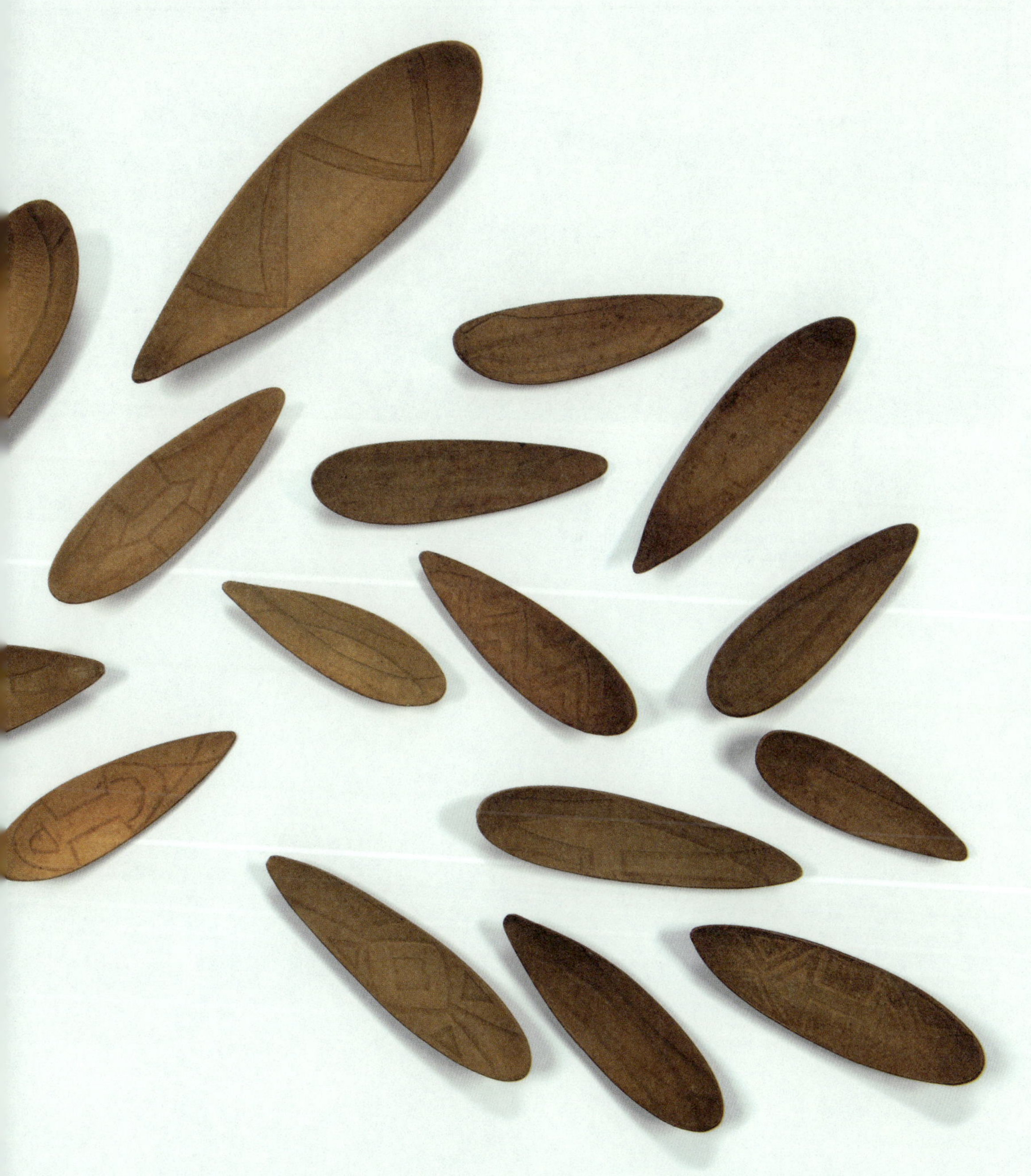

fig. 5 **Calabash rice spoons fashioned by Okanisi women, before 1883**

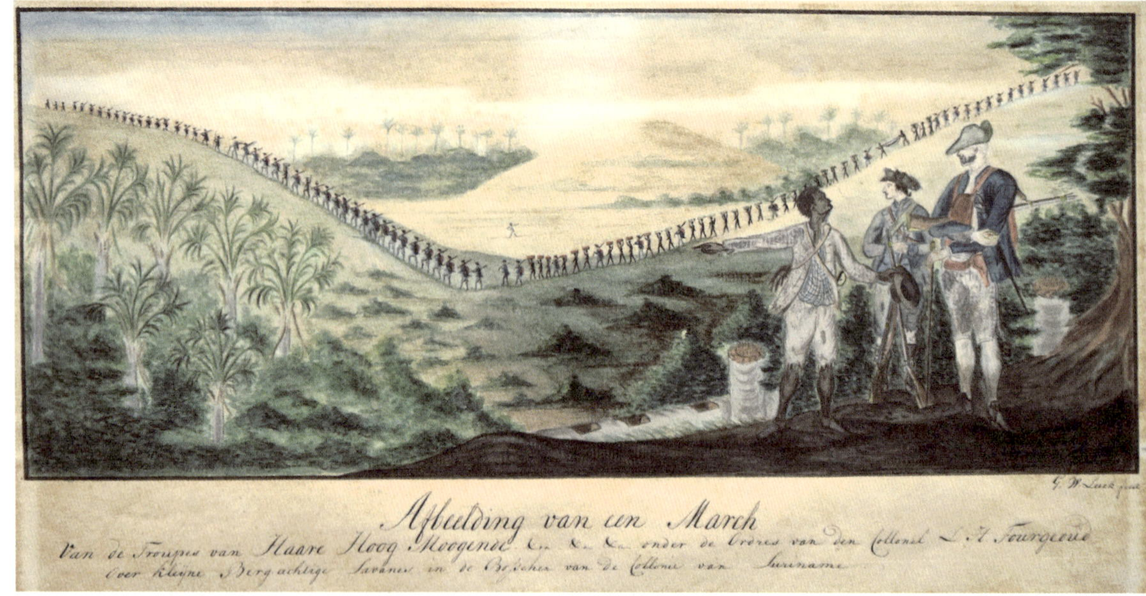

fig. 6 **Heavily armed colonial troops on the hunt for Maroons, G.W. Luck, c. 1773–1777**

eighteenth century, by which time the struggle against the Maroons had already been waged for a hundred years. Beginning in 1770, colonel L.H. Fourgeoud led an expedition against a group led by Boni. His troops included John Gabriël Stedman, who later wrote a book about Fourgeoud's exploits. The illustrations from this book, including that of a punished man hanged from a hook through his ribs, and a Maroon with a rifle, have been displayed in many exhibitions.

Less commonly shown is the work of G.W. Luck, which includes a landscape with a horizon lined with armed soldiers (fig. 6). This watercolour depicts the harsh reality experienced by people forced into slavery, as well as by those who tried to escape it. People in slavery were promised freedom if they took part in expeditions against the Maroons. The choice between the interests of others and one's own must have been a diabolical dilemma for people who were unable or did not dare to flee. It must also have been difficult for the Maroons to see former comrades collaborating with the oppressor. This was a guerrilla war that lasted centuries, in which complex choices had to be made between principled convictions and pragmatic considerations.

The relationship between European oppressors and the people they tried to keep enslaved was often paradoxical as well. A second watercolour by Luck, entitled *Afbeelding van een Camp* (Depiction of a camp) (fig. 7), again shows the importance of knowledge brought from Africa by enslaved people. It depicts how Africans had to provide the troops with food and ensure their health. One fascinating aspect is the snake under a soldier's hammock. The reptile was probably placed there because it was thought to have a protective and healing effect.[16] This demonstrates a faith in African knowledge, diametrically opposed to the work of European scholars who tried to prove that Africans were less evolved human beings.[17]

The knowledge of crops brought by people from Africa was recognized quite early as indispensable to survival in Suriname, in terms of food supply as well as medicinal applications. One powerful example is the *Hermann Herbarium*, which dates from 1687. This substantial book contains 50 dried plant samples from Suriname. Two of them originate from Africa: sesame and okra (fig. 8). These must have been brought across the Atlantic Ocean on board slave ships. Perhaps okra and sesame were taken along as provisions, and the captive Africans then smuggled the seeds onto land once in Suriname, where they grew these crops on their small farming plots for their own consumption. The specimens in the book were a gift for a fellow botanist and were probably collected by Hendrik Meyer; Paul Hermann himself never set foot in Suriname. This compilation – the oldest surviving collection of plants from Suriname – shows the great interest and care that went into conveying information of this kind.

The complexity of the relationship between Maroons and the colonial authorities is also reflected in the written correspondence between the government in Paramaribo and Ndyuka leader Boston Band, better known by his descendants as Adyáko Benti Basiton. Boston Band was brought in slavery from Jamaica to Suriname. He was multilingual and could read and write in English. That latter detail is remarkable, as people in slavery generally were not allowed to read or write. Band managed to escape slavery and, with others, led a major uprising in 1757. Through pamphlets, he let it be known that he

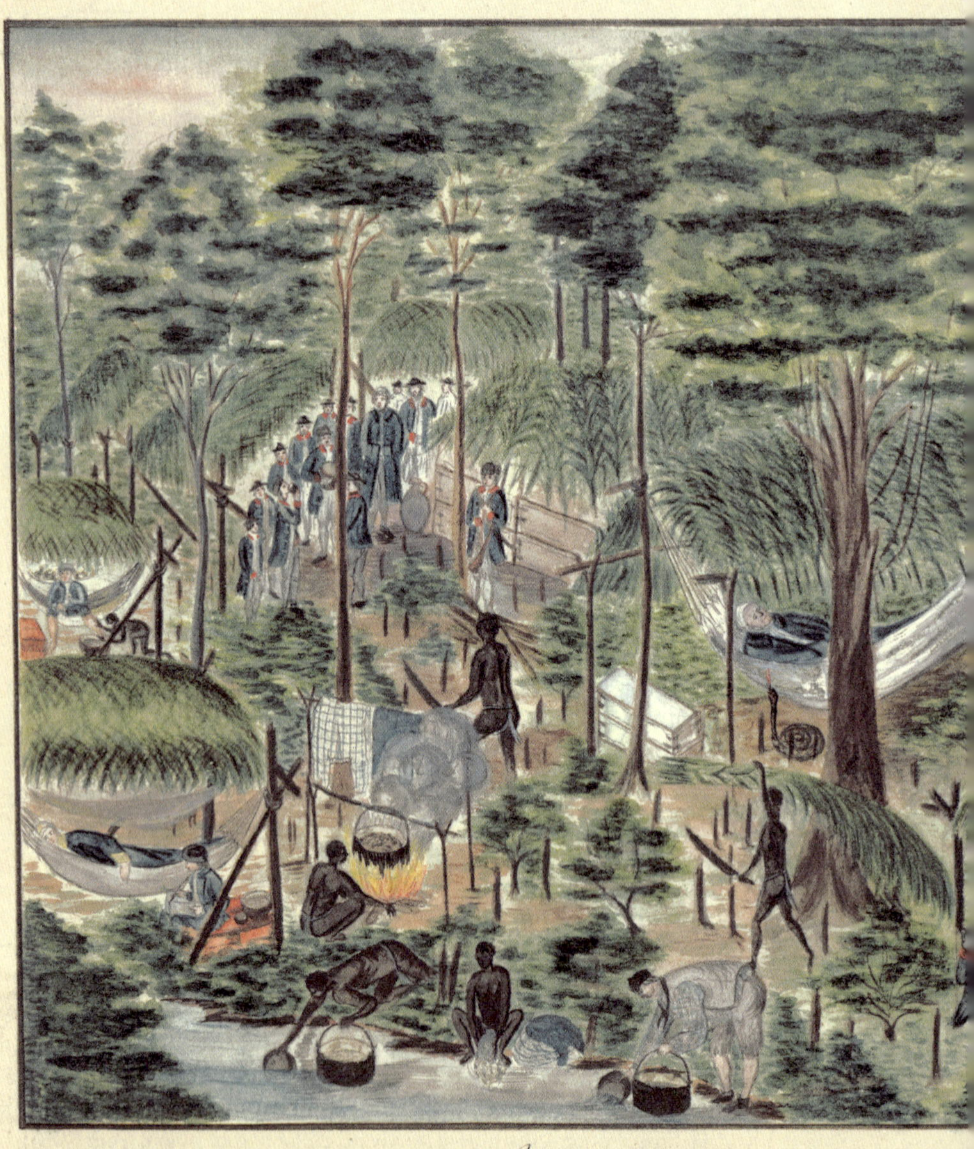

fig. 7 **Colonial military camp, G.W. Luck, 1773–1777. The snake under the hammock is probably there for the protective and healing effect it was thought to possess**

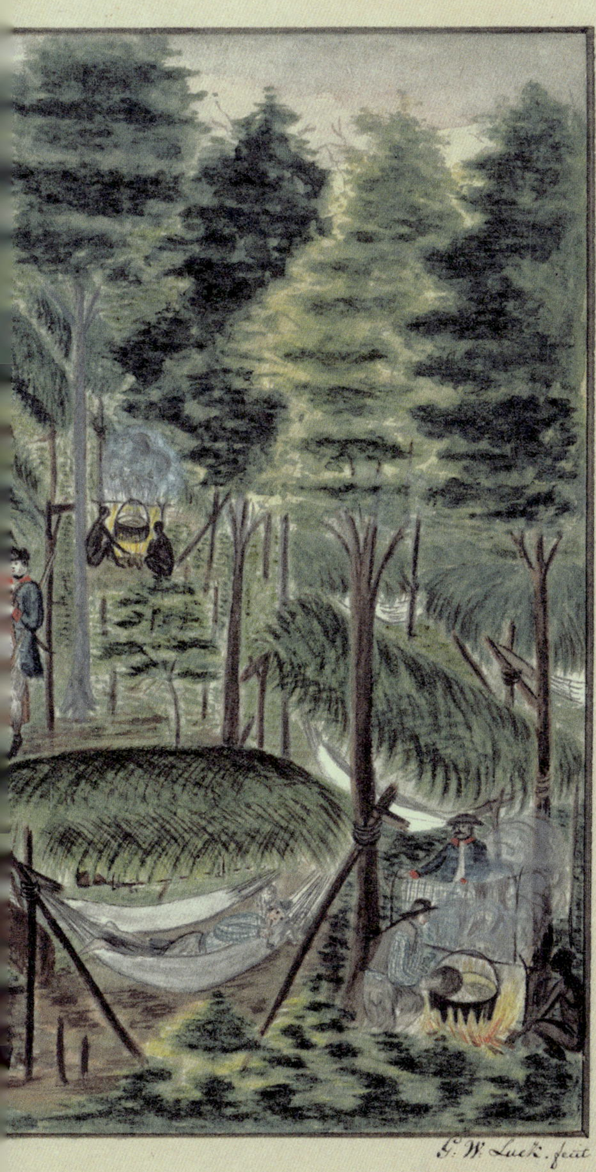
G. W. Luck. fecit
Hoog Moogende &a &a &a.
de Bosschen van de Colonie

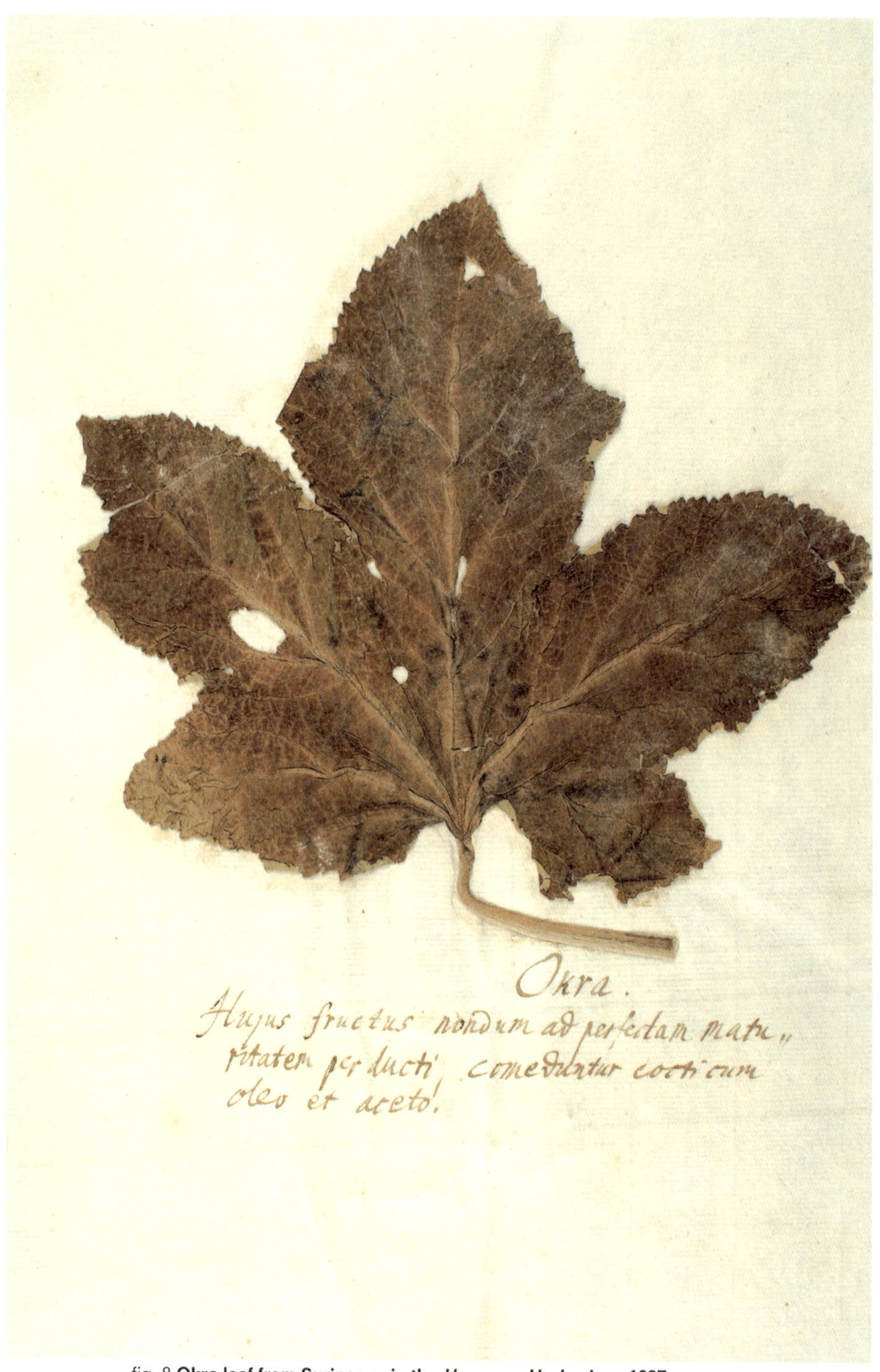

fig. 8 **Okra leaf from Suriname, in the *Hermann Herbarium*, 1687**

would cease the resistance only when his community was recognized as a free nation. At that moment, there were 3,000 to 4,000 Maroons in Suriname.[18] The colonial authorities felt they had no choice but to agree to the autonomy of Boston Band's group, and on 10 October 1760 a peace accord was signed (fig. 11). This treaty was preceded by years of written negotiations between Boston Band and governor Wigbold Crommelin. The correspondence was continued after 1760 because the colonial authorities had insisted on being able to set demands on how the peace was implemented. The Society of Suriname wanted to prevent more people from joining the free Maroons and thereby undermining the plantation system.

A letter from Boston Band dated 5 August 1761 shows how diplomacy and coercion went hand in hand (fig. 9). The letter is a reply to an official mandate to hunt down people who have recently escaped from plantations. Band replies that these people have already been captured by others and he is therefore able to evade the order. He then pleads for the people from his village who are being held by the governor in Paramaribo to be returned. Clearly, the colonial government did not shy away from threatening to use violence and even held people hostage.[19] In a subsequent letter, on 29 December 1761, the governor writes: 'We can ascribe these desertions to nothing other than your people ... running away as well in hopes of not being turned in again' (fig. 10).[20] This shows that even after the peace accord the Maroons were under constant threat. The colonial authorities did not see the slavery system as the reason people fled, blaming it instead on 'the bad example' given by the Maroons, purely and simply by living in freedom. (Incidentally, the letter pictured is a Dutch translation made for its recipients, the colonial authorities, who were not always conversant in English, the language in which Boston Band wrote. Band's original letters, unfortunately, have not survived.)

bringing together sources and perspectives

Until now, the history of the Maroons has often been represented in Dutch museums as that of a community located in Suriname. To many Dutch people, this was a history that had little to do with them. Can objects from the collection of the national museum of the Netherlands be relevant to Maroons? Susi and Simba Mosis are the first Maroon women to have entered the Rijksmuseum's archive to view and reflect on De Lavaux's map. This produced new insights into this centuries-old collection piece. The women said they were deeply affected to see that the struggle about which they had learned mainly through traditional stories, passed down from generation to generation, had also been turned into a printed depiction at the time. The map makes the history visible, palpable – it even has a smell. But what struck them above all was the contrast in the meaning of the object to different groups. What was made for the Society of Suriname as a showpiece is intensely confrontational for a descendant of the oppressed group. 'This map shows what we had to endure, how we had to try to survive. Our ancestors were freedom fighters. Their struggle made us who we are; it shapes our identity.'

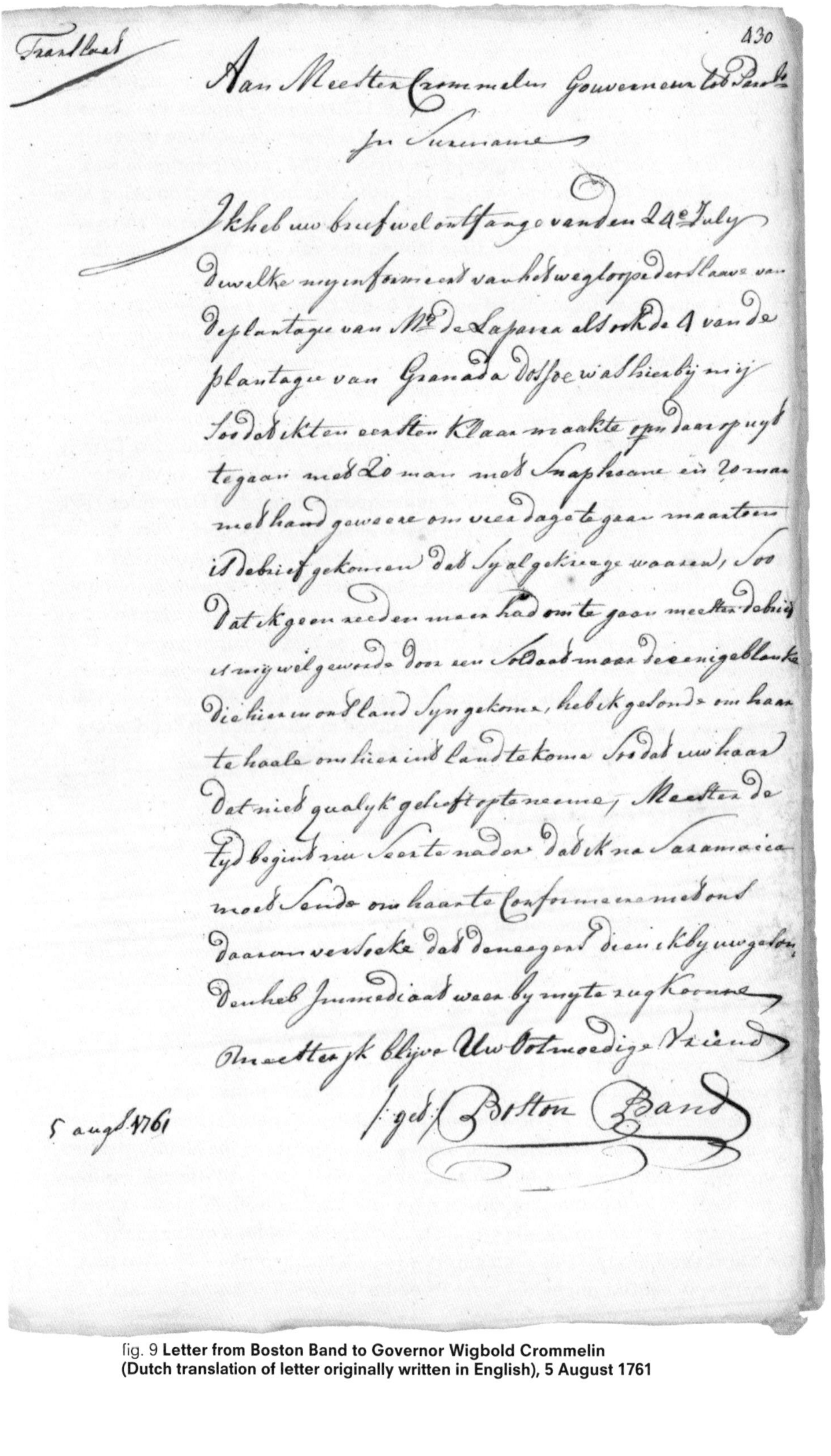

Translaat

Aan Meester Crommelin Gouverneur tot Par.bo
In Suriname

Ik heb uw brief wel ontfange van den 24e July
dewelke mij informeert van het wegloopen der slaave van
de plantagie van Mr. de Lapara als ook de 4 van de
plantagie van Granada dos hoe wal hierbij mij
soo dat ik ten eersten klaar maakte om daar op uyt
te gaan met 20 man met snaphaane en 20 man
met handgeweere om vier dage te gaan maar toen
is de brief gekomen dat sy al gekreege waaren, soo
dat ik geen reeden meer had om te gaan meester de brief
is mij wel geworde door een soldaat maar de eenige blanke
die hier in ons land syn gekome, hebik gesonde om haar
te haale om hier in't land te koma soo dat uw haar
dat niet qualyk gelieft op te neeme, Meester de
tyd begint nu kort te naderen dat ik na Saramacca
moet sende om haar te conformeeren met ons
daarom versoeke dat de negers die ik by uw gesonden
heb immediaat weer by myte rug koome
Meester yk blijve Uw ootmoedige Vriend

/:get:/ Boston Band

5 aug.t 1761

fig. 9 **Letter from Boston Band to Governor Wigbold Crommelin (Dutch translation of letter originally written in English), 5 August 1761**

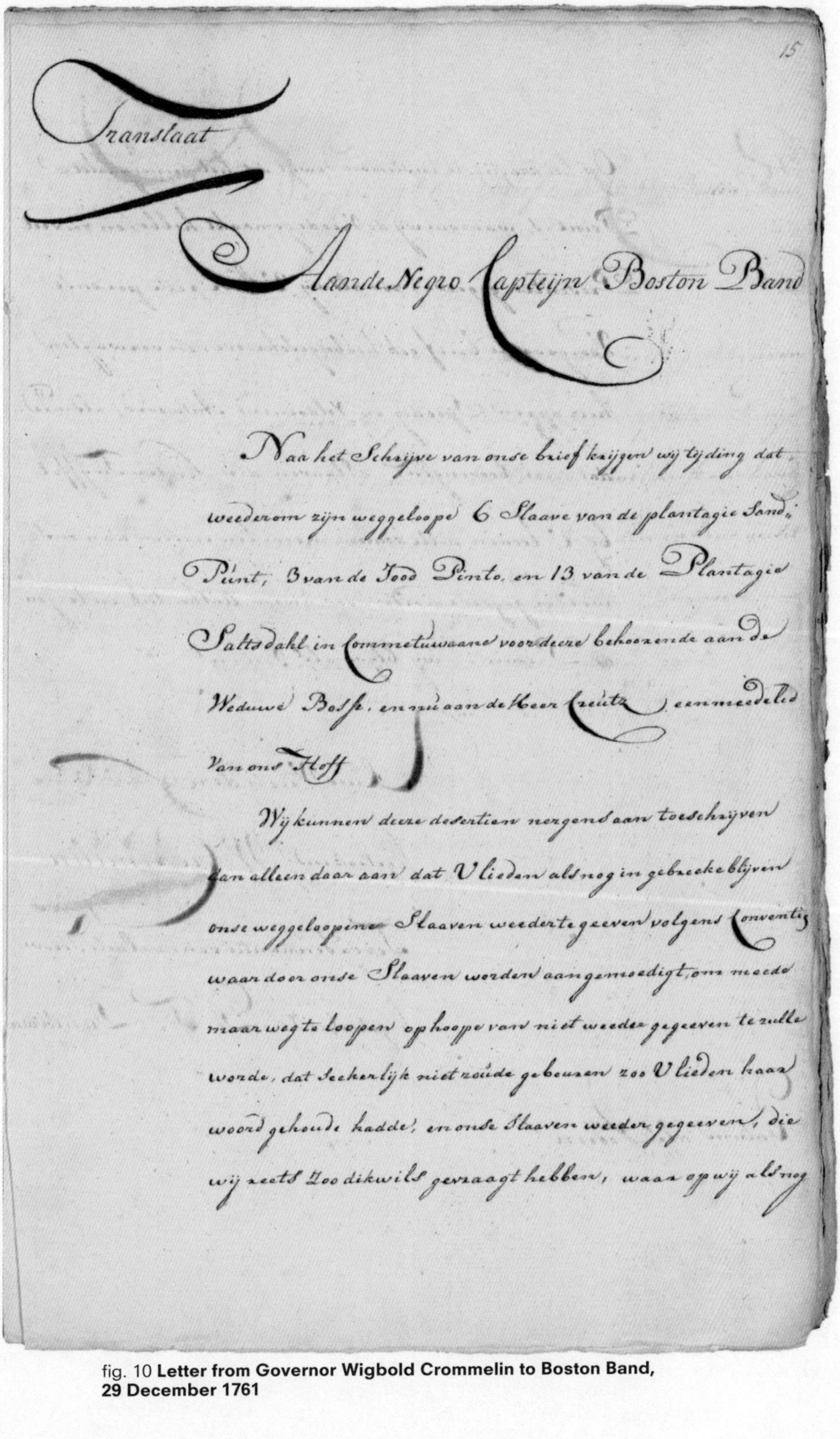

15

Translaat

Aan de Negro Capteijn Boston Band

Naa het Schrijve van onse brief krijgen wij tijding dat weederom zijn weggeloope 6 Slaave van de plantagie Sand„ Punt, 3 van de Jood Pinto, en 13 van de Plantagie Saltsdahl in Commetuwaane voor deeze behoorende aan de Weduwe Bosse, en nu aan de Heer Creutz een meedelid van ons Hoff

Wij kunnen deeze desertien nergens aan toeschrijven dan alleen daar aan dat U lieden als nog in gebreeke blijven onse weggeloopene Slaaven weeder te geeven volgens Conventie waar door onse Slaaven worden aangemoedigt, om meede maar weg te loopen op hoope van niet weeder gegeeven te zulle worde, dat Seekerlijk niet zoude gebeuren zoo U lieden haar woord gehoude hadde, en onse Slaaven weeder gegeeven, die wij reets Zoo dikwils gevraagt hebben, waar op wij als nog

fig. 10 **Letter from Governor Wigbold Crommelin to Boston Band, 29 December 1761**

fig. 11 **Peace treaty signed between the Society of Suriname and the Okanisi, 10 October 1760**

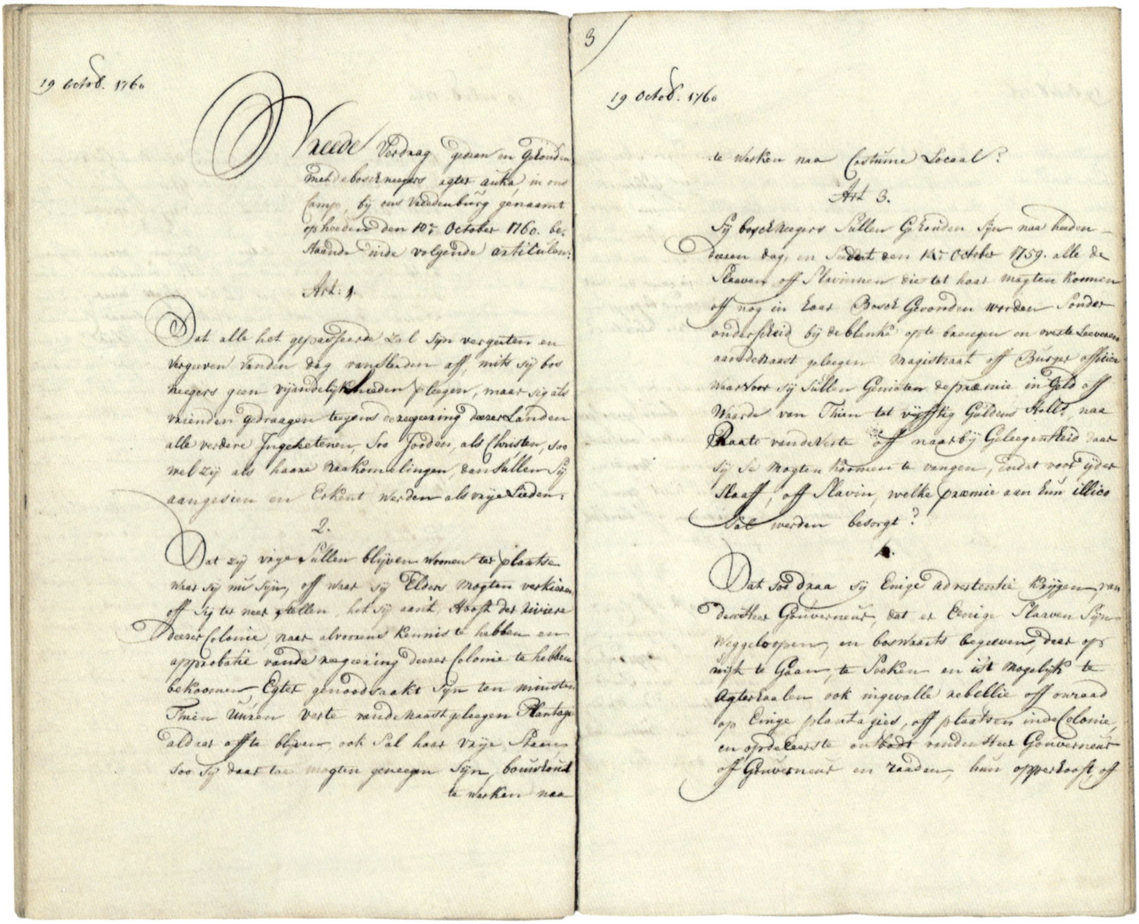

So a period that, to the Maroons, is primarily about a heroic struggle against injustice was documented by and for the people whose economic interests lay in the maintenance of oppression. For the museum, this is an important lesson in sensitivity regarding its own collection and how it relates to various groups in society. It is a new insight that contributes to awareness about the collection's layered nature; objects that were long seen as the legacy of colonial power can no longer be seen separately from the perspective of those who saw this power as illegitimate and who defended themselves against it. By combining museum objects and written sources with immaterial heritage, we arrive at a new historiography, in which divergent guiding threads from our colonial history are braided together. The result is a braid with a broader relevance that situates us on the way to building a new narrative about the Netherlands and its inhabitants today.

valika smeulders

tula

liberty, equality and fraternity

People in slavery resisted in many ways, for instance by escaping the plantation economy or by sabotaging it. There were also enslaved people who sought the solution in transforming the colonial system from the inside out. In the eighteenth century, a spirit of change was sweeping across Europe: people demanded greater equality between the classes and began to liberate themselves from the yoke of despotic leaders. In the Caribbean, the French island of Saint-Domingue (present-day Haiti) was the first place where local freedom fighters, following the French Revolution, declared the country independent as well as free of slavery. This was the example that Tula, a man forced to work on a plantation in Curaçao, wanted to follow in 1795. That year, the Netherlands fell under French rule, as the Batavian Republic. Tula reasoned that French law therefore applied to Dutch colonies like Curaçao, and that those who were enslaved were thus legally free. Tula's resistance and that of his 2,000 fellow fighters did not result in the end of the slavery system. The hope they cherished for a society in which everyone would ultimately be equal can be found in written sources, which show a substantial awareness of the reach of the colonial world, its political dynamics and the religious and philosophical voices within it. In addition, oral sources provide a glimpse of how injustice was experienced at this time. These sources attest to the preservation of human dignity and pride among those who were enslaved. Songs about liberty and equality would be sung long into the twentieth century. How did those who were not free conceive of freedom?

the 1795 uprising

Curaçao is a small island with a large natural harbour off what was then the coast of Spanish South America. In the colonial period, it was the ideal location for Dutch trade with the Americas – trade both in goods and in human beings. No large-scale plantations were established there; the enslaved people who worked on the island mainly had functions serving the local elite, in their houses, their gardens and around the harbour. There was a high rate of manumission – enslaved people obtaining their freedom in exchange for money. There were economic reasons for this: in times of drought and food shortage, slaveholders were keen to be relieved of providing for the people they regarded as their property. As a result, Curaçao had relatively large numbers of free inhabitants of colour in the eighteenth century. Colonial rulers would often complain of how 'insolent' such people were.[1]

Among enslaved people in Curaçao, uprisings had already been organized in 1716, 1750 and 1774, each followed by harsh reprisals.[2] Some of the insurgents were banished and sold to Saint-Domingue, where they spread information about the resistance on Curaçao.[3] And during the revolution on Saint-Domingue in 1793, many plantation owners fled to Curaçao, taking their enslaved labourers with them. The latter in turn shared the news of the freedom won on Saint-Domingue with enslaved people on Curaçao.[4] Ships' crews also supplied the Caribbean with news about the resistance to slavery and the political situation in other parts of the word. Both enslaved and free people of colour worked on the ships. And then there were escapees: between 1759 and

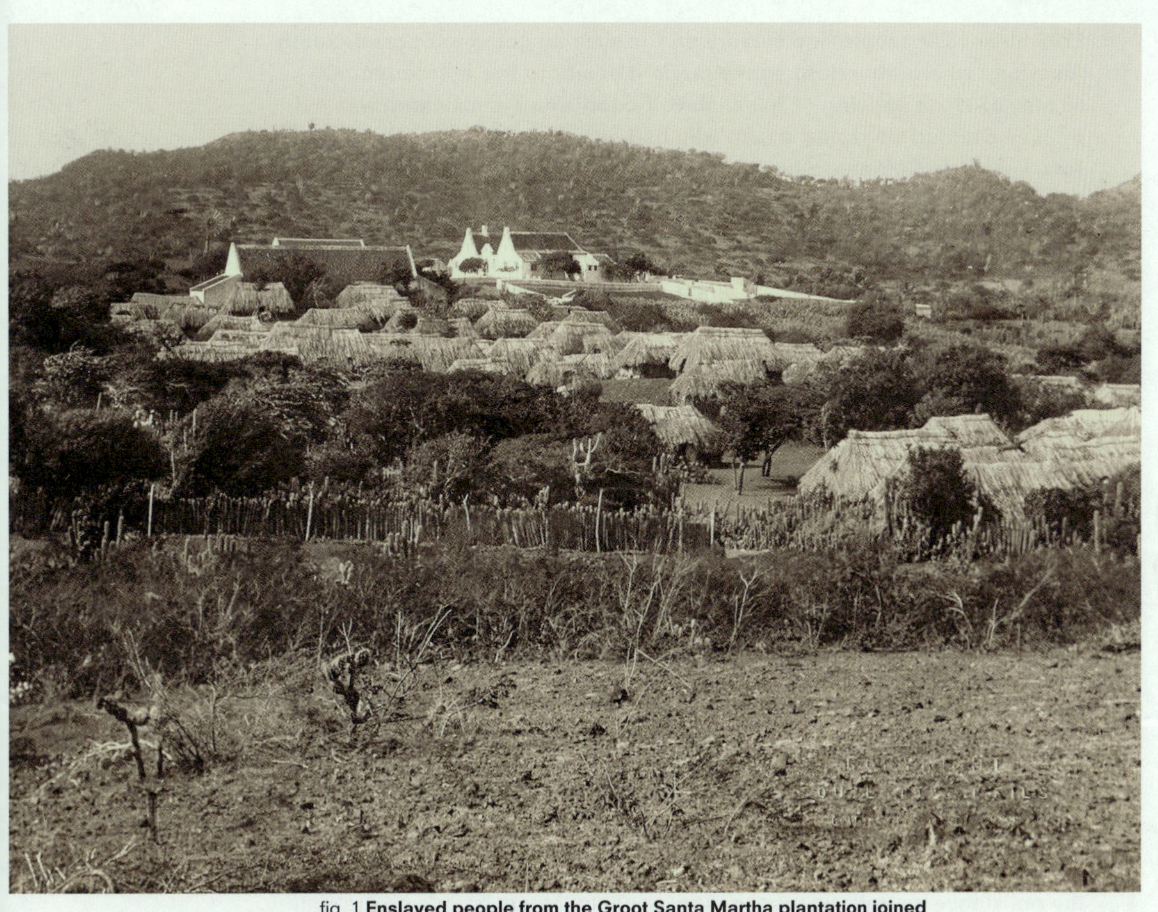

fig. 1 **Enslaved people from the Groot Santa Martha plantation joined the resistance in 1795. Detail of a photograph from c. 1890–1920**

1766 alone, 380 people fled slavery on Curaçao by going to Spanish South America,[5] where abundant space made it easier to live in freedom. On 10 May 1795, an uprising of 300 enslaved people on the mainland was led by José Caridad González, a man who had escaped slavery on Curaçao, and José Leonardo Chirinos, a black man with papers attesting to his freed status. When this uprising failed, a number of the insurgents fled to Curaçao.[6] Early that year the Netherlands had become part of France, as the Batavian Republic. The colonial elite, like the Dutch populace, was split between conservative Orangists who supported the stadtholder William V, who had fled to England, and pro-French patriots who championed liberty, equality and fraternity, the principles of the French Revolution. While the latter were not of one mind about the position that free people of colour should occupy in society, some had progressive ideas about the abolition of slavery.[7]

It is in this context of resistance and solidarity among individuals from different groups, free and enslaved, local and international, Black, brown and white, that Tula, on 17 August 1795, took the initiative to stop work on the Knip plantation on Curaçao.[8] He argued that, given the situation in the Netherlands and on Saint-Domingue, slavery was over on Curaçao as well. The landowner and slave holder, Casper van Uytrecht, refused to accept this reasoning, so Tula and his comrades decided to present their argument to the government of Curaçao. In the days that followed, they marched from plantation to plantation towards the city of Willemstad. More people joined at every plantation, until 2,000 people were participating in total – 15 per cent of all the enslaved people on the island (fig. 1). The insurgency lasted five weeks.

During those weeks, multiple confrontations took place with well-armed colonial soldiers. The insurgents were short of food and provisions. The government promised generous rewards for the tip that would lead to the arrest of the resistance leaders: 25 *johannesen*, equal to the governor's annual salary. Under these circumstances, Tula was ultimately betrayed by those close to him.[9] After being paraded on horseback, 'on display', he was put on trial.[10] Along with the other leaders of the uprising, including Bastiaan Carpatta, Louis Mercier and Pedro Waccaaw, he was sentenced to horrifying torture and death. Tula was stretched on the rack, his face was scorched, and his head chopped off with an axe and displayed on a pike.[11] The prosecutor noted that these punishments had already been abolished in the Netherlands and 'other civilized countries' but that he would impose them nonetheless. Afraid of the threat to the status quo, the colonial elite was keen to set a deterrent example.[12]

tula's thoughts on liberty

Archival documents are vital sources for the stories of people in slavery. Often, these documents, produced by people who were part of the colonial system, had an administrative or legal function. As a result, people in slavery appear in them only as 'property', as people without opinions of their own, or as transgressors or disruptors of 'order'. In order to get closer to the experience of the human being in slavery, it is important to read the archival documents critically, against the colonial grain. In Tula's case, fortunately, we have more than just the documents from his trial. During the insurgency, a garrison captain wrote down his reflections on the uprising, and there were negotiations with a priest. Via these reports, we have access to accounts from two different perspectives. Captain Baron van Westerholt describes what was in his eyes the hostile attitude of the 'rioters'. But the account by Father Jacobus Schinck shows that he found it difficult to reconcile his world view, in which slavery was justified, with the way in which Tula and his fellow fighters received him and spoke to him. Deeply upset, he asked to be allowed to leave the island in order to 'find my peace of mind again'.[13]

Father Schinck's meeting with Tula took place on 19 August, two days after the uprising began. On this day, Tula, with his 1,200 comrades, had won a first confrontation with colonial soldiers and they were spending the night at the Porto Marie plantation. The Franciscan priest had been dispatched there to persuade him to surrender. To the insurgents, especially given that successful first day, this was not a logical proposition. The people present with Tula for the conversation became agitated, and one of them said in French: 'the priest has come here to change our minds.'[14] Yet the group remained friendly; one of them gave the priest his entire supply of snuff tobacco. Tula then patiently explained their point of view, presented the priest with rational arguments and alluded to the political situation and the changes in authority and legislation in Europe and on Saint-Domingue:

> We have been too badly mistreated; we seek to hurt no one, but seek our liberty; the French Negroes have won their freedom; Holland has been taken over by the French, therefore we must be free here too.[15] (fig. 2)

Schinck did not respond to Tula's arguments about the Batavian Republic and said that the resistance fighters would not be able to survive as Maroons. As such he made it clear that the colonial authorities had no plans to abolish slavery or accept that Tula and his comrades could secede from colonial society. Whereupon Tula presented weightier moral arguments and managed to appeal to Schinck precisely in his area of expertise:

> Father, do not all people descend from a father Adam and Eve? ... Have I done wrong by freeing 22 of my brothers from the shackles in which they were unjustly placed? ... Father, the liberty of the French has been used to torment us: when one of us was punished, 'you're after your freedom too?' was flung at him. I was once bound, I cried out incessantly for mercy for a poor slave, until, when the bonds were undone, the blood flowed from my mouth, I fell to my knees and called out to God: 'O Divine Majesty! O Pure Spirit! Is it Your will that we be mistreated like this!' Ah, Father, a beast is more cared for, when a beast breaks a leg it receives treatment.[16] (fig. 3)

Tula thus spoke of the constant, structural calls for freedom among the enslaved people, and the violent repression of these. There is a perceptible ambivalence regarding the 'liberty of the French' to which Tula alludes, and the evolution of the Enlightenment in the eighteenth century. The Declaration of the Rights of Man and the Citizen had been drawn up in France in 1789. This was based on the ideas of philosophers John Locke and Jean-Jacques Rousseau, on natural law and tolerance and on the equality of all people, respectively, as well as Montesquieu's legislative elaboration of these. While this declaration can be read as a universal declaration of human rights, exceptions were made. Active citizenship was the prerogative of a small group, defined as the group that contributed financially to society. This led to bloody protest, in France mainly carried out by the reform-minded Jacobins, led by Robespierre. This violent reaction was an alarming spectre for many.[17]

Father Schinck was given food at the Porto Marie estate on Tula's orders, as well as a room for the night, where there was even a Bible at his bedside, but he remained gripped by fear. He wrote:

> [I] hear them from my room singing the current French songs, but very softly so as not to disturb my sleep; but I must confess that I was overwhelmed by such fear and anguish that I thought I was in the hands of the bloodthirsty Robespierre, and the guillotine hovered roughly before my eyes.[18]

A more broadly shared citizenship, in Schinck's perception, as well as that of many others, could degenerate into terror, both among people in Europe and among people who had been held in slavery. In regard to this latter group, moreover, the thinking developed during the Enlightenment had created a 'hierarchy of civilization', the idea that enslaved African men and women could claim the same rights but were not yet ready for them. They were not yet sufficiently 'enlightened'.[19]

Tula, however, imagined a society without racial hierarchy. He knew what had happened on Saint-Domingue. The people there who had freed themselves from slavery were now the leaders of an independent country. The central role that Tula played earned him the nickname Rigaud, after general André Rigaud, at the time the most important leader of the revolution on Saint-Domingue. Van Westerholt's report mentions that Tula and his men claim to have received a letter from Rigaud:

> they stubbornly refused to surrender and demanded their freedom and equality with the Whites, basing this on a Letter from General Rigaud in which liberty was promised them and saying that Holland and France now being one, the Slaves here, like in the French Colonies, must be free.[20] (fig. 4)

Rigaud was the child of a mixed relationship and he led an army of people from various ethnicities; in his experience, Black, brown and white worked together.

To what degree was Tula prepared to use violence to realize his ideal? Schinck's account of his meeting with the resistance fighters does not indicate that he was ever threatened. On the contrary, he was received with utmost

fig. 2 **In his conversation with Father Schinck, Tula refers to the situation in the Netherlands and Saint-Domingue, report, 1795**

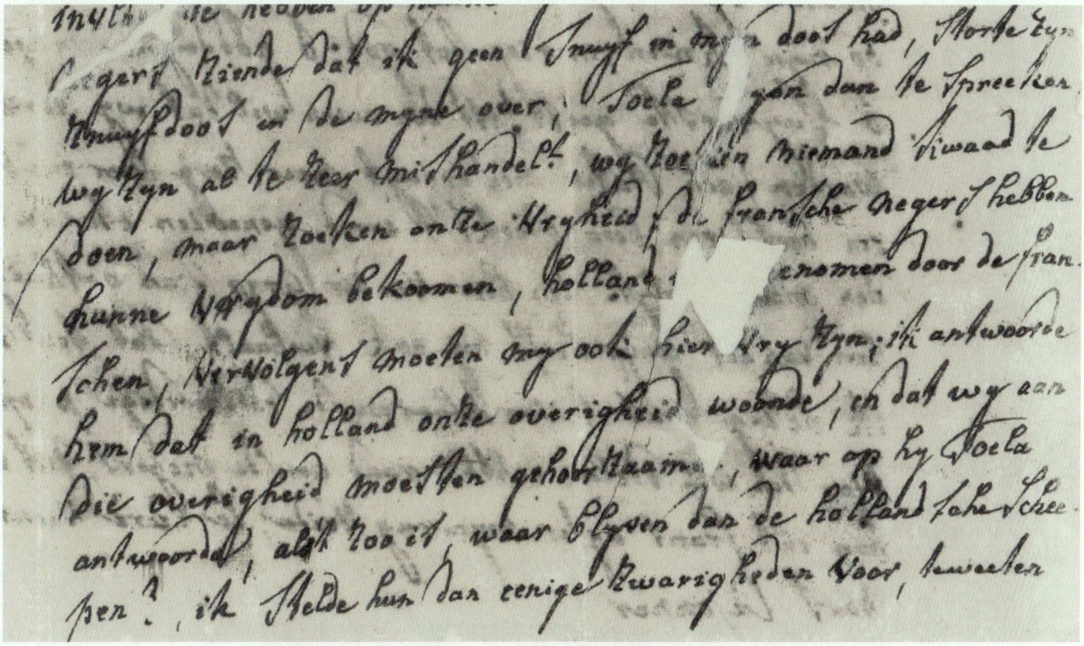

fig. 3 **Tula goes on to underpin his argument with moral considerations, report, 1795**

friendliness and even hospitality and returned to his companions the next morning unscathed. The fighters seem interested in negotiating and are disappointed when the priest showed so little openness to their verbal arguments. But the fighters were certainly not 'obedient sheep' either, as the priest wrote that he had expected.[21] Tula was a passionate orator and spoke fervently against injustice. Van Westerholt described him and his comrades as 'proud' and claimed that, after he indicated that there would be no mercy for them, they opened fire first. He wrote that after the confrontation that followed, the fighters let it be known that they were prepared to give up their lives: 'A certain TouSsaint, one of their officers, called out, among others, to the undersigned in French, *nous sommes ici pour vaincre ou mourir* [we are here to prevail or to die].'[22]

related heroes, portrayed heroes

The Toussaint mentioned by Van Westerholt was probably Louis Mercier; according to the documentation on the uprising, he was the property, like Tula, of the slaveholder Van Uytrecht of the Knip plantation.[23] Mercier too owed his nickname to a general on Saint-Domingue, Toussaint L'Ouverture. L'Ouverture was the grandson of a king from Dahomey (in present-day Benin) whose son had been taken into slavery and brought to the Caribbean. Once he obtained his freedom, L'Ouverture ran a coffee plantation. When the revolution broke out on the island, he initially proved reticent, and led a group of counter-revolutionaries. Only after the French revolutionaries also abolished slavery in 1793 did he join the side of the French Republic and the Jacobins, in 1794. In May 1795 he became the first Black French general, at the head of an army of Black soldiers. He later defeated Rigaud in a struggle for power on Saint-Domingue and took over his position as the most important leader; he proclaimed the island's first autonomous constitution. He was arrested under Napoleon's regime and deported to France, where he died in prison. During the bicentennial of the French Revolution in 1989, L'Ouverture was honoured with a plaque in the Panthéon in Paris.[24]

Toussaint and other revolutionaries and delegates of colour from the island in the Convention Nationale, the French parliament during the French Revolution, were immortalized in prints, etchings and paintings in the late eighteenth and early nineteenth centuries.[25] In this way, their likenesses were disseminated. In 1878, a small stipple engraving found its way into the collection of the Rijksmuseum (fig. 5). The description reads: 'Portrait bust of François-Dominique Toussaint L'Ouverture, French general and leader of the Haitian Revolution. He wears a uniform and a plumed hat.' The print was made by Govert Kitsen, a Rotterdam engraver, after a design by François Bonneville. This Frenchman published the original in 1802, as part of a four-volume collection of 200 *Portraits des personnages célèbres de la Révolution* (Portraits of famous people of the Revolution). The portrait was reused in various publications. As far as we know, the engraving is the only portrait of this French-Caribbean hero in a Dutch collection.

More portraits of Black heroes from the colonial period were preserved in France, however. One example is an engraving entitled *Toussaint Louverture,*

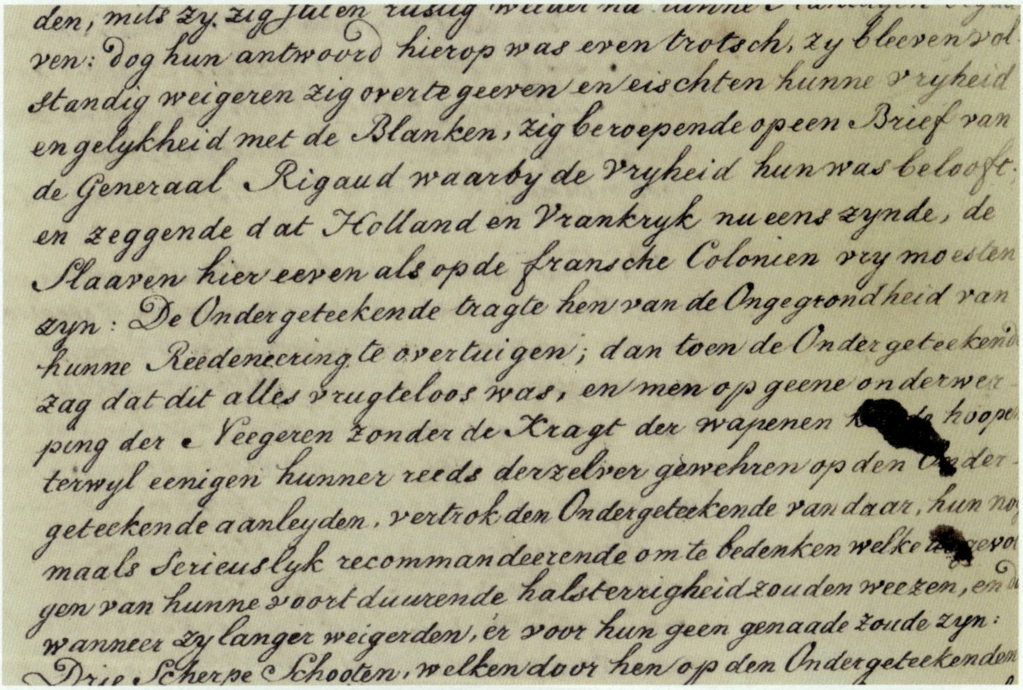

den, mits zy zig zulen rustig weeder na hunne [illegible]
ven: dog hun antwoord hierop was even trotsch, zy bleeven vol-
standig weigeren zig over te geeven en eischten hunne vryheid
en gelykheid met de Blanken, zig beroepende op een Brief van
de Generaal Rigaud waarby de Vryheid hun was belooft;
en zeggende dat Holland en Vrankryk nu eens zynde, de
Slaaven hier eeven als op de fransche Colonien vry moesten
zyn: De Ondergeteekende tragte hen van de Ongegrondheid van
hunne Reedeneering te overtuigen; dan toen de Ondergeteekende
zag dat dit alles vrugteloos was, en men op geene onderwer-
ping der Neegeren zonder de Kragt der wapenen [illegible] hoopen
terwyl eenigen hunner reeds derzelver geweeren op den Ondergeteekende aanleyden, vertrok den Ondergeteekende van daar, hun nog
maals serieuslyk recommandeerende om te bedenken welke [illegible]gevol-
gen van hunne voortduurende halsterrigheid zouden weezen, en
wanneer zy langer weigerden, er voor hun geen genaade zoude zyn:
Drie Scherpe Schooten, welken door hen op den Ondergeteekenden

fig. 4 **Referring to Rigaud, 'liberty and equality with the whites' was demanded, report, 5 October 1795**

chef des noirs insurgés de Saint Domingue (Toussaint L'Ouverture, leader of the insurgent Blacks of Saint-Domingue) produced around 1796 (fig. 6). In this colour portrait, the general is depicted on horseback. Some abolitionists saw the revolution on Saint-Domingue and L'Ouverture's position as the first Black head of state as important examples for the world.[26] In the historiography that followed in France, too, the French Revolution has always been seen as a crucial part of the nation's history. In the Netherlands, the Batavian period is seen as less significant; from 1815, with the advent of the first King of the Netherlands, the emphasis shifted to the Orangist story. The resistance of 1795 in the Dutch colonies was never recorded, visually or in writing, as part of the history of the Netherlands. As a result, there are no historical portraits of Tula.

oral history

Fortunately, oral sources have survived that can bring us quite close to the experience of people from Tula's time. There is a recording, for instance, in which we can hear the voice of Ma Chichi, who was interviewed on Curaçao in 1958 by Father Brenneker. Because of his interest in Afro-Curaçaoan oral history, the history of what was then called 'the lower classes', Brenneker recorded dozens of interviews with elderly people. Thanks to these recordings, we can still hear their voices today. Ma Chichi was one of the interviewees; she was 105 years old at the time of the interview and therefore born ten years before the abolition of slavery.

FB *E tempu ei, por a mira katibunan ainda?*
MC *Ai si pader.*
FB *hopi? ... tabatin katibu ainda?*
MC [whispering] *O! Tur kaminda.*
FB *Tur kaminda?*
MC *Tur e shonnan, no.*
FB *Nan ta'tin katibu.*
MC *Tur e shon. Ta'tin.* [louder, more emphatic]: *Ma AMI.*
Nos a lanta ... meskos ku yu 'i shon!
FB *A si. Si, si. M'a komprondé.*
MC *Pasobra, pader sa, mi tabatin un wela.*
FB *Si.*
MC *M'a hasi nunca manera e shonnan tabata ke.*
FB *Aha si.*
MC *Mi wela ku a kriami.*
FB *Si.*
MC *E n' hasi nunca manera e shonnan tabata ke.*[27]

FB Could you still see slaves at that time?
MC Ah, yes, father.
FB Many? Were there still many slaves?
MC [whispering] O! All over.
FB All over?

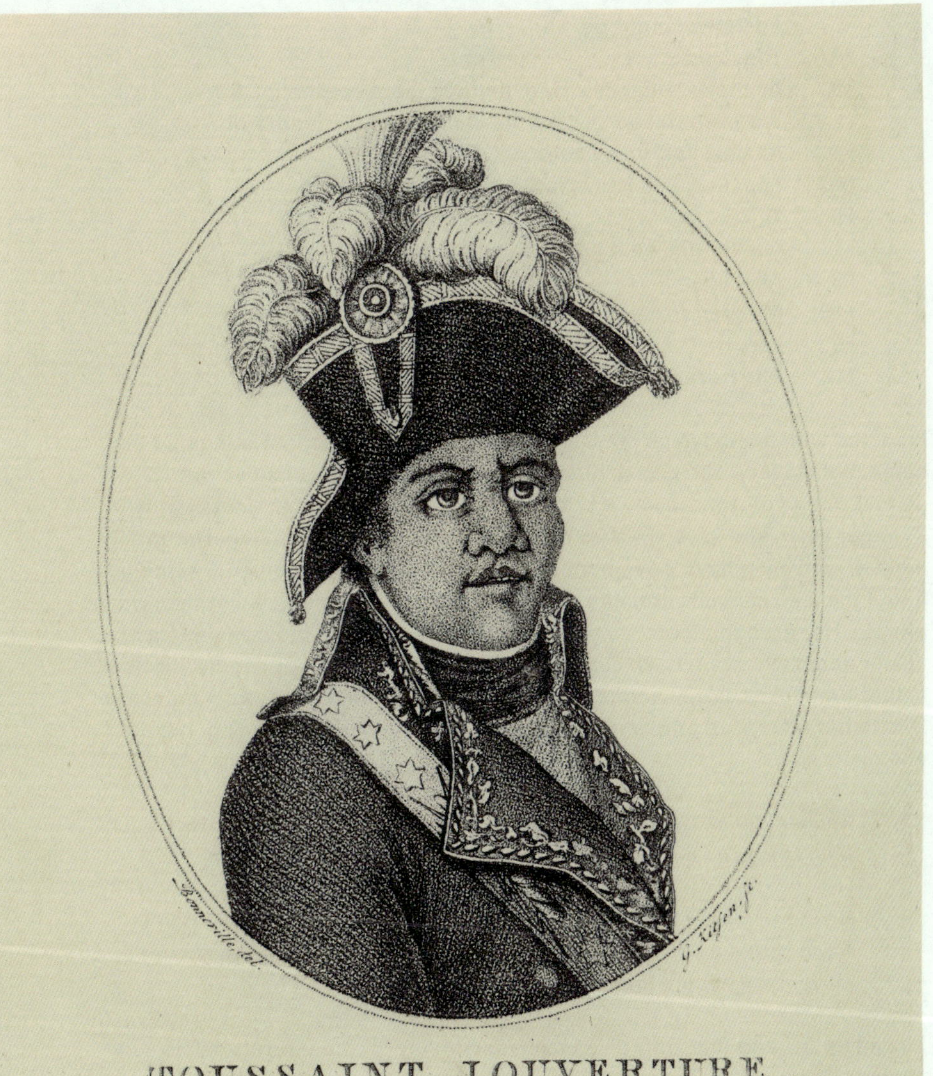

fig. 5 **Toussaint L'Ouverture, c. 1802–1810**

MC All those landlords, eh.
FB They had slaves.
MC All those landlords. Had. [louder, more emphatic]: But I.
We were raised. ... Like the children of the landlord!
FB Ah yes. Yes, yes. I see.
MC Because, you know, father, I had a grandma.
FB Yes.
MC I never did what the lords wanted.
FB Aha, yes.
MC My grandma, who raised me.
FB Yes.
MC She never did what the lords wanted.

From the whisper in which Ma Chichi speaks, when the priest brings up the subject of slavery, one can deduce that this subject is a sensitive one. She almost does not want to say it out loud. But her tone becomes noticeably stronger when she says she was raised as an equal human being. Her grandmother, who must have been born around the turn of the nineteenth century, about the time of Tula's uprising, taught her that she was not lesser than white people. Her grandmother was never submissive, just like the free people of colour about whom we have already read that they were supposedly 'insolent'. Father Brenneker asks whether Ma Chichi can still sing a song from that time. Due to her advanced age, she has to search her memory for a song, but then she recites:

> *Kaiman djuku. Djuku kaiman. ... Mi n' ta laba tayo. Mi n' ta laba komchi. Mi n'ta bari kas. Mi n' ta katibu 'i shon. Mi n' ta katibu 'i shon.*[28]
>
> No more yoke. Yoke is over. ... I don't wash plates anymore. I don't wash bowls anymore. I don't sweep the house. I am not the master's slave. I am not the master's slave.

The interview and the song give us an idea of how people in Tula's time saw slavery. There is a great awareness of one's own mental freedom, of the injustice of the system, and there is an unshakeable conviction that all people are equal. These ideas have been held on to through the centuries.

> *Libertat, galité*
> *La reina Victoria manda e kos pa nos!*
> *Libertat, galité*
> *Willem de derde manda e kos pa nos!*[29]
>
> Liberty, equality
> Queen Victoria, send it to us!
> Liberty, equality,
> William the Third, send it to us!

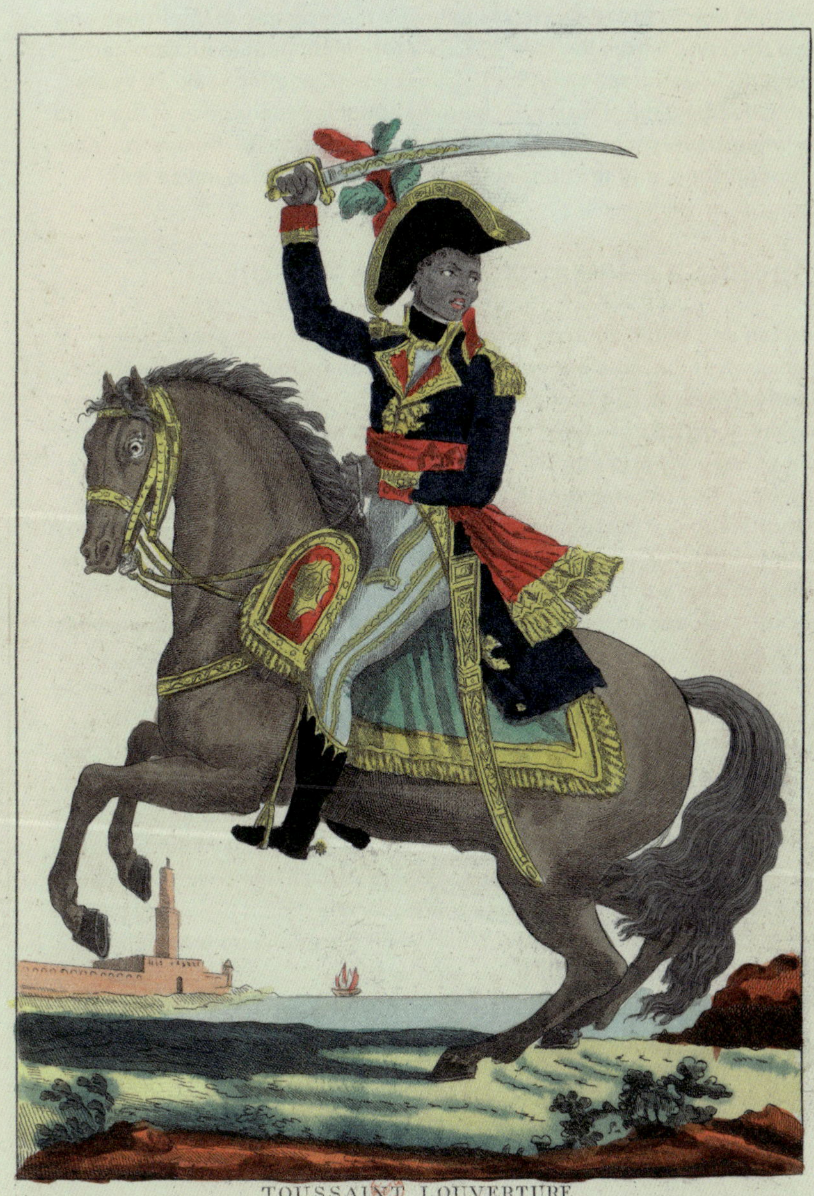

fig. 6 **Toussaint L'Ouverture, c. 1796–1799**

So the themes of 'liberty and equality' from the French revolutionary motto were still being sung about during the reign of Queen Victoria, who ascended the British throne in 1837, shortly after the abolition of slavery in British-held areas in 1834. William III became King of the Netherlands in 1849. It would take until 1863 before the Netherlands followed the example of the British and abolished slavery. So from the time of Tula's rebellion, people on Curaçao sang about their steadfast belief that slavery would end for some 70 years before abolition became a reality. By singing about independence of the mind in a time when slavery was legal, people inspired courage in themselves and others through song, and the consciousness of institutional injustice was passed on.

how tula's legacy was passed on

While written and visual sources from Tula's time can thus provide only a limited glimpse of the lives of people in slavery, anthropological collections assembled afterwards can accomplish this a bit better. In the first decades following the abolition of slavery, for instance, Antonius van Koolwijk produced a number of beautiful photographic portraits on Curaçao, Aruba and Bonaire, including one of an old man that is now preserved in the collection of the Netherlands Nationaal Museum van Wereldculturen (fig. 7).[30] Printed on almost transparent paper, it is a miracle that the photograph has remained relatively intact. What did not survive is information on who this man was and what his life was like. It is clear, however, that the man must have been born in the early nineteenth century. He must have heard about Tula's ideas at first hand.

Learning about these stories at first hand was no simple matter. People in slavery were not allowed to gather and exchange ideas freely. And they were forbidden to read or write. This made it difficult for them to organize, to rise in resistance against the system. Virtually no physical pieces of evidence of resistance have survived. In its collection associated with the Knip estate on which Tula was forced to work, the National Archaeological Anthropological Museum of Curaçao has a unique object: a bamboo stick that seems innocuous at first but in which a blade has been ingeniously concealed (fig. 8). Its precise age is unknown. It is known, however, that Black people were forbidden to carry sticks in the period around Tula's struggle.[31]

However, weapons are not the only physical evidence of resistance; in the context of colonial slavery, musical instruments can also qualify as such. In order to suppress unrest, people in slavery were only permitted to gather on special occasions. At these sporadic get-togethers, there was usually music and dancing. People made musical instruments from the materials they had at their disposal: from parts of garden tools to natural materials, more or less modified.

On Curaçao this produced a music genre called *muzik di zumbi*, music of the spirits. To play this music, six or seven different instruments were needed, together creating rhythms and melodies. One noteworthy instrument in this kind of music is the *benta*, the mouth bow (fig. 9). The bow is made from a branch, with a single string made from bark. The benta is played with a

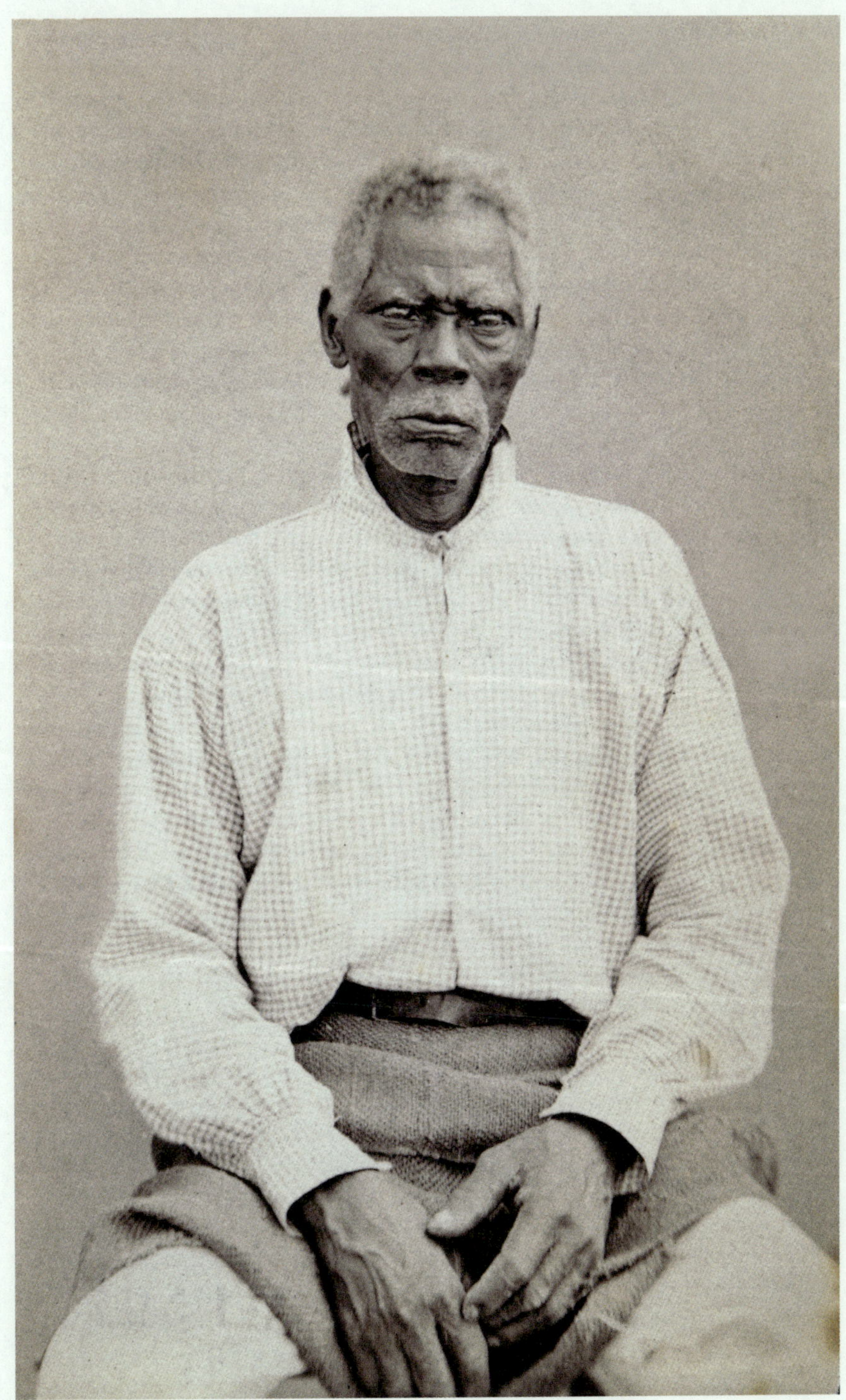

fig. 7 **Man, possibly a *tambú* player, photographed before 1887**

stick. The point of the instrument rests on the knee of the player, with the other end directly in front of their slightly open mouth, which forms the sound box.[32] This produces extended notes that seem to float back and forth. The association with spirits, preserved in the name of the music, must come from this ghostly sound. The name, however, also says something about the relationship between slaveholder and enslaved person: the lack of recognition of humanity and creativity on the one hand, and on the other how people in slavery, in spite of restrictive rules, managed to hold on to their resilience and humour.

Gathering to make music was used not only as an opportunity for relaxation and fun but also to talk about current events. For this, the *tambú* was most commonly used (fig. 10). The word *tambú* refers to a music genre and its associated dance and spiritual customs. Similar to musical practices in Haiti, it has West African, mainly Congolese, roots.[33] Tambú also refers to the most important, defining instrument used for this music, the drum. This drum is played sitting on a chair; the posture of the man in the photograph here looks a lot like that of a tambú player (fig. 7). It is an instrument made with a great deal of skill, and such drums were often given a name, such as 'Revolution of the People'.[34] The most meaningful aspect of a tambú gathering is the singing. There is one lead singer. He or she sings one line at a time, to which the choir responds. The song reflects the latest news: the singer gives his or her view of current events. In this way, news was disseminated and opinions shaped through song. This happened in Tula's time, but thereafter as well.

It is therefore not surprising that the authorities opposed tambú gatherings. Reasons given were that the tambú was 'of the devil', 'indecent' and 'uncivilized'. The tambú was in fact banned in 1936. Participants at gatherings were arrested for conspiracy. But individuals were also arrested for practising at home, entirely alone. The ban on tambú gatherings was lifted in 1952, but even thereafter these gatherings were subject to stricter rules than other parties for another 60 years. They were only permitted around the new year and could only last until midnight. This shows, on the one hand, how ingrained colonial ways of thinking are and, on the other, how oral history can survive only through a substantial awareness of its significance.

Tula's story was not previously afforded a place in the Rijksmuseum. The collection, largely composed of objects from the upper classes, did not at first glance lend itself to the telling of his story of challenging the colonial system. By bringing different collections and forms of information together, however, a clearer picture emerges of the world seen through Tula's eyes and of what Tula meant to people, during his lifetime and thereafter. By reading written sources in a different way, it becomes clear that he was a thoughtful, well-informed man with a world view according to which everyone, regardless of skin colour, was equal. Oral sources and knowledge about the history of music show that this world view sustained many in the long journey towards the abolition of slavery. From this, it becomes evident that people in slavery, in spite of the dehumanization upon which the system was based, were able to hold onto their dignity and the hope of equal citizenship. Acknowledging that the use of limited collections and source material produces an incomplete

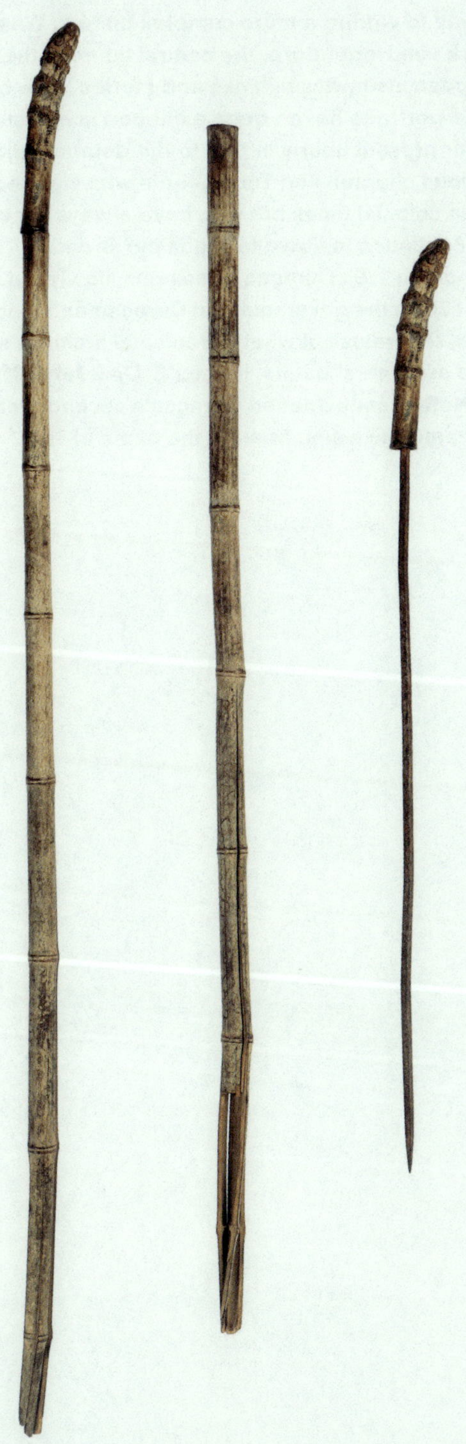

fig. 8 **A bladed cane from the Knip plantation: physical evidence of resistance, date of manufacture unknown**

picture of history opens the way to writing a more complex history. Was slavery ended by men like Dirk van Hogendorp, the central figure of the next chapter? By the efforts of European men whose names and stories have been immortalized in writing, whose portraits haven been exhibited in museums for centuries? Or do we owe our present liberty in part to the determination of people like Sapali, in the previous chapter, and Tula, people who were not immortalized in tangible form in colonial times but who have always lived on in spirit in the movement that continues to strive for equality? Broader recognition of the significance of the 1795 Curaçao uprising is slowly but surely emerging. On 17 August 2010, the government of Curaçao announced that Tula and his fellow fighters, regardless of what the colonial archives state, would no longer be referred to as 'rioters' but as 'heroes'.[35] On 2 July 2018, King Willem-Alexander of the Netherlands opened Curaçao's second pier for cruise ships, unveiling a commemorative sign bearing the name of Tula.

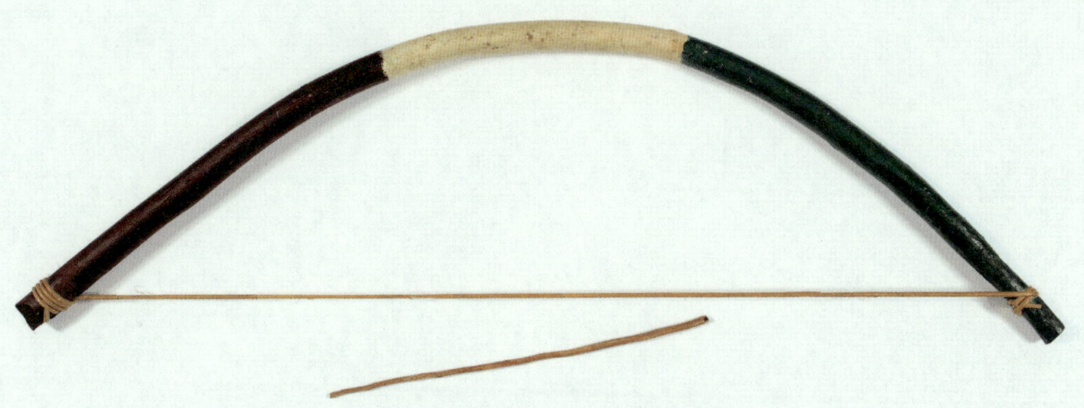

fig. 9 **A *benta* from Curaçao, a mouth bow used in the forbidden 'music of the spirits', before 1958**

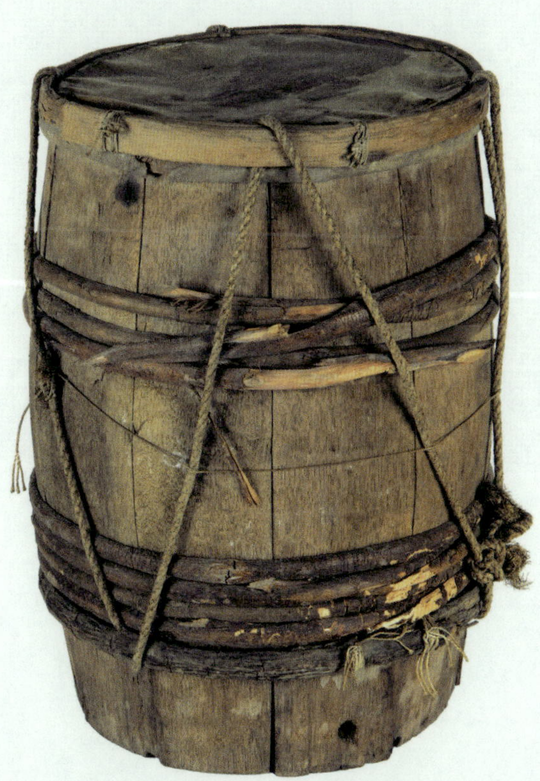

fig. 10 **Drum used in *tambú* music, in which current events were sung about, before 1885**

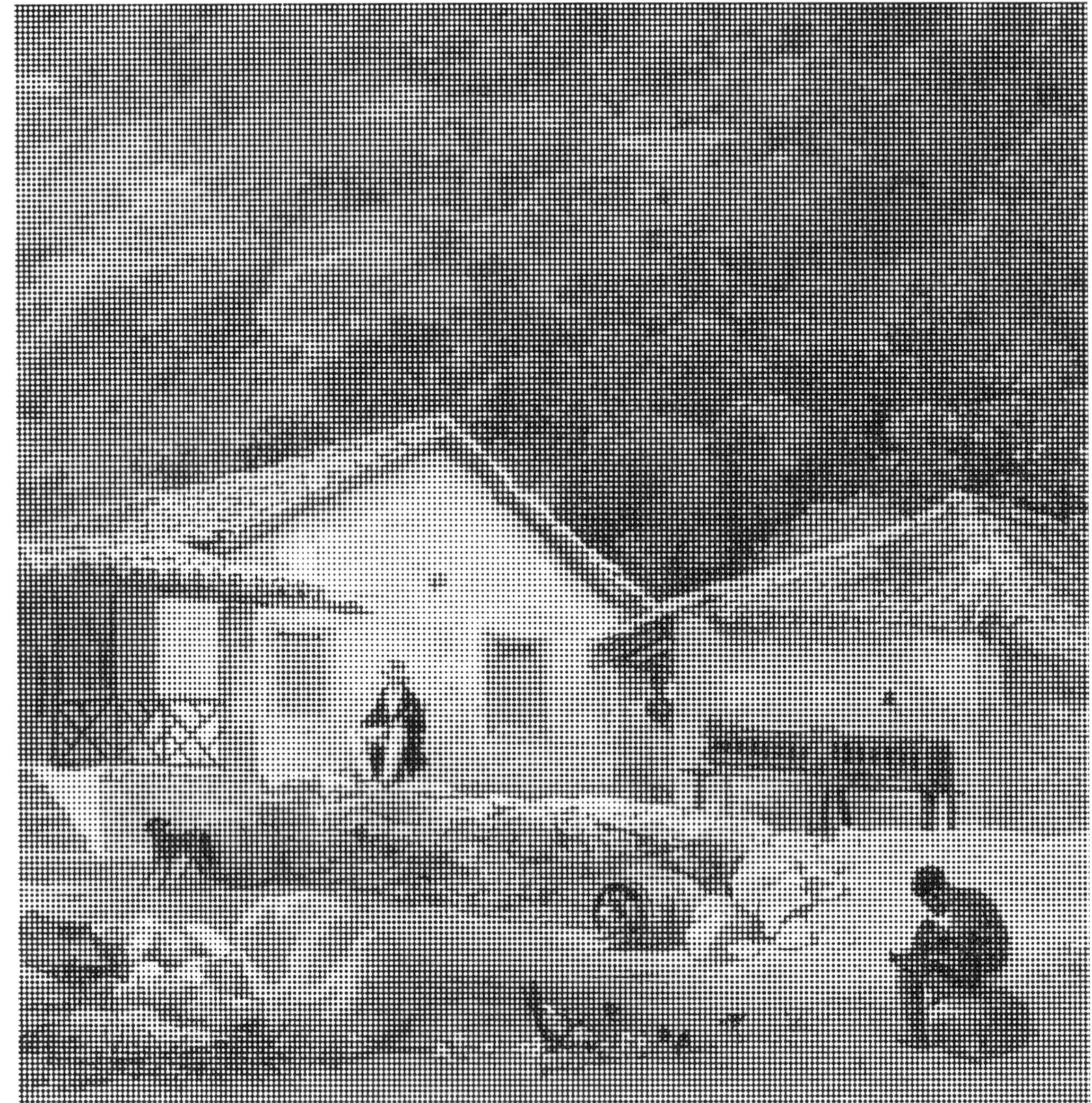

valika smeulders
lisa lambrechts

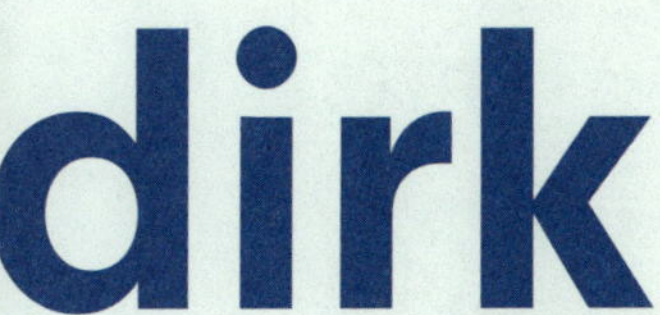

from abolitionist to slaveholder

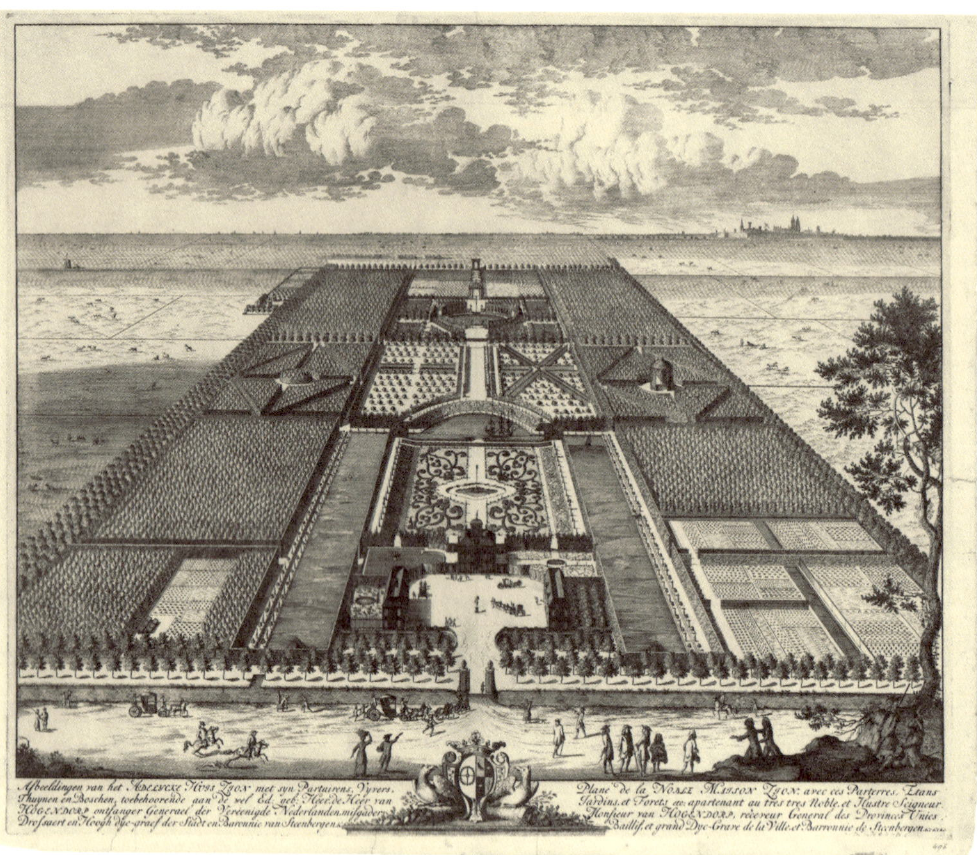

fig. 1 **The Van Hogendorp family's Sion estate in Rijswijk Pieter van Call (II), c. 1725**

Dirk van Hogendorp came from a family of high-placed, influential officials. He was critical of the slavery system, and he followed his father in speaking out about the excesses committed by slaveholders. In order to raise this issue he wrote a play based on his father's 1780 novella *Kraspoekol*, about a cruel female slave owner in Batavia (now Jakarta) on Java. He believed that the slavery system could be brought to an end within twenty years. His efforts to abolish slavery met with such great resistance that an attempt to perform the play in The Hague in 1801 was disrupted and had to be cancelled before the first act was finished. This lack of support for his ideals, which were partly inspired by the French Revolution, led Van Hogendorp to characterize himself as an 'oppressed Batavian'. Later, following the Battle of Waterloo, and twenty years after the publication of his play *Kraspoekol*, he turned his back on Europe and became a plantation owner in Brazil, where he made a number of disconcerting choices. His financial records reveal that he hired enslaved people from other plantations as day labourers and also bought people himself, reasoning, in his own words, that 'one certainly needs slaves ... to perform housework, because the free ones are too bad, and want to move or run away at any moment.'[1] Was the freedom argued for by European abolitionists the same freedom envisioned by enslaved people?

the elite and international power

Dirk van Hogendorp was born in 1761 into a Dutch ruling-class family that would later be elevated to the nobility. He lived for some of his youth in The Hague, the country's seat of government, and spent much of his time in this period at Sion, his great-aunt's country estate in present-day Rijswijk. A print made around 1725 shows the luxurious layout of the manor house, surrounded by formal gardens and ponds (fig. 1). Dirk clearly grew up in very privileged surroundings, and the circles in which he moved were very internationally oriented. As was customary among sons of the ruling classes in this period, honour and prestige were central to his upbringing.

The Van Hogendorp family had close connections in The Hague with the stadtholder's court,[2] whose residents included two young men of African descent who had started working there when they were children. Guan Anthony Sideron and Willem Frederik Cupido were about the same age as Dirk and they lived within walking distance of his home in the city.[3] It is quite possible that Dirk encountered them in the local area or saw them participating in parades and official appearances by the stadtholder. The court was proud to have Guan and Willem as servants: their presence gave the small Dutch Republic international allure.[4] They were not 'slaves' – colonial slavery was not legalized in the Dutch Republic itself – but servants whose loyalty was beyond doubt. The two men remained part of the stadtholder's inner circle for their entire lives, even accompanying him when he fled to Britain following the revolution that led to the Batavian Republic replacing the Dutch Republic in 1795. Possibly, it was these two young men who were Dirk's earliest inspiration for his ideas about slavery, freedom and social relations between people of different ethnicities and cultures.

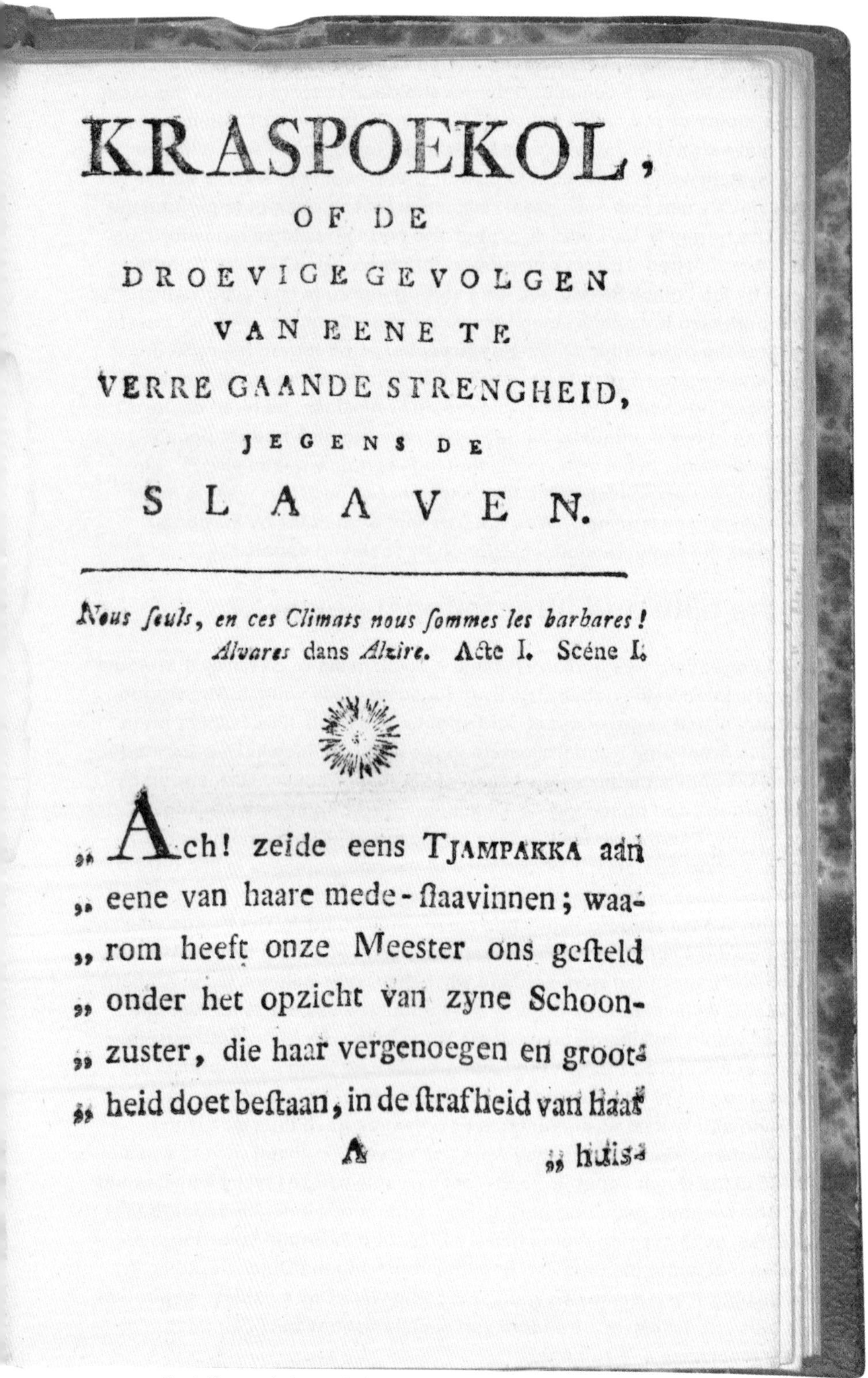

KRASPOEKOL,

OF DE

DROEVIGE GEVOLGEN

VAN EENE TE

VERRE GAANDE STRENGHEID,

JEGENS DE

SLAAVEN.

Nous ſeuls, en ces Climats nous ſommes les barbares!
Alvares dans *Alzire.* Acte I. Scéne I.

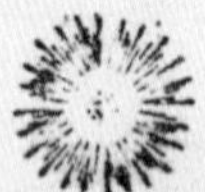

„ Ach! zeide eens TJAMPAKKA aan
„ eene van haare mede - ſlaavinnen; waa-
„ rom heeft onze Meester ons geſteld
„ onder het opzicht van zyne Schoon-
„ zuster, die haar vergenoegen en groot-
„ heid doet beſtaan, in de ſtrafheid van haar

A „ huis-

fig. 2 ***Kraspoekol***, **novella by Willem van Hogendorp, 1780**

Dirk's father, Willem van Hogendorp, was a doctor of law and held Dutch East India Company (VOC) posts at various locations in Southeast Asia from 1774 to 1784. As a VOC administrator he belonged to the very highest echelons of the company and colonial society. These posts were important to him because they were well paid – and he had debts to pay. Through the contacts he made in the course of his work he was also able to supplement his income by engaging in private business dealings. Such activities had actually been forbidden since 1724 but they happened nonetheless, and a blind eye was generally turned. He also did work for the public good, such as co-founding the Bataviaasch Genootschap voor Kunsten en Wetenschappen (Batavian Society for Arts and Sciences). He was furthermore committed to the broader well-being of people in Batavia, writing novellas about healthcare and the treatment of enslaved people (fig. 2). Willem was an example for Dirk, with the father's choices, lifestyle and ideas forming the building blocks for the son's convictions.

After a short military career in Prussia, in 1784 Dirk decided to follow in his father's footsteps and became a VOC official in Southeast Asia, where he hoped to make his name and fortune.[5] He soon realized, however, that progression to more senior positions was not going to be easy. Like his father before him, he made repeated appeals for recommendations from the stadtholder and other people, but to no avail. Senior positions were allotted to applicants with local and family connections, rather than networks in the Dutch Republic. Dirk felt aggrieved by this and expressed his frustration in letters to his politician brother, Gijsbert Karel van Hogendorp.[6] He realized that he would only have a chance at having a successful career if reforms took place in the colonial administrative apparatus. Dirk saw the VOC system as outdated and doomed to collapse under the weight of corruption, maladministration and unequal opportunities, and he was preoccupied with its reform throughout the sixteen years he spent mostly in Java.[7]

At the time, the spirit of revolution was sweeping across Europe. In 1795 a great shift took place in the Netherlands that followed the example of the French Revolution. The new Batavian Republic instated the ideals of freedom, equality and fraternity championed by that revolution. Dirk supported the principles of this new constitution.[8] Emboldened by the sense that the time for change and reform had come, he started to put his ideas about a new colonial administration to paper.[9] His writings show that, despite belonging to an elite that benefited from colonial property and sought to continue to profit from it, he believed that in an ideal colonial society underpinned by the fundamental principles of 'freedom and equality', there was no place for the slave trade or slavery.[10]

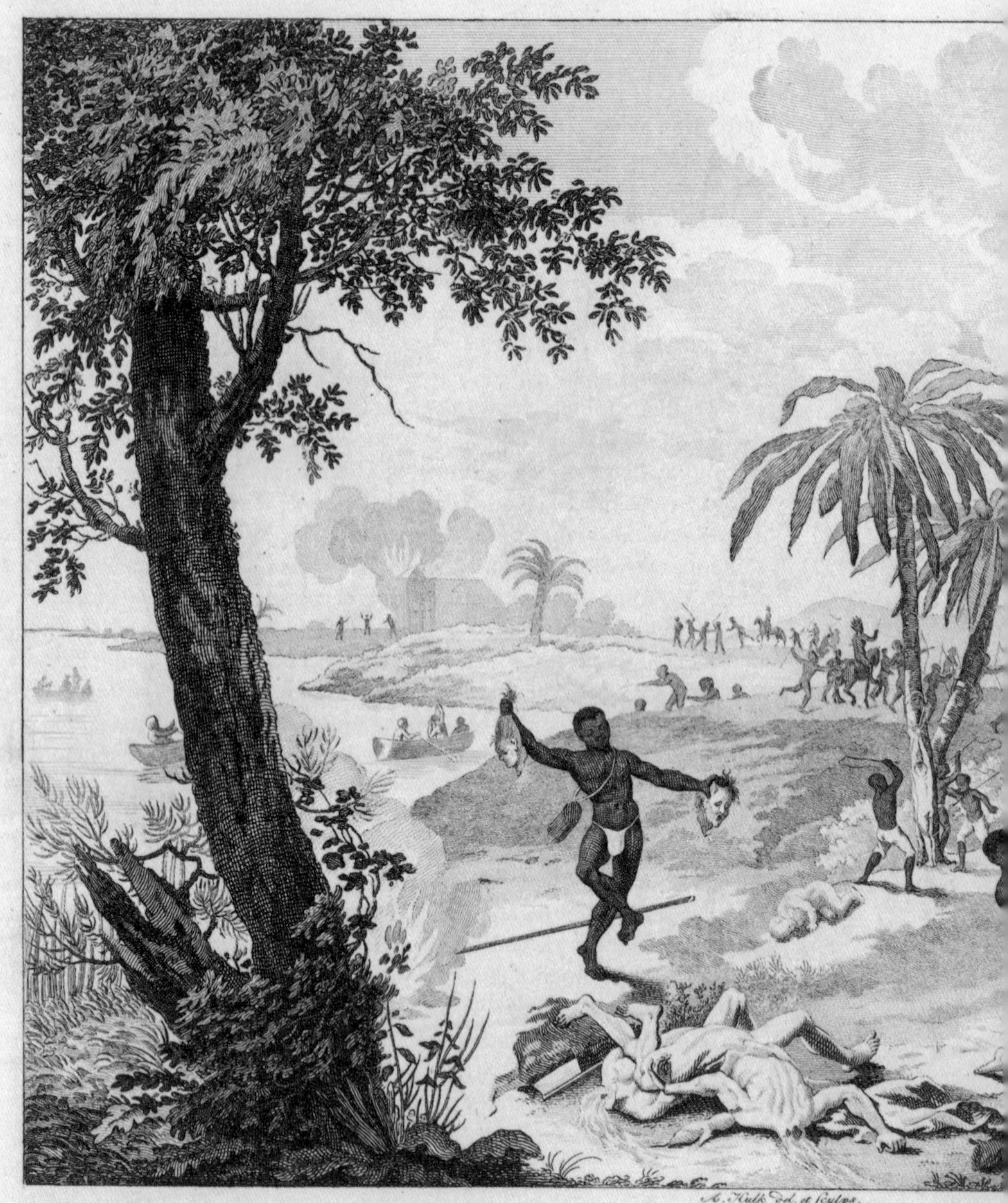

fig. 3 **Print depicting the uprising in Berbice, 23 February 1763, A. Hulk, c. 1763–1817**
Images such as this haunted the imaginations of many a slaveholder in the 18th century

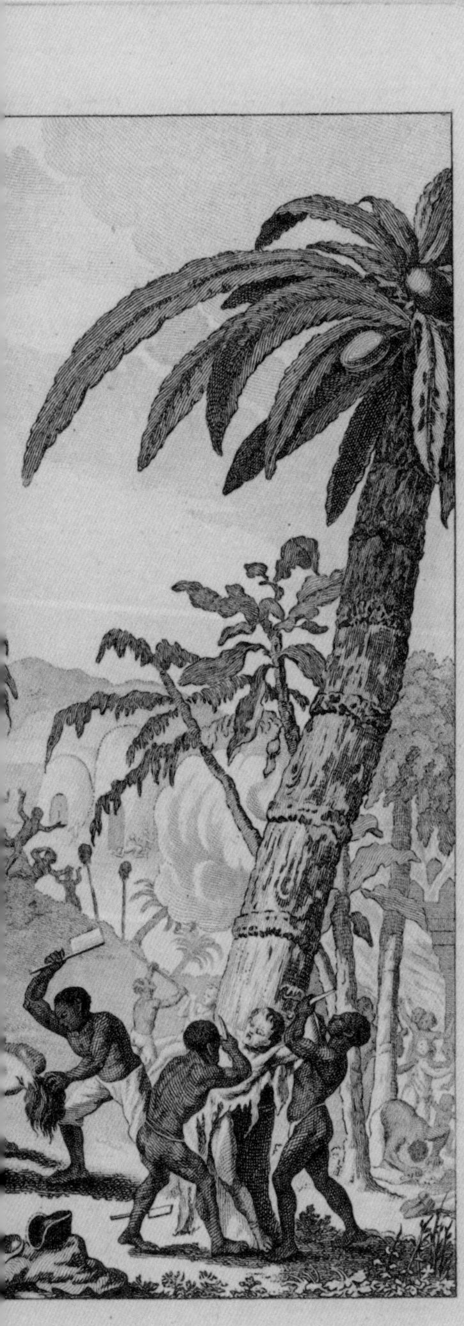
23 Feby Ao 1763.

violence, resistance, publications and theatre

Resistance to European rule was rife in colonized territories in the eighteenth century. In the Caribbean region, for example, there were at least a hundred small- and large-scale uprisings in this period. The 1763 insurgency in Berbice (in present-day Guyana) was one of the largest acts of resistance ever to take place in a Dutch colony; the enslaved population, led by Cuffy, escaped slavery and captured the entire colony. The resistance fighters took over the running of the region, and the colonizers fled the plantations. It was not until almost a year later that colonial reinforcements arrived from the Dutch Republic, and it took six months for them to reconquer the region.[11] Uprisings such as this struck fear into the hearts of those members of the upper classes with colonial interests, and horrific stories about such events circulated in the Dutch Republic and its colonies, as illustrated by a print showing the Berbice uprising (fig. 3). This Dutch print of the battle depicts the insurgents massacring the colonists. The extent to which this image reflects actual events is unknown, but given the excessive cruelties inflicted by slaveholders, it is not inconceivable that retaliation took place.[12] Taking that into account, the print conveys the stereotypical image of the 'primitive' and 'terrifying' Other that was used to legitimize colonization, slavery and the denial of self-determination for enslaved people.

Some responses were more moderate and empathetic, such as the play *Monzongo of de Koningklyke Slaaf* (Monzongo, or the royal slave), which was published in 1774 following the Berbice insurrection. Although the play's author, Nicolaas van Winter, conceals his message within a euphemistic narrative about Mexico under Spanish rule, in the foreword he notes that the play was inspired by events in the Dutch colony[13] and that his aim was to 'bring attention to the indecency of slavery, and to make heard the voice of humanity'.[14] It was rare in this period for criticism of the country's transatlantic system to be openly expressed. Readers of English could learn about the cruelty of slavery in Suriname from Aphra Behn's *Oroonoko; or, the Royal Slave*, published in 1688. A century later, books appeared by authors such as Ignatius Sancho and Olaudah Equiano, who had experienced slavery themselves. Theatre, however, was a more popular and accessible medium for members of the broader public wanting to find out more about what was going on in colonized territories. *Monzongo* attracted large audiences around the Dutch Republic.[15]

The authors of these plays were responding to the fact that the growing middle class in Europe harboured increasing numbers of people with sympathies for oppressed people. This bolstered the upper classes in their philanthropic efforts against injustice, and they visited the city theatres in great numbers.[16] Willem van Hogendorp was also critical of slavery, particularly in Batavia, where enslaved people were subjected to what he regarded as unreasonable violence. He was concerned by 'the danger of excessively cruel treatment'[17] and in his morality novella *Kraspoekol, of de droevige gevolgen van eene te verre gaande strengheid jegens de slaaven* (Kraspoekol, or the lamentable consequences of overly harsh treatment of slaves), he appeals for moderation of this behaviour because of its potential to lead to violent retribution.

In the years that followed, Dirk became increasingly convinced that enslaved people were resisting acts of excessive violence and duress. He believed that the solution lay in reform and that if these people gained personal freedom and could own land, national prosperity as a whole would grow, and the formerly enslaved people would no longer wish to withdraw from Dutch colonial rule.[18] When the Batavian Republic was proclaimed in 1795, Van Hogendorp was the colonial governor of Oosthoek in Surabaya. Emboldened by this political turn, he voiced his opinions increasingly loudly. This was not well received by the conservative colonial administration in Java. Dirk was prosecuted and imprisoned on charges of corruption, abuse of power, illicit trade, exploitation and violent repression of the local population.[19] Despite his criticism of the slavery system, it is certain that he owned at least 153 enslaved people.[20] In his defence plea he admitted to having given orders to carry out corporal punishment, but only if a crime had been committed.[21] Van Hogendorp wrote about his imprisonment that he felt himself to be an 'oppressed Batavian', and a 'slave ... forced to crawl before tyrants.'[22] In 1798, Dirk fled to the Netherlands, claiming that he would not receive a fair trial in Batavia. He left behind his wife, who would die there in 1801.

Upon his return to the Netherlands, he was determined to restore his honour and reputation, prove that the accusations made against him were false, and be exempted from prosecution.[23] He defended himself publicly through a series of texts, published over a short period, that set out his position and proposal for reforms.[24] In 1800 he published a theatre adaptation of his father's novella, which he titled *Kraspoekol; of de Slaaverny. Een tafereel der zeden van Neerlands Indiën* (Kraspoekol, or slavery. A morality play set in the Dutch East Indies). In this publication, Van Hogendorp advocates the gradual abolition of a system he believed should never have existed in the first place. He writes about this 'unnaturalness' in his introduction to the play:

> No people in the world have succeeded, or ever can succeed, in devising a good code of law for slavery. Slavery is in its essence so contrary to human rights, and in itself fundamentally absurd, that in seeking to establish it in law, no equitable or just codes or institutions can be based upon it.[25]

intercultural relations, disapproval and empathy

It is striking that both Willem van Hogendorp and his son Dirk attribute cruelty against enslaved people only to others, despite being slaveholders themselves.[26] Willem wrote that excesses were generally committed by 'people of the third and fourth grade'.[27] The administrative hierarchy of the VOC in Batavia comprised a European upper class and, below it, several social strata in which mixed relationships between European men and local and enslaved women were commonplace. The VOC encouraged such relationships and discouraged the importing of European brides, based on the idea that local women would be less financially demanding and would furthermore bind

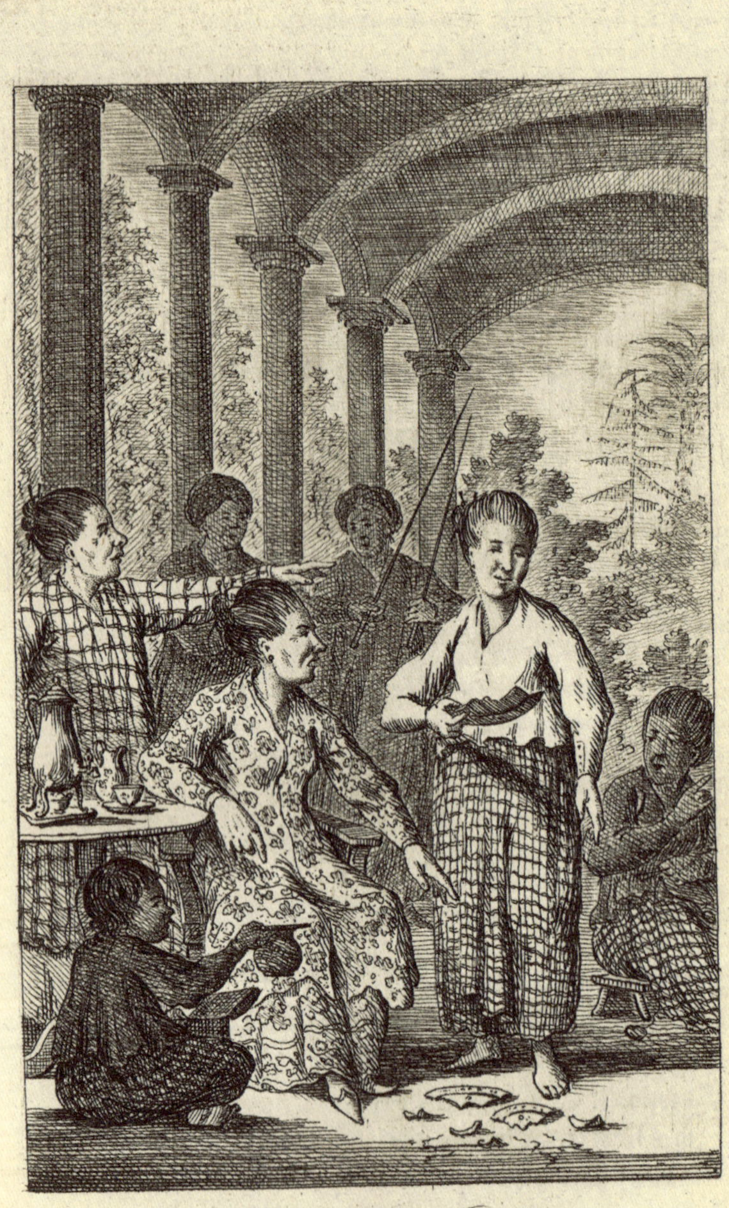

fig. 4 **Title page of *Kraspoekol*, the play by Dirk van Hogendorp, 1800**

the Dutch men to Batavia. These mixed relations led to the birth of bicultural children who were not easily accepted by either the Europeans or the Asians.[28] Sons, if they were lucky, would be sent to the Dutch Republic to receive an education that would later enable them to execute senior positions in the VOC.[29] Daughters, however, were often disregarded.[30] Most of these girls were brought up under the supervision of their Indonesian mothers, who saw maintaining an enduring relationship with a European man as a means to a better life. Dirk van Hogendorp believed that it was primarily these women and their daughters who were responsible for the maltreatment and violence against enslaved people.[31] He wrote that the woman's relationship with a European man led to her feeling superior to enslaved people, and passing on this attitude to her daughter or daughters, who 'learned to see [enslaved people] as far beneath them'.[32] He drew the conclusion that their lack of a 'moral' European upbringing awakened in them a competitive drive that was expressed in rage and jealousy towards the enslaved people in their household, particularly those women for whom the woman's husband or lover had a particular preference, Dirk claimed.[33]

The central villain in Dirk van Hogendorp's play, as in his father's book, is a woman of mixed Southeast Asian and European heritage named Kraspoekol, which means 'hit hard' in Malay. Her name is a reference to the pleasure she derives from having the women she keeps in slavery beaten.[34] The book's sole illustration shows a scene from the play, set in Batavia (fig. 4): Kraspoekol, dressed in sumptuous 'East Indies' style clothing, points sternly at a broken glass and porcelain plate that the enslaved woman Tjampakka ('fragrant flower' in Malay) has just accidentally dropped on the floor. Tjampakka's bare feet and checked cotton skirt clearly signal her status. The incident is the result of a devious plan, however. Kraspoekol wants a reason to punish Tjampakka because she has discovered that Tjampakka is of noble stock and has complained to other people about Kraspoekol's abusive behaviour. Tjampakka has praised Kraspoekol's European brother-in-law Wedano for his gentler treatment of the enslaved people in his household. This has caused Kraspoekol to become irritated and angry. On the left of the drawing, behind Kraspoekol, is the overseer, or *mandoresse*, who instructs the two enslaved men in the background to beat Tjampakka with a sjambok.[35] The beating is just prevented by the timely arrival home of Wedano, who subsequently grants Tjampakka her freedom.

Dirk created the Wedano character in his own image: like the play's author, Wedano is a chief merchant who speaks out against slavery, the slave trade and the cruel treatment of enslaved people.[36] Van Hogendorp contrasts Wedano's qualities with the negative traits of a new character he wrote into the play named Champignon, a nobleman. The playwright uses this character to highlight not only the arrogance and hubris of many senior VOC officials in Batavia but also their frequent incompetence. The Champignon character shares traits with the author's arch-enemy, the conservative commissioner general S.C. Nederburgh.[37] The play features frequent bragging about self-enrichment being the reason for going to a colonized territory. Champignon, for example, says, 'Conscience! Ha-ha! If we did not leave that behind us, few of us would

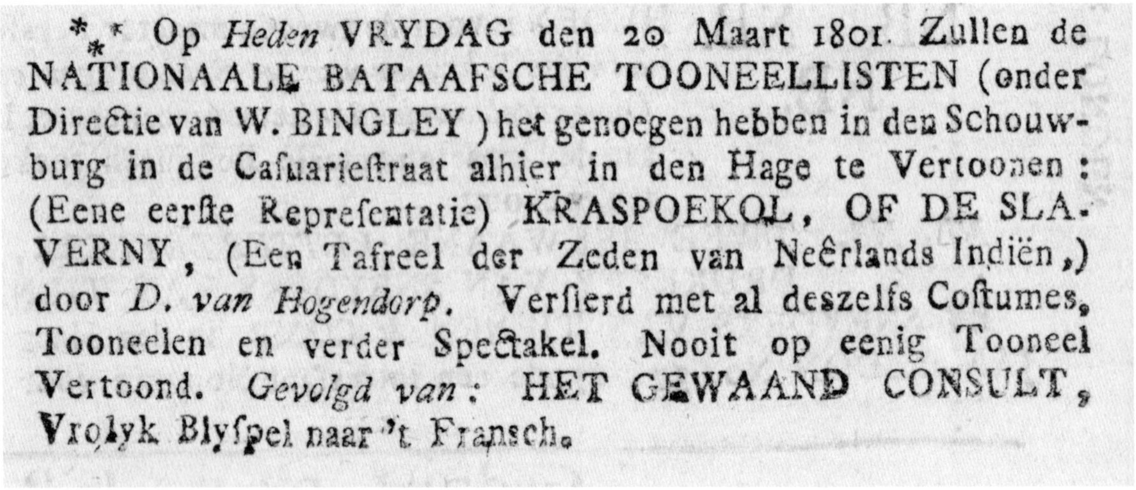

⁎ Op *Heden* VRYDAG den 20 Maart 1801. Zullen de
NATIONAALE BATAAFSCHE TOONEELLISTEN (onder
Directie van W. BINGLEY) het genoegen hebben in den Schouw-
burg in de Caſuarieſtraat alhier in den Hage te Vertoonen :
(Eene eerſte Repreſentatie) KRASPOEKOL, OF DE SLA-
VERNY, (Een Tafreel der Zeden van Neêrlands Indiën,)
door *D. van Hogendorp.* Verſierd met al deszelfs Coſtumes,
Tooneelen en verder Spectakel. Nooit op eenig Tooneel
Vertoond. *Gevolgd van:* HET GEWAAND CONSULT,
Vrolyk Blyſpel naar 't Fransch.

fig. 7 **Advertisement for the performance of *Kraspoekol* in the *Haagsche Courant* newspaper, 20 March 1801**

have made our fortune. I, at least, have never been bothered by it; I took what I could grab, and so became rich.'[38] By placing himself in a positive light through the Wedano character, and casting a woman as the main perpetrator of violence against enslaved people, Dirk deflects the accusations aimed in his direction.

It is striking that Dirk van Hogendorp links cruelty not only with a local upbringing but also specifically with women of mixed heritage. When he was looking for a wife, sixteen years earlier, education was one important factor he took into consideration. His first marriage, in 1785, was to Margaretha Elisabeth Bartlo. She was the daughter of a wealthy VOC undermerchant and probably of third-generation Eurasian heritage.[39] Dirk regarded her as a suitable candidate for marriage because as well as being the daughter of a prominent VOC official she had also, unlike other local young women, had a European upbringing and 'a better education than women in this country'.[40] A miniature portrait was painted of Bartlo around 1786, when she was thirteen years old, and Van Hogendorp sent it to his mother (fig. 5).[41] It is a clear display of cultural blending: while Margaretha is shown playing a European table piano in a clearly European setting, complete with classical column and Empire-style chair, her abundant jewellery – the band on her upper arm, the head ornament hanging from her veil and the large ring through her nose – all originate in Indian traditions.[42] This jewellery, the pearl bracelets on her wrists and the expensive muslin veil she is wearing were all local indicators of wealth and status.

Van Hogendorp had himself portrayed in a very different way: around 1813 he was painted in uniform, full-length and larger than life-size (fig. 6). By this time he was the governor of Hamburg. We know from the travelogue of the British author Maria Graham that the uniform conceals another aspect of the man: in her 1824 *Journal of a Voyage to Brazil* she describes 'Count Hogendorp': 'On undressing him after death, his body was found to be tattooed like those of the natives of the eastern islands.'[43] These were not images of anchors of the type many sailors in Europe had tattooed on their arm, but large, highly stylized body-covering patterns with a symbolic meaning, of the type made in Polynesia.

In 1801, six months after the publication in The Hague of *Kraspoekol*, Dirk Van Hogendorp collaborated with the Nationaale Bataafsche Tooneellisten theatre company on a performance of the play at the city's theatre (fig. 7).[44] It was to be a tumultuous evening, because in The Hague, as in Batavia, there were conservative forces who had no time for Van Hogendorp's proposals for immediate abolition of the slave trade and gradual abolition of slavery. And so it was that the performance of the play attracted saboteurs from local circles with interests in the colonized regions of Southeast Asia and the Caribbean.[45] In response to an article about the evening in the Hague periodical *Janus Janus-Zoon*,[46] John Carleton, the English translator of Van Hogendorp's *Berigt van de tegenwoordigen toestand der bataafsche Bezittingen in Oost Indien en den handel op dezelve*, (Account of the present state of Batavian possessions in the East Indies and the trade of the same, 1799), wrote:

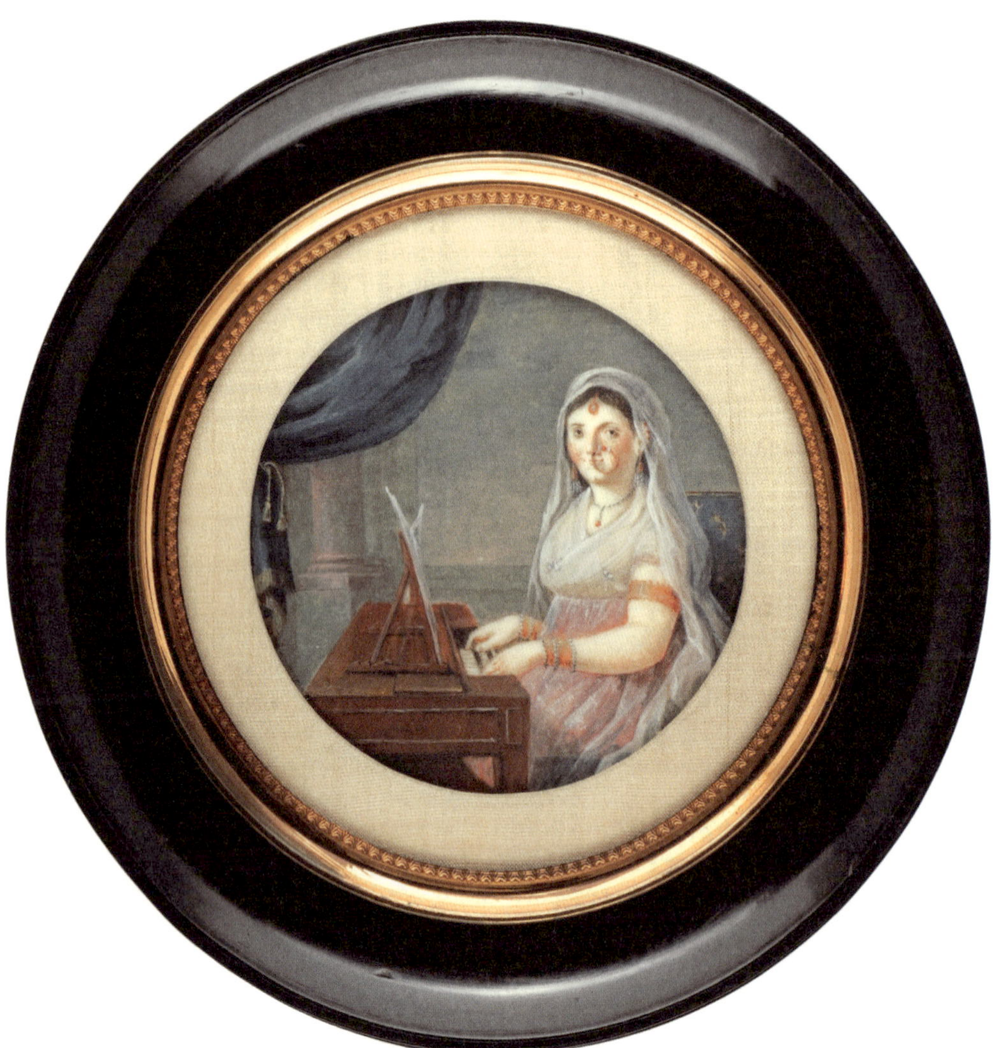

fig. 5 **Portrait miniature of Margaretha Elisabeth Bartlo, c. 1786**

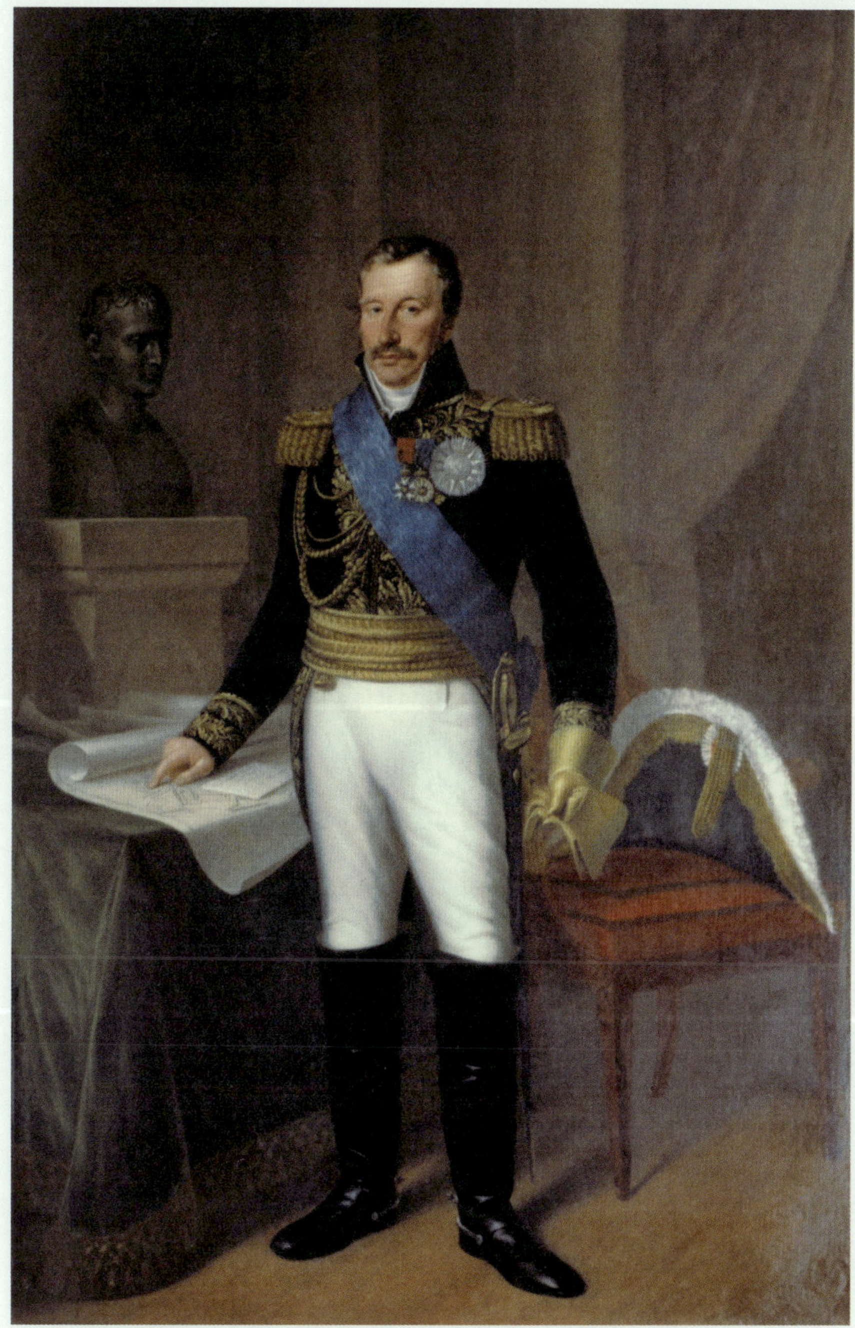

fig. 6 **Life-size portrait of Dirk van Hogendorp, with a bust of Napoleon Not visible are Dirk's Polynesian tattoos, Christoph Suhr, c. 1813**

> The East India Gentry, not thinking it proper to exhibit the most illustrious actions of themselves and their noble ancestors upon a stage to vulgar European spectators, went to the play provided with little half penny-whistles and trumpets, and kept up such a tremendous whistling and trumpeting from the very moment the curtain began to be drawn up, that not a single syllable of the play could be heard – and, if these Gentlemen could, they would also have extinguished the candles, to keep in darkness what themselves and their ancestors never intended for the light.[47]

The uproar in the auditorium meant it was impossible for the audience to hear the play, and it was halted before completion of the first act. Their curiosity piqued, members of the public rushed to the bookshop the following day and the published version soon sold out, with the result that Van Hogendorp reached a large audience after all.[48] We cannot be certain that the protest in the theatre was prompted exclusively by anti-abolitionist ideas. It is possible that Dirk's own controversial character and polemical behaviour also played a part. Whatever the case, *Janus* published a rectification in its following edition:

> Because JANUS, despite all the invectives, wishes to be just and remain so, it must now, having received information about what took place, in all openness concede that it is certain that the booing arose to a greater degree from a hostile disposition towards HOOGENDORP the person, rather than towards the play itself; because of the conviction [among the public] that HOOGENDORP himself had not treated his slaves in a kindly manner; this notion naturally led to disquiet. That the uproar reached such heights was due to the belligerent means deployed to disrupt [the play], which they believed they had a right to do. And if this is the case, it places the events in a very different light.[49]

Was Van Hogendorp a flawed idealist, someone who had the best interests of oppressed people at heart but who was incapable of critically assessing his own part in the system? Or was pointing to the proverbial speck in the eye of the other a tactic in order to put competitors on the back foot and so advance his own career?

orange bitter

Dirk van Hogendorp certainly envisaged for himself a senior position in the progressive system he advocated. After briefly serving as an envoy of the Batavian Republic to St Petersburg, he occupied various political, diplomatic and military posts under King Louis Napoléon Bonaparte of the Netherlands and, later, Louis's brother Emperor Napoleon himself, who in 1812 elevated Van Hogendorp to the rank of Comte de l'Empire (Count of the Empire). In 1813, Napoleon appointed him Governor of Hamburg. This is when the large portrait of Van Hogendorp in uniform was painted (fig. 6). It was a personal gift from Napoleon,[50] who appears on the left of the painting in the form of a bust.

Following Napoleon's first fall from power later that year, Van Hogendorp returned to the Netherlands and pledged allegiance to King William I of the Netherlands, who had been brought back to the country from England by Dirk van Hogendorp's brother, Gijsbert Karel. But when Napoleon rose from the ashes and returned to power, Van Hogendorp tried to join the French side once more. When Napoleon met his final defeat at the Battle of Waterloo in 1815, Van Hogendorp would not have been able to expect a warm welcome in the new Kingdom of the Netherlands. He decided to emigrate – to Brazil.

In 1817, Van Hogendorp leased a plantation located two hours from Rio de Janeiro, on the slopes of Corcovado, the mountain on which the iconic statue of Christ the Redeemer was later built. The plantation's name was Hope's Estate, but Dirk renamed it Novo Sion (New Zion) in memory of Sion, the Van Hogendorp family's old country estate.[51] The print depicting the original estate reflects the level of ambition he clearly must have had as a plantation owner in Brazil (fig. 1). Dirk set up Novo Sion as a coffee and orange plantation and had 30,000 new coffee trees planted. He sold the oranges and also produced wine, brandy and distilled liqueurs such as lemon liqueur and Curaçao liqueur. These alcoholic drinks were intended for export to Europe and Batavia, but this was a relatively unsuccessful enterprise. He also ventured into exporting butter, sugar and cured meat to the Dutch Republic.[52]

All these activities meant Novo Sion was a labour-intensive business, and Dirk, a single man, was keen to have help around the house. His surviving financial records and the travel journals written by Europeans who visited him give us some idea of who these workers were. It is more challenging to get a clear picture of their status. Some were enslaved by other plantation owners and hired by Dirk; others were free; and yet others were purchased by Van Hogendorp.[53] His accounts and cash books provide a record of the work carried out and who was paid for it – hired and free workers received payment. The absence of a family name in the records probably indicates that the person concerned was enslaved. There is mention, for example, of 'negro Epiphanio' and of the carpenters Fortunado and Pedro, who built a duck coop. It is noted of another man, Joaquin, that he 'created rebellion and was highly impertinent'. We can be fairly certain that 'the free negro Antonio', who appears in the cash book as 'Antonio Nègres', was a free man, but how free could he have been given the burden of a last name used to construct hierarchy? It is likely that those individuals who appear in the records without any accompanying payment for their work had been bought by Van Hogendorp. The cash book contains several names and, on the penultimate line, the words 'mes esclaves' (my slaves), followed by the figure '3'. Why would these three people be included without names in the 'Noms des Personnes' column?[54] (fig. 8)

fig. 8 **Three people are recorded in an 1822 cashbook from Dirk van Hogendorp's Novo Sion plantation as 'my slaves', with no names given**

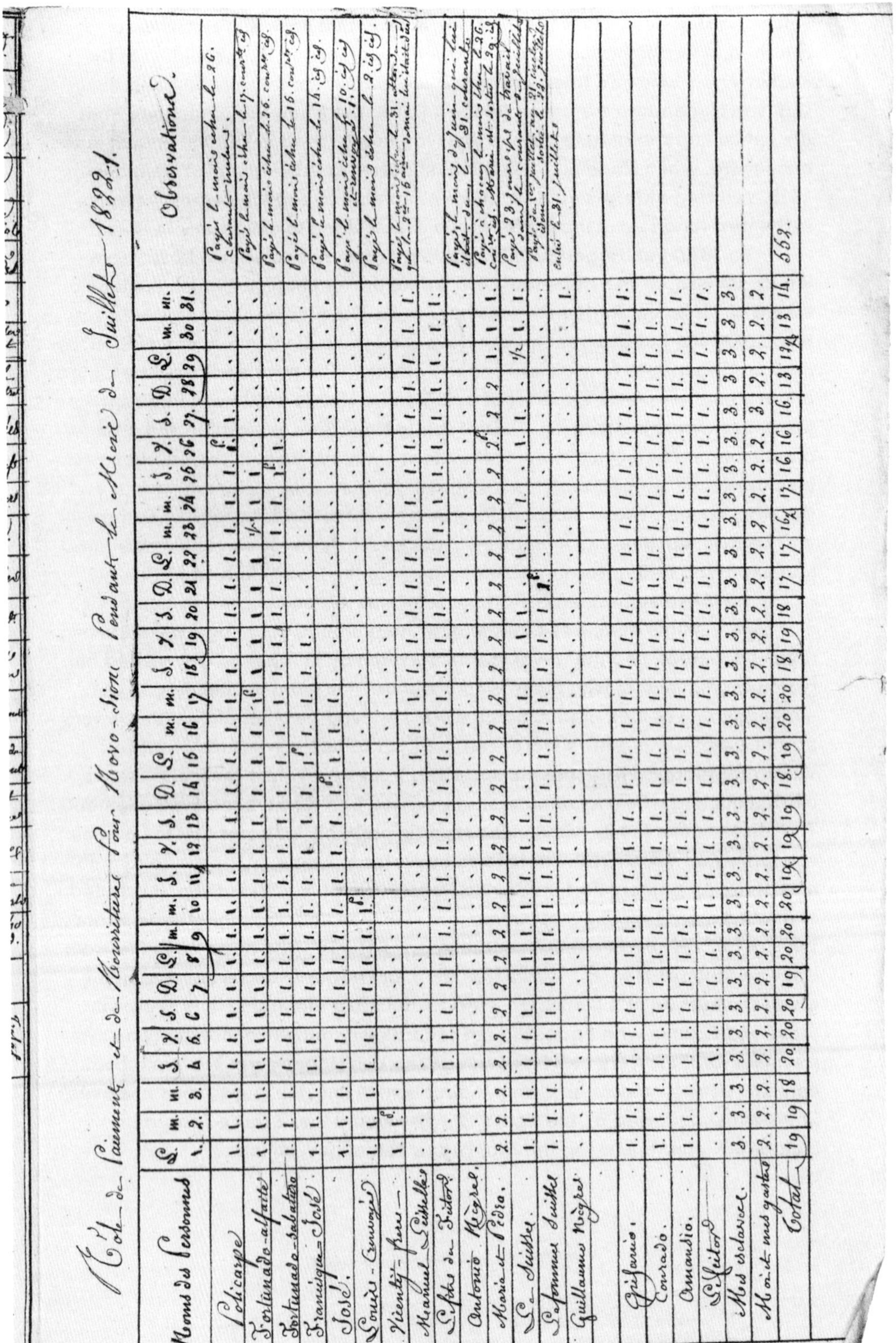

cezar and zinga

A possible explanation for making a single reference to three people is that they were all part of the same family: a father, mother and son. A visitor to the plantation named Theodor von Leithold mentioned in his travel journal that the smaller house next to his own was occupied by his gardener, his kitchen servant and their eight-year-old child.[55] Another visitor mentions in a letter that a man named Cezar and his spouse lived with Van Hogendorp, who had paid for their freedom.[56] Van Hogendorp himself writes that, 'The porter is a slave whose freedom I recently gifted. He is loyal and intelligent, they are different from ordinary negroes, because she even speaks French.'[57] These people ensured Van Hogendorp's life was very pleasant for him. On an occasion when Von Leithold decided on the spur of the moment to dine with Van Hogendorp at his home, they were treated to an extensive menu of poultry soup, spinach with eggs, fricassee of chicken, pepper sauce, leg of lamb with salad, and a desert of oranges and rusks, followed by port and Madeira wines, coffee and, to round it all off, liqueur.[58]

No record has been found that yields the name of Cezar's wife, but it seems that Van Hogendorp enjoyed looking at her. Maria Graham describes in her journal how,

> on returning to the house, he introduced to me ... his negroes, whom he freed on purchasing them: he has induced the woman to wear a nose jewel, after the fashion of Java, which he seems to remember with particular pleasure.[59]

Might Van Hogendorp have wished to be reminded of his first wife? Clearly, Dirk also very much enjoyed looking at himself: Von Leithold mentions in his travel journal that the central area of his by no means grand home was dominated by the almost 2.5-metre-tall portrait of his host: 'At the middle of the wall of this room, just above the front entrance, hung a painting depicting the general, life-size, that almost filled the full height of the room.'[60] Van Hogendorp liked to remind his visitors of the prestigious positions he had held, and to be addressed as 'General'.[61] Von Leithold also describes how the general loved to relax at the front of his house, under the eaves – he even had a picture painted of himself seated in front of the house (fig. 9). Is the figure in the right foreground of the painting perhaps Cezar? And is the figure between them, in the shade of the eaves of the smaller building, Cezar's wife? Did she choose voluntarily to work with her breasts uncovered, or did she do so at Van Hogendorp's behest? Whatever the reason for this choice, we do know that a watercolour of the same scene that he sent with a letter to his niece Mina in 1821 was a chastened version in which the female figure is portrayed wearing a dress (figs. 10, 10a).

The cash book does not appear to contain any record of payments to Cezar and his family. Is it possible that this group of three received a combined allowance and that this is the reason that they are referred to as 'my slaves'? It would seem that in Van Hogendorp's perception, freedom for people of

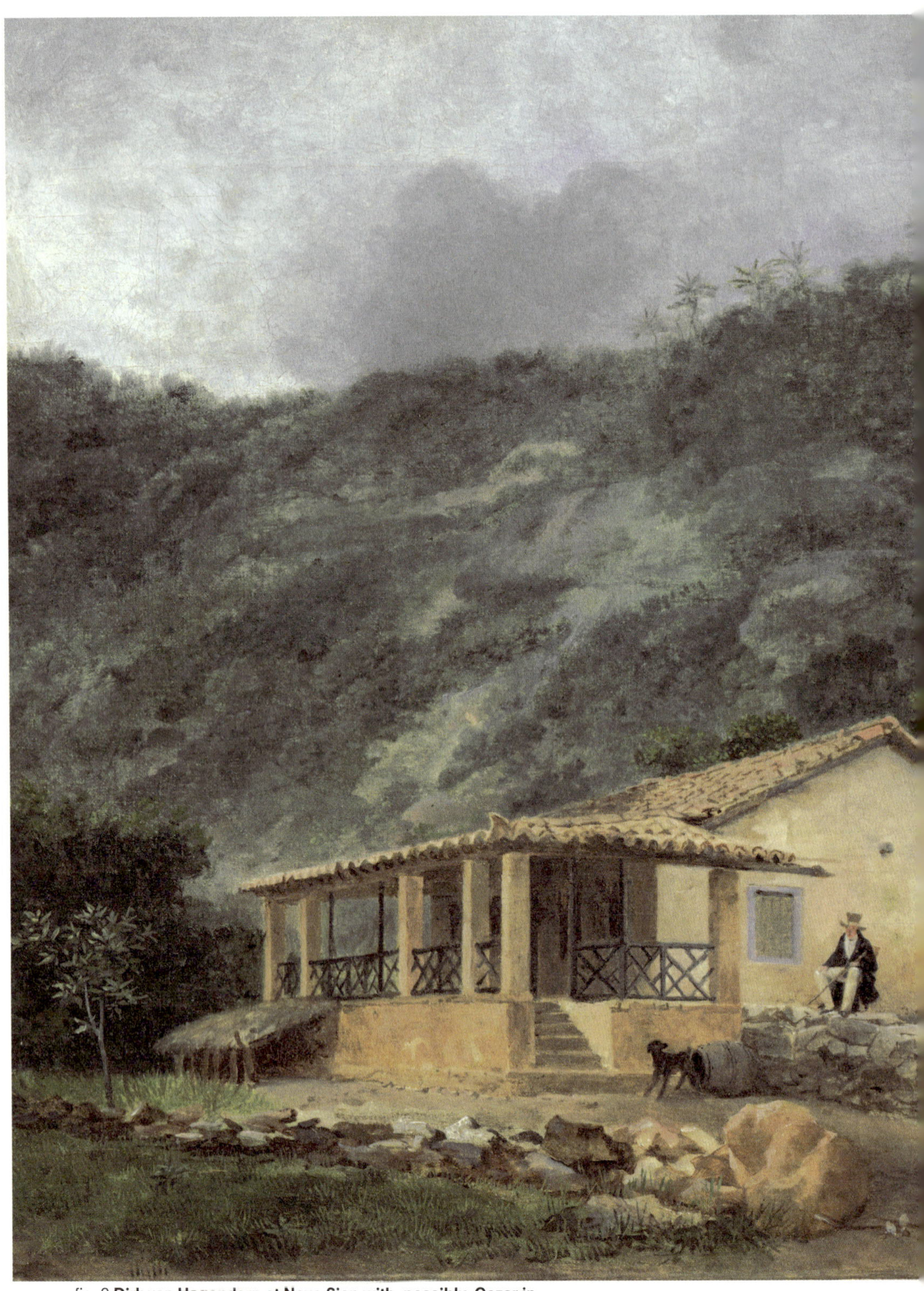

fig. 9 **Dirk van Hogendorp at Novo Sion with, possibly, Cezar in the far-right foreground and Cezar's wife in the right background, in the shade of the eaves of the smaller buidling, c. 1820**

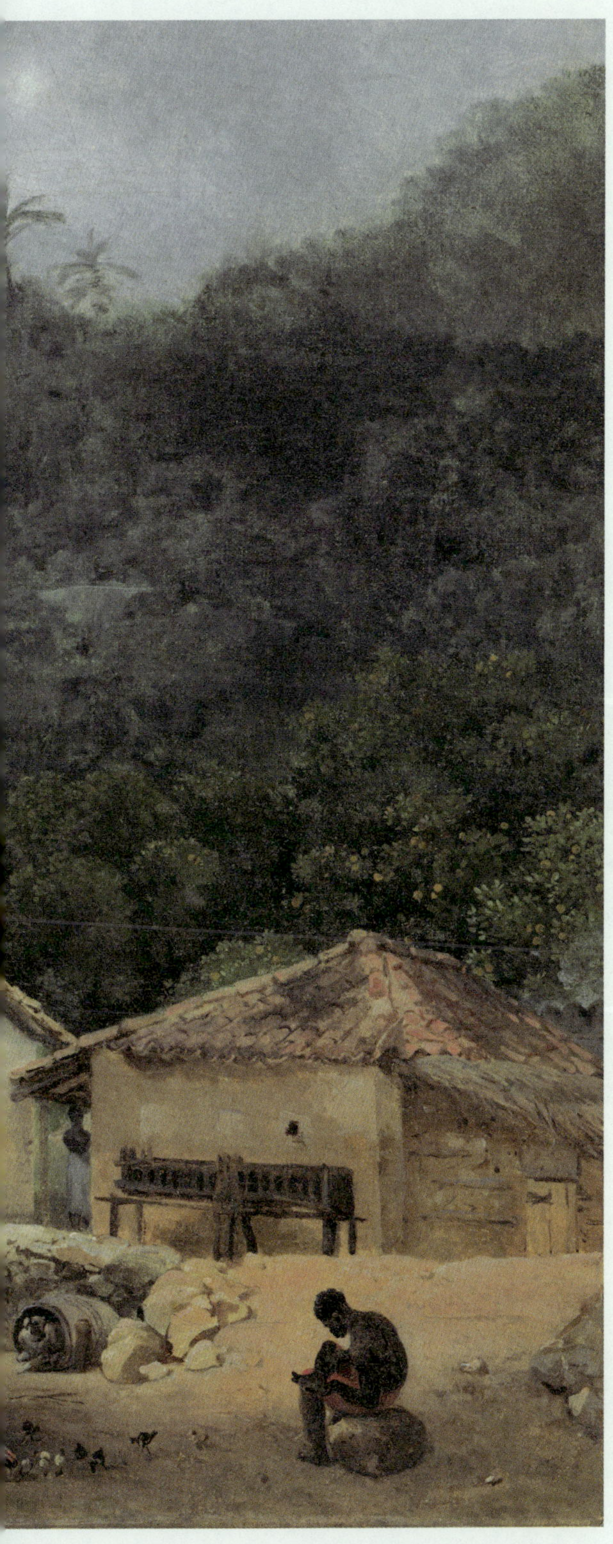

Het voorste Gebouw is myn woonhuis, en het Agterste de Keuken en Provisie kamer. Myn [illegible] zult Gy wel erkennen, en de twee Zwarten zyn myn Kok en zyn vrouw, die my redelyk wel oppassen, waarom Jk hun ook in 't vorige jaar, toen Jk, so onverwagts van Willem, die remise ontving, ieder een kleyne Neger en Negerin, tot hulp heb-aangekogt; want voor Huiswerk moet men hier absoluut Zwarten hebben, om dat de [illegible] al te slegt zyn, en alle ogenblik verhuisen, of wegloopen.

Zie daar, lieve Zuster, aan Uw verlangen voldaan. Jk wensche U van harten, al het huiselyk Geluk en Genoegen, hetwelk den Hemel U, in so ruime Mate schynt te schenken, en hetwelke Gy, en ook myn goede Broeder so heel verdient. Kusch alle Uwe lieve kinderen, regt hartelyk voor my. Jk omhelse U in Gedagten, en verblyve tot de dood,

Uw liefhebbende Broeder.

D:

Pour ma chère Soeur Mina.

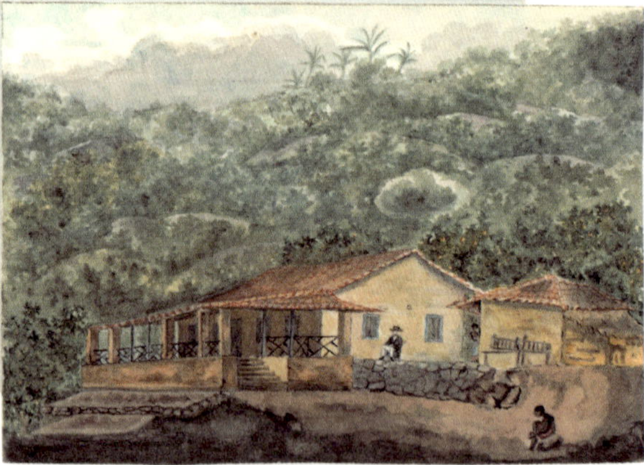

fig. 10 **Watercolour accompanying Dirk van Hogendorp's letter to his niece Mina, in which he writes that he has 'bought help' for his cook and his wife, 31 July 1821**

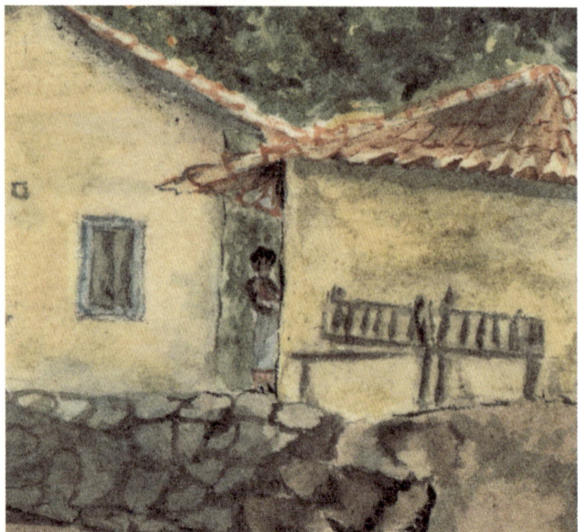

fig. 10a **Detail of the watercolour, where the woman is depicted wearing a dress**

colour did not necessarily mean that they were equal to other free people; that they were free to move and do as they chose. In his letter to Mina in 1821, Van Hogendorp bemoans the 'bad habit [of] freed slaves to run away':

> the two blacks are my cook and his wife, who look after me quite well, which is why also last year, when I unexpectedly received the permission from Willem, I bought for each of them a young negro and negress as help, since one certainly needs slaves here to perform housework, because the free ones are too bad, and are wont to move or run away at any moment.[62]

It is possible that one of these 'procured helpers' was Zinga, whose name we encounter in *Voyage autour du monde* (Voyage around the world), a travel journal by another of the general's visitors: Jacques Arago. He describes Van Hogendorp as being very attached to an Angolan woman named Zinga, lamenting, 'this is my negro, my brave Zinga, my only company in my lonely life'.[63] Did he perhaps never free Zinga in order to prevent her from leaving him?

in closing

The details of Dirk van Hogendorp's life combine to form a contradictory picture of the man. Like others of his time, he was mindful of injustice and idealistic in his judgement that slavery should be abolished. He nonetheless chose to buy human beings. He bemoans the fact that the people working for him would otherwise be disloyal, but never attributes this to the way he himself treats them. He expects those who are freed to remain eternally devoted to their liberators, envisaging an attitude encapsulated in his play *Kraspoekol* by the words spoken by the Tjampakka character: 'My benefactor! My saviour! My master! I shall serve you for all eternity, for all eternity; serve you and care for you with all my heart and soul. Thou hast liberated me from shame.'[64] Twenty years later, he still clung to the slavery system. He purchased human beings and called them 'my slaves' and 'my negro'. The historical account of the ending of slavery often attributes a prominent role to the leadership of European 'abolitionists' such as Van Hogendorp. Nonetheless, resistance fighters such as Tula had a very different notion of what 'freedom, equality and fraternity' would look like in a fair, post-slavery society.

valika smeulders

lohkay

beads versus laws

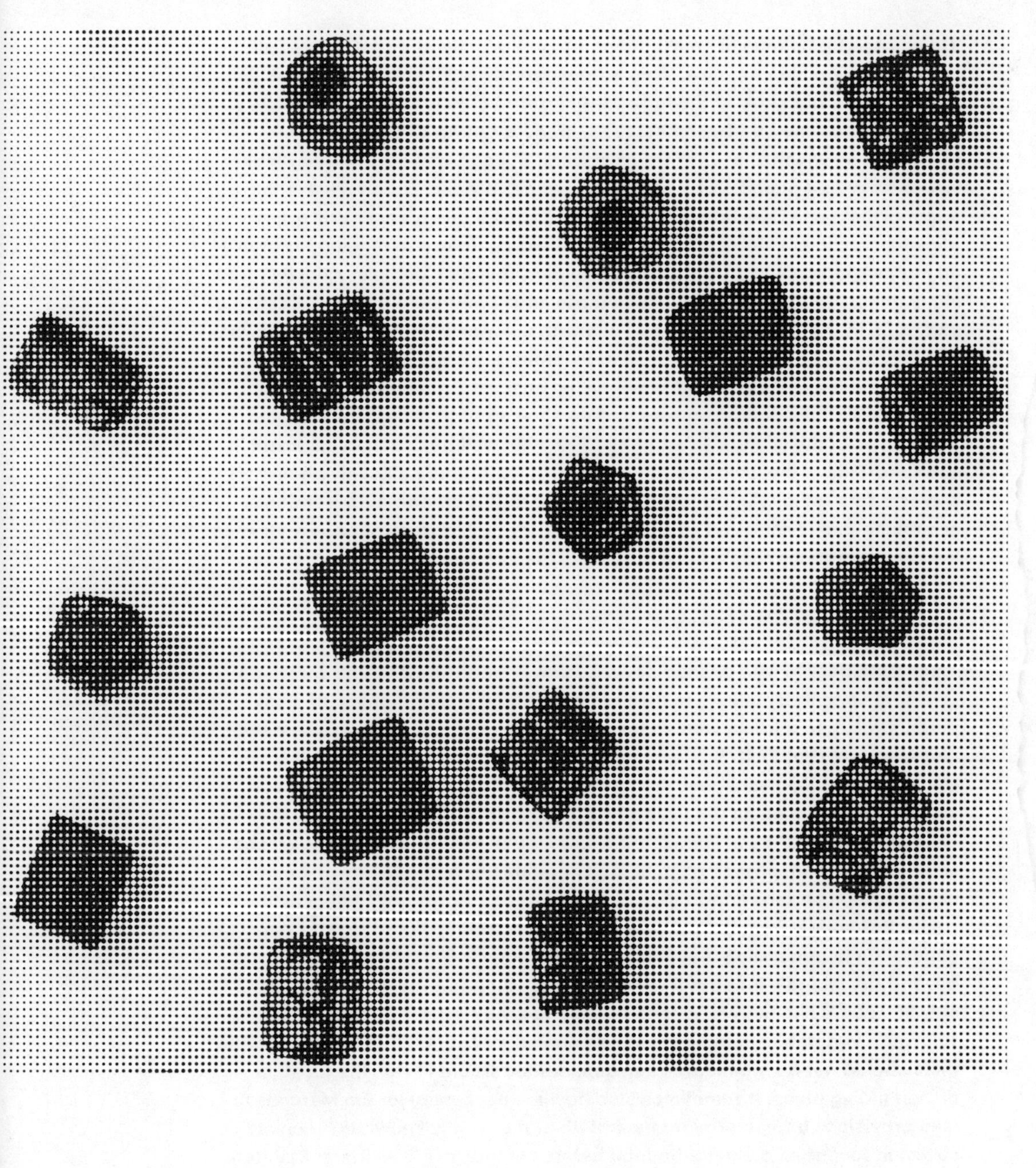

'Do you see that plume of smoke there, up on that hillside? That's One-Tété Lohkay, stoking her campfire.' This is how parents in Sint Maarten start telling their children the story of the legendary figure Lohkay. Oral tradition has it that Lohkay, who had been enslaved, made a daring escape from the plantation on which she was forced to work. But she was recaptured by her slaveholder and punished by having one of her breasts cut off. This is the origin of the name One-Tété Lohkay, or 'Lohkay with one breast'. This gruesome punishment did not stop Lohkay from escaping again and managing to survive on her own in the island's hills. Her unyielding rejection of the system inspired many generations of people living on the islands of Sint Maarten, Sint Eustatius and Saba in the Dutch Caribbean. Following a series of mass escapes (known as *marronages*) by enslaved people in Sint Maarten and Sint Eustatius, a decisive event took place in 1848, when all the enslaved workers on Diamond plantation fled. Plantation owners had no choice but to accept the de facto freedom of all the islands' inhabitants. This was well before the enactment in 1860 and 1863 of the laws through which the Netherlands officially abolished slavery. This raises the question of how we define freedom. Is freedom something that is achieved by making a law, through a stack of paper? Or is freedom something that is lived in spite of the circumstances?

my name is ...

Among the people who passed down Lohkay's story, she became known as One-Tété Lohkay. By talking to their children about a single plume of smoke, parents relate to a brave woman faced with a difficult choice. The islands of Sint Maarten, Sint Eustatius and Saba were too small to hide Maroon communities. Some escapees managed to reach nearby islands, but those who chose to remain on the island had to lead an isolated and lonely life. The telling of the story of One-Tété Lohkay's punishment, and the choice she made in spite of it, passes on to new generations both the reality of life in an unjust system and the importance of choosing one's own path within it.

It is known from the oral history that has been passed down from generation to generation that there were Maroons in Sint Maarten who lived beyond the island's inhabited regions, a very limited area on an island of only 85 square kilometres. To feed themselves they fished, hunted birds and cultivated vegetables and herbs. It was crucial, of course, that their vegetable plots should not be identifiable as such, or they would reveal the location of their hiding place. It sometimes also became necessary for the Maroons to take provisions from nearby farms and plantations. It is known that Lohkay collected food from the neighbouring estates of Industry, Saunders, St Peters, Marigot Hill and South Reward, all of which are located in an area of Sint Maarten called Cul de Sac.[1] This was the first substantial colonial settlement in the Dutch part of Sint Maarten (the island was split into French and Dutch territories in the seventeenth century), and in the eighteenth and nineteenth centuries a number of sugar plantations were located there. Industry plantation has now been renamed after its last occupant, Emilio Wilson.[2] Wilson is well-known in Sint Maarten for the part he played in making history visible. As a

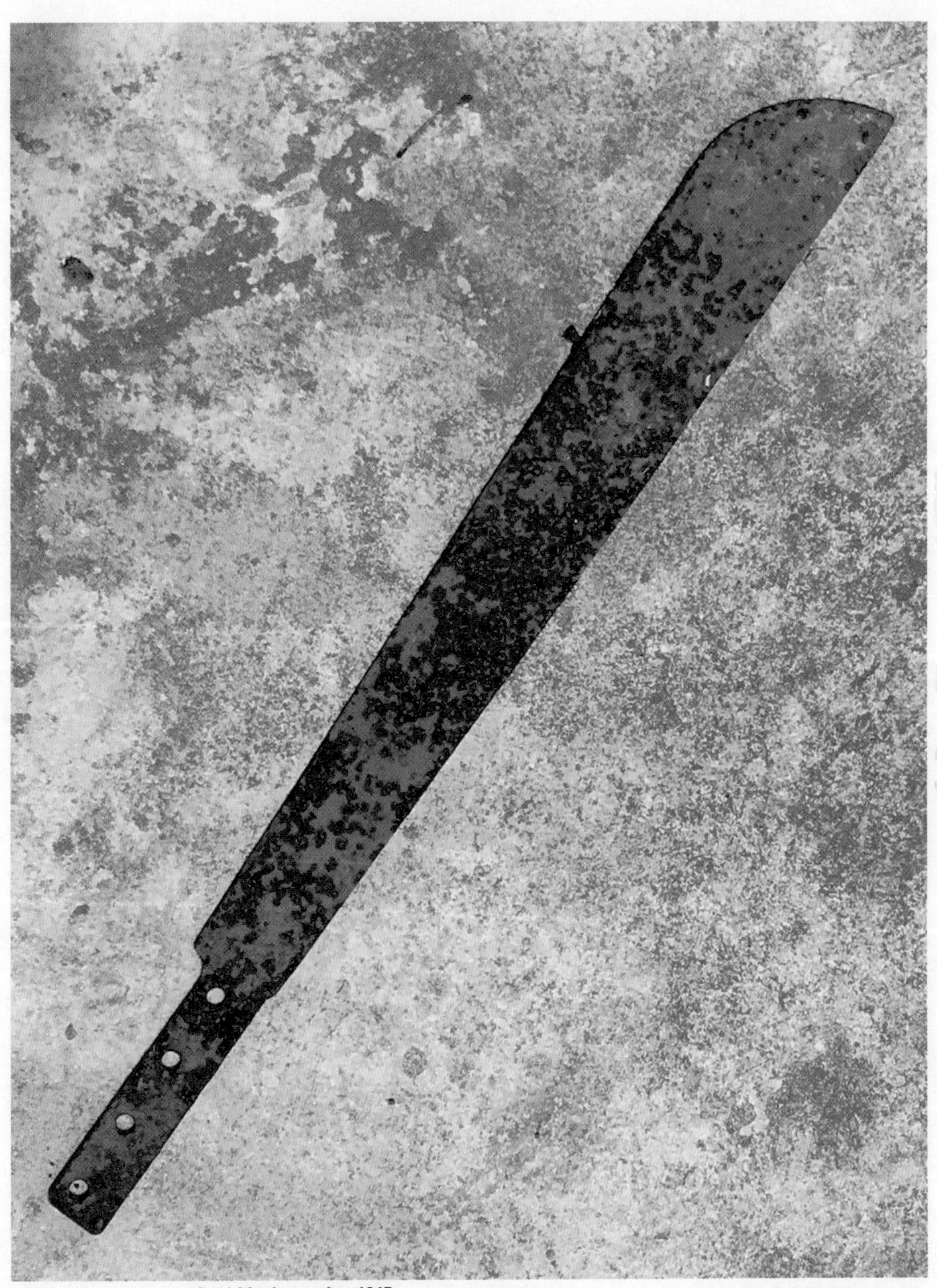

fig. 1 **Machete, after 1845**

descendant of enslaved people, he leapt at the opportunity to buy the estate on which some of his forebears had lived and worked. Initially he lived in the plantation's mansion, a grand residence that in 1740 was home to John Philips, the Scottish-Dutch vice commander of Sint Maarten after whom the capital, Philipsburg, is named. After the building was destroyed by hurricane Luis in 1995, Wilson moved into the 'boiler house', where the cane juice was boiled and where his ancestors must have worked. Wilson's aim was to ensure that the estate and the stories connected with it were preserved, protected and made accessible to visitors – not just the stories of those in power, such as John Philips, but also of enslaved people like Wilson's own ancestors. With this in mind, in 2002 he converted an area of the property into a public park, which now bears his name and contains a bust of him. The sugar-boiling house is now a restaurant. Thanks to Wilson, the many tourists who visit the island can experience its multifaceted history *in situ*.[3]

As more people became acquainted with Emilio Wilson's family history, more related data emerged. In 2005, the Sint Maarten Black History Awareness Foundation made an interesting discovery that was covered by the Sint Maarten newspaper the *Daily Herald*. The article concerned an archival record mentioning someone thought to be one of Wilson's ancestors. In this disturbing administrative document, human beings are described as company assets, with a monetary value added next to each person's name. Wilson's foremother is described thus: 'Also named Mary Ann. As an invalid, also of now having no leg 000.00'. For a slaveholder she, having lost a limb, had lost her value. How might she have lost her leg? Through an accident at work, perhaps, or as a result of disease? Or had she perhaps tried to escape? The law of 1734 permitted the shooting of escapees in the foot if they refused to be taken back to the plantation.[4] It is possible, therefore, that having attempted to escape she was shot in the foot, and that she lost her leg due to complications from the injury. The same document contains another entry that is pertinent to our story: 'a Negro girl named Lukey Two Hundred and Forty Guilders 240.00' (fig. 2).

For someone kept in slavery, the name Lukey, meaning 'lucky', has an ironic ring to it. The same can be said of other names that colonial slaveholders gave to enslaved people, such as those referencing powerful or mythological figures: names like Princes and Adonis, for example. It is highly unlikely that Lukey thought herself lucky to be living a life in slavery. The Sint Maarten Black History Awareness Foundation added a note to this name: 'One Tete Lukey', the same name as the legendary woman who managed repeatedly to escape her slaveholders. If this Lukey is indeed our protagonist Lohkay, then it is the only tangible historical evidence containing a reference to her. Unfortunately, the document was lost following its publication in the newspaper. This archival material gives us some indication of when Lohkay would have lived. Emilio Wilson was born in 1911, and if we assume that his great-great-grandmother who was named in the same document lived at the start of the nineenth century, we can place Lukey in the same period. This source also adds a new dimension to the oral history. Whereas the story that has been passed on by word of mouth focuses mostly on the part of her life she lived in freedom, this document offers a glimpse of the life from which she escaped: one that centred on her

later, the labor situation would be changed. The people   July 1, 1863.

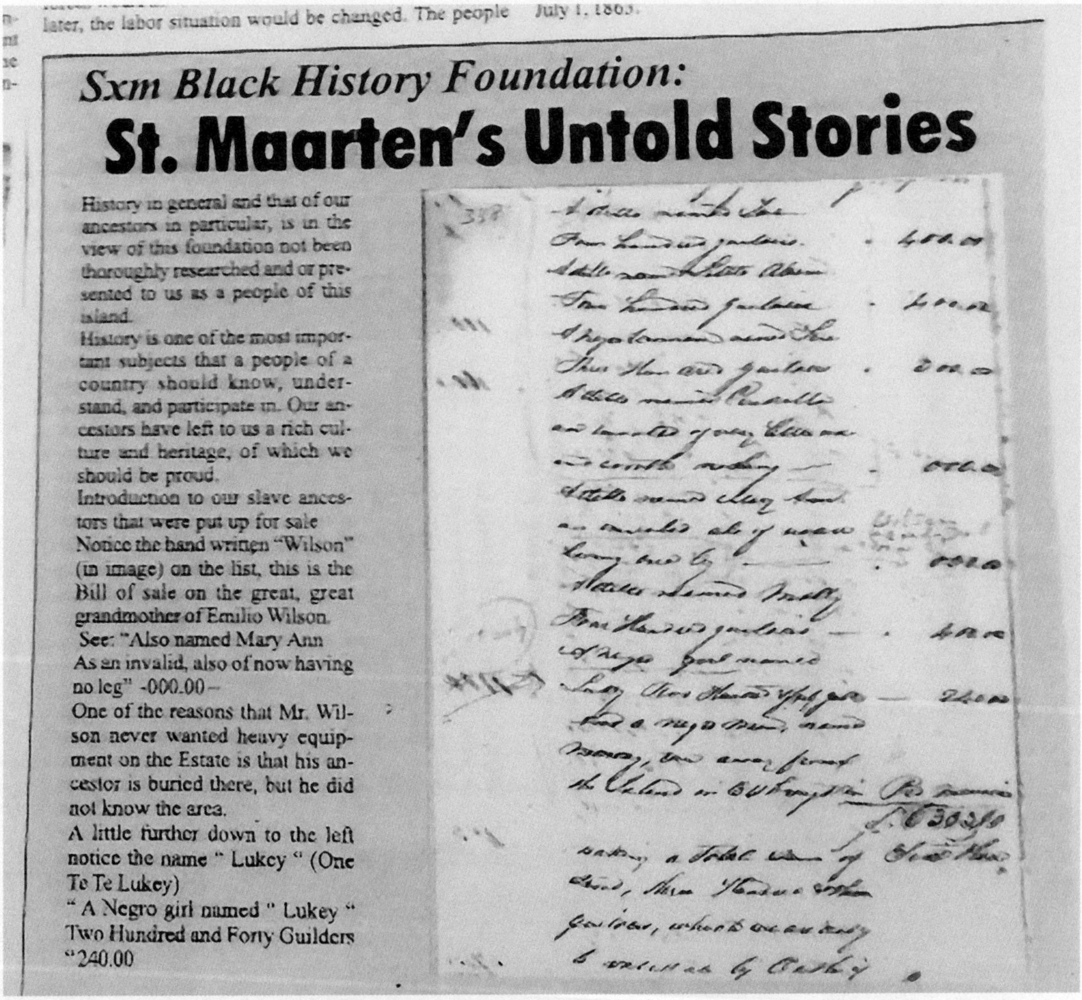

Sxm Black History Foundation:

St. Maarten's Untold Stories

History in general and that of our ancestors in particular, is in the view of this foundation not been thoroughly researched and or presented to us as a people of this island.

History is one of the most important subjects that a people of a country should know, understand, and participate in. Our ancestors have left to us a rich culture and heritage, of which we should be proud.

Introduction to our slave ancestors that were put up for sale

Notice the hand written "Wilson" (in image) on the list, this is the Bill of sale on the great, great grandmother of Emilio Wilson.

See: "Also named Mary Ann As an invalid, also of now having no leg" -000.00 –

One of the reasons that Mr. Wilson never wanted heavy equipment on the Estate is that his ancestor is buried there, but he did not know the area.

A little further down to the left notice the name " Lukey " (One Te Te Lukey)

" A Negro girl named " Lukey " Two Hundred and Forty Guilders "240.00

fig. 2 **Archival document containing a probable reference to One-Tété Lohkay: 'a Negro girl named Lukey Two Hundred and Forty Guilders 240.00', *Daily Herald*, 1 July 2005**

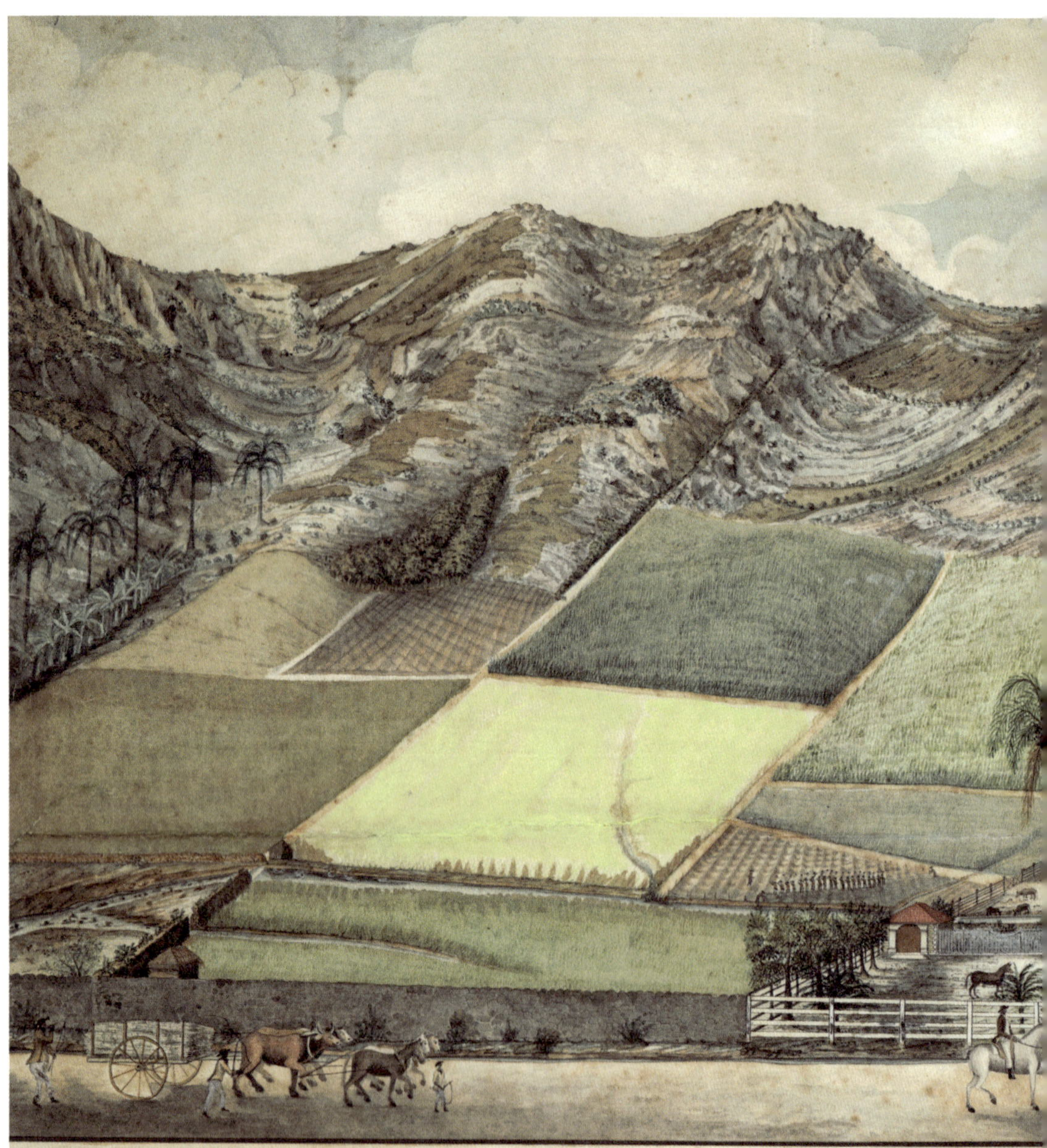

fig. 3 **The Retreat plantation in Cul de Sac**
Samuel Fahlberg, 1816

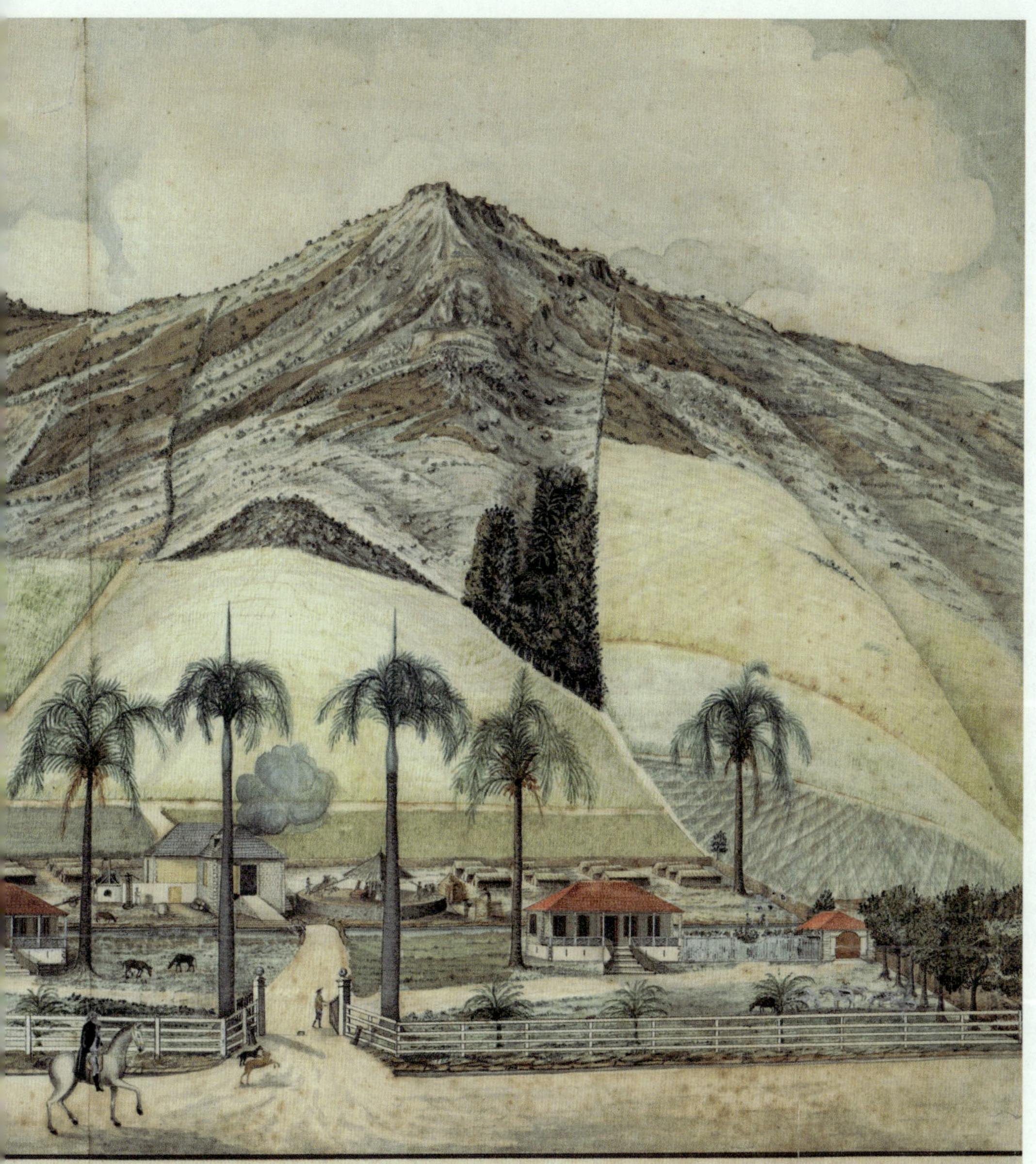
REAT
CUL DE SAC; THE PROPERTY OF
GOVERNOR OVER THE ISLANDs St MARTINS & SABA.
BY HIS GRATEFUL AND MOST OBEDIANT SERVANT
Samuel Fahlberg.
Colonial Surveyor

usefulness to a landowner, who on top of it all forced her to bear a name that suggested she should be happy with her lot.

The people who passed on her story modified her name from Lukey to One-Tété Lohkay. This modification encompasses an alteration of her enslaved name, as well as a reference to her struggle and the price she had to pay for her freedom. The use of breast amputation as a form of punishment also appears in the oral histories of places other than Sint Maarten. Suriname has a heroine named Alida whose story is similar: this enslaved woman was punished by Susanna du Plessis, a jealous plantation owner, because her husband was too fond of looking at Alida's breasts. Enslaved women in Suriname were often obliged to work naked from the waist up, as can be seen in a painting in the previous chapter (see pp. 260–261). The behaviour of the male slaveholders, who surrounded themselves with naked women and violated them, must have caused jealousy among their European spouses. It is likely, therefore, that this type of amputation was prompted by envy or rage, using tools that were at hand, such as the machetes that were used at the plantations at the time (fig. 1). The removal of breasts was not a legally defined punishment, and no mention of it appears in the archives, so some people cast doubt on whether it ever actually took place.[5] This reasoning can be countered by the fact that rape was seldom mentioned in official documentation, either. We can nonetheless be certain that it took place because of the many mixed children who were conceived under the oppressive and hierarchical colonial system.

In 2010, Sint Maarten became an autonomous country of the Kingdom of the Netherlands. As such, it can now make its own decisions about its commemorations, and a statue of One-Téte Lohkay is now part of those.[6] The statue portrays her running with a bundle of kindling for the fire that is referred to in the story told by parents to their children. It is obvious that beneath the simple wrap she wears, she is missing one breast. The figure radiates independence and strength, with the result that the amputation symbolizes her tenacity. Nonetheless, the way in which she is seen and represented is still evolving. A growing number of people in Sint Maarten are starting to call their heroine simply 'Lohkay'. Referring to her in this new way removes the connection between Lohkay's name and the injustice done to her. Now her name is more a reflection of the person she chose to be.

realizing freedom

Near Industry was another plantation in the Cul de Sac district named The Retreat. A surviving watercolour depicting this plantation offers us a rare insight into the way a sugar concern was laid out (fig. 3). The Retreat was the country home of Willem Hendrik Rink, Sint Maarten's commander from 1790 to 1801. His tenure overlapped with the period of French occupation of the Netherlands, during which neighbouring Haiti liberated itself from slavery and French Republicans took over plantations on Sint Maarten and freed enslaved people.[7] The watercolour was painted in 1816, two years after the Netherlands signed a treaty abolishing the international slave trade. Contrary to these developments, Rink and many other Dutch and French plantation owners in Sint Maarten still clung on to the use of slavery as part of their business operations, and evidence of this can be seen in the painting. In the foreground, on the nearside of the canal, is a stone-built living area for the owner (left) and the overseers (right). On the far side of the canal is the area where production took place, and where twenty dwellings for enslaved workers stood. These dwellings were generally timber-built, partly for which reason they have not survived. The largest building on the far side of the canal is the boiler house. The mill is also visible. This is where the sugarcane was pressed to obtain the sugarcane juice. The mill was powered by horses, oxen and sometimes people. Beyond the processing area are the sugarcane fields, where twenty people can be seen at work, supervised by an overseer.[8] People are also working at the mill and by the water, where we can see women during the wash. On the road, close to the entrance to the estate, two men on grey horses are visible – the owner and the overseer, perhaps? Behind them are people using a cart and pack animals to transport freight. The fact that these people are not wearing shoes indicates that they are enslaved.

This scene illustrates the contrast between the luxurious lifestyle enjoyed by the owner and the living and working conditions of the enslaved people. Despite living at such close quarters with the enslaved people, the slaveholder showed little concern for their humanity. This is evidenced by archaeological finds in Sint Eustatius, such as a shard of an eighteenth-century plate depicting the sugar production process (fig. 4). The idyllic image shows a mill in a natural landscape with birds flying free above it. The accompanying calligraphic text evokes a very different atmosphere: 'Bring more Cane to Mill Negro'. Enslaved people lived a reality in which they were considered a means of production and, moreover, despised. All the while, the hills and the promise of freedom were in constant view, as can be seen in the depiction of The Retreat. This proximity of freedom must surely have made it tempting to attempt an escape, but it is clear from the picture how difficult it would have been to hide – who would dare to flee when the chance of being recaptured was so great? This explains why it was meaningful to pass Lohkay's story on: it was made into a kind of mantra by which people instilled courage and hope in themselves and one another.

And hope did indeed endure. Saint Martin is a small member of the Leeward Islands, which form a compact arc in the Caribbean. Two watercolours from 1822 and 1823 show the capital Philipsburg from two sides: one is an inland view (fig. 5), the other faces out to sea (fig. 6). In the foreground of the latter, a figure can be seen carrying on their head a load that looks very much like a bundle of sugarcane. The man or woman appears not to be wearing shoes, which suggests that the person concerned is enslaved. In the distance is the neighbouring island of Saba and, to its left, on the horizon, Sint Eustatius. Besides Saba and Sint Eustatius there are several other neighbouring islands nearby, such as Saint Kitts, on the far left of the picture. These islands were ruled by various colonial powers, each with their own policy on slavery. In 1825, for example, the United Kingdom, which took a leading role in ending colonial slavery, decided that it would no longer extradite people who had fled into its territory from Dutch territory – to do otherwise would have equated to engaging in the slave trade. In the years that followed, the United Kingdom (1834), Sweden (1847), France (1848) and Denmark (1848) all abolished slavery. Consequently, enslaved people living in Dutch territories had increasing opportunities to escape. Now, as well as being able to choose to become a Maroon, they could find refuge on other islands where slavery had already been abolished.[9]

In Sint Maarten the colonial regime responded by imposing more regulations. Gatherings of enslaved people were banned to curb communications among them. And in a measure that constrained enslaved people in their ability to be self-sufficient, mutual trade and the cultivation of foodstuffs was also forbidden. Furthermore, to prevent escapes, unregistered boats were banned and an evening pass was introduced. Harsh punishments were imposed on those who failed to comply with these rules, including the aforementioned gunshot to the foot.[10] At the same time, in a seemingly contradictory move, the central government in the Netherlands enacted measures intended to improve living conditions, in the hope this would mitigate the motivations for enslaved people to flee.[11] And of course they also had a proverbial carrot dangled in front of them: the freedom that had already been introduced elsewhere kept alive their hopes that it would not be long before abolition was enacted in the Dutch colonies.[12]

While the Dutch colonial regime sought to prolong the duration of the slavery system, enslaved people in Dutch territories were becoming increasingly aware of the growing options for escape. The rising numbers of former slaves in British territories provided encouragement. In the preceding decades the prospect of a solitary life functioned as a deterrent to potential escapees, who were also concerned about the people they would leave behind: what kind of life would they have with a loved one gone? Would they be punished for their association with the escapee? But confidence in a positive outcome grew along with the size of the areas to which people in Sint Maarten could go, and the number of allies in them. They devised the remarkable and large-scale strategy of mass escapes of entire plantation communities. In 1840, for example, all the enslaved people on three plantations belonging to a single Dutch owner escaped.[13]

In 1848, slavery in the French part of Saint Martin was abolished. The people who gained their freedom were sympathetic towards their counterparts across the border, as witnessed by surviving song lyrics that were written down at the close of the twentieth century:

> *Obbey Ben'a here 'm long time, Bukkra hide 'm long time*
>
> Oh, we heard them for a long time, the white master hid them for a long time

Another version reveals that this sense of solidarity also led to action in the form of collaborating on marronages:

> Oh we benna here 'm long time. But we come then and we hide 'm, oh poor slave. And we get emancipation.[14]

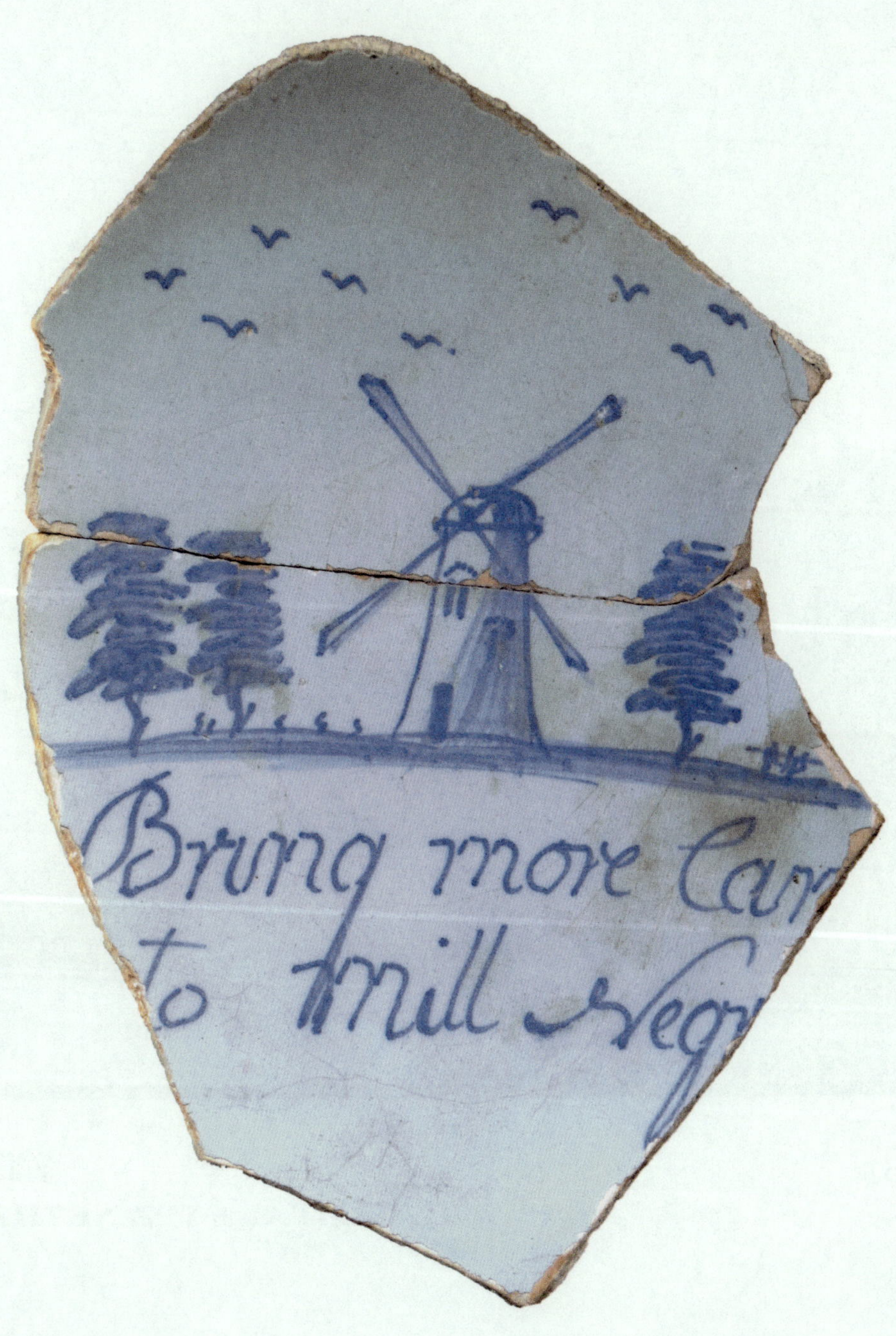

fig. 4 **Plate sherd with a text reading: 'Bring more Cane to Mill Negro'**
Sint Eustatius, 1750–1800

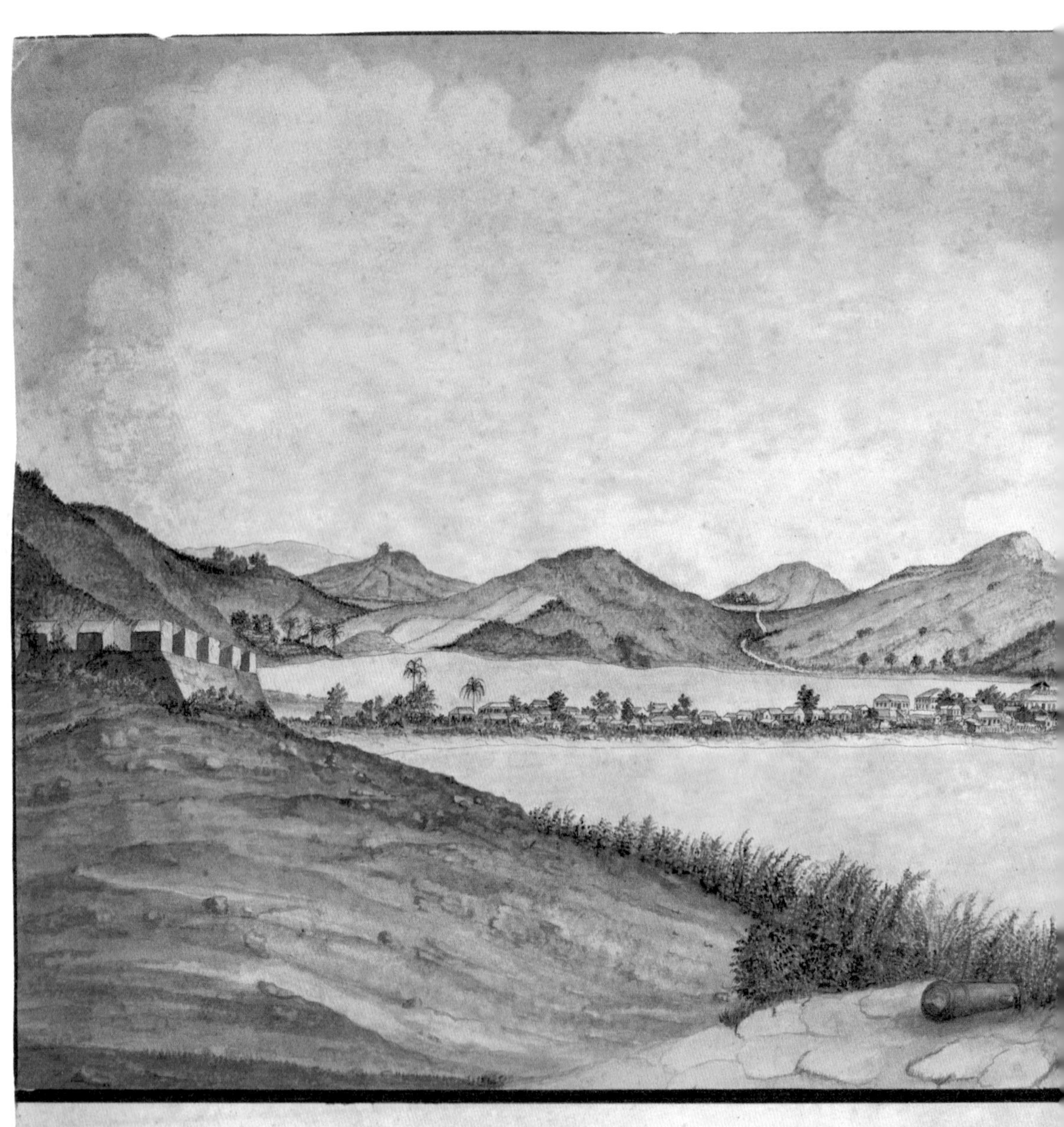

fig. 5 **Inland view of Philipsburg, 1823**

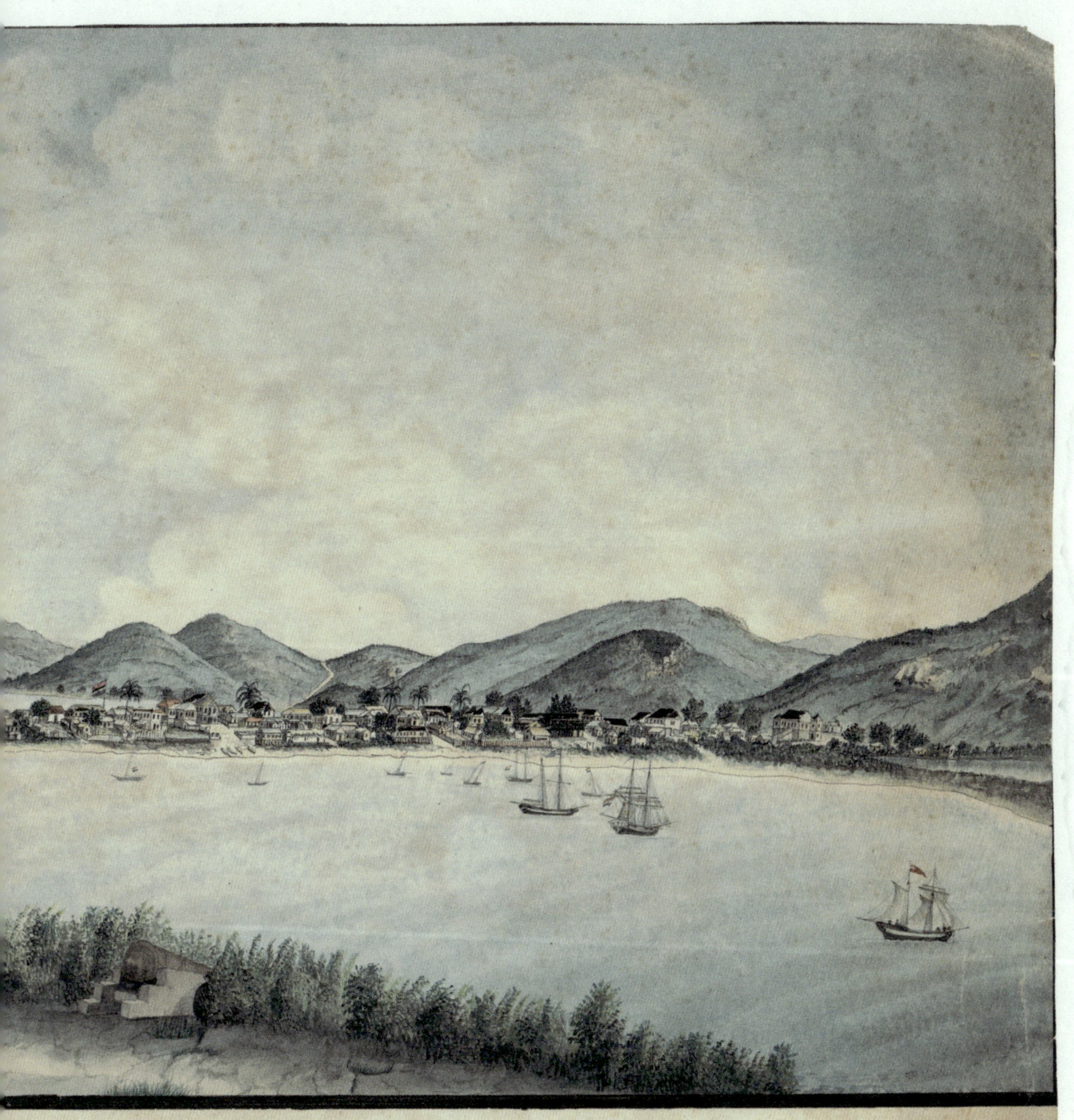

IPSBURG.
OF THE ISLAND SAINT MARTIN'S.
Amsterdam.
lberg

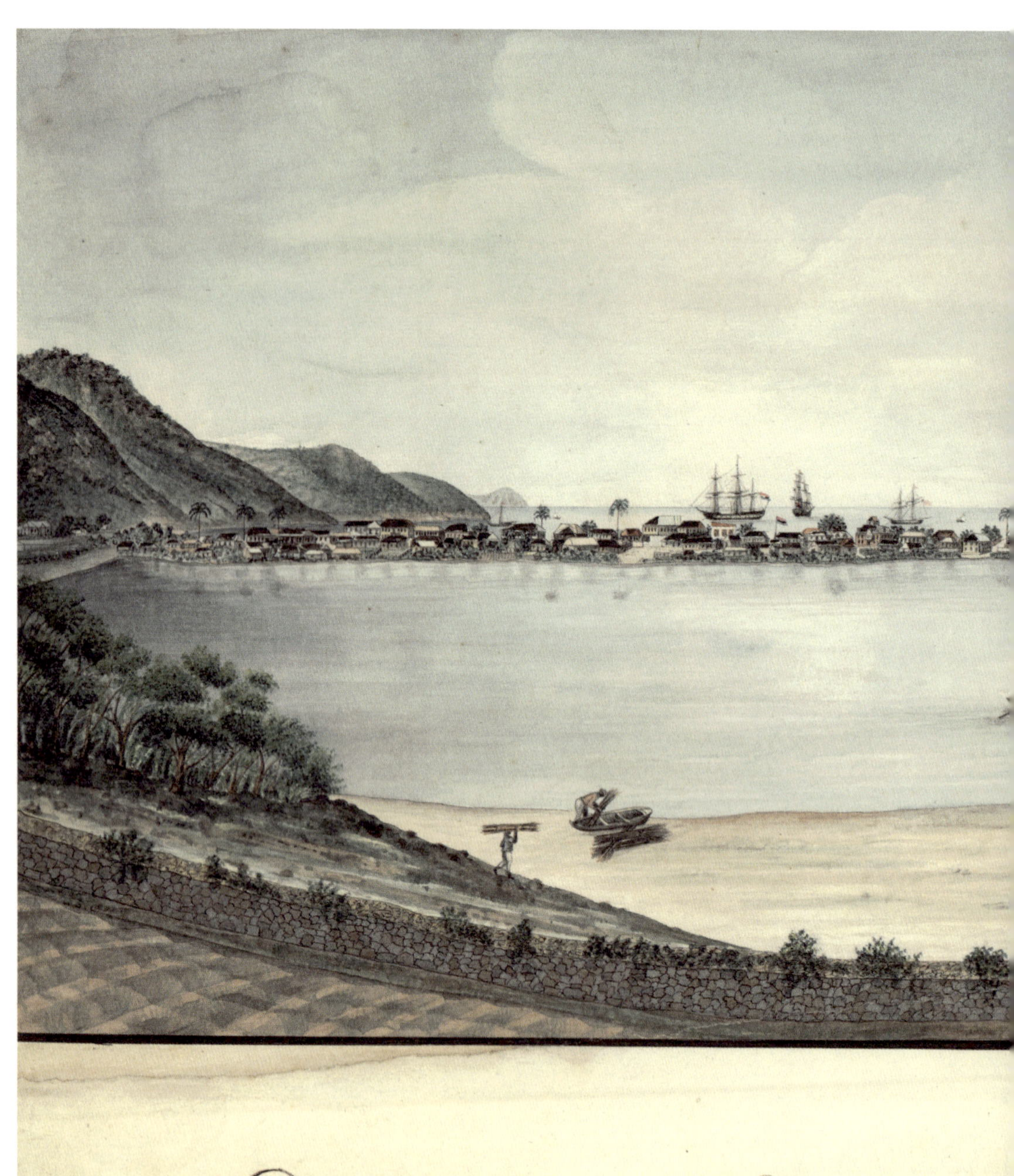

fig. 6 **View of Philipsburg facing out to sea, 1822**

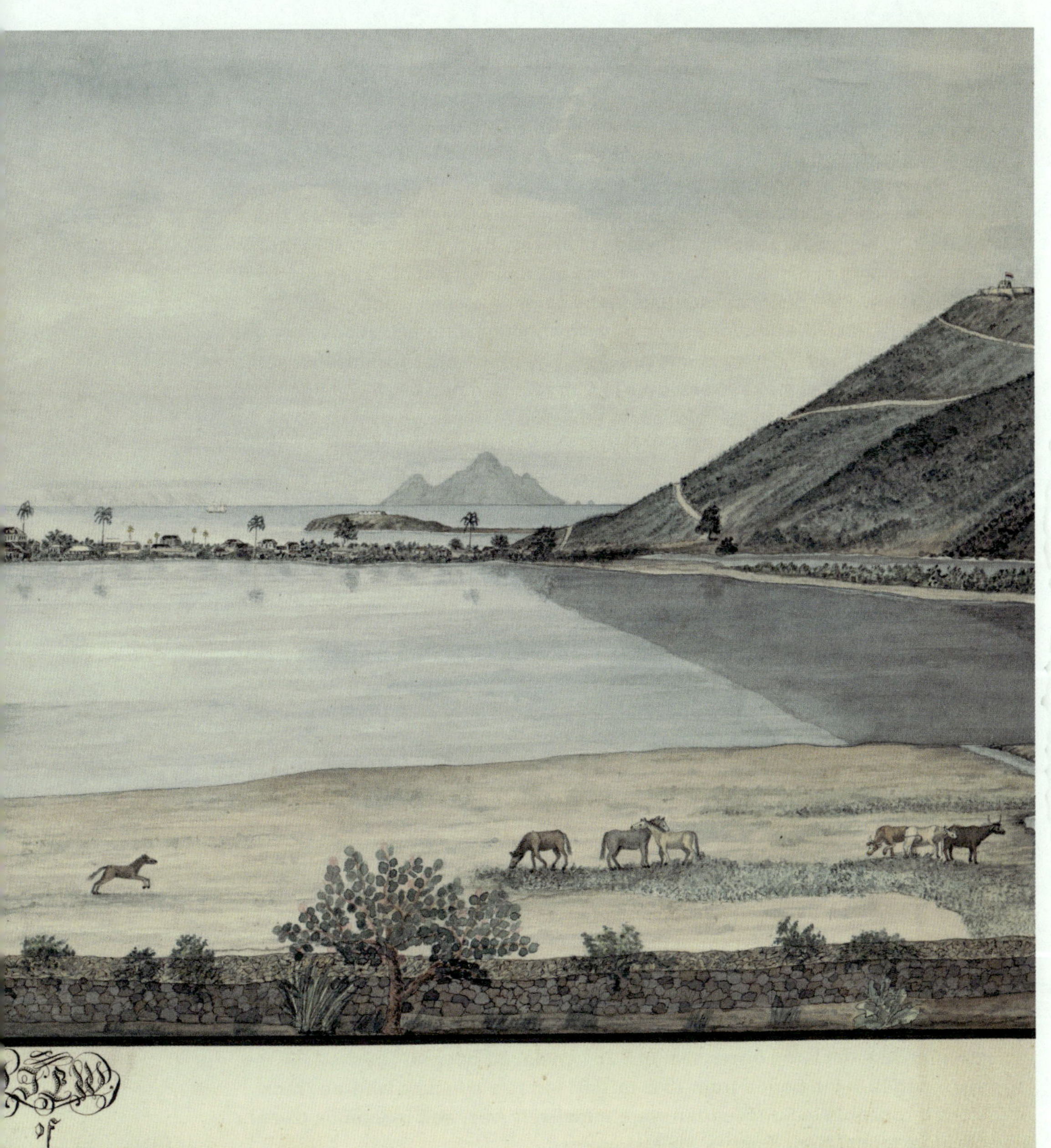

of
LIPSBURG.
part of the Island Saint MARTINS.
Former Governor of the Islands St MARTINS and Saba.
Most Obedient Humble
Samuel Fahlberg

What stands out in these lyrics is that they first refer to the injustice of the system, and then immediately afterwards to the autonomous actions taken to bring an end to that system. In 1848, all the enslaved people on the Diamond plantation fled to the French part of the island, where they found refuge with formerly enslaved people ('we come then and we hide 'm'). Only after these words does the song refer to the 'getting' of emancipation (the proclamation of freedom by the state), which took place fifteen years later. The historical record tends to focus on the statutory abolition of slavery by the Dutch in 1863, but in the oral history of Sint Maarten, the efforts of enslaved people are prioritized.

The written historical sources in the colonial archives only make it possible to trace the administrative path to abolition. Interpretations vary on which figures took the lead in this process. The researcher Jessica Roitman, for example, writes that slaveholders in Sint Maarten had been wanting to do away with the slavery system for some time due to declining profits, while the historian Alejandro Paula concludes in his archive study that slaveholders were very committed to the system – more even than the national government in the Netherlands.[15] What is certain, however, is that following the mass escape of the 'Diamond 26' – the colloquial collective name for the former enslaved workers who fled from the plantation – the slaveholders appealed in writing to the Crown in the Netherlands requesting the immediate ending of slavery. Several plantations had lost their entire labour force and could no longer function. Their owners made it clear that they wanted to be financially compensated for the loss of the labour force due to the abolition of slavery. It was due to this request for financial compensation that the Dutch state did not want to comply with the request for abolition in 1848. The years that followed were marked by a tug of war between the government in the Netherlands and on the islands (fig. 7).

When slavery was at last abolished in 1863, the compensation paid to the slaveholders in Sint Maarten was lower than elsewhere in the Kingdom of the Netherlands, at 100 guilders.[16] The Dutch state reasoned that the plantation owners on Sint Maarten incurred smaller losses because they had already been living for fifteen years with the reality that enslaved people could no longer be considered property. This is supported by figures from a census conducted in 1863 to determine the number of enslaved people for whom compensation would have to be paid: only 1,456 people were counted, while slaveholders declared ownership of 2,254 enslaved people.[17] In short, all the marronages in the period from 1848 to 1863 led to a situation whereby most enslaved people in Sint Maarten were effectively free, and plantation owners could no longer treat them as their property.[18]

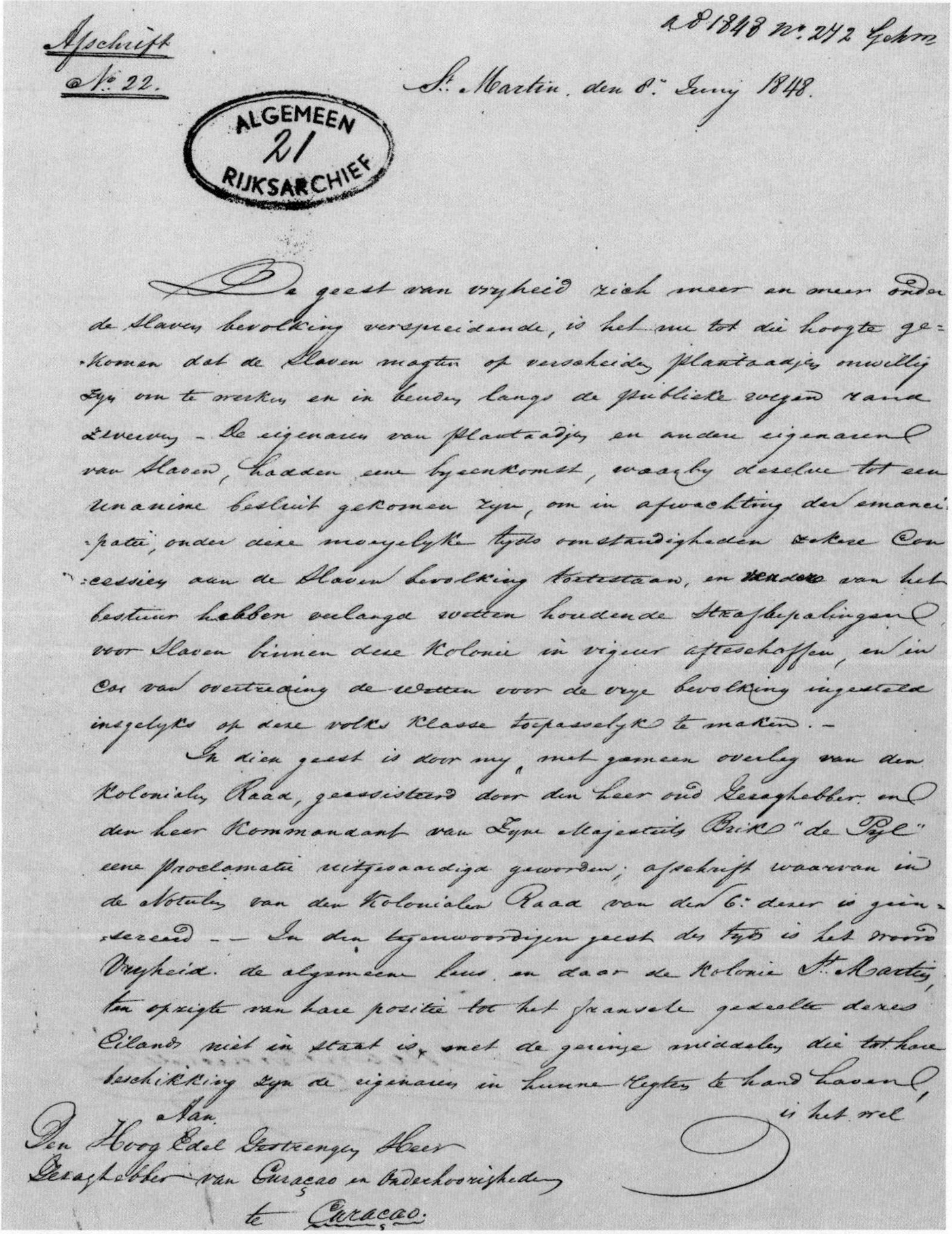

Afschrift
No. 22.

AD 1848 No. 242 Geh…

St. Martin, den 8e Juny 1848.

De geest van vryheid zich meer en meer onder de Slaven bevolking verspreidende, is het nu tot die hoogte gekomen dat de Slaven magten op verscheiden plantaadjes onwillig zyn om te werken, en in benden langs de publieke wegen rond zwerven. - De eigenaars van plantaadjes en andere eigenaren van Slaven, hadden eene byeenkomst, waarby deselve tot een unanime besluit gekomen zyn, om in afwachting der emancipatie, onder deze moeyelyke tyds omstandigheden zekere Concessies aan de Slaven bevolking toetestaan, en verder van het bestuur hebben verlangd wetten houdende Strafbepalingen, voor Slaven binnen deze Kolonie in vigeur afteschaffen, en in Cas van overtreding de Wetten voor de vrye bevolking ingesteld insgelyks op deze volks Klasse toepasselyk te maken. -

In dien geest is door my, met gemeen overleg van den Kolonialen Raad, geassisteerd door den heer oud Gezaghebber en den heer Kommandant van Zyne Majesteits Brik "de Pyl" eene Proclamatie uitgevaardigd geworden, afschrift waarvan in de Notulen van den Kolonialen Raad van den 6e dezer is geinsereerd -- In den tegenwoordigen geest des tyds is het woord Vryheid de algemeene leus, en daar de Kolonie St. Martin, ten opzigte van haare positie tot het Fransche gedeelte dezes Cilands niet in staat is, met de geringe middelen die tot haare beschikking zyn de eigenaars in hunne regten te handhaven, is het wel

Aan
Den Hoog Edel Gestrenge Heer
Gezaghebber van Curaçao en Onderhoorigheden
te Curaçao.

fig. 7 **Letter from the authorities of Sint Maarten to the authorities of Curaçao on changes to the slavery system, 8 June 1848**

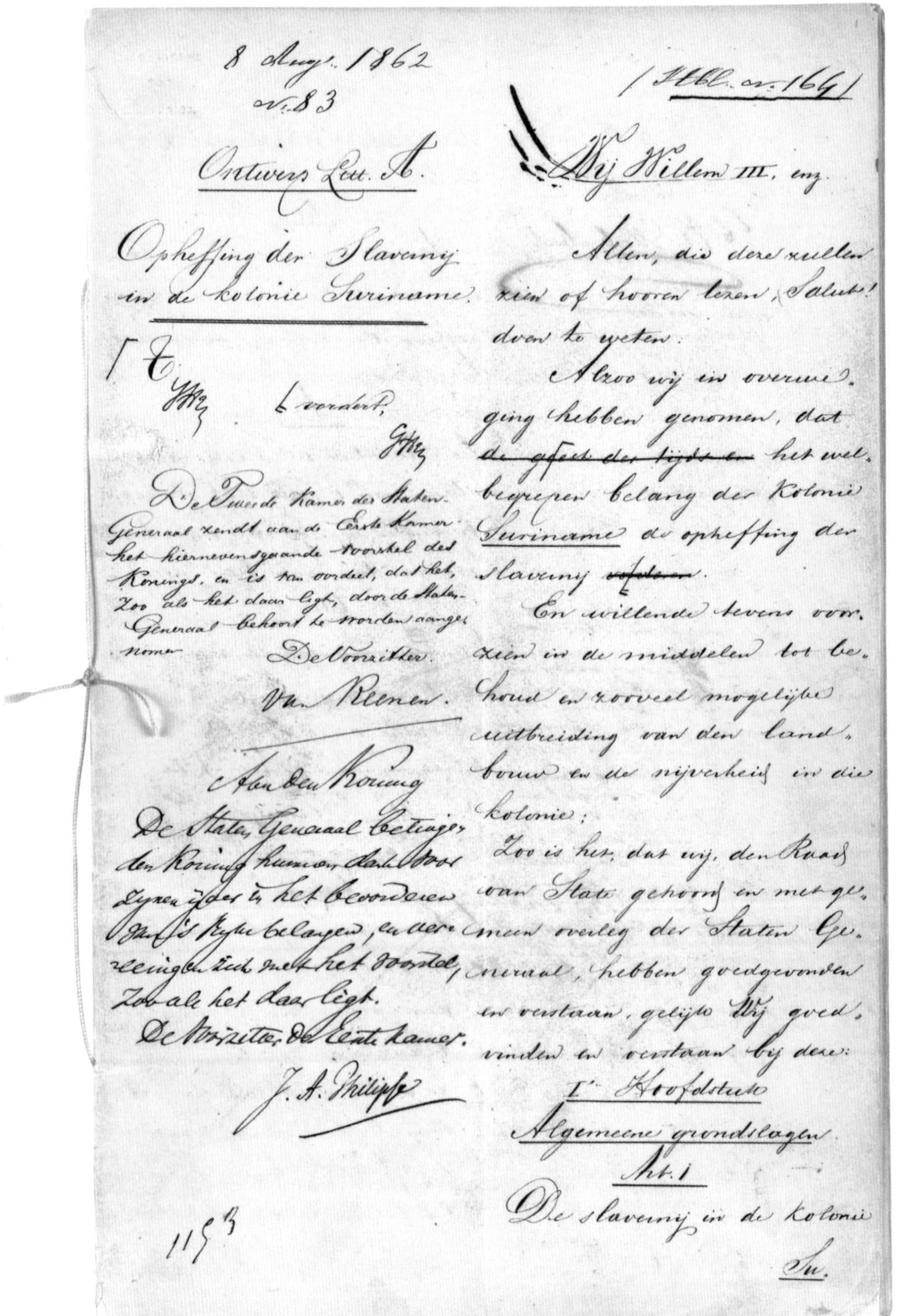

8 Aug. 1862
No. 83

Ontwerp Lett. A.

Opheffing der Slavernij in de kolonie Suriname.

vordert,

De Tweede Kamer der Staten-Generaal zendt aan de Eerste Kamer het hiernevensgaande voorstel des Konings, en is van oordeel, dat het, zoo als het daar ligt, door de Staten-Generaal behoort te worden aangenomen.

De Voorzitter.

Van Reenen.

Aan den Koning

De Staten Generaal betuigen den Koning hunnen dank voor Zijnen ijver tot het bevorderen van 's Rijks belangen, en vereenigen zich met het voorstel, zoo als het daar ligt.

De Voorzitter der Eerste kamer.

J. A. Philipse

1153

(Stbl. no. 164)

Wij Willem III, enz.

Allen, die deze zullen zien of hooren lezen, Salut! doen te weten:

Alzoo Wij in overweging hebben genomen, dat het welbegrepen belang der Kolonie Suriname de opheffing der slavernij [vordert].

En willende tevens voorzien in de middelen tot behoud en zooveel mogelijke uitbreiding van den landbouw en de nijverheid in die kolonie;

Zoo is het, dat Wij, den Raad van State gehoord en met gemeen overleg der Staten Generaal, hebben goedgevonden en verstaan, gelijk Wij goedvinden en verstaan bij deze:

1e Hoofdstuk

Algemeene grondslagen

Art. 1

De slavernij in de kolonie Su-

fig. 8 **Act for the abolition of slavery in the Dutch Antilles, enacted in 1863**

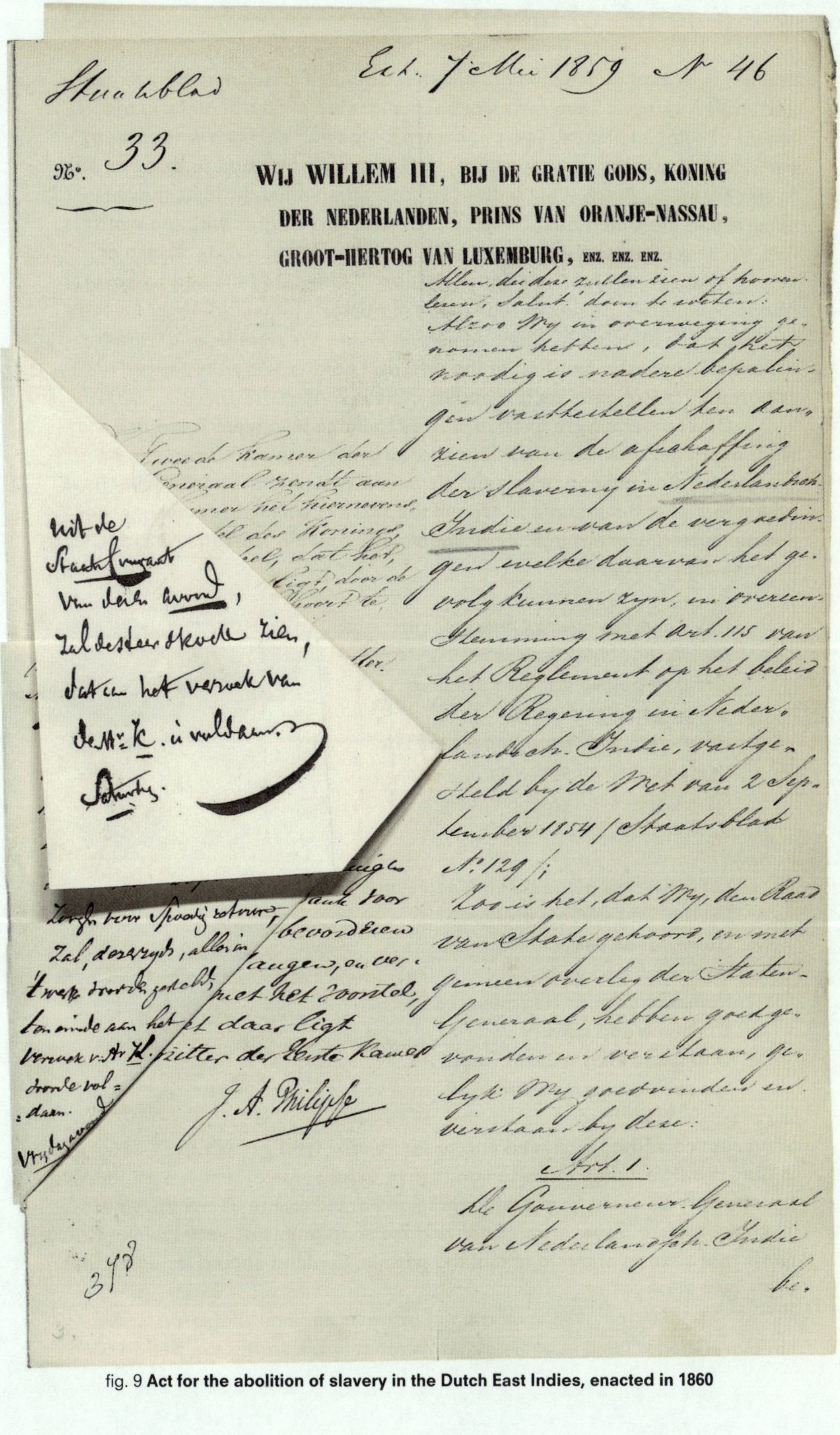

Staatsblad

Ext. 7 Mei 1859 No 46

No. 33.

WIJ WILLEM III, BIJ DE GRATIE GODS, KONING DER NEDERLANDEN, PRINS VAN ORANJE-NASSAU, GROOT-HERTOG VAN LUXEMBURG, ENZ. ENZ. ENZ.

Allen, die deze zullen zien of hooren lezen, Salut! doen te weten:

Alzoo Wij in overweging genomen hebben, dat het noodig is nadere bepalingen vast te stellen ten aanzien van de afschaffing der slavernij in Nederlandsch-Indië en van de vergoedingen welke daarvan het gevolg kunnen zijn, in overeenstemming met Art. 115 van het Reglement op het beleid der Regering in Nederlandsch-Indië, vastgesteld bij de Wet van 2 September 1854 (Staatsblad No. 129);

Zoo is het, dat Wij, den Raad van State gehoord, en met gemeen overleg der Staten-Generaal, hebben goedgevonden en verstaan, gelijk Wij goedvinden en verstaan bij deze:

Art. 1

De Gouverneur-Generaal van Nederlandsch-Indië be-

Uit de Staatscourant van deze avond, zal de heer [illegible] zien, dat aan het verzoek van de Hr. K. is voldaan.

J. A. Philipse

378

fig. 9 **Act for the abolition of slavery in the Dutch East Indies, enacted in 1860**

a sense of meaning

'History is written by the victors', Winston Churchill is reputed to have said, and written sources have certainly been allocated a central place in the record of colonial history. Two phenomena – 'power' and 'the written word' – come together in the abolition laws. In 1863 they were used to bring an end to slavery in the Dutch West Indies (fig. 8); a little earlier, in 1860, the same occurred in the Dutch East Indies (fig. 9). The text begins with the words 'We, William III, by the grace of God, King of the Netherlands, Prince of Orange-Nassau, grand Duke of Luxemburg'.[19] They are followed by several pages containing articles of legislation – articles that would never be read by the people affected by them. At no point were the people who were freed consulted about the wording of the law, and neither were they given an opportunity to evaluate the law and its consequences.

Other means were used to convey to those who were freed that they were expected to accept their fate and be grateful to the Crown – to be grateful for the abolition of colonial slavery, a system that should never have been created in the first place. One of the ways in which this message was communicated was through song. People in Suriname were instructed to sing the following words:

Des Konings naam zij hooggeacht
Den Koning dank gebracht
Komt, zingen wij tot prijs van hem
Met onverzwakte stem
Hij maakte ons, arme Negers vrij
Van schande en slavernij
God zegen koning Willem Drie
Voor zoveel gunstbewijs.

Let the King's name be high acclaimed
Let the King receive gratitude
Come, let us sing in his praise
With unabated voice
He made us poor Negroes free
Of shame and slavery
God bless King William Three
For such great generosity.

Songs conceived by enslaved and formerly enslaved people have survived in Curaçao. The words to these songs give expression to feelings for the king that are very different from gratitude. In one of these, the use of the words 'Long live Willem Three' is sarcastic, and the song goes on to say in unequivocal terms that instead of trying to fool the people, the king should try doing that to his own kin.[20]

The 1860 and 1863 laws did not bring to an immediate end to the structural inequalities in society that were instated during the period of

colonial slavery. On the contrary, in the nineteenth century the representation of history in museums and the public space soared, a narrative that placed a strong emphasis on the legitimization of colonial conquest and rule. This legitimization was further underpinned by pseudoscientific attempts to establish a hierarchy of ethnic groups. Colonial exhibitions were staged that exhibited not just products but also people from colonized regions. A photograph taken at the Amsterdam World's Fair in 1833, titled *Verschillende typen Surinaamse creolen* (Various types of Surinamese Creoles), shows how people were classified and essentialized (fig. 10)**. Twenty years after the abolition of slavery, these women were no longer objects in plantation records; now they were transformed into objects in an exhibition on Amsterdam's Museum Square.**

The expressions on the faces of the women looking into the camera convey many emotions, from resignation to the situation at that moment – one from which they saw no immediate way out – to self-awareness, self-esteem and mental freedom. In a world where, for centuries, Black people had been considered instruments of production, and where this injustice is far from universally acknowledged, the creation of meaning is in no sense a neutral process. The meaning imparted by institutions that were part of the system is diametrically opposed to that which was experienced in the past and in the present by descendants of enslaved people.

History is omnipresent in Sint Eustatius. While under colonial rule the island was an important trading post and slave market. The great wealth of the period is reflected in many remnants, which have led to the island becoming a major site for archaeological discoveries. These include many potsherds and beads (fig. 4)**. Beads were used as currency during the colonial period, and similar ones are to be found all over the world, wherever Dutch traders went: from South Africa to Indonesia, and from Alaska to Sint Eustatius. Relatively large quantities of blue glass beads are to be found on the island** (fig. 11)**, though why most of the beads found here are this particular colour is a mystery. The fact that many of them are found in the water is behind the often heard explanation that the beads were part of the cargo of a sunken ship. Over time, these beads have become unofficially incorporated into the marketing of tourism on the island. Tourists who visit the island to dive are told that finding a blue bead on the seabed will bring them good fortune: they have been chosen to find a bead and they will return to the island in the future. A more interesting phenomenon, however, is the connection that local people make in their oral history between the beads and slavery and freedom. This story is less frequently shared with visitors and is intended mainly for their own circles.**

The story goes that in the period of slavery and shortly thereafter the beads were used in Sint Eustatius as currency, specifically by people in slavery and their descendants. This would have been in line with the aforementioned rule that trade was forbidden in order to prevent people building their independence – they would not, after all, be able to use the beads to pay for everything that could be bought with hard cash. It is believed that the collecting of beads was also bound up with the right to marry, a right that all citizens had but which enslaved people did not. If a man possessed sufficient beads for

a string that he could tie around the waist of his intended wife, then he was permitted to marry her. The beads were also worn as jewellery, and African Caribbean priests used them as part of their spiritual attire. These forms of use maintain a relationship with Africa, where the wearing of beads is associated with beauty and aesthetics as well as status and identity. It is this latter function that is most pertinent to the story, which tells that, at the moment of emancipation, people threw their beads into the water en masse, in a collective rejection of the colonial system. Thus, the explanation now given for the presence of so many blue beads in the water represents a reclamation of equality with other citizens and the rejection of a separate currency. Nowadays, those inhabitants of Sint Eustatius who wear a blue bead do so to signal a connection with their ancestors, and their pride in those who took an independent stance with respect to colonial rules.[21]

From the colonial period until today, migration has been a common factor influencing the composition of the population of the Leeward Islands. Many inhabitants were born elsewhere, and these new islanders are joining those who came before them in a search for a common identity, a story that connects them. Traditions are constructs, the result of the meaning a society assigns to what they decide is common heritage. In the Leeward Islands, the focus is shifting towards resistance as part of a common identity. Although stories such as the one about the blue beads cannot be traced in a literal sense to historical documents, they do align with the reality of that period. The stories are therefore, as Felicia Fricke writes, 'qualitatively rather than literally true'.[22]

One of the first decisions taken by the government of the young country of Sint Maarten in 2010 was to establish an annual commemoration on 1 July. The focus on this day lies not on William III's law but on the flight of the 26 people from Diamond plantation in 1848. This mass escape is re-enacted as living history. Imbuing liberty with meaning in this way represents a conscious decision to prioritize what Lohkay has taught us, through her independent stance towards the system and her confidence in her own resourcefulness.

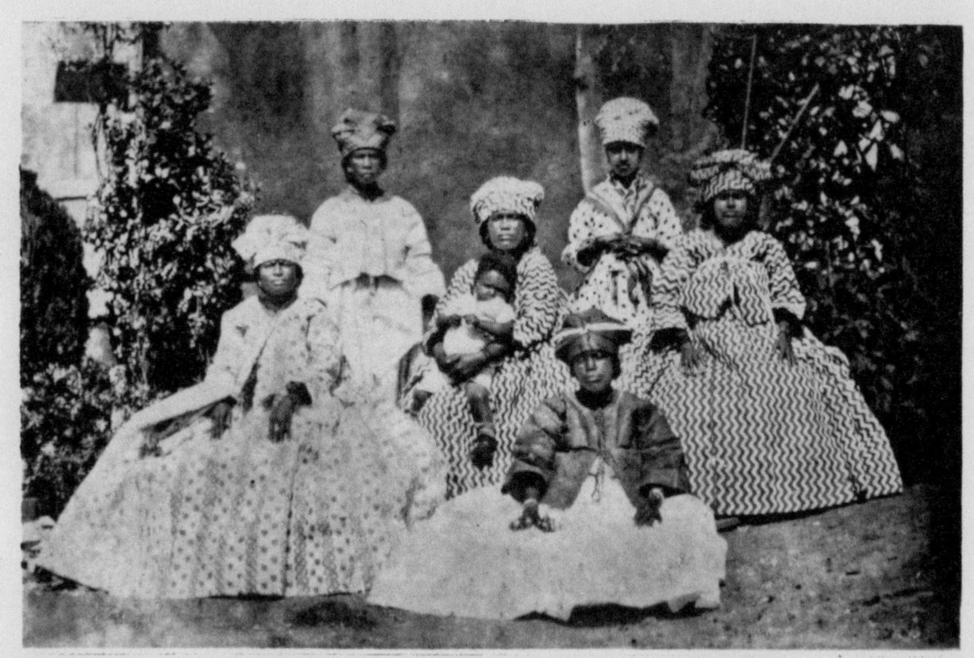

fig. 10 **Photograph of Surinamese women at the World's Fair in Amsterdam, 1883**

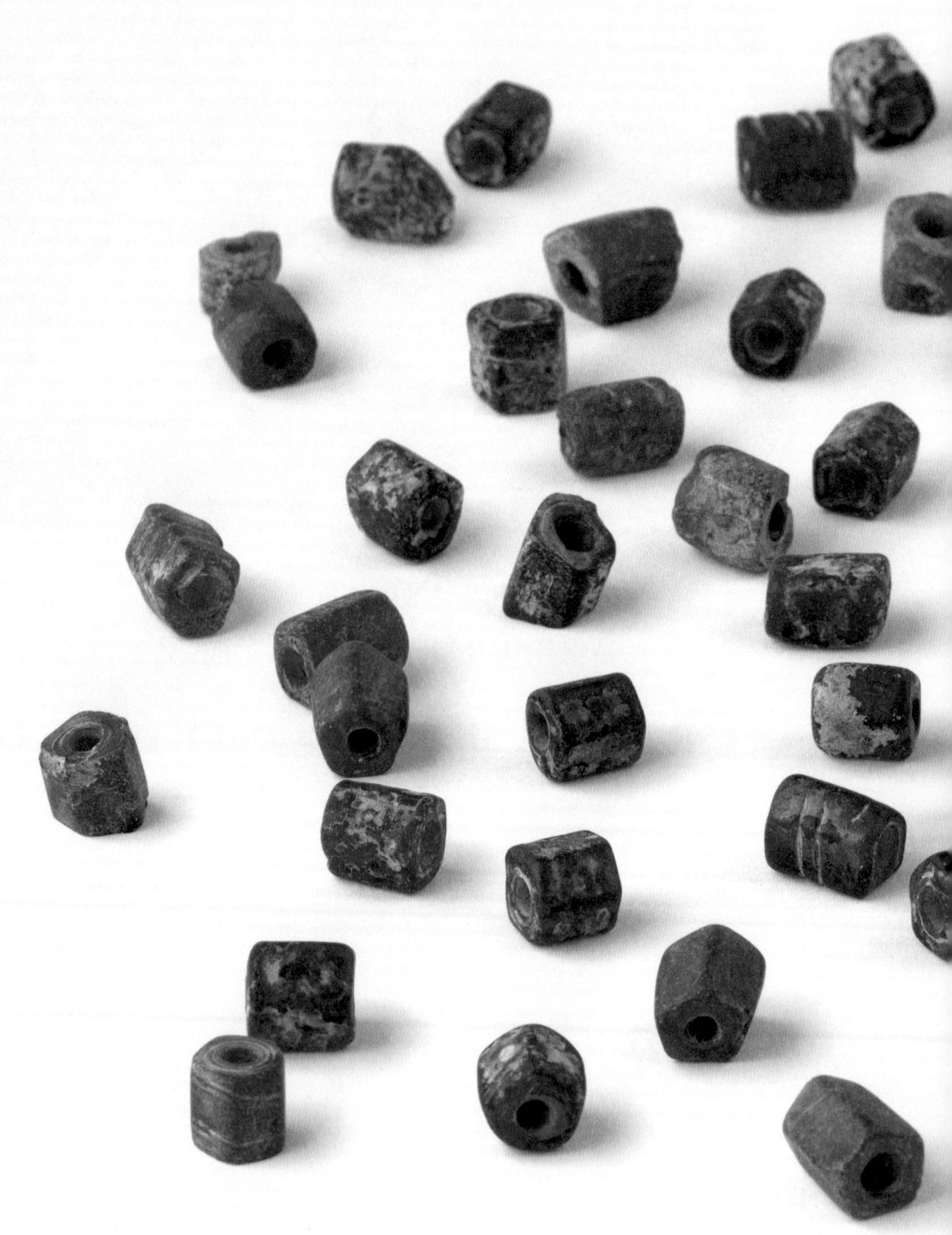

fig. 11 **Beads from Sint Eustatius, 18th and 19th centuries**

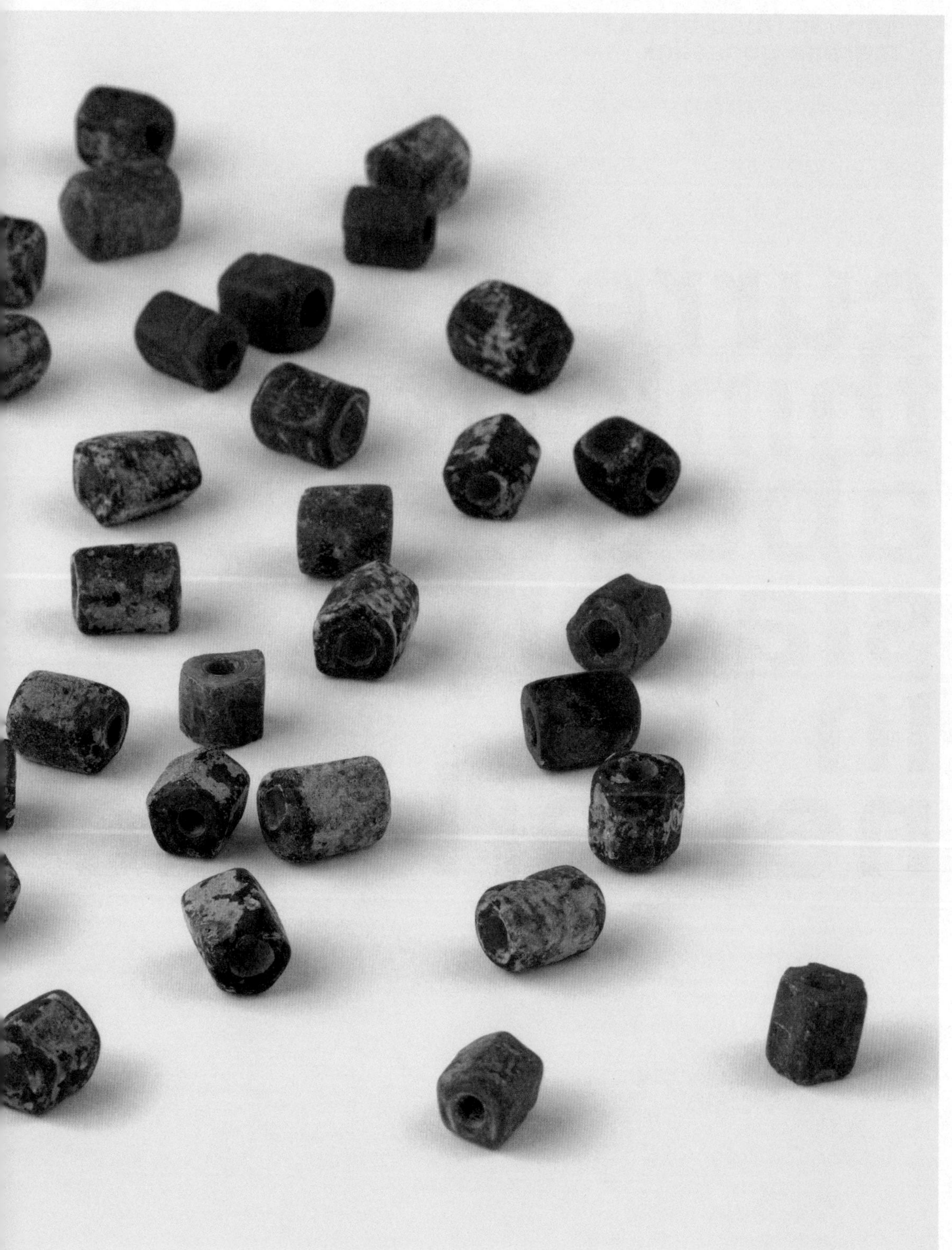

karwan fatah-black
martine gosselink

current thinking about slavery in the netherlands

In this concluding chapter, nine writers and scholars are asked about what slavery means to them and what their perspective is on the role slavery plays in the present. They all possess extensive knowledge of the subject and have usually devoted decades to it. What spurred them to study the slave trade and slavery? Do they perceive a change in their own involvement and in how society deals with the history of slavery? How is the legacy of slavery viewed in the Netherlands? Which angles dominate and which are lacking in Dutch scholarship on slavery? How might we do justice to this history? Is there consensus, or are opinions polarized? The paths of these people, who together form a community of researchers, have crossed multiples times already. The chapter opens with the biographies of the nine researchers, focusing on their personal history with the study and understanding of historical slavery.

living with the history of slavery

Reggie Baay (b. 1955, Leiden) specialized in colonial and postcolonial literature and history during his studies at Leiden University. He was editor of the journal *Indische Letteren* and has written numerous articles on colonial history. Since 2005, Baay has published a number of books and novels on the Dutch East Indies, several based on his own family history. In the literature and historiography of the Dutch East Indies, there was often little attention paid to slavery, and this spurred Baay to do greater justice to this aspect of its history in his own work – not through protest, as he puts it, but by giving lectures and writing books. Baay received widespread praise for his *Daar werd wat gruwelijks verricht* (Something gruesome was done there, 2015), about slavery in the Dutch East Indies.

Piet Emmer (b. 1944, Haarlem) developed a fascination for the history of slavery during his studies in history at Leiden University. In one of his dissertations, Emmer analyzed a slave transport from Middelburg to Africa and Suriname. It was the last slave transport undertaken by the Middelburgse Commercie Compagnie (MCC) and quite possibly the last (legal) slave transport originating in the Netherlands. In 1814, Dutch subjects were prohibited from taking any further part in the slave trade. This is not to the credit of the Dutch political elite, in Emmer's view; abolition of the slave trade, after all, took place under pressure from the British. Emmer obtained his doctorate in 1974 with a research thesis on the abolition of and campaigns against the Dutch slave trade. In 2000 he published a successful general-audience book, *De Nederlandse slavenhandel 1500–1850* (The Dutch slave trade, 1500–1850), of which a fourth, revised edition was published in 2019.

Cynthia McLeod-Ferrier (b. 1936, Paramaribo) grew up in Suriname when the country was still under Dutch rule. Her father, Johan Ferrier, was Suriname's first president. At home, his daughter Cynthia was expected to think in and speak Dutch, to dress and feel Dutch. 'I must not speak Negro English', was the line she most often had to write as punishment at school. As a girl she read popular Dutch children's books, and she could imagine herself perfectly as a

Dutch child. At the same time, she only had to look in the mirror to understand that her ancestors had lived in slavery. When she asked about this, she received no answer. It was not spoken of, either at home or anywhere else in Suriname. This changed when the first Surinamese students returned to Paramaribo after their studies in the Netherlands, where they had experienced being seen not as Dutch but as Surinamese. They had (re-)discovered their Surinamese identity. These role models, who often became teachers, no longer forbade their students to identify as Surinamese. As a result, Suriname became itself. In *A Distant Mirror: The Calamitous 14th Century* by Barbara W. Tuchman (1978), McLeod read that a people without access to its own sources about its own history has a self-image based on myths and stereotypes. She realized that this also applied to Suriname and wanted to set the history straight. McLeod has since written ten historical novels and multiple studies on Suriname.

Wayne Modest (b. 1972, Jamaica) came to the Netherlands in 2010 to become head of the curatorial department of the Tropenmuseum in Amsterdam (now part of the Nationaal Museum van Wereldculturen). In Jamaica, the country of his birth, Modest earned a doctorate with a research thesis on the historical evolution of museums in relation to the history of slavery. Prior to obtaining his doctorate, he worked as head curator of anthropology at the Horniman Museum in London and as director of the department of Museums of History and Ethnography at the Institute of Jamaica in Kingston. From 2014–2020 Modest was director of the Research Centre for Material Culture, the Nationaal Museum van Wereldculturen's research institute; in January 2021 he was appointed director of content of the museum. He is also professor (by special appointment) at the Vrije Universiteit Amsterdam. In these roles he has focused and continues to focus on slavery and colonialism, how their effects continue in the present, and how they are presented. Interwoven with his working life, and therefore with his ever-present interest in slavery, is Modest's 'other life', a semi-professional career in theatre and music. He investigates such topics as how religious musical traditions are part of the music of today, and whether songs sung during funeral rites, for instance, help us to understand slavery. Which forms of resilience and resistance can be 'read' in this ritual music, and what aspects of it can be found in current reggae or dancehall music?

Gert Oostindie (b. 1955, Ridderkerk) did not know during his studies in social sciences and history at the Vrije Universiteit Amsterdam that the history of slavery would become a guiding thread in his professional life. Research for his doctoral dissertation on nineteenth-century Cuba confronted him with the plantation slavery there. He subsequently wrote *In het land van de overheerser II: Antillianen en Surinamers in Nederland, 1634/1667–1954* (In the land of the overlord II: Antilleans and Surinamese in the Netherlands, 1634/1667–1954; 1989), with Emy Maduro. Only afterwards did he choose slavery in Suriname as the subject of his dissertation. His Surinamese father-in-law, Frank Koulen, was a descendant of enslaved people and had participated in the liberation of the Netherlands as a soldier in the Second World War. Koulen tested Oostindie, the latter realized in hindsight, as to whether he had too 'white' a gaze on history. Not just as a researcher but also through his inlaws, Oostindie thus learned about being Black in the Dutch colonies and in the Netherlands and the legacy of the history of slavery. Since his dissertation in 1989, Oostindie has published about 30 books and hundreds of articles on the subjects of colonial history, slavery in Suriname and the Antilles, decolonization, and the legacies and present-day significance of the colonial past. As director of the KITLV/Royal Netherlands Institute of Southeast Asian and Caribbean Studies and Professor of Colonial and Postcolonial History at Leiden University, Oostindie plays a prominent role in the academic research and public debates on colonialism and slavery.

Matthias van Rossum (b. 1984, Maarn) studied history at the Vrije Universiteit Amsterdam, began teaching at Leiden University in 2012 and earned his doctorate in 2015 with a dissertation on the relations between European and Asian sailors working for the Dutch East India Company (VOC) in Asia. With Karwan Fatah-Black he wrote 'Beyond Profitability: The Dutch Transatlantic Slave Trade and its Economic Impact' in 2014, on the contribution of the Dutch slave trade to the Dutch economy. This article, published online, was inspired by his dissatisfaction with debates in which the history of slavery was placed at a remove: the Dutch Republic, with its free labour market, was praised as the first modern economy, while the history of Atlantic slavery was seen as something that took place overseas and was therefore not part of the history of the Republic itself. The history of Dutch slavery, in Van Rossum's view, has been dismissed as marginal, and the Netherlands as a 'minor colonizer'. Asian slavery in particular interests Van Rossum, and he obtains much of his information from court archives in Batavia. Van Rossum attaches great importance to the thorough exploration of such archives from the bottom up. This allows him to study the everyday historical realities, which leads to a different and broader understanding of the slavery system than is the case in the existing historiography. With his book *Kleurrijke tragiek* (Colourful tragedy, 2015) he was one of the first scholars to make a significant contribution to the domain of research into slavery under the VOC.

Valika Smeulders (b. 1969, Curaçao), at seven years of age, migrated with her parents from the Netherlands to Suriname, which had just become independent. On the way, sailing past numerous different islands, she became acquainted with the region from which her family came. The luxurious life on board stood in stark contrast to the poverty on the islands. Smeulders wondered where the poverty and differences came from. Among her ancestors were slaveholders as well as enslaved people and contract labourers: a family in which the national history of Suriname, Curaçao and the Netherlands is reflected in all its facets. Back in the Netherlands, Smeulders studied Latin American languages and cultures. She participated in a research project into the presence of slavery in museum collections and subsequently worked on the first permanent exhibition of the newly founded NiNsee (National Institute for the Study of Dutch Slavery and Its Legacy). For her doctoral dissertation, she studied the ways museums deal with the history of slavery in Ghana, South Africa, Suriname and Curaçao. Since then, via research projects, publications and city tours, Smeulders has worked on how the public relates to and comes to terms with the history of slavery. In 2017 she started work as one of the curators of the *Slavery* exhibition at the Rijksmuseum. Since 1 July 2020 she has been head of the museum's Department of History.

Alex van Stipriaan (b. 1954, Ghent) has been Professor of Caribbean History at Erasmus University Rotterdam since 1997 and was previously a curator at the Tropenmuseum, Amsterdam, for about ten years. The year before independence, he visited Suriname in 1974 as a nineteen-year-old student. He now calls that country, along with the Netherlands, 'his land and his life', the place to which he has always returned, and he has also acquired a great familiarity with the Dutch Caribbean. His discovery in 1975 that he was white, and how it is possible to speak the same language and yet mean something completely different, was a revelation to Van Stipriaan. For his dissertation he researched the development of the Surinamese plantation economy during slavery during the colonial period. Since then he has concentrated on the cultural history and legacy of slavery, which he does as a scholar, a maker of exhibitions and documentaries, an adviser on numerous projects and as an activist. For instance, he was one of the co-founders of the National Slavery Monument in Amsterdam and of NiNsee, and has written, among other publications, a report for the Netherlands Council of State on the untenability of Zwarte Piet (Black Pete) from a historical perspective. He is among those charged with conducting an exploratory investigation commissioned by the government that is to result in a national slavery museum in Amsterdam. In his book *Rotterdam in slavernij* (Rotterdam in slavery), published in 2020, he describes in detail how this city's society was deeply intertwined with the slavery system for centuries and how this was evident in Suriname and Curaçao as well.

Gloria Wekker (b. 1950, Paramaribo), raised in the Netherlands, became the first Black woman professor at Utrecht University, in 2001. *'Peroen, Peroen mi patron ... Ingrisiman sa tjari pranga go na jobo pran'* (Peronne Peronne, my commander ... I will send those Englishmen back to the sea on the wrecks of their ships), Wekker's grandfather would play on his guitar, an eighteenth-century song about defending Paramaribo against the return of the English; and *Faya siton*, a song about a man called Mr Jantje (also called Jansen, see p. 23) who has murdered someone's child. As a child, Wekker understood little of this, but a seed was planted. At eighteen she travelled to Normal, Illinois, as an exchange student. With 1,400 other students she was taught about history and sociology, and therefore about slavery as well. When Jesse Jackson gave a talk at the college, the Black students could sit at the front, the white students at the back. She had to choose, asking herself: Am I Black or white? The seed germinated. Wekker chose Black, a moment as clarifying as it was shocking, for at home the Wekkers spoke of themselves as 'Brown', and there was little visibly 'Black' about her light-complexioned, Jewish father. Wekker studied anthropology at the University of Amsterdam and obtained a doctorate from the University of California, Los Angeles on the sexuality of Surinamese women, with a link to slavery. After becoming a professor emeritus, she made a breakthrough in the public debate on racism: her book *White Innocence: Paradoxes of Colonialism and Race* (2016), published in Dutch as *Witte onschuld* in 2017, opened up a great deal of discussion about white privilege in the Netherlands.

guilt, shame and other dilemmas

'In the world of colonial slavery, the absolute concepts of "right" and "wrong" work less well as moral indicators,' Alex van Stipriaan believes – and not just in that context, incidentally. 'Most people want to be counted among the good guys and not the bad guys. That is why many Dutch people are proud of their country as a model of tolerance, even as a leading light in the world. And that of course collides with something as inhumane as slavery. The idea of being on the wrong side does not fit the national self-image, and that contributes to a limited view of history. The argument is often: "you cannot look at history through the lens of today." Yet you never hear this about positive perceptions of history. Liberation from Spanish occupation, that brilliant seventeenth-century painter or inventor, the resistance against the Nazis – it all gets gladly appropriated in terms of "we" and "us". But you cannot shop around in history and select only what makes you look good. Look at national history as a human life. No one's life consists solely of high points. That is not credible. Yet many would prefer to identify only with the high points of history.'

'Unwillingness to face this history is sometimes expressed in far-reaching trivialization and relativism,' says Gert Oostindie. 'A statement such as "slavery has always existed", usually expressed to gloss over this history, is an example of such relativism. It is true, but so what? It does not mean that the enslaved people did not mind being enslaved.'

A sense of guilt is often involved in confronting and examining this history in depth. But guilt is not a relevant concept for most researchers in this discussion. Reggie Baay, and many with him, feels that we are not guilty of the actions of our ancestors: 'What matters is to look at what this history has done to us, for the legacy of slavery does exist.' Cynthia McLeod agrees: 'No one living now is guilty, except if you are still racist, whether you are white or Black.' Oostindie also considers guilt a difficult concept in discussing individuals of today, but one can talk about institutional guilt: 'We are heirs to a society that was responsible for this. So first of all you can never pretend it did not happen. Our States General were fine with it. Our monarchy was fine with it. Our democracy, our churches were fine with it.' Everyone will say that slavery is repugnant, says Valika Smeulders; we should 'acknowledge that fact and move forward as a society. That history includes more than just victims: there is also a great deal of strength to be discovered in it; new cultures have come out of it. It has formed our present society. Acknowledge that beautiful and that ugly side. This is crucial in order to make progress.' And, Baay adds, we should 'acknowledge also that ugly side to show that around the world today, there are still people who give themselves the right to turn other people into property and take away their freedom.'

So much for the question of guilt. Now to shame. The nine researchers were asked to reflect on the critical reactions that followed a statement once uttered by Martine Gosselink in the *NRC* newspaper: 'shame is my compass'. The crux of these reactions was that some historians consider shame not to be a useful premise for scholarship. Gosselink said that the shame that she sometimes experiences when she comes across yet another example of human cruelty in history and realizes what humanity is capable of is an emotion that drives her to want to understand *why* people do certain things to one another. The examples Gosselink mentioned were not, incidentally, deeds from Dutch history as such, but human behaviours in general. The reactions of our nine researchers present a broad palette of thoughts: 'There is plenty of reason for shame about slavery,' says Gloria Wekker, 'but shame can also lead to paralysis. I would prefer to see it lead to action. Surely it cannot be that only Black people have to explain what racism is and what privileges are.' Van Stipriaan agrees: if shame or anger moves you to do something with it, that is useful. The word 'shame' elicits an entirely different memory for Cynthia McLeod, one from her childhood: 'the shame, as a Surinamese, of talking about slavery. People simply did not do that then. You ignored your being Black or Surinamese.' For Piet Emmer: 'I have never wondered whether guilt is anything other than shame. Sure, you can be ashamed about something without bearing any guilt for it. Given our present norms and values, a substantial part of our past is something to be ashamed of.'

Valika Smeulders feels shame about one of her ancestors, a Scottish director and owner of several plantations; he had 200 people in his possession and was even convicted twice for his horrific mistreatment of them. 'It's not nice, but it is the reality,' she says. 'I am ashamed that he is my ancestor, for what he did to those people. I know someone who is a descendant of a woman who had to work under him. I have apologized to her. I felt the need to do that, even though I fully realize that there is nothing I can do about it. But from the moment I discovered that this link existed between us, I had to share it with her. I feel that being able to talk about it brought us closer together. But it might be easier for me to do so because I also share her experience: I am also a descendant of an enslaved woman who worked under him.'

Wayne Modest also considers emotions a necessary element in addressing historical injustice. They are important to how we relate to one another, as individuals but also as a society, and how this society provides answers to its citizens. 'Shame is part of the ethical compass by which we address historical injustice in the present. Not shame and guilt as a sense of culpability, but as a sense of responsibility to create a better world. Hope has a place here as well. We remind ourselves of the way people, despite the violence, against the current, were able to fashion a future.'

who writes this history?

Are emotion and research at odds with each other? 'It is simply not possible to deal with this history without emotions,' says Valika Smeulders, who sees slavery as a basic element of the history of the Netherlands. It may have taken place several centuries ago, but it is nonetheless 'the foundation upon which our societies of today are built, however regrettable that is. You cannot link one single emotion to this; a whole gamut of emotions is involved. Furthermore, the point is not to remain stuck in the past; what matters is what you *do* with that past.'

Personal involvement with the subject as a researcher sometimes elicits suspicion among the public at large. Are there ideological motives, for example, at work behind the fact that some in the public debate place emphasis on the extremely substantial role of slavery in the history of the Netherlands, or the opposite, when some argue that slavery played an entirely negligible role? And can someone whose ancestors served in the Dutch East Indies look objectively at its colonial history? The discussion about the emotional involvement of researchers sometimes leads to the conclusion that people in certain societal positions are necessarily incapable of conducting accurate research. Among the group of nine researchers, however, none would defend the idea that someone is or is not capable of carrying out proper research into the history of slavery based on his or her origins. As Emmer says: 'In scholarship, the geographical, economic and social background of the researcher should make no difference.' Gloria Wekker agrees, in a general sense: 'Anyone should be able to study anything, otherwise we are dealing with epistemological apartheid.' This does not resolve the question entirely, however. According to Wayne Modest, the public debate around the question of who writes history sometimes goes drastically off the rails: 'We have been misinterpreting the question "who produces history?" quite a bit lately, as an obstacle to white scholars and curators being able to tell this history. That is not the point, however. What matters is that we are able to reflect critically on our positions as researchers and on those of research institutions, as well as the authority this confers. Complexity and layeredness are best served by a less hierarchical academic and popular history environment.' Wekker adds: '[The production of knowledge] is going to have to be more equitably distributed in the Netherlands than it is today. There are too few Black scholars in this field, at a time when we are long past the first generation. But you do see that other "newcomers" are researching their own history and pursuing fields of study besides always law, economics or medicine.' It is important that all groups be represented within the field of historical research. But this is not the end of the matter, according to Modest and Wekker, who see a crucial connection between history and power. Like the Haitian researcher Michel-Rolph Trouillot, they argue that different groups and individuals do not have the same power to have historical viewpoints adopted by society, something that should be desirable in an equitable society.

method

Thinking about their emotional involvement and reflecting on their own positions is second nature to the researchers. It is a stepping stone to in-depth discussions on the collection of evidence (which sources are used?) and methodology (how do you set up your research, and from what perspective do you interrogate your sources?). Central questions here include how we might uncover a history that has long been shrouded in silence; what perspectives we take; and which questions we actually ask. Is the history of slavery defined by the slave traders and the plantation owners whose records are well preserved? Or is the history of slavery instead the history of the enslaved people, of those who escaped and of the emergence of anti-Black racism? And do these two perspectives meet? This happens often, as recent research has increasingly revealed. Formerly enslaved people, for example, sometimes became slaveholders themselves, and plenty of descendants of enslaved people count plantation owners among their ancestors: Valika Smeulders, Reggie Baay and Cynthia McLeod know this from researching their own family histories.

Elaborating new perspectives and making audible voices that were silenced for centuries requires fresh thinking that takes researchers out of their traditional conceptual furrows. For Gloria Wekker, the American poet and feminist Adrienne Rich was an important inspiration. Rich wrote: 'Re-vision – the act of looking back, of seeing with fresh eyes, of entering an old text from a new critical direction – is for women more than a chapter in cultural history: it is an act of survival. Until we understand the assumptions in which we are drenched we cannot know ourselves.' Wekker explains: 'That means we have to approach history in a new, conceptual way, if only because it means our own survival. I feel this way not just about women's history, but also in relation to slavery and race.' Her drive and her sense of urgency prove to be crucial to doing such work, precisely because it goes against the grain of the conventional, the usual pattern. At the same time, Wekker sees the limitations of her anthropological approach, in which the traditional historical sources are not normative but rather where the experiences and testimonies of people themselves are taken seriously, such as the cultural production of food, clothing, sayings and so forth – a view in which everyday life takes centre stage: 'This produces an incomplete picture, but we have to gather as much information as possible in order to speculate about what we do not or cannot know. The alternative would be: we cannot know about it so let us not bother with it.'

Starting in 2001, Valika Smeulders participated in a research project for the Museumvereniging, the Dutch association for museums. She investigated the collections of museums, archives and libraries for the presence of items related to the history of slavery. She wrote a report, later published as a book, entitled *Op zoek naar de stilte. Sporen van het slavernijverleden* (In search of the silence: traces of the history of slavery, 2007), with Waldo Heilbron, Alex van Stipriaan and Aspha Bijnaar. This book is still relevant and continues to inspire new researchers to look for the silences and gaps surrounding the history of slavery. The concept of 'historical silence' was originally coined by Trouillot in 1995 to describe why certain perspectives on history are often left out of the discussion. It is not just a matter of deliberate ignoring it is also a question regarding the way historical knowledge comes about, how professional historians guard the boundaries of their craft and sometimes simply from a cultural inability to acknowledge a different perspective. *Op zoek naar de stilte* was published at the beginning of the period when Dutch museums first began to deal with the history of slavery. 'I encountered surprise, ignorance, curiosity, interest,' Smeulders says about this. Since her research, the silence has gradually been broken further. The growing consciousness about the silence surrounding the history of slavery has resulted, in the Netherlands, in historians in other domains beginning to wonder what kinds of silences might still exist and whether or not to help break them.

It is precisely in the research into the history of slavery that a great deal of inspiration can be found for the way in which inaudible voices can break a silence. Wekker explains: 'A good example is the publication *First-Time: The Historical Vision of an Afro-American People* (1983) by the American anthropologist Richard Price, in which he presents two views of the history of the Saramaka [a people in Suriname descended from people who escaped plantations]: the stories of the Saramaka themselves as well as the written sources of the colonizers.' In that respect, the history of research on the subject of slavery resembles women's and gender studies, where a great deal of conceptual thinking had to be done initially on the question of how these histories could be told in a way that did justice to the past and to the new interests of the present. Moreover, these histories overlap: the history of sexual violence and of slavery cannot be considered separately. Wekker says, 'It is absurd that all those sexual activities of mainly white men with women of colour in the colonies have been virtually erased, especially given the large proportion of the Surinamese population that resulted from them.'

There are clearly differences of opinion among the researchers. Gert Oostindie, for instance, sees limitations in the use of oral history: 'We are, after all, a couple of centuries too late to interview people and use their direct experiences or family stories as reliable sources about the past.' Yet he does not entirely reject oral history, primarily because a great deal can be learned from such stories of emotions and cultural resistance, handed down from generation to generation. 'Songs and oral traditions, for instance, can be used as sources; they are still sung today and often express feelings about life on the plantations. They give an indication of how people perceived the system. But they are few, and they reveal few concrete facts. Good examples are oral traditions that indicate why ancestors fled from the plantations: because the regime was intolerable. There is continuity in these songs. But they speak mainly of feelings, of how certain events were perceived; seldom of concrete facts.' This nuanced attitude seems to apply for most of our researchers: critical and constructive, instead of shooting from the trenches in which the public debate often becomes mired.

astonishment and nuance

Historical research is often driven by astonishment about the past. The causes of this sense of astonishment among our nine slavery scholars are diverse, although the question of how it is possible for colonial slavery to have taken place for so long and on such a massive scale is pervasive. For Reggie Baay, 'astonishment about what a human being is capable of is my motivation for doing research and writing. Always those instances of cruelty, however often and wherever they occur.' In historical research, this human cruelty can be observed from a distance and examined carefully. It then becomes clear that a great deal has remained the same between then and now, but also that there are crucial differences. The difference between the slavery period and today's society alone forms a source of curiosity for many of our interviewees, although this difference often leads to two extremes, and this is not correct. Our present-day existence is not, after all, entirely free or without violence, and nor was the past a time of nothing but extreme oppression; even without the codification of modern human rights, human dignity has always existed. In other words, some of the universal, human values we uphold today were equally valid at the time.

At the same time, the researchers realize that the caricature of slavery as an all-encompassing, one-sided act of oppression, as it was portrayed by the anti-slavery activists of the eighteenth and nineteenth centuries, does not match the layered world revealed by the archives. It is precisely this layeredness of the slavery society that most of the researchers aim to document. Gert Oostindie gives an example in his dissertation *Roosenburg en Mon Bijou: Twee Surinaamse plantages, 1720–1870* (Roosenburg and Mon Bijou: Two Surinamese plantations, 1989): 'after the Emancipation of 1863, most of the "emancipated", mainly the young, left the plantation in search of better opportunities. The older people remained behind. One missionary notes the bitter words of an old sisa [sister] in 1878: "*Da liebi vo wi na den pikin gron kom pori moro moro*", "Our life here on our garden plots keeps getting worse". This is not because they liked their life in slavery, but because afterwards their everyday life fell apart. This environment was of course defined by slavery, but also by a sense of community built up over a century and a half.'

Piet Emmer also provides a bit of nuance: 'An exhibition on slavery will never be able to count on general agreement. You have to discard the illusion that you can please everyone from the start. Surprise people: make them think, Oh, you can look at it that way, too? The attention given in the NTR television documentary series *De Slavernij* (Slavery) in 2011 to forms of slavery other than that in the Caribbean was a revelation to many people. Apparently, few viewers knew that tens of thousands of European sailors had been enslaved by North African pirates (the Barbary pirates). Even fewer people were aware of the fact that there were more enslaved people in the possessions and trading posts of the Dutch East India Company (VOC) in Asia and South Africa than in all the Dutch colonies in the West combined. Furthermore, the series also highlighted present-day forms of involuntary labour.'

Cynthia McLeod gives an example of one of the countless lives in slavery of which many do not immediately think in relation to this subject: 'Imagine,

there is an enslaved woman, a Black woman; she has a child with a white man. This daughter is a *mulatta*. Later the daughter also enters into a relationship with a white man, whose household is run by enslaved people. What does this woman say to her husband? "Buy my mother too, and buy my mother's other children; buy my mother's sister, my aunt, my brother." Officially, these people are *her* slaves too, but at the same time they are her family. She buys them in order to give them a better life.' So there *were* possibilities within slavery to resist and to help one another.

Matthias van Rossum wants to move beyond the dismissive relativism of some fellow historians by opposing it with a more critical, contemporary and more understanding historiography: 'What used to dominate colonial historiography was a relativist perspective: that the colonial activities of the Dutch were not as bad as those of other Europeans.' The trivialization of the scale and significance of this history does not match the world being revealed by a lot of 'new' archival research material. On the one hand, there is a great deal of visibility in the primary material – letters, plantation records, governmental archives and so on – but on the other hand much remains invisible in the historiography and public consciousness. Social and economic history, Van Rossum's domain, is also changing its perspective. He argues that the role of slavery within socio-economic history has often been considered something that unfolded outside the Netherlands: 'The Netherlands of the seventeenth and eighteenth centuries, the Dutch Republic, is seen as the first modern economy, with high wages and free labour. This obscures the fact that slavery was an essential part of it.' Socio-economic history has paid scant attention to the link between colony and colonizer. This shift in both disciplines, colonial studies as well as socio-economic history, is spurring a great deal of new research, and this is not limited to the history of Atlantic slavery. Van Rossum argues that in general, 'we in the Netherlands do not have a long tradition of looking at the dark sides and the negative aspects of our past. In order to develop new narratives and perspectives, and to have them flourish, we need space in the landscape of culture and the humanities.'

asia and the atlantic region

Thanks to the self-aware and vast international community of descendants, there has been a great deal of research done and discussion conducted on the history of slavery in the Atlantic region. This is not the case for Asia. The ubiquitous presence of the history of Asian slavery in the sources in contrast to the public and professional silence about it was an important motivation for Reggie Baay: 'It started with my research into the *njai*, 30 years ago. When the first Dutch people set foot on Indonesian soil, the first forced sexual relations with njais, enslaved women, began. I was continually surprised that no one here had done research about this recently. These forced sexual relationships are mentioned in the eighteenth-century books of Jacob Haafner and François Valentijn. And there were even debates in parliament about them. So it was not something we could not have known.' That sense of an unjust silence also moved Matthias van Rossum to document the history of Asian slavery. For his study into the way everyday life and work were organized in the world of the VOC, he conducted research into the colonial judicial archives in Batavia: 'in no fewer than one in three court cases did I come across questions involving enslaved people.' Although his first research project was not about slavery, the subject attracted his attention as a result of it. He continued to encounter evidence of the enormous scale of slavery in the VOC operation, a scarcely known fact until then.

How does the museum world of today handle the new insights about colonial slavery in Asia? The visibility and lingering legacy of our history of slavery are constantly growing and receiving increasing attention. For instance, there are plans for the establishment of a Slavery Museum in Amsterdam; museums have joined forces through the platform Musea Bekennen Kleur (Museums show their true colours); and for the first time in its history an exhibition on the subject is taking place at the Rijksmuseum, the national museum of the Netherlands. In the discussions surrounding the establishment of the Slavery Museum, but also in the elaboration of the aforementioned exhibition, differences often emerge in the perception of slavery and its legacy among descendants of enslaved people in Asia and in the transatlantic region. This was also the case among the nine researchers we interviewed. Indo-European Dutch people usually do not know that their ancestors may have been enslaved. In Suriname and the Antilles, the civil status of the inhabitants is well documented, making it a simple matter to trace someone's ancestry, in contrast to the situation in Southeast Asia, where children of enslaved people blended into the wider community and were not identifiable as descendants based on their physical features, resulting in a different, less determinate racial legacy than in the Americas, where anyone with a darker skin colour knows that he or she is descended from an enslaved person from an African country and only a few generations removed from this history. Anti-Black racism and the structural subordination associated with it are concrete social legacies of the history of transatlantic slavery. The situation is different in Southeast Asia. Even before the arrival of the Europeans, slavery was an integral part of Southeast Asian societies. The relation of a white slaveholder and an enslaved person of colour would have been slightly less notable, as the practice of slavery had long existed there. In Asia, the offspring of multiracial marriages also secured a societal status earlier; in Suriname, for example, this did not begin until the nineteenth century.

With this preamble, the researchers were asked whether the future Slavery Museum should provide room for both histories. 'Of course,' says Baay, 'if you leave out that part, you are falsifying history again.' Gloria Wekker agrees: 'it is *one* story; you cannot divide it artificially. Descendants from the Americas are afraid that, now that it is finally "their turn" to be in the spotlight, that descendants from Southeast Asia will steal this attention when they have placed the subject on the public agenda and obtained success with it. I am exaggerating, of course, but basically it does come down to that. In anthropology we call this "the image of the limited good": there is only a small quantity of a given, desirable good, and if this is taken by another there is little left for me.

It's very understandable, but that is not how we should approach it.' Baay agrees: 'Afro-Dutch descendants need not fear that an Indo-European community is going to come forward en masse to celebrate the abolition of slavery, or make all sorts of claims on the history of slavery, because the community that would have to organize this simply does not exist.'

perspective

From what perspective is the subject of slavery discussed? Many of the arguments expressed in past debates have since been refuted, such as 'slavery was primarily a thing of the ruling class': we now know that all levels of the population were directly or indirectly involved. Likewise, the idea that 'slavery was considered quite ordinary at the time; people did not know any better': we now know that there were always voices of protest, and sometimes they were even in chorus. Or, 'fortunately, that dark chapter was closed on 1 July 1863': we now know that the Netherlands is still grappling with the mental legacies of this history. The silence is being broken and perspectives are shifting. That silence in history, according to the researchers, is also an indication of the degree of Dutch research on the subject: what exists in the primary sources can only be found if one actually has an eye for it. The perspective used to be of 'standing on a Dutch ship, looking out at the rest of the world', as Alex van Stipriaan puts it. 'This is not a metaphor; it is literally how the popular television series *Nederlanders overzee* (Dutchmen overseas, broadcast on the channel Veronica) visualized the Dutch history in the 1980s. They went around the world on a ship, in search of artefacts left behind by the brave and inventive men of the VOC and WIC.' From the deck of the ship, certain questions were simply not posed, for instance whether there is a relationship between colonial history and present-day racism. For Piet Emmer, the answer to this question is clear: he argues that 'racism preceded [the colonial period of] slavery, so there is not a unique connection. For instance, the most dangerous form of racism in Europe, anti-Semitism, already existed in the early Middle Ages, so long before the beginning of colonialism and the slavery associated with it.' According to some, however, that forms of racism existed before the advent of transatlantic slavery does not preclude the notion that it took on a different form and meaning during the colonial period. 'There *is* a connection between slavery and racism,' says McLeod. 'Slavery has indeed existed since time immemorial, but the enslavement of people with a dark skin colour created a very different form of slavery. Black people were enslaved by white people because they were Black. The first Europeans who enslaved Africans were Catholic and lived by the principle "Love thy neighbour". But that principle made slavery impossible, so they came up with a solution: "The Black is not your neighbour, for a Black is not a human being". To prove this, the human features of Black people were taken away and they were ascribed "animal" features: people said that they have no intelligence; they can think, but at most at the level of an eight-year-old child. They have no feelings; they feel less physical pain and they do not know higher emotions like love or faith. According to eighteenth- and nineteenth-century race theories, all races were ordered in a vertical line, with the superior race at the top: the white race! The white race was therefore allowed to dominate the world, take possession of African and Asian lands and turn them into colonies. The superior white civilization was imposed on all races, for the way things were done among the whites in western Europe was best for everyone. This is racism. Slavery has been abolished, but that thinking still exists.'

What role does traditional historiography play in this racism? According to Van Rossum, the traditional colonial historiography, in which topics such as colonial violence and racism are trivialized or dismissed, has significantly shaped the public perception of slavery. 'It is a perspective steeped in colonial interests, lacking a critical or reflexive gaze on this past: these histories look at the slave trade, ships, conquests and trade conflicts as part of the classical interpretation of colonial and maritime history, from a limited national colonial perspective, without a proper understanding of the operation and impact of the history of slavery.'

In other parts of the Afro-Atlantic diaspora, this domain has been taken further, and often started earlier as well. The American researcher Allison Blakely published the book *Black in the Dutch World* in 1993. In the introduction he expresses his surprise at the limited interest of Dutch historians in this question. Gloria Wekker experienced during her studies in the United States how differently race and skin colour were discussed there from what she was used to in the Netherlands. In the 1970s, the Surinamese-Dutch sociologist and cultural anthropologist Humphrey Lamur was one of the first to take a new look at the plantation economy. In the 1980s, when Gert Oostindie came across other Atlantic slave societies during his research in Cuba, he saw that the research that was being done there did not yet exist at all in the Netherlands. It inspired him to write a dissertation about the Dutch plantation economy in Suriname. Internationally, this history was placed on the public agenda by organizations like UNESCO. A lot of international 'preliminary work' later led to research at home, such as the comparative research of Valika Smeulders into the way people dealt with this history in four parts of the Afro-Atlantic diaspora: Ghana, South Africa, Suriname and Curaçao. She visited former Ghanaian slave forts with African American descendants of enslaved people: they made contact with their ancestors, and they talked, sang, danced and wept; all of which provided her with a new perspective on dealing with the history of slavery.

Great progress was made in the United States, in particular, with the development of new lines of questioning and research methods. This meant that a larger community of researchers was formed there as well. Piet Emmer was also inspired by what was taking place abroad; by the camaraderie of an academic community exploring a new field of research: 'Thanks to international connections, an infrastructure of periodicals, congresses and book series emerged, especially around the Atlantic region.' That does not mean, however, that the Netherlands is doing well in that international field; only in terms of furnishing quantitative data on the extent of the slave trade does the Netherlands contribute at a high level. There is a palpable wish among many of the interviewed researchers to raise the level of the research and debate at home by encouraging engagement with conceptual and methodological discussions. This would make it possible to research the legacy of slavery as well as cultural histories on the assessment of slavery in a more structural way.

It is clear that a new generation of researchers has emerged in the fields of history and anthropology, producing knowledge from different premises, a mixed field, in terms of gender as well as race and ethnicity. Matthias van Rossum says that it would be positive if more 'global history' were conducted in the future, as well as more historiography focusing on people themselves and everyday life. He would like to see a consciousness emerge both in society and in scholarship about the interconnectedness: how Asian and Caribbean histories coincide with the history of the Netherlands. Van Rossum feels that we have a great deal to gain from setting up exchanges with scholars in the countries involved in this history: Suriname, Indonesia and India, as well as other European countries. Scholarship on slavery, in that regard, is currently very segmented. Van Rossum wants to understand that past in a broader European and global perspective. Smeulders, while not wanting to ignore the African slave traders entirely, counters that we must realize that transatlantic slavery was really a European system of an entirely different nature, form and extent than traditional African slavery had been. Too often the African slave traders are trotted out as an excuse not to have to deal, as Dutch people, with the history of slavery and its legacy.

Gert Oostindie agrees: 'You hope that you are contributing to the creation of a more balanced picture of history, that it becomes part of a broader historical consciousness. Denial – the stubborn refusal to talk about it, seeing it as Netherlands-bashing – is the wrong approach. We must not prevaricate, and at the same time we must seek connection. A significant portion of society still does not want to know anything about it, although that portion is shrinking. But in any case, that is where we have to focus our efforts. I hope and believe that all of colonial history, and therefore the inherent racism and violence as well, will become acknowledged and socially acceptable subjects in our national history. If we succeed in building a society in which there is room for this diversity, we will look back on a period in which we fought the good fight.'

the future

How do we do justice to the past? What sort of future do our nine writers and researchers envision? When asked about her vision of what is to come, Cynthia McLeod paints a positive picture. She has seen the increase in attention paid to and curiosity about the history of slavery with her own eyes. She ignores the suggestion that she is partly the cause of this. 'Slavery was a horrible system. A lot of people did not survive it. Only the strong. Contract labour was also a horrible system. There too only the strong survived. Who are the strong? *We are!* Let's feel like victors! As a victor you can do anything. We are not victims. Show yourself.'

For Wayne Modest, scholarship does justice to the past by looking at the ways in which enslaved people refused or resisted, and how creative they were. Without intending to minimize addressing the issue of violence in the colonial past, Modest is striving to seek out the humanity, the hope and the small joys of those people who were enslaved. In this way we are able to reflect on how people survived situations and circumstances that many of us would not survive today.

Surviving slavery and contract labour is also an important subject for McLeod. As a Surinamese descendant of survivors, she feels it her duty to 'develop our country, our territory, a beautiful land with all kinds of possibilities, fertile soil, clean drinking water, gold, oil, bauxite, wood. We are only half a million people! We have to make that land flourish. We have the opportunity. I say this in Suriname as well. With good leaders we will get there. So that all Surinamese can have a good life. The Netherlands do not need to pay us homage. We can do it ourselves, with a new leader, too. Absolutely.'

Gloria Wekker emphasizes the importance of materiality, which is why she cheered the arrival of Erwin de Vries's National Slavery Monument in the Oosterpark in Amsterdam, 'a beautiful, moving image of people in all sizes, from small children to adults, free at last'. She is also curious to see what the planned Slavery Museum will be like, and she considers it important that slavery be given the attention it deserves, starting in primary school – a sentiment shared by many others, too. There has to be, Wekker says, a more reflective way of thinking, a way to think critically. She would like to see more data based on ethnicity in healthcare, given that, as she points out, social and institutional racism take a toll on mental and physical health: 'When I look at the people who have died in my circle of Black friends, I think that these early deaths of Black women could well be the consequence of slavery and its lingering effects. Such continuing effects are classified by the American writer and scholar Saidiya Hartman under the term "the afterlife of slavery".' There is a lot more to achieve, according to Wekker: the inequality in the guidance for secondary-school options given to Dutch children at age twelve, which determines their future and is connected to their future social position, has to stop; the fact that in prisons almost all guards are white; the automatism of the white norm.

Piet Emmer finds it 'quite elegant that the Rijksmuseum is devoting attention to the historical misery of a small minority group in our country. The exhibition will undoubtedly be seen by many visitors who know little or perhaps even nothing of the subject.' Reggie Baay also sees the exhibition at the Rijksmuseum as a way of doing justice to the history of slavery – in a way that tells the story well, not just because slavery is far more extensive than most of us think, but also because the phenomenon still exists. Though he would prefer to see the story be told in a more permanent way.

In 1997, Gert Oostindie wrote in *Het paradijs overzee* (Paradise overseas) that it was very odd that there was no slavery monument in the Netherlands. He is glad that one has since been erected. 'An honourable symbol now would be for the king to present an apology, not just because of his family connection to the history but also in the broader symbolic context in particular: only then will we truly understand that slavery and its consequences are part of the canon of the Netherlands. And if the Netherlands would just stop with Zwarte Piet, that would mean great progress too. For that matter, however, apologies are less interesting than what follows, because apologizing is only the beginning.'

For Alex van Stipriaan, justice will be done to the history of slavery as soon as that history – in all its facets and legacies – becomes as self-evidently 'our' history in education and in the historical consciousness of all Dutch people as the Second World War, the Holocaust and the Resistance, and the legacies thereof.

The museum world has been making good progress when it comes to slavery, especially over the last several years. Yet Matthias van Rossum calls for an even greater, more significant contribution to the museum and academic knowledge infrastructure of the international history of slavery and related issues, in which Asia, Europe and the Atlantic region, as well as both present and past, come together – starting with schoolbooks.

Valika Smeulders mentions the importance for the future that genuine, focused attention be paid to colonial slavery, so that you can explain that racism today is tied to that phenomenon. She too suggests that a museum could be useful in this regard. But she also points out that you can always avoid a building if you want. Public space is far more compelling, more direct. Would it not be wonderful if at the National Monument in The Hague, erected in 1869, where we celebrate the freedom of the Dutch people after French occupation, we also celebrated the freedom of enslaved people in 1863? Smeulders wants slavery in the streetscape, in our national memory. 'Make Keti Koti [a holiday on 1 July celebrating the abolition of slavery] a national holiday! In Suriname, all ethnic groups come together on that day. People sometimes combine elements of each other's traditional attire – a sari with an *anjisa* [Creole headwrap] for example – as a sign of unity among many ethnicities, a national history.' Could something like the Tomb of the Unknown Soldier and eternal flame on the Champs-Elysées in Paris serve as a model for an eternally burning flame for the unknown enslaved person? 'Yes,' replies Smeulders, 'keeping a flame like that burning takes care and attention. Then you would really acknowledge that slavery is a significant part of our history. It is a beautiful symbol that you would take care of such a monument as a part of your family. And a flame also radiates light, something positive. If you go together towards the light you are working on the future from a positions of strength and positivity.'

This essay was made possible by the generous time given by nine researchers and writers who shared their knowledge with us. The interviews were conducted from 21 October 2019 to 29 January 2020, prior to the resurgence of the long-running Black Lives Matter movement. The audio recordings and transcripts of the interviews have been entered into the exhibition archives of the Rijksmuseum.

notes

slavery
pp. 8–19

1 Van der Ham 2013, pp. 213–216; Van der Ham 2016, pp. 15–17.
2 Sint Nicolaas 2018, p. 33.
3 Hulsman 2015.
4 Dragtenstein 2010.
5 Ferdinand 2018.
6 Sint Nicolaas 2020, pp. 274–275.
7 The audio tour was produced in close collaboration with Jörgen Tjon a Fong.

dutch colonial slavery
pp. 22–57

For this chapter, grateful use was made of the many publications that have been issued on the subject of slavery in recent years, including Van Rossum 2015; Van Rossum 2020a; Van Rossum et al. 2020; Fatah-Black 2018; Baay 2015. With thanks to Doreen van den Boogaart for her help in writing this chapter.

1 Cairo 2007, p. 78; Ferdinand 2018, pp. 205–206.
2 Worden and Groenewald 2005, pp. 350–352.
3 According to the inscription, the founder Johannes Borchhardt cast the bell in the Artisan Quarter of Batavia, where enslaved labourers and prisoners primarily worked.
4 Van de Wall 1943, p. 86; De Bruijn and Kist 2001, pp. 56–57; Passchier 2005, pp. 209–210.
5 Van de Wall 1943, p. 90.
6 For the successive owners of the Santa Catharina plantation, see Langenfeld 2013 (consulted on 8 September 2020). At the time of the Emancipation (legal abolition of slavery) in 1863 there were twenty enslaved people working on the plantation. At this time, the plantation was owned by J.E. Price. See the slave registers of Curaçao on the website of the National Archives of the Netherlands, The Hague: afbeeldingen.gahetna.nl/naa/thumb/3000x3000/c116c42b-b376-ed78-86e6-81acd0512b7d.jpg.
7 The estate was owned by the Van Breda family from 1731 to 1901, see Gosselink, Holtrop and Ross 2017, p. 124 (fig.).
8 See 'Bell Will Be a Focus for Honest Discussion and Reflection', www.caths.cam.ac.uk/about-us/news-and-events/bell-will-be-focus-honest-discussion-and-reflection, 10 May 2019 (accessed 12 May 2019). The bell was donated to the college in 1960 by an alumnus who had found it in a riverbed in Guyana. The similarity of the name of the plantation to that of his former college inspired the donation. As there was no other connection between the college and the plantation, the college began looking for a new location for the bell, where the historical context could be better presented. After the exhibition in the Rijksmuseum, the bell will be donated to the Guyana National Museum in Georgetown. With thanks to professor Sir M. Weland and Dr C. Higgins of St Catharine's College, Cambridge.
9 The Wederzorg plantation is located in the Commewijne region of Suriname. In 1745, surveyor P. Gardin mapped out the coffee plantation for its founder, the widow of Abraham Vereul. Around 1753 the plantation was bought by Anna Hedwig Meijer (?–1772). The plantation bell probably dates from her time. See the file on the Wederzorg plantation on the Commewijne River by Philip Dikland, via www.suriname-heritage-guide.com (accessed 13 January 2020, in Dutch). There was also a noteworthy case of sexual abuse on this plantation in the mid-nineteenth century, see '1841 Seksueel Misbruik', www.amsterdam.nl/stadsarchief/themasites/amsterdam-slavernij/1841-seksueel-misbruik, 15 June 2020 (accessed 14 August 2020).
10 The Middelburgse Commercie Compagnie (MCC) was a major player in the slave trade from 1732 to 1807. The MCC was founded in 1720 and existed until 1889. The MCC archives are part of UNESCO's World Heritage list and are housed in the Zeeuws Archief in Middelburg.
11 See, among others, Green 2020.
12 Salpeter was used as a raw material for gunpowder shipped from Bengal by the VOC. Gunpowder was an important means of payment within the slave trade, including for the MCC. See Fatah-Black and De Windt 2018.
13 Van Rossum 2015, p. 9.
14 A. van Stipriaan addressed the paradox of slavery extensively in his lecture 'The Contested African Body: Historical Paradoxes of Black and White in Suriname during Slavery', held at the Conference on Slavery, Indentured Labour, Migration, Diaspora and Identity Formation, 18–23 June 2018, Paramaribo, Suriname; Oostindie 1993, p. 95; Patterson 1982.

15 Van der Chijs 1885–1900, pt. 1, p. 172, cited in Van Rossum 2015, p. 73.
16 The term is derived from the Latin legal term *manumissio*, literally 'release from the hand'. See Fatah-Black 2018, pp. 13–14, and Neslo 2016, p. 97.
17 Fatah-Black 2018, p. 13.
18 See the story of Horij van Bengalen, p. 159 in the 'Van Bengalen' chapter of this book.
19 Bartels 1993, pp. 65–72; Green 2020.
20 The extensive Tempatie uprising in Suriname in 1757 followed a decision by the slave-holder to move some of the enslaved labourers from the La Paix timber plantation to a sugar plantation. See Sint Nicolaas 2018, p. 83.
21 Boshof and Du Plessis 1918, p. 22. Kanaldorp is the present-day District Six in Cape Town. See also Winberg 1992, p. 87. In South Asia and Southeast Asia the legacy of slavery is, to our knowledge, found not so much in lyrics but rather in melodies and instruments.
22 *Bolla* refers to the hairstyle of European women, namely in a bun with a cap. With thanks to Niki de Wolf for the translation and Marieke van der Wal for sharing her knowledge of South African songs.
23 Coolhaas 1960, pp. 46–47.
24 For the early debate on slavery, see Van Rossum 2020b.
25 Stevens 2015, pp. 23–25.
26 Statement by Middelburg pastor Bernardus Smytegelt, in Smytegelt 1747.
27 Genesis 9:18–27.
28 Archangel et al. 2020, pp. 76–77.
29 Tang 2013, pp. 82–88.
30 For the slave fund from Zierikzee, founded in 1735 and still in use, see www.slavenkas.nl (accessed 17 September 2020).
31 Geelen 2018, p. 26; Van Rossum et al. 2020.
32 Archangel et al. 2020, p. 14.
33 Ibid., p. 16.
34 See p. 113 in the 'Oopjen' chapter of this book; Van Groesen 2017.
35 Karwan Fatah-Black drew my attention to the similarity of the image of sugar mills in the book *Beschryvinge van de volk-plantinge Zuriname* by J.D. Herlein and the rendering by Frans Post. Herlein's illustration also found its way onto engraved glass, including that of Siparipabo, see p. 92 in the 'Wally' chapter of this book.
36 In the course of the seventeenth century, the prohibition on slavery in the Netherlands was specifically included in printed legislation. From 1644, for example, the charters of Amsterdam explicitly stipulate that the city does not recognize slavery and that every person in Amsterdam is free. This legislation also implied that enslaved people who came to the Dutch Republic could claim their freedom. See p. 126 in the 'Paulus' chapter of this book.
37 See Van Stipriaan 1993b and Van Stipriaan 2020 for an overview of the voices of protest.
38 Van Rossum 2020a, p. 3.
39 In Van der Ham 2016, extensive attention is devoted to the slave trade by the Dutch on the west coast of Africa. For smuggling, see Paesie 2008.
40 Daalder et al. 2013, p. 29.
41 The Trans-Atlantic Slave Trade Database provides insight into the registered slave trade and cites a figure of 554,336 people, see www.slavevoyages.org (accessed 3 July 2017). Because many illegal slave traders were also operating, an estimate of over 600,000 people has been made.
42 The Hague, National Archives of the Netherlands, Sociëteit van Suriname, 1.05.03, inv. no. 215. The ship's log is presented and discussed in Dragtenstein 2017.
43 For the relations between Jan Wils and Joris Ernsthuijs and the role of director general Sweerts at Elmina, see Dragtenstein 2017, pp. 88–89; for a map with the places along the Gold Coast where the ship stopped, ibid., p. 111.
44 Ibid., pp. 96, 113.
45 Dragtenstein points out the shortcomings of the oft-cited book by Willem Bosman, slave merchant for the WIC, published in 1704, which claimed that the Dutch did not buy sick and weak Africans and behaved better than other European traders. See Dragtenstein 2017, p. 114.
46 An average of 16 per cent of the enslaved Africans died during the crossing as a result of dehydration or diseases like dysentery, scurvy and the pox, see www.slavevoyages.org; see also Daalder et al. 2013, p. 153.
47 Dragtenstein 2017, p. 133.
48 Ibid., p. 127, n. 178.
49 Van der Linde 1963.
50 Cape Town, Western Cape Archives, Miscellaneous 49, Serrurier papers, transfer deeds of slaves; a stiver is a Dutch currency unit that was also used in the country's colonies.

51 The document states: 'Siladana, van de leeteeren casta' (Siladana of the *leeteeren* caste; which caste is meant is not clear).
52 Baay 2015, pp. 57–60, 170; Van Rossum et al. 2020, p. 16.
53 Why this specific 12-stiver document was used as the deed of sale and did not remain in the VOC archives in India is unknown.
54 The slave registers can be consulted via 'Curaçao: slaven- en emancipatieregisters 1839–1863', www.nationaalarchief.nl/onderzoeken/zoekhulpen/curacao-slaven-en-emancipatieregisters-1839-1863.
55 The letters 'GWC' shown in fig. 12 probably represent the logo of the Geoctroyeerde West-Indische Compagnie (West India Company).
56 Herlein 1718, p. 91, reports that each slaveholder had a new brand applied.
57 The servant Trijntje Pieters, for example, bought a share of stock in the VOC for 75 guilders, see Van der Ham 1998, p. 56.
58 The Hague, National Archives of the Netherlands, Oude West-Indische Compagnie (OWIC), minutes of the Zeeland Chamber of the Dutch West Indies Company, 5 November 1637, inv. no. 1.05.01.01-2. With thanks to Dienke Hondius.
59 'Lyst der Fabricquen en Producten, welke uit deese Landen getrokken werden ter versending na onse Westindische Colonien', in *Nieuwe Nederlandsche Jaerboeken van het Koningrijk der Nederlanden*, Amsterdam 1770. With thanks to Alex van Stipriaan.
60 Brandon and Bosma 2019, p. 5.
61 Quoted in ibid., pp. 8–9.
62 The inventory of the Overveen farm in South Africa is a striking example of this. There were 21 enslaved people with very diverse geographic origins, see p. 169 in the 'Van Bengalen' chapter of this book; Gosselink, Holtrop and Ross 2017, pp. 124–125; Ross 1983, pp. 15–16. Slaveholders often preferred men because of the hard work required.
63 Van Rossum 2015, p. 44; see also the licence of Francina van Bengalen, p. 160 in the 'Van Bengalen' chapter of this book.
64 Halberstadt 1856, p. 74.
65 In South Africa, for the greater part of the eighteenth century, a community of escaped enslaved people lived in the caves of Hangklip, above False Bay. See Gosselink, Holtrop and Ross 2017, p. 127; see also the escaped Balinese people in the 'Surapati' chapter of this book, pp. 186–187.
66 For the significance of the uprising on Haiti, see Trouillot 2015. Karwan Fatah-Black also discussed this in his lecture 'Waar de ketenen begonnen te breken', Keti Koti Lecture 2020, Pakhuis de Zwijger, Amsterdam, 30 June 2020.
67 The basis for scientific racism was laid at the end of the eighteenth century and can be found, for example, in the work of the Groningen scholar Petrus Camper and that of father and son Gerard and Willem Vrolik, whose anatomy collection forms the basis of the Vrolik Museum at the Academic Medical Centre (AMC) in Amsterdam.
68 Van Stipriaan 2020, also for the debate on abolition in the first session of the national parliament of the Batavian Republic.
69 Baay 2015, p. 177.
70 See, among others, the 'Lohkay' chapter of this book, pp. 264–289.
71 Baay 2015, pp. 179–184
72 Ferdinand 2018, p. 88.
73 Baay 2015, pp. 205–214.
74 For the varying compensations received by slaveholders in the Dutch East Indies, see Baay 2005, pp. 198–211.
75 Ellen Neslo calls this the 'hollowing out of the system from the inside out', see Neslo 2016.
76 In Suriname the compensation was 300 guilders per person, in the Antilles 100 guilders, see p. 280 in the 'Lohkay' chapter of this book.

joão

pp. 62–83

1 Ferrão and Soares 1997, p. 195.
2 Green 2020, p. 113.
3 Den Heijer 2011, p. 41.
4 Boxer 1977, p. 66.
5 Ibid., p. 211.
6 Barleus 1923, p. 296.
7 Van der Eijk, 2006, p. 16.
8 The Hague, National Archives of the Netherlands, Oude West-Indische Compagnie (OWIC), 1.05.01.01, inv. nos. 60, 61, 62, 65 and 66; interrogation of João Mina, inv. no. 62, fol. 61.
9 Ferrão and Soares 1997, p. 175.
10 Klooster 2016, p. 63.
11 The Hague, National Archives of the Netherlands, OWIC, 1.05.01.01, inv. no. 62, fol. 61.
12 Ibid.
13 Ferrão and Soares 1997, p. 174.

14 Ibid.
15 Boxer 1977, p. 104.
16 Ibid., p. 97.
17 Ibid., p. 98.
18 Van den Tol 2018, p. 250.
19 Meuwese 2012, p. 8.
20 Do Lago and Do Lago 2007, p. 379.
21 See p. 113 in the 'Oopjen' chapter of this book.
22 See p. 94 in the 'Wally' chapter of this book.
23 The Hague, National Archives of the Netherlands, OWIC, 1.05.01.01, inv. no. 62, fol. 61.
24 Van den Tol 2018, p. 248.
25 Ibid., p. 249.
26 Ibid.
27 Van Groesen 2017, p. 108.
28 Meuwese 2012, p. 2.
29 Meuwese 2018, p. 233.
30 Van der Ham 2016, p. 48.
31 Ibid.
32 Green 2020, p. 112.
33 The Portuguese sourced enslaved people from Nigeria and Benin in this period.
34 After the official abolition of the slave trade by the Dutch Republic in 1815, Elmina remained an important post for the Dutch, partly for the recruiting of African soldiers for the Royal Netherlands East Indies Army. The last Dutch slave ship from Elmina to the Americas sailed in 1803.
35 Van den Tol 2018, p. 248; The Hague, National Archives of the Netherlands, OWIC, 1.05.01.01, inv. no. 53, fol. 22.
36 Visser 2001, p. 31.
37 Trans-Atlantic Slave Trade Database, see www.slavevoyages.org/HXgOHVrj; Visser 2001, p. 31.
38 Visser 2001, p. 30.
39 Marees 1602 (1912), p. 183.
40 Ibid.
41 Ferrão and Soares 1997, p. 174.
42 Visser 2001, p. 30.
43 Meuwese 2012, p. 1.
44 The Hague, The Royal Collections of the Netherlands, A4 1454, fol. 196, no date, but probably 1640, cited in Françozo 2014, p. 109.
45 The Hague, The Royal Collections of the Netherlands, A4 1454, fol. 203, 31 October 1642.
46 These portraits are part of four albums with drawings, titled *Theatrum rerum naturalium brasiliae*, in Kraków, Jagiellonian Library, Libri Picturati 34, fols. 1, 3, 5.
47 Fromont 2014, p. 125.
48 Wiesbaden, Hessian State Archives, 1642, Abt. 171 Z 4305.
49 Ibid. In 1491, during the period of Portuguese expansion, the Congolese kings had converted to Catholicism. See Bostoen 2018, p. 207.
50 Wiesbaden, Hessian State Archives, 1642, Abt. 171 Z 4305.
51 Ibid.
52 Françozo 2014, pp. 110–112.
53 Thornton 1998, pp. 189–213.
54 Van den Tol 2018, p. 250.
55 Ratelband 2003, p. 43.

wally

pp. 84–105

1 The Hague, National Archives of the Netherlands, Sociëteit van Suriname, 1.05.03, inv. no. 234.
2 For a comparable story about Manuel, an enslaved man, see Fatah-Black 2018, ch. 1.
3 The Hague, National Archives of the Netherlands, Sociëteit van Suriname, 1.05.03, inv. no. 234, fol. 254. The spelling of Wally varies: Walij is also used. For the events at Palmeneribo, see also Dragtenstein 2004.
4 The Hague, National Archives of the Netherlands, Sociëteit van Suriname, 1.05.03, inv. no. 234, fols. 254–260.
5 Ibid., fols. 261–262.
6 Quoted in Van den Bel, Hulsman and Wagenaar 2014, p. 26. Original letter in French and Zeelandic, Middelburg, Zeeuws Archief, 2.1, inv. no. 2035, letter 332.
7 The enslavement of other indigenous peoples, such as the Tiriyó (Trio) and Wayana, was permitted; see Hoogbergen 2013, p. 152.
8 Trans-Atlantic Slave Trade Database, see www.slavevoyages.org/voyages/HXgOHVrj.
9 For a detailed explanation of the administrative structure of the Society of Suriname, see Fatah-Black 2019 and Van Stipriaan 1993a.
10 The Hague, National Archives of the Netherlands, Aanwinsten Eerste Afdeling, 1.11.01.01, inv. no. 409, apparently unpublished. With thanks to Philip Dikland, who alerted me to this document.
11 Enslaved Africans who managed to escape slavery and founded their own settlements in the forest, and their descendants.
12 Van Stipriaan 2006, p. 408.
13 See p. 113 in the 'Oopjen' chapter of this book.

14 In Zandvliet et al. 2006, Nicolaas Witsen is placed sixteenth in the list of the 250 richest people of the seventeenth century.
15 Amsterdam City Archives, 5075, Notarissen ter Standplaats Amsterdam, inv. no. 190, Stephanus Pelgrom, no. 4775, fol. 201. Egidius van den Bempden signs off on behalf of Jonas Witsen. Like Witsen he belonged to a powerful family of Amsterdam patricians with interests in city government as well as business. Van den Bempden was mayor of Amsterdam but also an administrator of the Dutch East India Company (VOC) and one of the directors of the Society of Suriname. Witsen knew him from his role as a municipal clerk.
16 Tom van der Molen, 'De andere Verhalen rond Plantage Waterlant', www.hart.amsterdam/nl/page/640910, 29 November 2018 (accessed 30 November 2018). Trawatte is taken from the house of Jonas Witsen to be buried on 24 November 1705.
17 Ibid.
18 Van Eeghen 1946.
19 Amsterdam City Archives, 5075, Notarissen ter Standplaats Amsterdam, inv. no. 140, Henrick Outger, no. 3369, 133, fols. 1147–1149.
20 Ibid.
21 The Hague, National Archives of the Netherlands, Sociëteit van Suriname, 1.05.03, inv. no. 234, fol. 257.
22 Ibid., inv. no. 234.
23 Ibid.
24 Ibid.
25 Ibid.
26 Ibid.
27 Ibid.

oopjen

pp. 106–121

The author wishes to thank Jonathan Bikker, Bianca du Mortier, Suzanne van Leeuwen, Mark Ponte and Monique Rakhorst.

1 Calculated using Internationaal Instituut voor Sociale Geschiedenis, Amsterdam, see www.iisg.nl/hpw/calculate-nl.php.
2 In many cases there was a domestic residence adjacent to the refinery premises, see Van Nierop 1958; Reisig 1793.
3 Daarnhouwer 1967, p. 224: 'Hier is de Hel. Daar is het wel. Al is het wat duur. Nog is het beter hier als in 't Vagevuur.'
4 Jan Soolmans was also known as Hans: 'Hans Solemans, koopman', *poorter* act, 8 March 1591, see Daarnhouwer 1967, p. 228.
5 Ibid.
6 Equivalent in modern terms to 65 million euros, see www.iisg.nl/hpw/calculate-nl.php.
7 Van Groesen 2013, p. 744.
8 Thanks to Elmer Kolfin and his research into seventeenth-century newspapers.
9 Poelwijk 2003, p. 107.
10 Ibid., p. 257.
11 Amsterdam supplied sugar to France, England, Poland, Sweden, Denmark, Bohemia, Austria, the German Empire and the Baltic region, see Poelwijk 2003, p. 56.
12 Jan Soolmans's first wife was Ida Baster; Willemina Salen's first husband was Guillaume van Kleef, bailiff of Mijdrecht.
13 Poelwijk 2003, p. 231, n. 102.
14 Grave no. 158, Poelwijk 2003, p. 225, n. 80.
15 Bikker 2016, p. 22; Erfgoed Leiden en omstreken, 0506, Oud Notarieel Archief, inv. no. 316, notaris Cornelis Dircxz van Grotelande, 1624–1641, fol. 208, 24 October 1630. The amount concerned was 300 guilders.
16 Bikker 2016, p. 28.
17 Ponte 2019; M. Ponte, 'Zwart in Amsterdam rond 1650', in Archangel et al. 2020, p. 55.
18 Rembrandt, *Two African Men*, 1661 (possibly mentioned in the 1656 estate inventory), The Hague, Mauritshuis, bequest of Abraham Bredius.
19 De Laet 1937. For the notice of marriage, see Bikker 2016, p. 30.
20 Zandvliet et al. 2006, p. 257.
21 These hearing transcripts also record the name João Mina, although it is unclear who conducted the interrogation; see pp. 65–69 in the 'João' chapter of this book.
22 The Hague, National Archives of the Netherlands, Verspreide West-Indische Stukken, 1.05.06, inv. no. 1408. With thanks to Mark Ponte.
23 Ibid.: 'the child was so big when it was presented for Holy baptism that it could walk'. We can conclude from this that the girl was old enough to walk by the time the baptism took place. The name Elunam has no meaning as far as we know; it is an anagram of Manuel, a common Portuguese name for boys.
24 See Van Eeghen 1956, p. 86: 17 May and 10 September 1634.
25 See Van Eeghen 1956, and Pijzel-Dommisse 2000, pp. 392–393.

paulus

pp. 122–145

The authors wish to warmly thank for their contributions to this chapter Annemieke van der Vegt, for her archival research, and Alissandra Cummins, for her reflections and insights.

1 Amsterdam, Rijksmuseum, inventory card BK-NM-5144.
2 See, for example, the Zoninus collar, an iron neck ring with a bronze tag attached, reading, 'I have run away; hold me. When you have brought me back to my master Zoninus, you will receive a gold coin' ('Fugi, tene me. Cum revoc [a] veris me d[omino] m[eo] Zonino, accipis solidum'). Rome, National Roman Museum, Baths of Diocletian, Museo Epigrafico, inv. no. 65043.
3 'Alexr. Steuart found guilty of death for theft at Perth the 5th of December 1701, & gifted by the Justiciars as a perpetual servant to Sir Jo. Areskin of Alva'. Edinburgh, National Museums Scotland, inv. no. H.MR 3.
4 See p. 33 in the chapter 'Dutch Colonial Slavery' of this book.
5 See Goris 1923, pp. 541–544.
6 See Maduro 1986, pp. 151ff.
7 See, for example, Simon Gikandi's analysis of the symbolism associated with Black servants and secondary figures in the American and European context, which includes an examination of the meaning of the slave collar, Gikandi 2011, p. 172.
8 Slavery also had no legal basis in Britain, but it was a common phenomenon nonetheless. The use of a collar to indicate that the wearer was the property of another person was a ubiquitous practice, as evidenced by the many seventeenth- and eighteenth-century advertisements giving notice of the escape of enslaved people. See www.runaways.gla.ac.uk/; Mtubani 1983, p. 72; Anonymous 1891.
9 See Maduro 1986, pp. 155, 157.
10 See note 8 above.
11 For the crests of the Nassau, Vianden and Dietz families, see Van de Venne 1937, p. 118.
12 'op 14 december is gedoopt paulus Maurus de Moor van de vrou vanderleck.' The Hague, Haags Gemeentearchief, Doop-, trouw- en begraafboeken 's Gravenhage, 0377-01, inv. no. 340, p. 9; Veldhuijzen 2003, p. 11.
13 This Jesuit-run chapel was situated between Nobelstraat and Juffrouw Idastraat. After closing in the early eighteenth century, in 1763 the church records were transferred to the French ambassador's Chapel on Casuariestraat.
14 Ponte 2019, p. 41; Blakely 1993, p. 58.
15 Kpobi 1993, pp. 12–129; Hondius 2010.
16 McGrath 2012, p. 17.
17 Blakely 1993, p. 105; In the seventeenth century, the compositional juxtaposition of a young Black man and a white woman was regarded as constituting a contrast in colour and position that enlivened paintings. In his 1678 introduction to painting, *Inleyding tot de Hooge Schoole der Schilderkonst* (Introduction to the Noble School of the Art of Painting), the influential artist Samuel van Hoogstraaten advised that: 'it may also give pleasure to the eye for maidens to be joined by a Moor sometimes', Otte 1987, p. 7.
18 'verbeeldende in zyn geheel, den ganschen omslag van een proper, ordentelyk en welgeschikt Huishouden', Anonymous 1798–1808.
19 The doll's house that Petronella Oortman commissioned in the late seventeenth century is believed to have cost somewhere between 20,000 and 30,000 guilders; as a comparison, Nicolaes Witsen purchased his residence at Herengracht 603 for 28,000 guilders, see Ter Molen 1994, pp. 123–125; Ter Molen 2017, p. 131.
20 Pijzel-Dommisse 2000, pp. 25, 28.
21 Ibid., pp. 49–50.
22 Ter Molen 1994, p. 125.
23 Von Uffenbach, who viewed the doll's house in 1718, describes this room – the most prestigious reception room – as the 'best room', see Pijzel-Dommisse 2000, p. 285.
24 Ibid., pp. 45, 50.
25 The parrot depicted in the overmantel in the doll's house (fig. 3) does not appear in the painting of it by Jacob Appel, see Pijzel-Dommisse 2000, pp. 287–288.
26 For the landscape illusion, see Pijzel-Dommisse 2000, pp. 262, 285; Ter Molen 2017, p. 133.
27 Ter Molen 1994, pp. 127–128, 133.
28 Other men of African origin who married in the seventeenth, eighteenth and early nineteenth centuries include Willem Frederik Cupido, Jacobus Capitein and Christiaan Congo Loango; see also Doortmont 2015.
29 'Herpaucker van [de] Comp[agni]e Lijffguardes te Paert van Sijne Hoogh[eit],

met Maria Sauls, jonged[ochte]r, beijde woonende alh[ie]r in den Hage', The Hague, City Archives, Rechtelijke archieven 's-Gravenhage, 0351-01, inv. no. 752, p. 91; Veldhuijzen 2003, p. 11.
30 Sypesteyn and De Bordes 1850, p. 83; Van Aalst 1985, p. 13.
31 Willem Adriaan, Count of Nassau-Odijk, was highly favoured by William III. The count succeeded him as the senior nobleman (*Eerste Edele*) of Zeeland province, and consequently as member of the States of Zeeland (the provincial parliament) and the States General of the United Provinces (the national parliament), as well as Extraordinary Ambassador to the courts of England and France, see Van Heuven-van Nes 2015, p. 140; Van Aalst 1985, p. 13.
32 See Rembrandt's drawing *Two Drummers*, 1638, London, British Museum, inv. no. Oo,10.122; Paulus Constantijn la Fargue, *Cavalerist met trommels en trommelstokken*, The Hague, City Archives, inv. no. kl. A 2844; Schreuder 2017, p. 211; Plate IV in *Atlas of verzameling van teekeningen de inrichting voostellende van het Artillerie-Materieel ten tijde van Prins Willem III, koning van Engeland (1691–1072)*, Soest, National Military Museum, inv. no. 00148297.
33 Anonymous 1688.
34 Kolfin 2008, p. 263; Schreuder 2017, pp. 208–209.
35 Schreuder 2017, pp. 207–208.
36 Several portraits exist of individual servants in Europe, including that of Angelo Soliman at the Habsburg court in Vienna, see Northrup 2002, pp. 151–153; Waterfield 2003, p. 145.
37 Schreuder 2008, p. 264; Northrup 2002, p. 153; Seelig 2005, p. 208.
38 Said 1978.
39 Eyres 2011, p. 46.
40 Otte 1987, p. 9; McGrath 2012, p. 15.
41 Molineux 2012, p. 21.
42 The chapel on Assendelftstraat (also known as Lorrestraat) was run by Carmelites who founded a mission in The Hague in 1649 and were based from 1664 onwards at the Assendelftstraat chapel, also known as the French Church, where services were held in French. In the eighteenth century a charitable institution called 't Hooftshofje was built next to it. In the 1820s, the building was converted and renamed Sint- Willibrordus-kerk. After falling into disrepair, it was demolished in 1972.
43 'Ce Jourdhuy 24e Avril 1690 Jay baptizé le fils de Mre. Paul Maurice Agulard, et de Marie Sauls. Il a eu par Maraine Madame Anne Elisabeth de Scaick, dame de Lalech. Il a esté renu[?] par les fonds au nom de la d[i]t dame par Elisabeth Weltins, sa femme de chambre et a esté nommé Maurice. Il est né le 23e du d[i]t mois ... que dessue', The Hague, City Archives, Doop-, trouw- en begraafboeken 's Gravenhage, 0377-01, inv. no. 355, p. 87; Veldhuijzen 2003, p. 11.
44 Ainsworth et al. 2015, p. 6.
45 Ibid., pp. 7–8, 41.
46 See, for example, the descendants of Cupido in Schreuder 2017, and the descendants of Elisabeth Samson: Verseput family, in Van Stipriaan et al. 2007.
47 Annemieke van der Vegt, who was unaware that her roots were anything other than European, is an example of this phenomenon: in the course of genealogical research she was surprised to discover an ancestor named Christiaan van der Vegt, who was born in Africa and had been put to work as a child in the Dutch Republic. In her research, Van der Vegt examines the country in the eighteenth century through Christiaan's eyes, demonstrating that the application of empathy and the ability to consciously take multiple perspectives can lead to new insights into the past and thus a more complex understanding of Dutch history and identity, see www.hoeheettechristiaan.nl.

van bengalen

pp. 146–175

With thanks to Doreen van den Boogaart for her help in writing this chapter.

1 Wouter Schouten's *Oost-Indische voyagie*, Amsterdam 1676, as quoted in Breet 2003, p. 326.
2 Ibid.
3 The equivalent of about 230–300 euros today, according to the calculation model of the International Institute of Social History, Amsterdam, see www.iisg.nl/hpw/calculate-nl.php.
4 Breet 2003, p. 327.
5 Oliver 1838, p. 1880, quoted in Baay 2015, p. 101.
6 Sen 1932, pp. 23–24.
7 Subramanian 1999, p. 83.
8 See p. 32 in the chapter 'Dutch Colonial Slavery' of this book.
9 Van Galen 2008, pp. 222–223.
10 Ibid., pp. 224–226; Subrahmanyam 1997, pp. 209, 213–214.

11 Transcript of the *firman* issued to Jan Luijnenburgh, 1642, The Hague, National Archives of the Netherlands, Verenigde Oost-Indische Compagnie (VOC), 1.04.02, inv. no. 1143, fols. 619–620.
12 Van Galen 2008, pp. 225, 235–236.
13 Van Dijk 2008, p. 16; Van Galen 2008, p. 216.
14 General Missives of the VOC, 3 February 1626, in Coolhaas 1960, pp. 185–186, 196, 199, 201, as quoted in Niemeijer 2005, p. 54.
15 Van Galen 2008, pp. 236–237.
16 Chakraborty 2019.
17 Van Rossum 2015, pp. 17, 33, 45–48.
18 At the time, about three months' salary. The Bengali silver sicca rupee was worth 33 Dutch stuivers (20 stuivers equalled a guilder). See Instituut voor Nederlandse Geschiedenis, *VOC Glossarium*, The Hague 2000, htttp://resources.huygens.knaw.nl/pdf/vocglossarium/VOCGlossarium.pdf.
19 The equivalent of 57.75 guilders, see note 18 above and www.iisg.nl/hpw/calculate2-nl.php.
20 Jakarta, Arsip Nasional Republik Indonesia (ANRI), Familiepapieren van Bloys van Treslong Prins, no. R178.
21 Furthermore, during the recording of the sale, Maart's subjugated position may have been cited and questioned. The seller would be asked whether Maart was his property, and Maart had to answer whether Plusker was her 'master'. The deed had to be preserved with care because it served as proof of ownership. Every new sale and transfer was added to it, see Van Rossum 2015, p. 44.
22 Ibid., p. 66.
23 The Hague, National Archives of the Netherlands, Schepenbank te Batavia, 1.04.18.03, inv. no. 11982.
24 Van Rossum 2015, pp. 72–77.
25 Mardijkers were formerly enslaved people who had been freed and converted to Christianity.
26 Jakarta, Arsip Nasional Republik Indonesia (ANRI), Archives of the Schepenbank of Batavia, 1620–1809, no. 1522. This document was found by Matthias van Rossum, who generously directed my attention to it.
27 As quoted in Hagen 2018, p. 487.
28 See pp. 32–33 in the chapter 'Dutch Colonial Slavery' of this book.
29 Niemeijer 2005, pp. 50–55.
30 Ibid.
31 Baay 2015, pp. 30–35.
32 Jakarta, Arsip Nasional Republik Indonesia (ANRI), Archief van de Gouverneur-Generaal en Raden van Indië (Hoge Regering) van de Verenigde Oostindische Compagnie en Taakopvolgers, 1612–1812, no. 2491, fol. 74, 23 January 1682.
33 Baay 2015, pp. 52–53; Mbeki 2018, p. 48.
34 Niemeijer 2005, p. 51.
35 Van der Chijs 1885–1900, pt. 3: 1678–1709, pp. 75–77.
36 Van Rossum 2015, p. 56.
37 Voskuil-Groenewegen et al. 1999, pp. 45–46.
38 Van de Wall 1934, p. 531; Van Rossum 2015, p. 22.
39 The Hague, National Archives of the Netherlands, VOC, 1.04.02, inv. no. 1595, fol. 177.
40 Valentijn 1724–1726, pt. 4, p. 10.
41 Ibid., p. 11.
42 Loth 1995, p. 27.
43 See www.iisg.nl/hpw/calculate-nl.php.
44 Boëseken 1977, pp. 9, 14, 22, 29, 65, 79–81, 95, 103.
45 Ibid., p. 79.
46 Dooling and Worden 2017, p. 121.
47 Boëseken 1977, p. 79.
48 Today, the slave lodgings serve as the slavery museum, under the name Slave Lodge (Iziko Museums of South Africa).
49 Cape Town, Western Cape Archives, CJ 1, criminal and civil cases, 1652–1673, 11-12-1669, p. 51A.
50 Ibid.
51 Upham 2012.
52 Dooling and Worden 2017, p. 131.
53 Slotsboo 1918, p. 121, quoted in Dooling and Worden 2017, p. 123.
54 See pp. 24–25 in the chapter 'Dutch Colonial Slavery' of this book.
55 Ross 1983, pp. 14, 118.
56 Ibid., pp. 15–16.
57 Cape Town, Western Cape Archives, MOOC 7/1/39, no. 49.
58 Cape Town, Western Cape Archives, MOOC 7/1/45, no. 52.
59 Resolutions of the Council of Policy of Cape of Good Hope Cape Town Archives Repository, South Africa, V.C. 12, pp. 219–220, Monday 11 April 1689.
60 Ibid.
61 Alkmaar, Regionaal Archief, Doop- Trouw en Begraafboeken, no. 10.3.001, Alkmaars Doopboek 1686–1694, inv. no. 09.
62 *Leeuwarder Courant*, 20 October 1879, p. 1.
63 Zijlstra 2012, p. 14.
64 Van der Chijs 1885–1900, pt. 2: 1642–1677, pp. 108–109.
65 Ibid., pp. 250–251.
66 See p. 126 in the 'Paulus' chapter of this book.

67 Leeuwarden, Tresoar, Description of Families in Friesland ('Volkstelling'); Towns, inv. no. 1631, p. 2, deed no. 22, period: 1744, see www.tresoar.nl and www.allefriezen.nl.

surapati

pp. 176–193

With thanks to Doreen van den Boogaart for her help in writing this chapter.

1 Leonard Blussé identified the male servant in Jacob Coeman's painting as Untung. Blussé describes him as senior merchant Pieter Cnoll's favourite servant, see Blussé 1986, pp. 195, 267.
2 Christomy 2003, p. 39.
3 Kumar 1976, pp. 5–7.
4 Ibid., pp. 8–17. The West Javanese *Surapati babad* is *lontar* manuscript no. 240 in the collection of the Royal Netherlands Academy of Arts and Sciences (KNAW) at Leiden University Library, Acad. 240. The East Javanese *Surapati babad* is the Kartasura babad of Leiden University Library, Cornelis Christiaan Berg collection, no. 143, CB 143, from a copy by a poet at the court of Surapati or that of one of his sons. The East Javanese *Surapati babad* is manuscript no. 585 in the Brandes collection of the Museum Pusat Kebudayaan Indonesia (National Museum of Indonesia), Jakarta, and dates from the nineteenth century. The Balambangan babad is part of the Oriental Manuscripts collection at Leiden University Library, Or. 3704.
5 Kumar 1976, pp. 379–384.
6 Ibid., pp. 319–384.
7 Paasman 2010, p. 96.
8 Valentijn 1724–1726, pt. 4-1, p. 125.
9 Meister 1692, pp. 292–294.
10 Valentijn 1724–1726, pt. 4-1, p. 123.
11 Kumar 1976, p. 19.
12 Ibid., pp. 313–314.
13 Blussé 1986, p. 19.
14 Van der Chijs 1885–1900, pt. 2: 1642–1677, p. 405.
15 Schulte Nordholt 1996, pp. 42–43.
16 Jakarta, Arsip Nasional Republik Indonesia (ANRI), Huysman legal archive, 15 February 1672, fol. 22.
17 Meister 1692, p. 292.
18 Kumar 1976, p. 378.
19 Ibid., p. 60.
20 As quoted in Paasman 2010, p. 95.
21 As quoted in De Jonge 1875, p. 165.
22 Kumar 1976, pp. 24–25.
23 Valentijn 1724–1726, pt. 4-1, p. 124.
24 As quoted in Paasman 2010, p. 96.
25 De Haan 1910–1912, p. 268.
26 Jakarta, Museum Pusat Kebudayaan Indonesia, Brandes collection, *Surapati babad*, no. 585, as quoted in Kumar 1976, p. 142.
27 Rickleffs 1993, pp. 87–92.
28 Leiden University Library, CB 143, Kartasura babad.
29 Kumar 1976, p. 211.
30 Ricklefs 1993, pp. 95–98, 100.
31 Valentijn 1724–1726, pt. 4-1, pp. 50, 196.
32 Kumar 1976, pp. 35–42.
33 Busken Huet 1882–1884, p. 346.
34 To earn this title, one must have undertaken acts described as heroic and remembered as an example to the people of Indonesia. For people who died before 1945, there is the added stipulation that they must have fought against colonialism in an area now belonging to Indonesia.
35 Busken Huet 1882–1884, p. 346.
36 The book was published as a serial between 1911 and 1913.
37 Bakker 1987, p. 1; Klooster 1984–1985, pp. 3–4.
38 Klooster 1984–1985, pp. 5–8.
39 Moeis probably knew Melati van Java's book from the 1898 Malay translation by Ferdinand Wiggers.
40 Klooster 1984–1985, pp. 8–11; Bakker 1987, p. 1.

sapali

pp. 194–219

This chapter could not have been written without the many people who shared their knowledge, mostly obtained through oral sources, with me. This is knowledge that, given the nature of the source, cannot be listed in a bibliography. I have therefore opted to name all of these individuals in the text. My heartfelt thanks go out to them, for their valuable contributions and their trust.

1 In this chapter, the appellation Ndyuka is used in relation to historical documents.
2 Van Andel 2018.
3 With thanks to Liesbeth Peroti and Ida Does for the recordings, and Margot van den Berg for her help with the orthography.
4 Van Brummelen, De Haan and Alexander 2018.

5 '"Wij willen onze vrijheid": Verzetshelden tijdens de slavernij', lab.nos.nl/projects/slavernijverzet/index.html (accessed 4 November 2020).
6 Carney 2004, p. 1.
7 Van Andel et al. 2019; Sikkema 2019.
8 Carney 2004, p. 7.
9 Van Andel et al. 2016; Van Andel et al. 2019; Sikkema 2019.
10 Veltman et al. 2019, p. 18.
11 Sint Nicolaas 2018, p. 73.
12 Hoogbergen 1992, p. 39.
13 De Groot 2009, p. 85.
14 Buve 1966, p. 24.
15 Van der Sijs 2003.
16 Hilkhuijsen 2012–2013, p. 202.
17 See, for instance, De Rooy 2014.
18 Dragtenstein 2010, p. 44.
19 The Hague, National Archives of the Netherlands, Sociëteit van Suriname, 1.05.03, inv. no. 313, p. 430.
20 Ibid., inv. no. 315, p. 15.

tula

pp. 220–239

1 Oostindie 2011, p. 2.
2 Gibbes 2002; Jordaan 1999.
3 Oostindie 2011.
4 Ansano 2017; Dufour 2019, p. 97.
5 Oostindie 2011.
6 Cain 2009.
7 Oostindie 2011, p. 12; see also Koekkoek 2013.
8 Reinier Salverda, via Aimé Césaire and Wendela Parkinson, cites another example of flows of information concerning resistance and freedom: that Toussaint L'Ouverture had read about uprisings in Suriname, Salverda 2015, p. 228.
9 Oostindie 2011; Cain 2009; Gibbes 2002.
10 The Hague, National Archives of the Netherlands, *Journaal gehouden door de schrijver J.G. Hummen aan boord van 's lands fregat* Ceres *onder commando van de kapitein Anthony d'Amers, 15 december 1793–12 augustus 1796*, Archief Marine, Aanhangsel II, 2.01.29.03, inv. no. 164, p. 166.
11 The Hague, National Archives of the Netherlands, *Bijlagen Resolutiën van Directeur (Comissarissen) en Raden, nr 55, d.d. 2 okt 1795*, Curaçao, Oude Archieven tot 1828, 1.05.12.01, inv. no. 121.
12 Oostindie 2011, p. 10.
13 The Hague, National Archives of the Netherlands, *Verslag Pater Schinck, 1794*, Curaçao, Oude Archieven tot 1828, 1.05.12.01, inv. no. 105.
14 Ibid.
15 Ibid.
16 Ibid.
17 James 1938.
18 The Hague, National Archives of the Netherlands, *Verslag Pater Schinck, 1794*, Curaçao, Oude Archieven tot 1828, 1.05.12.01, inv. no. 105.
19 Koekkoek 2013.
20 The Hague, National Archives of the Netherlands, Curaçao, Oude Archieven tot 1828, 1.05.12.01, inv. no. 106.
21 The Hague, National Archives of the Netherlands, *Verslag Pater Schinck, 1794*, Curaçao, Oude Archieven tot 1828, 1.05.12.01, inv. no. 105, last page.
22 The Hague, National Archives of the Netherlands, *Rapport Westerholt 5 oktober 1795*, Curaçao, Oude Archieven tot 1828, 1.05.12.01, inv. no. 106.
23 Oostindie 2011, p. 10.
24 Dufour 2019, pp. 52, 96–97.
25 See multiple examples in Dufour 2019; Bender and Dubois 2011.
26 Dufour 2019.
27 Willemstad, National Archives, Fundashon Zikinzá Collection, no. 607.
28 *Kaiman djuku* is Guene, a language spoken exclusively by enslaved people on Curaçao. In his reconstructive research, Martinus Arion has shown that this expression must be derived from Cape Verdean Creole and Portuguese; Martinus 2004, p. 285; Willemstad, National Archives, Fundashon Zikinzá Collection, no. 607.
29 Sung by a woman born in 1903, Willemstad, National Archives, Fundashon Zikinzá Collection, no. 607; included on the CD: Juliet, Lopez and Weeber 2002. Translation and interpretation by Rose Mary Allen, Allen 2007, pp. 110–111.
30 Coomans 1997, p. 104.
31 See for example Jordaan 2003, p. 241.
32 See Brenneker 1974.
33 Ansano 2017.
34 Brenneker 1974.
35 'Tula awor ofisialmente heroe nashonal', see youtube.com, uploaded by TeleCuracao Multimedia, 18 August 2010 (accessed 20 May 2020).

dirk

pp. 240–263

1 The Hague, National Archives of the Netherlands, Collection 049 G.K. van Hogendorp, 2.21.006.49, inv. no. 167.
2 Timmer 1988, p. 19; Van Meerkerk 2013, p. 28.
3 From 1767 to 1772 the Van Hogendorp family lived on Noordeinde, at the corner with Scheveningsebrug. Cupido and Sideron lived on Molenstraat until 1772.
4 See Schreuder 2017.
5 Van Hogendorp 1887, pp. 56–57; Du Perron-De Roos 1943, p. 141.
6 Du Perron-De Roos 1943, pp. 156–157, 173–174, 178, 199–200; Timmer 1988, pp. 46–49.
7 Du Perron-De Roos 1943, pp. 131, 134–138, 141, 170.
8 See Dirk van Hogendorp's letter to Gijsbert Karel van Hogendorp, 21 January 1797, Surabaya, and the short biographical text he wrote in Surabaya in 1798, Du Perron-De Roos 1943, pp. 188–189, 202–203.
9 Van Hogendorp 1887, p. 93.
10 On 2 July 1796 Hogendorp wrote *Proeve over den slaavenhandel en de slaaverny, in Neerlands Indie*, in which he set out his ideas pertaining to the abolition of the slave trade and slavery, see Van Hogendorp 1801b, p. 453.
11 Brommer, Den Heijer et al. 2011, p. 105; Kars 2016, p. 49.
12 Later publications showed this, such as the book by John Gabriël Stedman *Narrative of a Five Years Expedition against the Revolted Negroes of Surinam* (1796). In 1799 a Dutch version was published, titled *Reize naar Surinamen en door de binnenste gedeelten van Guiana*.
13 'When, in the year 1763, the Colony of Berbice by the slaves was ended, and the astonishing punishments for it meted out, I found the feelings of some of my compatriots, and even several of the most competent among them, differed greatly from my own', Van Winter 1774, foreword.
14 Ibid.
15 Adams 2015, p.11.
16 Adams 2018, pp. 147–148.
17 Van Hogendorp 1780, p. iv.
18 See letter of Dirk van Hogendorp, 8 October 1794, Du Perron-De Roos 1943, p. 180; Van Hogendorp 1799b.
19 Turksma 2005, pp. 32–33; Van Hogendorp 1801a, pp. 2, 8, 38, 107–108.
20 Du Perron-De Roos 1943, pp. 135, 148–149, 166–168, 244, 248; Van Hogendorp 1887, pp. 65, 115; Timmer 1988, p. 61; The Hague, National Archives of the Netherlands, Collection 069 Van Hogendorp, 2.21.08.69, inv. no. 64.
21 Van Hogendorp 1799a, p. 25, Du Perron-De Roos 1943, pp. 212, 234–235.
22 The Hague, National Archives of the Netherlands, Collection 019 Van Alphen en Engelhard, 2.21.010, inv. no. 4; Du Perron-De Roos 1943, p. 214.
23 Van Hogendorp 1887, pp. 123, 128; Van Hogendorp 1799a, pp. 17–18, 24; Du Perron-De Roos 1943, pp. 210, 214; The Hague, National Archives of the Netherlands, Collection 019 Van Alphen en Engelhard, 2.21.010, inv. no. 4, p. 11.
24 He published two successive editions of *Berigt van de tegenwoordigen toestand der bataafsche Bezittingen in Oost Indien en den handel op dezelve* (Account of the present state of Batavian possessions in the East Indies and the trade of the same; 1799, 1800. See note 47 for publication details of the English translation); *Kraspoekol; of de Slaaverny (Een tafereel der zeden van Nederlands Indiën)* (Kraspoekol, or slavery. A morality play set in the Dutch East Indies; 1800); *Ontwerp om de Oost-Indische Compagnie dezer landen in haren vorige bloei, en welvaart, ... te herstellen*, 1801; *Verzameling van stukken, rakende de zaak van Dirk van Hogendorp, opperkoopman in diens der Oost-Indische Compagnie, en gezaghebber van Java's Oosthoek*, 1801; *Stukken, raakende den tegenwoordigen toestand der Bataafsche bezittingen in Oost-Indië en den handel op dezelve*, containing *Proeve over den slavenhandel en de slavernij in Neerlands Indie*, 1801.
25 Van Hogendorp 1800, p. v.
26 Dirk van Hogendorp's father Willem owned enslaved people when he took up his post as colonial administrator (*resident*) of Rembang, Java, in 1774, see Timmer 1988, p. 11.
27 Van Hogendorp 1780, foreword.
28 Van Hogendorp 1800, p. vi; De Jong 2000, pp. 124, 148; Gelman Taylor 1983.
29 The two brothers of Dirk van Hogendorp's first wife Margaretha Elisabeth Bartlo were sent in 1785 to study in Holland, where Dirk's brother, Gijsbert Karel, and his mother would keep an eye on them. In 1788, he sent his fourteen-month-old son to the

Netherlands, believing the boy would receive a better upbringing in the country, see Du Perron-De Roos 1943, pp. 136, 152, 155, 198; Van Hogendorp 1887, p. 73.

30 De Jong 2000, pp. 131–132.

31 He already developed this idea in *Proeve over den slavenhandel en de slavernij in Neerlands Indie*, published in 1796, in Van Hogendorp 1801b, p. 457.

32 Van Hogendorp 1800, pp. vi–vii.

33 'There are certainly some people, particularly women, who treat their slaves very badly; by both harsh corporal punishments and the withholding of necessary clothing and foodstuffs, but especially by making them suffer the effects of their evil tempers, even more so if envy or the jealousy of love leads the women to believe that her husband or lover favour a particular [female] slave, then she may be merciless in making said slave suffer, and cruelly mistreat her.', Van Hogendorp 1801b, p. 457; Van Hogendorp 1800, p. vii.

34 Adams and Van der Haven 2016, p. 6; Van Hogendorp 1800, pp. 13, 16.

35 Van Hogendorp 1800, pp. x, 13–19, 22–24; Van Hogendorp 1780, p. 5.

36 Van Hogendorp, 1801b, p. 25; Van Hogendorp 1800, pp. ix, 73–74, 82, 109.

37 In 1793 the government in The Hague dispatched S.C. Nederburgh to the Dutch East Indies to tackle corruption within the VOC, which was leading to year-on-year losses. Nederburgh quickly became a focus for Van Hogendorp's criticism, however, for behaving like a monarch rather than combating corruption, see Van 't Veer 1958, p. 23; Van Meerkerk, 2013, p. 128; Nieuwenhuys 1978, p. 73.

38 Van Hogendorp 1800, p. 86.

39 Elisabeth Margaretha Bartlo was born in Batavia, as were her mother, grandmother and great-grandmother. Her great-grandmother's name was Sio Nio Lim, see 'Afstammelingen van Gerard Van der Voorden', gw.geneanet.org/johanniswijken?lang=nl&iz=931&m=D&p=gerard&n=van+der+voorden&siblings=on¬es=on&t=T&v=6&image=on&marriage=on&full=on (accessed 10 April 2020. Her father, Sirardus Bartlo, was a VOC undermerchant (Gesworen klerck generale secretarie VOC), a municipal officer (*schepen*) and municipal vice president in Batavia. A respected and wealthy man, he was also owner of the Angkee and Kapok estates near Batavia, see gw.geneanet.org/johanniswijken?lang=nl&iz=943&p=sirardus&n=bartlo (accessed 10 April 2020).

40 See Van Hogendorp 1887, p. 57.

41 The Hague, National Archives of the Netherlands, Collection 049 G.K. van Hogendorp, 2.21.006.49, inv. no. 9.

42 Du Perron-De Roos 1943, p. 132; Van Meerkerk 2013, p. 89.

43 Maria Graham visited Novo Sion on two occasions, see Graham 1824, p. 172.

44 *Haagsche Courant*, 20 March 1801, p. 1.

45 *Janus Janus-Zoon: Suum Cuique* 38 (1801), pp. 281–283.

46 Ibid., pp. 281–286.

47 London, The British Library, India Office Records and Private Papers, John Carleton, *Important Extracts from a Dutch book entitled Account of the Present State of Batavian Possessions in the East Indies and the Trade of the Same*, 1 May 1801, Mss Eur C22, p. 14; Nieuwenhuys 1978, p. 72; Van 't Veer 1955, p. 59.

48 The day after the performance of the play in 1800, the M. Roelofswaert bookshop in Delft sold more copies of *Kraspoekol* than in the entire previous six months since its release, see Van 't Veer 1955, p. 59.

49 *Janus Janus-Zoon: Suum Cuique* 39 (1801), p. 292.

50 Van Meerkerk 2010, p. 39.

51 Timmer 1988, p. 96.

52 Ibid., pp. 96–97; The Hague, National Archives of the Netherlands, Collection 069 Van Hogendorp [1922 Acquisition], 2.21.008.69, inv. no. 59.

53 In July 1822, Dirk Van Hogendorp had seventeen enslaved people working for him, sixteen in August and fifteen in October. In an 1821 letter to his niece Mina he indicates that he intends to buy two people to work for him, see pp. 262–263 in this chapter; Timmer 1988, p. 97; The Hague, National Archives of the Netherlands, Collection 049 G.K. van Hogendorp, 2.21.006.49, inv. no. 30; Von Leithold 1821, p. 188.

54 The Hague, National Archives of the Netherlands, Collection 049 G.K. van Hogendorp, 2.21.006.49, inv. nos. 30, 31.

55 Von Leithold 1821, p. 186.

56 Timmer 1988, p. 97.

57 Ibid.

58 Von Leithold 1820, p. 187.

59 Graham 1824, p. 172.

60 Von Leithold 1820, p. 185.

61 See Graham 1824, p. 172.

62 The Hague, National Archives of the Netherlands, Collection 049 G.K. van Hogendorp, 2.21.006.49, inv. no. 167.
63 Arago 1839, p. 83.
64 Van Hogendorp, 1800, p. 31.

lohkay

pp. 264–289

1 Sekou 1996.
2 'Emilo Wilson Park', see http://stmartin-stmaarten.com/st-maarten-sightseeings/emilio-wilson-park-st-maarten (accessed 22 July 2020).
3 'Emilio Wilson's History', 2017, see http://emilios-sxm.com/emilio-wilsons-history (accessed 22 July 2020).
4 Sekou 1996.
5 See, for example, Roitman 2020 and De Haas 2014.
6 Smeulders 2016.
7 Sekou 1996, p. 41.
8 Barka 1993.
9 Smeulders 2016, p. 44; Roitman 2016.
10 Smeulders 2016, p. 45; Sekou 1996.
11 Smeulders 2016, p. 45; Paula 1993.
12 Smeulders 2016, p. 45; Sekou 1996.
13 Voges 2006, p. 9.
14 Sypkens Smit 1995.
15 Roitman 2016; Paula 1993.
16 Raders 1863; Van Sypesteyn 1866, p. 18.
17 Van Sypesteyn 1866, p. 54.
18 Paula 1993, p. 115.
19 'Wij Willem III, bij de gratie Gods, koning der Nederlanden, Prins van Oranje-Nassau, Groot-Hertog van Luxemburg.'
20 Allen 2007, p. 110.
21 Fricke 2019.
22 Ibid.

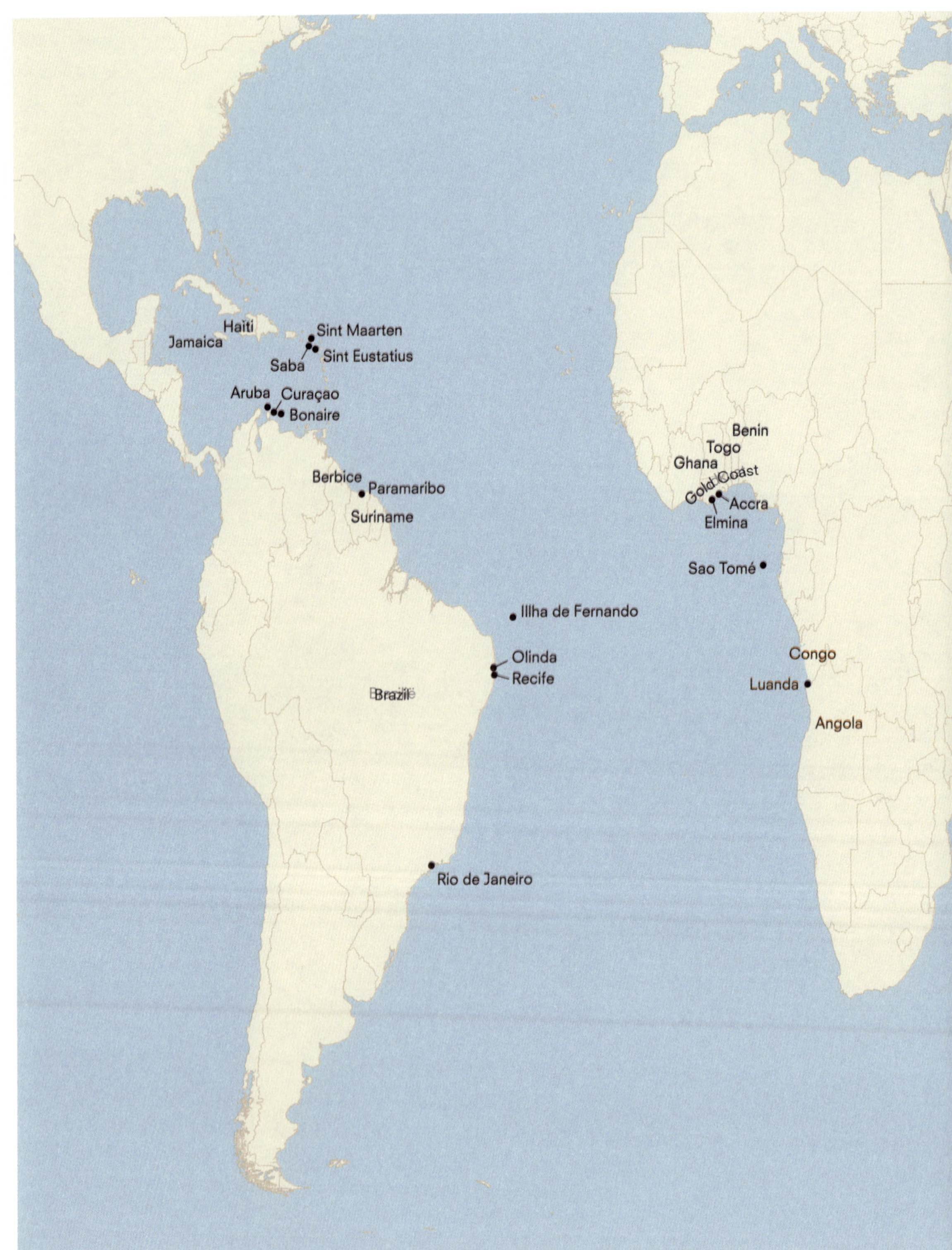
Haiti
Jamaica
Sint Maarten
Sint Eustatius
Saba
Aruba
Curaçao
Bonaire
Berbice
Paramaribo
Suriname
Benin
Togo
Ghana
Gold Coast
Accra
Elmina
Sao Tomé
Illha de Fernando
Olinda
Recife
Brazil
Congo
Luanda
Angola
Rio de Janeiro

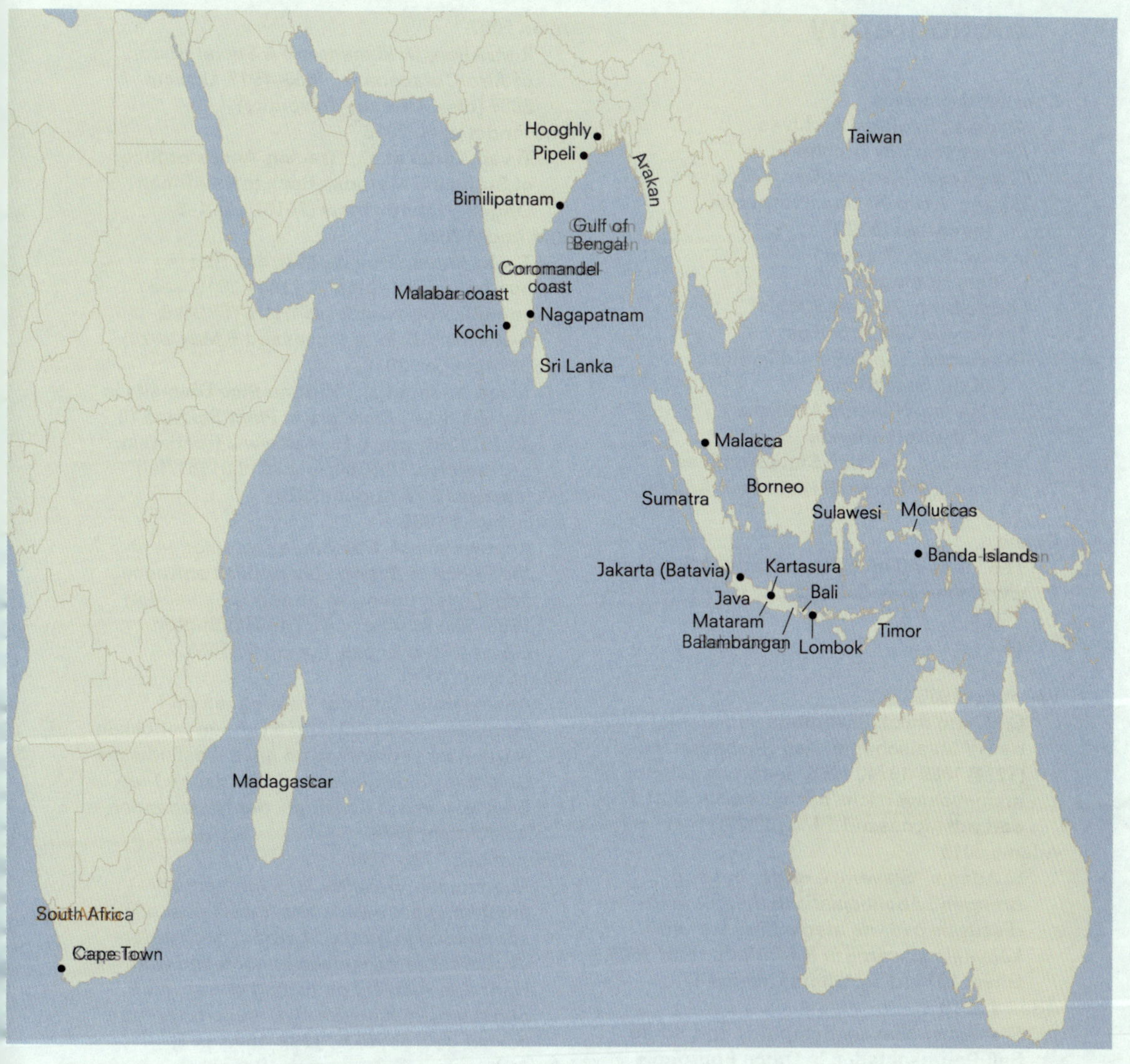

Details from the Gall-Peters projection of the world map. The countries and places indicated play a role in the lives of the protagonists of this book.

bibliography

Consulted Archives
Alkmaar, Regional Archives
Amsterdam City Archives
Cape Town, Western Cape Archives
Jakarta, Arsip Nasional Republik Indonesia (ANRI)
Leeuwarden, Treasor
Leiden, Heritage Leiden
Middelburg, Zeeuws Archief
The Hague City Archives
The Hague, The Royal Collections of the Netherlands
The Hague, National Archives of the Netherlands
Wiesbaden, Hessian State Archives
Willemstad, Centraal Historisch Archief

Online
The Trans-Atlantic Slave Trade Database: www.slavevoyages.org

a

Van Aalst 1985
G.M. van Aalst, 'Inventaris van archief van de NV Maatschappij Van Nassau la Lecq, (1274) 1888–1974', 1985, see www.gahetna.nl/archievenoverzicht/pdf/NL-HaNA_3.21.12.ead.pdf (accessed 1 May 2020)

Adams 2015
S. Adams, *'Slavernye onder het oog [...] brengen'. Abolitionistisch theater in de discussie over de afschaffing van de koloniale slavernij in Nederland rond 1800*, Ghent 2015 (diss. Ghent University)

Adams 2018
S. Adams, 'Slavery Sympathy and White Self-Representation in Dutch Bourgeois Theater of 1800', *Early Modern Low Countries* 2 (2018), pp. 146–168

Adams and Van der Haven 2016
S. Adams and K. van der Haven, '"Er is geen recht voor ons...". Van Hogendorps abolitionistisch toneelstuk Kraspoekol (1800) als proces tegen de slavernij', *Internationale Neerlandistiek* 54 (2016) 1, pp. 1–17. For abstract, see biblio.ugent.be/publication/ 7241019 (accessed 28 August 2020)

Ainsworth et al. 2015
M. Ainsworth, S. Hindriks and P. Terjanian, 'Lucas Cranach's Saint Maurice', *The Metropolitan Museum of Art Bulletin* 72 (2015) 4, pp. 3–46

Allen 2007
R.M. Allen, *Di ki manera? A Social History of Afro-Curaçaoans, 1863–1917*, Utrecht 2007 (diss. Utrecht University)

Van Andel et al. 2016
T. van Andel et al., 'Tracing Ancestor Rice of Suriname Maroons Back to its African Origin', *Nature Plants* (2016), pp. 1–5

Van Andel 2018
T. van Andel, 'Hoe de Marrons rijst in hun haar verstopten', 24 May 2018, see youtube.com/watch?v=4H1IbY6PGIk&-feature=emb_logo (accessed 6 May 2020)

Van Andel et al. 2019
T. van Andel et al., 'Hidden Rice Diversity in the Guianas', *Frontiers in Plant Science* 10 (2019) 1161, pp. 1–15, see www.frontiersin.org/articles/10.3389/fpls.2019.01161/full (accessed 28 August 2020)

Anonymous 1688
Anonymous, *A True and exact relation of the Prince of Orange his publick entrance into Exeter*, unknown newspaper, London 1688, San Marino, CA., The Huntington Library, Rare Books, inv. no. 227661

Anonymous 1770
Anonymous, 'Lyst der Fabricquen en Producten, welke uit deese Landen getrokken werden ter versending na onse Westindische Colonien', in *Nieuwe Nederlandsche Jaerboeken van het Koningrijk der Nederlanden*, Amsterdam 1770

Anonymous 1798–1808
Anonymous, *Beschryving van een uytmuntendt konst-werk. Van 't welk naar alle vermoeden in gansch Europa, noch elders eene weêrga zal kunnen aangetoond worden: waar aan ruim vijf en twintig jaaren, met ongelooflyke moeyte, vlyt, en verbaazende kosten gearbeydt is*, 1798–1808, p. 3, Amsterdam, Rijksmuseum Research Library, N.M. 1010

Anonymous 1891
Anonymous, 'Silver Collars for Slaves', *Daily Alta California* 84, no. 152, 1 June 1891, see cdnc.ucr.edu/?a=d&d=DAC18910601.2.39&srpos=1&e=-------en--20-DAC-1--txt-txIN-slave+collar-------1 (accessed 28 August 2020)

Ansano 2017
R. Ansano, *Vlémayo ta vle ma yo: influensha di kreyol haitiano den gueni i papiamentu di kòrsou*, 2017, see www.academia.edu/33425574/Vl%C3%A9mayo_ta_vle_ma_yo_influensha_di_kreyol_haitiano_den_gueni_i_papiamentu_di_k%C3%B2rsou (accessed 28 August 2020)

Arago 1839
J. Arago, *Voyage autour du monde. Souvenirs d'un aveugle*, Paris 1839
Archangel et al. 2020
S. Archangel et al., *Zwart in Rembrandts tijd*, Amsterdam (Rembrandthuis)/Zwolle 2020

b

Baay 2015
R. Baay, *Daar werd wat gruwelijks verricht. Slavernij in Nederlands-Indië*, Amsterdam 2015
Bakker 1987
M. Bakker, *Het verhaal achter het verhaal: een vergelijking van drie romans over Surapati*, Leiden 1987 (diss. Leiden University)
Barka 1993
N.F. Barka, *Archaeological Survey of Sites and Buildings, St. Maarten, Netherlands Antilles: I, St. Maarten Archaeological Research Series Report* no. 3 (1993)
Barleus 1923
C. Barleus, *Nederlandsch Brazilië onder het bewind van Johan Maurits Grave van Nassau, 1637–1644. Historisch – geographisch – ethnographisch* (translated into Dutch by S.P. L'Honoré-Naber), The Hague 1923
Bartels 1993
L. Bartels, 'De trans-Atlantische slavenhandel, wat betekende dit voor Afrika?', in B. Brommer (ed.), *Ik ben eigendom van ... Slavenhandel en plantageleven*, Wijk en Aalburg 1993, pp. 65–72
Van den Bel, Hulsman and Wagenaar 2014
M. van den Bel, L. Hulsman and L. Wagenaar (eds.), *De reizen van Adriaan van Berkel naar Guiana*, Leiden 2014
Bender and Dubois 2011
T. Bender and L. Dubois, *Revolution! The Atlantic World Reborn*, London 2011
Bikker 2016
J. Bikker, *Marten and Oopjen. Two Monumental Portraits by Rembrandt*, Amsterdam 2016
Blakely 1993
A. Blakely, *Blacks in the Dutch World. The Evolution of Racial Imagery in a Modern Society*, Bloomington 1993
Blussé 1986
L. Blussé, *In Strange Company. Chinese Settlers, Mestizo Women and the Dutch in VOC Batavia*, Dordrecht 1986
Boëseken 1977
A.J. Boëseken, *Slaves and Free Blacks at the Cape, 1658–1700*, Cape Town 1977
Boshoff and Du Plessis 1918
S.P.E. Boshoff and L.J. du Plessis, *Afrikaanse volksliedjies. Deel 1. Piekniekliedjies*, Pretoria, Amsterdam/Cape Town 1918
Bostoen 2018
K. Bostoen and I. Brinkman (eds.), *The Kongo Kingdom. The Origins, Dynamics and Cosmopolitan Culture of an African Polity*, Cambridge 2018
Boxer 1977
C. Boxer, *Nederlanders in Brazilië 1624–1654*, Alphen aan den Rijn 1977
Brandon and Bosma 2019
P. Brandon and U. Bosma, 'De betekenis van de Atlantische slavernij voor de Nederlandse economie in de tweede helft van de achttiende eeuw', *TSEG/Low Countries Journal of Social and Economic History*, 16 (2019) 2, pp. 5–46; for abstract, see doi.org/10.18352/tseg.1082 (accessed 25 September 2020)
Breet 2003
M. Breet, *De Oost-Indische voyagie van Wouter Schouten*, Zutphen 2003
Brenneker 1974
P. Brenneker, *Sambumbu. Volkskunde van Curaçao, Aruba en Bonaire*, vol. 3, Willemstad 1974
Brommer, Den Heijer et al. 2011
B. Brommer, H. den Heijer et al., *Grote atlas van de West-Indische Compagnie dl. 1, De oude WIC 1621–1674*, Voorburg 2011
De Bruijn and Kist 2001
M. de Bruijn and B. Kist, *Johannes Rach 1720–1783, Artist in Indonesia and Asia*, exhib. cat. Jakarta (National Library of Indonesia)/Amsterdam (Rijksmuseum) 2001
Van Brummelen, De Haan and Alexander 2018
L. van Brummelen, S. de Haan and T. Alexander (directors), film *Stones Have Laws (Dee Sitonu a Weti)*, 100 min., The Netherlands/Suriname 2018
Busken Huet 1882–1884
C. Busken Huet, *Het land van Rembrand. Studiën over de Noordnederlandsche beschaving in de 17de eeuw*, 2 vols., Haarlem 1882–1884
Buve 1966
R. Buve, 'Gouverneur Johannes Heinsius. De rol van Van Aerssen's voorganger in de Surinaamse Indianenoorlog, 1678–1680', *Nieuwe West-Indische Gids* 45 (1966), pp. 14–26

c

Cain 2009
A. Cain (ed.), *Tula, slavenopstand van 1795 op Curaçao*, Amsterdam 2009

Cairo 2007
A. Cairo, *Hebi Sani. Mental Well Being Among the Working Class Afro-Surinamese in Paramaribo, Suriname*, Lexington KY 2007 (diss. University of Kentucky)

Carney 2004
J.A. Carney, '"With Grains in her Hair": Rice in Colonial Brazil', *Slavery and Abolition. A Journal of Slave and Post-Slave Studies* 25 (2004) 1, pp. 1–27

Chakraborty 2019
T. Chakraborty, 'Slave Trading and Slave Resistance in the Indian Ocean World: The Case of Early Eighteenth Century Bengal', *Slavery & Abolition. A Journal of Slave and Post-Slave Studies* 40 (2019), pp. 706–726

Van der Chijs 1885–1900
J.A. van der Chijs (ed.), *Nederlandsch-Indisch Plakaatboek, 1602–1811*, 17 vols., Batavia/The Hague 1885–1900

Christomy 2003
T. Christomy, *Signs of the Wali. Narratives at the Sacred Sites in Pamijahan, West Java*, Canberra 2003 (thesis Australian National University)

Coolhaas 1960
W.Ph. Coolhaas (ed.), *Generale missiven der V.O.C. Deel 1, 1610–1628*, The Hague 1960

Coomans 1997
H.E. Coomans 'Nieuwe archeologische gegevens uit oude bronnen', in L. Alofs et al. (ed.) *Arubaans Akkoord. Opstellen over Aruba van vóór de komst van de olie-industrie*, Bloemendaal 1997, pp. 101–111

d

Daalder et al. 2013
R. Daalder, D.J. Tang and L. Balai (eds.), *Slaven en schepen in het Atlantisch gebied*, Leiden/Amsterdam 2013

Daarnhouwer 1967
F. Daarnhouwer, 'Waar stonden de suikerbakkerijen 't Vagevuur en 't Groot Hemelrijck?', *Maandblad Amstelodamum* 54 (1967), pp. 222–230

Dapper 1668
O. Dapper, *Naukeurige beschrijvinge der Afrikaensche Gewesten, van Egypten, Barbaryen, Libyen, Biledulgerid, Negroslant, Guinea, Ethiopiën, Abyssinie*, Amsterdam 1668

Van Dijk 2008
W.O. van Dijk, 'An End to the History of Silence? The Dutch Trade in Asian Slaves. Arakan and the Bay of Bengal, 1621–1665', *IIAS Newsletter* (2008) 46, p. 16

Dooling and Worden 2017
W. Dooling and N. Worden, 'Slavery in South Africa', in Gosselink, Holtrop and Ross 2017, pp. 119–129

Doortmont 2015
M. Doortmont, 'Marriages Between White and Black in the Netherlands. Legal and Social Issues from the Early Nineteenth Century', 2015, see gcdb-doortmontweb.blogspot.com/2015/11/marriages-between-white-and-black-in.html (accessed 1 May 2020)

Dragtenstein 2004
F. Dragtenstein, 'De opstand op Palmeneribo', *OSO Tijdschrift voor Surinamistiek* (2004) 2, pp. 214–235

Dragtenstein 2010
F. Dragtenstein, *Alles voor de vrede. De brieven van Boston Band tussen 1757 en 1763*, Amsterdam 2010

Dragtenstein 2017
F. Dragtenstein, *Van Elmina naar Paramaribo. De slavenhaler*, Zutphen 2017

Dufour 2019
A. Dufour (ed.), *Le modèle noir. De Géricault à Matisse*, Paris (Musée d'Orsay et de l'Orangerie) 2019

e

Van Eeghen 1946
Chr.P. van Eeghen, 'Dirk Valkenburg-boekhouder-schrijver-kunstschilder voor Jonas Witsen', *Oud Holland* 91 (1946), pp. 58–69

Van Eeghen 1956
I.H. van Eeghen, 'Marten Soolmans en Oopjen Coppit', *Maandblad Amstelodamum* 43 (1956), pp. 85–90

Van der Eijk 2006
C. van der Eijk, *Ketenen en Kanonschoten. De bewegingsruimte van Afrikanen in zeventiende eeuws Brazilië*, Amsterdam 2006 (diss. Social History, Vrije Universiteit Amsterdam)

Eyres 2011
P. Eyres, 'British Warfare and The Blackamoor. A Patriotic Celebration of Victory and Trade', in P. Eyres (ed.), *The Blackamoor & The Georgian Garden. New Arcadian Journal* (2011) 69/70, pp. 25–95

f

Fatah-Black 2018
K. Fatah-Black, *Eigendomsstrijd. De geschiedenis van slavernij en emancipatie in Suriname*, Amsterdam 2018

Fatah-Black 2019
K. Fatah-Black, *Sociëteit van Suriname 1683–1795. Het bestuur van de kolonie in de achttiende eeuw*, Zutphen 2019

Fatah-Black and De Windt 2018
K. Fatah-Black and M. de Windt, 'De ontbrekende schakels tussen compagnie en consumptie. Wie waren de grote opkopers bij de veilingen van de VOC in Zeeland in de achttiende eeuw?', *Tijdschrift voor geschiedenis* 131 (2018) 3, pp. 475–499

Ferdinand 2018
F. Ferdinand, *Toontaal. Sprekende Surinaamse liedjes van 1650–1950*, Volendam 2018

Ferrão and Soares 1997
C. Ferrão and J.P. Soares, *Dutch Brazil: The Thierbuch and Autobiography of Zacharias Wagener. Volume II*, Rio de Janeiro 1997

Françozo 2014
M. Françozo, 'Global Connections. Johan Maurtis of Nassau-Siegen's Collection of Curiosities', in M. van Groesen (ed.), *The Legacy of Dutch Brazil*, New York 2014, pp. 105–123

Fricke 2019
F.J. Fricke, *The Lifeways of Enslaved People in Curaçao, St Eustatius, and St Maarten/St Martin. A Thematic Analysis of Archaeological, Osteological, and Oral Historical Data*, Canterbury 2019 (diss. University of Kent)

Fromont 2014
C. Fromont, *The Art of Conversion. Christian Visual Culture in the Kingdom of Kongo*, Chapel Hill, NC 2014

g

Van Galen 2008
S. van Galen, *Arakan and Bengal. The Rise and Decline of the Mrauk U Kingdom (Burma) from the Fifteenth to the Seventeenth Century AD*, Leiden 2008

Geelen 2018
Alexander Geelen, *Defining Slavery in Cochin, Social Backgrounds, Tradition and Law in the Making of Slaafbaarheid in Eighteenth-Century Dutch Cochin*, Leiden 2018 (unpubl. diss. Leiden University)

Gelman Taylor 1983
J. Gelman Taylor, *The Social World of Batavia. European and Eurasian in Dutch Asia*, Madison, WI 1983

Gibbes 2002
F.E. Gibbes (ed.), *De bewoners van Curaçao vijf eeuwen lief en leed 1499–1999*, Willemstad 2002

Gikandi 2011
S. Gikandi, *Slavery and the Culture of Taste*, Princeton, NJ 2011

Goris 1923
J.A. Goris, 'Uit de Geschiedenis der vorming van het Antwerpsch Stadsrecht. Slavernij te Antwerpen in de XVIde eeuw', *Bijdragen tot de Geschiedenis* 15 (1923), pp. 541–544

Gosselink, Holtrop and Ross 2017
M. Gosselink, M. Holtrop and R. Ross (eds.), *Good Hope. South Africa and the Netherlands from 1600*, Amsterdam/Nijmegen 2017

Graham 1824
M. Graham, *Journal of a Voyage to Brazil, and Residence There, During Part of the Years 1821–1823*, London 1824

Green 2020
T. Green, *A Fistful of Shells. West Africa from the Rise of the Slave Trade to the Age of Revolution*, London 2020

Van Groesen 2013
M. van Groesen, '(No) News from the Western Front. The Weekly Press of the Low Countries and the Making of Atlantic News', *Sixteenth Century Journal* 44 (2013) 3, pp. 739–760

Van Groesen 2017
M. van Groesen, *Amsterdam's Atlantic. Print Culture and the Making of Dutch Brazil*, Philadelphia, PA 2017

De Groot 2009
S.W. de Groot, *Agents of their own Emancipation. Topics in the History of Surinam Maroons*, Amsterdam 2009

h

De Haan 1907
F. de Haan, *Dagh-register gehouden Int Casteel Batavia vant passerende daer ter plaetse als over geheel India. Anno 1678*, Batavia 1907

De Haan 1910–1912
F. De Haan, *Priangan. De Preanger-Regentschappen onder het Nederlandsch Bestuur tot 1811*, 4 vols. Batavia, 1910–1912

De Haas 2014
A. de Haas, 'Plessis, Maria Susanna du (1739-1795)', 13 January 2014, see resources.huygens.knaw.nl/vrouwenlexicon/lemmata/data/Plessis,%20Susanna%20du (accessed 22 July 2020)

Hagen 2018
P. Hagen, *Koloniale oorlogen in Indonesië. Vijf eeuwen verzet tegen vreemde overheersing*, Amsterdam 2018

Halberstadt 1856
A. Halberstadt, *Vrijmaking der slaven in Suriname en de opheffing van het meesterschap, volgens de Staatscommissie*, Amsterdam 1856

Van der Ham 1998
G. van der Ham, *Geschiedenis van Nederland*, Amsterdam 1998

Van der Ham 2013
G. van der Ham, *De geschiedenis van Nederland in 100 voorwerpen*, Amsterdam 2013

Van der Ham 2016
G. van der Ham, *Tarnished Gold. Ghana and the Netherlands from 1593*, Amsterdam/Nijmegen 2016

Van der Ham 2018
G. van der Ham, *Tachtig jaar oorlog. De geboorte van Nederland*, Amsterdam 2018

Heerma van Voss et al. 2018
L. Heerma van Voss et al. (ed.), *Wereldgeschiedenis van Nederland*, Amsterdam 2018

Den Heijer 2011
H. den Heijer, *Geschiedenis van de WIC (1621–1790)*, Zutphen 2011

Herlein 1718
J.D. Herlein, *Beschryvinge van de volk-plantinge Zuriname*, Leeuwarden 1718

Van Heuven-van Nes 2015
R. van Heuven-van Nes, *Nassau en Oranje in gebrandschilderd glas 1503–2005*, Hilversum 2015

Hilkhuijsen 2012–2013
J. Hilkhuijsen, 'In de Bosschen van de colonie van Suriname', *Armamentaria* (2012–2013), pp. 202–205

Van Hogendorp 1780
W. van Hogendorp, *Kraspoekol, of de droevige gevolgen van eene te verre gaande strengheid, jegens de slaaven. Zedekundige vertelling*, Batavia 1780

Van Hogendorp 1799a
D. van Hogendorp, *Brief van Dirk van Hogendorp, aan alle vryheid en vaderland lievende Bataaven in Nederlandsch Oost-Indien*, Bombay 1799

Van Hogendorp 1799b
D. van Hogendorp, *Berigt van den tegenwoordigen toestand der Bataafsche bezittingen in Oost-Indiën en den handel op dezelve*, s.l. 1799

Van Hogendorp 1800
D. van Hogendorp, *Kraspoekol; of de Slaaverny. Een tafereel der zeden van Neerlands Indiën*, Delft 1800

Van Hogendorp 1801a
D. van Hogendorp, *Verzameling van stukken, rakende de zaak van Dirk van Hogendorp, opper-koopman in dienst der Oost-Indische Compagnie, en gezachhebber over Java's Oosthoek*, The Hague 1801

Van Hogendorp 1801b
D. van Hogendorp, *Stukken, raakende den tegenwoordigen toestand der Bataafsche bezittingen in Oost-Indië en den handel op dezelve*, The Hague/Delft 1801

Van Hogendorp 1887
D. van Hogendorp and D.C.A. van Hogendorp, *Mémoires du général Dirk Van Hogendorp, comte de l'empire*, The Hague 1887

Hondius 2010
D. Hondius, '"No Longer Strangers and Foreigners, but Fellow Citizens". The Voice and Dream of Jacobus Eliza Capitein, African Theologist in the Netherlands (1717–47)', *Immigrants & Minorities* 28 (2010) 2-3, pp. 131–153

Hoogbergen 1992
W.S. Hoogbergen, *De Bosnegers zijn gekomen! Slavernij en rebellie in Suriname*, Amsterdam 1992

Hoogbergen 2013
W. Hoogbergen, 'De binnenlandse oorlogen om Suriname in de achttiende eeuw', in V. Enthoven, H. den Heijer and H. Jordaan (eds.), *Geweld in de West. Een militaire geschiedenis van de Nederlandse Atlantische wereld, 1600–1800*, Leiden 2013, pp. 175–198

Hulsman 2015
M. Hulsman, *Verhalen van vrijheid. Autobiografieën van slaven in transnationaal perspectief 1789–2013*, Hilversum 2015

j

James 1938
C.L.R. James, *The Black Jacobins. Toussaint l'Ouverture and the San Domingo Revolution*, London 1938

De Jong 2000
J.J.P. de Jong, *De waaier van het fortuin. Van handelscompagnie tot koloniaal imperium. De Nederlanders in Azië en de Indonesische archipel 1595–1950*, The Hague 2000

De Jonge 1875
J.K.J. de Jonge, *De Opkomst van het Nederlandsch Gezag in Oost-Indië*, vol. 8, The Hague 1875

Jordaan 1999
H. Jordaan, 'De veranderde situatie op de Curaçaose slavenmarkt en de mislukte opstand op de plantage Santa Maria in 1716', in H. Coomans et al. (ed.), *Veranderend Curaçao. Collectie essays opgedragen aan Lionel Capriles ter gelegenheid van zijn 45-jarig jubileum bij de Maduro & Curiel's Bank N.V.*, Bloemendaal 1999, pp. 473–501

Jordaan 2003
H. Jordaan, *Slavernij en vrijheid op Curaçao. De dynamiek van een achttiende-eeuws Atlantisch handelsknooppunt*, Zutphen 2013

Juilet, Lopez and Weeber 2002
E. Juilet, W. Lopez and L. Weeber, CD *Muziek, sleutel tot de geschiedenis van Curaçao (Músika, yabi pa historia di Kòrsou)*, Amsterdam 2002

k

Kars 2016
M. Kars, 'Dodging Rebellion. Politics and Gender in the Berbice Slave Uprising of 1763', *The American Historical Review*, 121 (2016) 1, pp. 36–69

Klooster 1984–1985
H.A.J. Klooster, 'Abdoel Moeis' roman over Surapati', *Jambatan. Tijdschrift voor Indonesische geschiedenis*, 3 (1984–1985) 1, pp. 3–15

Klooster 2016
W. Klooster, *The Dutch Moment. War, Trade, and Settlement in the Seventeenth-Century Atlantic World*, Leiden 2016

Koekkoek 2013
R. Koekkoek, 'Revolutie en de beproeving van radicaal burgerschap', NEMO Kennislink (2013), see nemokennislink.nl/publicaties/revolutie-en-de-beproeving-van-radicaal-burgerschap/ (accessed 28 August 2020)

Kolfin 2008
E. Kolfin, '61. Portret van Willem III', in E. Kolfin and E. Schreuder (eds.) *Black is Beautiful. Rubens tot Dumas*, exhib. cat. Amsterdam (De Nieuwe Kerk)/Zwolle 2008

Kpobi 1993
D.N.A. Kpobi, *Mission in chains. The Life, Theology and Ministry of the Ex-Slave Jacobus E.J. Capitein (1717–1747) with a Translation of his Major Publications*, Zoetermeer 1993

Ter Kuile 1896
O. ter Kuile, *Koper en brons*, The Hague 1986

Kumar 1976
A. Kumar, *Surapati. Man and Legend*, Leiden 1976

l

De Laet 1937
J. de Laet, *Iaerlyck verhael van de Verrichtinghen der Geoctroyeerde West-Indische Compagnie in derthien Boecken. Deel 4* (S.P. L'Honoré Naber and J.C.M. Warnsinck eds.), The Hague 1937 (Werken van de Linschoten-Vereeniging, vol. 30)

Do Lago and Do Lago 2007
B.C. do Lago and P.C. do Lago, *Frans Post 1612–1680. Catalogue Raisonné*, Recife 2007

Langenfeld 2013
E. Langenfeld (comp.), *Plantages, tuinen en 'kanoekjes' met hun eigenaren tussen 1780 en 1885*, see archiefvriend.com/index.php/bronnen/62-kanoekjes2 (updated May 2013)

Von Leithold 1820
T. von Leithold, *Mijn uitstap naar Brazilië, of Reize van Berlijn naar Rio de Janeiro en van daar terug, enz.*, Amsterdam 1821

Van der Linde 1963
J.M. van der Linde, *Ballade van de slavenhaler*, Nijkerk 1963

Loth 1995
V. Loth, 'Pioneers and Perkeniers. The Banda Islands in the 17th Century', *Cakalele* 6 (1995), pp. 13–36

m

Maduro 1986
E. Maduro, 'Nos A Bai Ulanda. Antillianen in Nederland 1634-1954', in G. Oostindie and E. Maduro, *In het land van de overheerser, dl. 2 Antillianen en Surinamers in Nederland 1634/1667–1945*, Dordrecht 1986, pp. 135–244

Marees 1602 (1912)
P. de Marees, *Beschryvinghe ende historische verhael, vant Gout Koninckrijck van Gunea* (S.P. L'Honoré-Naber ed.), Amsterdam 1912 (first edition 1602)

Martinus 2004
E.F. Martinus, *The Kiss of a Slave. Papiamentu's West-African Connections*, Curaçao 2004

Massing 1995
J.M. Massing, 'From Greek Proverb to Soap Advert. Washing the Ethiopian', *Journal of the Warburg and the Courtauld Institutes* 58 (1995), pp. 180–291

Mbeki 2018
L. Mbeki, *Building Life Histories of Cape Town's Enslaved, 1700–1850. An Archival and Isotopic Study*, Amsterdam 2018

McGrath 2012
E. McGrath, 'Caryatids, Page Boys, and African Fetters. Themes of Slavery in European Art', in E. McGrath and J.M. Massing (eds.), *The Slave in European Art. From Renaissance Trophy to Abolitionist Emblem*, London/Turin 2012, pp. 3–38

Van Meerkerk 2010
E. van Meerkerk, 'De ingestudeerde natuurlijkheid van Gijsbert Karel. Sporen van de gebroeders Van Hogendorp', *Biografie bulletin* 20 (2010) 1, pp. 37–43

Van Meerkerk 2013
E. van Meerkerk, *De gebroeders Van Hogendorp. Botsende idealen in de kraamkamer van het Koninkrijk*, Amsterdam 2013

Meister 1692
G. Meister, *Der Orientalisch-Indianische Kunst- und Lust Gärtner*, Dresden 1692

Meuwese 2012
M. Meuwese, *Brothers in Arms, Partners in Trade. Dutch-Indigenous Alliances in the Atlantic World, 1595–1674*, Leiden 2012

Meuwese 2018
M. Meuwese, 'Braziliaanse Indianen in de Republiek', in Heerma van Voss et al. 2018, pp. 231–235

Ter Molen 1994
J.R. ter Molen, 'Een bezichtiging van het poppenhuis van Petronella Brandt-Oortman in de zomer van 1718', *Bulletin van het Rijksmuseum* 42 (1994) 2, pp. 120–136

Ter Molen 2017
J.R. ter Molen, *Een plezierreis in de zomer van 1718. De familie Von Uffenbach in de Nederlanden*, Zwolle 2017

Molineux 2012
C. Molineux, *Faces of Perfect Ebony. Encountering Atlantic slavery in imperial Britain*, Cambridge, MA 2012

Mtubani 1983
V.C.D. Mtubani, 'Afican Slaves and English Law', *Botswana Journal of African Studies* 3 (1983) 2, pp. 71–75

n

Neslo 2016
E. Neslo, *Een ongekende elite. De opkomst van een gekleurde elite in koloniaal Suriname 1800–1863*, De Bilt 2016

Nieuwenhuys 1978
R. Nieuwenhuys, *Oost-Indische spiegel. Wat Nederlandse schrijvers en dichters over Indonesië hebben geschreven vanaf de eerste jaren der Compagnie tot op heden*, Amsterdam 1978

Niemeijer 2005
H. Niemeijer, *Batavia. Een koloniale samenleving in de 17de eeuw*, Amsterdam 2005

Van Nierop 1958
L. van Nierop, 'De Jordaan in 1731 en 1742. Suikerraffinaderijen', *Maandblad Amstelodamum* 45 (1958), pp. 151–160 and 179–181

Northrup 2002
D. Northrup, *Africa's Discovery of Europe 1450–1850*, New York/Oxford 2002

o

Oliver 1838
J. Oliver, *Tafereelen en merkwaardigheden uit Oost-Indië*, vol. 2. Amsterdam 1838, p. 1880

Oostindie 1993
G. Oostindie, 'Slavenleven', in B. Brommer (ed.), *Ik ben eigendom van ... Slavenhandel en plantageleven*, Wijk en Aalburg 1993, pp. 95–113

Oostindie 2011
G. Oostindie, 'Slave Resistance, Colour Lines, and the Impact of the French and Haitian Revolutions in Curaçao', in W. Klooster and G. Oostindie (eds.), *Curaçao in the Age of Revolutions, 1795–1800*, Leiden/Boston, MA 2011, pp. 1–22

Otte 1987
M. Otte, '"Somtijts een Moor". De neger als bijfiguur op Nederlandse portretten in de zeventiende en achttiende eeuw', *Kunstlicht* 8 (1987) 22, pp. 3, 6–10

p

Paasman 2010
B. Paasman, 'Reynier Adriaensen, fantastische getuige van de bloedige Bantamoorlog', *Indische letteren* 25 (2010), pp. 91–100

Paesie 2008
R. Paesie, *Lorrendrayen op Africa. De illegale goederen- en slavenhandel op West-Afrika tijdens het achttiende-eeuwse handelsmonopolie van de West-Indische Compagnie, 1700–1734*, Amsterdam 2008

Parker Brienen 2006
R. Parker Brienen, *Visions of Savage Paradise. Albert Eckhout, Court Painter in Colonial Dutch Brazil*, Amsterdam 2006

Passchier 2005
C. Passchier, 'Het huis Reinier de Klerk, een voormalige buitenplaats in Jakarta', *Bulletin KNOB* 104 (2005) 6, pp. 207–213.

Patterson 1982
O. Patterson, *Slavery and Social Death. A Comparative Study*, Cambridge, MA 1982

Paula 1993
A.F. Paula, *'Vrije' slaven. Een sociaal-historische studie over de dualistische slavenemancipatie op Nederlands Sint Maarten 1816–1863*, Zutphen 1993

Du Perron-De Roos 1943
E. du Perron-De Roos, 'Correspondentie van Dirk van Hogendorp met zijn broeder Gijsbert Karel', *Bijdragen tot de Taal-, Land- en Volkenkunde van Nederlandsch-Indië*, vol. 102, 1/2th instalment (1943), pp. 125–273

Pijzel-Dommisse 2000
J. Pijzel-Dommisse, *Het Hollandse pronkpoppenhuis. Interieur en huishouden in de 17de en 18de eeuw*, Zwolle/Amsterdam 2000

Poelwijk 2003
A.H. Poelwijk, *'In dienste vant suyckerbacken'. De Amsterdamse suikernijverheid en haar ondernemers, 1580–1630*, Hilversum 2003

Ponte 2019
M. Ponte, '"Al de swarten die hier ter stede comen". Een Afro-Atlantische gemeenschap in zeventiende-eeuws Amsterdam', *TSEG/ Low Countries Journal of Social and Economic History* 15 (2019) 4, pp. 33–62

r

Raders 1863
R.F. van Raders, *Onderzoek naar de beweerde vrijverklaring der slaven op het Eiland St. Martin in 1848*, The Hague 1863

Ratelband 2000
K. Ratelband, *Nederlanders in West-Afrika 1600–1650*, Zutphen 2000

Reisig 1793
J.H. Reisig, *De Suikerraffinadeur, of volledige beschrijving van het suiker, deszelfs aankweking, bereiding en verzending, met de opgaave der verschillende bewerking, molens, fabrieken enz. In en buiten Europa*, elfde stuk van de *Volledige beschrijving van alle konsten, ambachten, handwerken, fabrieken, trafieken, derselver werkhuizen, gereedschappen, enz.*, Dordrecht 1793

Ricklefs 1993
M.C. Ricklefs, *War, Culture, and Economy in Java, 1677–1726. Asian and European Imperialism in the Early Kartasura Period*, Sydney 1993 (*Southeast Asia Publications Series*, vol. 24)

Roitman 2016
J.V. Roitman, 'Land of hope and dreams. Slavery and abolition in the Dutch Leeward islands 1825–1865', *Slavery and Abolition 37* (2016) 2, pp. 375–398

Roitman 2020
J.V. Roitman, 'Blog: The Mystery of the Missing Mammary', 25 February 2020, see www.kitlv.nl/the-mystery-of-the-missing-mammary-musings-on-mutilations-as-meaningful-memories/ (accessed 22 July 2020)

De Rooy 2014
P. de Rooy, '"Je gaat het pas zien als je het doorhebt". Ras als ideaaltype in de 19de eeuw', in *Op het eerste gezicht. Het veronderstelde verband tussen uiterlijk en innerlijk*, Haarlem (Teylers Museum)/Tielt 2004, pp. 38–51

Ross 1983
R. Ross, *Cape of Torments. Slavery and Resistance in South Africa*, London 1983

Van Rossum 2015
M. van Rossum, *Kleurrijke tragiek. De geschiedenis van slavernij in Azië onder de VOC*, Hilversum 2015

Van Rossum 2020a
M. van Rossum, *The Dutch East India Company and Slave Trade in the Indian Ocean and Indonesian Archipelago Worlds, 1602–1795*, Oxford Research Encyclopedia, Asian History, online, February 2020, https://doi.org/10.1093/acrefore/9780190277727.013.403 (accessed 12 November 2020)

Van Rossum 2020b
M. van Rossum, 'De VOC, Van Amsterdam naar Azië', in P. Brandon and G. Jones (eds.),

De slavernij in Oost en West. Het Amsterdam-onderzoek, Amsterdam 2020, pp. 52–61

Van Rossum et al. 2020
M. van Rossum et al., *Testimonies of Enslavement. Sources on Slavery from the Indian Ocean World*, London 2020

S

Said 1978
E.W. Said, *Orientalism*, New York 1978

Salverda 2015
R. Salverda, 'Raynal and Holland. Raynal's Histoire des deux Indes and Dutch Colonialism in the Age of Enlightenment', in C.P. Courtney and Jenny Mander (eds.) *Raynal's Histoire des deux Indes. Colonialism, Networks and Global Exchange*, Oxford 2015, pp. 217–235

Schouten 1676
W. Schouten, *Oost-Indische voyagie: vervattende veel voorname voorvallen en ongemeene vreemde geschiedenissen, bloedige zee- en landt-gevechten tegen de Portugeesen en de Makassaren* [etc.], Amsterdam 1676

Schreuder 2008
E. Schreuder, '64. Portretstudie van een zwarte bediende of muzikant', in E. Kolfin and E. Schreuder (eds), *Black is Beautiful. Rubens tot Dumas*, Amsterdam (De Nieuwe Kerk)/Zwolle 2008, pp. 264–265

Schreuder 2017
E. Schreuder, *Cupido en Sideron. Twee Moren aan het hof van Oranje*, Amsterdam 2017

Schulte Nordholt 1996
H. Schulte Nordholt, *The Spell of Power: A History of Balinese Politics, 1650–1940*, Leiden 1996 (Verhandelingen Van Het Koninklijk Instituut Voor Taal-, Land- En Volkenkunde, no. 170) 12, pp. 42–4

Schutte 2001
G.J. Schutte, *Het Calvinistisch Nederland. Mythe en werkelijkheid*, Hilversum 2001

Seelig 2005
L. Seelig, '"Christoph Jamnitzer's "Moor's Head". A Late Renaissance Drinking Vessel', in T.F. Earle and K.J.P. Lowe (eds.), *Black Africans in Renaissance Europe*, Cambridge 2005, pp. 181–209

Sekou 1996
L.M. Sekou, *National Symbols of St. Martin. A Primer*, Philipsburg 1996

Sen 1932
D.C. Sen, *Eastern Bengal Ballads*, vol. 4, Delhi 1932

Van der Sijs 2003
N. van der Sijs et al., *Uit Oost en West. Verklaring van 1000 woorden uit Nederlands-Indië*, Amsterdam 2003

Sikkema 2019
A. Sikkema, 'Rice varieties found of slaves in Surinam', 5 October 2019, see resource. wur.nl/en/show/Rice-varieties-found-of-slaves-in-Surinam.htm (accessed 21 July 2020)

Sint Nicolaas 2018
E. Sint Nicolaas, *Shackles and Bonds. Suriname and the Netherlands since 1600*, Amsterdam/Nijmegen 2018

Sint Nicolaas 2020
E. Sint Nicolaas, 'Acquisition no. 1: Multiple pillory, used to shackle enslaved people', *The Rijksmuseum Bulletin* 68 (2020) 3, pp. 274–275

Slotsboo 1918
J.K. Slotsboo, *The Reports of De Chavonnes and His Council*, Cape Town 1918

Smeulders 2016
V. Smeulders, 'Slavernij, erfgoed herdenken en identiteit in het Koninkrijk', *OSO Tijdschrift voor Surinamistiek en het Caraïbisch gebied* 35 (2016) 1+2, pp. 39–53

Smytegelt 1947
Bernardus Smytegelt, *Des Christens eenige troost in leven en sterven*, Middelburg 1747

Stevens 2015
H. Stevens, *Bitter Spice. Indonesia and the Netherlands from 1600*, Amsterdam/Nijmegen 2015

Van Stipriaan 1993a
A. van Stipriaan, *Surinaams contrast. Roofbouw en overleven in een Caraïbische plantagekolonie 1750–1863*, Leiden 1993

Van Stipriaan 1993b
A. van Stipriaan, 'Stemmen van protest', in B. Brommer (ed.), *Ik ben eigendom van … Slavenhandel en plantageleven*, Wijk en Aalburg 1993, pp. 117–131

Van Stipriaan 2006
A. van Stipriaan, 'Suriname. Somerszorg. De plantages', in M. Prak (ed.), *Plaatsen van herinnering. Nederland in de 17de en 18de eeuw*, Amsterdam 2006, pp. 400–411

Van Stipriaan et al. 2007
A. van Stipriaan et al., *Op Zoek naar de Stilte. Sporen van het slavernijverleden in Nederland*, Leiden 2007

Van Stipriaan 2020
A. van Stipriaan, 'Het Nederlandse slavernij-debat in de zeventiende en achttiende eeuw', in Brandon et al. (ed.), *De Slavernij in Oost en West. Het Amsterdam onderzoek*, Amsterdam 2020, pp. 300–307

Subrahmanyam 1997
S. Subrahmanyam, 'Slaves and Tyrants. Dutch Tribulations in Seventeenth-Century Mrauk-U', *Journal of Early Modern History* 1 (1997), pp. 201–253

Subramanian 1999
L. Subramanian, *Medieval Seafarers*, New Delhi 1999

Van Sypesteyn 1866
J.C.A. van Sypesteyn, *Afschaffing der slavernij in de Nederlandsche West-Indische kolonien uit officiële bronnen zamengesteld*, The Hague 1866

Van Sypesteyn and De Bordes 1850
J.W. van Sypesteyn and J.P. de Bordes, *De verdediging van Nederland in 1672 en 1673. Bijdragen tot de staats- en krijgsgeschiedenis van het vaderland*, The Hague 1850

Sypkens Smit 1995
M.R. Sypkens Smit, *Beyond the Tourist Trap. A study of St. Maarten culture*, Amsterdam 1995

t

Tang 2013
D.J. Tang, *Slavernij. Een geschiedenis*, Zutphen 2013

Thornton 1998
J. Thornton, *Africa and Africans in the Making of the Atlantic World, 1400–1800. Studies in Comparative World History*, Cambridge 1998

Timmer 1988
F.M. Timmer, *Pour la besoin de sa cause. Dirk van Hogendorp 1761–1822*, Amsterdam 1988 (diss. Amsterdam University)

Van den Tol 2018
J. van den Tol, 'De Portugese slavenlobby in Nederlands-Brazilië' in Heerma van Voss et al. 2018, pp. 248–252

Van den Tol and Van Groesen 2015
J. van den Tol and M. van Groesen (eds.), *The Legacy of Dutch Brazil. De Zeventiende Eeuw. Cultuur in de Nederlanden in interdisciplinair perspectief*, Cambridge 2015

Trouillot 2015
M-R. Trouillot, *Silencing The Past. Power and Production of History*, Boston, MA 2015

Turksma 2005
L. Turksma, *Wisselend lot in een woelige tijd. Van Hogendorp, Krayenhoff, Chassé en Janssens, generaals in Bataafs-Franse dienst*, Westervoort 2005

u

Upham 2012
M. Upham, 'Consecrations to God: The "nasty, brutish, and short" life of SUSANNA from BENGAL otherwise known as "ONE EAR" – 2nd recorded female convict at the VOC-occupied Cape of Good Hope', *Uprooted Lives: Unfurling the Cape of Good Hope's Earliest Colonial Inhabitants (1652–1713)* 8, 2012, pp. 7–10, see e-family.co.za/ffy/ui66.htm (accessed 28 August 2020)

v

Valentijn 1724–1726
F. Valentijn, *Oud en nieuw Oost-Indiën, vervattende een naaukeurige en uitvoerige verhandelinge van Nederlands mogentheyd in die gewesten*, 5 vols., Dordrecht/Amsterdam 1724–1726

Van 't Veer 1955
P. van 't Veer, 'Kraspoekol of het aakelig lot der slaaven', *Indonesië* (1955) 1, pp. 59–63

Van 't Veer 1958
P. van 't Veer, *Geen blad voor de mond. Vijf radicalen uit de negentiende eeuw*, Amsterdam 1958

Van de Venne 1937
J.M. van de Venne, *Geslachts-register van het vorstenhuis Nassau (Walramsche en Ottosche lijnen)*, Maastricht 1937

Veldhuijzen 2003
S.E. Veldhuijzen, 'Aantekeningen over "gekleurde inwoners" in Den Haag, vanaf ca. 1621. "De moren van Patras - vroege allochtonen in Den Haag"', The Hague: City Archives. OV 18 Aantekeningen Haagse Geschiedenis diverse personen – 037

Veltman et al. 2019
M.A. Veltman et al., 'Origins and Geographic Diversification of African Rice (Oryza glaberrima)', *PLoS ONE* 14 (2019) 3, pp. 1–28. For abstract, see pubmed.ncbi.nlm.nih.gov/30840637/ (accessed 28 August 2020)

Visser 2001
W. de Visser, *Piet Hein en de Zilvervloot. Oorlog en Handel in de West*, Hilversum 2001

Voges 2006
M.S. Voges, *Cul-de-Sac People. A St. Martin Family Series*, Philipsburg 2006

Voskuil-Groenewegen et al. 1999
S.M. Voskuil-Groenewegen et al., *Zilver uit de tijd van de Verenigde Oostindische Compagnie*, Zwolle 1999, pp. 45–46

W

Van de Wall 1934
V.I. van de Wall, 'Bijdrage tot de geschiedenis der Perkeniers, 1621–1671', *Tijdschrift voor Indische Taal-, Land- en Volkenkunde* 74 (1934), pp. 516–580

Van de Wall 1943
V.I. van de Wall, *Oude Hollandsche Buitenplaatsen van Batavia, deel 1*, Deventer 1943

Waterfield 2003
G. Waterfield, 'Black Servants', in G. Waterfield et al., *Below Stairs. 400 Years of Servants' Portraits*, London (National Portrait Gallery) 2003, pp. 139–151

Wiesebron 2003
M.L. Wiesebron (ed.), *Brazilië in de Nederlandse Archieven*, Leiden 2003

Winberg 1992
C. Winberg, 'Satire, Slavery and the Ghoemaliedjies of the Cape Muslims', *New Contrast* 19 (1991) 4, pp. 78–96

Van Winter 1774
N.S. van Winter, *Monzongo, of de Koninklijke Slaaf. Treurspel*, Amsterdam 1774

Worden 2002
N. Worden, 'Ethnic diversity at the VOC Cape', in T.M. Eliëns (ed.), *Domestic Interiors at the Cape and in Batavia, 1602–1795*, The Hague (Gemeentemuseum)/ Zwolle 2002, pp. 129–139

Worden and Groenewald 2005
N. Worden and G. Groenewald (eds.), *Trails of slavery. Selected Documents Concerning Slaves from the Criminal Records of the Council of Justice at the Cape of Good Hope, 1705–1794*, Cape Town 2005

Z

Zandvliet et al. 2006
K. Zandvliet et al., *De 250 rijksten van de Gouden Eeuw*, Amsterdam 2006

Zijlstra 2012
H. Zijlstra, 'Het mysterie van de maaltijd te Dokkum verder ontrafeld', *De Sneuper. Officieel orgaan van de Historische Vereniging Noordoost-Friesland* 25 (2012) 112

index

of relevant people and places

a

b

c

l

m

n

o

p

r

Z

works in the exhibition

supplemented by supporting illustrations in this book

supporting illustrations
'slavery. an exhibition of many voices'

Jean Saint (attributed to), *Box Depicting the Trade in Ivory, Gold and People Carried out by the Dutch West India Company (WIC) in Africa, Presented to Stadtholder Willem IV*, 1749
see p. 10 and 'gallery 2'

Group photograph of participants in Jennifer Tosch's Black Heritage Amsterdam Tour in front of the militia company portrait by Bartholomeus van der Helst from c. 1640–1643
see p. 12

Georg Sturm, *Self-Sacrifice*, 1885
Painting in the Great Hall of the Rijksmuseum
Amsterdam, Rijksmuseum
see p. 16

Visualization of one of the *Slavery* exhibition galleries by Afaina de Jong
see p. 18

Portrait of Tirzo Martha and David Bade
Photo: Kiem Loon Elvis John Chen
see p. 18

supporting illustrations
'dutch colonial slavery'

Samuel Daniell, *Boer House in South Africa with Slave Bell on the Right*, 1804
Hand-coloured aquatint, 56 × 40 cm
London, British Library, inv. no. 458.h.14, part 1, p. 16
see p. 25

Anonymous, Bell on the Wederzorg plantation in Commewijne, Suriname, 18th century
see p. 27 and 'atrium'

Anonymous, *Dutch Merchant and His Wife with Enslaved Men in Hill Landscape*, 1700–1725
Oil on canvas, 48 × 57.2 cm
Amsterdam, Rijksmuseum, inv. no. SK-A-4988
see p. 29

Anonymous, *Slave Market, Possibly in the Environs of Batavia*, 1700–1725
Oil on canvas, 57.5 × 78 cm
Christie's
see p. 29

Gesina ter Borch, *Two African Boys*, 11 September 1654
Page 35 from a family album she compiled, 1654
Watercolour and ink on paper, 24.3 × 36 cm
Amsterdam, Rijksmuseum, inv. no. BI-1887-1463-35; purchased with the support of the Rembrandt Association
see p. 37

Hendrik van Schuylenburgh, *The Trading Post of the Dutch East India Company in Hooghly, Bengal*, 1665 (detail)
see p. 37 and 'van bengalen'

Pieter de Wit, *Director-General of the Gold Coast Dirk Wilre in the Fort of Elmina*, 1669
Oil on canvas, 103.2 × 141.4 cm
Hong Kong, The Mari-Cha Collection Limited, inv. no. MCCL#887
see p. 39

Jan Wils, Journal and daily log of the slave ship *d'Coninck Salomon*, 1686
see p. 41 and 'gallery 3'

Romuald Hazoumè, *La Bouche du Roi*, 1997–2005 (details)
London, British Museum, inv. no. AF2006,20.1-405; purchased from the October Gallery in 2006 with the support of the Art Fund and the British Museum Friends
Photos: © Romuald Hazoumè
see p. 45 and 'gallery 3'

Archives of Jan Serrurier, 'transport deeds' of enslaved people, 1763–1766
see p. 47 and 'gallery 4'

Branding iron with the letters 'GWC', date of manufacture unknown
see p. 49 and 'gallery 4'

Anonymous, *View of the Leeverpoel Plantation in Suriname, 'Plantagie Leeverpoel Geleegen Rievier Cottica linksop vaarende'* (title on object), 1772–1792
Pen in grey, brush in colours in watercolour, pencil, 42.8 × 64.3 cm
Amsterdam, Rijksmuseum, inv. no. RP-T-1959-119; purchased with the support of the F.G. Waller-Fonds
see p. 51

Andries Beeckman, *The Castle of Batavia*, c. 1661 (detail)
see p. 53 and 'van bengalen'

atrium

Johannes Borchhardt, Bell of the Reinier de Klerk estate, Batavia, 1772
Bronze, wrought iron, h. 60 cm, diam. 48 cm
Amsterdam, Stichting Werkspoormuseum, inv. no. d00008
Photo: Rijksmuseum, Albertine Dijkema
see p. 20

Anonymous, Bell of the Santa Catharina estate on Curaçao, before 1750
Cast iron, red paint, 45.5 × 54 × 44 cm
Leiden, Stichting Nationaal Museum van Wereldculturen, coll. no. TM-5872-1a
see p. 20

Anonymous, Bell of the Wederzorg plantation in Commewijne, Suriname, 18th century
Bronze, h. 45 cm, diam. 45 cm
Commewijne, L. Tjin-A-Djie jr Family, Wederzorg Plantation
Photo: William Tsang
see p. 20

Anonymous, Bell of the De Catharina plantation in Demerara, in present-day Guyana, 1772
Bronze, h. 61 cm, diam. 63 cm
Cambridge, St Catharine's College
see p. 20

Anonymous, Bell of the Oranjezicht farm near Cape Town, c. 1775
Bronze, h. 55 cm, diam. 55 cm
Cape Town, Iziko Museums of South Africa, inv. no. SACHM 1309
see p. 20

gallery 2

Jean Saint (attributed to), *Box Depicting the Trade in Ivory, Gold and People Carried out by the Dutch West India Company (WIC) in Africa, Presented to Stadtholder Willem IV*, 1749
Gold, tortoiseshell, velvet (interior), 5.8 × 18 × 11.9 cm
Amsterdam, Rijksmuseum, inv. no. NG-NM-824
see p. 10

gallery 3

Jan Wils, Journal and daily log of the slave ship *d'Coninck Salomon*, 1686
Manuscript, 36 × 24 × 12 cm (closed)
The Hague, National Archives of the Netherlands, 1.05.03, inv. no. 215
see p. 41

Romuald Hazoumè, *La Bouche du Roi*, 1997–2005
Multimedia installation with plastic and glass objects, cowrie shells, beads, tobacco, spices, amongst others, variable dimensions, c. 1150 × 285 cm
London, British Museum, inv. no. AF2006,20.1-405; purchased from the October Gallery in 2006 with the support of the Art Fund and the British Museum Friends
Photos: © Romuald Hazoumè and photo: Georges Hixson (pp. 60–61)
see pp. 58–61

gallery 4

Archives of Jan Serrurier, 'transport deeds' of enslaved people, 1763–1766
Manuscript, 23 × 42 cm
Cape Town, Western Cape Archives, Miscellaneous 49
see p. 47

Branding iron with the letters 'GWC', date of manufacture unknown
Iron, l. 23 cm; branding iron: 3.7 × 2.2 cm
Amsterdam, De Nederlandsche Bank Nationale Numismatische Collectie
see p. 49

joão

Anonymous, Foot stocks designed for the constraint of multiple enslaved people, with 6 separate shackles, c. 1600–1800
Foot stock: wood, 265 × 37.5 × 23 cm; chain: iron, l. 300 cm
Amsterdam, Rijksmuseum, inv. nos. NG-2019-502 and -503; gift from Mr J.W. de Keijzer, Gouda
see pp. 72–73

Hans Propheet, *View of the Fort and Harbour of Elmina*, 1629
Pen on paper, 44 × 63 cm
The Hague, National Archives of the Netherlands, Verzameling Buitenlandse Kaarten Leupe, 4.VEL, inv. no. Vel0771
see p. 76

Hans Propheet (attributed to), *Map of the Gold Coast, 'Caert vande Gout cust in Guines waer in verthoont werden de afdeelinge van haer paercken, alsoo die vande prinsipalste swarten hobbe onder vracht, en ayn met stipeilen van een gescheyden en by onse volck op deese mannier bevonden en bekent'* (title on object), c. 1629
Pen and brush on paper, 47.5 × 69.5 cm
Paris, Bibliothèque nationale de France, GE DD-2987 (8198 B)
see p. 78

Frans Post, *Sugar Mill, Driven by Oxen, 'Anotatie der figuure ende wercke in den ingenio ofte suijckermoole hoe de selve met osse werd gedreeven'* (title on object), 1640
Pen and brush on paper, 22.5 × 31 cm
Rotterdam, Atlas van Stolk, inv. no. 46440
see p. 70

Anonymous, Basin. Gift of Garcia II to Johan Maurits, Potosí, 1586
Gilt silver, diam. 53.5 cm
Siegen, Evangelische Nikolai-Kirchengemeinde, inv. no. HStAD, R 4, 5461 UF
see p. 82

Letter from Garcia II, King of Congo, to Johan Maurits, stadtholder in Brazil, 1586
Manuscript, 30.5 × 20.5 × 9 cm
Wiesbaden, Hessian State Archives, HHStAW Bestand 3036, No. HHStAW, Abt. 171, No. Z 4305

Letter from Pieter Mortamer, Director at Luanda, to Johan Maurits, 31 October 1642
Manuscript, 36 × 53 cm (open)
The Hague, The Royal Collections of the Netherlands, inv. no. A04b-1454, folio 203–204

Anonymous, *Vrijburg Palace, Mauritsstad, Brazil*, c. 1642–1652
Parchment, mounted on silk and backed with paper, 19 × 62.5 cm
Amsterdam, Rijksmuseum, inv. no. NG-1053

Transcript of the interrogation of João Mina, from the letters and papers repatriated from Brazil in the archives of the Dutch West India Company, conducted 4 October 1646
Manuscript, 33.5 × 46 cm
The Hague, National Archives of the Netherlands, 1.05.01.01, inv. no. 62, folio 61
see p. 68

Georg Marcgraf, *Map of Dutch Brazil*, 1664
Burin and watercolour on paper, 117 × 157.5 cm
Rotterdam, Maritime Museum Rotterdam, inv. no. WAE598
see p. 74

Pieter Nason, *Portrait of Johan-Maurits van Nassau-Siegen 1604–1679 with a Young Black Man Holding a Map*, c. 1666–1675
Oil on canvas, 134.5 × 107 cm
Brussels, Royal Museums of Fine Arts of Belgium, inv. no. 142

Pieter de Wit, *Director General of the Gold Coast Dirk Wilre in the Fort of Elmina*, 1669
Oil on canvas, 103.2 × 141.4 cm
Hong Kong, The Mari-Cha Collection Limited, inv. no. MCCL#887
see p. 39

Congolese *mpu* cap, before 1674
Natural fibre, 20 × 15 cm, diam. 18 cm
Copenhagen, The National Museum of Denmark, inv. no. Dc.123
Photo: Arnold Mikkelsen, The National Museum of Denmark/CC-BY-SA
see p. 80

Olfert Dapper, *Naukeurige beschrijvinge der Afrikaensche gewesten van Egypten, Barbaryen, Lybien, Biledulgerid, Negroslant, Guinea, Ethiopiën, Abyssinie, vertoont in de benamingen ... met lantkaerten en afbeeldingen van steden, drachten, &c. na 't leven getekent, en in kooper gesneden; getrokken uyt verscheyde hedendaegse lantbeschrijvers en geschriften van bereisde ondersoekers dier landen door O. Dapper* (Descriptions of Africa), 1676
Book, 33 × 49.5 cm (open)
Amsterdam, Rijksmuseum Research Library, 327 I 29
see p. 80

supporting illustrations

Zacharias Wagener, *The Slave Market in Recife*, in Z. Wagener, *Thierbuch*, c. 1637–1641
Watercolour, 21.2 × 33.5 cm
Dresden, Staatliche Kunstsammlungen, MS. C 2269, folio 106r
Photo: bpk|Staatliche Kunstsammlungen Dresden|Herbert Boswank
see pp. 66–67

Jean-Baptiste Debret (draughtsman) and Thierry Frères (engraver), *Enslaved People in Brazil, Constrained in Foot Stocks, 'Negres ao Tronco'* (title on object), c. 1830, in J.B. Debret, *Voyage pittoresque et historique au Brésil*, plate 45, Paris 1834–1839
São Paulo, Instituto Itaú Cultural
see p. 70

wally

Anonymous, *Portrait of the Painter Dirk Valkenburg*, c. 1685–1721
Pencil, brush in brown and grey on paper, 19.9 × 16.3 cm
Amsterdam, Rijksmuseum, inv. no. RP-T-1940-322

Dirk Valkenburg, *The Waterland Plantation in Suriname*, c. 1698–1718
Oil on canvas, 31.5 × 47.5 cm
Amsterdam, Amsterdam Museum, inv. no. SA-35413
see pp. 98–99

Dirk Valkenburg, *Plantation in Suriname*, 1707
Oil on canvas, 52.5 × 45.5 cm
Amsterdam, Rijksmuseum, inv. no. SK-A-4075

Dirk Valkenburg, *Gathering of Enslaved People on One of Jonas Witsen's Sugar Plantations*, 1708
Oil on canvas, 58 × 46.5 cm
Copenhagen, SMK, The National Gallery of Denmark, inv. no. KMS 376
see p. 100

Dirk Valkenburg, *View of the Mill and the Boiling House of the Waterland Plantation*, 1708
Pen and brush, 19.6 × 34.1 cm
Amsterdam, Rijksmuseum, inv. no. RP-T-1905-103; purchased with the support of the Rembrandt Association
see p. 95

Dirk Valkenburg, *View of the Surimombo Plantation in Suriname*, 1708
Pencil, pen and brush in grey, 18 × 25.5 cm
Amsterdam, Rijksmuseum, inv. no. RP-T-1905-104; purchased with the support of the Rembrandt Association

Dirk Valkenburg, *View of Three Houses on the Surimombo Plantation in Suriname*, 1708
Pen and brush in grey, black chalk, 18.2 × 36 cm
Amsterdam, Rijksmuseum, inv. no. RP-T-1905-105; purchased with the support of the Rembrandt Association

Dirk Valkenburg, *Sluice on the Palmeneribo Plantation in Suriname*, 1708
Pen and brush in grey, black chalk, 23.9 × 35.8 cm
Amsterdam, Rijksmuseum, inv. no. RP-T-1905-106; purchased with the support of the Rembrandt Association

Dirk Valkenburg, *View of the Residence on the Palmeneribo Plantation in Suriname*, 1708
Pen and brush in grey, black chalk, 20.7 × 36.9 cm
Amsterdam, Rijksmuseum, inv. no. RP-T-1905-107; purchased with the support of the Rembrandt Association
see p. 103

Dirk Valkenburg, *Residence and a Barn on the Surimombo Plantation in Suriname*, 1708
Pen and brush in grey, black chalk, 17.6 × 34.8 cm
Amsterdam, Rijksmuseum, inv. no. RP-T-1905-108; purchased with the support of the Rembrandt Association

Contract between Jonas Witsen and Dirk Valkenburg drawn up by notary H. Outgers, 24/27 February 1706
Manuscript, 34 × 56 × 17 cm
Amsterdam City Archives, Archief van de Notarissen ter Standplaats Amsterdam 5075, nr. 133/1147, inv. no. 3369

Transcript of the interrogation of Wally from the archives of the Society of Suriname, 1707
Manuscript, 35 × 34 × 9 cm (closed)
The Hague, National Archives of the Netherlands, Sociëteit van Suriname, 1.05.03, inv. no. 234
see p. 87

J.D. Herlein, *Beschryvinge van de volk-plantinge Zuriname* (Description of the Suriname Colony), 1718
Book, 23 × 54 cm (open)
Amsterdam, Rijksmuseum Research Library, 318 C 19

Anonymous, Ceremonial glass bearing the inscription *''t Welvaren van Siparipabo'* (The Prosperity of Siparipabo), c. 1725–1750
Lead glass, h. 17.8 cm
Amsterdam, Rijksmuseum, inv. no. NG-2010-133; purchased with the support of the Johan Huizinga Fonds/Rijksmuseum Fonds
see p. 92

Jacob Houbraken, *Portrait of Jonas Witsen*
c. 1749–1780
Engraving, 17.7 × 11.7 cm
Amsterdam, Rijksmuseum,
inv. no. RP-P-OB-48.396

Kappa, 19th century
Cast-iron, h. 51 cm, diam. 137 cm
Amsterdam, Rijksmuseum, inv. no. NG-2020-5
Photo: William Tsang
see p. 95

Sugar cane machetes, c. 1800–1850
Iron, wood, l. resp. 62, 63, 63, 67, 67 and 63 × 5 cm
Oudeschild, Museum Kaap Skil,
inv. nos. V12-M26 t/m M30
see p. 91

Anonymous, *Enslaved Men Digging Trenches*, c. 1850
Watercolour, 32.5 × 25.4 cm
Amsterdam, Rijksmuseum, inv. no. NG-2013-22-19; purchased with the support of the Johan Huizinga Fonds/Rijksmuseum Fonds
see p. 93

Brush used in invocations, before 1893
Wood, cowrie shell, hair, pigment, 22 × 23 × 3.5 cm
Leiden, Stichting Nationaal Museum van Wereldculturen, coll. no. RV-926-1

Musical instrument made out of a calabash, used in Winti rituals, before 1938
Wood and cotton, 32 × 11.5 cm
Leiden, Stichting Nationaal Museum van Wereldculturen, coll. no. RV-2363-96
see p. 101

oopjen

Rembrandt van Rijn, *Portrait of Oopjen Coppit*, 1634
Oil on canvas, 207.5 × 132 cm
Paris, Musée du Louvre, inv. no. RF 2016-2; joint acquisition by the Dutch State and the French Republic, collection Rijksmuseum/ collection Musée du Louvre
see p. 109

Rembrandt van Rijn, *Portrait of Marten Soolmans*, 1634
Oil on canvas, 207.5 × 132 cm
Amsterdam, Rijksmuseum, inv. no. SK-A-5033; joint acquisition by the Dutch State and the French Republic, collection Rijksmuseum/ collection Musée du Louvre
see p. 108

Earthenware sugar funnel and collecting jars, archaeological finds, c. 1575–1700
Earthenware, h. 45.5 cm, diam. 33.5 cm; h. 20 cm, diam. 13.5 cm; h. 23.4 cm, diam. 15 cm; h. 25 cm, diam. 15.5 cm; h. 41 cm, diam. 21.2 cm
Amsterdam, Collectie Monumenten en Archeologie, TU15-1,SST-20-3, 6, 8 and 10
see p. 112

Minutes of the church council in Paraíba, begun 1 October 1635
Manuscript, 22 × 29.5 × 0.5 cm (open)
The Hague, National Archives of the Netherlands, Verspreide West-Indische Stukken, 1.05.06, inv. no. 1408
see p. 120

supporting illustrations

Romeyn de Hooghe, *Brazilian Sugar Workers*, before 1682
Etching, 21.2 × 29.9 cm
Amsterdam, Rijksmuseum, inv. no. BI-1972-1043-43
see p. 112

Interior of a Sugar Refinery with Boiling Kettles and Tools for Reduction Process, in Jan Hendrik Reisig, *De suikerraffinadeur*, plate VII, 1793
see p. 116

Interior of a Sugar Refinery with Jars and Tools for Tilling Them, in Jan Hendrik Reisig, *De suikerraffinadeur*, plate V, 1793
see p. 117

paulus

Anonymous, *Portrait of Maurits, Count of Nassau La Lecq*, c. 1670
Oil on canvas, 273 × 260 cm
Amersfoort, Cultural Heritage Agency, inv. no. C250
Photo: Margareta Svensson
see p. 142

Baptism and marriage record maintained by Georg van der Schueren, 14 December 1674
Manuscript, 20.5 × 33 cm (open)
The Hague, City Archives, 0377-01, inv. no. 340, p. 9
see p. 127

Marriage banns, 's-Gravenhage, 11 June 1684
Manuscript, 41.2 × 35.4 cm (open)
The Hague, City Archives, 0351-01, inv. no. 752, p. 91

Anonymous, Collar with the Nassau crest, 1689
Brass, h. 2.8 cm, diam. 12 cm
Amsterdam, Rijksmuseum, inv. no. BK-NM-5144; gift of Preuyt, Terheyden
see p. 125

Baptismal record, chapel in the Assendelftstraat, 24 April 1690
Manuscript, 16 × 20.3 cm (open)
The Hague, City Archives, 0377-01, inv. no. 355, p. 87
see p. 145

John Nost the Elder, *Bust of an African Man,* 1701
Marble, h. 100 cm
London, The Royal Collection/HM Queen Elizabeth II, inv. no. RCIN 1396
Photo: Royal Collection Trust / © Her Majesty Queen Elizabeth II, 2020
see p. 141

Jacob Appel (I), *Petronella Oortman's Doll's House (1655/56–1716),* c. 1710
Oil on parchment on canvas, 87 × 69 cm
Amsterdam, Rijksmuseum, inv. no. SK-A-4245; transfer from Nederlandsch Museum voor Geschiedenis en Kunst
see p. 131

Anonymous, Spittoon, painted with scenes from the tobacco harvest, c. 1715–1725
Faience, 8.9 × 12.4 cm
Amsterdam, Rijksmuseum, inv. no. BK-NM-12400-403; gift of the heirs of J.F. Loudon, The Hague
see p. 133

Cornelis Troost, *Inspection of a Cavalry Regiment, Possibly by Willem van Hessen-Homburg,* 1742
Oil on canvas, 47.5 × 66 cm
Amsterdam, Rijksmuseum, inv. no. SK-A-4023; purchase 1960
see pp. 136–137

supporting illustrations

Romeyn de Hooghe, *Portrait of Willem III with a Black Servant at his Side,* 1668–1688
Etching and engraving, 55.5 × 44 cm
Amsterdam, Rijksmuseum, inv. no. RP-P-2007-742; gift of H. van Leeuwen, Amerongen
see p. 139

Romeyn de Hooghe, *Life and Deeds of Willem III, 'Orangien wonderspiegel vertoonende Willem Hendrick de III prince van Orangie'* (title on object), 1675
Etching, 46.4 × 56 cm
Amsterdam, Rijksmuseum, inv. no. RP-P-1885-A-9007; purchase 1885
see p. 139

Anonymous, Petronella Oortman's Doll's House, c. 1686–1710
Oak cabinet, lined with tortoiseshell and tin, 255 × 190 × 78 cm
Amsterdam, Rijksmuseum, inv. no. BK-NM-1010; transfer 1875
see p. 130

van bengalen

Wouter Schouten, *Study with Construction Labourers,* c. 1660
Pen and brown ink, c. 27 × 21 cm
Amsterdam, Rijksmuseum, inv. no. RP-T-1964-364-8(V); gift of the heirs of N.P. van den Berg
see p. 158

Andries Beeckman, *The Castle of Batavia,* c. 1661
Oil on canvas, 108 × 151.5 cm
Amsterdam, Rijksmuseum, inv. no. SK-A-19
see p. 160

Johannes Vinckboons (attributed to), *Two Views of Dutch East India Company Trading Posts: Lawec in Cambodia and Banda in the Southern Moluccas, 'Gezicht op Banda, zuidelijke Molukken Neyra'* (title on object), c. 1662–1663
Oil on canvas, 97 × 140 cm
Amsterdam, Rijksmuseum, inv. no. SK-A-4476
see p. 164

Hendrik van Schuylenburgh, *The Trading Post of the Dutch East India Company (VOC) in Hooghly, Bengal,* 1665
Oil on canvas, 203 × 316 cm
Amsterdam, Rijksmuseum, inv. no. SK-A-4282
see pp. 154–155

Sentence of Susanna van Bengalen, 11 December 1669
Manuscript, 58 × 38.5 × 10 cm
Cape Town, Western Cape Archives, Cj 1, criminal and civil cases, 1652–1673, p. 51A
see p. 168

Anonymous, *Enslaved Bengalis Sold to the Dutch*, 1676
Print, 19.4 × 15.4 cm
Amsterdam, Rijksmuseum,
inv. no. RP-P-OB-47.475, in Wouter Schouten, *Wouter Schoutens Oost-Indische voyagie ...*, 2 pts., Amsterdam 1676, pt. 2, pp. 10–11
see p. 152

Baptismal record of Magdhalena de Baron, the daughter of Baron van Bengalen and Rosetta van Sambauwa, January 1690
Manuscript, 20.5 × 33 × 9 cm
Alkmaar, Regional Archives, Doopregister Grote Kerk Alkmaar, January 1690, archive no. 10.3.001, inv. no. 09
see p. 172

Anonymous, *Map of the Ganges River taken from a Moorish Map*, c. 1695
Pen on paper, 52.5 × 74.5 cm
The Hague, National Archives of the Netherlands, 4.VEL, inv. no. 259
see p. 148

Isaac de Graaff, *Map of Bengal, from P. Palmeris to Martavan (Pegu)*, c. 1695
Pen on paper, 52.5 × 74.5 cm
The Hague, National Archives of the Netherlands, 4.VEL, inv. no. 257
see p. 150

Gerard Wigmana, *Dinner with Julius Schelto van Aitzema, Sara van den Broek, Guests and Servants*, 1697
Oil on canvas, 117 × 180 cm
Dokkum, Gemeente Noardeast-Fryslân, inv. no. 475/41
Photo: Hans Knijff
see p. 174

Francina van Bengalen's certificate of freedom, 6 July 1746
Manuscript, 33 × 41 cm
Jakarta, Arsip Nasional Republik Indonesia (ANRI), familiepapieren van Bloys van Treslong Prins, no. N31
see p. 160

Will and possessions of Angela van Bengalen, 1720
Manuscript, 43 × 55 × 9 cm (open)
Cape Town, Western Cape Archives, MOOC 13/1/2, inv. no. 1722–1727, no. 1

Mention of Abraham van Bengalen in the inventory of the Overveen farm of Hendrick Willem van der Merwe and Aletta Keijser, 6 October 1750
Manuscript, 34 × 24 × 13 cm
Cape Town, Western Cape Archives, MOOC 8/7.11

Hendrik Rennebaum, *Sirih* box, 1775–1780
Silver and velvet (interior), 5 × 15.4 × 11.1 cm
The Hague, Kunstmuseum Den Haag, inv. no. 0154568
see p. 162

Robert Jacob Gordon (attributed to), *Panorama of Cape Town and its Surroundings as seen from the Sea*, 1778
Pen in ink over a drawing in pencil, brush in watercolour, 41.5 × 770 cm
Amsterdam, Rijksmuseum, inv. no. RP-T-1914-17-21
see pp. 166–167

Anonymous, *The Enslaved Augustus van Bengalen Holding the Pipe of Hendrik Cloete*, c. 1788
Graphite, 21 × 33 cm
Sint Maarten (NH), Swellengrebel-Boekee Archive
see p. 170

Tool for harvesting nutmeg, consisting of a bamboo stick with two sharp wooden hooks, above a basket in which to catch the picked nuts, before 1897
Bamboo and wood, 114 × 9 × 10 cm
Leiden, Stichting Nationaal Museum voor Wereldculturen, coll. no. RV-1130-102b
see p. 164

surapati

Jacob Coeman, *Pieter Cnoll, Cornelia van Nijenrode, their Daughters and Two Enslaved Servants*, 1665
Oil on canvas, 132 × 190.5 cm
Amsterdam, Rijksmuseum, inv. no. SK-A-4062; purchase 1961
see pp. 178–179

Georg Meister, *Die orientalisch-indianische Kunst und Lustgärtner; das ist, eine aufrichtige Beschreibung der meisten indianischen, als auf Java Major, Malacca und Jappon, wachsenden Gewürtz- Frucht- und Blumen-Bäumen ... wie auch noch andere denckwürdige Anmerckungen,*

was bey des Autoris zweymahliger Reise ... gesehen und fleissig observiret worden (book with description of the life of Surapati), 1692
Book, 21.5 × 30.5 cm (closed)
Leiden, Leiden University Libraries, 465 B 1

François Valentijn, *Oud en nieuw Oost-Indiën, vervattende een naauwkeurige en uitvoerige verhandelinge van Nederlands mogentheyd in die gewesten* (book with description of the life of Surapati), pt. 4, 1726
Book, 35 × 22.5 × 4.8 cm
Amsterdam, Rijksmuseum Research Library, 302 D 5

Anonymous, Balambangan babad, 1730–1740
Manuscript on dried palm leaf, 30 × 50 cm (rolled out); 30 × 3.5 cm (rolled up)
Leiden, Leiden University Libraries, no. Or 3704; Van der Tuuk Bequest

Gerard van Keulen (publisher), Adriaan Reland (surveyor/cartographer), Jacob Keyser (engraver/etcher), *Pasuran, the Region over which Surapati Ruled, 'Insulae Iavae Pars Occidentalis Edente Hadriano Relando'* (title on object), 1734
Coloured copper print, 52 × 118 cm
The Hague, National Archives of the Netherlands, 4.VELH, inv. no. 213A
see pp. 184–185

Anonymous, West Javanese *Surapati babad,* c. 1750
Manuscript on dried palm leaf, 35 × 50 cm (rolled out); 35 × 3.5 cm (rolled up)
Leiden, Leiden University Libraries, no. Acad. 240
see p. 181

Anonymous, *The Attack on Captain Tack at Kartasura by Surapati in 1684 under Susuhunan Amangkurat*, 1900–1950
Paint on glass, 37 × 45 × 2 cm
Leiden, Stichting Nationaal Museum van Wereldculturen, coll. no. 7082-S-465-133
see p. 189

Anonymous, Mask representing Surapati, before 2003
Wood, 21.5 × 16.8 × 11 cm
Leiden, Stichting Nationaal Museum van Wereldculturen, coll. no. TM-6148-4-1
see p. 193

Anonymous, Mask representing François Tack, before 2003
Wood, 20.6 × 16.5 × 16 cm
Leiden, Stichting Nationaal Museum van Wereldculturen, coll. no. TM-6148-4-2
see p. 193

supporting illustrations

Melati van Java, *Van slaaf tot vorst. Historisch-romantische schets uit de geschiedenis van Java* (From slave to ruler. Historical romantic sketch from the history of Java), 1907 edition
Book, h. 23 cm
Amsterdam, Rijksmuseum Research Library, no. 803 E 79
see p. 191

Anonymous, *The Murder of Captain Tack in Kartasura*, 1890–1900
Paint and ink on linen, 67 × 123 cm
Leiden, Stichting Nationaal Museum van Wereldculturen, coll. no. TM-H-796
see p. 189

Abdoel Moeis, *Surapati*, 1965 edition
Book, h. 19 cm
Leiden, Leiden University Libraries, no. 824 B 32
see p. 191

sapali

Stalk of a rice variety named after Ma Sapa or Sapali
On loan from Mrs T. van Andel, Amsterdam
Photo: Marlies Lageweg
see p. 200

Paul Hermann and Hendrik Meyer, *Hermann Herbarium*, c. 1687
Book containing 50 dried specimens from Suriname, 56 × 65 × 5 cm (open)
Leiden, Naturalis Biodiversity Center, inv. no. L.2077646
see p. 214

Alexander de Lavaux, *Map of Suriname, 'Generale Caart van de Provintie Suriname Rivieren & Districten met alle d Ondekkingen van van Militaire Togten mitsgaders de groote der gemeetene Plantagien gecarteert op de naauwkeurigste waarneemingen'* (title on object), 1737
Silk, 186.5 × 215.5 cm
Amsterdam, Rijksmuseum, inv. no. NG-539; purchased 1966
see pp. 202–204

Peace treaty, 10 October 1760
Manuscript, 34 × 48.5 cm (open)
The Hague, National Archives of the Netherlands. Sociëteit van Suriname, 1.05.05, inv. no. 152
see p. 218

Dutch translation of a letter in English from Boston Band to Governor Wigbold Crommelin, 5 August 1761
Manuscript, 34.5 × 52 cm (open)
The Hague, National Archives of the Netherlands, Sociëteit van Suriname 1.05.03, inv. no. 313, p. 430
see p. 216

Letter from Governor Wigbold Crommelin to Boston Band, 29 December 1761
Manuscript, 34 × 45 cm (open)
The Hague, National Archives of the Netherlands, Sociëteit van Suriname 1.05.03, inv. no. 315, p. 15
see p. 217

G.W. Luck, *Depiction of a Military March led by Colonel L.H. Fourgeoud, 'Afbeelding van een March Van de Troupes van Haare Hoog Moogende ... onder de Ordres van den Collonel L.H. Fourgeoud over kleijne Bergachtige Savanes in de Boschen van de Collonie van Suriname'* (title on object), c. 1773–1777
Watercolour, 35.5 × 20 cm
E. van Drecht collection
see p. 210

G.W. Luck, *Depiction of a Military Camp, 'Afbeelding van een Camp. Zoo als hetzelve gemaakt werd door de Troupes van Haare Hoog Moogende ... onder de Ordres van den Collonel L. H. Fourgeoud in de Boschen van de Colonie van Suriname'* (title on object), c. 1773–1777
Watercolour, 17.5 × 26.5 cm
Soest, National Military Museum, inv. no. 00268996
see pp. 212–213

John Gabriël Stedman, *Map of Suriname with Early Maroon Settlements ('verblijfplaats der Oucas') and a Rice Paddy ('veld met rijst bezaait')*, 1799
Engraving, 20 × 43 cm
Zeist, Museum Het Hernhutter Huis
see p. 206

Comb from Suriname, before 1817
Bone, 14.8 × 4 × 0.18 cm
Middelburg, Zeeuws Museum, KZGW collection, inv. no. 3600-BEV-Z-89
Photo: Ivo Wennekes
see p. 208

Rice spoons, before 1883
Calabash, 17 pieces, variable dimensions, 3.8 × 12.2 cm, 11.2 × 40.4 cm, 12.4 × 40.1 cm, 4.3 × 14.5 cm, etc.
Leiden, Stichting Nationaal Museum van Wereldculturen, coll. nos. RV-370-381a-q
see p. 209

tula

Governor's journal of Johannes de Veer, 15 July 1795 – 3 October 1795
Manuscript, 34 × 77 × 8 cm (open)
The Hague, National Archives of the Netherlands, 2.01.28.01, inv. no. 139

Journal kept by the writer J.G. Hummen aboard the frigate *Ceres* under the command of Captain Anthony d'Amers, 15 December 1793–12 August 1796
Manuscript, 32.5 × 41 cm
The Hague, National Archives of the Netherlands, 2.01.29.03, inv. no. 164

Report by Father Schinck, 1795
Manuscript, 36 × 52 cm (open)
The Hague, National Archives of the Netherlands, 1.05.12.01, inv. no. 105
see p. 227

Report by Captain Van Westerholt, 5 October 1795
Manuscript, 36 × 52 cm (open)
The Hague, National Archives of the Netherlands, 1.05.12.01, inv. no. 106
see p. 229

Journal of Captain Albert Kikkert, commanding the Batavian frigate *Ceres*, 18 February 1795 – 3 July 1799
Manuscript, 32.5 × 41 cm
The Hague, National Archives of the Netherlands, 2.01.29.03, inv. no. 73

Carl de Vinck, *Toussaint Louverture, chef des noirs insurgés de Saint Domingue*, 1796–1799
Etching, 32 × 23 cm
Paris, Bibliothèque nationale de France, inv. no. N-2 (TOUSSAINT-LOUVERTURE, 1743–1803)
see p. 233

Govert Kitsen after a design by François Bonneville, *Portrait of Toussaint Louverture*, c. 1802–1810
Etching and dot engraving, 16.2 × 12.4 cm
Amsterdam, Rijksmuseum,
inv. no. RP-P-1878-A-2156; purchased 1878
see p. 231

Bladed cane from the Knip plantation, date of manufacture unknown
Bamboo, wood, 91 × 4 cm (2 parts)
Willemstad (Curaçao), National Archaeological Anthropological Memory Management (NAAM)
Photo: Carlo M. Wallé
see p. 237

Drum, before 1885
Wood, sheep skin, 40.5 × 23 cm
Leiden, Stichting Nationaal Museum van Wereldculturen, coll. no. RV-472-2
see p. 238

A. J. van Koolwijk (photographer), *Man from Aruba*, before 1887
Paper, cardboard, 12.6 × 7.8 cm
Leiden, Stichting Nationaal Museum van Wereldculturen, coll. no. RV-A53-4
see p. 235

Benta, before 1958
Natural fibre, 78 cm
Leiden, Stichting Nationaal Museum van Wereldculturen, coll. no. TM-2675-1a
see p. 238

supporting illustration

Soublette et Fils (photo studio), *House and Village Belonging to the Groot Santa Martha Plantation*, 1890–1920
Gelatin printing-out paper, 11 × 18.3 cm
Leiden, Stichting Nationaal Museum van Wereldculturen, coll. no. TM-60019497
see p. 223

dirk

Pieter van Call (II), *Bird's-Eye View of the Sion Estate*, c. 1725
Etching, 53 × 63.4 cm
Amsterdam, Rijksmuseum,
inv. no. RP-P-1907-2112; purchased 1907
see p. 242

A. Hulk, *The Uprising in Berbice, 'Opstand der Neger-slaven in de Berbice, 23 februari 1763'* (title on object), c. 1763–1817
Print, 18.1 × 22.9 cm
Dordrecht, on loan from Huis Van Gijn, Atlas Van Gijn, inv. no. VG2998
see pp. 246–247

Willem van Hogendorp, *Kraspoekol, of de droevige gevolgen van eene te verre gaande strengheid jegens de slaaven: zedenkundige vertelling*, 1780
Book, 19 × 13 cm
Leiden, Leiden University Libraries, inv. no. 1210 H 41: 2
see p. 244

Anonymous, *Portrait miniature of Margaretha Elisabeth Bartlo*, c. 1786
Watercolour on ivory base in wooden frame, diam. 7.4 cm; wooden frame: 16.4 × 16.4 cm
Rotterdam, Museum Rotterdam, inv. no. 11393
see p. 254

Dirk van Hogendorp, *Kraspoekol; of de Slaaverny. Een tafereel der zeden van Neerlands Indiën*, 1800
Book, 17 × 11 cm
Amsterdam, Allard Pierson Museum, Archaeological Museum of the University of Amsterdam, inv. no. OK 63-9118
see p. 250

Christoph Suhr, *Dirk van Hogendorp as Governor of Hamburg with a Bust of Napoleon*, c. 1813
Oil on canvas, 240 × 140 cm
Leiden, Leiden University Libraries, inv. no. KITLV 52V12
see p. 255

Anonymous, *General Dirk van Hogendorp at Novo Sion*, c. 1820
Oil on canvas, 36.5 × 45 cm
Leiden, Leiden University Libraries, inv. no. KITLV 52V14
see pp. 260–261

Letter from Dirk van Hogendorp to his niece Mina, with an anonymous watercolour based on the painting of Novo Sion, 31 July 1821
Manuscript and watercolour, watercolour: 18 × 12.5 cm; letter: 21.4 × 30.5 cm (open)
The Hague, National Archives of the Netherlands, 2.21.006.49, inv. no. 167,
p. 262

Ledger and monthly accounts of the Novo Sionplantation (Brazil), July 1822
Manuscript, 46 × 36.5 cm (open)
The Hague, National Archives of the Netherlands, 2.21.006.49, inv. no. 31
see p. 258

supporting illustration

Advertisement in the *Haagsche Courant*, 20 March 1801
The Hague, Royal Library of the Netherlands, signatuur KW C 94, no. 34
see p. 252

lohkay

Fragment of a plate depicting the sugar production, with the words: 'Bring more Cane to Mill Negro', 1750–1800
Earthenware, 16.5 × 11.7 cm
Oranjestad, Sint Eustatius, Collectie St. Eustatius Historical Foundation
see p. 275

Samuel Fahlberg, *The Retreat Plantation, 'The Retreat. Situated In The Quarter Cul de Sac; The Property Of William Henry Rink Esquire Formerly Governor Over The Islands St. Martins & Saba'* (title on object), 18 October 1816
Watercolour, 51.5 × 77.5 cm
The Hague, National Archives of the Netherlands, 4.MIKO, inv. no. 320
see pp. 270–271

Samuel Fahlberg, *View of Philipsburg, 'View of Philipsburg. The Capital of the Netherland part of the Island Saint Martins'* (title on object), 1822
Watercolour, 43.5 × 74 cm
The Hague, National Archives of the Netherlands, 4.MIKO, inv. no. 319
see pp. 278–279

Samuel Fahlberg, *View of Philipsburg, 'View of Philipsburg. The Capital of the Netherland-Part of The Island Saint Martin's'* (title on object), 1823
Watercolour, 45 × 75 cm
The Hague, National Archives of the Netherlands, 4.MIKO, inv. no. 318
see pp. 276–277

Machete, after 1845
Iron, 57 × 6 cm
Oranjestad, Sint Eustatius, Collection St. Eustatius Monuments Foundation
see p. 267

Minutes (Transcript) by citizens and proprietors of the Dutch part of Sint Maarten (in English), 1 June 1848
Manuscript, 25 × 20 cm
The Hague, National Archives of the Netherlands, 2.10.01, inv. no. 4349, folio 23

Letter from the authorities of the Dutch part of Saint Martin to the authorities of Curaçao on changes to the slavery system, 8 June 1848
Manuscript, 25 × 20 cm
The Hague, National Archives of the Netherlands, 2.10.01, inv. no. 4349, folio 21
see p. 281

Act of 7 May 1859, on the implementation of the abolition of slavery in the Dutch East Indies, 7–12 May 1859
Manuscript, 34.5 × 22 cm
The Hague, National Archives of the Netherlands, 2.02.04, inv. no. 1190
see p. 283

Royal Decrees of 8 August 1862 no. 84 certifying legislation for the abolition of slavery in the Dutch Antilles
Manuscript, 34 × 21 cm
The Hague, National Archives of the Netherlands, 2.02.04, inv. no. 1383B
see p. 282

Roland Napoleon Bonaparte, photo with caption: 'No 3. Verschillende typen Surinaamse creolen', in *Les Habitants de Suriname. Notes recueillies à l'Exposition Coloniale d'Amsterdam en 1883*, 1884
Amsterdam, Rijksmuseum, inv. no. RP-F-1994-12-3
see p. 287

Selection of blue beads from Sint Eustatius, 18th–19th century
Glass, various dimensions
Oranjestad, Sint Eustatius, private collection
Photo: Rijksmuseum, Staeske Rebers
see pp. 288–289

supporting illustration

Article in *The Daily Herald*, 1 July 2005
Photo: Valika Smeulders
see p. 269

This book was published on the occasion of the exhibition *Slavery* at the Rijksmuseum in Amsterdam.

The exhibition *Slavery* was made possible, in part, by the Mondriaan Fund, Blockbuster Fund, Fonds 21, DutchCulture, Democracy and Media Foundation, Stichting Thurkowfonds, Scato Gockinga Fonds/ Rijksmuseum Fonds, Fonds de Zuidroute/ Rijksmuseum Fonds, Zusjes Nieuwbeerta Fonds/ Rijksmuseum Fonds, Fonds Dirk Jan van Orden/ Rijksmuseum Fonds, Henry M. Holterman Fonds/ Rijksmuseum Fonds and Boomerang Agency.

The documentary *Nieuw licht – het Rijksmuseum en de slavernij* (New Light – The Rijksmuseum and slavery), directed by Ida Does and produced by Memphis Features, follows the makers of the exhibition.

authors
Stephanie Archangel, junior curator of history, Rijksmuseum
Karwan Fatah-Black, assistant professor of Dutch colonial history in the department of social and economic history, Leiden University
Martine Gosselink, director of the Mauritshuis, The Hague, formerly head of the history department, Rijksmuseum
Maria Holtrop, curator of history, Rijksmuseum
Lisa Lambrechts, curator of history in training, Rijksmuseum
Eveline Sint Nicolaas, senior curator of history, Rijksmuseum
Valika Smeulders, head of the history department, Rijksmuseum

translation
Pierre Bouvier (Foreword, Slavery: An Exhibition of Many Voices, Dutch Colonial Slavery, Wally, Van Bengalen, Surapati, Sapali, Tula, Current Thinking about Slavery in the Netherlands)
Steve Green (João, Paulus, Oopjen, Dirk, Lohkay)

editing
Geri Klazema, Barbera van Kooij, Rijksmuseum

english text editing
Sophie Kullmann

image research
Ellen Slob, Rijksmuseum

index
Miekie Donner

photography
Image Department of the Rijksmuseum and other institutions and individuals as indicated in the list of exhibited works (pp. 340–350). For the maps on pp. 322–323, the following should be added: Carto Studio BV, Utrecht.

cover
Modified version of *Enslaved Men Digging Trenches*, c. 1850
see p. 92

design
Irma Boom

lithography
BFC, Bert van der Horst

printing and binding
Drukkerij Wilco

publisher
Atlas Contact, Amsterdam/Antwerp

ISBN 978 90 450 44279
NUR 688

FOUNDER

PHILIPS

MAIN SPONSORS

BankGiroLoterij

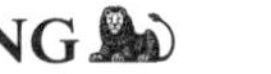